THE SWORD AND THE OLIVE

MARTIN VAN CREVELD

THE SWORD
AND THE OLIVE

A CRITICAL HISTORY OF THE
ISRAELI DEFENSE FORCE

PublicAffairs
New York

PHOTO CREDITS: Zionist Archive, *Chapters 1 and 4*; Hagana Archive, *Chapter 2*; Israel Government Press Office, *Chapters 3, 5, 6, 7, 8, 9, 10, 11, 12, 13, 14, 15, 16, 17, 18, 19, 21, and The Good*; French Press Agency, *Chapter 20*; Dvora Lewy, *And the Evil.*

LIBRARY OF CONGRESS CATALOGING-IN-PUBLICATION DATA

Van Creveld, Martin L.

  The sword and the olive : a critical history of the Israeli defense force / Martin van Creveld.

   p.   cm.

ISBN 1–58648–155–X (pbk.)

   1. Israel. Tseva haganah le-Yiśra'el—History.   2. Israel—Armed Forces—History.   I. Title.

UA853.I8V373   1998

355'.0095694—dc21   *98-21872*

                                                                                                                    CIP

10   9   8   7   6   5   4   3   2   1

In memory of Miki Levanon (1971–1992),
who died by friendly fire.

Contents

PART III: RUNNING OUT OF STEAM, 1974–1997

MAPS

Note on Sources, Translations, Transliterations, and Acronyms

As necessarily follows from the nature of the subject, the great majority of sources used in this study are in Hebrew. Some of them, notably the memoirs of such famous personalities as Moshe Dayan, Yitschak Rabin, and Ariel Sharon, have been translated into English. Nevertheless I have normally made use of, and referred to, the Hebrew originals—the reason being that they are often much more detailed and contain important documentary material that has been omitted from the English editions. To give the non-Israeli reader at least an idea of the nature of the source in question I have quoted each Hebrew title and provided it with a translation. Those translations are my own and by no means always correspond to the "official" English titles that are carried on the front pages and that all too often sacrifice accuracy for literary effect. It is my hope that this system will enable the non-Israeli reader, if not to check on my facts, then at least to obtain some kind of feel for the sources that I have used.

As foreigners driving around Israel and trying to read the road signs will note, transliteration represents a problem; occasionally it seems there are as many transliterations as there are people, if not more. I tried to be as simple, consistent, and phonetically correct as I could, even if this meant ignoring the normal system (e.g., *kibbuts* instead of "kibbutz," Chayim instead of Haim) and substituting one of my own.

Finally, and for consistency's sake, I have treated Hebrew acronyms as I would English ones: for example, in writing TSAHAL (for Tsva-Hagana Leyisrael) rather than the more normal Tsahal (let alone Zahal, which does not correspond to the way in which the word is pronounced); and PALMACH (for Plugot Machats) rather than Palmach. The reason for this is to make the informed reader, who may well have heard these terms before, aware that they *do* in fact represent acronyms. And indeed acronyms are something that the Israeli armed forces, like their opposite numbers in other countries, have been spouting forth in prodigious numbers.

Still there is no denying that, for all but Hebrew-speakers, access both to the numerous Hebrew terms and to the sources remains difficult if not impossible. Therefore, as in any good restaurant, please feel free to ignore the kitchen and enjoy the meal.

Glossary of Acronyms and Hebrew Terms Used in the Text

Achdut Ha-avoda Unity of Labor; a left-wing activist party led by Yisrael Galili and Yigal Allon

AEW airborne electronic warfare

AFV armored fighting vehicle

aluf, alufim **(pl.)** brigadier (later major) general

APC armored personnel carrier

APSDFS armor-piercing, sabbot-discarding, fin-stabilized ammunition

BAKUM (Basis Klita U-miyun) Recruit Absorption and Classification Base

Bar Giora first Jewish self-defense organization in Palestine (1907)

Betar right-wing nationalist organization founded in 1925

chalutsim pioneers

chared, charedim **(pl.)** "the anxious ones"; non-Zionist orthodox Jews

chatatsit gravel thrower; a contraption dreamed up by TAAS for combating Palestinian demonstrators

CHEN (Chel Nashim) Women's Army Corps

Cherut Freedom; a right-wing political party, the ancestor of the modern Likud Party

Chets Arrow: (1) type of elongated, armor-piercing ammunition developed for the Merkava tank; (2) antiballistic missile developed by IAI

CHIM (Chel Mishmar) Garrison Force; Hagana's stationary force

CHISH (Chel Sadeh) Field Force; one of Hagana's strike forces

Chok Sherut Bitachon National Service Law of 1949

CIC commander in chief

CO comanding officer

COS chief of staff

dunam a parcel of land measuring 1,000 square meters

en brera "no choice"; the ideological justification for Israeli wars until 1973

ECM electronic countermeasures

ETSEL (Irgun Tsvai Leumi) National Military Organization; pre-1948 right-wing terrorist organization

fashla, fashlot **(pl.)** slang for "blunder"

FLIR forward-looking infrared; a night-vision system for aircraft and helicopters

FOSH (Plugot Sadeh) Field Companies; organized by Hagana in 1937–1938

GADNA (Gdudei Noar) Youth Battalions; a paramilitary organization for youths run by the IDF

gafir, gafirim **(pl.)** Jewish police officer working for the British authorities

Galil Israeli-made assault rifle

garin, garinim **(pl.)** "cores" of NACHAL youths earmarked for new settlements

gesher ha-glilim roller bridge used in the 1973 October War to cross the Suez Canal

GHQ general headquarters

Gush Emunim Bloc of the Faith; a group of extreme right-wing nationalist Jews in the Occupied Territories

hachshara, hachsharot **(pl.)** PALMACH training group

HAGA (Hagana Ezrachit) Civil Defense Organization

Hagana Defense; the Jewish self-defense force in Palestine before 1948

hagana merchavit territorial defense

Ha-shomer The Guard; the second Jewish self-defense organization in Palestine after Bar Giora

Histadrut Labor Federation

IAF Israel Air Force

IAI Israel Aircraft Industries

IDF Israeli Defense Force

KABA (Kvutsat-echut) Quality Group; a system of classifying recruits by quality

KABAN, KABANIM **(pl.)** *(ktsin beriut nefesh)* mental health officer

Kfir Lion Cub; the Israeli-built light fighter-bomber

kibbuts, kibbutsim **(pl.)** communal settlement where all property is held in common

kippot sruggot literally, "knitted yarmulkes"; the nickname for right-wing nationalist orthodox Jews

Knesset the Israeli parliament

kofer ha-yishuv the *Yishuv*'s ransom; the tax imposed by the Jewish community in Palestine in 1929

Lavi Young Lion; the Israeli-built fighter-bomber that never flew

LECHI (Lochame Cherut Yisrael) Israel's Freedom Fighters; a pre-1948 right-wing terrorist organization

LIC low intensity conflict

Likud Unity; the right-wing political party that has dominated Israel during most of the years since 1977

Maarachot Campaigns; the IDF's periodical (monthly)

maarav, maaravim **(pl.)** ambush

MABAT (Mifalim Bitchoniyim) Defense Plants; an arms-manufacturing subsidiary of IAI

MADAS, MADASit (fem.) Madrich Sport; a physical training instructor

maoz, meozim **(pl.)** bunker

MAFCHASH (Mifkedet Kochot Ha-sadeh) ground forces headquarters

MAFDAL (Miflaga Datit Leumit) National Religious Party

MAPAI (Mifleget Poale Erets Yisrael) Workers' Party of the Land of Israel; ancestor of the modern Labor Party

mateh staff

MATKAL (Mateh Klali) General Staff

mechdal oversight

Merkava Chariot; an Israeli-built tank

milchemet brera "war of choice"; the biblical term sometimes used in modern Israel to describe a war in which it took the initiative

mirdaf, mirdafim **(pl.)** pursuit

Mishmar Ha-gvul Frontier Guard

Mispenot Yisrael Israeli Shipyards

mistanen, mistanenim **(pl.)** infiltrators

Moav (Moab) long-range UAV reportedly being considered by the IDF for combating surface-to-surface missiles

MLRS multiple rocket launching system

MOS military occupation specialty

moshav different types of communal settlements in which the land, but not agricultural implements, are owned in common

Mossad Institution; Israel's foreign secret service

NACHAL (Noar Chalutsi Lochem) Fighting-Pioneer Youth, the army's corps of pioneers in uniform

NAGMASH, NAGMASHim (pl.) (*nose geyasot meshuryan*) armored personnel carrier

NAGMASHA, NAGMASHot (pl.) (*noset geyasot meshuryenet*) heavy armored personnel carrier on tank chassis

NCO noncommissioned officer

NILI (Netsach Yisrael Lo Yeshaker) Israel Will Live Forever; Jewish espionage ring in Palestine during World War I

noter, notrim **(pl.)** Jewish police officer working for the British authorities

Ofek Horizon; generic name for Israeli satellites

PALMACH (Plugot Machats) Hagana's pre-1948 strike force

PALYAM (PALMACH-YAM) PALMACH's naval company

PAZAM (pesek zman minimali) minimum periods between promotions

PGMs precision-guided munitions

pkida plugatit, pkiddot plugatiyot **(pl.)** company clerk (female)

POUM (1) Plugot Meyuchadot (Special Companies); Hagana intelligence organization set up in 1941; (2) Pikkud U-mateh (Command and General Staff College)

PTSD posttraumatic stress disorder

RAFAEL (Rashut Le-pituach Emtsaei Luchama) Weapon Development Authority

RAFI (Reshimat Poalei Yisrael) Israeli Workers' List; a party founded by Ben Gurion after his resignation as prime minister in 1963

Rechesh Acquisition; Hagana's arms-procurement organization

Reshef Spark; a class of Israeli missile boats

rosh mateh klali chief of the General Staff

rosh mifkada artsit chief of country headquarters, the title carried by Hagana's chief of staff

RPV remotely piloted vehicle

Saar Tempest; a class of Israeli missile boats

sabra "the fruit of the cactus," a nickname for Israeli-born Jews *sayarot* commando units

SAM surface-to-air missile

Shavit Comet 2, an (unsuccessful?) surface-to-surface missile built by RAFAEL during the early 1960s

Sherut Aviri Air Service; PALMACH's underground air arm

Sherut Zehirut Prudence Service; Hagana's security service

Shin Bet (Sherut Bitachon) Israel's domestic Security Service

shomer, shomrim **(pl.)** guard

SIGINT signals intelligence

siyur, siyurim **(pl.)** patrol

slik, slikkim **(pl.)** an underground chamber where arms were hidden

SNS Special Night Squads; commando units organized by Capt. Orde Wingate during the disturbances of 1936–1939

TAAS (Taasiya Tsvait) Israel Military Industries Ltd.

tachkir, tachkirim **(pl.)** debriefing

tadrich, tadrichim **(pl.)** briefing

taoz, teozim **(pl.)** bunker

timsach, timaschim **(pl.)** crocodiles; code name for rafts used in crossing the Suez Canal in 1973

TOW tube-launched, optically tracked, wire-guided antitank missile

TSAHAL (Tsva Hagana Le-Yisrael) IDF

tsva keva standing forces

UAV unmanned airborne vehicle

ugda division

Uzi Israeli-made submachine gun

YAMACH, YAMACHim (pl.) *(yechidat machsanei cherum)* emergency depot

yeshive, yeshivot **(pl.)** talmudic high school

yeshivot hesder arrangement yeshives; Talmudic high schools in which students split time between the military and study

Yishuv pre-1948 Jewish community in Palestine

zroa ha-hachraa the decisive arm; applied to each arm and service to itself

Preface to the Paperback Edition

The autumn of 1998 was perhaps the most hopeful moment in the entire hundred-year history of the Arab-Israeli conflict. At Wye Plantation, Maryland, Israeli, Palestinian, and American representatives were hard at work. Their purpose was to hammer out an agreement that would enable the Israel Defense Force (IDF) to withdraw from parts of the City of Hebron. At the head of the Israeli delegation to the talks was Prime Minister Benjamin Netanyahu, political hardliner and leader of the Likud Party. Many observers believed that should the negotiations succeed, the most important obstacle to peace would have been overcome and the end of the conflict would be in sight.

The negotiations did succeed, but the conflict did not come to an end. Whether because the Israelis refused to continue working toward a final agreement, which would have entailed more withdrawals, or because the Palestinians did not meet their obligations under the agreement by gathering illegal arms and ending incitement of violence against Israel, the peace process stalled. Disappointed with Mr. Netanyahu's inability to make progress, Israeli voters ousted him in favor of Ehud Barak, but even the latter's offer to surrender 96 percent of the occupied territories and establish a Palestinian state did not persuade Mr. Arafat to make peace under conditions that Israel felt it could accept. In particular, most Israelis considered the Palestinian demand that Israel grant the refugees who had fled the country during the 1948 War the "right of return" as tantamount to the destruction of their state. As it was probably meant to be.

In September 2000, the Second Palestinian *Intifada*, or Uprising, got under way. It was much more violent than the *Intifada* of the late 1980s and early 1990s. Hundreds of Israelis died. The Israel Defense Force responded by using force on a scale that only a few years earlier would have made its commanders shake their heads in disbelief. As these lines are being written, the conflict is still raging and, indeed, intensifying. Israeli forces have entered and are conducting operations in many of the towns surrendered to the Palestinians under the 1993 Oslo Agreement; whomever carries weapons and refuses to surrender, they simply kill. The Palestinians continue to wreak havoc in Israel. By the use of suicide bombers, the most hateful tactic of all, they are killing men, women, and children indiscriminately and further stoking the fire.

It is impossible to say where it will all end. Soldiers are so afraid of lightly armed terrorists that they try to pursue them in sixty-ton tanks. Others prefer spending time in prison rather than serving in the territories and becoming involved in what they see as atrocities; still others, instead of keeping a stiff upper lip, openly weep over their dead comrades' graves. The media runneth over with signs of Israeli weakness. Visiting Tel Aviv and noting the thousands who besiege foreign embassies in order to look into the possibility of emigrating—although, so far, few have actually taken that step—an observer might be forgiven for thinking that Israel is coming to the end of its tether.

As this book explains in considerable detail, such an impression would have some truth to it. But this weakness is only part of the story, and to believe in it entirely would be misleading and, therefore, as dangerous as dangerous can be. Not far behind the impotent weeping and wailing and the shameful lack of courage, a powerful combination of rage and despair is gathering force. The following figures illustrate the trend as nothing else can. In the summer of 2000, before the start of the current Uprising, only 7 or 8 percent of Israelis felt that it would be necessary to repeat the events of 1948 and expel the Palestinians into Jordan in order to secure Israel's future. By February 2002 the number had risen to 33 percent, and in April of the same year it stood at 44 percent. Desperate times will lead to desperate measures. Should the present hostilities continue to escalate, the time when Israelis will unite behind a leader who will do *anything* for their safety cannot be far off.

That leader may well be Ariel Sharon. In the past, he has often said that Israel's policy of propping up the Hashemite regime in Jordan was a mistake and that Jordan, which according to him has a Palestinian majority even now, is the true Palestinian state, the inference being that the Palestinians should go there. A few weeks ago, when a journalist asked him whether he was contemplating ethnic cleansing, he said he did not think in such terms. Those who believe him are welcome to their illusions. Sharon's entire career shows that he is the last man to charge ahead without a plan. Though it is impossible to be sure, his intention in allowing the conflict to escalate may well be to create the conditions for doing what, in the past, he has often hinted he wanted done. The fact that he does not seem to have a plan makes it all the more likely that he does.

Should Sharon judge that the time for implementing his plan has come, then may God help the Palestinians. As hard as it may be for some to believe, the IDF has essentially been wearing kid gloves. To expel the

Palestinians will require only a few brigades, and second-rate ones at that; meanwhile, the bulk of the Israeli forces, armed and equipped as never before, will deploy on Israel's borders to deal with possible attempts at intervention by the neighboring Arab states. Should such intervention be attempted, the main role in repelling them will be played by the Israeli Air Force. It too is armed and equipped as never before. In 1982, the last time the Israeli Air Force engaged in large-scale operations, it destroyed all the Syrian antiaircraft defenses in Lebanon and shot down about a hundred Syrian aircraft with hardly any losses. Syrian commanders of armored divisions charged with taking the Golan Heights or Egyptians preparing to drive a unit across 150 miles of open desert might do well to recall Isaiah 5:26–30 (author's translation):

> And He will lift up a sign . . . and shall hiss unto them from the end of the earth; and, lo, they shall come with speed swiftly. None of them shall be weary nor stumble; none shall slumber or sleep. Neither shall the girdle of their loins be loosed, nor shall the latchet of their shoes break. Whose arrows are sharp, and all their bows bent for shooting; their horses' hoofs shall be counted like flint, and their wheels like a tempest; their roaring shall be like a lion, and they shall roar like young lions; yea, they shall roar, and pounce upon the prey, and devour it and belch, and no one shall deliver it.

What is it to be? Are the two sides going to withdraw from the brink of the abyss and agree on some kind of compromise? Or will the conflict escalate, leading Israel to rise and smite its enemies? Outsiders, however good or bad their intentions, cannot answer this question; it is up to the Palestinians and the Israelis themselves. The former should finally forget about doing away with Israel, even if they euphemistically call that goal "the right of return." The latter should finally forget about retaining much of the Territories that were occupied in 1967. Whatever the answer, it is clear that the IDF is going to play a critical role in events to come. It is for those who seek to understand that powerful force—its origins, growth, mentality, modus operandi, and capabilities—that this book is intended.

MARTIN VAN CREVELD
Mevasseret Zion, Israel
April 17, 2002
Israel's fifty-fourth Independence Day

INTRODUCTION

EVER SINCE IT OFFICIALLY emerged out of the prestate Hagana during Israel's War of Independence in 1947–1949, the Israeli Defense Force (IDF) has become one of the world's leading armed forces. Time and again it has captured global headlines by fighting, and usually winning, wars against Israel's Arab neighbors. Time and again it has come up with innovative concepts, beginning with the conscription of women (the only time in history this has been done) and more recently with the development of new weapons systems such as active tank armor and remotely piloted vehicles (RPVs), unveiled for the first time during the 1982 invasion of Lebanon. Even as these lines are written, and regardless of the ongoing peace process, the IDF remains the ultimate guarantor of the country's existence and a critical component in the balance of power in one of the world's strategically most important regions.

This book will trace the history of the IDF from its origins—the organizations known as Bar Giora and Ha-shomer, which date to the time when Palestine was part of the Ottoman empire—to the present day. It lies in the nature of things that the greatest attention will be devoted to military questions, that is, war and preparations for war; yet as far as space permits, political, economic, social, and cultural issues must also be considered. The longtime forces that shaped the IDF will be examined, but so will the outstanding and often highly colorful leaders who were responsible for making the day-to-day decisions. Analysis will combine with narrative, the general with the specific. Only in this way, and by taking as comprehensive a point of view as possible, can one hope to do justice to the subject as a whole.

With these objectives in mind, the volume falls into three main parts. Part I will take us from the beginnings past World War I, past the time when Hagana was founded during the period of British rule as a self-defense organization, past the establishment in 1941 of PALMACH as the first full-time fighting force, past the start of the underground struggle against the British in 1944–1947, and all the way through Israel's War of Independence, which lasted from November 1947 to January 1949. Part II will trace the IDF's growth from the War of Independence to the 1973 Arab-Israeli War inclusive, the period when it fought its most celebrated campaigns and also turned itself from a popular militia equipped with infantry weapons into one of the world's most modern and most powerful armed forces. Part III will examine the slow but steady decline of the IDF from the end of the October War to the present day, a period characterized above all by the introduction of high technology (including, according to foreign reports, nuclear weapons and their delivery vehicles) on the one hand and the increasing shift from interstate war to antiguerrilla and antiterrorist operations on the other.

For the reader who is not an Israeli and does not know Hebrew, a word concerning the sources used in writing this volume may be in order. Partly for understandable security reasons, partly because of the eastern European political tradition of which they were the carriers, Israel's leaders have traditionally made it rather hard to gather information on defense in general and the IDF in particular. During recent years the situation has tended to improve: Parts of both the state archives and those of the IDF itself are now open through to the period of the 1956 Suez Campaign, as are various prestate archives. Still, the extent of the change should not be exaggerated. Especially compared to what we have come to expect of Western democracies with their various freedom of information acts, much— including much that is critically important to the Israeli state's existence— remains inaccessible to the public.

In trying to close the gap I have drawn on the enormous body of material represented by the secondary literature, the press (both the general one and that which is published by the IDF itself), memoirs, diaries, and interviews. In doing so I have not been wary of footnoting the volume very heavily; the reason being that, since so much is censored, I wanted to make sure that I could point out my sources for each fact cited. Also, I wanted to give the reader at least an idea concerning the enormous body of material that is available, and that, in previous full-length, English-language accounts of the subject written by either foreigners or Israelis, for the most part has remained either untouched or unmentioned.

MARTIN VAN CREVELD
Jerusalem, Israel

THE SWORD AND THE OLIVE

What is good? You ask. To be brave is good.

FRIEDRICH NIETZSCHE, *Thus Spake Zarathustra*

I

THE SURGE, 1907–1949

A T THE BEGINNING of the period covered by this part, the first
Jewish self-defense groups, consisting of a few dozen loosely
organized, inexperienced, and ill-armed men and women in the
northern part of Erets Yisrael (Land of Israel), had just been founded. By the
time it ended there already existed a regular, state-owned, Jewish armed force
with almost 100,000 men and women under arms. It included, besides a dozen
ground combat brigades, at least embryonic air and naval arms as well as a
general staff, a logistic service, an intelligence service, a communications service, a technical service, and even a "psychological research service"
employing 62 people.[1] These forces, as well as the rudimentary military industries by which they were supported, had to be constructed under exceptionally difficult circumstances. On the one hand the work had to be carried out
against the background of constant skirmishes with the local Palestinian population; on the other, much of it had to take place underground and in the
teeth first of the Ottomans who ruled the country and then of the British
mandatory authorities.

"Battle-Worthy Guards": Ha-shomer members dressed up as Arabs, ca. 1910.

CHAPTER I

"BATTLE-WORTHY GUARDS"

A
T THE BEGINNING of the twentieth century, Palestine—even the country's borders had yet to be defined, let alone marked on the ground—was merely a remote and neglected province of the Ottoman empire. Neither in the towns nor in the countryside were there any wheeled vehicles. The former had alleyways with steps and narrow turns designed for pedestrians and donkeys; the latter did not have any metalled roads at all. For example, when Napoleon campaigned in Palestine in 1798–1799 the state of the roads prohibited him from taking his siege artillery along; having been shipped from Alexandria to Acre, it was intercepted by the British navy and lost. When the British philanthropist Sir Moses Montefiore visited the country half a century later he discovered that his carriage was useless and that the only way to get the heavy metal parts of a windmill he was building to Jerusalem was on the backs of mules.

The very first wheeled vehicle, appropriately nicknamed "Pharaoh's chariot," was introduced in 1869. Even so, at the end of the century the journey from Jaffa to Chadera—a little more than forty miles—took nine hours to accomplish by cart.[1] The journey by horse-drawn carriage to Jerusalem, though similar in length, took even longer. Normally people would leave during the early afternoon. Nighttime being too dangerous for travel, they would spend the night in a caravansary at Shaar Ha-gai (The Gate to the Valley) some thirty miles away. They would start again in the morning and arrive around noon after having driven up and down the mountain tracks.[2] Even after a railroad between the two towns was built in 1892 the trip still took four to six hours. There were stretches where the train, winding its way along the mountain track, could be overtaken by a galloping horse.

Owing to the absence of paved roads, as late as 1913 there was only a single motorcar in the entire country.[3] Telecommunications, too, were few and far between. Influenced by the Muslim priesthood or *Ulema*, the Ottomans had been notoriously slow to adopt the art of printing, and it was only in 1727, almost three centuries after Gutenberg, that the first press was established at Constantinople.[4] The first telegraph line linking Constantinople with Beirut and from there via Haifa to Jaffa was inaugurated in 1865; a year later it was extended to Jerusalem.[5] Which other towns were hooked up is not known, but in 1919 the British operated a network that included, besides the above, Ramla, Afula, Hebron, Gaza, Tul Karem, Acre, Nazaret, and Tiberias.[6] As for telephones, in 1914 there were none—this at a time when a well-developed country such as Germany or England already had tens of thousands.

This area of approximately 10,000 square miles between the Jordan and the Mediterranean was populated by perhaps 55,000 Jews[7] and up to 600,000 Arabs (mostly Muslims, but including a Christian community amounting to perhaps 10 percent of the total) and Druze.[8] Politically speaking the country was considered part of Greater Syria and also included what was later to become known as Transjordan. Governed from Damascus, from north to south, it was divided into the three regions (*sanjaks*) of Acre, Nablus, and Jerusalem. However, in practice the poor infrastructure only enabled the government to assert itself inside the towns where police forces were stationed. In some of these towns the presence of foreign consuls also helped protect their countrymen, if not against robbers then at any rate against the authorities.

Outside the towns, all of which were walled and closed at night, the countryside was largely left to its own devices. Much of it was dominated by a number of clans, that is, *very* extended families (the number of members often ran into the thousands) with a loose social structure and a recognized, though normally largely ritual, sheik, elder, or chief. Each clan was named after some long-deceased sheik and lived on its own territory, which might be measured in hundreds of square miles. Each one skirmished with the rest, raided neighboring farms, and, by demanding protection money, rendered the roads unsafe. For example, the village of Abu Gosh west of Jerusalem, now a place where motorists stop for a meal, used to be a notorious robbers' den. Until the 1870s, when things started slowly improving, clans even engaged each other in regular battles in which several hundreds of warriors on each side sometimes took part. Except at harvesttime, when it called a truce and sent its heavily guarded officials in to collect taxes, the government rarely interfered.[9]

During the 1880s the "old" Jewish population began to be joined by newcomers who made their way out after the pogroms that followed the assassination of Czar Alexander II in 1881; twenty years later they were joined by another wave, in turn driven out by the pogroms that shook Russia's Jewish community after the country's defeat in the war against Japan.[10] The total number of immigrants may have been around 40,000, though it is estimated that only half of them stayed. Forming part of the great Jewish emigration movement that was leaving eastern Europe during those years, many belonged to the poorest classes. Others were members of the intelligentsia, a Russian term referring to people who were generally well educated (e.g., professionals) but not property-owning. Having alienated their families by attending non-Jewish high schools and even university, upon graduation many also found themselves rejected by their gentile environment, which refused to accept them on equal terms. As in all emigration movements aiming to settle in underdeveloped countries, males predominated. Almost all who arrived in Palestine were young and unmarried, a fact by no means insignificant in determining the kinds of lives that they took up and the ideals they entertained.

Whereas less than 20 percent of the Arab population was urban, more than 80 percent of the Jews, both old and new, lived in the towns. The most prominent was Jerusalem, half its population (50,000 total) being Jewish. Others were Safed, Tiberias, Haifa, Jaffa, and Tel Aviv (the latter a purely Jewish town that was founded in 1909 and grew very rapidly). The remaining 20 percent or so of Jews, however, went out to the countryside. The land on which they settled was mostly waste, such as the malaria-bearing swampland in the Valley of Esdraelon and around the settlement of Chadera in the center of the Sharon Plain. It had been purchased, often from absentee landlords, first by the Parisian Rothschilds, who donated large sums of money for the purpose, and later by the Jewish Colonization Association, the first bank founded by the Zionists. Settlements such as Rosh Pina (the earliest of the lot), Sejera, Yavniel, Merchavia, Tel Adashim, Rechovot, Rishon Le-tsion, Nes Tsiona, Gedera, and others came into being (see Map 1.1); most only numbered a few dozen inhabitants although the largest, Petach Tikva, already had 700 in 1897. It was in these settlements that a "security" problem first arose between Jews and Arabs (see Map 6.1).

Although joined by some recent immigrants, especially from Egypt, Lebanon, and Algeria,[11] most of the Arab population had been living in the area for centuries. Although not in possession of formal title,[12] it had often been using the land in question for hunting, grazing, wood-gathering, and the like, a problem not at all unique to Palestine but one with consequences felt equally in countries such as Canada, Australia, and New Zealand. In fact, the difference between the formal, individual, Western landowning system and the antiquated, informal, family- or clan-based one prevailing in much of the Ottoman empire persists in much of the West Bank and even in parts of the Negev Desert, where it sometimes gives rise to conflicts. At that time it often led to quarrels over grazing rights, water holes, rights to fruit-

MAP 1.1   JEWISH SETTLEMENTS IN PALESTINE, 1914

bearing trees, and the like, as well as plain theft and robbery.[13] The unsettled conditions created a demand for guards—who in the best Ottoman tradition themselves sometimes turned robber and blackmailed their employers. Many of them were Circessians, members of a Muslim people who had left their native Caucasus during the 1870s to avoid coming under Russian rule. Though they had since become acclimatized, they still retained their separate identity, as they do to the present day.

Apart from the desire to escape pogroms and poverty, the newly arrived Jewish settlers also brought with them certain ideas. Prominent among them was the need to leave the traditional Jewish occupations such as inn-keeping, small-scale trading, lending, and the like, into which they had been driven by centuries of persecution as well as the prohibition on owning land. This situation had supposedly created a race of *Luftmenschen* (Yiddish for air men), that is, a race of petty hagglers whose souls were as arid, as cramped, and as devoid of wider vistas as the *shtetels* in which they spent their lives.[14] Taking up the anti-Semitic stereotypes created by the societies in which they were born, some early Zionists even went so far as to claim that Jews did not know how to dress, walk, or behave themselves.[15] In any case they dreamed of taking up agriculture, both as a way to earn an honest living without the need for intermediaries and to regenerate individually and as a community.

Along with the declared preference for an agricultural way of life came socialist and even communist ideas. (Throughout the period between 1880 and 1917, Jews, hoping that a brave new society would do away with discrimination, were prominent in the movements that led to the Russian Revolution.)[16] Some of these ideas derived from books—first those of Saint Simon and Fourier—whose solution to the problems of this world was the establishment of self-contained agricultural communities—and later those of Marx. However, probably the most important motive behind the adoption of socialism and collective forms of settlement such as the *moshavim* and *kibbutsim* was the fact that the purchasing agencies normally made land available to groups rather than to individuals. Another was the practical problems that the immigrants faced in their new country. Young, penniless, and often acquainted with each other from back home, they clustered together in search of work and a place to live. This was carried to the point that entire families might occupy a single shanty and two people shared a pair of boots.

Although the Old Testament has plenty to say about war and warfare, during the period of the Diaspora (starting in 70 A.D.) any idea of organized Jewish military action appeared almost entirely preposterous. Hence, and beginning already around 200 A.D., a long line of scholars had begun removing all reference to it from Jewish thought, even to the point where their exegesis turned King David from a commander into a scholar and his band of champions from soldiers into *yeshive* students.[17] During the first half of the nineteenth century, however, the wind began to change. In Thessaloniki and elsewhere, a few rabbis came under the influence of the Greek and Italian struggles for independence. They started looking forward to the day when the Jews too would set out to reconquer their ancient country, weapons in hand.[18] After midcentury such ideas were no longer rare. In 1862 the well-known Pomeranian rabbi Tsvi Kalisher followed up his Palestinian journey by publishing *Greetings from Zion*, drawing up a comprehensive and, as he claimed, divinely inspired plan for the Jewish resettlement of Palestine. In the process, "battle-worthy guards" would have to be mounted to prevent the "tent-dwelling" sons of Yishmael from "destroying the seed and uprooting the vineyards."[19]

But whereas Kalisher and his followers were strictly orthodox—much later, they were to found the MAFDAL (National Religious Party)—many of the Zionists who followed him had freed themselves from their parents' religious beliefs and were strongly secular-minded, even atheistic. In their hands the longing for settling the country, including the establishment of some kind of Jewish army, did not link up with the *Torah* but with Jewish history, particularly during the Hellenistic and Roman periods with which many of them were familiar from their school days. Hence, for example, the sudden popularity of "Maccabee" (Maccabean) and "Bar Kochva" (after the leader of an anti-Roman Revolt in 132–135 A.D.) as names for Jewish student associations and the like—to say nothing of a Viennese sports club known simply as Ha-koach (The Force). It was in this context, too, that the story of Masada was resurrected.[20] Of all the ancient sources that describe the Jewish revolt against Roman rule in 66–73 A.D., Jewish as well as non-Jewish, the only one to mention Masada is Josephus. During the Diaspora centuries the episode was all but ignored by Jewish scholarship, which did not approve of suicide under any circumstances. In the hands of the *chalutsim* (pioneers) it was revived, however, until it became inflated into a symbol of national heroism—"again Masada will not fall."

When the *Biluyim*, whose role in Zionism is akin to that of the *Mayflower* Pilgrims in the English settlement of North America, arrived in 1882, their "constitution" already included a clause concerning the need to master the use of weapons for self-defense.[21] A few years later one of their number, Yaakov Cohen, wrote a poem about the need to "deliver our country by the force of arms." Having fallen "by blood and fire," Judaea would likewise rise "by blood and fire."[22] In this way he unwittingly coined a slogan that would be adopted by some of the ancestors of today's Likud Party.

From 1880 on, the contrast between the supposedly cowardly "Diaspora Jew" who "avoided the ranks of heroes"[23] and the courageous Israelites depicted in the biblical Books of Joshua, Judges, Samuel A, and Samuel B became a stock-in-trade of Hebrew literature. Thus, in 1905, the poet Chayim Bialik was sent by the Zionist organization of his native Odessa to report on the pogroms that had taken place in the Ukrainian town of Kishinev. The outcome was a famous poem named "Be-ir Ha-hariga" ("In the City of Slaughter"). While wasting few words on the gentile rowdies it described the Jewish victims as "hiding in shitholes." Not only did they refuse to move a finger even when their wives were raped in front of their eyes, but later they came running to the rabbis to ask whether those same wives could still be sexually approached or not. Another poet, Shaul Tshernichovsky, wrote ballads celebrating the heroism of King Saul on the eve of his death in the Battle of Gilboa. Yet another, Yehuda L. Gordon, sang the praise of Jewish paragons from King David through the Maccabeans all the way to the rebels of 67–70 A.D., whom he depicted as fighting the lions in the Coliseum. Later the work of all three poets, but the former two in particular, formed part of the official curriculum and were studied by generations of schoolchildren. All three still have streets named after them in every major Israeli city, as does Max Nordau, the best-selling Zionist author who invented the term *yahadut shririm* (muscular Jewry) to describe the type of person he dreamed about.

The scion of an assimilated bourgeois family in Vienna and a dyed-in-the-wool liberal, Theodor Herzl, as the founder of modern Zionism, was less enthusiastic about arms, armies, and heroic deeds. In *The Jewish State*, his most important programmatic work, he did not envisage the people's return to their country as an enterprise to be carried out by force. Instead he emphasized the role of Jewish capital and Jewish know-how; indeed when he visited Palestine in 1898 he could see for himself that they were already beginning to revive the country. Concerning the military, all he had to say was that the coming state would be neutral (presumably he had Switzerland in mind) and would only need a small army that, however, would be provided "with every requisite of modern warfare" for keeping internal and external order.[24] Still, in the privacy of his diaries even he took a different line and allowed his imagination to run wild. As a young man he had enjoyed the pseudo-martial strutting associated with student life;[25] now he noted that the new state should permit dueling so as to help restore the Jews' long-lost sense of honor.[26] A born impresario, he discussed the military ceremonies, tattoos, and parades that would be held to uplift the masses and imbue them with the proper martial spirit[27] and speculated about the color of the breeches to be worn by the Jewish cavalry force.

Prior to their arrival, a few of the immigrants had been members of improvised gangs in their Russian hometowns. They did their best to put up some kind of resistance to the pogroms and also engaged in what they called "national terror"—meaning occasional assassination attempts directed at prominent anti-Semites.[28] Convinced that force could be met only with force, it was these people who, in 1907, established the two earliest self-defense organizations: Bar Giora (after a leader in the Great Revolt against the Romans in 67–73 A.D.) and Ha-shomer (The Guard), into which the former was later absorbed. Their leader was one Joshua Chankin, then aged forty-three, who had lived in the country since 1881. With his black beard and haunted look he bore a faint resemblance to Rasputin; as a land-purchasing agent working for the Jewish Colonization Association (JCA) he had access to funds. His closest comrades were one Yisrael Shochet and one Yitschak Ben Tsvi. The former was a charismatic character, a strict disciplinarian, and possessed of a strongly independent mind; this last quality would cause him to be pushed aside when Jewish self-defense became institutionalized after World War I. The latter, a mild and scholarly man, proved a better survivor and lived to become Israel's second president in 1952.

Self-defense apart, the first concern of the *shomrim* or "guards" was to put as much distance as possible between themselves and the small towns from which they came and that, to them, stood for everything that was base, cowardly, and weak. Accordingly they modeled themselves on the Circassians, who enjoyed a reputation for bravery and whose place, after all, they sought to take. They grew mustaches and put on Arabic dress including *kefiye* (headgear), *shabariye* (a curved hunting knife with grooves to take the blood), and a bullet-studded bandoleer. Some also set out to acquire at least a smattering of Arabic language and culture—including the establishment in many settlements of a *madfa* (guest room) where visiting Arabs would be served coffee and engaged in long, leisurely, conversations.[29] Precisely because they represented a vital part of the Guards' attempt to create a new self-image, these affectations were by no means universally welcomed by the established Jewish population. To them, the attempt to replace a crowd of real Arabs with their Jewish imitators seemed either reprehensible or ludicrous.[30]

Partly by persuasion, partly by less reputable methods such as mounting raids and thus displaying the inadequacy of the existing security arrangements, Ha-shomer was able to take over guard duties in a considerable number of Jewish settlements. As is apt to happen in such situations, it was by no means always entirely clear whether the sums they received (usually very paltry, but often combined with room and board) represented wages or protection money; on at least one occasion they even threatened to kill some farmers who would not take them on.[31] Riding horses and carrying rifles, pistols, sabers, and sometimes merely sticks, the *shomrim* engaged in occasional skirmishes—brawls might be a better term—with Arab intruders, horse thieves, and the like. From time to time there were casualties on both sides. However, the *shomrim* understood that the objective of Arab "warfare" during those years was booty rather than blood. Hence overall violence was held within bounds and the matter was usually settled by holding a *sulcha* or "reconciliation ceremony."

A highly secretive, elitist organization—it held its initiation rites in dark caves lighted by candles[32]—at peak Ha-shomer itself numbered approximately a hundred members. Its hard core, some ten or twelve in number, originated in Chankin's own hometown, Gomel, and were related to each other by blood or marriage. However, it did not admit "ordinary" people—including, as it happened, a black-haired, stocky, recent immigrant by the name of David Gruen (later David Ben Gurion), who apparently refused to swear unconditional allegiance to the organization and its leaders.[33] Ha-shomer was by no means sufficient to mount guard over the Jewish agricultural settlements that, though small and comparatively few in number, were already coming to be scattered all over the country. Accordingly, the nucleus of true *shomrim* was supplemented by several hundred others who were not members but whom the organization, acting as a contractor, hired and put to work. Funding came from the various Jewish land-acquisition companies that, through their agents, advanced money for purchasing arms. For example, a rifle cost 120 French francs and a horse 400; a major item of expenditure consisted of an insurance fund of 7,000 francs, which was meant to cover any claims for compensation that might arise from the Guards failing in their duty. Conversely, the farmers who hired the organization's services undertook to pay it 40–120 francs a month for each Guard (payment varying on whether or not he was mounted). In addition, one *mejida* (a small Turkish coin) was owed in case the farmer himself proved negligent by leaving gates open and the like.[34]

The organization's name notwithstanding, even at this early stage the line separating defense from offense proved difficult to maintain. In addition to its declared task of guarding the settlements, Ha-shomer provided escorts for men and women traveling from one place to another. Chasing away intruders and recovering stolen property such as horses, mules, and livestock easily translated into hot pursuit, ambushes, and the like.[35] It also translated into vendettas (*gum* in Arabic) with neighboring clans, who sought to avenge their members who had been wounded or killed by the *Jahud* (Jews). Gaining confidence—also as a result of self-designed training exercises—the organization's members sometimes initiated punitive expeditions or simply raids in order to acquire arms from their enemies. They also helped settlers clear newly acquired or disputed plots, an oper-

ation that then and later was known under the grandiloquent name of
"conquering [i.e., settling] the land."

A typical "conquest" took place in the summer of 1909 at Kfar Tabor
near the mountain of that name.[36] Twenty-five Ha-shomer members—a
huge force for those days—were concentrated together with arms, plows
(for opening the land and thus marking it), and draft mules. A morning
parade was held and those present took an oath to conquer or die; equally
important, a field kitchen was improvised and staffed by the men's sisters,
girlfriends, and wives. In fact, a handful of women had been members of
Ha-shomer from the beginning; others were brought in as dependents of
individual *shomrim*. In both capacities they took their share of the primitive life, not seldom at the cost of considerable physical hardship that in
turn led to miscarriages. Nevertheless, they were almost entirely confined
to auxiliary tasks such as cooking, doing the laundry, nursing (and, in the
person of Shochet's wife, Manya, bookkeeping), a situation about which
they not infrequently complained.[37]

Arriving on the spot, the Guards followed their preprepared plans and
divided into two groups. While the one plowed, the other engaged in a
rock-throwing exchange with some members of the local Zbich clan and,
displaying their weapons, drove them off. Next the two groups reunited
and sat down to a picnic that, to judge by the loving detail in which it is
described, was by no means the least important part of the proceedings.
The Arabs watched from a safe distance. Later they returned, claiming
and, in the end, obtaining[38] pecuniary compensation for land on which
they had been living for centuries but that, having been sold beneath their
feet, they could no longer defend. Throughout the operation, which from
beginning to end lasted six days, not a Turkish soldier or policeman
appears to have presented himself.

Not all "conquest" operations were so cozy or ended without bloodshed. In February 1911 another group of Ha-shomer members sought to
establish themselves in a place named Merchavia in the Valley of
Esdraelon. Ten thousand *dunam* (ten square kilometers) of land having
been purchased by Chankin in his capacity as a JCA agent, a force of
twenty Guards set out. The head of the local Sulam clan tried to make
them pay protection money; failing this, harassment began, and the next
three months witnessed a number of skirmishes. After an incident in which
two Arabs died and a Guard's horse was wounded, their fellow clansmen
("hundreds" of them, if the Jewish participants' memoirs may be trusted)
assembled and mounted an attack. Conducted mainly with old-fashioned
rifles and accompanied by much shouting, demonstrations of horseman-
ship, and the like, the "battle" lasted for six hours; at that point Turkish

policemen arrived from Nazareth, rescued the Jews by arresting them, and left the Arabs to plunder what remained of the settlement. An investigation was launched and, after more than a year, led to the release of the *shomrim* and the reestablishment of Merchavia. According to an anonymous quote in the official Hagana history,[39] supposedly the episode "proved to the Arabs that Jews could not simply be robbed; people spoke admiringly of the Jew who heroically resisted a whole bunch of robbers."

Originally based in the north of the country, Ha-shomer gradually spread to the rest as well, reaching as far as Gedera some thirty-five miles south of Tel Aviv. However, in the absence of a developed infrastructure of roads and telecommunications the distances between one settlement and another seemed enormous. This in turn made the construction of a centralized command structure impossible. Instead the organization acted as a sort of clearinghouse for Guards including those engaged in day-to-day duties and those who were occasionally assembled for larger operations. It provided both members and nonmembers with arms, appointed them to the places where they were needed, and switched them from one settlement to another as needed. It also looked after financial affairs including, by this time, a mutual sickness fund that covered the expenses of the many who were wounded in action. By 1914 its assets, most of them in the form of horses and weapons, stood at 17,000 francs; its debts to the JCA and to private individuals amounted to 27,000 francs. Then as now, obtaining economic self-sufficiency was not exactly the strongest point of the Jewish community (*Yishuv*).

Though no figures are available, by 1912–1913 Ha-shomer seems to have gone a considerable way toward its goal of replacing the Circassian Guards with Jewish ones in many of the settlements. The original hunting arms had been replaced by pistols and bolt-action rifles, some of them purchased legally from merchants in Haifa, Beirut, and Damascus and others stolen from the Ottoman army. Most were old and could only take a single bullet in the breech; a few, however, were magazine-loaded and, regarded as a great innovation, much feared by the Arabs who called them *Abu Hamsa* (father of five).[40] Then as later the greatest advantage that the organization possessed was the members' education and the ties that they maintained with their former homeland. This even enabled them to obtain and put into operation a machine for filling spent cartridges with gunpowder, something entirely beyond the capacity of their Arab opponents. In 1912 these achievements apparently made Shochet feel confident enough to present the Jewish Agency with a proposal for creating a countrywide defense organization for the entire Jewish community. Its core was to be formed by an unspecified number of "regulars" provided by Ha-shomer; around them would cluster a much larger number of part-time "reservists," that is, workers and farmers who would receive training, acquire or be provided with arms, and be available in the emergency.[42] Given the technical obstacles, particularly the near-total lack of telecommunications, the proposal was premature.

In December 1914 a new military governor, Jamal Pasha, had arrived in Jaffa, where he doubled as commander in chief of the 4th Ottoman Army. As it happened, this was not his first encounter with the energetic Jews from Erets Yisrael, some of whom, including, besides Yisrael Shochet and Yitschak Ben Tsvi, David Ben Gurion, had been studying law in Constantinople during 1912–1913. When the Balkan wars broke out a number of them tried to volunteer for the Ottoman army, the idea being to prove their loyalty to the empire as a way of obtaining greater autonomy for the Jewish community. Understandably in view of the fact that Russia was supporting Turkey's enemies, the idea was not well received. It fell to Jamal, a leading "Young Turk" who at that time was serving as the town's military governor, to have them arrested on suspicion of being Russian spies. Their comrades complained to the Russian ambassador, who quickly obtained their release; however, suspicion remained.[42]

At the outbreak of World War I, the capitulations system, under which the citizen of foreign powers living in Palestine enjoyed certain privileges and immunities, had been abolished. This enabled Jamal to proclaim martial law and apply it to the entire population, regardless of which passports they held. He also prohibited all associations, political movements, newspapers, flags, as well as the parades to which the Guards, riding their horses in their exotic dress and firing into the air in the Arab fashion, were much addicted.[43] His attitude to the Jewish community was governed by the fact that many of its members were Russian citizens and thus enemy aliens, as indeed were many of its leaders. Specifically, Ha-shomer was suspected of engaging in pro-British activities.

In fact opinions within the organization, as within the Jewish community as a whole, were divided. Some *shomrim*, notably Ben Tsvi with his excellent Arabic and genuine admiration for Arab culture, saw the war as an opportunity to prove their loyalty to the Ottoman empire; as in 1912–1913, they proposed to take out Ottoman citizenship and create an "Ottoman Legion" that would fight in its ranks. Others, to the contrary, thought the time had come to rid the country from a hopelessly backward, corrupt, and rapacious government—including not least the impositions of Jamal himself.[44] In the spring of 1916 Shochet and a few of his comrades-in-arms even hatched a fantastic plot to capture Jerusalem and deliver it to the British as an Easter present.[45] Overcome by gratitude, the latter, it was hoped, would help the Jews realize their own nascent national aspirations.

In any event these plans came to naught. American and even German protests to the contrary, Jamal set out to banish as many Russian immigrants as he could lay hands on; some 7,500 of them, mostly young ones, eventually reached Egypt. An order to surrender all arms went out and was, of course, disobeyed; Ha-shomer, however, was forced underground. All three of its leaders were deported, along with a considerable number of their followers. Some of the deportees got as far as eastern Turkey, from where they moved into the Caucasus and on to Russia; a few died under the harsh conditions.

In September–October 1917 the Ottomans unearthed a pro-British Jewish espionage ring known as NILI (short for *Netsach Yisrael Lo Yeshaker*, roughly translatable as "Israel Will Live Forever"), which was operating in Zichron Yaakov to the south of Haifa. The two organizations, though not identical, were connected, because the same people were sometimes members of both. Repeatedly, messages were passed between NILI and Ha-shomer's diaspora in Egypt. Persecution was intensified and many of the remaining members were arrested, taken to Damascus, and tortured.[46] By the time the war ended in late 1918 the entire country was occupied by the British, the organization was in ruins, and attempts to revive it did not prove successful.

As Moshe Dayan once said, the sum total of Ha-shomer's deeds could easily have been carried out by a single squad of TSAHAL (Tsva Hagana-Le-Yisrael, the "Israel Defense Force") at its best. Its members, though individually brave, are better described as a gang than an army. They had no uniforms but imitated the dress worn by their Circassian competitors; were not clearly distinct from the population at large, many of them doubling as agricultural laborers; and of course did not obey a government that was still decades away. Yet they were the first to take the military road not merely as a means to a military end but with the explicit goal of shedding the supposed characteristics of the Wandering Jew, replacing him with a new, hardy, and courageous type who would take up arms in defense of himself, his settlement, and his country. For many decades thereafter, the determination to do so was perhaps the most important factor that made for the success of this and later Jewish armed forces in Erets Yisrael. To coming generations of Israelis it provided a source of inspiration as well as a number of leaders who went on to greater things.

Founding Hagana: group of Hagana commanders in Jerusalem, 1929.

CHAPTER 2

FOUNDING HAGANA

I N PALESTINE DURING the nineteenth century most people identified themselves—and were identified by the government for the purpose of military service, taxation, and the like—by the religion to which they belonged. Hence the early clashes between the Arab and Jewish communities had little to do with nationalism; instead they were due to the prevailing unsettled conditions as well as growing Jewish economic power. Supported by the Zionist organization abroad, that power was already enormous in comparison and quite capable of buying up entire tracts of land with or without the inhabitants' consent; nor were those inhabitants, who overnight turned from "owners" into undesirables, always well treated once the change in ownership had taken place.[1] Another bone of contention was formed by the different social systems that characterized the two peoples. Specifically, this included the much greater freedom granted to Jewish women, who, according to the Arabs, went around half-naked and did not shrink from using their charms to obtain favors from the government.[2]

Arab nationalism did, however, become more important after the Young Turk revolution of 1908 promised modernization and, with it, greater rights to the empire's various peoples. Initially the new government was liberal-minded; it partially lifted censorship and permitted political discourse to be broadened.[3] As part of this awakening an Arab-language press came into being for the first time, and during the last years before World War I it began to characterize Zionism as "an enemy who in the future will usurp them in an area which they believe to be purely Arab."[4] In the port cities of Haifa and Jaffa, the first associations dedicated to combating Zionism were established. Their objectives were to prevent the ongoing sale of Arab-owned lands and persuade the government to put an end to Jewish immigration.[5]

This early nationalism was stimulated by several factors: the collapse of Ottoman rule during World War I; the 1917 Balfour Declaration, in which His Majesty's government promised Dr. Weizman, head of the Zionist organization, to provide a national home for the Jews in Palestine; and the arrival of a third wave of Jewish immigrants in the wake of the Russian Revolution. Above all, however, there was the mandate system, the brainchild of the South African prime minister, Ian Smuts. In this system the League of Nations "mandated" Turkey's former Middle Eastern provinces to Britain and France, thereby enabling those two powers to rule the area. For their part, the Arabs regarded the system as a violation of the promises that the British Foreign Office had given them in 1916–1917 in return for agreeing to rise against their Ottoman overlords.

The upshot was an Arab uprising that shook Palestine, as well as neighboring Syria and Egypt, from the autumn of 1919 on. From Damascus to Cairo there was sporadic violence, rioting in various cities, and, in the countryside, small-scale guerrilla warfare organized and directed by the clans. Particularly in eastern Galilee, a remote area with wide-open borders with the neighboring French-ruled countries of Lebanon and Syria, there were attacks by armed gangs on a number of isolated Jewish settlements that had been set up in the area during World War I. With a combined population of a few hundred people those settlements could barely be reached, let alone protected, by the colonial power.

Of these attacks the best known was against the village of Tel Chai—in reality, barely more than a reinforced compound built of stone—on March 1, 1920. The defense consisted of fifteen men under Yosef Trumpeldor, a dashing, one-armed veteran of the 1905 Russo-Japanese war who also happened to be exceptionally handsome and something of a ladies' man. Tales of the group's heroism in clinging to this remote outpost—once established a Jewish settlement will never be surrendered, as one slogan had it—began circulating even before the main assault. When the attack finally came it brought about the deaths of seven defenders and the evacuation of the settlement. Among those killed was Trumpeldor himself, who supposedly died with the Hebrew equivalent of "sweet and becoming it is, to die for one's country . . ." on his lips.[6] By so doing, he provided the *Yishuv* (pre-1948 Jewish community in Palestine) and the yet-to-be-formed IDF with their first memorable martyr for the cause, inspiring a number of jingles (poems would be too complimentary) that were written in his honor and that children were made to sing even thirty years later.

These disturbances seem to have taken the British by surprise. The huge armies created during the war were already being demobilized as fast as possible, causing shortages of manpower. Palestine at the time was merely a small part of an enormous Middle Eastern empire, most of it newly acquired as a result of the war, that now reached from the Libyan border through Transjordan and Iraq down to Kuwait on the Persian Gulf. Most of the area in question had even fewer roads, railroads, telecommunications, and other modern amenities than Palestine did; then as now, the Jewish presence in the latter was already giving it a comparatively modern character.[7] Overwhelmed by their commitments, the British took the best part of two years to restore order.

From 1919 on members of Ha-shomer as well as other Jews deported by Jamal began drifting back from exile. In Palestine they were joined by newcomers, most of them Russians belonging to a younger generation that had left the country in the wake of the revolution when the borders were still open. The preceding years had enabled members of both groups to gain a modicum of military experience. Of the Jews who now lived in Palestine—including Trumpeldor, Ben Tsvi, and David Ben Gurion—some 5,000 had served in the Jewish battalions the British established on the model of the Czech, Polish, and Finnish legions (although of the four battalions that existed at one time or another, only two had seen any real action during the winter of 1918).[8] Other members of the Jewish community had served either on the eastern front during World War I or in the Russian civil war and Russian-Polish wars that followed it; a few even dated as far back as the Russo-Japanese war. Even so, many of Ha-shomer's veteran members were now married with children to look after. Their wives understandably objected to their resuming a lifestyle that required them to move from one settlement to another as duty called, either by cart or camelback through country that was by no means secure.[9]

This combination of domesticity with greater military experience—as well as the nature of the very loosely coordinated Arab uprising that took place simultaneously throughout the country—called for a new type of military organization. In May 1920 Ha-shomer was formally disbanded. Of its leaders, Chankin resigned himself to the decision and continued with his land-purchasing activities for the Jewish Agency; not so Shochet and his strong-willed wife. Together with a select group of followers they retreated to *kibbuts* Kfar Giladi near Tel Chai in the far north, where they pursued independent arms-collecting activities for years to come. The group's assets, such as they were, were passed on to Hagana, which took its place.

Hagana's first head—commander would be too strong a term—was a twenty-eight-year-old veteran of the Jewish battalions named Yosef Hecht. His outstanding qualities seem to have been obstinacy and an obsession with secretiveness, so much so that he all but removed himself from the pages of history and is not even mentioned in Hagana's *Who Is Who*.[10] Militarily he was neither more nor less experienced than his comrades. He was flanked by a committee of five men plus two "candidate" members on the Soviet communist model. The most important committee members were Eliyahu Golomb, head of the largest section (in Tel Aviv), and Levi Shkol-

nik; the latter subsequently changed his name to Eshkol and served as
Israel's prime minister from 1963 to 1969. Both men were primarily politicians and organizers and only marginally knowledgeable about military
affairs proper, this being a telling comment on the way the *Yishuv* did business then and later.

Unlike its predecessor, Hagana was not an elitist organization but a
popular militia whose ranks were open, at least in principle, to any member of the Jewish community. Also unlike Ha-shomer, it was not a private
association accountable only to itself (although some Ha-shomer leaders
had also been up to their necks in left-wing politics, founding and refound-
ing microparties, all of which used "workers" in their names). Instead it
was born as the result of a deliberate decision to set up a Jewish armed
force that would operate in the service of the community as a whole. As
such it came under the authority of the newly founded National Labor
Federation, or Histadrut Ha-ovdim Ha-leumit.

Then and for decades thereafter, Histadrut was much more than a trade
union. Headed by a secretary general and the Acting Council, both of
which were democratically elected by the membership (women, too, had the
vote from the beginning), it was the closest thing to a government that the
Jewish community in Erets Yisrael possessed. It played the role of a trade
union by representing workers vis-à-vis employers, but it also owned and
ran a range of economic enterprises. Among them were a food-packaging
and -producing plant for the agricultural settlements, a range of light
industries, a construction firm, a road-building firm, truck and bus companies, a bank, retail stores, and the like. In time these assets turned it into the
largest employer in the country—a strange thing to say of any trade union,
especially one that to this day has significant consequences for Israel's economy. Histadrut also ran a huge variety of cultural associations, newspapers,
schools, clinics, sickness and unemployment insurance systems, sports
clubs, and even entire residential areas built by, and for, members.

As in other places where anticolonial resistance movements asserted
themselves, these interlocking organizations were ideal cover for the military arm that during most of its existence remained illegal in the eyes of
the British government—the more so because, although Histadrut did not
constitute a government and did not possess coercive power, its leadership
talked of "the duty of volunteering." In the collective settlements membership started virtually at birth; but even in the towns the social and economic pressure it could bring to bear was usually sufficient to bring
recalcitrant individuals to heel. The means used included publishing their
names, firing them from their jobs, and expelling them from the ranks,
which automatically put an end to any form of social insurance and bene-

fits that they might have accumulated. When all else failed, the use of violence was not excluded.[11]

No sooner had Hagana been founded than it underwent its first test. In May 1921, following the British decision to separate Palestine west of the River Jordan from the area to the east, rioting started in the center of the country between Chadera and Nes Tsiona. The largest single outbreak was in Jaffa, whose inhabitants threatened to storm Tel Aviv, at the time a small "town" of mainly one- and two-story houses numbering fewer than 10,000 people, many of them recent immigrants. There were bloody casualties, including a few dead. The local Hagana organization was not very well prepared: The eight rifles, twenty pistols, and five hand grenades that the local Hagana branch had buried in the dunes to the north (then and later, a place for lovers' trysts) could not be found under the shifting sand. Some three hundred Hagana members, most of them youngsters with little organization and less training, faced the Arabs with sticks in hand.

If the situation had not been serious—the outlying neighborhoods were in danger of being overrun and some of their inhabitants had to be evacuated—it might have been comic. Following three days of skirmishing Tel Aviv was saved by a detachment of Jewish constables whom the British had been training at a camp near Ramla, some fifteen miles away. Alerted by telephone, eighteen men deserted their posts and marched to the sound of the guns. Upon arrival they were issued ancient Turkish rifles by the British official in charge of Jaffa Harbor. Thus armed, they paraded in martial splendor through the streets of Tel Aviv, where inhabitants are said to have cheered madly. Apparently this demonstration of overwhelming force sufficed to drive the Arabs—a mere disorderly mob with even less organization than the Jews—back to the city of Jaffa. It also convinced the British that their Jewish auxiliaries could not be trusted, and they were accordingly dismissed.

Hagana's operations in response to the rioting that took place elsewhere in the country were on an even smaller scale, often no more than five or six men seeking to stop a crowd while armed with pistols with or without ammunition. The last skirmish took place in Jerusalem's Jewish quarter in November 1921, where approximately 5,000 Jews lived and where Hecht, normally based in Haifa but happening to be present, took charge. Five Jews were killed and forty wounded in the narrow alleyways. Though the assailants possessed hardly any firearms, they compensated with edged weapons; eyes were gouged out, breasts and testicles cut off, and the like. Next, however, Hagana asserted itself. Some ten members, armed with pistols and hand grenades, took up positions and managed to hold off an Arab mob for forty minutes until the arrival of the British police.

From that point on, calm was restored. Thanks in part to the moderate policies of the high commissioner, Sir Herbert Samuel,[12] the years between 1922 and 1929 were perhaps the most enjoyable for the British in Palestine and were, from a security point of view, almost absolutely quiet. Jews immigrated at an unprecedented rate, and though the number of those who left was almost equally great, the *Yishuv* managed somehow to increase the Jewish population from 84,000 in 1922 to 175,000 nine years later.[13] The British, fearing they would alienate the Arab population, took few practical steps to implement the Balfour Declaration of November 1917, in which they had promised a "national home" for the Jews in Palestine. On the contrary: In 1921–1922 the territory east of the River Jordan was detached from Palestine, and a new interpretation of the document was published that specifically excluded the possibility of creating an eventual Jewish state. Nevertheless, the community felt it could rest secure in the bosom of a civilized imperial power that delivered peace and, until the onset of a recession in 1927, unprecedented economic prosperity as well.

As the *Yishuv* devoted its resources to building new settlements, the development of Hagana was excruciatingly slow. In theory Hagana was centralized, countrywide, and solely responsible for overseeing the defense of the entire Jewish community. In practice it was a "primitive confederation"[14] between the three main branches, that is, those located in the cities of Jerusalem, Tel Aviv, and Haifa as well as many smaller ones in settlements all over the country. The organization being illegal, communication among its parts was difficult and sometimes dangerous. Hence each of the rural branches was often forced to look after itself in purchasing arms, organizing guards, mounting patrols, and so on. Moreover, the organization's left-wing, socialist ideology was not shared by the entire Jewish community that, then as now, was sharply divided along political lines. This led to the establishment of several rival organizations. Some were so ephemeral that their very existence was barely noted and can be documented only through the memoirs of their few members. Others, though invariably much smaller and less well developed than Hagana (on which they modeled themselves), were destined to prosper.

By the late twenties, the time it was destined to undergo (and, let it be said immediately, fail) its second test, Hagana must have had a few thousand members. In Haifa, for example, there were some three hundred members out of a Jewish population of 16,000; the 16,000 Jews formed about a third of the city's total population. Virtually all were part-timers, and only about half could be supplied with arms of any sort.[15] Training was in the hands of former sergeants and corporals who had served in various World War I armies. It was carried out during the members' free time, normally twice a week, at various secret locations that had to be constantly guarded against discovery. Time was taken up largely with drills and familiarization with weapons as well as intellectual exercises ("What would you do if an Arab came at you up front and two more on the left?"). To acquaint the members with the country, hiking tours were held, perhaps with the odd pistol carried along in great secrecy. In 1925, Hagana even conducted an experimental squad commanders course, totaling around twenty men, in the woods on Mount Carmel near Haifa. That, however, was as far as things went. With a few exceptions—notably Yochanan Ratner, a professor of architecture at Haifa's Technical Institute and a former Russian army officer who later became the first chief of staff (COS)—military experience at any level above enlisted was entirely absent.

Either because Ha-shomer had been driven underground during the war and was incapable of looking after its own—as its leaders said—or because it deliberately hid its best equipment—as its enemies claimed—what arms it did pass on to Hagana were almost useless. Even so, the collapse of the Ottoman empire had resulted, as such events will, in large numbers of weapons being abandoned or sold by the retreating Turkish soldiers. When that source dried up, Hagana members, strapped for cash and taking advantage of the still unsettled conditions, sometimes "exed" (short for expropriated) money from Jewish and other "capitalists," particularly those who were engaged in illegal activities such as smuggling and who could not therefore turn to the authorities for protection.[16] More funds were made available by the various Zionist organizations abroad and used for buying arms in Europe, chiefly Vienna, where arms were cheap. They were packed into suitable containers—the favorites were refrigerators, which could be reassembled and sold upon arrival, and earth-moving equipment—and smuggled into the country by way of Beirut, where French control over the port was relatively lax. From there they were taken overland into Galilee.

The resulting stocks, mostly pistols and rifles but already including the occasional machine gun, were stored in underground chambers, later to be known as *slikkim* (hideaways), all over the country. Given the great variety in types of weapons, getting hold of ammunition represented a problem; attempts were made to manufacture it, though with what success can no longer be established.[17] The largest single *slik* was at Kfar Giladi in the far north, where, as already mentioned, the Shochet family and a number of former Ha-shomer members had made their homes[18]—and where previously unknown caches are being unearthed to the present day. Presumably selected because it was close to the Lebanese border and out of the government's way, eventually it turned out to be equally remote from the places where the arms were needed.

Provided thus with organization and arms, Hagana designated a commander for each town and settlement. Particularly in the smaller places the cadres in question were part-timers, barely distinguishable from the majority of the working population among which they lived. Perhaps in the entire country only a dozen or two were full-time "soldiers"; even many of those were primarily *askanim* (Hebrew for the Russian party activist) who combined their work for Hagana with their political activities. Each commander was responsible for drawing up a defensive plan; selecting the relevant positions to be occupied in case of an emergency; storing and distributing such arms and other kinds of equipment as were to be had; and allocating his men among the positions. Communications between the various positions were to be maintained by means of whistles, flags, flashlights, and messengers selected among high-school students as well as female Hagana members. Under British ground rules the latter were immune to searches and were therefore often used as ambulant *slikkim*. This was a role in which women and their male comrades were inordinately proud. Only a very few women actually fought, and then only in self-defense.

Under British rule the existence of Hagana and many of its activities were, in principle, illegal. Those caught bearing arms without license incurred long jail sentences. Nevertheless the authorities, well aware that their own forces were thinly spread, were prepared to tolerate at least some kind of Jewish self-defense organization. Throughout the twenties repeated discussions were held between the British authorities and Ben Tsvi, who was acting as the chief Hagana representative and whom his interlocutors described as a "perfect Bolshevik." The objective seems to have been to find some way in which the more remote settlements in particular might keep their arms *and* at the same time put them under British control by means of an extended licensing system. Though no formal agreement was reached, the fact that the talks were held at all indicated the British willingness to close an eye to some of Hagana's activities; in Jerusalem, so long as arms were kept out of sight, Hagana was even able to organize maneuvers and hold them openly, right under the government's nose.[19] Then and later, had this not been the case, the organization probably could not have existed.

Such, roughly, was the state of Hagana when the second Arab uprising broke out in 1929. This time it started in Jerusalem, where Jews and Arabs had been bickering over the former's right to pray at the Wailing Wall.[20] The Arab leader was the mufti or chief Muslim priest, Haj Amin al Hussayni, the head of a prominent clan whose members had held the position since the middle of the nineteenth century. From the beginning of the year there were repeated incidents as Jews mounted parades to demonstrate their presence and Arabs tried to stop them by rock-throwing and knifings.

Massive Arab rioting began on August 23 under the usual battle cry *itbach al Yahud* (slaughter the Jews). Thanks to ten years' development under British supervision the country's infrastructure was now much more advanced, to the point that telegraphs were already being replaced by a network of some 3,000 telephones.[21] Though the Arabs, unlike the Jews, did not have any countrywide leadership and were only very loosely coordinated, this network enabled the uprising to spread like wildfire to Jaffa, Haifa, Safed, Tiberias, and numerous smaller places.

Once aroused, the forces of order turned out to consist of 142 British policemen, half of whom were stationed in Jerusalem. The army is said to have had 77 troops, nine armored cars, four pickups, and a handful of patrol aircraft that had been equipped with machine guns for strafing; they were assisted by 169 Jewish and 1,063 Arab policemen.[22] Since both the high commissioner and the chief of police were out of the country on leave, command devolved to their subordinates, lowly majors and captains.

Since the British forces were so small, the task of defending the *Yishuv* during the critical first four days fell almost entirely on Hagana. Individual commanders reacted quickly, taking up positions and attempting to hold them. However, the organization as a whole did not, nor in fairness could it have done so. Seeking to fragment the uprising and to prevent it from spreading, the British authorities promptly suspended all newspapers, halted rail traffic, blocked the main roads, and cut the civilian telephone network (but because most of the operators were Jewish, this last measure was only partially effective and tended to work against the Arabs and in favor of the *Yishuv*).

In Haifa, where Hagana did better than anywhere else, the disturbances started on August 25 and lasted for three days. At the peak, 3,000 Jews were driven from their homes, some of which were looted by rampaging Arab mobs. In the face of this a number of "strategic" positions were occupied and held.[23] On the second day a force of ten men, commanded by one Nachum Levin, actually commandeered a bus, drove it down the slopes of Mount Carmel into the Arab neighborhoods, and opened fire—quite an innovation for the time. Meanwhile a call for help went out to that old warhorse, Shochet's wife, Manya, in Kfar Giladi. Ultimately she was able to bring in reinforcements, including seven men and, much more important, thirty rifles. Some were smuggled in an ambulance; Ms. Shochet went so far as to slice the hands and face of a companion with a razor in order to simulate (if that is the term) a wounded person in need of medical attention. Others were carried in the back of a Buick specially modified for the purpose.[24] By that time, though, the riots had already subsided.

Elsewhere things went less well for Hagana. The worst outbreak took place in Hebron, where the ancient, strongly orthodox Jewish population trusted in their neighborly relations with the Arabs and where no self-defense organization existed at all. On August 24 an Arab mob broke in and massacred sixty-five people with clubs, agricultural implements, and knives. The remaining 300 or so escaped (from then until the years after 1967 no more Jews lived in the city). Smaller massacres, accompanied by looting and burning, took place in Safed and in the village of Motsa near Mount Kastel to the west of Jerusalem. A car was sent from Jerusalem, and its occupants succeeded in extricating the remaining inhabitants; next the settlement was abandoned, plundered by the Arabs, and set on fire (as were a number of other settlements throughout the country, including Mishmar Ha-emek and En-Zetim in the north, Ramat Rachel near Jerusalem, Chulda near Ramla, and Beer Tuvia in Philistia). According to Hagana history, in Beer Tuvia the women were begging to be poisoned when three British aircraft appeared and saved the situation.[25]

In Tel Aviv, at that time a more sizable town with a population of about 50,000, some 230 Hagana members immediately obeyed orders and presented themselves. The men were issued what arms were to be had—rifles, pistols, and a couple of light machine guns—and sent out to occupy positions in the various neighborhoods. There they were joined by small groups of vigilantes, often consisting of citizens who had served in the Jewish battalions or else of high-school students. Some brought along their own unregistered and unlicensed pistols, whereas others came with homemade swords, axes, and the like. The two "armies" faced each other across the agricultural space then separating Tel Aviv from Jaffa. From time to time a British armored car would appear on the scene, firing into the air and causing both Jews and Arabs to run for cover before it moved somewhere else. Later these patrols became more frequent, putting a cap on the disturbances, which became increasingly limited to potshots.

In fact the British, even though taken by surprise and requiring time to get organized, reacted credibly enough. On the afternoon of August 27 the first reinforcements in the form of 400 Royal Marines aboard the warship *Barham* reached Haifa from Malta; their arrival sufficed to overawe the city, which quickly began returning to normal. Elsewhere, too, the appearance of disciplined British units, even those with few troops, was usually enough to disperse the crowds. At the end of six days 133 Jews and 116 Arabs had been killed, 339 and 232 wounded; whereas almost all Jewish casualties were caused by Arab rioting and sniping, most Arab casualties were inflicted by organized units of British and British-commanded troops. Order in the towns was quickly restored, although operations aimed at suppressing small-scale guerrilla activity in the countryside took much longer and were ongoing six months later. Eventually some 1,300 people were put on trial, most of them Arabs but including a few Jews as well. Twenty-six Arabs and three Jews were sentenced to death, but most of the sentences were later commuted; three Arabs actually hanged.

The events of 1929 were to prove a turning point in the history of Hagana and, with it, of the yet to be born Israeli Defense Force. Speaking in public, the *Yishuv*'s leaders, many of whom were conveniently out of the country at the time the troubles broke out, were ecstatic about the heroism displayed by their fellow citizens; thus, Ben Gurion as chairman of Histadrut claimed that Hagana "had saved our people from destruction" and demanded that it be "further fortified." In private, however, they were much less laudatory, savaging it for failing to protect Hebron and Safed in particular. Organization, training, armaments, and readiness all came under critical fire—by the same politicians, needless to say, who throughout the twenties had starved Hagana of funds.

After two years of ugly squabbling, including a minor "commanders' revolt," these criticisms finally led to Hecht's forced resignation (although in practice without real authority, as the organization's titular head he was the natural scapegoat; at the same time, paradoxically, he was blamed for trying to do too much on his own without consulting the rest). Control of Hagana passed from the Histadrut to the Zionist executive as the highest directing body both of the Jewish Agency and of world Zionism. From 1935 on, the head of both bodies was David Ben Gurion, who thus assumed overall responsibility for the community's political and military fortunes. Day-to-day control was exercised by a five-man committee; two members represented Histadrut, two the towns, and one the collective settlements. The guiding spirit remained Eliyahu Golomb, the archtypical party activist who had thus rid himself of his principal rival. Yet however modest Hecht's achievements, his term of office marked the real foundation of the first Jewish armed force to serve the Jewish people in nearly two thousand years.

"Beyond the Fence": Hagana detachment searching Arab marauder, 1938.

CHAPTER 3

"Beyond the Fence"

For Britain the events in Palestine, a small province that straddled British communications between the Suez Canal and their much more important holdings in Iraq, acted as a warning. The number of troops stationed in the country was increased to two battalions; additional British policemen were also recruited until their number reached 744 in 1935, in addition to 1,452 Arab and 282 Jewish auxiliary police. New roads were built, particularly one linking Acre with Safed that for the first time opened western Galilee, heretofore an area crossed only by goats, to the movements of modern armed forces. A professional police officer named Herbert Dowbigin was brought in from Ceylon to investigate and submitted a new plan for policing the country.[1]

These and other measures notwithstanding, the British were aware that they could not be everywhere at once. They therefore once again engaged Hagana in talks to see how the *Yishuv* might be made to do more in its own defense without, of course, endangering imperial rule. Various plans were discussed but, in the end, came to very little. The only measure actually taken was to distribute 585 rifles, each with 50 rounds, to various Jewish settlements throughout the country; considering that there were already well in excess of a hundred settlements, this didn't amount to much. The rifles and rounds were contained in sealed boxes and, to make sure they were still there, inspected by British officers who came by once a year. The idea was that they should be used only in an emergency.

Thus left to its own devices, Hagana set out to rebuild and expand its forces. Galvanized into action by the riot emergency, Zionist organizations abroad launched a fund drive. By the end of 1929 they had collected 800,000 Palestinian pounds, equivalent to the same sum in British pounds and to five times that sum in U.S. dollars (and this at a time when the average annual income of an Arab peasant family stood at 27 pounds).[2] The money was well spent. Destroyed settlements were rebuilt and others fortified by adding patrol roads, fences, searchlights, shelters, and the like. Attempts were made to analyze the lessons of the recent events including, in particular, the need for better training, an efficient intelligence organization, and improved communications between Hagana headquarters and the settlements and among the settlements themselves.

While the rest of the world was caught in the Great Depression, for the Jewish community in Palestine the early thirties were once again years of unprecedented economic and demographic growth. In 1924 the United States had imposed its immigration law, effectively closing the most important country in which Jews had been settling since the late nineteenth century. The shadow of national socialism was darkening Europe, and hundreds of thousands were leaving. Between 1931 and 1936 the Jewish population in Palestine grew from 175,000 to 400,000. Not only were the newcomers better educated and wealthier than their predecessors, but most of them were younger, with the result that the proportion of males of military age (fifteen to forty-nine) was actually larger than that among the Arabs.3 Eighty percent of the immigrants went to the three large towns of Haifa, Jerusalem, and especially Tel Aviv, which tripled its population to 150,000 and thus accounted for 40 percent of the total population.4 Outlying areas also benefited. Between 1920 and 1937 an additional 683,000 *dunam* of land passed into Jewish hands. Consequently all Jewish holdings combined now amounted to 1.33 million *dunam*, approximately 5 percent of the total area west of the River Jordan and perhaps 8 percent of the area that eventually would become the state of Israel.5

In 1931, after a two-year hiatus, Hagana once more received a titular head in the person of Saul Avigur (originally Meirov). Russian-born like the rest, thirty-two years old at the time, he had been raised in Tel Aviv and gained his spurs by helping guard various northern settlements during the twenties as well as smuggling arms from Syria and Lebanon. He set up his headquarters in Room 33 of Histadrut's main building on Allenby Street, Tel Aviv, a handy arrangement for communicating with other activists and for avoiding prying Britons. A list of members and an inventory of available resources were drawn up. It brought to light an incredible assortment of arms, many of them antiquated or in bad repair, with or without ammunition to match. Though regularly updated thereafter, the inventory even under the best circumstances was by no means complete. Many settlements concealed their assets not only from the British but also from their superiors in Hagana.6 This was not a surprising reaction, given Hagana's recently demonstrated inability to move resources around the country or provide aid in an emergency.

The tendency to conceal arms reflected a deeper dilemma already familiar from Ha-shomer days, namely, whether Hagana was to be a countrywide, centralized, and disciplined organization under a single command or merely a loose coalition between local self-defense groups, each of which looked after the needs of its own settlement or town. Avigur, needless to say, stood for the former interpretation. In 1934 he drafted a document known as "The Foundations of Defense" (*Oshiot Ha-hagana*). In it he emphasized that Hagana was the sole organization responsible for Jewish self-defense as well as the need to combat any attempt to set up alternative groups. It was to be run along military lines, with a recognized chain of command, bottom-to-top accountability, and strict discipline.[7]

However sensible these demands might be in theory, in practice they could not be realized. Not being a government in the formal sense of the word, the Zionist Agency did not have the authority to prevent other groups from organizing themselves; nor was the imposition of strict military discipline practicable under the prevailing conditions, in which the organization was semilegal at best. The root of the problem went deeper. Most of the leaders of Hagana and the *Yishuv* originated from eastern Europe, where they had lived under czarist rule. Jews traditionally regarded military service, indeed any kind of laws—enacted by governments usually bent on persecuting them—as things to be evaded by every possible means. Coming to Palestine, they took these qualities along; it is said that no recruits were ever as undisciplined as the volunteers for the Jewish battalions in 1917–1918.[8] The tendency to play games with the law worked at crosscurrents with a penchant for self-help (made all the more necessary by Hagana's lack of funds and the settlements' isolation with an almost total lack of telecommunications in the countryside).

These factors created a unique military lifestyle that, whatever the manuals might say, always combined a spirit of high enterprise with rather lax discipline. A typical example was Moshe Dayan—who during his lifetime was revered partly for that very reason. Born in 1915, he was a natural warrior possessed of exceptional courage under fire, a certain peasant cunning, and many excellent ideas about how to outwit and beat the enemy. However, he and his comrades-in-arms were also quite prepared to fill their stomachs by breaking into chicken coops belonging to the neighboring *kibbutsim*;[9] indeed, "a tendency to disregard questions of law and order"[10] was said to be characteristic of Hagana commanders down to the 1948 war and beyond. So long as motivation remained strong, as it was bound to be at a time when first the Palestinian Arabs and later the much larger and more populous Arab states constituted a mortal threat to the community's very existence, this combination of qualities proved irresistible. Still, in principle one could foresee the day when, as the intensity of the threat and with it motivation diminished, it would become positively dangerous.

During 1930–1935, though, such a situation was still very far in the future. Under its new leader, Hagana's overriding purpose was to obtain additional arms. Agents were sent to Belgium, France, and Italy, the former two because controls were lax and the last because the fascist government was often prepared to overlook Jewish activities that it judged to be anti-British. (In 1935–1937 the port of La Spezia even hosted the first-ever course for naval personnel to be held by Hagana.) Arms and ammunition were purchased and packed into crates and suitcases as if forming part of the baggage of new immigrants; others were stored in barrels marked "cement." Shipped to Jaffa and later to the new port at Haifa, they were smuggled through customs by Jewish officials who cooperated and by Arab ones who were bribed. From time to time there was a leak, either an accidental one as a case hit the floor and broke or when somebody noticed and told. The resulting interruptions were, however, seldom serious and did not halt the flow for long.

All of the arms in question required maintenance. Others were in need of repair, and for others still no ammunition was available. These problems led to the first attempts to set up an independent arms industry, in reality little more than carefully concealed underground rooms where a handful—originally fewer than ten—of technically gifted men spent hours tinkering around and improvising solutions. Primitive hand grenades, bombs, and similar devices were also produced and tried out during the hikes that Hagana kept organizing for members. For example, by 1935 more than a hundred grenades were being manufactured per day—first under primitive conditions in outlying settlements, then in a more comfortable if well-concealed workshop in Tel Aviv. The arms thus produced or purchased had to be transported and stored in the *slikkim*, all under the nose of the British Central Intelligence Division (CID). The latter had a good general idea of what was going on but was unable to put an end to Hagana's activities; in such a situation specific intelligence is everything, and specific intelligence was rarely forthcoming.

Meanwhile training and organization proceeded along lines already familiar since the 1920s. Hagana members—in Tel Aviv alone they now numbered around a thousand—continued to devote Saturday mornings and one evening a week. According to surviving accounts these were highly formal occasions; lacking real coercive authority, commanders sought to substitute by means of parades, salutes, and a show of secrecy that had as much to do with self-esteem as with the need to keep the British at bay.[11] With the aid of foreign military manuals, a training course of 120 hours was devised. It included, besides drill—which accounted for one-quarter of the total— fieldcraft, minor tactics, weapons handling, and, by way of a supreme achievement, firing perhaps ten to fifteen rounds of ammunition each. Exercises were held with the aim of trying out covert approaches to outlying settlements that might require help in an emergency. In these "maneuvers," no arms could be carried openly (yet a few were secretly carried as a precaution against the ever-present threat of marauders). So the burden of carrying a machine gun, for example, would be simulated by five bricks; enemy shots were simulated by the blowing of whistles, whereupon the men were supposed to take cover or disperse or assault the "enemy" as appropriate.

Taking office, Avigur had brought with him a one-man team of accountants, who soon put order into Hagana's funds, previously a weak point due to prevailing collectivist ideas making little distinction between the organization's property and that of individual members. Regular if extremely limited funding—all salaries combined amounted only to some 2,500 British pounds a year—in turn permitted the establishment of a medical department, a legal department, an intelligence service, and a counterintelligence service (known as Sherut Zehirut, literally "Prudence Service"). In all these activities the Tel Aviv branch, incomparably larger and possessing greater financial means than the rest, took the lead. Others followed, with or without guidance from general headquarters.

Hagana's plans in regard to the future also showed some progress compared to the pre-1929 years. In the cities and the rural settlements the most important task remained the preparation of blocking positions that would be occupied in case Arab mobs emerged from their residential areas and tried to storm Jewish neighborhoods and settlements. During the early thirties a handful of so-called *nodedot* (patrols, literally wanderers) were set up.[12] A typical *nodedet* consisted of perhaps a dozen men—the few surviving sources do not mention any women. With or without orders from general headquarters, they met every week to practice such activities as patrolling, minor tactics, river crossings, and the like. In Tel Aviv some of the members of the local *nodedet* even brought along private cars and motorcycles. As a result, the unit was considered highly mobile by the standards of the day.

Throughout these years the *Yishuv* and its leaders failed to understand, or perhaps merely pretended not to understand,[13] the intense hatred that their growing presence in the country seemed to inspire among the Arab population. Writing *Altneuland*, a utopian novel that contains a description of the future Jewish community in the land of Israel, Theodor Herzl addressed the question by introducing a sympathetic Arab character named Rashid Bey. No, Rashid explained to his newly arrived Jewish friends as he showed them around in his luxurious touring car, he did not mind more of them coming in. On the contrary, was not the arrival of immigrants from Europe precisely the factor that in a mere twenty years had turned the country from a neglected backwater into a bustling center of trade and industry? As to social differences between the two peoples, no problem either. Rashid's "happy and contented" wife, Fatma, did not mind remaining at home, and all the party got to see of her was "a lovely feminine hand" waving a handkerchief.[14]

So long as Ottoman rule lasted, and clashes with the Arabs were localized, it was possible to dismiss Arab resentment as occasioned by social and economic factors only. But the countrywide disturbances of 1919–1921 made it necessary to look for a new explanation. Some sought it in anti-Semitism, arguing that the "events" were merely local variations of the pogroms familiar in their native countries, with the British taking the place of the czar in refusing to protect Jews.[15] Others thought that the Arab masses were being deliberately incited by their "feudal" masters, that is, the heads of clans, rich landowners, and "capitalists" who feared less their inferiors would become infected by the Jewish socialist community arising in front of their eyes.[16] Blame was also placed on fanatical religious leaders out to conserve Islam's traditional ways while consolidating their own positions.

In this context, it should not be overlooked that many of *Yishuv's* left-wing leaders were left-wing intellectuals, past masters in using history in order to bolster their theories and adapt them to shifting reality. The one possibility that most of them did not dare contemplate: that Arabs understood Zionism only too well; in other words, Arab resistance to the movement, far from being a by-product of some conspiracy or terrible misunderstanding that could be taken care of, was merely a mirror image of their own attempt to take over a country from its long-established inhabitants. To admit that the two sides were similar would be tantamount to saying that both of their causes (or none) were, objectively speaking, equally just. Better to close one's eyes and go on with the self-imposed task of "building our country in the teeth of all those who seek to destroy us," as the lyrics to one popular song went.

Not that closing one's eyes was easy during those years. Even at its best, Palestine under British rule remained a mildly violent country with occasional attempts at cattle rustling, attacks on isolated individuals, ambushes of cars driving on deserted roads, and the like. For example, on April 5, 1931, three members of Yagur, a *kibbuts* not far from Haifa, were waylaid and murdered. Similar attacks took place on January 16, March 5, May 1, and December 22, 1932. Some of the assailants were hunted down and put on trial, others not (and no wonder, given that the Palestine police was itself made up of Arabs who formed an absolute majority among the personnel). In October 1933, Jaffa and Nablus even witnessed small-scale repetitions of the events of 1929, except that this time the British authorities were ready and put down the disturbances at the cost of several dozen Arab dead. In

November 1935, British forces hunted down and killed Sheik Izz a-Din al Kassam, a Haifa schoolteacher-turned-terrorist who, some fifty years later, was destined to become the patron saint of the Hamas fundamentalist organization.[17] All these clashes took place against a continuous background of smaller incidents as members of both communities sought to prevent the other from plowing land, uprooted or burned citrus trees, blocked wells, destroyed agricultural equipment, and the like.

Sunday, April 19, 1936, was an ordinary working day, what with the Muslim weekly holiday falling on the previous Friday and the Jewish one on Saturday. Signs of rising tension had been multiplying for some time as both sides attacked individuals belonging to the other. Nevertheless Jewish workers, many of them employed in the port, went to Jaffa as they always did. Just what happened next has never been thoroughly investigated.[18] Apparently there was a rumor that Jews had killed a woman and three *Choranis* (laborers originating in the Choran, a district of Syria), who, as usual, were clustering around the port in search of work. Rioting started, and by the end of the day sixteen Jews had been killed and dozens wounded; some of the corpses were so mangled they could not be identified. Six Arabs had also been killed, all of them by police.[19] As news of the riots spread, Palestinian Arab leaders met in Nablus. On April 25 they set up their first countrywide leadership in the form of a ten-member Supreme Arab Committee. Its president was Amin al Hussayni, whom we have already met.

On May 15 the committee declared a general strike among the Arab community. It was to last for 172 days and serve as the background for many terrorist attacks. Throughout the country, roads were blocked, railroads cut, agricultural workers waylaid, and urban targets attacked with rocks, knives, firearms, and homemade bombs; British police stations were also targeted. Fauzi al-Kauji, an Iraqi officer of Syrian descent, was invited by the committee to take charge. He brought along three companies—approximately 200 men made up of Iraqi, Syrian, and Druze volunteers; once in Palestine he set up a fourth company of locals. Lacking any logistic organization, they installed themselves in the villages of Samaria, whose inhabitants were made to feed the warriors and provide additional arms—whether they wanted to or not, it should be added. From there they attacked British convoys making way toward Nablus and other cities.[20]

These were the days before the British army, and the armies of other imperialist countries, had learned that their roles were to proceed from one defeat to the next. Over the next few months some 20,000 British troops were dispatched to Palestine and took charge. They returned fire, blew up the houses of suspected terrorists, and, aided by spotter aircraft, systematically hunted down rebel gangs in their mountain hideouts. By October 1936 hundreds of Arabs must have been killed; among the Jews there were 80 killed and 400 wounded.[21] Militarily and economically the Arab Palestinians were at the end of their tether. "At the request of the Arab Kings"—there were three at the time—the Supreme Arab Committee met and called off the strike. Kauji and most of his men were able to withdraw to the Jordan and leave the country unmolested, though whether this was part of some secret deal is unknown.

The lull, however, proved temporary. In September 1937 the British governor of Galilee was murdered. The authorities took the occasion to arrest 300 leading Arabs, including Amin Hussayni (who escaped and was able to leave the country). This signaled renewed troubles. By spring 1938 the number of Arab guerrillas was estimated at 15,000. Of those, perhaps 10 percent moved about in small "strike forces" while the rest remained in their villages and joined the fighting as the occasion called.[22] Against them were arrayed British forces complete with armored cars, artillery, and aircraft. The climax came in March 1938, when 2,000 troops commanded by Gen. Archibald Wavell—destined to become British commander in chief of the Middle East—fought a regular battle in the hills around Jenin. From this time on, order was gradually restored as the British systematically hunted down their enemies. After April 1939, when the British succeeded in killing "Supreme Commander" Abd Al Rachim Al Haj Muhamad, the uprising gradually collapsed; individual acts of terrorism were still occurring when World War II broke out in September 1939.

Contrary to the situation in 1929, these events did not catch Hagana off-guard. Forewarned by its intelligence service, the Tel Aviv branch had acted swiftly, sending members to take up blocking positions to the north of Jaffa all the way from the beach, which was fenced off, to the east. Similar measures were taken in other cities; as a result, only in Jerusalem was it necessary to evacuate the Jewish quarter until the construction of a new police station permitted evacuees to return. Meanwhile in the countryside the preceding seven years had been used to provide the settlements with underground bunkers, barbed-wire fences, searchlights, and internal and external communications in the form of buzzers, signaling lamps, and the like—all paid for by an unofficial taxation system known as *kofer ha-yishuv* (the *Yishuv*'s ransom). In 1938 it covered about 70 percent of Hagana's operating expenses[23]—this at a time when the Arab High Council was barely able to pay for its telephone bills. As a result, when the attacks came, not one *kibbuts*, *moshav*, or *moshava* had to be evacuated.

Faced with the common enemy, Hagana and the British authorities drew closer than ever.[24] As many as 3,000 Jews, selected from a list of "reliable" personnel submitted by the Jewish Agency, were taken into the newly established Supplementary Police. With their pay of 3 pounds a month provided partly by the government, partly by Hagana, the *notrim* or *gafirim*, as they were variously known, were issued arms and uniforms. They were trained by British personnel and dispatched to mount guard wherever needed—including roads, railroads, ports, and airports. Not content with this, the British also sought to make use of the remaining Hagana forces. The country was divided into ten regional commands, each under the authority of an army officer. Supported by a Jewish Agency representative, in an emergency he had the authority to call up the local Hagana members. In time, almost the entire Hagana was incorporated into the so-called Jewish Settlement Police and was thus presented with an invaluable opportunity to carry arms openly and receive professional training.

The most important innovations between 1936 and 1939 were, however, tactical. In the days of Ha-shomer, Jewish Guards had often engaged in offensive operations, hot pursuit, and the like. In 1919–1921, as in 1929, such operations had been few and far between; but with the British now supporting Hagana or at least prepared to close an eye to Hagana activities, things changed. Already in 1936 the *nodedot*, now operating openly and in uniform, started mounting patrols in the hills around Jerusalem—no mean feat, given that the standard Jewish reaction to Arab rioting heretofore had been to take shelter. By 1938 the *nodedot* totaled some 400 men, divided into sixty squads. Many squads came complete with a pickup truck—some even covered by bullet-proof plating—and a light machine gun. According to the fashion of the time, this was immediately translated into the lyrics of a popular song, "the *tender* [i.e., pickup truck] drives along."

In the autumn of 1936 there arrived in Palestine a British officer named Orde Wingate. Wingate at that time was thirty-three years old. The son of an officer who had been known as "the Terror of the Sudan," he had gained his spurs (and learned Arabic) while serving in that country from 1928 to 1933; in addition he was a student of the Bible and something of a mystic who believed that Zionism had been preordained by God. Quickly earning a reputation for being a friend to the *Yishuv*, he met with its leaders, including Chayim Weizman, David Ben Gurion, and Eliyahu Golomb. In the autumn of 1937 he persuaded his superiors to allow him to study the modus operandi of the Arab gangs, and in June 1938 he submitted his report, "Ways of Making His Majesty's Forces Operate at Night with the Objective of Putting an End to the Terror in Northern Palestine."

Forty British infantrymen and four trucks were put at Wingate's disposal. He also received permission to recruit seventy-five Jewish *notrim* (the list, as usual, was provided by Hagana). He organized both groups into

Special Night Squads (SNS). After a short period of organization and training the SNS started operating in July 1938, patrolling the oil pipeline between Iraq and Haifa and launching attacks on Arab villages suspected of harboring terrorists. In the first month alone they allegedly killed sixty terrorists; Wingate himself was wounded, then recovered and went back into action with his men. With interruptions, his activities lasted until May 1939, when his intimacy with the *Yishuv*'s leaders excited his superiors' ire and he was transferred out of the country.

Much later, Wingate's contribution to the nascent Jewish army was summed up by David Ben Gurion. According to him, "The Hagana's best officers [including Moshe Dayan] were trained in the Special Night Squads, and Wingate's doctrines were taken over by the Israel Defense Force."[25] Those doctrines included a preference for night action as best suitable for the belligerent whose firepower was weak; a heavy emphasis on good reconnaissance and intelligence, in turn based on an intimate familiarity with the countryside and the relevant languages; longish approach marches (as much as twenty to thirty miles in a single night) intended to take the enemy by surprise; a variety of tricks, such as raising a ruckus at one point and attacking at another, meant to confuse the enemy and put him off-balance; and finally the short, sharp attack delivered with all the firepower that the available troops could muster.[26]

Wingate's departure did not mark the end of Hagana's attempts to set up a mobile strike force. In the winter of 1937–1938 it decided to establish the Plugot Sadeh or "Field Companies" (FOSH). Some experience was already available in the form of the *nodedot*, which were going out on the initiative of local commanders; but now it was a question of fusing them into a unified strike force with a central headquarters and regional branches. The FOSH commander was Yitschak Sadeh. A Russian like the rest, Sadeh, according to his own subsequent and not always consistent accounts, seems to have spent the years 1914–1919 successively fighting for the czar, serving in the St. Petersburg police, and doing hatchet jobs for various White and Red organizations. Later he joined a group that was led by Trumpeldor (like his master he was a ladies' man and sufficiently handsome to pose as a Greek god) and left for Erets Yisrael, where he arrived in 1922. There he had joined Hagana as a "candidate" member of its Directing Committee. However, it was only during the events of 1936–1939 that this burly man, who was unable to earn a decent living, began to make his mark.[27]

A hopeless administrator, Sadeh was a born leader. He and his fellow organizers were able to assemble around 300 men, divide them into six regionally based companies, and give them a short period of training before going into action in the summer of 1938. Unlike those of the SNS, their operations were semilegal and merely tolerated by the British; tactically, however, they were very similar. Small units—rarely more than a platoon at a time, armed with rifles and grenades and perhaps a light machine gun—set up ambushes and mounted patrols in areas reaching from the Lebanese border in the north to the outskirts of Tel Aviv in the south. Their stated objective was to intercept marauders before they could reach the Jewish settlements; occasionally they also attacked the terrorists' bases and places of refuge, a great innovation for those days. To overcome the natural squeamishness of new recruits, care was taken to expose them to enemy dead.[28] It did not amount to much, and yet some of the IDF's most senior future commanders—including, besides Moshe Dayan, Yigael Yadin and Yigal Allon—gained their initial military experience by passing through Sadeh's organization.

By the summer of 1939 the uprising was subsiding as attacks by large gangs almost ceased and those by smaller ones became increasingly rare. This was one of the last times when an armed force belonging to a "developed" country booked a real success in what, much later, was to become known as low-intensity conflict (LIC); hence the methods used by the British and their Jewish allies are worth studying in a little more detail. Perhaps the single most important step was the erection of a fence that separated Palestine from Lebanon to the north, thus cutting off reinforcements and the flow of arms. Next, as already mentioned, there were aggressive patrolling and ambushes as well as extensive use of troops to guard sensitive spots. All this required good intelligence, often acquired by unconventional methods—as when Wingate lined up prisoners and executed one out of every ten to make the others talk. From time to time there were also acts of spectacular brutality, as when British troops, seeking to improve access and open up fields of fire, blew up much of the ancient city of Jaffa.[29]

In retrospect, nevertheless, one suspects that the real causes behind the demise of the uprising were not so much military as political and psychological. The question as to how the promises contained in the Balfour Declaration could be reconciled with the rights of Palestine's Arab population had preoccupied the British from the beginning of the mandate. Various schemes had been floated, including one that provided for the partition of the country (the Peel Committee's Report of 1937). Now, pressed to the wall, they produced the White Paper of May 1939; in it any intent of setting up a Jewish state was flatly denied. Jewish rights to purchase land were limited to 5 percent of the total area, mainly in the Plain of Sharon and around Haifa. Immigration was restricted to 15,000 a year for the next five years, when it would stop. Last but not least, the Palestinian Arab community was promised "evolution toward independence" at the end of ten years.

With World War II and the Holocaust just around the corner, from the Jewish point of view the White Paper could not have come at a worse time, and indeed they lost no time in denouncing it. Palestinian Arabs, claiming a victory over their Jewish opponents, gave in to exhaustion and laid down their arms for the time being. When war did break out, it was soon followed by the arrival of tens of thousands of British and Commonwealth troops from Australia, New Zealand, India, and South Africa. The military buildup increased the amount of manpower available for security purposes many times over. Perhaps more important, it also ushered in another period of exceptional economic prosperity. As imperial spending increased by a factor of three or four,[30] a whole series of new industries was founded to supply the British forces with everything from food to medicines to water bottles. Both Arabs and Jews, but particularly the latter, exploited the situation by alternately working for the British and stealing from them—which they seem to have done on a truly heroic scale.

Meanwhile FOSH, like Ha-shomer before it, was disbanded. A mantle of secrecy surrounds these events; Hagana headquarters ordered all FOSH papers to be destroyed.[31] Possibly the decision was due to the desire of local Hagana commanders to repossess their best men. Possibly, too, Ben Gurion, Golomb, and the rest did not reconcile themselves to the existence of a unified strike force wholly devoted to its charismatic commander, over whom they had no effective control.[32] Neither explanation is entirely convincing, the more so since such suspicions as may have existed evidently did not apply to Sadeh himself. As most of his men went home, he was put in charge of a new unit known as POUM (Plugot Meyuchadot or "Special Companies"). Operating covertly and on a much smaller scale than their predecessors, they represented a police organization, an intelligence service, a counterintelligence service, and a special operations command all rolled into one.

Missions entrusted to the unit and its handful of men—as usual, women, among them Sadeh's lover, Margot, were given auxiliary tasks such as maintaining communications, smuggling arms, photographing targets, and the like—included hunting down individual Arab terrorists, executing Jewish informers, and attacking British patrol boats that stood in the way of ships carrying illegal immigrants.[33] They also coordinated the voyages of those very ships; one of them, *Patria*, arrived at Haifa only to have Sadeh's men sabotage it with considerable loss of life in order to prevent the British from sending its passengers to Mauritius.[34] Finally, the anti-British character of some of Sadeh's operations did not prevent him from cooperating with the British in mounting raids against Axis targets throughout the eastern Mediterranean and as far away as Ploesti, Romania. Some of his men went on to build Mossad, Israel's answer to the U.S. Central Intelligence Agency (CIA). Others took part in the construction of Hagana's budding arms industry, whereas at least one, Chayim Laskov, rose to become IDF chief of staff.

In the summer of 1939 a party of forty-three members, including Moshe Dayan,[35] was caught under arms while taking part in an exercise at Yavniel, near Tiberias. They were arrested, tried, and sentenced to ten years in prison; more searches, arrests, and trials followed, all resulting in sentences much heavier than those meted out during the previous three years.[36] The British were no longer prepared to close an eye to Hagana's activities; any idea that Zionism could achieve its objectives by peaceful means had to be abandoned, and from this point on it was entertained only by a few academics. The publication of the White Paper hastened the decline of so-called political Zionism, which hoped to achieve those objectives with British aid and was represented principally during the previous two decades by Chayim Weizman. Its place has now been taken by a more "activist" line represented by Ben Gurion as leader of the *Yishuv*. Not accidentally, his favorite attire was not the evening dress of British aristocrats but plain khaki.

As to Hagana itself, it had passed out of infancy and into childhood. In 1937 the five-man political caucus that had run the organization was disbanded. Yochanan Ratner, the Haifa architecture professor, was appointed as the first *rosh mifkada artsit* (chief of country headquarters, his official title). Two years later he was replaced by Moshe Sneh, an urbane physician who was to hold the post until 1946 and who much later became head of Israel's Communist Party. An ex officio member of the Jewish Agency Executive, the *rosh mifkada* had under him a *rosh mateh klali* (chief of the general staff). The latter in turn consisted of a planning division, a training division, a technical division, and an intelligence division.[37] The organization was anything but perfect; in particular, a manpower division and a logistics division were still absent. Yet it was light years in advance of anything possessed by the Palestinians, who were still acting exclusively in locally based bands. Funded partly by the Jewish Agency and partly by Histadrut, Hagana now had perhaps 200–300 persons—almost all male—working for it full-time; they included, besides the leadership and Sadeh's men, technicians who manufactured arms, "quartermasters" in charge of the *slikkim*, and fund-raising and weapons-purchasing agents in various countries. Membership had grown to 15,000. Not counting the arms carried by the *notrim*, it could boast 6,000 rifles, 1 million rounds of ammunition, 600 light machine guns and submachine guns, 24,000 hand grenades, and 12,000 rifle grenades.[38] With or without the authorities' permission, Hagana had been able to hold regular training courses for thousands of personnel of different kinds, including recruits, squad commanders, sergeants, signal men, and paramedics. Whether in action with SNS or FOSH, some units had now been bloodied in action. Among its field commanders, a few had now reached the point where they were capable of leading a platoon in defensive and offensive operations against the enemy. With his keen eye for personnel, Sadeh in particular had already identified some individuals destined to go on to much greater things. For all that, however, the story of the IDF had barely begun.

CHAPTER 4

TOWARD STATEHOOD

T HE SPRING OF 1940 was a dark period for the British war effort. Beginning on May 10, 1940, the Germans attacked in the west. By the end of the month Dunkirk was being evacuated, and on June 10, Italy, whose Mediterranean possessions at the time reached as far east as the Dodecanese, entered the conflict. In September 1940 the Italian army invaded Egypt from Libya, driving some sixty miles before halting at Sidi Barrani. These events were followed by the British advance to Tripoli in the winter of 1940–1941; the dispatch of a German corps to Libya in February 1941; the launching of a German counterattack that, in May and June, seemed about to drive the British from Egypt; and the abortive Greek campaign that ended with Axis occupation not only of the Greek mainland but of Crete as well. As a result, during late spring 1941 it appeared as if the British position in the Middle East was being threatened by a pincer movement coming from the south and north.

Thus pressed, the British once again became willing to accept whatever Hagana had to offer—indeed it might almost be said that whenever there was trouble His Majesty's government in Palestine turned to the Jews, only to bite the hand offered in friendship when the danger had passed. As already mentioned, Sadeh as commander of POUM (the special companies) had been providing the British with personnel—some of whom were German- or Arab-speaking—for carrying out commando raids against Axis targets. The largest of these was launched on May 18, when twenty-three men took to the sea in a boat with the objective of reaching the Vichy French–owned oil refineries in Tripoli, Lebanon, and sabotaging them. This operation was a complete failure as the boat, along with its crew, disappeared without a trace—possibly because some of the training had been carried out around Haifa Harbor, which was swarming with spies.[1] Refusing to be discouraged, Sadeh again sent his best men when the British set out to conquer Lebanon and Syria from the French early the next month. Thirty-five Jewish guides went ahead of Australian troops, their mission being to cut telephone wires, occupy bridges, and so on. The best known

Toward Statehood: the wreckage of a bridge that was blown up by PALMACH, 1946.

among them was Moshe Dayan, who along with his comrades had been released from jail and who lost an eye in the operation.[2]

These operations, though, only represented the cutting edge of a much greater organizational effort. In summer 1940, Hagana's leaders met to start planning for the establishment of a regular Jewish force that would attempt to fight and delay an eventual Axis invader. Some nine months later preparations went into high gear. As usual, the greatest obstacle was financial; not being a state, the *Yishuv* did not yet have a regular taxation system at its disposal, and voluntary contributions were insufficient. It was surmounted by means of an extraordinary arrangement between Hagana and the *kibbuts* movement. In return for two weeks' labor every month, the latter undertook to maintain the troops.[3]

Since few *kibbutsim* had housing to spare, the new force, known as PALMACH (for Plugot Machats, literally "shock companies," possibly a translation of the German *stosstruppen*), was made to live in tents among the eucalyptus trees that surrounded many settlements; so spartan were living conditions that, as legend has it, only one person in the entire organization even possessed a bathrobe.[4] These arrangements may explain why, then and later, PALMACH looked and felt much like a youth movement complete with campfires, singsong, pranks played among the members, and the like. They also fostered an extremely strong team spirit that, as outsiders thought, was not always compatible with loyalty to Hagana as a whole.[5]

PALMACH's commander in chief (CIC) was once again Yitschak Sadeh, now fifty-one years old, bald, and, though with a heavy paunch and suffering from a heart condition, apparently the only senior Hagana member qualified for the task. He selected his company commanders from among former *nodedot*, SNS, and FOSH personnel, including above all Yigal Allon and Moshe Dayan. Six companies were established, including both male and female; though no precise figures are available, something about the relative size of the two groups may be gathered from the fact that when the first class of recruits completed its training in May 1942, the passing-out parade included 427 men but only six (some say eight) women.[6] Later the organization expanded until it could muster 1,000 troops in 1943 and around 1,500 in 1944. Operating with British permission, they engaged in intensive training, including sniping, reconnaissance, and demolition work. After two years the recruits were released, and others took their place; some of the veterans, instead of going home, organized in so-called *hachsharot* (preparatory groups) and set out to found new *kibbutsim* where, of course, they remained active as Hagana members. In time PALMACH, an enterprising lot if ever there was one, was even able to maintain a naval company (PALYAM) and a handful of aircrews who operated under the guise of an aerial sports club.

Originally PALMACH was intended to fight the Germans in case Palestine should be evacuated by the British, leaving the Jewish population unprotected. According to a plan coordinated with British military intelligence, known as the Palestine Post Occupation Scheme, the area around Mount Carmel was to be turned into a sort of national redoubt and used as a base for guerrilla operations. The topography appeared favorable and included, besides the cover provided by the woods, a large number of hillside caves, some of which had already served as hideouts in prehistoric times. Now plans were laid for storing arms and ammunition, destroying roads and communications, blowing up bridges, sowing mines, laying booby traps, and the like, all in order to delay the Wehrmacht for as long as possible while allowing the British to make good their escape.

In the next year, heartened by Germany's failure to seize the Libyan port of Tobruk, the leaders of Hagana became more ambitious. They even negotiated with the British for the construction of a four-division force (thirty-six battalions) that would try to hold the entire northern part of the country, including Haifa with its modicum of industry, heavy earth-moving equipment, airstrip, and port.[7] Apparently the fact that the loss of Egypt would effectively bring about the end of the Royal Navy in the eastern Mediterranean was overlooked; ever the optimist, Sadeh at one point believed—or pretended to believe—that his well-trained men could take on 500 German tanks with Molotov cocktails.[8] This, of course, was a gross exaggeration. Yet it also overestimated the size of the force that the Wehrmacht, now fully occupied in grinding its way toward Stalingrad, could deploy in the Middle East. When the Afrika Korps arrived at El Alamein in late July 1942, it was down to exactly nineteen operational tanks.

As usual, British connivance with Hagana's activities did not survive the period of greatest danger. The Battle of El Alamein opened on October 23, 1942, and ended with mostly British forces driving the Germans out of Egypt. The invasion of French North Africa followed in November, and by the end of 1942, at the latest, it was clear that any danger from that quarter had definitely passed. The British Foreign Office, as well as the military and intelligence authorities deployed in Palestine itself, started contemplating the possibility of a Jewish revolt after the war.[9] They were aware of Ben Gurion's growing power and the "activist" line that he took. They also consistently overestimated the forces of Hagana and occasionally invented Jewish paramilitary organizations when in fact there were none.

As part of this policy, plans were made to reinforce the British military presence in Palestine. Raids and searches were resumed but rarely yielded considerable results. For example, in October 1943 *kibbuts* Chulda was surrounded and searched. More than eighty mortar rounds were unearthed, a loss by the standards of those days but one that did not affect the operations of Hagana countrywide.[10] Meanwhile PALMACH in its camps defied the British and continued to train. In 1941 a platoon commanders course was held at Juara, a remote hilly district south of Esdraelon; it became the first in a long series of courses that produced a number of future IDF chiefs of staff. Three years later Sadeh already felt sufficiently confident in his commanders' ability to consolidate his eleven companies, plus a headquarters company, into four battalions.

Nor were PALMACH and Hagana the only organizations that provided Jewish soldiers with training during those years. Given the horrible rumors that were beginning to reach the *Yishuv* from Nazi-occupied Europe, many of the *Yishuv*'s members felt they could do better than to spend their time raising cucumbers for the *kibbutsim* and playing with pistols when no British troops were nearby. With or without permission from the Jewish Agency—the latter, fearing that its own forces would become depleted, initially attempted to resist the movement—they volunteered for the British armed forces. Eventually the number of volunteers approached 30,000, a little more than 10 percent being women. Numerically speaking and relative to its size, the *Yishuv*'s contribution to fighting the Axis was thus as great as that of any other country at the time.

Almost all the volunteers served in various second-line units—in particular, women from Palestine were used to drive trucks along the endless supply routes of the 8th Army across the Sinai, Egypt, and Libya. Others spent their careers digging trenches, guarding bases, or carrying out quartermaster duties far in the rear. Some 500 were even organized into a Palestinian Coast Guard and positioned in a chain of watch stations; initially without arms, their job was to alert the authorities in case German or Italian ships presented themselves.[11] Still, a select few found their way into combat forces, including signals, engineers, sappers, and artillery, as well as the Royal Air Force and the Royal Navy.[12] By pressing the British to set up a Jewish brigade on the model of the World War I battalions, Ben Gurion and his "foreign minister" at the Jewish Agency, Moshe Shertok (later, Sharet), hoped to derive the maximum benefit from the volunteer movement. The authorities dragged their feet, and it was not until the winter of 1944–1945 that a Jewish brigade, with the Star of David as its symbol, was formed. By the time it reached the front in northern Italy (March 1945) the war was all but over.[13]

When members of the British and Jewish forces reencountered one another in Hagana after 1945, they discovered that their differences could not be greater.[14] From "Chinese" Gordon to T. E. Lawrence the British military has always had a sprinkling of brilliant eccentrics; Wingate him-

self used to conclude each SNS operation by sitting stark naked in the dining room and munching an onion.[15] In the main, however, they consisted
of regular soldiers with a powerful bureaucratic structure and an emphasis
on uniforms, hierarchy, drill, punctiliousness, ornamental swords, and
swagger sticks. Like all good soldiers (their own favorite term was *lochem*
or "fighter") PALMACHniks also liked to swagger; but *their* idea of doing
so was to wear carefully cultivated forelocks, formless home-knit headgear
known as "socks," wide-open shirts, and so-called palm-length khaki
shorts with the whites of their pockets dangling out below. Their "stumpy,
dumpy" women also wore shorts, making for an interesting anatomical display that did not escape foreign observers.[16] Young, ingenious, and inde-
pendent-minded, they were a disorderly lot and proud of it. Informality
reached the point where subordinates addressed commanders by their
nicknames; thus Rechabam Zeevi (who was to command the central front
in 1970–1973) became "Ghandi," David (Elazar) "Dado," Mordechai
(Gur) "Motta," Refael (Eytan) "Raful," and one particularly tall officer
"Guliver." All of this not seldom degenerated into simple sloppiness.

Both traditions were carried into the IDF, where they competed for
decades thereafter, particularly in regard to questions of organization,
training, and the amount of drill required of troops. PALMACH commanders rejected formal discipline, salutes, and even the insignia of rank;
to their former British rivals such attitudes bordered on sacrilege. As the
Yishuv's leader and the highest civilian authority in charge of defense matters, Ben Gurion was inclined to favor the members of the British school—
the more so because, not being associated with the *kibbuts* movement, they
were considered politically neutral and more amenable to discipline. It is
true that few of them had gained much command experience; Laskov, who
was the highest-ranking, had been a major in charge of two platoons.[17]
Still, to Ben Gurion's mind it was they and not the PALMACH rabble who
knew how to run an army and thus represented "real" soldiers.

Nevertheless, a few years after Israeli independence had been achieved,
the PALMACH veterans came out on top. One reason may have been that
they systematically trained for leadership; for example, Sadeh had insisted
that every qualified PALMACHnik go through a squad commanders
course in addition to basic training. At a time when the rest of Hagana still
thought in terms of part-time volunteers, PALMACH commanders
already led a regular strike force that was organized first in battalions and
then in brigades, albeit ones that were increasingly forced to operate
underground as the mandate entered its last years and anti-British operations and persecution intensified. Last but not least, the native-born
PALMACH approach was better adapted to the spirit of a people who,

then and later, distrusted formality as well as spit and polish. One way or another, and except for the years of Chayim Laskov (1958–1961) and Tsvi Tsur (1961–1964), from 1953 to 1983 *all* IDF chiefs of staff were former PALMACH personnel, as were many of its generals.

Once World War II had ended and the servicemen returned, Hagana could muster about 30,000 men and women in various degrees of training and readiness. The core consisted of the 2,000 mobilized members of PALMACH. Its new commander, Yigal Allon, was the first native-born Israeli to reach such a high position in Hagana; a surprisingly gentlemanly character for a man of his background (he had been born in 1918, the son of an out-of-luck peasant in Kfar Tabor), in time he proved to have a first-class strategic mind. He molded the troops into a highly motivated fighting force, "deployed from the sea to the desert" and "always ready to take orders," as their anthem proudly proclaimed. The remaining Hagana members were reservists available in an emergency. Some 4,000 had passed through PALMACH and constituted *its* reserve—throughout the period PALMACH tended to look upon itself as a separate corps d'elite, an attitude fraught with implications for the future. An additional 3,300 were organized in CHISH (Chel Sadeh or "Field Force") and represented the direct descendant of the old *nodedot* and FOSH. The bulk of the force, however, was known as CHIM (Chel Mishmar or "Home Guard"). As its name indicates, it consisted of personnel—units would be too strong a word—who were intended for stationary self-defense should the places in which they lived be attacked.

Just as important as organization was the acquisition of additional arms. As had been done previously, some arms were smuggled into the country by various means—a favorite method was to conceal them inside construction and earth-moving equipment—or else procured locally by buying or stealing them from the British. Moreover, Hagana's own military industries (Taasiya Tsvait, TAAS) had been expanding to the point that, between 1939 and 1944, its size increased sixfold.[18] By 1944 twelve "institutions," scattered all over the country, were turning out explosives, detonators, hand grenades, mortars, submachine guns, and various types of ammunition—including, on the eve of independence, as many as 20,000 rifle rounds per day. Often located in or near *kibbutsim*, the institutions were staffed by a core of specialists as well as a larger number of youths, both male and female, who volunteered for the task. From time to time the British discovered a workshop and raided it. These raids, however, represented isolated reverses and never disrupted TAAS for long.

In autumn 1945, TAAS's chief, an engineer named Chayim Slavin, was sent to the United States on a subsistence budget of $9 per day.[19] With funds from the Zionist organization and making use of the postwar glut, he bought up machines for manufacturing ammunition at a fraction of their original cost. They were dismantled into small parts and shipped home in 800 separate crates—the reassembly instructions are said to have taken up an index consisting of 70,000 cards. By the time the War of Independence broke out in November 1947, Hagana possessed 754 mortars of all calibers, 16 antitank rifles, 980 machine guns, 3,662 submachine guns, 17,642 rifles, 3,830 pistols, and 53,751 hand grenades.[20] Once they had been taken out of the *slikkim* and distributed to the units, these weapons turned out to be more than sufficient to take care of the homegrown Palestinian Arab militias. They were, however, hopelessly inadequate for fighting the regular forces of neighboring Arab countries possessing armor, artillery, and aircraft.

In 1945, however, it was the British and not the Arabs who most concerned Hagana. As already mentioned, World War II had brought about a lull in Jewish-Arab relations. Heavily decimated in 1936–1939—as much by their own gangs as by the British and the Jews—many Arab leaders were already beginning to realize that their last hope of survival vis-à-vis the growing Jewish forces depended upon continued British occupation of the country; in fact those who could afford to do so were already beginning to sell property and move elsewhere.[21] In any case the Arabs were relatively quiescent. This enabled Jews and Britons to turn against one another on a scale and with a fury unequaled since the beginning of the mandate.

Both sides did, in fact, have much to complain about. Intent on maintaining their imperial presence in the Middle East, the British regarded the activities of Hagana—even its very existence—as illegal and were concerned with limiting its operations as much as possible. For their part, Hagana and the *Yishuv* behind it were furious at what they saw as the British breach of the promises contained in the Balfour Declaration; from 1941 on, Ben Gurion, as the leading personality, was determined to create an independent Jewish state despite anything the government in London might say or do. Other, more immediate bones of contention included restrictions that had been placed on the purchase of land as well as continuing constraints on immigration—the latter becoming a major issue during the years immediately following the Holocaust, when hundreds of thousands of survivors were desperately trying to get into the region.

Against this background, Hagana, heretofore concerned primarily with defending the *Yishuv* against the Palestinian Arabs and not seldom cooperating with the British, opened operations against the occupiers. The first "action" took place on October 9, when a PALMACH unit numbering a hundred men (it is not known whether there were women among the participants) broke into the camp at Atlit, south of Haifa, where two hundred illegal immigrants were being held. The infiltrators knocked out the Arab guards, and a British police car that appeared on the scene was attacked with grenades and machine guns; it overturned, killing one of its occupants. The internees were smuggled to nearby *kibbuts* Bet-Oren, which in turn was surrounded by thousands of Haifa residents who came out to demonstrate against the British. Fearing a major clash, the latter desisted.

From now on such attacks multiplied. Hagana's stated preference was for a bloodless struggle; normally it was only when British personnel sought to interrupt the operations (participation in which naturally carried the death sentence) that they were subjected to direct fire. Thus, on November 1, 1945, Palestine's railway net was sabotaged at no fewer than 153 places, and three patrol boats in the ports of Haifa and Jaffa were sunk. On November 24 two observation posts that had been intercepting immigrant ships were demolished (and like the Irish Republican Army years later, Hagana would call the British ahead of time to let them know that bombs had been planted). All these operations were carried out by PALMACH members who, in their minds, thereby justified the long years of preparation and training. The first months of 1946 saw more attacks on observation posts, a radar station, and four police stations. The climax came on June 17. Several hundred troops set out simultaneously and dynamited ten out of eleven border bridges, causing 250,000 pounds' worth of damage and temporarily halting traffic between Palestine and the neighboring countries.[22]

Not all operations were completely successful, and there were casualties on both sides. Moreover, Hagana was not the only Jewish organization fighting the British during these years. The need to use armed force—at least for self-defense—had been acknowledged by the nascent *Yishuv* since the arrival of the second wave of immigrants in 1900. However, to the mind of the socialist majority such force was only one element in the Jewish awakening. At least as important was the need to "settle the country" and "liberate" (*li-geol*, a term that also carried apocalyptic connotations) it from its "desolation." Incidentally this was not a uniquely Zionist argument but was one that echoed late-nineteenth-century imperialist ideas concerning Europe's "civilizing mission."[23] From the beginning, though, there were those who disagreed. The most important of the "dissenters" or "revisionists," as they were known, was Zeev Jabotinsky, a bespectacled, highly cultured, and charismatic journalist from Odessa.

Having served in the Jewish battalions during World War I, Jabotinsky in 1920 helped defend the Jewish community in Jerusalem, for which the British gave him fifteen years in jail. Granted amnesty, he found himself at odds with the *Yishuv*'s leaders. Unlike most of them he was no socialist and regarded the communal settlements as secondary—important, perhaps, but hardly the highway to independence and statehood. Instead, and acting on the belief that the British would support such a course, he emphasized the need to prepare a Jewish armed force to take over Palestine from its Arab inhabitants once the British gave the green light. In retrospect Jabotinsky's belief in British benevolence, which he shared with others such as Dr. Weizman, appears naive, whereas his own craving for things military—including insignia, uniforms, salutes, parades, and certain affectations of behavior that he called *hadar* (glory)—was merely childish. Still, arguably these weaknesses were balanced by a better understanding of the Arab-Jewish conflict. Unlike his socialist opponents, Jabotinsky was ready to admit that the Arab resistance did not result from some terrible misunderstanding. Instead they too were building an embryonic national movement that had right on its side; hence the issue could be settled only by force of arms.[24]

In 1925 the Zionist revisionist movement, as well as its youth movement Betar (after the site where the Jews had made their last stand against the Romans in the revolt of 132–135 A.D.), was founded. Its members recited Cohen's poem about the need to redeem Judaea with "blood and fire" as well as Jabotinsky's own poem about "dying or conquering the mountain." In 1931 the dissidents, perhaps 10–20 percent of the entire *Yishuv*, set up their own military organization with the objective of taking a more aggressive line against the Arab gangs as well as the British. During the late thirties, ETSEL (Irgun Tsvai Leumi, or "National Military Organization") made its presence felt by launching attacks on Arab civilians—a bomb was planted amid a crowded Haifa market, for example—as well as sabotaging government targets such as telephone wires, railways, and a Jerusalem radio station. In response the authorities took action and on September 1, 1939, were able to achieve something of a coup by arresting the entire ETSEL leadership.

Once World War II broke out, Jabotinsky, who was organizing Betar from abroad, announced that ETSEL would suspend its struggle against the British in favor of cooperating with them against the Nazis. ETSEL's two leaders, David Raziel and Abraham Stern, were released from prison; in May 1941 the former was even sent on a commando operation to Iraq, where he was killed. The truce was maintained, more or less, until December 1941, when the ship *Struma*, a 180-ton Danube cattle boat, limped into Constantinople harbor with 769 Jewish refugees aboard. For two months the Jewish Agency, the Turkish authorities, and the British engaged in negotiations as the latter refused to grant the passengers entry visas to Palestine; finally the Turks lost patience and ordered the ship to sea, where it promptly sank. Whether this was due to its own condition or to an attack by a German submarine, as has been claimed, remains unclear to the present day. In any case almost all its crew and passengers, including 250 women and 70 children, were lost.

Jabotinksy had died in August 1940 and ETSEL, already torn between those who favored continuation of the truce and those who wanted to resume the struggle against the British, split. Seeking revenge for the *Struma* episode one group, led by Abraham Stern, broke away to found LECHI (Lochame Cherut Israel, Israel's Freedom Fighters), an even more extreme organization. Stern himself was a classics student at Hebrew University. Later he studied in Italy, where he was influenced by fascism; like his master, Jabotinsky, he was a gifted poet whose dark, solemn verses are laced with obedience, duty, and death. He was soon hunted down and killed in a shoot-out, but his followers refused to give up. Unlike Hagana they did not have either the Jewish Agency or Histadrut behind them. Unable to set up even an unofficial taxation system, they were compelled to obtain funds by raiding banks, post offices, and the like as well as by door-to-door collections. They resumed operations against the British, albeit on a very small scale as LECHI probably numbered no more than a few dozen activists.

By early 1944, ETSEL too was prepared to resume operations against the British. From 1943 on it was commanded by Menachem Begin, a fire-eating orator from Poland, where his organizational skills had taken him to the head of the local Betar movement. Young—he was born in 1913—Begin, unlike Jabotinksy, was incapable of creating a coherent political ideology. Even more than Jabotinsky he was in love with things military and worshipped force for force's sake, to the point that, after he had expostulated on the subject at a meeting held in Warsaw just before World War II, Jabotinsky told him to "go and drown yourself in the Vistula."[25] Between them the two organizations launched a terrorist campaign, attacking and demolishing government offices, capturing arms, and even temporarily occupying the government broadcasting station in Ramallah, north of Jerusalem. In August 1944 Sir Harold MacMichael, the departing high commissioner whom extremists blamed for the *Struma* affair, narrowly escaped an assassination attempt. Two months later two LECHI members killed Britain's resident minister in Cairo, Lord Moyne.

When World War II ended there were thus three separate Jewish "armies" intent on fighting the British. Of the three, Hagana was semilegal—its role in defending outlying settlements continued to be grudgingly recognized by the British—and by far the largest. The other two were strictly outside the law and only numbered a few thousand (ETSEL) and a few hundred (LECHI) members respectively. Ideologically speaking they differed very sharply, Hagana being socialist, ETSEL nationalist, and

LECHI—to which belonged the future prime minister, Yitschak Shamir—
a terrifying amalgam of the two.[26] As important, Hagana acted as the military arm of the Jewish Agency. Not so the "dissident" LECHI and
ETSEL, which went their separate ways and refused to recognize the
agency's authority. From September 1944 to May 1945 their antagonism
was carried to the point where the three organizations burned the others'
vehicles, raided the others' hiding places for arms, and kidnapped and
interrogated the others' members. To forestall British retaliation for the
assassination of Moyne, Hagana even tortured its rivals and turned them
over to the authorities—an episode that became known as the *saison* (a reference to the hunting season) and left bitter memories on both sides.[27]
Indeed, so much did Ben Gurion personally hate Begin that for decades
thereafter he refused to call him by name, always referring to him as "the
man sitting next to [fellow] Knesset member Bader."

As in other antioccupation struggles that took place in various countries
during World War II, the internecine fighting among the separate resistance
movements diverted time, men, and resources away from the anti-British campaign. Yet it tended to make the authorities' position even more difficult, since
there was no single, sovereign, and authoritative Jewish leadership to negotiate with. Internally Ben Gurion sought, though he did not succeed, to concentrate all authority in his own hands and rule with an iron fist. Facing the
Yishuv's external enemies, however, he could always blame extremists over
whom he had no control, thanks in part to the authorities' own refusal to allow
his organization a free hand. This ambiguity was not lost on the British on
the various occasions that they negotiated with him.[28] Nor was it to be the
last one of its kind in the bloody history of the Arab-Israeli conflict.

In October 1945, only two months after World War II had ended, the
British fear of a Jewish uprising became true as the three organizations
began to coordinate their activities under what was known as the United
Front of the Revolt. With Sneh as Hagana's commander acting as the coordinator in chief, a semiofficial division of labor was established—the more
easily because he and Begin knew each other from back home in Poland and,
in spite of their pronounced political differences, got along well enough. As
always, Hagana displayed a marked preference for bloodless operations
such as bringing in immigrant ships, building new settlements in districts
that were officially closed to Jews, and, of course, organizing the ubiquitous,
noisy, and rowdy demonstrations against this or that aspect of mandatory
policy. Less squeamish, ETSEL attacked British targets and deliberately set
about killing security personnel by mounting ambushes and planting
bombs; LECHI for its part specialized in pinpoint assassinations of selected
persons, including Jewish "traitors."[29]

In practice these fine distinctions tended to break down. Despite their ideological differences, LECHI and ETSEL worked so closely together as to be virtually indistinguishable. Whatever Hagana's intentions, many of its operations also resulted in British—let alone Arab—casualties, particularly when things went wrong. Finally, Sadeh and his POUM emulated LECHI and also went after Jewish traitors. However, all three organizations differed from counterparts in other countries in one important way: Dependents of British officials and servicemen—in other words, women and children—were never targeted. Perhaps this was because, having come to Palestine with no intention of settling in it, dependents were not regarded as *colons* in the classic sense of that term.

Through 1946 and 1947 one terrorist operation followed another; for that period the average was calculated at precisely 17.285 "incidents" per month.[30] Police stations and military offices were attacked, communications cut, oil refineries set ablaze, railway crossings demolished, trains derailed, air bases bombed, and cafes catering to British personnel blown up, often with heavy losses of life. From time to time the British CID succeeded in uncovering a terrorist hideout. This would lead to firefights and casualties on both sides (e.g., on June 16–17, 1946, eleven LECHI members were killed and twenty-three more captured, a heavy blow to such a small organization). As would happen in later liberation movements, such as those of the Croats in Bosnia and the Kurds in Iraq, operations tended to spread beyond the borders of the homeland. Both Hagana and ETSEL sent agents to Europe, where they lobbied governments. In Belgium, France, Italy, and Yugoslavia it was possible to find officials who, with or without payment, were prepared to close an eye to what was going on. While in Europe they also raised funds among the local Jewish communities, purchased arms, and bought or leased ships for smuggling immigrants into Palestine.

Like the ill-fated *Struma*, most of the ships were old and barely seaworthy. As one story has it, PALYAM personnel who were responsible for purchasing them were issued screwdrivers and told to stick them in the sides of the ships and see how far they would go.[31] They were disguised as fishing boats or freighters, provided with false papers, packed chockablock with illegal immigrants, and shoved off to make their way toward Palestine's shores as best they could. A few of the ships escaped detection and unloaded their passengers, who were promptly taken to the neighboring *kibbutsim*, where they would be at least temporarily safe from British eyes.[32] Most ships, however, confronted by an efficient naval service that was provided with aircraft and radar, were intercepted during the voyage.

The authorities' normal way for dealing with *olim* (immigrants) was to intern them in Palestine or, increasingly, Cyprus, where more than 17,000 people eventually came to live in camps. Later, to demonstrate the government's determination to not give in, Foreign Secretary Ernst Bevin hit on the brilliant idea of sending one ship (*President Warfield*) all the way back to Hamburg, whence it had come. When it returned the passengers refused to go ashore, and the ugly scenes of soldiers beating men, women, and children were repeated. In the face of this even the British press lost patience, calling the operation "a stupid decision," "a manifest blunder," and "the ultimate stage of lunacy."[33] Meanwhile the Cyprus camps were infiltrated by Hagana agents, who threatened to extend the terrorist campaign to that country as well.[34]

At peak the British deployed 100,000 men in Palestine.[35] This represented one-tenth of their entire armed forces; the annual cost to the taxpayer was estimated at 40 million pounds. Besides the uniformed and nonuniformed police, two-and-a-half divisions were brought in, complete with tanks, armored cars, artillery, patrol aircraft, and, at sea, naval vessels as large as cruisers.[36] Since Palestine's Arab population sided with the British, even providing auxiliary manpower for guard duties and the like, this represented one of the highest ratios of troops to population ever deployed in any modern counterinsurgency (the French in Algeria never deployed more than 600,000 men to hold down 9 million or so people).[37] In the authorities' favor it should be said that they never deliberately fired into crowds. Although there were two or three occasions when troops panicked and a few demonstrators were killed, a Jewish large-scale massacre never took place and entire Jewish settlements were not demolished with explosives (much to the Arabs' regret, it must be added). Thanks to the British recognition that Jews constituted a "semi-European" race,[38] the struggle over Palestine was, relatively speaking, almost gentlemanly. By comparison, in Yugoslavia under the German occupation almost 1 million are said to have died.

Yet the British used their long experience in colonial policing to launch virtually every type of antiterrorist operation imaginable.[39] In 1945 the Defense (Emergency) Regulations were issued, suspending civil liberties, such as freedom from arbitrary arrest, and giving the security forces a free hand.[40] Thereupon they engaged in overt and covert surveillance, employing their own personnel as well as the rare member of the Jewish community who could be forced or persuaded to cooperate; mounted guards, many of them Arab, over sensitive installations throughout the country; fenced off entire areas (the center of Jerusalem was turned into "Bevingrad") with barbed wire; imposed curfews; and set up roadblocks (the "checkpost" intersection near Haifa still exists) in hope of catching suspects traveling from one district to another.

The core of British counterinsurgency consisted of a policy known as "cordon and search," divided into small searches, large searches, cordon searches, snap searches, countrywide searches, and ordinary searches. On top of this there were restorations of law and order, individual arrests, group arrests, mass arrests, trials, incarcerations, hangings, and deportations to such places as Mauritius and Somalia—where a number of captured ETSEL personnel promptly escaped. Whether with or without authorization from above, some British security personnel also set up death squads that kidnapped and tortured and murdered suspects, some of them mere teenagers. All these activities were crowned by executions and, as it turned out and inevitably had to turn out, made no difference whatsoever.

The largest antiterrorist operation took place on June 29, 1946. Known as "Operation Agatha," in the words of Field Marshal Bernhard Montgomery, chief of the Imperial General Staff, its purpose was "to smash [the Jews] forever."[41] After careful preparation three British divisions went into action all over the country; they arrested almost 3,000 "ringleaders" and "instigators" and took them to a camp at Latrun some twenty miles to the west of Jerusalem.[42] Not only that, but more than 200,000 people—one-third of the entire Jewish community—were put under curfew and had their houses systematically searched for suspects, arms, and information. Outlying settlements suspected of containing *slikkim* were surrounded with troops and subjected to extensive searches. A major hideout was discovered at *kibbuts* Yagur near Haifa and, according to Hagana's own figures, yielded 325 rifles, 100 mortars, 10,000 hand grenades, and several hundreds of thousands of ammunition rounds.[43] By a stroke of good luck the British captured a list of PALMACH members but could not decipher the code in which it was written. Consequently they failed to identify individuals who, forewarned by Hagana's intelligence service,[44] escaped by merging into the civilian population. Nor did the dragnet destroy the underground organizations of ETSEL or LECHI, though Begin himself spent four days in a waterless hole that had been dug below his house and came within a hair of being caught.

"Black Saturday"—the Jewish nickname for the British sweep—caused Hagana to suspend its attacks on British personnel and concentrate on bloodless operations such as bringing in immigrants.[45] Not so ETSEL, which only three weeks later and with Sneh's connivance[46] carried out its bloodiest operation yet. A bomb was planted in British police headquarters in Jerusalem, which were located in the southern wing of the King David Hotel. It killed dozens, including some Jews who were in the building. Acting with or without their superiors' permission, British agents later retaliated by blowing up the houses on Ben Yehuda Street, also in the center of Jerusalem. Besides the hotel proper, two entire apartment buildings went up in a column of dust; forty-eight people were killed and 200 or so wounded. However, in this case the operation, far from serving a useful purpose, only served to illustrate the way in which the government was losing control and itself turning terrorist.

Meanwhile anti-British operations, including in particular some daring prison escapes, continued. During a single week in July 1947, LECHI claimed to have carried out no fewer than twenty-two operations in places as far apart as Jerusalem and Haifa.[47] At about the same time, a crescendo of hatred was reached when the British started hanging captured ETSEL members. In retaliation Begin and his men kidnapped two British sergeants (one of whom later turned out to be part Jewish). They were hanged in defiance of world opinion as well as the *Yishuv*'s own leadership. For example, Golda Meir claimed to be "shocked" by the ETSEL action; as was her wont on such occasions, however, she did nothing. In a macabre touch the corpses were suspended from trees in a nearby grove. The ground between them was booby-trapped, and a British policeman was severely injured when he tried to cut them down.[48]

This is hardly the place to inquire which of the two principal paramilitary forces—Hagana with its organization and bloodless operations or ETSEL with its acts of terrorism—did more to drive out the British. Since ETSEL developed into Likud and Hagana was run by the Labor Party, the echoes of this question continue to influence Israeli politics to the present day. Nor can we examine the relative roles played by military, political, and diplomatic events in Palestine, London, and the world arena, where decolonization and the Cold War had just begun.[49] Suffice it to say, facing determined opposition the authorities' will to resist was broken. The turning point probably came in December 1946, when Britain's Labor government, having failed to reach agreement with the Palestinian Arabs, decided to submit the question of Palestine to the United Nations (UN). On November 29, 1947, after an investigating committee (UNSCOP) had come and gone, the UN voted to partition the country. Next day the British announced they would evacuate by August 1948, a date later moved up to June 30. This was only four years after ETSEL and LECHI resumed the struggle and three since the assassination of Lord Moyne. Counting all forces combined, at bottom it was the handiwork of a few thousand activists armed with little more than high courage and their people's near-unanimous support. Taking advantage of the international situation as well as Britain's own domestic crisis during the postwar years, they took on and defeated one of the most powerful empires the world has known.

When it was all over the usual analyses emerged, and excuses for failure were sought and found:[50] The Palestine insurgency had caught the British armed forces amid the post–World War II demobilization, with the result that there was very great personnel turbulence, and stability could not be achieved. This factor affected operational readiness and training, which in turn caused troops and commanders to resort to repetitive, often routinized and unimaginative tactics. Instead of acting, the British forces reacted—sometimes so slowly that they took an entire night to decide whether or not to mount a search after a police station had been attacked.[51] In doing all this they suffered from inadequate intelligence, which in turn resulted from insufficient familiarity with the country, its language, and its culture. Although the police and especially the CID were better at gathering intelligence than the army, cooperation between them was defective, owing to the latter's reluctance to study and adopt police methods. There was a lack of political guidance from above, which led to the division and duplication of effort; it also prevented the authorities on the spot from developing an effective counterpropaganda line. The need to operate in full view of British and world media constituted another handicap, since it compelled the forces to forego the use of the harshest (and presumably most effective) methods. And so on, and so on, ad infinitum if not ad nauseam.

In retrospect, each of these very different explanations probably contained an element of truth. Yet each overlooks the critical factor, namely, that war is a moral and physical struggle by means of the latter.[52] Physically speaking, British losses in the struggle were so small as to be almost negligible. From summer 1945 to summer 1947 British losses amounted to a little less than 400, including 125 dead and 259 wounded[53]—far fewer than those claimed by a single day of battle during World War II or a single night of bombardment during the Blitz. In any event, it was precisely the "victories" won by the security forces that ended up working against them. Perhaps most damaging to the British was the repeated spectacle of immigrants, many of them former concentration camp inmates with numbers still tattooed on their arms, being manhandled, wounded, and sometimes killed by troops who sought to transfer them to prison camps or else to other ships prior to internment. As early as 1942 the train of events that led to the sinking of *Struma* had been called "stupid, callous, and inhuman" in the House of Lords.[54] Now the unedifying events in Palestine were being displayed all over the world by newspapers and newsreels. Some stories were deliberately spread by the Jewish Agency as part of a well-coordinated propaganda campaign, whereas others were produced by journalists sent to cover the events.[55]

The outcome was a public-relations disaster that could not but affect the British people and the troops themselves. To watch five fast destroyers escort a rickety, 420-ton steamer, *Chayim Arlozorov*, until it hits a rock and sinks is bad enough (the occupants were rescued); to have to board the ships and fight it out with their miserable human cargoes is worse. As one soldier remembered, "When you went alongside they were out of control . . . you used to get badly attacked. . . . Some of the blokes got knocked on the ground and women put knitting needles into their testicles, so we had pads. They used to bombard us with tins of fruit . . . and everybody used to grab them."[56] As humiliation followed humiliation even Winston Churchill, an acknowledged expert on such matters, accused the British troops of not knowing how "to behave like men."[57] At one point ETSEL kidnapped and flogged a number of British officers in retaliation for the flogging of its own men. Thereupon a French newspaper published a cartoon showing a member of His Majesty's forces holding his tin hat behind him. The caption explained that since "the threatened area" had moved from the head to the buttocks the salute too should be similarly transferred.

The British government was learning that under certain circumstances and given sufficient time Thucydides's words in the Melian dialogue may become inverted. It is not always "they who are strong do what they can, they who are weak suffer what they must."[58] Instead, and no less frequently, it is the weak who do what they can, the strong who suffer what they must. Though much weakened by World War II, the British at the time still constituted a world empire. As such they found themselves "fighting" the weak, the helpless, the pregnant, and the semistarved. They were damned if they "lost" and twice damned if, as usually happened, they "won" and "succeeded" in restoring order, arresting suspects, and even stopping immigrants from reaching their destination. Although their lives were seldom in very great danger—the more so because they tended to spend a growing part of their time on base—the British troops found the experience "repugnant" and "frustrating"; the struggle ended by taking away their self-respect, whereupon they turned tail and left. It was a lesson that others, not least the Israelis themselves, were destined to learn later and to their cost.

CHAPTER 5

AT WAR FOR INDEPENDENCE

DESPITE THE considerable roles that ETSEL and LECHI played in ejecting the British, both were strictly underground organizations with extremely limited capacities for overt military action. This was much less true of Hagana, which, thanks in part to the semilegal status it had enjoyed during various periods of its existence, was already preparing to wage a conventional war against the Arabs even as it was struggling against the British. In PALMACH it possessed a strike force of exceptional quality; in CHISH and CHIM it possessed at least a pool of trained or semitrained personnel, most of whom, however, were not yet formed into units let alone assembled and exercised. Accordingly the period between 1945 and 1948 was one of large-scale military construction and organization.

No sooner had V-E Day arrived (May 8, 1945) than Ben Gurion went to the United States.[1] Within weeks he succeeded in getting together a committee of twenty Jewish millionaires who were willing to help—"the best Zionist meeting ever" he noted in his diary.[2] Funds, now already measured in millions of dollars per year, were made available and put at the disposal of Hagana agents such as Teddy Kollek, who later was to become mayor of Jerusalem and was destined to make his early mark in this field. Since many countries had laws against the export of arms to the Middle East, ruses had to be used, including one occasion when light bombers (Beauforts) were purchased under the pretext of making a movie. Some of the arms were shipped to Erets Yisrael, as already related. However, most were stored abroad in anticipation of the day when the British mandate would end.

As those components of Hagana not engaged in the day-to-day task of defending against the Arabs or fighting the British expanded, it became necessary to set up an office that would coordinate its now very far-flung and multitudinous activities. With war clearly approaching, Ben Gurion wanted to have his hand firmly on the helm. Accordingly, late in 1946 he created a defense portfolio in the Jewish Agency with himself at its head. The chain of command now went from Ben Gurion as head of the Agency

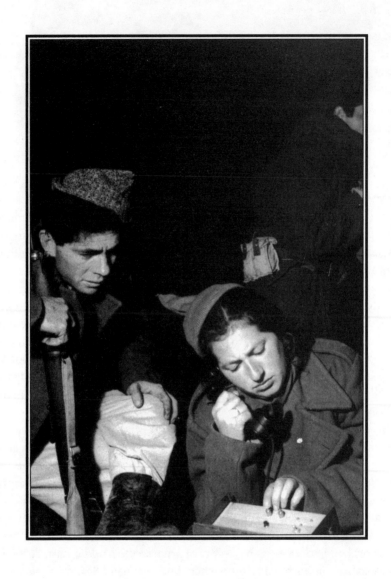

At War for Independence: Hagana members defending
Kibbuts *En Charod, February 1948.*

to Ben Gurion as minister of defense (although, as he used to say later on, with him it was often the prime minister who went to see the minister of defense instead of vice versa). Next in line was Yisrael Galili, a Hagana veteran and a representative of the *kibbuts* movement who had taken over from Sneh as *rosh mifkada artsit* and who in turn commanded Yaakov Dori as chief of the General Staff.

In April 1948, Ben Gurion, using Hagana's failure to break the siege of Jerusalem as his excuse, pointed out that *two* Jewish Agency representatives in charge of defense were one too many.[3] Galili, a political rival, was fired. So was Sadeh, the founder of PALMACH and thus the natural candidate for the job (however, the previous year he had displeased Ben Gurion— who sometimes acted as a tin-pot dictator—by penning an article where he denied the need for unconditional obedience under all circumstances).[4] While Sadeh was sidetracked to command a brigade, Galili became an *eitses geber* (Yiddish for adviser), a position that as leader of a left-wing party and member of several cabinets (and, later, as Golda Meir's reputed lover) he retained on and off for the next twenty-five years. From then on the minister of defense for the Jewish Agency dealt directly with the chief of staff or, since the latter was ailing, with his deputy, Yigal Yadin. Later, when the Agency's executive turned itself into the government of Israel, that arrangement remained in force.

At a lower level, these reforms were followed by the construction of a proper general staff. Various blueprints were submitted, mainly by former members of the British armed forces. Another key figure was Yisrael Beer, a Russian-born, horse-toothed veteran of the Spanish civil war with a reputation as a theoretician (he claimed to have earned a Ph.D. in military history) who acted as Ben Gurion's personal military adviser. The fundamental choice was between the Franco-American model and the German model, which, earlier in the century, had been transmitted to Britain by way of military writer Spencer Wilkinson.[5] The former system united operations, intelligence, training, and doctrine in a single division, known as the General Staff Division; the latter had one division each for operations, intelligence, personnel, and supply. By adopting the Anglo-German model the IDF thus put much greater emphasis on operations as opposed to the other two divisions, namely, personnel (comprising manpower administration, discipline, and justice) and supply (which took care of stocks and armaments as well as financial matters). Over the years these arrangements have often been modified in detail, but the basic idea—where the head of the General Staff Division unites operations, intelligence, training, and doctrine and acts as a *primus inter pares* under the chief of staff (COS)—still persists.

Actual preparation for conscripting manpower and building an army got under way in late 1947. A decree for military registration was issued on November 28; by the middle of 1948 a total of almost 50,000 men and women aged seventeen to thirty-five had been called up. Besides 27,000 previous Hagana members, they included perhaps 7,000–10,000 recent immigrants who, as they were being concentrated in transit camps in various European countries, had been mustered even before they reached their new homeland. As the figures indicate, so long as the British presence continued, the response made by members of the *Yishuv* was modest, and indeed there was much talk about "deserters" and "shirkers." Once they left, it became possible to put state authority behind the mobilization process, however, and the numbers it produced became much larger. By the end of 1948 almost 200,000 persons, of whom 164,000 were male, had been registered for service.[6]

The task of classifying the conscripts, organizing them in units, issuing them equipment, training them, and preparing them for battle was enormous—the more so since it had to be carried out by beginners. (In the entire *Yishuv* there was probably not one person who had commanded as much as a battalion in action, and the British did in fact comment on the "amateurishness" of the organization.)[7] Moreover, so far from obtaining any breathing space, it was already engaging in hostilities with the Palestinians.

During the last months of 1947 the other side too had been making preparations for the conflict. The Arab population living west of the River Jordan must have numbered 900,000–1.2 million; the higher estimate is probably the most accurate. Of those, rather fewer than 10,000 had some kind of formal training, having served with various British units, mainly police. Organization was still limited to bands, that is, loose associations based either on the village or, on a slightly larger scale, the clan; in the towns there also were a number of *jihadias* (associations of holy warriors). The largest *jihadia* was centered in Jaffa and may have counted perhaps 2,000–3,000 men.[8] Here and elsewhere, the warriors brought along their own arms, complete with fifty to seventy rounds of ammunition. However, they did not possess heavy weapons or a logistic infrastructure, let alone the kind of bureaucratic organization that is the backbone of any modern army. The "arms industry" was limited to the manufacture of primitive bombs.

These "modest"[9] forces were joined by several thousand more who had infiltrated from the neighboring countries—according to the British authorities, by March 1948 their number reached 5,000.[10] Known somewhat grandiloquently as the Arab Salvation Army, they were divided into several bands that are best described as paramilitary. The largest band was poised to enter Palestine from southern Syria. The troops were much better armed than their Palestinian brethren, being provided with military-type vehicles as well as some artillery originating in the Arab armies and paid for by the Arab League. Their commander was Fauzi al Kauji, who gained fame during the 1936–1939 uprising. In May 1941 he had taken part in the abortive Rashid Ali uprising against the British; driven into exile, he had somehow contrived to reach Germany where he attended the Berlin war academy. He was also said to have done rather well out of the previous episode and may have hoped to repeat the experience.

Another force to reckon with was the Arab Legion, that strange amalgam of army cum police force that the British had established in Transjordan. During 1936–1939 some of its units had been sent to help put down the third Arab uprising, a task that they carried out with considerable brutality and also a certain gusto.[11] Paid for by the British Treasury and commanded by fifty or so British officers, during most of its history it took orders more from the British ambassador to Amman than from the Hassemite king, Abdullah. In 1946, Transjordan was granted its independence, however, and in any case bringing as much of Palestine as possible under the control of King Abdullah, as an imperial ally, was an objective over which he and his British paymasters could see eye to eye. Of its 20,000 men, slightly under half were available for duty in the war. Unlike the Palestinian levies, moreover, this was a regular force provided with a proper organization as well as artillery and armored cars. It also turned out to be better trained and motivated than all the rest.[12]

During the final months of the mandate some of the Arab Legion forces were already deployed in the Arab part of Palestine where they formed part of the British garrison. This fact may have encouraged King Abdullah of Transjordan to open negotiations with the *Yishuv*. Since Moshe Shertok (Sharet), the head of the Agency's political department, was working with the United Nations at Lake Success, New York, the person on the spot was the formidable Ms. Meir. Trying to stop the authorities in Haifa from deporting illegal immigrants, she had once slapped a British officer in full view of the world press; in November 1947, dressed as a man, she went to Naharayim on the River Jordan. No written agreement was produced, but the Jewish side came away with the distinct impression that the king, who of all the Arab leaders was the most peacefully inclined (and also most in need of Jewish capital and know-how to develop his desert kingdom), agreed not to join an eventual Arab-Israeli war. In return, the agency promised to favor the king's occupation of the Arab part of Palestine, that is, the area corresponding roughly to the West Bank.[13]

Assuming continued peaceful relations between the *Yishuv* and Abdullah, the agreement made excellent sense. Apart from the four villages composing Gush Etsion, about twelve miles southwest of Jerusalem, there were no Jewish settlements in this mountainous, densely inhabited, and, on the whole, not very fertile area. (Hence Hagana, whose strike forces were only just being formed, would probably have been unable to defend it anyhow.) But should war develop between the two sides then enemy troops would be positioned on the hills within a few miles of the Mediterranean, putting Israel in an impossible strategic situation. One way or another, probably no other single event did as much to shape the state's borders and, with them, the fate of the holy land as a whole. Nevertheless all the negotiations were kept secret, to the point that they were still not mentioned when the IDF's official history of the 1948 war was published in 1959 (not that this is unusual in a country where censorship serves mainly to prevent its own citizens from learning what everybody else already knows).

With the stage thus set, the show could get under way. In its early phases it took the shape of riots (in Jerusalem, Tel Aviv, and Haifa during the first week of December). Whereas these outbreaks were easily met by the local Hagana organizations, their place was soon taken by less spectacular but more effective forms of attack such as car bombs, sniping, and small-scale assaults on outlying neighborhoods—a task made easier by the fact that all over the country Jews and Arabs often lived close to one another. As will happen when fighting is conducted at extremely close quarters, both sides soon found themselves wading in blood and gore; still, and thanks largely to small company–sized PALMACH and CHISH units being rushed about like firehoses, none seems to have led to the loss, on a temporary or permanent basis, of a Jewish neighborhood. From November to March, attacks were mounted against outlying settlements all over the country, which too held out and were not lost. They included, from north to south, Kfar Szold, Tirat Tsvi, and Gesher in the upper Jordan Valley (the latter two came under attack by Kauji and the Arab Salvation Army), Nve Yaakov and Har Tuv in the vicinity of Jerusalem, and Nistanim, Kfar Darom, Revivim, Nvatim, and others in the Negev (see Map 6.2).

From December 1947 on, LECHI, ETSEL, and Hagana responded in kind—as Israeli accounts have it—by raiding Arab neighborhoods throughout the country. The almost purely Arab town of Jaffa was attacked by ETSEL, Arab villages in Galilee by Hagana; the latter also blew up a number of bridges in the northern part of the country with the objective of slowing down the arrival of additional volunteers from the neighboring countries. Nor were the Jewish organizations less inclined than their enemies to bomb Arab civilian targets such as markets, movie theaters, buses, and the like. The largest "operation" of this kind took place in Haifa. On January 15 a party of Hagana members disguised themselves as British soldiers. They took a truck into a street described as housing "the headquarters of the local bands" and blew it up with great loss of life.[14]

As would happen in other similar conflicts—Bosnia is a good recent example—these skirmishes resulted in heavy casualties. In the first four months 1,200 Jews lost their lives; the number of Arab dead is unknown but must have been at least as high and probably much higher. However, the skirmishes did little if anything to upset the balance or promote strategic objectives. Arab attacks on Jewish communications arteries, uncoordinated though they may have been, did threaten to gradually cut the *Yishuv* into several disparate parts. Then as now the real Jewish heartland was in the southern half of the Plain of Sharon between Tel Aviv and Chadera. Throughout winter 1948 the roads leading from there north to Haifa, northeast to Lake Tiberias and Galilee, and south toward the Negev Desert came under sporadic attack. In any event the northern part of the country was never completely cut off, there being always the alternative road or bypass. Not so in the south, where repeated attacks by bands centering on Majdal (modern Ashkelon) caused all traffic to be suspended from March 26 on and where communications with the settlements in the Negev could be maintained only by light aircraft.

With or without strategic intent, from late January on, the Battle of the Roads, as it was later called, tended to coalesce along the highway from Tel Aviv to Jerusalem. Particularly vulnerable were the Ramla-Lyddia area, which, although almost purely Arab, could be bypassed to the south; and the fifteen-mile-long mountain stretch from Shaar Ha-gai to the city for which, as the name indicates, there was no alternative and which accordingly saw some of the heaviest fighting. Except for a handful of settlements—desperately poor *kibbutsim* and *moshavim*—Jerusalem itself was isolated in the hills. It was entirely dependent on outside supplies, having no agricultural hinterland to speak of and barely enough water to sustain the population. Moreover many of its almost 100,000 Jews were orthodox and thus all but useless for any purpose but praying. Hence the Hagana organization in the city was exceptionally weak—just a few dozen men, as the PALMACH operations officer responsible for the area, twenty-five-year-old Yitschak Rabin, bitterly wrote in his memoirs.[15]

From January 1948 on, conditions along the road deteriorated to the point where Jerusalem could be accessed only by convoys of trucks—some of them with homemade armor—under armed escort provided by PALMACH. Climbing the hills of Judaea, the convoys were likely to encounter roadblocks made of stones, manned by hundreds of Arabs with rifles and grenades (and, later, also booby-trapped); the same applied to the return journey. Ben Gurion, who traveled the road on December 23, 1947, noted in his diary that they got through only at the cost of four wounded and a wrecked bus.[16] All this took place right under the noses of British garrisons that were using the road to evacuate Jerusalem. Depending on the whims of local commanders and the way they interpreted their instructions, British behavior was inconsistent. On some occasions they confiscated Hagana's arms, leaving the escorts defenseless. On others they intervened and extricated the occupants of beleaguered convoys, albeit usually on condition that they surrender their armored cars.

On February 23, 1948, the British withdrew from the area, leaving the two sides to fight it out. This is hardly the place to follow every twist and turn in the Battle for Bab al Wad (the Arab name for the road to Jerusalem), which lasted from late February to the end of April and has since given rise to much controversy in Israel.[17] Conducted almost solely with the aid of small arms—the heaviest weapons at Hagana's disposal at this time were a number of self-manufactured 3-inch (81 mm) mortars—it claimed a comparatively large number of casualties; even worse, the armored cars were being lost at an unacceptable rate. An early attempt to temporarily occupy some villages near the road in order to secure it was made at the end of March but ended in failure owing to bad planning and insufficient coordination. By that time, one of the darkest periods in the entire war, it looked as if the battle was being lost as two large convoys tried to get through but failed.

Yet the continuing British evacuation finally enabled Hagana to start operating in the open. In the first days of April, three battalions totaling 1,500 men—an enormous force for an organization that had never used more than a company in action—were concentrated in *kibbutsim* to the south and west of Shaar Ha-gai. Since the *Yishuv* remained desperately short of arms, 200 rifles and four light machine guns were flown in from Czechoslovakia aboard an American-piloted Constellation aircraft that landed at an improvised airstrip. It was the kind of operation that, however primitive the conditions under which it took place, perfectly illustrates the *Yishuv*'s advantage over Palestine's Arab population at the time: Here were two communities, one backward and one modern, locked in mortal combat. Economically speaking, the *Yishuv*, though small and poor by Western standards, was far ahead of the Arabs. For example, out of a total of 59.5 million pounds in bank deposits, 50.2 million belonged to Jews and only 9.3 million to Arabs.[18] A Jewish municipality of comparable size had ten times the budget of its Arab counterpart.[19] Man for man the Jews were better armed, better led, and, something that proved decisive, possessed countrywide organization, both political and military. Scant wonder they came out on top, albeit the price they paid for learning often proved exceptionally heavy both on individual occasions and for the war as a whole.

"Operation Nachshon" (named after a biblical hero) opened on April 6. Its commander was Shimon Avidan, who like the rest had been trained by Sadeh. Its objective was to permanently occupy the villages on both sides of the road—the first time such an objective had been set to any Hagana unit and thus representing a new phase in the war. Proceeding from west to east the troops easily took the hills flanking the first few miles of road, occupying villages (most were found empty) and blowing up the houses in them so as to open fields of fire for the subsequent defense. Farther along the road, however, heavy fighting developed. Attacks and counterattacks centered on Mount Kastel, a commanding position that blocked the road and passed from hand to hand several times. In one of those attacks the leader of the local band, Abd-al Kadr al Hussayni, was killed. His death signaled the end of the beginning. Whatever organization the Arabs possessed disintegrated (having occupied Kastel for the last time they simply went home in order to celebrate a wedding, as legend has it). From the middle of the month on, this final stretch of the road to Jerusalem was definitely open—no more convoys failed to get through—although much more fighting was needed to keep it open.

Around Jerusalem proper much had changed. On April 9 the local branch of ETSEL stormed Dir Yassin, an Arab village near the city's western outskirts that had long served as a departure base for the local bands (from Dir Yassin to Mount Kastel it was less than three miles as the crow flies). As Begin later recounted the episode, a pickup truck carrying a loudspeaker went ahead of the troops to warn the population;[20] as at the King David Hotel, however, ETSEL's warnings had a way of going unheeded. When the village was entered its houses were found to be occupied, the inhabitants ready for defense. In the subsequent heavy fighting, ETSEL men, penetrating the narrow alleyways, systematically demolished houses with explosives. When the day ended some 100–200 people, including many women and children, were dead. Four days later the Arabs committed their share of atrocities by attacking a Jewish convoy to Mount Scopus, Jerusalem. As the British troops in the area looked on, seventy-seven people were killed and another twenty wounded. Most of them were Hebrew University faculty and medical personnel on their way to work in the Hadassa hospital.

Whereas news of the Mount Scopus attack merely reinforced Jewish determination—after all, Jews had nowhere to go—the effect of the Dir Yassin attack among the Palestinians was just the reverse. Previously only a trickle of well-to-do Arabs had been leaving the country for neighboring ones, many hoping to return when hostilities ended; now the news of the atrocity triggered a mass flight. These events seem to have taken the Jewish leadership by surprise. Although there had long been some vague talk about the possibility of changing the "demographic balance," up to this point there had been scarcely any offensive plans—holding out and retaliating was all that Hagana had prepared for—and consequently no detailed schemes for dealing with any noncombatant Arab population that might come under Jewish rule. Needless to say, once the mass flight got under way it was almost always welcomed. Often, as in Lyddia and Ramla later in the war, it was assisted by any means, including the most brutal. Over the next six months or so the result was the uprooting of perhaps 600,000–760,000 people from their homes. This was 75–85 percent of the non-Jewish population in the area that later became part of Israel.[21]

Not to be outdone, Hagana for its part followed up on "Operation Nachshon" by reinforcing its hold over the road to Jerusalem and the city itself by clearing Arab villages in the area. The task was entrusted to a newly established PALMACH brigade, Harel; its commander was the newly promoted Yitschak Rabin. Like the rest, Rabin had gained considerable experience in small-unit and underground operations; with Dayan he helped spearhead the British invasion of Syria in 1941. Like the rest, too, he had never gone through anything more advanced than a platoon commander's course conducted under somewhat irregular conditions. To the last night of his life he would recall "the good-looking boys" with whom he had fought in this area, and so many of whom had died.

During April 19–22 Rabin's men passed four major convoys into Jerusalem, though the last one was attacked and badly mauled. These reinforcements were used in "Operation Yevusi" (after the biblical, pre-Israelite inhabitants of the area) in order to extend the Jewish-controlled part of Jerusalem north and south. Fighting, conducted almost exclusively with small arms and at very close quarters, was heavy; in the south the dominating monastery of Saint Simon, held by a company that counted among its ranks *two* future chiefs of staff (David Elazar and Refael Eytan), came within a hair of being overrun.[22] The follow-up on "Operation Yevusi" was "Operation Kilshon (Pitchfork)," which opened during the first half of May and extended the Jewish hold on the western part of the city.

Even so, not all objectives were achieved. In particular, the overlooking hill of Nebi Samuel and the Arab neighborhood that links Jerusalem with Hebrew University on top of Mount Scopus could not be secured, the former because the attack on it failed and the latter because the British, in one of their last acts, made Hagana return it to the Arabs (in whose hands it remained until 1967). More serious, Hagana did not succeed in breaking the siege of the Jewish Quarter of the Old City. Surrounded by walls that proved impregnable to available weapons, fewer than 2,000 Jews were fighting for their lives against an Arab population ten times as large. The latter were assisted by a battalion of the Arab Legion, some 600 strong with artillery, which, contrary to the understanding achieved in the previous year, had joined the fighting.[23]

Although ultimately successful in securing West Jerusalem, more or less, Hagana was unable to hold on to Gush Etsion, which fell to the Arab Legion on May 12 after several attempts to reinforce it failed.[24] The next month would witness continued fighting in the city proper and in the corridor leading to it. The latter could be extended to a maximum width of perhaps twenty miles, but in the former no further progress was made by either side. Although casualties were heavy, geographically speaking the scale of the fighting may be gauged from the fact that one "major" Transjordanian armored advance was halted a few hundred yards from its starting point at Nablus Gate. The surrender to the Legion of the Jewish Quarter (May 28) marked the hardening of the battlelines. After that there would be no more great changes until the conclusion of the armistice agreements later in the year, the Legion being content to hold their positions.

Not so in the rest of the country, where there was usually less dependence on individual roads, much greater room for maneuver, and, in most places, no well-organized and well-commanded Arab Legion to limit what Hagana and its PALMACH spearhead could do. Calling in reservists, PALMACH was expanded to eight battalions, although not all of them were as well trained and cohesive as the original force. During the second week of April some of these forces underwent their baptism of fire by taking on Kauji's forces in the Valley of Esdraelon. Having been repulsed at Tirat Tsvi and Gesher, Kauji crossed the Jordan farther south and, finding himself unopposed, moved into his old stomping ground of Nablus, Tul Karem, and Jenin. From there he moved west toward Mishmar Ha-emek, a strategically positioned *kibbuts* in the Valley of Esdraelon. Next he may have planned to continue to Haifa in a pincer movement on both sides of Mount Carmel (at any rate that is what strategy would dictate).

Sadeh commanded the opposition, an assortment of PALMACH companies and local Hagana forces totaling between two and three battalions. He used the kind of flexible tactics that would become PALMACH's specialty: In the face of Kauji's superiority in artillery his men abandoned positions by day but reoccupied them by night, thus holding their own at comparatively low cost. A battle of attrition developed that lasted for a few days—strangely enough under the eyes of the British, who at first tried to mediate but later threw in the towel. It ended when Sadeh ambushed a major advance by Kauji's forces (April 11–12), outflanked him from the south, and, by threatening to cut him off from his base near Jenin, forced him to retreat northeast toward Nazaret. At the time these events took place neither the

Syrians nor the Lebanese regular forces had as yet entered the war. With the British withdrawal continuing apace, practically the only obstacle standing between the Jews and full control over the northern part of the country was the local Palestinians.[25]

Even more so than in the area around Jerusalem, Palestinians who were on their own were in no position to withstand the onslaught of the much stronger Hagana forces. The first town to come under attack was Tiberias, which fell on April 17–18, its 2,000 Arab inhabitants (facing perhaps three times as many Jews) being evacuated by the British. Next was Haifa, where the two sides had been sniping and car-bombing each other for months; on April 21 it became clear that the British were going to evacuate their positions early, opening the door to a Hagana offensive. Five CHISH companies made their way down the mountain from the Jewish neighborhoods into the Arab ones below, causing all but 3,000 of the Arab inhabitants to flee.

Next, one PALMACH and one CHISH battalion were concentrated in the upper part of the Jordan Valley (north of the Sea of Galilee); fighting all the way, they made their way west into the mountains toward Safed. Here the local militias were assisted by a part of the Arab Salvation Army, which had infiltrated from Lebanon. Its commander, Adib Shishakli, was a Syrian regular army officer who later rose to become his country's dictator. Like those of Kauji farther to the south, his troops wore uniforms (they even carried gas masks)[26] and were provided with vehicles and artillery.

The fighting for Safed lasted about a week; in terms of casualties suffered by both sides it was one of the most bitter chapters in the war. Concentrating all available forces for a single blow—even at the risk of denuding the Jewish settlements in the area[27]—Yigal Allon used his PALMACH battalion to outflank the town from the north, thus interposing his forces between Shishakli and the Lebanese border. With Hagana's homemade mortars in support, he stormed the city on the night of May 10–11, an operation that culminated in hand-to-hand fighting in the vaults of the ancient citadel. Almost simultaneously, other forces advanced north from the area east of the Gilboa Mountains to Bet Shean, which they took. The last northern city to fall was Acre; on May 17–18 it came under attack by a force that drove north some eight miles from Haifa. Here, however, the Arab population was not forced to flee, and once the first few chaotic days were over it was able to continue life in comparative security.

Thus, during a period of approximately five weeks, units belonging to several different Hagana brigades—the largest formation actually employed in any single operation seems to have been the battalion—cleared almost the entire northern part of the country, including the Valley of Esdraelon, Haifa, and upper Galilee (both east and west). Meanwhile around Tel Aviv other forces were planning to occupy Jaffa, the largest single Arab town in the country. During preparations they were forestalled by ETSEL units; the latter had hijacked a British train[28] and helped themselves to mortars and ammunition. On April 25 they opened their attack and were joined by Hagana two days later. Known as "Operation Chamets (Leavened Bread)," it ended with the clearing of the entire area around Tel Aviv of Arab inhabitants. In the aftermath the largest British army camp in the country, built for 30,000 men and located at Sarafand, some ten miles east of Tel Aviv, was also taken under the noses of Arab Legionaries who had been sent to occupy it.

By the middle of May, Jewish forces had occupied about one-third of the total area allocated to the Israeli state under the UN partition plan. Militarily the Palestinians had nearly ceased to exist. Following events at Dir Yassin and elsewhere, hundreds of thousands were already on their way to exile, whereas the rest could do little more than pray for assistance from outside. On May 13 even the road to the Negev was temporarily opened, though the forces that carried out the operation were promptly recalled to fight at Latrun, on the way to Jerusalem, thus opening the way to the Egyptian army, which was soon to advance from Gaza. Yet Hagana's victories should not be allowed to hide the desperate nature of the struggle, as it made evident the loss of Jerusalem's Jewish Quarter and Gush Etsion, the near disaster at Mishmar Ha-emek, the tough fighting around Safed, and of course the large number of casualties. The casualties were in fact an indication of the troops' determination to conquer or die. Nor was it by any means the end of the story. Instead, just when they had more or less overcome the Palestinians and their allies from the Arab Salvation Army, Israel faced the much more formidable challenge of invasion by armies of neighboring countries.

Repelling Invasion: half-track column, Golani Brigade, October 1948.

CHAPTER 6

REPELLING INVASION

THE INTERNAL AND external political events that led to the declaration of the Jewish state do not concern us here. Suffice it to say, although the British withdrawal had not yet been completed, the creation of the new state was formally announced by Ben Gurion in Tel Aviv on May 15, 1948. This announcement was followed promptly by a declaration of war on the part of the neighboring Arab countries of Lebanon, Syria, Transjordan, Iraq, and Egypt. The Arab Legion was already taking part in the fighting in the area around Jerusalem. The rest now sent their armies into action.

The possibility, indeed probability, of having to fight not only the local Palestinian population but also the regular forces of the above-mentioned countries had preoccupied the leadership of the *Yishuv* for some years past.[1] According to information recorded in Ben Gurion's diary, in mid-1947 the Arab states could muster a total of 160,000 men as well as four hundred tanks and armored cars.[2] However, by no means did all of these forces take part in the invasion of Palestine. Some Arab regimes, notably in Syria and Jordan, could not bring their full weight to bear owing to internal security concerns, a problem that, then and later, affected Israel only to a marginal extent. The geographical positions of Egypt and Iraq meant that they would have to operate their armies at the ends of long and, as it turned out, vulnerable lines of communication.

In the event the invading forces were limited to approximately 30,000 men. The strongest single contingent was the Jordanian one, already described. Next came the Egyptians with 5,500 men, then the Iraqis with 4,500 who, as they deployed in the Nablus area, were joined by perhaps 3,000 local irregulars. The total was thus around eight rather under-strength brigades, some of them definitely of second- and even third-rate quality. To these must be added approximately 2,000 Lebanese (one brigade) and 6,000 Syrians (three brigades).[3]

Thus, even though the Arabs countries outnumbered the *Yishuv* by better than forty-to-one,[4] in terms of military manpower available for combat in Palestine the two sides were fairly evenly matched. As time went on and both sides sent in reinforcements the balance changed in the Jews' favor; by October 1948 they had almost 90,000 men and women under arms, the Arabs only 68,000.[5] Not so, however, in terms of equipment. According to Ben Gurion's strategic adviser, Yisrael Beer, the Egyptian army entered the conflict with 48 guns, 25–30 armored cars, 10–20 tanks, and 21–25 combat aircraft (another source puts the total number of Egyptian aircraft at 177, but many of them were not serviceable). The Iraqis had 48 guns, 25–30 armored cars, and 20 aircraft; Syria, 24 guns, 36 armored cars, 10–20 tanks, and 14 aircraft; Jordan, 24 guns and 45 armored cars; and Lebanon, 8 guns and 9 armored cars.[6] The somewhat schematic nature of these figures makes one suspect that they were calculated from tables of organization rather than counted in the field—the more so because the Arab forces, like their Jewish opponents, rarely operated in forces larger than a brigade. Accordingly it is hard to say whether they corresponded to reality, particularly when readiness is taken into account.

Against these forces Hagana, thanks to the British blockade, initially possessed nothing heavier than home-built armored cars (in reality, trucks with two steel plates with a layer of concrete between), 2- and 3-inch mortars, and PIATs (light antitank weapons). Some progress, however, had been made during the last months of the mandate; retreating armies have a habit of leaving equipment behind. Some arms were diverted from bases as they were being evacuated; others were purchased from corrupt British personnel, enabling Hagana to acquire a few light aircraft as well as a couple of tanks. Additional arms had been ordered abroad, and their escorts, Hagana's representatives abroad, were waiting for the opportunity to ship them to Haifa. The United States having placed the Middle East under an arms embargo that was efficiently enforced, the principal sources were Italy and Yugoslavia, both of which showed some sympathy for the *Yishuv*. Even more important was Czechoslovakia, which had just fallen into Stalin's clutches. Soon it began selling comparatively large amounts of weapons and equipment; priced at $12 million (U.S.), this brought in one-quarter of Czechoslovakia's entire foreign currency income for the year.[7]

Arriving before May 15 or shortly thereafter, the Czech arms included 25 fighters (Messerschmidt ME–109s), 200 heavy machine guns, 5,021 light machine guns, 24,500 rifles, and no fewer than 52,540,000 rounds of ammunition[8]—with the result that by June there were enough small arms to equip all units. Heavy arms, however, were still desperately short. Military vehicles such as jeeps, command cars, and half-tracks arrived in dribs and drabs. The same applied to artillery, tanks, and aircraft—the latter including a handful of former American B–17 bombers as well as some Dakota trans-

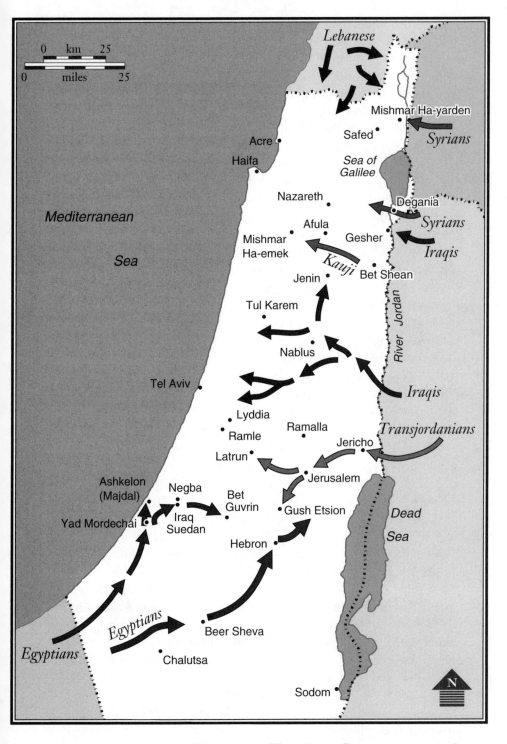

MAP 6.1   THE ARAB INVASIONS, 1948

ports. Much of the materiel that did arrive had been sold as scrap and was antiquated, such as pre–World War I 65mm French mountain guns, which were promptly nicknamed "Napoleonchiks." Inexperienced Hagana personnel did not always know how to maintain and operate the many different types of new arms. By the time the war ended, the heavy-weapon gap between the two sides was decreasing, but it had not yet been closed.[9]

The departure of the British also allowed for accelerated construction of a regular army. During the last years of the mandate Hagana had operated a few light aircraft under the guise of an aero-sports club.[10] Emerging from the underground, the Sherut Aviri (PALMACH's underground air arm) had 37 pilots including, besides the self-trained PALMACHniks, a few former Royal Air Force personnel (the most prominent of whom was Ezer Weizman)[11] and a few Jewish and gentile volunteers from various countries. The main base was at Sdeh Dov, north of Tel Aviv. However, as hostilities expanded, several other bases were improvised around the country; these were the days when fighters, if not bombers, could still operate from dirt airstrips. During the first two weeks after the establishment of the Jewish state the Egyptian air force sent out its Dakota transports to bomb Sdeh Dov and Tel Aviv proper. The Israeli pilots for their part took to the air and flew reconnaissance, liaison, strafing, and bombing sorties countrywide, even though some "bombs" were no more than pieces of pipe filled with explosives and dropped by hand. On June 3 they scored their first kills on two Egyptian planes that attacked Tel Aviv, thereby bringing the enemy "strategic bombing" campaign to an end.

What was true of the air force also applied to the navy, which comprised an incredible gathering of antiquated hulks. Most of them were former immigrant-carrying vessels that had been seized by the British, taken to the port of Haifa, and abandoned; one had started life as an icebreaker in the U.S. Coast Guard and was sold to Hagana for the princely price of $10. At first none were armed, though two were later provided with 65mm and 75mm field guns. Officers and men were inexperienced. The former were mostly PALYAM personnel who had previously been in charge of immigrant ships (although they did not themselves sail, a task left to hired crews); the latter were a miscellaneous lot of landlubbers who might have sailed a boat at some point in their lives.[12] In spite of its obvious shortcomings, this improvised force as early as June 4 fought a naval engagement off the coast of Tel Aviv. Supported by a few aircraft from Sdeh Dov, the two available Israeli ships—one of which was armed with wooden guns—took on an Egyptian force of one destroyer and three landing craft. The enemy was forced to turn tail and desist any offensive operations he may have been planning.

Finally, the weeks immediately following independence were used to disband the various existing military and paramilitary organizations and place them under a single, unified command. TSAHAL (that is, the IDF) was officially brought into being on May 28 by means of a decree signed by the provisional government; from then on it was to be the sole regular force in charge of fighting Israel's external enemies. For Hagana personnel, commanders, and staffs this involved a mere change in nomenclature. The situation was different in regard to ETSEL and LECHI, which had heretofore been beyond the pale but had to be brought under central government control. Although, as the future was to show, LECHI had one last spectacular terrorist act up its sleeve, the integration of its personnel proceeded smoothly. Not so ETSEL, which proved a much tougher nut to crack.

On June 2, five days after the IDF had been formally established, ETSEL concluded an agreement with the provisional government. Begin agreed to dissolve his organization, hand over its arms, and send its members to join the IDF.[13] What followed next is subject to an intense and politically heated dispute. ETSEL's 5,000 men joined the IDF not as individuals but in seven battalions of troops who were concentrated in Jerusalem and who operated under their own command. Meanwhile an ETSEL ship carrying nine hundred volunteers and a relatively large quantity of arms was on its way from Port de Bouc near Marseilles.[14] Apparently Ben Gurion and Begin could not agree how to distribute the arms among their men. The former insisted that all be handed over to the IDF; the latter wanted to retain 20 percent for the ETSEL battalions, which was roughly their proportion in the army. Fearing, or pretending to fear, that ETSEL was engineering a coup, Ben Gurion ordered Hagana to shell the ship as it was anchored opposite Tel Aviv on Monday, June 21. *Altalena* caught fire and went to the bottom with the loss of sixteen lives as well as all the arms onboard. The intensity of the feelings raised by this episode may be gauged from the fact that, then and later, Ben Gurion used the epithet "sacred" when referring to the gun that had done the shooting.

While the provisional government was using these somewhat brutal methods to put its house in order, the war had been under way for more than a month. Although the various Arab invasions took place almost simultaneously, their coordination was more apparent than real. Probably the one thing on which the Arabs could agree was the need to aid the Palestinians. This in turn may have reflected their fear of the extremely dynamic Jewish community and Israel's capacity for future expansion—a subject that had come up at the Cairo meeting of Arab prime ministers in December 1947.[15] That apart, the invaders were often at cross-purposes. Proceeding clockwise on the map, the Lebanese were simply aping the

Syrians. The Syrians may have dreamed about reestablishing Greater Syria (i.e., the pre-1914 situation in which both Palestine and Transjordan were ruled from Damascus), yet if such was their goal the steps they took toward its realization were totally inadequate. The Iraqi motive in sending an expeditionary force to Palestine—a country with which they had no common border—was probably to frustrate the Syrians. The same was true of King Abdullah, who as we have seen had his own designs on at least part of Palestine and may even have dreamed of offering his "protection" to the Jews and annexing it in its entirety.[16]

Finally, the Egyptians probably wanted to prevent a situation whereby a stretch of Israeli-owned land, the Negev Desert, would cut them off from the rest of the Arab world. Nor could they afford to see parts of Palestine occupied by other Arab states without seeking compensation for themselves (and, of course, vice versa). Thus, reflecting these divergent objectives, there was no common military headquarters, no attempt at coordinating the offensives of the Arab armies, and, apart from embassies maintained in the others' capitals, not even a regular liaison service for sharing enemy intelligence.[17] Accordingly, once the road network inside Palestine had been more or less secured and the Israeli command-and-control problems solved, the IDF was able to operate on internal lines and beat the Arabs in detail.

Preliminary skirmishes with the Syrians had taken place since the previous November; on May 18, 1948, after two days of shelling, a brigade-sized force came down the Golan Heights and occupied Tsemach on the southern shores of Lake Galilee. The Hagana commander in charge happened to be Moshe Dayan, then thirty-three years old and native to the area. The local *kibbutsim*, Degania A and Degania B, had been fortified for defense and reinforced by a PALMACH battalion. On May 19 Syrian forces crossed the Jordan and gingerly moved west. Supported by artillery and a few tanks, they tried to overrun the settlements, which fought back with PIATs and Molotov cocktails. The battle climaxed during the afternoon of May 20, when the Jews positioned four Napoleonchiks on the overlooking hills to the west and opened fire. As Dayan later wrote, no sooner did the Syrian troops hear the shells whistling overhead than they fled, leaving Tsemach strewn with bodies, weapons, and vehicles.[18] Only once more did the Syrian army try to invade Palestine proper, when in the first week of June a brigade-sized force struck north of Lake Chule and occupied Mishmar Ha-yarden—a purely local operation that led nowhere (see Map 6.1).

Farther south, the vanguard of the Iraqi expeditionary force had arrived in the Jordan Valley after marching almost a thousand miles from Baghdad. On May 14 it occupied the electricity works at Naharayim; what equipment could be moved was stolen, the rest was demolished, and it has remained in ruins. Finding the bridges across the river likewise demolished, they established a pontoon bridge and crossed toward *kibbuts* Gesher, the neighboring police fort, and the overlooking Crusader fortress of Belvoir blocking the road to the interior. If Ben Gurion's diary can be believed, the defenders had, apart from rifles and Stens (British light submachine guns), only one PIAT and two mortars.[19] Nevertheless the Iraqis, repulsed in turn at each main point of attack, decided to withdraw after a week's fighting.

Meanwhile other Iraqi forces had entered Palestine farther south. Concentrating in the Nablus area, they collected any of Kauji's warriors that were still around and attempted attacks to the west and south. During the end of May and beginning of June there was heavy fighting on both sides of the Iraqi enclave as IDF units, basing themselves at the local settlements, contained the breakout attempts and even mounted an offensive toward Jenin. Wadi Ara, the most important corridor connecting the Plain of Sharon to the Valley of Esdraelon, was captured by the Golani infantry brigade, and inhabitants abandoned most of the Arab villages on either side. However, the Iraqi forces in the area remained undefeated and were to make their presence felt during the summer months, when they succeeded in breaking the Israeli hold on the hills around Jenin.

In central Palestine things did not go as well. As the defenders of Jerusalem's Jewish Quarter were approaching the end of their tether during the second half of May, the center of gravity shifted twenty or so miles west to Latrun. Here a strategically positioned police fort dominated the road toward the city; like others of its kind it had been built after the 1929 uprising and was designed to withstand, if not a regular army attack, at any rate the worst that lightly armed bands could muster. Somehow Hagana's intelligence service missed the fact that Abdullah's Legionaries, and not merely Palestinians, were positioned in the fortress—and that they possessed heavy machine guns and light artillery in addition to small arms. Hence preparations for the assault seem to have been somewhat haphazard.

Originally planned to start before midnight, the approach march was delayed.[20] By the time the troops, two crack battalions, reached their jumping-off positions on the morning of May 23, it was already daytime. Coming under murderous fire from machine guns and artillery positioned on the station's roof, they did their best but were beaten back with heavy losses; abandoned in the sweltering heat, the stench of decomposing bodies spoiled the air for weeks thereafter.[21] Among the wounded was twenty-year-old Ariel Sharon, who commanded the lead platoon of one battalion (even though he had never gone through officer school). He and a few comrades barely made it back, crawling some 1,200 meters over the stone terraces while under fire all the way.

The next attempt to recover Latrun took place on May 30. This time the infantry was supported by Napoleonchiks, armored cars, a few half-tracks, and even a couple of Cromwell tanks that had been illegally sold by British personnel. However, inexperience and faulty coordination caused this assault to be no more successful than the first.[22] Some of the infantry consisted of untrained personnel who had been mustered in the European refugee camps and were thrown into the battle a few days after their arrival with hardly any time to acclimatize themselves. Among the tank crews, one consisted of former British soldiers—mercenaries, to call things by their name—and the other of Russian immigrants who claimed to have operated tanks in the war against Germany. The two were thus unable to communicate; when the former withdrew due to mechanical failure the latter turned tail and returned to the assembly area without having fired a shot. This and similar incidents were typical of a motley, ill-organized, and ill-trained—but on the whole highly motivated—force.

Having failed to capture Latrun, the IDF, as it now was, solved the problem by improvising a road that bypassed the salient to the southwest, thereby allowing the convoys to resume their journey to Jerusalem and saving the western part of the town from sharing the fate of the Jewish Quarter. Over the next week or so—until the first truce went into effect on June 11—both sides shelled the other sporadically across the hills that separated the fortress from the road. Meanwhile the brunt of the fighting shifted even farther south. Following the lead of the Arab Legion, a battalion of Muslim Brotherhood volunteers commanded by Lt. Col. Abd al Aziz did not wait for the proclamation of the Jewish state, starting its invasion on May 10. Its attempt to capture Kfar Darom, south of Gaza, failed. However, it did occupy Iraq Suedan, another stout, British-built police station, which dominated the coastal road to the south.

Five days later the regular Egyptian army joined the invasion with two division-size task forces. One prong followed Abd al Aziz and, basing itself at Gaza, took the coastal road. It bypassed Kfar Darom, overran *kibbuts* Yad Mordechai, and drove toward Tel Aviv. By May 29 it had reached as far as Ashdod, only twenty-five miles south of the main Jewish city; there, however, it was brought to a halt after a bridge had been demolished and the advance columns were attacked by four of the IDF's newly arrived Messer-schmidt fighters. The other prong entered Erets Yisrael after crossing Sinai by a different road farther south. Basing itself at Rafah, it advanced southwest and occupied Beer Sheva before driving northeast into the West Bank, reaching as far as the outskirts of Jerusalem, where it linked up with Abdullah's troops (see Map 6.1).

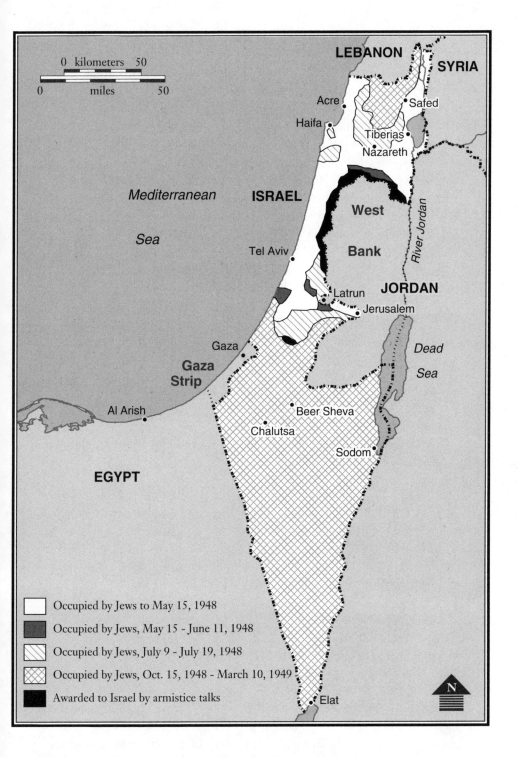

Occupied by Jews to May 15, 1948

Occupied by Jews, May 15 - June 11, 1948

Occupied by Jews, July 9 - July 19, 1948

Occupied by Jews, Oct. 15, 1948 - March 10, 1949

Awarded to Israel by armistice talks

MAP 6.2   PHASES IN THE WAR OF INDEPENDENCE, 1948–1949

Like the rest of the Jewish territory, the southern front was defended partly by the settlements—all of which were more or less fortified and provided with arms—and partly by two understrength Hagana (IDF) brigades that seldom if ever operated as complete units. Early attempts to halt the Egyptians failed; settlements with defenses that proved good enough to repel Palestinian irregulars and halfhearted Syrian and Iraqi attacks were either bypassed or proved incapable of halting a full-scale assault by the Egyptian army. Attacked on all fronts simultaneously, usually the best that the former Hagana forces could do was to send platoon-size reinforcements to settlements as they came under attack. In the meantime it desperately improvised a main line of defense from Ashdod to Bet Guvrin in the east.

On June 11 a four-week truce mandated by the UN Security Council came into effect. While enabling both sides to recuperate, it worked in favor of the Jews, who had just about reached the end of their tether. Accustomed to having their armies fed by the British, Arab countries had made no special efforts to build arms acquisition organizations. Not so the *Yishuv*, which now began to reap the results of three years' efforts buying arms and preparing them for transport to Erets Yisrael. The most spectacular acquisition was the B–17s—the famous "Flying Fortresses" used by the Allies in World War II. They arrived from Czechoslovakia on July 17, having bombed Cairo, Al Arish, and Gaza along the way;[23] other aircraft, including British Spitfire and American Mustang fighters bought in Europe, followed in the summer months.

Meanwhile the ground forces, which carried the brunt of the war, received a small number of tanks, half-tracks, and 75mm guns. Although not all of these arms proved serviceable—for example, a handful of Sherman tanks had perforated barrels and could not be reconditioned—they enabled the IDF to establish its first "armored" brigade—with Sadeh as commanding officer. Since there were not nearly enough tanks to go around, only part of one battalion was in fact provided with them. The rest of the troops rode an ill-matched assortment of armored cars, half-tracks, and jeeps with medium machine guns affixed to their hoods. These were good enough to beat the Egyptians, as it turned out.

While Abdullah toured the Arab capitals, vainly seeking to establish a unified command with himself at its head, Ben Gurion held a series of meetings with his commanders in which the lessons of the war were discussed and strategy for the next stage laid down.[24] Perhaps most important, the four weeks of cease-fire were used to rebuild and train the formations (very necessary given that gunners, for example, received six days' training before being sent to the front).[25] A top-level reorganization was carried out and divided the country into four fronts (north, east, center, and south). Although no permanent divisions were established, for the first time Supreme Headquarters appointed commanders at levels higher than that of brigade. When the IDF returned to action it did so not as a loose federation of twelve improvised brigades (plus equally improvised air and naval forces) but as a cohesive, disciplined force capable of coordinating operations on a countrywide scale.[26] To symbolize the change the previous improvised stripes, known as blue band ranks (after a brand of margarine), were abolished. Insignia of rank were introduced for the first time, with the names of the various grades taken from the Bible.[27]

When fighting reopened on July 7, the IDF's first objective was to eject the Syrians out of Mishmar Ha-yarden. A force of four battalions—approximately 2,000 men—concentrated in neighboring *kibbutsim*. Surprising the Syrians, it carried out the task with relative ease; however, a nighttime attempt to cross the Jordan to take the Syrian rear suffered delays and was met by a counterattack when morning broke. Several days of heavy fighting ensued, during which the IDF, feeling itself inferior in firepower, adopted its standard method: Take cover by day while engaging mobile operations by night. Despite the intervention of the B–17s, which bombed the Syrians, these battles ended in a stalemate that would last until the end of the war.

Not so in lower Galilee, into which Kauji had retreated after his April defeat. Rebuilding his forces with volunteers from Lebanon, on July 12 he debouched southward intending to cut the road leading northeast from the Valley of Esdraelon, thus preparing for the eventual reoccupation of Tiberias. The ensuing battle had much in common with the earlier one at Mishmar Ha-emek; for eight days the Arab Salvation Army, supported by artillery, faced an Israeli infantry battalion engaged in a flexible defense. In the event these engagements proved to be a useful cover for "Operation Dekel (Palm Tree)," directed into Kauji's rear from its jumping-off positions on the Mediterranean coast north of Haifa. The movement started on the night of July 15 and proceeded almost without resistance, thus proving how far the IDF had already gone in breaking the Palestinians. Nazaret surrendered on July 16, forcing Kauji to suspend his attacks and retreat north.

Meanwhile on the central front, operations during the Ten Days—that is, the period until the next truce entered into force—were equally hard-fought. Two brigades widened the corridor that led to Jerusalem, one in the region south of Latrun and the other farther west in the Ramla-Lyddia area. As the Arab Legion stood by, the town of Lyddia was cleared by an "armored" battalion—in fact, half-tracks spearheaded by a former British armored car—commanded by Moshe Dayan.[28] Like an old-fashioned cavalry regiment charging a line of infantry, it drove through the main street and reversed direction, firing wildly into houses on both sides. The psychological shock caused the fall not only of Lyddia; neighboring Ramla surrendered immediately, and the IDF had captured the most important airfield in the country.

With the areas west and south of Latrun now firmly in Israeli hands (see Map 6.2), Allon as the front commander determined that the time had come to make another attempt on the police fortress. Once again, poor intelligence concerning the strength of the Arab Legion in the area failed to register the presence of two armored cars; the Israelis had also neglected to provide the leading company with antitank weapons. In addition, and as happened during the previous attacks against the same objective, coordinating forces at night proved beyond the capability of headquarters—which for some reason was located much too far in the rear.[29] This failure was followed almost immediately by an equally abortive attempt to reconquer the Jordanian-held Old City. Mounted on July 17–18, just before the second truce went into effect, the operation was repulsed with heavy losses; its commander, David Shealtiel, was relieved.[30]

In the south, the truce had caught the Egyptian army on the eve of a major attempt to bypass Ashdod to the east by driving farther inland. Breaking the truce twenty-four hours early, the Egyptians attacked the settlement of Negba; it was their single largest operation, conducted with the aid of a reinforced brigade with three infantry battalions, an armored battalion, an armored car battalion, an artillery battalion, antitank weapons, and air support. The battle culminated on July 12 when 4,000 artillery rounds came down on the *kibbuts*—inflicting few casualties, however, since the civilian population had long been evacuated and the entire defense put underground.[31] Negba held out and the Egyptian attempt, the last one of the war, to break through the line that led from Ashdod on the Mediterranean coast to Bet Guvrin in the Judaean foothills failed. Yet the IDF's attempt to retake Iraq-Suedan was also repulsed with losses, earning the fort its nickname—"The Monster."

The first truce had come to the IDF "like manna from heaven," enabling it to recuperate and reorganize. Not so the second truce of July 18, which found the IDF in a much stronger position. In the north the Syrians had been definitely repulsed; only parts of eastern upper Galilee were still in the hands of Kauji, who nevertheless would be thrown out with little difficulty during "Operation Chiram" in late October. In the center, along what would become the Israel-Jordan border, large-scale fighting between the Iraqis and Jordanians had ended, except for the area around Bet Shemesh, southwest of Jerusalem, which had been reached by an

Egyptian force from Hebron. In the south the last and most powerful Egyptian offensive had been broken. By contrast the Israelis, now with a rapidly growing army and in full offensive swing, were poised to take the initiative and carry it through to the end of the war.

On September 17, 1948, while the second truce was still in effect, a party of LECHI men murdered the UN mediator, Count Folke Bernadotte, and one of his assistants. The previous day he had submitted his proposals to resolve the conflict, which included redrawing the borders to establish a much smaller Jewish state than that provided in the UN resolution of November 29, 1947 (the entire Negev Desert was to be taken away) and granting the right of return to Arab refugees. His murder was roundly condemned by the government, which nevertheless used the opportunity to put the Jewish house in order. During the next few days two hundred LECHI men were arrested, and the dissolution of the IDF's former ETSEL battalions was ordered. Having lost their troops, former ETSEL leaders were deprived of any participation in power and consigned to the opposition (from which they would emerge, to everybody's amazement, following the 1977 elections).

In the short run, much more significant was the decision to dismember PALMACH. As the *Yishuv*'s main strike force, PALMACH had borne the brunt of the fighting between December 1947 and May 1948; subsequently, when it was swamped by newly raised IDF formations, it continued to act as the latter's cutting edge. Elite formations have a way of looking down on the rest of the forces and disobeying orders; PALMACH was no exception (to the point that Allon felt obliged to apologize for his men's arrogance).[32] Early in the war PALMACH brigades, engaged in desperate fighting all over the country, expressed their lack of confidence in Yadin and the general staff, repeatedly refusing to carry out orders unless they had been transmitted to them by way of PALMACH's own central headquarters.[33] Subsequently entire groups of PALMACH men deserted their assigned units to rejoin their comrades.[34] On another occasion PALMACHniks stopped an IDF convoy, beat its occupants, and "confiscated" a jeep and seventy-six rifles—resulting in a complaint that found its way to Ben Gurion himself.[35]

According to Ben Gurion's U.S. adviser, Col. David Marcus, PALMACH in the meantime had developed into "the best-motivated infantry in the world."[36] Though the incidents were indicative of the organization's superb cohesion and fighting spirit, they also presented a challenge that no defense minister or well-run armed force could tolerate; perhaps, as often claimed, they were seized upon merely to rid a force affiliated with the prime minister's left-wing political rivals. In any case the order to disband PALMACH went out on October 7—first its headquarters and then—after the war ended—its fighting formations. With that, the integration of the IDF as the Jewish state's sole armed force for use against external enemies was accomplished. It was a move that the PALMACHniks never forgot or forgave, and many of them left the IDF en masse as soon as the war ended.

Thus the stage was set for the final act in the great drama that, starting on November 29, 1947, had already claimed so much blood. During the second truce Ben Gurion received conflicting advice as to which enemy, forces under King Abdullah or the Egyptians, should be the target of the forthcoming Israeli offensive. In the end, however, it was decided to leave the Arab Legion where it was rather than attempt the conquest of the most densely settled Arab areas of Erets Yisrael—a decision that may have been motivated in part by fear of British intervention.[37] Allon, now in command of a comparatively enormous force of four brigades, was given the green light. On October 15, 1948, the IDF broke the truce and started its attempt to roll up the Egyptian front from east to west. On that day everything seemed to go wrong, including, besides the IDF's usual inability to coordinate infantry, artillery, and armor,[38] the failure of the air force to carry out its operations on time. Allon, however, refused to give up. Instead he used his initial attack as a feint, rapidly redeploying his forces and throwing them against Chuleikat in the center. The fact that the other fronts remained quiet allowed yet another brigade to be brought up, and the combined force attacked during the night of October 18–19.

Allon could not be suspected of having studied armored operations in any depth,[39] but Sadeh, commanding the Eighth Brigade, certainly had.[40] This may explain why operations proceeded almost set-piece according to the teachings of Basil Liddell Hart, the famous British military critic; another model might have been Rommel at Gazala (May–June 1942), where he stuck his head between two British forces and "threatened" to surround both.[41] Whatever its strategic origins, once the breakthrough had been achieved an "expanding torrent" was formed. One Israeli force turned west, threatening to cut off the Egyptians along the coast and forcing them into a fifteen-mile retreat on Gaza; had it not been for their engineering service, which improvised a new road, the Egyptians would have been surrounded and annihilated. The other arm drove south to Beer Sheva. So surprised were the Egyptians that, when Allon's units approached the town on October 20, they had not even been put on alert. Beer Sheva's fall meant that the communications of the Egyptian eastern prong, running from Hebron to the Suez Canal, were cut.

Isolated in the hills of southern Judaea and receiving barely a trickle of supplies, the eastern forces were no longer able to play an active role in the war. Not so the western forces, still occupying the Gaza Strip—that term did not yet exist—as well as some areas farther east and southeast. With Allon still in command, the IDF now husbanded its forces for one last effort centering around the capture of "The Monster" at Iraq Suedan. The first step was to create an unprecedented concentration of firepower. It included, besides the now standard 75mm field guns, improvised flamethrowers and an experimental 160mm mortar—the last a TAAS weapon that proved more dangerous to its operators than to the enemy. Personally reconnoitering the terrain, Sadeh discovered an approach route that would hide the attackers from the eyes of the garrison for as long as possible. This was followed by a week's training, during which tanks (the two that were available), half-tracks, jeeps, artillery, infantry, and combat engineers all rehearsed their appointed roles to prevent further failures in coordination.

The attack started at 2:00 P.M. on November 9, the time being selected so that the setting sun would interfere with the defenders' sight as the afternoon wore on. The preceding weeks' preparations and training paid off; there were no further errors, and all operations functioned like clockwork. Though the Egyptians put up a stout resistance, two hours' bombardment—heavier than anything seen during the war—not only wrecked the fort but also provided cover for IDF infantry and combat engineers, who were able to breach the fences and plant dynamite charges under the walls.[42] Still, the defenders refused to surrender and had to be ferreted out by means of tear gas. As Iraq Suedan surrendered, the road to the Negev was definitely opened. During the next few weeks the IDF occupied its eastern part, including Sodom at the southern end of the Dead Sea, which had been isolated almost since the beginning of the war.

A two-month truce imposed by the UN Security Council followed, during which Israelis and Egyptians tried unsuccessfully to negotiate a settlement. When no agreement could be reached, however, Allon developed a typically sophisticated plan to defeat the remaining Egyptian expeditionary forces by means of a well-coordinated strike against the rear. The operation started on the night of December 22 when an infantry brigade was sent to attack the Gaza Strip from east to west; to make sure that Egyptian attention would indeed be directed to that sector, air and naval forces bombed and shelled Gaza. Meanwhile the bulk of Allon's forces, moving mainly by night and in great secrecy, were concentrated in the Beer Sheva area to the southeast. From there they took an old, barely passable Roman road to Chalutsa south on the Palestinian-Egyptian border.

Arriving at Chalutsa on December 27 after a grueling march, Allon's leading force—a battalion from the Negev brigade riding jeeps—crossed the border into the Sinai. There it easily overran the local Egyptian positions at Abu Ageila and captured a military airfield. Next, in classic "expanding torrent" fashion, the offensive split. One brigade drove north-northwest toward Rafah, at the southern extremity of the Gaza Strip. There, however, it met with stout resistance; the Egyptians not only held their own but counterattacked with tanks and machine gun carriers, thus showing they still had plenty of fight.

Whether or not it had been planned in this way, the reverse caused the center of gravity to shift to Allon's other brigade. Advancing northwest from Abu Ageila, by December 29 it had reached Al Arish on the Mediterranean, thus cutting the road from Rafah back to Port Said. It was a classic "indirect approach" operation carried out against little opposition and with barely any loss. However, when the British government presented an ultimatum and threatened to intervene, Ben Gurion decided to retract this particular horn.[43] The order to retreat was given, and by December 31 the "armored" brigade that had carried out the move was on its way back to Chalutsa.

During the next week, last-ditch attempts to capture the Gaza Strip by means of renewed attacks from the south and east failed as the Egyptians, though surrounded from all directions, held on by the skin of their teeth. An armistice with Egypt was concluded on January 7, 1949, but not before five British Spitfires, sent out as a warning to the IDF to desist from its attempts to reduce the Egyptians, had been shot down by the Israel Air Force (IAF). All that remained was to send a brigade due south from Beer Sheva to occupy Elat on the shores of the Red Sea, a move justified by the fact a formal armistice with Jordan had not yet been signed. Encountering weak opposition, the brigade reached its objective on March 10. Lacking a proper Israeli flag, the men painted a sheet with ink and hung it from a mast planted in a barrel. This patriotic act is a fitting metaphor for a war that, from beginning to end, was conducted with much improvisation against a background of inadequate means.

CHAPTER 7

THE ACHIEVEMENT AND THE PRICE

W HEN THE WAR of Independence ended in 1949, less than a
year had passed since Hagana had fully emerged from the
underground—even as late as May 1948 its available striking forces only numbered around 16,000 men.¹ Its successor, the IDF, was
no more than seven months old and had to organize itself amid the most
intense hostilities. Yet it had already proved itself more than a match not
only for the Palestinian Arabs, who after the middle of May 1948 were little more than hapless victims of much stronger forces, but also for the
combined regular armies of the neighboring countries.

Their starting positions located in the north, far from Israel's demographic centers, the Lebanese and the Syrian forces never presented much
of a threat. Both were beaten back, if not exactly with ease then at any rate
before they could advance very far from the borders—meaning, in the Syrian case, perhaps a mile or two west of the River Jordan. The Egyptian
expeditionary force, thanks mainly to the absence of opposition in the
comparatively large, virtually empty area of the Negev Desert, had penetrated much deeper. However, cooperation between its eastern and western arms was always deficient if not nonexistent; when the western arm
came under attack from October on, the eastern arm, sitting in the hills,
did not stir. In the end the latter force was also defeated and had its lines
of communications cut. But for Ben Gurion's decision to heed the UN
Security Council resolution and let it go, it would have been annihilated.

As the last armistice agreements were signed in July 1949 only the Iraqi
expeditionary forces and the Arab Legion remained intact. Even more so
than the Egyptians, who at least had to overrun a couple of settlements that
stood in their way, both owed their presence in Erets Yisrael to the fact that
they had entered unopposed—the former as part of the British imperial forces
and the latter in an area where there were no Jewish settlements after its disgraceful failure at Gesher. The armistice found them in occupation of the
West Bank, including not least the salient of Latrun. Isolated and far from
home, the Iraqis withdrew by their own accord without further fight

The Achievement and the Price: knocked-out Syrian tank, 1948.

(though Iraq refused to sign an armistice and is thus technically still at war with Israel). As for Abdullah's Arab Legion, it had fought better than any other Arab force. Yet on scarcely any occasion had the Arab Legion attempted to conquer territory allocated to the Jews by the partition plan, preferring to stay on the defensive. By the end of the war it remained where it did solely on sufferance and could have been kicked out at any time had Ben Gurion been willing to issue the order.

Then as later, much of this achievement was the result as much of Arab weakness as of Israeli strength. Poor, underequipped, and unorganized, the Palestinian irregulars did what they could, threatening to close the roads and inflicting many casualties between December 1947 and April 1948. Theirs, however, was little more than a loose association of locally based bands; once the British withdrawal was more or less complete and Hagana had the opportunity to flex its muscles, the *jihadias* did not stand a chance against the Jewish steamroller with its companies, battalions, and brigades. As the failure at Mount Kastel in particular indicated, the Palestinian Arabs, following a centuries-old tradition, were capable merely of ambushing and raiding. By contrast the Jews, who from April 1948 on were waging a modern war, overran and conquered (after which, seeking to create fields of fire, they invariably demolished).

Though the Arab armies were better organized and equipped, they also suffered from weaknesses. Hardy, abstemious, and seldom inclined to independent action, Arab troops generally fought quite well as long as they were made to occupy fixed positions and told to defend them to the death—situations in which their superiority in artillery (often the case) could be exploited.[2] Their weaknesses came to the fore when they tried, or were forced, to maneuver; indeed in the majority of cases they could hardly be made to advance without cover from artillery and tanks. As the fall of Beer Sheva in particular shows, the more rapid the pace of operations the more inclined they were to lose their balance and fall apart. During the next twenty-five years these weaknesses resurfaced time and again.

The Arab armies also labored under other problems. Perhaps the most important was a crippling shortage of ammunition, owing to the international arms embargo—which they were unable to overcome for lack of preparation—as well as, in the case of the Egyptians and the Iraqis, long lines of communications.[3] For example, after February 25, 1948, the Arab Legion received no new ammunition for its 20mm guns. Some of the ammunition used by the Iraqi artillery was more than thirty years old; the Syrians had no ammunition for their heavy 155mm guns.[4] Whereas Jewish stockpiles were growing all the time, enemy stocks were so depleted they stole ammunition shipments earmarked for each other. In addition they were ill-coordinated, technically incompetent, slow, ponderous, badly led, and unable to cope with night operations that, willy-nilly, constituted the IDF's expertise.

As might be expected in a situation so unevenly matched, shortcomings in the air and at sea were more apparent than on land. On paper the Arab air forces, having been formed before the war, outnumbered the nascent Israeli one considerably. In practice, however, poor maintenance meant the great majority of Arab aircraft were unserviceable, and the role they played after the first few weeks of war was all but negligible. With the Israelis, too, maintenance left something to be desired; near the end of the war only four out of eleven transports, and thirteen out of twenty-four fighters, were serviceable.[5] However, as the clash with Britain's Royal Air Force proved, aircraft that did take to the air were flown by first-class pilots, either foreign volunteers (the majority) or members of the *Yishuv* who had somehow managed to find the necessary training. Having put an end to the Egyptian attacks on Tel Aviv and gained air superiority over Erets Yisrael, their most important contribution was perhaps maintaining contact with isolated areas, such as the Negev, at times when no other communications existed. During the last months of the war they also bombed and strafed almost unhindered, though operations were seldom decisive due to lack of numbers.

These are technicalities, as events proved. Perhaps most decisive was the fact that the Zionist attempt to cast away Jewish history and create a new race that would be distinguished by its fighting qualities had proved a brilliant success. The IDF's conduct of the War of Independence was certainly anything but perfect. However, as far as can be determined, the blunders often committed, and the unnecessary casualties sometimes suffered, almost always resulted from lack of training and inexperience rather than from cowardice. To quote Ariel Sharon, "There was so much we did not know."[6] In Ben Gurion's words, "Our men in the Army are good Zionists but they have yet to become soldiers."[7] These problems were evident during the attempts to pass convoys into Jerusalem and assist the isolated settlements at Gush Etsion; the same is true in regard to the desperate but ill-starred fighting for Latrun. There, in the face of a disciplined, well-commanded, and well-positioned enemy, one failure followed another until the IDF threw in the towel and, in typical fashion, simply bypassed the problem.

At the heart of the difficulty was a persistent inferiority in firepower. From the time of Mishmar Ha-emek (April 1948) on, this factor forced the Israelis to operate in a dispersed manner, flexibly, and at night so as to close the range between its weapons and those of the enemy. Such operations require good coordination, however, and it was here that command experience, or its lack, was absolutely critical. Thus, a vicious cycle: The very means that were used to overcome one weakness led to another. As time went on and these problems were overcome, operations tended to become better organized and bolder. After several failures, the final attack on Iraq Suedan was as well orchestrated as available means permitted. The occupation of Beer Sheva was like a stroke of lightning, whereas Allon's subsequent drive into the Sinai represented a brilliant if small-scale copy of the 1940 German breakthrough at Sedan, France. As we shall see, this boldness—the most important quality needed by any army—often made up for deficient training, lax discipline, and the sometimes imperfect command-and-control and communications systems. Such boldness would keep the IDF in good stead for perhaps three decades. After that, the situation changed.

From a different perspective, though, the determination to develop a new kind of Jew was carried out at the cost of the cultural blight of an entire generation. Ben Gurion, Ben Tsvi, and many lesser-known comrades—including, in spite of his rough exterior, Yitschak Sadeh—had been remarkably literate. Ben Gurion knew his Bible, collected books, studied ancient Greek, and dabbled in Plato (imagining himself the philosopher king, no doubt). Ben Tsvi was an acknowledged expert on things Arabic and wrote extensively on the history and geography of Erets Yisrael. Sadeh not only knew several modern languages—having been home-tutored by an important early-twentieth-century Jewish intellectual, Hillel Zeitlin—but also had a surprisingly good understanding of art history that resulted from his lifelong habit of collecting reproductions of great artists. He certainly knew how to pull heartstrings; when he published his memoirs, *Ha-pinkas Patu-ach* (The Notebook Is Open), in the early fifties, they became a best-seller.

Among their juniors, Moshe Dayan had a poetic soul, as his memoirs and other writings show. A few such as Shimon Peres—who for that very reason never quite made it in Israeli elections[8]—were even interested in learning. This did not apply to their contemporaries, the young generation of Israeli-bred or *sabra* soldiers. Inside they may have been soft, as the cliché told; but on the outside they were prickly and not seldom boorish. Many were raised on farms (like Sharon) or attended agricultural boarding schools (like Rabin). Some, like Refael Eytan, grew up in extreme poverty among the chicken coops of a godforsaken *moshav*—of which he once said that, unlike ears, they did not have to be cleaned every day. Others spent their youth not with their parents but in the communal dormitories of the *kibbutsim*. Prevailing economic conditions dictated spartan living; even clothes were owned in common, laundered in the communal laundry, and distributed on a first-come, first-wear basis. Children bathed in cold water year-round, slept on wooden boards, and underwent courses in wrestling and hand-to-hand fighting in a deliberate and, as it turned out, only too successful attempt to instill them with hardihood and courage.[9]

In this generation, wrote Arthur Koestler in 1946, "the humanistic hormones of the mind are absent."

> Their parents were the most cosmopolitan race of the earth—they are provincial and chauvinistic. Their parents were sensitive bundles of nerves with awkward bodies—*their* nerves are whip-cords and their bodies those of a horde of Hebrew Tarzans roaming in the hills of Galilee. Their parents were intense, intent, over-strung, over-spiced— they are tasteless, spiceless, unleavened and tough. Their parents were notoriously polyglot—they have been brought up in one language which had been hibernating for twenty centuries before being brought artificially back to life. . . . They speak no European language except a little English on the Berlitz school level; the not too numerous and not too competent translations of world classics strike no chords in them. . . . As against this they know all about fertilizers and irrigation and rotation of crops; they know the names of birds and plants and flowers; they know how to shoot, and fear neither Arab nor devil.[10]

Others held a somewhat different view: "Pacifism is a pipe dream. . . . No human conflict has ever been solved by debates and reasoning. . . . Never did a people voluntarily surrender their country, or rights, or property. . . . No conflict has been solved without a real struggle." This was not some reactionary adherent of Bismarck ranting about history being made by iron and blood; it was Yitschak Tabenkin, renowned socialist leader and the principal ideologue of the Achdut-Ha-avoda Party, as far back as 1942. Addressing teachers on the topic of "School and the War," he urged them not to "look down upon it" but to include it in their program of studies.[11] Whatever the differences between the Israeli right and left at this time, they shared a feeling of contempt for the learned—yet supposedly unmartial and cowardly—"diaspora Jew." They combined this with the absolute determination to fight and bleed for the "state on the way." The outcome was a unique blend of belligerence and insouciance that was carried over into the IDF, and, owing to the latter's influence as perhaps the single most important institution in the country, to much of Israeli society at large.

Meanwhile the price paid for this bellicosity was heavy indeed. The number who died in the war approached 6,000 (5,682 to be exact)[12]—far more than in any other of Israel's subsequent wars and amounting to almost one-third of all those killed since the end of 1947 to the present day. Of those 5,682, 2,000 or so fell between November 1947 and May

1948, 1,200 in the period May 15–June 10, 1948, and the rest between July 1948 and January 1949. Allowing for the size of the *Yishuv*'s population and the duration of hostilities, the blood bath was more intense than that undergone by either Britain or Germany in 1914–1918 and did not fall far short of the demographic disaster experienced by France during the same years (although it is true that, starting already during the war itself, massive immigration more than compensated for the losses).

As is probably true of all wars, those aged eighteen to thirty were over-represented (64.8 percent of the dead compared to 47.1 of the general population). Six percent of those aged seventeen to twenty and more than 5 percent of those aged twenty-one to twenty-five died; this served as the theme for a famous poem, "Magash Ha-kessef" ("The Silver Platter"), which honored the "boys and girls" who had given their lives. Two other groups were also somewhat overrepresented: the well educated (high school and over) and those with proven leadership capabilities (officers and NCOs). Contrary to the subsequent legend of the "lost generation," these excess losses were not serious enough to justify talk of the serious blow to the "quality" of Israeli society. Yet the casualties may indicate the forces' high fighting power and their willingness to sacrifice their lives.[13]

The total of 5,682 dead includes 4,520 military personnel (79.5 percent) and 1,162 civilians (21.5 percent). Of 5,213 male dead, 801 were civilians (15 percent); of 469 female dead, 361 were civilians (76.9 percent). Though women constituted 10.6 percent of the armed forces in December 1948, 108, or 2.4 percent of the above-mentioned 4,520, were killed. Among the 383 IDF members who died during the attacks on Latrun were three women; one was a wireless operator, the other two were nurses.[14] It is thus clear that, relative to their share of the population, far fewer women died than men. Moreover, female casualties were greatly overrepresented among civilians and greatly underrepresented among the military. This of course is not to disparage the heroism displayed by women—who were killed weapon in hand (there were a few, including an American-trained pilot), died while on active service or while defending their settlements against attack, or carried out the no less important and no less difficult tasks of ordinary life in a time of total war.

Statistics, however, cannot fully convey the pain and the sorrow of this war, by far the most difficult fought by the state of Israel and the only one in which it may have come close to defeat, if not physical extinction. As in the United States after the Civil War and in Britain after World War I, war became the formative experience for entire age groups. For years thereafter myths were woven around the dead, poems composed in their honor, and books published in their memory (by 1953, there were at least 320).[15] As any casual visitor will notice, the Israeli countryside is packed with war memorials. Some are old, some new, but all are decorated with lists of names (many overlapping, as different organizations commemorated *their* fallen ones without waiting for authorization from above). Generations of warriors have made their mark, not seldom leaving more than one family member behind as fathers, husbands, brothers, sons, and nephews visited and revisited the same battlefields. Perhaps poet Uri Tsvi Greenberg says it best in remembering one casualty, a former LECHI member (my translation):

> *Mourn, oh daughters of Israel*
> *The radiant robber, his brothers' hate*
> *Who finally achieved that what he longed for*
> *When setting forth to rob freedom for Zion's sake*
> *Now fallen on honor's field.*

II

THE YEARS OF GREATNESS, 1949–1973

T HE MILITARY organization that fought and won Israel's War of Independence was, by world standards, a small and disorganized force. Apart from small elements of "armor"—in reality little but leftover half-tracks and jeeps mounted with machine guns—almost the entire force consisted of infantry armed with World War I–era rifles and badly made, unreliable, homemade submachine guns and mortars. On land the largest permanent formation was the brigade; the much smaller air force and navy were not only motley and inexperienced but depended on an incredible assortment of antiquated weapons, many bought as scrap after World War II. Though self-confident and battle-hardened, the commanders were almost entirely self-taught. With only a year or so having passed since they had emerged from the underground, they possessed no formal military education. Indeed probably not a single IDF officer had gone through so much as a company commanders course during peacetime.

Worse, the years immediately following the war (starting in 1947, it ended in 1949) witnessed considerable demoralization. When the Korean

War broke out, Prime Minister Ben Gurion finally and irrevocably decided to throw in Israel's lot with the West.[1] Consequently the state lost the support of the Soviet Union, which, by allowing the Czechs to supply Israel with weapons, had done much to make victory possible. However, the quest for new "Western" allies did not prove successful at first, since Washington and the other governments were wary of driving the Arabs into Soviet arms. Furthermore, the war severed the economic ties that had linked Erets Yisrael to the Middle East, and Israel's foreign currency holdings were wiped out at a stroke when Britain, in an act of vengeance, expelled its former colony from the sterling block.[2] As the country struggled to repay its war debt—less than 20 percent had been funded by taxes—it was swamped by a wave of immigration that by 1951 had more than doubled the population. Most of the immigrants came from "Oriental," that is, non-European, countries. Whatever their virtues, they had not achieved anything close to the educational standards and technical skills of the pre-1948 *Yishuv*. All these factors weighed heavily on the population—and could not but affect the IDF.

By 1973, once again, the situation would be entirely changed. The IDF had been transformed from a dirt-poor, demoralized force armed with cast-off weapons into a comparatively well-endowed, self-confident, and technologically sophisticated pocket juggernaut. Whereas the world's leading armed forces saw their freedom of action increasingly constrained by the proliferation of nuclear weapons,[3] the IDF remained relatively free of such considerations. As a result it became the envy of the world, especially during the years immediately following the Six Day War. From June 1967 on, every Israeli citizen seemed to have turned into his own Superman. As Winston Churchill might have said, seldom had so (comparatively) few achieved so much within such a (comparatively) short time.

CHAPTER 8

THE ARMY OF THE STATE

T HOUGH THE WAR of Independence ended with the decisive defeat of the combined Arab armies (which, as already noted, could have been annihilated had the political decision been made), it proved but one stage in the history of the Arab-Israeli conflict. Although during the years immediately following independence there were attempts to negotiate with the rulers of Jordan, Syria, and Egypt,[1] it soon became clear they would make peace (if at all) only in return for territorial concessions, which Ben Gurion adamantly refused to make. Whatever their personal feelings, the Arab rulers' reluctance probably rested on fear of public opinion. Even before 1947 the public had been fiercely anti-Israeli; now, inflamed by the spectacle of defeat and the arrival of hundreds of thousands of Palestinian refugees, it became incensed to the point that it regarded any attempt to negotiate as treachery. Against this background, even the more peacefully inclined Arab leaders, such as King Abdullah and the Syrian dictator Husni az Zaim, felt themselves unable to proceed. Abdullah even paid with his life after being accused of negotiating with the Jews.

Whatever the reasons for the continuing conflict, during the first half of the 1950s it was obvious to Israeli leaders that a *hasibuv ha-sheni* (second round) had to be prepared for; indeed a children's war game was sold by that name in shops and was quite popular at the time. The fundamental objectives always remained survival of the state and defense of its territorial integrity[2]—in other words a defensive aim. This, however, did not preclude offensive-minded thinking among various circles. Most radical in its opposition to the 1949 armistice agreements was Menachem Begin's opposition Cherut Party, which contended the partition of the country represented "not a tactical error, neither a strategic error, but a historical crime." Harkening back to biblical times when the Kingdom of Israel reached Amman and beyond, Begin and his Myrmidons regarded not only the West Bank but also Transjordan itself as legitimate targets for Israeli expansion;[3] in fact the party newspaper used quotation marks when referring, for example, to the "Jordanian" government or "Jordanian" soldiers.

The Army of the State: officer school passing-out ceremony, 1955.

Then and later, neither Israeli public opinion nor government shared Begin's designs on the East Bank (after 1967 such ambitions were quietly dropped by Cherut itself). Still, there was no denying that the Israel-Jordan border established by the armistice agreements was totally illogical, not simply because of the very difficult strategic situation it created for Israel but because it upset the country's economy, severed its transportation network, and created new barriers where previously there were none. No less than Ben Gurion once described the loss of the West Bank and Jerusalem as *bechia le-dorot* (a weeping matter for generations). As early as March 1949, Allon, then at the peak of his glory as the most outstanding field commander of the War of Independence, expressed regret at not having been ordered to throw the Arab Legion out, adding that if it had depended on him the war would have ended differently.[4] A similar so-called activist line was adopted by Moshe Dayan, former PALMACH company commander and Ben Gurion's favorite general, who took over as IDF chief of staff in 1953.[5] During his term the General Staff produced contingency plans for the occupation of all or part of the West Bank.[6] In the end, though, they remained no more than that—contingency plans should minor hostilities along the border (and there were many) escalate.

Against this background, the new state's fundamental politico-strategic doctrine began to take shape.[7] One of the first attempts to sum up the lessons of the war was made in 1950 by the new chief of the General Staff, Yigael Yadin. Only thirty-two years old, he could rightly be regarded as Israel's top-ranking and most experienced soldier. Some of his points might have been taken straight from Stalin's "Five Permanently Operating Factors."[8] Others sounded as if they had been hijacked from Basil Liddell Hart (but there is no evidence that Israeli commanders had studied him before 1947). Yadin contrived to marry this combination of grand strategic ideas and strategic-operational principles with an emphasis on Israel's permanent geographic and demographic inferiorities vis-à-vis the Arab countries—as well as the Arabs' much greater military potential (should they succeed in mobilizing their resources).

To be specific, Yadin's first "lesson" was the "utmost importance of the factor of the morale of the country"; second, the need for "total utilization of the war potential of the Jewish community"; third, "the outstanding importance of unity of command" as a basis for concentration and maneuver; and fourth, the importance of such age-old principles of war as surprise, the offensive, concentration, mobility, and the indirect approach.[9] At the root of the entire structure were Israel's geographic and demographic weaknesses and its supposed inability to sustain a war of attrition; hence everything hinged on moving operations into enemy territory at the earliest possible moment to deliver a sharp, concentrated blow. The objective was not so much to bring about complete victory, which was regarded as impractical, but to smash the Arab armed forces and gain territory that could then be used in bargaining. Since the international arena was perceived as favoring oil-rich Arabs against the Jewish state, speed in the field was essential to forestall UN cease-fires (which happened twice before, in July and November 1948). Even so, it was considered that Israel would need the passive or, if possible, active political support of at least one major power when it went to war.[10]

Since then these points have often been presented as some particular proof of genius on the part of IDF founders—*ha-avot ha-meyasdim*, as the Hebrew saying goes.[11] In fact they were rather obvious and applicable to any modern country in Israel's geostrategic situation. Had not Prussia's Frederick the Great instructed his generals in the eighteenth century to wage short, lively wars not too far away from its own borders?[12] To the informed the similarity between the IDF's doctrine and that of the pre-1945 German army, though necessarily unacknowledged, has always been striking. Less well known is the fact that the doctrine was by no means universally accepted at first. Though himself a regular soldier in charge of the IDF, Yadin in his analysis had emphasized the role played by "the border settlements" in "containing the enemy's advance." By so doing he put his finger on an issue that, owing to its continuing political implications, requires some explanation.

The vulnerability of outlying Jewish settlements to Arab attacks during prestate days has already been discussed. Then, however, it was a question of defending each settlement on its own to prevent it from being overrun; whereas in 1947–1949, settlements came to be seen as important not only in and of themselves but also in strategic terms, as obstacles to invading Arab forces. But the performances of the settlements in regard to this strategic role had been mixed. In the north, Mishmar Ha-yarden, the two Deganias, Tirat Tsvi, and Gesher had fought very well and played important roles in halting the Syrian and Iraqi invasions, although Mishmar Ha-yarden was occupied and the other four were saved only when regular Hagana (mainly PALMACH) units rushed to their aid. In the center, Gush Etsion, geographically isolated and lacking reinforcements, failed to hold out against the Arab Legion, and repeated attempts to save it exacted a heavy price as reinforcements were wiped out and convoys forced to turn back. Finally, in the south the Egyptian army had overrun one settlement, bypassed several others, and failed to conquer at least one (Negba, which was supported by regular Israeli forces). Perhaps a fair judgment would be that the settlements did in fact successfully resist invasion so long as they could not be bypassed and *so long as they were not on their own.* Indeed to expect farmers, however well armed and motivated, to do more in the face of heavily armed regular forces borders on the preposterous.[13]

During the early fifties the question of rural settlement and defense was heavily loaded with political and ideological overtones. In the eyes of the ruling socialist parties the settlements, as much as the IDF, were the key to the possession of Erets Yisrael; although the army could conquer territory, only the *kibbutsim* and *moshavim* had the power to "liberate" it from desolation and convert it to Jewish land. Thus the left-leaning members of Israel's government, like the political parties they represented, were inclined to exaggerate the military role played by the *hagana merchavit* (territorial defense) before independence and during the War of Independence itself and to insist that *hagana merchavit* be allowed to play a role in the defense of the country. As is always the case, the fact that settlements were provided a role also meant that resources had to be allocated to them—much to the resentment of the IDF.[14]

The argument as to the respective advantages of a regular, centralized armed force on the one hand and those of territorial defense on the other went on for years after the 1949 cease-fire. So long as conditions remained unsettled and infiltrators represented a major problem—which continued to be the case until the 1956 Sinai campaign discussed later—the two schools wrestled one another without arriving at a clear decision. After all—regardless of what the IDF might say—one could hardly leave settlements to their fate without causing demoralization and despair. Next, the period between 1956 and 1967 appeared to have brought about the victory of the TSAHAList school. The Suez campaign brought home to the Arab rulers the dangers of allowing infiltrators to cross the border into Israel. As they took measures to control the situation, day-to-day security tended to improve, and the settlements' arrangements for self-defense were gradually allowed to decay.

The entire question of territorial defense was reopened with the 1967 war and the subsequent expansion of Israel's borders. Since then public opinion has remained divided. In a curious reversal of roles, the right—particularly the national religious right—now insists that the "settlements" (meaning those located in the Occupied Territories) were a vital aid to the country's defense. By contrast the left, denying what had previously been a pillar of its own thought, insists only settlements in the Jordan Valley are of any value and that the rest merely represent "a strategic burden" that itself requires protection by the IDF. The debate, which has profound implications for the future of Israel and its security, persists (see Chapters 12 and 20).

In the early 1950s, however, this role reversal was in the future. Meanwhile the government implemented Yadin's basic lessons in regard to the need for a single organization with a unified command and strict top-to-bottom authority. Ben Gurion's 1948 victory over Galili, as well as the dismemberment of the *Yishuv*'s other fighting organizations (ETSEL and PALMACH), had ensured that the Jewish state would have a single army unreservedly subordinate to a single civilian government. Although that relationship was not explicitly embodied in law until 1976,[15] it has never been questioned. In the half-century since the Israeli state was established it is virtually impossible to find a case where the military openly challenged the civilian authorities.[16]

In theory the top-level chain of command was and remains clear, running from prime minister to minister of defense to chief of staff. In practice, however—the Agranat Commission investigated the question in the wake of the 1973 war[17]—the exact division of labor among the three has never been clearly defined. The result is that much depended on personalities. Some prime ministers (David Ben Gurion, Levi Eshkol, Menachem Begin, Yitschak Rabin during his second term, and Shimon Peres) preferred to act as their own ministers of defense. Others inserted a third person between themselves and the COS; he in turn might be civilian (Pinchas Lavon, Shimon Peres, Moshe Arens) or former military (Moshe Dayan, Yitschak Rabin, Ezer Weizman, Ariel Sharon, Yitschak Mordechai). Some prime ministers felt confident about defense matters and kept the military on a short leash (Ben Gurion, Eshkol until 1967, and Rabin). One (Golda Meir) refrained from doing so while frankly admitting she did not know exactly what a division was.[18] Another (Menachem Begin) kept meddling even though his military knowledge had been acquired during his kindergarten years and barely developed thereafter.

The fact that the IDF obeyed its political masters did not mean it was without influence on defense planning and, through it, Israeli policy as a whole. In fact the opposite was the case. Defense minister Ben Gurion had a weakness for uniformed personnel and was inclined to belittle the importance of the civilian ministry itself. The Israeli defense ministry had grown haphazardly out of Rechesh, Hagana's arms-acquisition agency, and Ben Gurion at least initially saw it as no more than an organization charged with providing whatever the IDF wanted;[19] during 1952–1954 he even received proposals aimed at abolishing the ministry and transferring its functions to the General Staff. Though these ideas were rejected, compared to its modern counterparts Israel's civilian defense establishment remained rather underdeveloped. Thus, it was not until 1958 that the defense ministry succeeded in wrenching control of the defense budget from the General Staff financial department.[20] Even then, long-range planning and force development continued to be the responsibility of the IDF. The latter in turn entrusted those tasks to relatively junior officers—

lieutenant colonels and lower—who were not even members of the Plenary General Staff (*forum* MATKAL).

Worse, Israel does not have a national security council or an intelligence czar responsible for coordinating internal and external, civilian and military, and strategic, political and economic intelligence. As a result, the IDF's intelligence division not only is the principal provider of enemy intelligence—along with Mossad (Institution), Israel's foreign secret service—but also is responsible for preparing the National Intelligence Estimate. In fact the head of military intelligence is a frequent participant in Cabinet meetings, a situation unheard of in other democratic countries. Imagine if Pres. George Bush, preparing for Desert Storm, had nobody to turn to for advice except the chairman of the Joint Chiefs of Staff—who in turn entrusted his G–2 (chief of intelligence) to produce not only the services' but the *national* intelligence estimates.

Such arrangements—as demonstrated by the IDF's surprise by the 1973 October War and again by its preparations for the unsuccessful 1982 Lebanon War—did not always make for sound planning. In fact it could be argued that but for the undisputed (if not always clearly defined) authority of the prime minister and minister of defense the IDF during much of its history has been all but immune to civilian criticism and control. Information on defense matters is provided by the prime minister and minister of defense only to the Knesset Foreign Affairs and Defense Committee. Not only is that committee sworn to secrecy; it lacks any sort of independent research organization. Furthermore, and unlike the U.S. Congress, for example, Israel's legislators do not have authority to subpoena officials (or anybody else) to testify under oath or otherwise. Hence even today neither the Knesset nor the committee exercises effective control over the defense budget; indeed so clueless was the committee that as late as February 1974 Dayan told it that Israel did not possess nuclear weapons.[21] Nor has the committee ever been able to seriously oversee issues such as orders of battle, organization, arms procurement, research and development, personnel, contingency plans, foreign deals of the arms industry, and the like.

In this supposedly democratic country the situation was routinely justified by referring to *ha-medina be-matsor* (the idea that the state was permanently under siege and could not afford to stoop to the kind of parliamentary controls that are common elsewhere). Israel's Declaration of Independence, which contains ringing phrases about the equality of all citizens regardless of gender and religion, does not say a word about the freedom of information. Enforcing the public's duty not to know is the job of the IDF officer in charge of military censorship. This institution was originally established by the British mandatory authorities under the Defense (Emergency) Regula-

tions of 1945 with the intent of combating the unfolding terrorism of those
years; once the state was founded Ben Gurion found them so to his taste that
he left them unaltered and never got around to replacing them with a more
democratic system. The censor exercises draconian power over content in
the media, licenses newspapers, and fines and suspends newspapers if, in his
view, they have violated secrecy. He does not have to explain the reasons for
his decision; indeed one paragraph in the law obliges newspapers to publish
free ads by the military censor denying or correcting information that the
papers themselves published.[22]

From time to time the law savagely bares its fangs. In 1986 a technician
named Mordechai Vanunu leaked nuclear secrets to a British newspaper.
He was kidnapped by Mossad agents, brought home, put on trial behind
closed doors, and sentenced to sixteen years' solitary confinement (none of
which prevented him from being put on the shortlist of candidates for the
1996 Nobel Prize). His case represents the best-known but by no means
sole instance of this kind. Yet the veil of secrecy would never have stayed
in place had not most of Israel's media cooperated. From the early fifties
on, Vaadat Ha-orchim, a forum of leaders in the print and broadcast
media, would regularly meet to receive private briefings from top officials,
from the prime minister down. In return they undertook *not* to inform
their audiences, a unique arrangement that reflected the public consensus
concerning the need for censorship and the goals it strives to achieve.[23]
Naturally the arrangement did not apply to foreign journalists who, in
practice if not in theory, were nearly free to write and broadcast what they
pleased; in the worst scenario they would lose their accreditation. Thus
one of the censor's main functions is to keep Israelis ignorant of what
everybody else already knows. This practice applied to the numerous
armed reconnaissances of the Sinai and West Bank during the fifties; the
decision of the 1965 Arab summit at Rabat to consider the construction of
a nuclear reactor at Dimona as a casus belli; the talks held with King Hussein of Jordan during the years after 1967;[24] and, to this day, numerous
incidents that take place in Lebanon and elsewhere.

Another factor that enabled the IDF to play a major (some would say
excessive) role in national decisionmaking is its unified structure.[25] In countries such as the United States, Britain, and Germany the ground forces and
navy grew separately. Often each one had a centuries-old tradition behind
it—thus not only creating problems coordination but enabling political
masters to divide and rule. Not so in Israel, where the air force and navy
originally formed an integral part of PALMACH and, through it, Hagana.
While speaking for all three services, the IDF's General Staff was also in
charge of ground forces, which incidentally has meant that to date, ground

officers only have held the position of chief of staff. The commanders of the air force and navy are responsible for looking after their services in peacetime and have considerable latitude in planning, force development, manpower organization, logistics, and intelligence. In wartime they command in accordance with the directives of the COS. They also participate in the meetings of the Plenary General Staff, where rank and status are no different from that of the front and division commanders. However, it has never been made clear whether they do so primarily as General Staff members or as representatives of their respective services.

As this structure indicates, and indeed as was the case during the War of Independence, the bulk of the IDF was formed by the ground forces, which were also regarded as the decisive arm—*zroa ha-hachraa* in Hebrew. They were divided into three regional commands—north, central, and south. In peacetime the commanding officers were responsible for their respective regions. In wartime they turned into operational commanders, taking charge of forces assigned them by the General Staff. As during 1948–1949 the largest permanent formation was the self-contained brigade, the idea being that divisions—let alone corps—were too cumbersome for a comparatively small army. At first there may have been some confusion as to exactly how these forces were to be used. As doctrine crystallized, however, from at least 1954 on they were systematically developed with an eye toward waging offensive or blitzkrieg-style warfare even though the means for doing so were at first primitive and inadequate.[26]

Given Israel's small size—300 miles long, nowhere more than 80 miles wide—inevitably the air force was centralized, subject to a single command, and given control over "everything that flies," including helicopters. Though much smaller than the ground forces, in terms of budget and owing to the high quality of its personnel the air force claimed priority, hence the considerable rivalry between the "greens" and the "blues" among the ground forces that has characterized the IDF during much of its history. Initially the air force was compelled to use whatever machines Hagana's foreign agents could lay hands on. This included an incredible assortment of light aircraft (British Austers, American Piper Cubs and Harvards); fighters (German Messerschmidts, British Spitfires and Mosquitoes, American Mustangs), and transports (American-built Constellations, Dakotas, and Stratocruisers). Thanks especially to the U.S. arms embargo (enforced against Israel in 1948 due to political factors), many were purchased not at source but from scrap yards where they had been left at the end of World War II. For example, no fewer than 250 twin-engine Mosquitoes were cannibalized to put together an operational force of some twenty aircraft. In what was to become a grand old IDF tradition, others were modified to carry out missions for which they were never intended; the B–17s ended their days as naval patrol aircraft, a suitable role by virtue of their long ranges.

The paramount mission of the air force has always been to maintain air superiority within Israeli airspace; the importance of this task was made clear by the Egyptian bombing campaign of May 1948, and until the Gulf War of 1991, Israel has been almost completely successful in it. With this goal achieved, it was designed, as the German Luftwaffe had been,[27] to dominate the battlefield. Early doctrinal statements still spoke of "strategic bombing," but that mission was later dropped, and the IAF became an almost purely operational force meant to strike the enemy's armed forces and lines of communication.[28] Short distances and the nature of the terrain, much of which consists of desert and does not offer cover, favored these missions. After the early bombers were retired the result was a force that centered almost entirely on its squadrons of fighter-bombers plus maritime patrol, transport, and light aircraft for liaison, rescue, and other missions.

Once the War of Independence ended, foreign-born pilots who had flown for Israel went home, leaving the IAF desperately short of personnel. Aharon Remez, who had been a warrant officer in the Royal Air Force and gained considerable combat experience, was selected as its first commander. Evidently the General Staff felt it had no other qualified airmen,[29] and hence his first replacement was a navy man (Shlomo Shamir, 1950), the second a ground man (Chayim Laskov, 1951). Nevertheless, it did not degenerate into a handmaiden of the ground forces.[30] Instead it argued for a considerable degree of autonomy to conduct its own campaigns and allocated only a limited number of sorties to the ground commanders, who used them as they saw fit by way of their air liaison officers. On the whole, and as long as the opponent consisted of regular forces, these arrangements have worked admirably and enabled the IAF to play a major, even critical role in each of Israel's major wars. (It should not be forgotten, however, that in 1973 on the southern front, air-to-ground coordination was initially almost absent and that IAF attacks on Israeli units—meaning friendly fire—took place in both the 1956 and 1982 campaigns.)

Though its organizational status was similar to that of the air force, the navy has never approached the latter's size and importance; indeed air force officers on occasion argued that their aircraft could reach and fight enemy ships long before the navy could and that the navy should be abolished. That advice was not heeded, but the navy clearly was the smallest and least important of the three services. During the early fifties its main vessels were two or three World War II corvettes to which were added a number of equally antiquated torpedo boats and landing craft acquired secondhand. These small vessels scarcely gave Israel any considerable operational reach—neither then nor later could there be any question of a "blue water" navy. Worse, because the Suez Canal was closed to Israeli shipping the available forces had to be divided between the Mediterranean and the Red Sea (only light craft, transported overland, could be shifted from one theater to the next). Reflecting the Mediterranean's greater importance, the main base was always at Haifa, to which the new port of Ashdod was added during the early sixties.

Since Israel is absolutely dependent on foreign trade, it is vulnerable to naval blockades of both the Mediterranean and the Red Sea. In practice, though, most of the wars that it has fought were so short and the condition of the Arab navies so deplorable that a serious attempt to cut its Mediterranean trade routes has never been made. Not so in the Red Sea, which was closed to Israeli shipping from 1949 to 1956 and again in 1967; however, in both cases geography dictated that the Straits of Tyran should be opened not by the navy but by the land forces following their campaigns in the Sinai. Accordingly, in peacetime the role of the Israeli navy has been limited to patrolling the coast, gathering intelligence of various kinds, shelling the coast (terrorist bases), and the like. In wartime it has fought a few engagements, first destroyer against destroyer and then—for the last time in 1973—missile boat against missile boat. On various occasions it has also supported the IDF by means of landing operations, albeit always on a small scale and never with more than mediocre success. Finally, on several occasions it sent submarines and frogmen to attack enemy ports, particularly in Egypt.

With a sensible doctrine and a unified organization thus in place, it was time to decide on the kind of armed forces that the state would maintain. On the one hand the new state found itself in extreme financial difficulty, made worse by the need to cater to a very large number of immigrants, who for the most part were penniless. On the other hand was the extreme demographic asymmetry between Israel and its Arab neighbors. Between them the two factors precluded any thought of a large, professional standing army. Not only was it too expensive; as Yadin pointed out there was no alternative to making full use of all available manpower. A Swiss-like militia system (in which practically all forces consist of citizens in arms) was apparently considered[31] but rejected because it would provide neither adequate training for large-scale warfare nor forces to address current security problems (which the Swiss, of course, did not have).[32] The solution ultimately adopted and incorporated into the Chok Sherut Bitachon (National Service Law) of 1949 was well suited to Israel's needs.[33] Contrary to what has sometimes been claimed it was also rather unoriginal, representing but a local variant of the model most advanced countries adopted after the

Prussian victories of 1866–1871 and that, having served countries such as France and Germany and Italy during most of the years since, now reached the Middle East.

According to this model, the armed forces of the state comprise three parts, a triangle if you will. The first, core force is formed by a relatively small number of professionals, officers, and noncommissioned officers (NCOs) who plan, organize, administrate, train, and maintain the force during peacetime. Their units consist of conscripts, who are the second element of the triangle. *Yeshive* students aside, young men (including members of the Circessian and Druze minorities but excluding Arabs) are inducted at eighteen. They are put through a battery of physical and mental tests[34] and made to serve two years; when the service period was later increased to two and a half years it was the longest of any country. For generations of Israelis, the day their child actually joins the army has become something of a transition point in life, one akin to but much more serious than American parents sending children off to college.

After basic training conscripts are sent to their units. They participate in advanced training courses and maneuvers and undertake such "current" security tasks as guard duty, border patrolling, combating infiltrators, and the like; together with the professionals they constitute the peacetime army. At the end of 1949 that army numbered almost 40,000 men and women;[35] perhaps two-thirds were conscripts. One out of every twenty-five Israelis thus served in the army, a remarkably high proportion. For example, before World War II, Germany, the most militarized country in Europe, maintained only one citizen out of every one hundred in uniform; perhaps the only country that could stand comparison with Israel in this respect was Prussia under Frederick the Great.

When their period of service is over the conscripts are discharged into the reserves. Representing the third element of the triangle, the reserves constitute neither a separate organization (such as the British Territorials or the U.S. National Guard) nor a general pool of manpower; instead they are organized in companies, battalions, brigades, and, beginning in 1967, entire divisions. Regularly called up for refresher training, the younger classes (up to age thirty-nine) are considered first-line units, whereas the remainder are assigned to civil defense, garrison duty, and the like. Apart from a small core of professionals who carry out administrative functions and look after equipment in peacetime, officers also are reservists (through 1973 two out of seven division commanders). These skeleton units can and will be called up in an emergency. In that case they are taken to the YAMACHim (emergency depots), processed into the army, issued uniforms and arms, and dispatched to the front as soon as the situation requires and transportation permits.

As in other armed forces that adopted this model, the importance of the three components within each service varies. Professionals on long-term contracts are proportionally most numerous in the air force. Being Israel's first line of defense it must be in a state of permanent, near-instant readiness; apart from this it also owns and operates more than its share of high technology, which requires a long time to study and master. Thus, in the air force, the simpler tasks are left to conscripts. Much the same applies to the navy. And though the navy and air force have reservists, including pilots called up in emergencies, the ground forces have the largest number of reservists, which indeed account for about three-quarters of wartime strength.

In theory this heavy dependence on reservists constitutes a weakness. In spite of regular refresher training (as many as thirty-five days per year and more for officers), mentally and especially physically the men can hardly be as well prepared as the conscripts. Moreover, since they serve only temporarily and maintain lives outside the military, exercising strict discipline can be a problem; indeed reserve units often assume a decidedly informal, unmilitary appearance. Yet for much of the IDF's history things have tended to work the other way around. The reserve units experience little personnel turbulence, so the men who constitute them remain together for many years on end. Meeting regularly for maintenance, training, and operational service, they form extremely cohesive units—complete with all the shared worldview, bonhomie, and mutual aid that implies.[36] For example, during the June 1967 war some of the personnel forming the armored *ugda* (division) in the center of Israel's Egyptian front had served together for five or six years.[37]

In some of this the IDF, building itself almost from scratch, wittingly or unwittingly took other armed forces as its model. For example, in Germany before 1914 and again before 1939 the younger classes of reservists were also considered first-line troops (though they did not receive nearly as much refresher training); as such, they were committed to battle very soon after mobilization and deployment. As in other countries, the system could operate only on the basis of a modern, integrated, countrywide network of transportation and telecommunications, which then as now constitutes one of Israel's most important advantages over its larger and more populous, but economically less developed and technologically less sophisticated, Arab neighbors.[38] The system did, however, include some elements that were almost entirely original. Perhaps foremost is the officer selection and training system.

The regular armed forces of most other countries—*militia perpetua*, as the seventeenth-century saying went—originated during times of absolute rule. Since they were intended for internal and external use—police forces in the modern sense developed after 1780 or so—the first concern of the rulers was to select officers in a way that ensured their loyalty. Even in the United States, never subject to absolute rule, this implied selecting officers mainly from the upper classes for specialized military academies; there, far from civilians and lesser ranks, officer candidates could be thoroughly imbued with the military spirit.[39] Not so Hagana and especially PALMACH. Initially they took any person with military experience they could find. Later they selected junior commanders from among the rank and file. They trained these commanders as best they could, leaving practical experience to fill in the rest.

Once the state was founded the ministry of defense opened one school (later a second) that took in fourteen-year-olds with military aspirations and trained them as officer candidates; both schools continue to operate and provide the IDF with a disproportionate number of its midgrade officers. Yet the great majority of future commanders continued to come via the rank and file. At entry level no distinction was made between prospective officers and anybody else. Soldiers who distinguished themselves during their conscript service were sent to the squad commanders course, long reputed to be the toughest in the army, and the most physically demanding on the students. Upon graduating they were made to play the NCO role for a while; volunteers underwent officer-qualification tests on the basis of superiors' recommendations.[40] Although the air force and navy maintain their own officer schools, the ground forces have only a single comprehensive course, so there is no segregation by arm. The specialized training of infantrymen, armor, and the like would follow later.

The upshot is that ground officers start their careers in common with enlisted personnel. Having commanded some of the latter as an NCO, each spends another period with fellow ground officers before going on to specialize. Contrary to that in many other armies, this system has ensured that commanders have a good understanding of their troops. It also put a greater emphasis on proven military competence and leadership as opposed to social origin or education—the latter being something of a sore point for the IDF.[41] There can be no doubt that from 1949 to 1973 this system served the IDF well. It not only produced first-class platoon commanders—the highest position soldiers could hold during their period of conscript service—but also provided an excellent pool from which senior officers could be selected. Whether this remains true is debatable, however; the issue will be discussed elsewhere (see Chapter 18). For the moment we will continue analyzing the officer corps.

Israeli officers traditionally have been younger than officers in other armed forces. In part this was the result of the War of Independence, which, as revolutionary wars often will, caused a winnowing-out of elderly personnel and the rapid promotion of outstanding young officers. Thus Yadin became chief of staff at thirty-two, his successor Mordechai Makleff at thirty-two, Dayan at thirty-seven, and Laskov—a true antediluvian by the standards of those days—at thirty-nine. If only because these young-sters did not want their subordinates to be older than they, what had begun as the product of circumstance turned into a matter of principle, and thus the IDF developed an officer corps that was much younger than those in other armies.

Having entered the IDF as conscripts, Israelis often served less than two years before being promoted second lieutenant, for there was no four-year academy that offered the equivalent of a university education. Once com-missioned, and assuming they signed up for the *tsva keva* (standing forces), promotion was fast. As in all armies there are minimal periods, known as PAZAM, to be spent in each rank. And whereas thirty years of total service is common elsewhere, the vast majority of Israeli officers who did not rise higher than major (later lieutenant colonel) could expect to retire in their late thirties or early forties.[42] At that point they were expected to take up a second career—usually in politics, government, or business.[43] Compared to those of other armies, the Israelis' system has probably produced a cer-tain originality and freshness of approach,[44] though whether that is still true is questionable. At the same time, however, it has also meant a large and growing burden of separation and pension payments.

The feature that has attracted the greatest amount of attention—and which is the subject of the worst misunderstandings—is the conscription of women. Throughout history, war has been the manly activity par excel-lence; women participated, if at all, almost exclusively as eggers-on, auxil-iaries, spectators, and victims. The advent of modern warfare did not change that situation to any great extent. Unlike men, women in modern times have rarely been subject to conscription. If called upon to volun-teer—as in many countries during World War I and World War II—they were assigned almost entirely to auxiliary tasks such as rear-echelon com-munication, administration, nursing, liaison, driving motor vehicles, and the like. With very few exceptions, only in extremis were women allowed to enter combat, as in World War II Britain, where women operated heavy home-based antiaircraft batteries, carrying out every task but pressing the firing button; and the USSR, where three regiments of female pilots were formed to fight the Nazis.[45]

In pre-1948 Israel, as in many other revolutionary societies, the situa-tion was entirely different. Much military activity took place in the coun-tryside, where conditions were primitive and something resembling a frontier society existed. Feeling exposed, men and women naturally joined to defend their homes against attack, which meant that women became Hagana members, receiving training with what weapons there were to be had. But as Hagana became institutionalized over time, women were mostly confined to ancillary tasks such as nursing, communications, and the like. As the first mobile striking force, Sadeh's *nodedot* included one woman who, not accidentally, was the sister of a senior Hagana commander; there were no women in the SNS.[46] The short shrift given females in Hagana generally is illustrated by an episode in the memoirs of the first chief of staff, Yochanan Ratner. At 3:00 A.M. after a particularly exhausting day, when Ratner and a fellow activist were ready to drop into bed, they were asked to discuss the problems of female *chaverot* (comrades)—to which they reacted by doubling up with laughter.[47]

Hagana's full-time striking force, PALMACH, took in volunteers of both sexes (at peak women formed about one-fifth of the total).[48] The vast majority were young and unmarried; many, having grown up in *kibbutsim*, had spent their entire lives in co-ed dormitories. The resulting force was perhaps more fully integrated than any other in history. Men and women—to be precise, little more than boys and girls in their late teens— lived in adjacent tents. They ate meals together and even took showers together in roofless shacks, separated by nothing more than a corrugated iron partition. The housing shortage even required married couples to live with a third person, who was expected to respect conjugal privacy.

Unlike other armed forces, as in Britain and the United States during World War II, neither PALMACH nor Hagana developed a separate women's corps. Before 1948 many of their operations were directed against the British. Men and women were often sent out in teams, with the latter acting as cover and carrying the illegal arms. Moreover, men occupied virtually all command positions—the higher one went, the more true this became—and women were always regarded as auxiliaries whose task was to assist the men.[49] Furthermore, even before independence, during "active" operations—such as blowing up a bridge—women, though they received weapons training in common with the men, were normally used only in support.[50]

No sooner did the War of Independence break out than the situation changed. After one incident in the Negev when a mixed patrol was attacked, its members killed, and their bodies mutilated, Hagana headquarters ordered all women out of combat units.[51] Given the shortage of personnel and the fact British presence continued, the order was not always obeyed, and a typical PALMACH company with an authorized strength of 140 or so men might yet contain two or three women.[52] From December 1947 to March 1948 a number of women, with pouches for hand grenades and pistols sewn under their dresses, helped take convoys into beleaguered Jerusalem as well as Gush Etsion. Acting as communicators and first-aid personnel, they often came under fire, returned fire when the opportunity presented itself,[53] and took their share of casualties; of 1,200 PALMACH dead, nineteen were women.[54] A few other women participated in the ferocious fighting for Safed and in the area around Latrun, where one of them, Netiva Ben Yehuda, most likely earned her reputation as "the Blonde Devil" of Arab myth. Whether accidentally or not, one of her tasks was to cover up some of the atrocities committed by male comrades, untying the hands of dead Arab prisoners to disguise the fact they had been shot in cold blood.

The fighting days of Ben Yehuda and most of her female comrades ended almost immediately after the proclamation of the state when, much to her resentment, she was permanently removed from the combat forces. Such was the impression of these few months that she has vowed to write no fewer than fifteen books; only three have materialized to date. Meanwhile, even in PALMACH units women were reduced almost exclusively to seeing men off to action and welcoming them upon their return—having dully cleaned rooms and prepared meals.[55]

When the War of Independence ended in early 1949, 10,632 women were in the IDF ranks, many of them in responsible noncombat but subordinate positions.[56] Except in PALMACH, where they had been active before 1948, women had not done well during the war, mainly because the selection process had been defective, mobilization haphazard, and training inadequate or absent.[57] Nevertheless the IDF, mindful of the much larger demographic and military potential of Israel's neighboring countries, wanted to retain their services to free male soldiers for the front. Accordingly they were subjected to conscription—against a storm of opposition from religious parties, which then as now consider it contrary to the rules of female modesty. In the end a compromise was struck, and women who declared themselves to be orthodox (as well as Circassian and Druze women) were exempted (as were women who were married, pregnant, or had children). Obvious practical considerations apart, Ben Gurion held motherhood to be "a sublime and sacred thing." A man, he said, might serve in the army and get married afterward; but taking an eighteen-year-old newlywed from her husband's embrace was little short of a crime.[58]

Women served twenty-four months, the same as men; but when male service time was increased to thirty months, that for women stayed the same. The period of reserve service for females extended only to the age of thirty-four. However, in practice discharged women were rarely called up for reserve duty, enabling them to concentrate on family, study, and career.

Moreover, the prestate system in Hagana and PALMACH—whereby women were fully integrated with the forces—was not retained. Instead CHEN (Chel Nashim, the Women's Army Corps; the acronym also happens to mean grace) was established, on the British model, in June 1948.[59] To the women of PALMACH the change represented a humiliation—the more so because former British army personnel were put in charge. Consequently morale dropped, and many women vented their resentment by getting married and leaving the service.[60]

Once the war was over, CHEN, guided by the General Staff, went to work. PALMACH members—particularly the kibbutsniks among them—had been fairly promiscuous[61] (the underwear of "conquered" female comrades were suspended from tent poles, and undesirable consequences—read: sexually transmitted disease—were taken care of quietly and efficiently by the network of Histadrut-affiliated clinics). Now, to show anxious parents that the army was not simply a vast "brothel"[62] as critics alleged, a much more puritan note set in. Eventually entire volumes of regulations were produced that treated every male soldier as a potential rapist. To protect women, male military police were prohibited from touching, male military doctors from examining (unless another woman was present), and male military judges from passing judgment. It became necessary to construct a double chain of administrative command, one for each sex, with the result that the main job of about 20 percent of women was to look after other women in the army.[63]

These arrangements certainly did not always suffice to prevent what today would be called sexual harassment, but the IDF, during most of its history, preferred to ignore or treat the problem by transferring female soldiers; after all a state that really needs its male warriors will be inclined to overlook their indiscretions (sexual and other). Nor were these arrangements able, or indeed intended, to prevent a situation where a great many Israeli youngsters first meet their partners, and acquire sexual experience, during military service. Strictly speaking, engaging in sexual intercourse on base is prohibited. Needless to say, the rule is constantly violated; normally those caught in the act are regarded with benevolent amusement. In early 1997 the Women's Lobby in the Knesset even demanded that the IDF provide female conscripts with free contraceptives, since buying them was too expensive.

Since it needed fewer women than men, the IDF, when conducting its entry-level examinations, applied higher psychological and educational standards to females.[64] Once inside, women did their five-week basic training in segregated bases, where they learned how to stand at attention and make beds modus militaris. In addition they went on marches and fired a few rounds from almost always second-class weapons; it was not until after the 1973 war that modern small arms became sufficiently plentiful to issue them to everybody; even then women often found it hard to carry the long M–16 or heavy Galil assault rifles. Tourists who visit Israel will, if they are lucky, glimpse female recruits on hikes. Their columns look disorderly— but, it must be admitted, hardly more so than those of the men.

After basic training women were assigned almost exclusively traditional tasks. They became administrators, secretaries, communicators, welfare workers, and medical auxiliaries in noncombat units as well as instructors in charge of teaching the basics to students inside and outside the army. At any one time, most women worked in bases close enough for them to go home at night whereas only a minority lived with combat units in so-called closed bases. There, inhabiting separate quarters, they are adored by the hordes of young males who surround them; those who know how to han- dle the situation live like princesses. Strangely enough, female military occupation specialties (MOS) did not include lorry driving (for which other armed forces assigned women during World War II). It is not clear whether this was due to physical reasons or because in the dirt-poor soci- ety that was Israel during the early fifties, driving a lorry was too presti- gious a job to entrust to a mere female.

As late as the Suez campaign it was still possible to find the very rare female piloting a transport aircraft and dropping paratroopers; by the early sixties, though, they too had disappeared without giving rise to any partic- ular comment.[65] Afterwards, there were isolated attempts to train women for other tasks, such as navy diver. These, however, led nowhere: The men's resentment caused many to drop out of the course, and few female graduates were used in their specialty.[66] Such occasional viragoes apart, up to 1973 most female soldiers could aspire to occupy clerical positions in the air force—"the best [women] for the pilots" was the slogan coined by none other than Ezer Weizman, a notorious womanizer during his youth. Other enlisted women were selected for the monotonous if important job of folding parachutes; wearing the red beret, their reward was to be kissed by heroic paratroopers. As we shall see, it was only during the great man- power comb-out of the mid-seventies that the position of IDF female sol- diers began to undergo significant change, the number of MOS open to them expanding. But by then, and not accidentally, the days of the IDF's greatness were also coming to an end.

Women have been able to attain NCO and officer status along with men, the selection procedures for both sexes being similar. Female NCOs and cadets are, however, trained at a separate base; once commissioned they are either assigned to CHEN—where their task is to train and administer other women—or to staff positions in administration, intelligence, welfare, and the like. As has been the case in most modern armed forces since at least Napoleon, the IDF manpower division develops officers by systematically rotating them through command, training, and staff positions. Except inside CHEN, however, during most of IDF's history women were excluded from two of these fields. As a result, the authority, responsibility, and prospects for promotion of female officers have always been rather limited. Not until 1982 was the post of CHEN commander—who commands far more women than most male officers will ever command men—transformed into a brigadier general's slot; outside CHEN, the only woman who attained that rank has been Shulamit Ligom, who in 1994 was appointed to look after public complaints.[67] Barred as they are from the rank of major general, female officers have yet to obtain a seat on the General Staff. Normally, the only woman present at its meetings is the chief of staff's secretary.

Thus, during most of its history the IDF's treatment of women has been backward- rather than forward-looking. In a society where anyone rejected for military service was—and, to some extent, still is—automatically suspect, its policy of conscripting proportionally fewer women than men helped marginalize large numbers of Oriental women, whose schooling standards were lower. They were not only stigmatized but also prevented from making use of IDF educational facilities.[68] In an army whose overriding purpose was combat, the women whom it *did* take were assigned almost entirely to second-rate posts. Except in staff positions, no woman was able to reach a slot where she would command men.

All this took place in a society that, being socialist and to some extent modeled on the USSR of the 1920s,[69] always granted women rather greater freedoms than did most other Western countries. Women serving in Ha-shomer, Hagana, and PALMACH might complain about not being made *truly* equal. Still, in Israel there was never any need for women to fight for the vote, given that they participated in all elections from 1920 on; or for state-subsidized kindergartens; or for the right to enter the universities and the professions, let alone open their own bank accounts and sign a check. Contrary to normal Western beliefs, which are shaped by pictures of busty girls in short skirts and with submachine guns at the ready, as modern feminism reached Israel during the eighties and nineties it suddenly became clear that the IDF had become an island of backwardness in respect to its treatment of women. In it male chauvinist attitudes and discrimination still persisted to a greater extent than anywhere else. And, as we shall see, the more select the arm or service the more true this became.

Thus, militarily speaking the feature usually seen as the single most original characteristic of the IDF—the conscription of women—has in reality been less important than is commonly thought. It has also given rise to many misunderstandings, which is why I have discussed it at some length. Somewhat less original, but much more important, was the system of officer selection, training, and promotion, including its heavy emphasis on proven competence, military experience, and youth and its corresponding neglect of social origin, formal education, and military affectations (such as shoulder straps and gloves). These characteristics apart, the IDF represented not so much an original creation as a typical modern armed force modeled on, and in many ways resembling, those of the principal twentieth-century European states (although, owing to a combination of inexperience and poverty, during the first half of the fifties its organization and equipment still left much to be desired).

Like the forces of other developed countries the IDF was trinitarian, that is, a corporate entity clearly separate from the government on the one hand and the people on the other. Like the forces of other developed countries it was supported by a ministry of defense; its principal role, small by comparison with some others, was to organize the civilian aspects of defense and procure arms for it. Less than the forces of most developed countries it was subject to civilian, particularly parliamentary control. More than them it took overall responsibility for the country's security including, in particular, intelligence; to be routinely called to report to the Knesset Foreign Affairs and Defense Committee is a privilege that no other Western military intelligence chief enjoys. More than them, too, it had a unified general staff in full command of the three services. Unable to support large forces in peace, it was divided into long-serving professionals, short-serving conscripts, and reservists—an arrangement typical of the majority of the world's greatest armed forces (Britain and the United States alone excepted) from 1871 on.[70] From the early 1950s on, it also developed a strategic-operational doctrine that, in light of the enemies it was facing, was designed to use all these characteristics to the best effect.

Nevertheless, in the end analysis these are matters of detail. Overshadowing them, and making the entire system possible, was the unique position of the IDF in the eyes of Israeli society. It is comparable, if at all, only to the status the armed forces held in Germany from 1871 until 1945.[71] The IDF was seen as the one great institution around which a young and heterogeneous nation could rally. This included not only old inhabitants and new immigrants but also right- and left-wing parties; and the situation where the latter were suspicious of the military for reasons of class (as in France around the turn of the century) hardly arose. Though differences in emphasis did exist, perhaps the only Israelis who resolutely opposed the military and all it represented were the *charedim* (non-Zionist orthodox Jews). Then as now they formed a world apart—in no small measure for that very reason.

The attempt, dating back two or three decades but only now getting into high gear, to create a new type of Jew who would be prepared to defend himself—not to say trigger-happy—had been only too successful. The War of Independence represented the first Jewish victory in more than two thousand years. No wonder Israeli public opinion happily rid itself of traditional Jewish pacifism and fell madly in love with everything military; particularly in *kibbutsim* the social pressure on young males to join combat units and distinguish themselves was well-nigh intolerable, driving some who did not measure up to suicide.[72] When the new state celebrated its first anniversary, in May 1949, the 300,000 people (one-third of the entire population!) who gathered to watch the IDF parade in Tel Aviv were so enthusiastic that they blocked the route, prevented the march-past from being completed, and turned the festivities into a mess.[73] Lesson learned, the next time the IDF put itself on display the troops looked and acted like tin soldiers, as one newspaper proudly proclaimed.[74] From then until 1968 every single Yom Atsmaut (Independence Day) centered around the inevitable march-past. It was held in various cities in rotation and often welcomed by elevating messages such as "Rejoice Tel Aviv, at TSAHAL entering thine gates."

Enthusiasm for things military also manifested itself on a day-to-day basis. Anthologies of Jewish heroic deeds, past and present, were printed and often went into many editions owing to their popularity as bar-mitsva presents and the like.[75] Martial songs, many of them with Hebrew words fitted to Russian tunes, were constantly broadcast on civilian and the IDF's radio stations. "How beautiful is the squad, marching through the mountains," one of them went. "Go out into the streets of the *moshava*, girls, soldiers are coming!" constituted almost the entire lyrics of another. A third took its inspiration from the colorful language used by NCOs to address their soldiers. One should not underestimate the importance of mere songs. On the contrary, given the massive immigration of those years, they were widely seen and deliberately used as vehicles for creating social cohesion where none had previously existed.[76] Doing so was among the missions of the military entertainment troupes that amused civilian and military audiences with songs and sketches about army life. For many years thereafter membership in these troupes (a phenomenon entirely unknown in other Western countries, where military entertainment stands to entertainment as military cooking stands to the chef's art) was often considered a good visiting card for youngsters seeking to enter Israeli show business.

Besides the standard fare of roses, rainbows, and kissing couples, the greeting cards Israelis sent on New Year's Day (Rosh Hashanah) often carried pictures of IDF soldiers, jeeps, tanks, combat aircraft, and warships (as

did packs of chewing gum, matchbox covers, cigarette packs, etc.). As happened, for example, in the United States after the Civil War and in Germany after World War I, elders used their onetime heroism to lord it over
youngsters. The latter, branded first as *brarah* (offal) and later as the
"espresso generation," sought to emulate the former, perhaps most notoriously by means of unauthorized hikes into enemy territory, during which
a number were killed. Two journalists published a collection of "Tall
PALMACH Tales" in 1953, which quickly became a best-seller.[77] At
Purim, the Israeli equivalent of Halloween, no costume was more popular
than that of an IDF soldier. The greatest compliment anyone could receive
was that he was a "fighter." Military-style boots were known, somewhat
sarcastically, as "heroes' shoes."

Far from being mere spontaneous manifestations of popular culture,
these attitudes were systematically fostered by the authorities. In the Knesset, Ben Gurion thundered about the need to use the army as a vehicle for
creating a race of warrior-settlers who would work the land by day and
stand guard at night.[78] At a less elevated level, the mayor of Ramat Gan
near Tel Aviv used to address hundreds of graduates every year. He was a
big-bodied Hagana veteran (while serving in the Ottoman army during
World War I he had distinguished himself by stealing the molds of a hand
grenade, thus permitting self-manufacture to get under way). In his heavily Russian-accented Hebrew he wished for his audience that they would
"become soldiers—heroes—good luck!"

Combined, as they frequently were, with the usual Israeli penchant for
indiscipline and slovenliness, in retrospect many of the manifestations of militarism that were characteristic of those years appear ludicrous. At the time
they reflected and created exceptionally high morale, which, as Napoleon
said, is to the physical aspects of war as three to one. The IDF's successes,
like those of armed forces in other countries, can never be understood without reference to its exalted position in the public mind. The public mind
itself was the product of the feeling of *en brera* (no choice), the importance
of which in Israeli history cannot be exaggerated.

En brera rested on the balance of forces. That balance was summed up
in the twin concepts of *i katan be-toch yam arvi* (a small island in an Arab
sea) and *meatim mul rabbim* (the few against the many), both born before
independence and serving the state well thereafter. It is true that as of late
1948 the IDF outnumbered all its enemies combined; and since then it has
often possessed superior weapons and firepower. Yet during much of
Israel's history the perceived ratio of its armed forces to those of neighboring countries has been on the order of one to three. Behind the myth,
carefully cultivated by Ben Gurion[79] and others, of a small and hopelessly

exposed state surrounded by potentially much stronger enemies—enemies bent on destroying it, no less—there existed a solid reality. For decades on end it was not so much doctrine, organization, training, technology, or whatever but *en brera* and the sense of utter determination that it generated that provided the real dynamo behind Israeli military prowess. Perhaps it was predictable that, if it went, everything else would go as well.

CHAPTER 9

TRIALS BY FIRE

HOUGH THE 1949 armistice agreements put an end to large-scale warfare with the Arab countries, small-scale fighting with the Palestinians—principally those who had recently become refugees—continued. The forced flight of approximately 600,000 people had left entire districts more or less empty. Even before the war ended, abandoned fields were being taken over by Israeli individuals and communal settlements (which often claimed and usually obtained Arab-owned plots and the crops they contained) and the government. Watching the process from improvised camps in Lebanon, Syria, the West Bank, and the Gaza Strip, the former owners could not but feel resentment and anger at the great material and physical losses. Yet the fact that most of the state's newly established borders did not rest on any geographical features and were, indeed, often unmarked on the ground encouraged infiltration.

Then and later, the motives of the *mistanenim* (infiltrators) varied.[1] Some were armed, but the majority were not. Some merely made brief journeys across the border to visit relatives who stayed behind or to save property such as crops, livestock, and whatever else survived expropriation and could be readily removed. Others planned to make a more permanent return to former homes, and still others came with the deliberate intent of taking revenge. The latter stole livestock, destroyed agricultural equipment, blocked wells, and attacked people; there were woundings, killings, mutilations (to bring back proof of their actions), and, very occasionally, rapes. The establishment of Israel had severed some of the region's traditional trade routes, particularly those between Egypt and Jordan, which were now separated by the Negev Desert. For this reason, and because in Israel basic foodstuffs were subsidized and therefore much cheaper than in neighboring countries, many infiltrators smuggled goods. Finally, although most acted on their own initiative, a certain percentage worked for the intelligence services of Syria, Egypt, and Jordan in particular.

However understandable the infiltrators' motives, no state can tolerate a situation whereby its borders are violated hundreds of times a year by

Trials by Fire: marking the road into Sinai, 1956.

thousands of people,[2] particularly if some are armed and attack property and citizens. From 1949 to 1956 two hundred to three hundred Israelis were killed by *mistanenim*, most in border settlements near the Gaza Strip or along the Israel-Jordan border, but some in the very heart of the country—which in any case was never very far from one border or another.[3] The number of Israelis wounded was 500–1,000; though no authorized figures estimate damage suffered, it must have amounted to many millions of Israeli pounds (an Israeli pound was worth $.55).[4] Even greater were the costs of security measures put in place, working days lost, and the general disruption and demoralization that followed.

The Israelis responded on three levels. The first, elementary response was to establish new settlements on the border—on the theory (promoted by Ben Gurion)[5] that the presence of Jewish populations would deprive infiltrators of freedom of movement. Most of the settlements were inhabited by new immigrants, but a few were founded by so-called *garinim* (cores) of young IDF conscripts. The latter were inducted into a special corps known as NACHAL (Noar Chalutsi Lochem, or Fighting-Pioneer Youth). After basic training they spent their military service working on a *kibbuts* and, after discharge, usually stayed on as civilians.

As commonly done before 1948, border settlements were prepared for defense. Fences were erected, searchlights installed, mines laid, booby traps set, personal arms distributed, training provided, and guard duties imposed. These and similar measures may have helped limit the damage caused by attacks, but apparently they did little if anything to reduce frequency. Furthermore, over time the infiltrators became more sophisticated and responded with measures of their own, such as blowing up an agricultural installation and ambushing the Israelis who came to see what happened. Meanwhile on the Israeli side, security became an intolerable burden as people were expected to stand guard at night and work by day. In 1952–1953, these problems became so severe that some settlements, particularly in the corridor leading to Jerusalem (many populated by new immigrants), came close to being abandoned.

In addition to helping the settlements defend themselves—territorial defense put into practice—there arose the question of whether to use the Israeli armed forces to combat infiltrators. As might be expected, the IDF vehemently opposed the idea of setting up a special organization, claiming that troops best qualified for the mission were its own;[6] however, its stance was rejected and a special force, known as Mishmar Ha-gvul (Frontier Guard), established. The Frontier Guard took volunteers who had already completed military service. Many were members of minority groups such as Bedouins, Druze, and Circessians who proved especially well suited for this kind of work, possessing mastery in the use of small arms, fieldcraft, track-ing skills, and a good command of Arabic; squeamishness was definitely not included in the job description. Organizationally speaking the Frontier Guard was part of the police, as it remains. In theory the Frontier Guard was responsible for day-to-day operations such as *siyurim* (patrolling) and *maaravim* (laying ambushes), the IDF standing in reserve in case of emer-gency. In practice the two organizations were almost interchangeable, as both wore military uniforms, engaged in all kinds of activities (save that the Frontier Guard was not supposed to cross the border and retaliate against Arab countries), and were called upon to deal with incidents as availability dictated.

Finally, to avenge past incidents and deter future ones, already in 1949 the IDF began to mount raids across the border. On occasion the identity of perpetrators, as well as their place of refuge, was known so that direct action could be taken against them; then and later, however, the real pur-pose of the raids was so-called indirect deterrence, meaning that the Arab civilian population and the Arab governments were to be punished for fail-ure to stop the infiltrators. As early as mid-1950, Dayan, then serving as CIC Southern Command, claimed that this kind of retaliation, however "unjustified and immoral" it might be, was the only "effective" way to put an end to infiltration.[7] Over the next few years he and other leaders repeated this argument time and again.

Initially the government of Israel denied that its forces had mounted border raids, insisting that they had been carried out by "irregulars" and "vigilantes." Later this masquerade, never very convincing either to the Arabs or to foreign observers, was dropped, and the IDF for the most part not only admitted responsibility but also proudly proclaimed it. During the early days—1950 to 1953—most of the raids were directed against Arab villages that supposedly served as the infiltrators' starting bases and refuges upon their return. The villages were attacked by mortar fire (occa-sionally, as hostilities escalated, artillery fire as well), strafed from the air, and attacked by units that fired on the villagers and demolished their houses; when Egyptian and Jordanian troops tried to interfere they were frequently ambushed. The proceedings were rather unappetizing, the IDF responding to civilian killings by indiscriminately killing infiltrators—including, on at least some occasions, some who were unarmed or had sur-rendered—torturing captives, and mutilating bodies. As if to emphasize that war, if prolonged, becomes an imitative activity that will cause two sides to resemble one another, the IDF increasingly resorted to attacks on property (livestock was expropriated and taken across the border, electric-ity and telegraph poles were uprooted, etc.).

The effect of the IDF's activities on the neighboring Arab populations and governments is debatable. Some Arabs reacted with fear, others with frustration, others with anger. At times the raids encouraged Egyptian and Jordanian authorities in particular to try reining in the infiltrators; on other occasions the outcome was just the reverse, that is, spurring them to acts of revenge. Whatever the Arabs' reaction, successive years of raids and counterraids proved that the IDF had no effective response to the problem and was incapable of guaranteeing the lives and property of Israeli civilians not only along the border but also, to a lesser extent, in the heart of the country. As Dayan would argue—without a shred of evidence and obviously attempting to justify a policy for which he bore a considerable share of the responsibility—at best the measures only prevented the situation from becoming worse.[8]

Meanwhile the combination of atrocities committed—news of which occasionally reached the Israeli public in spite of strict censorship—and the IDF's apparent inability to achieve their objective was beginning to erode the IDF's fighting power. Surviving evidence shows that through roughly 1951, commanders considered the raids beneficial for the morale of the participating units (one reason for undertaking them in the first place)[9] as well as useful for training;[10] later the wind changed and one failure began to follow upon another. Thus, in 1952, raids were mounted at Wadi Fukin, Bet Sira, Bet Awa, Idna, Rantis, and Bet Jalla among other places. According to an IDF intelligence division report, all "ended in failure" and caused the IDF to lose prestige in the eyes of its Arab enemies[11] (not to mention the effect on Israel's civilian authorities).[12]

Then came the Falame village raid on January 25–26, 1953. First, the battalion mounting the operation repeatedly lost its way in the dark. Next, having found its objective, it attacked but was repulsed by a Jordanian force consisting of just twelve riflemen—not Arab Legionaries, mind you, but members of the decidedly second-class National Guard. An attempt to reenter the village on January 28–29 was equally unsuccessful. This failure was followed by a series of others (in one case a navy ship sent to gather intelligence in the Red Sea committed a navigation error, ran aground on the Saudi coast, and had to be rescued). One platoon, sent to blow up a well in the Gaza Strip, lost its way, wandered all night, and finally discovered it had not even crossed the armistice line—whereupon a squad commander hid behind a rock and killed himself with a hand grenade.[13] On another occasion an IDF unit, apparently believing it was in the West Bank, attacked a camp of Israeli Bedouin. They killed a seventy-year-old man, two women, three camels, and twenty sheep.[14]

Facing these and other failures,[15] the IDF first tried to restore morale by fiat. Acting as head of the General Staff Division, Dayan, for example, harangued the troops about the need to abandon "Jewish cleverness" (as if there had been anything clever about the recent debacles) in favor of frontal attacks. Missions were to proceed according to plan unless and until at least 50 percent of the men had become casualties.[16] When those stirring words failed to produce results, Makleff, as chief of staff, decided to set up a special unit that would take over the task of carrying out reprisals. Its designated commander was twenty-seven-year-old Maj. Ariel Sharon. Like Allon, Sharon was the son of a not-too-successful farmer.[17] Unlike Allon, he did not grow up a gentleman; at several points during his career he found his integrity questioned by superiors and subordinates alike. Though he had never gone to officer school, he rose in the service and in 1950 went through a battalion commanders course, commanded by then Lt. Col. Yitschak Rabin. For two years he served under Dayan while the latter was CIC Northern Command. Subsequently he left the IDF for civilian life, studying history at Jerusalem's Hebrew University.

Back in the army, this "daring and clever" (according to Dayan) officer was given a jeep and a free hand, touring the country while looking for men who would be suited for the new unit. His catch constituted a mixed lot, some of them veterans who had left the forces in the wake of the War of Independence and others who were still on active service. One man brought in another: Militarily the ones with the brightest futures were Mordechai Gur and Refael Eytan, rough-hewn fighters who perfectly fit Koestler's description of their generation and who were destined to rise to chief of staff. Two or three others would become generals. Dayan, however, reserved his esteem for one Meir Har Tsion, whom he considered "the greatest Jewish warrior since Bar Kochva."[18]

Known simply as Unit 101, the new force began with twenty men, which gradually increased to forty-five as one friend brought in another. Some of the men were outlandish characters, seldom bothering to wash, change clothes, or comb their hair; others were quiet and introverted. Trained at Sataf, near Jerusalem, they launched their first operation on August 29 following the killing of an Israeli man and the wounding of a woman two weeks earlier. Two teams entered the village of Burej in the Gaza Strip, searching for the local chief of Egyptian intelligence considered responsible for sending the infiltrators; failing to find him they killed some forty Palestinian civilians at the cost of two Israeli wounded. Even more murderous raids followed, culminating on the night of October 15. By that time Sharon's men had been merged with Battalion 890, a paratrooper unit that had heretofore failed to distinguish itself but that he, in a remarkable demonstration of leadership, pulled out of its lethargy. Now a mixed force of 101 men and paratroopers, Unit 202 stormed the Jordanian village of Kibiya and killed no fewer than sixty-nine people, mostly women and children.[19] Predictably, this operation also failed to end the hostilities along the border, which resumed after a few weeks. Moreover, the sharp international reaction convinced Dayan that, in the future, military bases rather than civilians would have to be targeted.[20]

In December 1953, Ben Gurion resigned as prime minister and minister of defense. Before leaving office he had pushed through the appointment of his hawkish protégé, Moshe Dayan, as IDF chief of staff; by so doing he undermined his successor, the mild-mannered, highly cultured, but ultimately weak-kneed Moshe Sharet. Russian-born like the rest, Sharet differed from Ben Gurion in that he was fully familiar with Arab language and culture; politically he was a dove who believed that Israel could achieve more by paying attention to its neighbors' psychology and national sensibilities.[21] Unlike Ben Gurion, he was primarily a diplomat and did not feel sufficiently at home with defense matters to take that portfolio for himself. Instead Pinchas Lavon, a veteran Labor Party intellectual, was appointed defense minister. Before and after 1948, Lavon had been known as a dove after Sharet's own heart, having, for example, resisted all ideas of deporting Israel's remaining Arab population. Suddenly he reversed his stance, becoming more aggressive than anybody else in government.

In spite of Sharet's good intentions, during his term of office the problem of infiltration remained much as it had been; in 1954 there were three times as many clashes along the border with Jordan than in 1953.[22] Patrols were fired upon, buses attacked, agricultural workers waylaid and murdered, and property destroyed or stolen in a succession of minor hostilities that seemed to have neither beginning nor end; conversely, Israeli settlers in the Jerusalem corridor organized their own hunting expeditions, mounting patrols, driving off livestock, and sniping at "living targets."[23] Whereas Sharet was in favor of restraint, seeking to influence the Arabs by way of diplomatic action in London and Washington, D.C., the IDF's commanders demanded action. Every so often the cup would run over; then, having extracted permission from a reluctant prime minister, they mounted operations far larger than those authorized by him. A pained Sharet repeatedly protested to them and in his diary, but in public he had to accept (and justify) the raids ex post facto.

Against this unseemly background, the factor that saved the IDF from drowning in a sea of self-contempt was probably neither the establishment of Unit 101 nor the new tactics that Sharon devised for overrunning

enemy strongholds—however brilliant they may have been.[24] Instead it
was the decision—taken willy-nilly under pressure from international public opinion—to switch from killing helpless civilians to attacking the Jordanian armed forces as an enemy more worthy of respect. From early
1954, orders for raids regularly included the phrase "women and children
are not to be hit under any circumstances"[25] (though figures on such questions are notoriously unreliable; those gathered by Israeli historian Morris,
who is unsympathetic to the IDF, from Jordanian and foreign sources bear
out this interpretation).[26] Thus, when the paratroopers stormed the village
of Nachlin on March 19, 1954, the result was seven Jordanian military
dead and only one civilian. At Chirbat Jinba in May of the same year three
out of four Arab dead were soldiers (National Guard); at Azun in June it
was three out of three, and at Bet-Laki in September at least three out of
four or five. Other raids, also directed against the Arab Legion rather than
civilians, brought in prisoners who were exchanged for Israeli ones. Moreover, once the General Staff ordered units firing across the border during
clashes with the Jordanians to refrain from targeting villages, no more villages were, in fact, hit.[27]

Although the decision to focus on military targets made the raids
"increasingly complicated and difficult,"[28] IDF morale, which had been
threatened by years of cruel and useless skirmishes with *mistanenim*, suddenly
soared.[29] Previously even some of Sharon's own men had been wondering
whether the poor villagers whom they were raiding really constituted "the
enemy";[30] now, they were able to mount an impressive display of captured
weapons for the benefit of visiting foreigners.[31] Israel's paratroopers found
themselves basking in public adulation similar to that which in France during the same years was giving rise to the so-called para myth.[32] As Shimon
Peres was to later write, "Children want to emulate them, mothers pray for
their safety, rural settlers admire their achievements, and youth regards
them as the embodiment of all its own virtues."[33]

Whereas ground forces were made to wear heavy, black, hobnailed
boots, paratroopers were given comfortable, red, American-style combat
boots with rubber soles. Whereas other troops were still burdened by cumbersome, World War I–vintage bolt-action rifles, the paratroopers sported
the new homemade Uzi submachine gun (named after its inventor but also
happening to mean, in Hebrew, my strength). Not only was the Uzi well
suited for the heroics of close combat, but with its short temper (when
falling or being hit it tended to fire bursts without anyone pressing the
trigger) it almost acted as a metaphor for the IDF. The original paratrooper force of one battalion was expanded three times over until it
reached a full brigade. Their previous commander, Lt. Col. Yehuda Harari,

was sacked; Sharon took over as commanding officer, and some of his more prominent subordinates became battalion chiefs. To ensure that the message got through, Dayan ordered all senior officers to take a jump course. As of this writing that practice remains in force even though it has been thirty years since any Israeli soldier leaped into enemy territory from an airplane.

Meanwhile the attention of Israel's security establishment was shifting away from the border with Jordan—troublesome, but owing to the kingdom's weakness never any danger to Israel's basic security—toward the Egyptian border. Gamal Abdel Nasser's rise to power in 1952–1953 had been closely watched by the Israeli government. Gingerly, attempts were made to see whether the new Egyptian president would be more inclined than his predecessors to conclude peace with Israel.[34] Although these led nowhere, the Egyptians' prime concern during those years was to rid the country of the British troops still occupying the Suez Canal Zone. Isolated from the heart of the Arab-Israeli conflict by the Sinai Desert, Egypt was much less affected by the border incidents that took place than were Israel and Jordan. Moreover, except for the Gaza Strip, it did not have to harbor large numbers of Palestinian refugees. The Gaza Strip constituted administered territory, and throughout the nineteen years of occupation (until 1967) its inhabitants were kept under military rule and systematically prevented from maintaining too much contact with Egypt proper.

In the middle of 1954 this troubled but essentially stable relationship was disturbed by the Lavon affair (*essek bish*, or unfortunate business).[35] As far back as 1951, Israeli military intelligence had set up an espionage network in Egypt. The approaching British evacuation of the Canal Zone caused the chief of intelligence, Benjamin Gibli, to fear the future; with the British gone, Nasser's hands might be untied. The network was activated, and small quantities of incendiaries (contained inside eyeglass cases!) were set off against British and American targets in Cairo and Alexandria, the objective being to sow discord and postpone or prevent the evacuation. In the event the explosions caused some minor physical damage but no casualties.

Shortly thereafter the ringleader, a dubious character named Evri Elad, who had been selected on the basis of his ability to pose as a German businessman, apparently betrayed the remaining members to Egyptian counterintelligence. Having stood trial, on January 31 several were executed. Inevitably, inside Israel a search for scapegoats got under way, and a commission of investigation was established. To cover his tracks Gibli had his secretary, a nineteen-year-old female soldier named Dalia Carmel, retype some documents to point the finger at Lavon as the perpetrator. Though Lavon vehemently denied that he had ordered the action, the investigating commission, misled by Gibli's testimony and the documentary "evidence" that he produced, failed to clear the minister of defense. With Sharet still in power, Lavon was forced to resign, his replacement being—who else— Ben Gurion.

No sooner had Ben Gurion come back to the ministry of defense than an opportunity for action presented itself. One, possibly two teams, working for Egyptian military intelligence, entered Israel from the Gaza Strip and broke into a secret installation—reputed to be an institute for biological warfare—in Nes Tsiona, south of Tel Aviv. On their way back they also killed a civilian cyclist. Retaliation against the Egyptians was inevitable. When it came it far exceeded anybody's expectations, including those of Sharet, who had warned against "large-scale bloodshed."[36] In the event Sharon's paratroopers killed one Palestinian civilian and no fewer than thirty-nine Egyptian soldiers. Some died when their base was stormed, others when they rushed to their comrades' aid and were ambushed.

Though the Egyptian border had never been quiet, matters now escalated. Teams of *mistanenim* crossed the border incessantly, mining and waylaying and destroying and killing. In response, highly placed Israeli officials, including some of Sharet's close advisers, suggested that the IDF occupy all or part of the Gaza Strip.[37] Though that advice was rejected, the paratroopers were sent in. Repeatedly they attacked targets along the border (not just in the Gaza Strip), inflicting dozens of casualties. From time to time things went out of control, and the two sides battled with few holds barred, including artillery (May 30) and aircraft (September 1). Previously most clashes had been the product of local initiatives. Now Egyptian intelligence organized a battalion of *fedayeen* (heroic fighters), many of them Palestinian jailbirds released on condition they take part in the murderous raids into Israel. Hostilities spread to the border with Syria, where several small demilitarized zones were left over from 1949 and where Israel engaged in a "forward" policy, insisting on its right to cultivate the fields "right to the border line," as the official line stated. They culminated in December 1955, when an IDF force demolished a chain of Syrian strongholds east of the Sea of Galilee, killing fifty-four (including six civilians) and taking thirty prisoners at the cost of six dead and fourteen wounded.

During this period, the IDF was not a tame instrument in the government's hands. At a minimum, lower-level commanders such as Sharon— who commanded the raid against Syria from a boat—systematically exceeded their instructions.[38] Claiming to have met with unexpected opposition or the need to extricate their own men, time after time they killed far more enemy troops and wrought far more damage than Sharet thought advisable or they themselves had forecasted when submitting plans. They were backed up by Dayan, who would receive each returning force with congratulations and alcohol; neither then nor later did he leave any doubt about his sympathies.[39] From January 1955 on he in turn was supported by the formidable figure of Ben Gurion. By the time of "Operation Sea of Galilee," the latter was back in the driver's seat, having ousted Sharet the previous month and reoccupied his prime minister's post.

As their high casualty lists indicate, the Egyptian armed forces at this time were no match for Sharon's men who repeatedly stormed their bases. As for training and motivation, they showed little progress since 1948–1949; their equipment was antiquated, much of it dating to World War II. To this was added the fact that both Britain and the United States refused to sell Nasser large quantities of new weapons—even if he could have afforded them. In summer 1955 the stalemate was broken when Western intelligence agencies got wind of a new arms deal between Egypt and Soviet-dominated Czechoslovakia. Israeli intelligence estimated that the deal involved 90–100 MIG–15 jet fighters (famous for their success during the Korean War); 48 twin-engine Ilyushin–28 light bombers; 230 tanks (including T–34s and the heavier Joseph Stalin III models); 440 field guns of various calibers; 34 heavy antiaircraft guns; and two destroyers, four minesweepers, twelve torpedo boats, and six submarines. Israel itself at the time had fewer than 50 jet fighters—British Meteors and French Ouragans, both models markedly inferior to the Soviet MIGs—and 130 tanks, including 100 World War II Shermans and 30 light, French-built AMX–13s.[40] Compared with this the deal constituted a revolution, both qualitatively and quantitatively.

As in 1967, Nasser's intentions as to his new might may never be known—though cynics could add that on both occasions his intentions remained unknown solely because he was preempted by the IDF.[41] Clearly news of the deal sent the Israel's government, armed forces, media, and public into something very close to a panic. Having spent time in London during the Blitz, Ben Gurion himself was particularly worried about the damage bombers might do to Israel. Previously there had been occasional talk about a preventive war;[42] now launching such a war became the persistent demand of the General Staff under Dayan.[43] The hawkish COS worked on the assumption that six to eight months would be needed by the Egyptian army to absorb the new arms. Thus each passing month diminished the Israeli superiority on which he had relied.

From early 1956 on, Israeli preparations for an eventual war against Egypt started in earnest. However, large parts of public opinion—including the left-wing parties on which Ben Gurion's coalition depended—refused to catch on to the idea that the General Staff was planning an *offensive* campaign. Instead they reverted to old ideas about territorial defense, insisting that the border settlements be prepared for such defense.⁴⁴ Against its will the IDF was forced to divert resources, conducting a survey to identify the 150 most critical settlements, providing them with weapons and training, as well as earmarking regular forces for protecting them.⁴⁵ Fortifications were built, antitank ditches dug, fields of fires prepared, and mines sown. Much of this huge effort was financed and mounted not by the IDF, whose plans were entirely different, but by civilian organizations that volunteered labor and contributed money. Much of it was wasteful and some of it bordered on the ridiculous, as when the craftsmen's association "purchased" a jet fighter (by donating its equivalent in money according to the official, government-published price list) and the employees of one bank purchased a tank.⁴⁶ On the positive side, it certainly showed the extent to which the people identified with their state.

By way of a more purposeful response to the Czech arms deal, the defense budget was almost doubled—from 126 million to 246 million Israeli pounds; additional sums were spent on civil defense, roads, and the like.⁴⁷ In late 1955 an acquisition list, including forty-eight F–86 Saber jet fighters and sixty M–48 Patton tanks, was presented to the U.S. government. Then and later, however, the State Department feared overt support of Israel would drive the Arabs into the arms of the USSR. Accordingly it led the Israelis by the nose; having taken several months to consider the matter, in March 1956 Secretary of State John Foster Dulles formally refused the most important items.⁴⁸ Washington ended up delivering no more than five helicopters, twenty-five half-tracks, and 110 heavy machine guns.

Meanwhile the main Israeli procurement effort had already switched to France, where there existed a certain sympathy for Israel in connection with the unfolding Algerian war. Negotiations were conducted by Shimon Peres, the thirty-two-year-old director general of the ministry of defense who on this and subsequent occasions proved himself a master of secret diplomacy. They led to the conclusion of an agreement whereby the French agreed to supply another sixty AMX–13 tanks, 400 Sherman tanks, 500 bazooka (antitank) launchers with 10,000 rockets, as well as 1,000 SS–10 (also antitank) missiles;⁴⁹ these arms, plus 200 6x6 lorries, were used to equip a total of fourteen ground combat brigades. The only element still needed by the IDF to launch its offensive campaign was new jet aircraft to counter the Egyptian MIG–15s. These came in the form of seventy-two French Mystère IV fighters, of which only 37 reached Israel prior to the outbreak of the campaign.⁵⁰ Flown across the Mediterranean by way of Brindisi, the first batch found the prime minister and half the government waiting in typical Israeli fashion when it landed.⁵¹

The story of the negotiations that led Israel, France, and Britain to a tripartite agreement to take offensive action against Egypt is well known.[52] Throughout the first half of 1956, tentative talks were held between intelligence officers on all sides, and a measure of cooperation was established.[53] Then, on July 26, 1956, Nasser provided the much-sought-after casus belli, proclaiming the nationalization of the Suez Canal before 100,000 people gathered to celebrate the revolution's third anniversary. Visiting Paris in early August, the chief of the IDF General Staff Division, Brig. Gen. Meir Amit, was asked quite bluntly whether Israel would agree to cooperate in case they (i.e., the French) and the British launched military operations against Egypt. While Washington advised caution,[54] Shimon Peres and Gibli's successor as chief of intelligence, Brig. Gen. Yehoshaphat Harkavi, were put in charge of the preliminary negotiations.

With the plans taking shape, cooperation between the IDF and the French armed forces intensified. In return for the weapons they received, the Israelis provided their ally with aerial photographs of the Canal Zone as well as information on the IDF's ability to support an operation against Egypt should France decide to launch it.[55] It remained to bring in the British, who had been secretly planning an operation for months but, faced with domestic opposition to the adventure, were inclined to be more cautious. After some diplomatic maneuvering they finally joined the bandwagon at a top-secret conference at Sevres, near Paris, October 22–24. To solve the question of responsibility, French General Maurice Challes hatched a plan whereby the French and British would be called in *after* the beginning of the Israeli attack in order to safeguard the Suez Canal against both the IDF and the Egyptian armed forces.[56] It was a highly unsavory plot that cast Israel in the role of the aggressor. In the end Ben Gurion, prodded by Dayan, accepted it only because the British refused to base their intervention on any other rationale—and without the British, the French would not move.

Militarily, too, the final form of "Operation Kadesh" (its Hebrew code name) was not exactly what the IDF had hoped for. Having no interest in the Sinai Peninsula per se, its objectives originally had been to occupy the Gaza Strip and the Straits of Tyran. The former was a wasp nest of *fedayeen*; the latter had been closed to Israeli shipping since 1949 and to Israeli overflights since September 1955. However, the agreement with France and Britain dictated a different modus operandi. The original plan to cut off Egyptian communications with the Gaza Strip by means of a seaborne landing at Al Arish was canceled, as was another plan for a drive on Sharm al-Sheikh. Instead the IDF was obliged to conduct the campaign from west to east, dropping paratroopers in an undefended zone near the canal to pro-

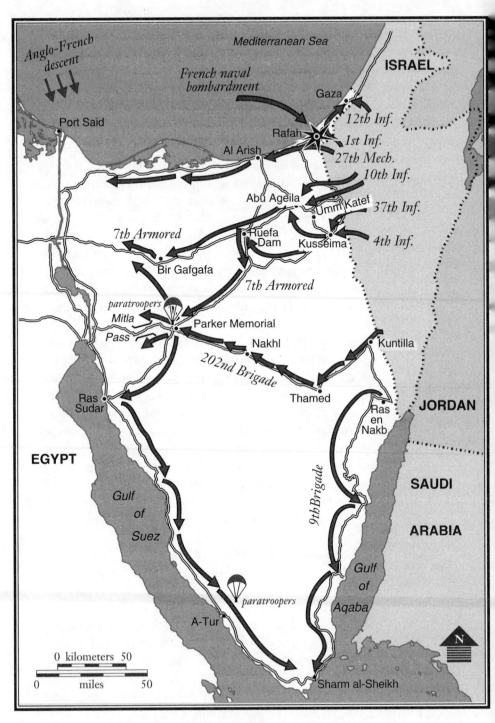

MAP 9.1   THE SINAI CAMPAIGN, 1956

vide London its much-needed pretext while also keeping open the option of withdrawing the force in case Israel's allies failed to live up to their words. The plans now spoke of "collapsing" the Egyptian military organization in the Sinai rather than simply killing their troops or occupying territory.[57] This in turn was based on Dayan's notion that Arab troops, unlike Western troops, would not fight but turn tail when their lines of communications came under threat—something that in fact did not happen.

To ensure that the operation proceeded in the desired sequence it was decided to unleash Israel's armored forces no earlier than thirty-six hours after H-Hour (see Map 9.1). The IAF too was compelled to violate its own doctrine—based, with the usual lack of acknowledgment, on the Luftwaffe's operations in 1939–1941—and cancel its plans for attacking the Egyptian airfields (most of which were located west of the canal).[58] Instead its main mission was defensive—maintaining air superiority over Israel proper—and providing air cover to the paratroopers near the canal, dropping supplies, and mounting strikes against Egyptian forces on the ground.[59] Ben Gurion did not yet feel fully confident in his pilots; he asked for and received the aid of four French squadrons (three fighter, one transport) as well as ten additional Dakota aircraft, which were simply put on loan.[60]

All these events took place against a background of continual clashes along the Israel-Jordan border. Not wishing to obstruct France's delivery of arms, Israel refrained from its usual punitive actions for most of the summer. In September, however, the paratroopers were unleashed no fewer than three times, killing dozens of Jordanian soldiers but also losing fairly heavily themselves as they tried to repeat their by now well understood tactics. Hostilities, fueled by diplomatic contacts that seemed to foreshadow the entry of Iraqi troops into Jordan, culminated on the night of October 10–11, when the paratroopers stormed the Arab Legion's strongholds at Kalkiliya on Israel's narrow "waist." A force that had been sent farther east to block eventual Jordanian reinforcements was itself ambushed and had to be extricated by means of heavy fighting.[61] Eventually the paratroopers, having killed some 70 Arab Legionaries, were able to return home before it became necessary to escalate by activating the IAF. They carried with them seventeen of their dead, however, causing Dayan to ask himself how long this kind of thing—to all appearances, useless as well as costly—could be carried on.[62]

In any event the troubles with Jordan proved instrumental in helping the IDF disguise its true designs against Egypt. Preparations for mobilization, in the form of registration exercises and the like, had been ongoing throughout the summer, and when the signal was given on October 24 the men and the units were ready. The first stage of the call-up was conducted on an individual basis, employing messengers who went around to "addresses" and without using the public media. Two days later, the masquerade was dropped and a public call-up went out by way of radio (there was as yet no television) and newspapers. As they would in 1967, the Israeli people, frustrated by years of border hostilities and believing themselves in imminent danger, responded enthusiastically. More than 100,000 men streamed to the colors, and some units actually got more troops than were authorized in their tables of organization[63] (the balance consisting of discharged personnel who nevertheless volunteered). As also in 1967, this overwhelming response—more than any particular strategic genius—was the secret to victory.

The Israeli mobilization caught the Egyptians at an inopportune moment, given that they had just withdrawn half of their forces from the Sinai in order to deal with the growing Anglo-French threat.[64] Against the 45,000 men deployed by the Israelis they had only 30,000, about a third being decidedly second-rate. From north to south, 8th Palestinian Division with two Palestinian brigades (86th and 87th) and one Egyptian National Guard brigade (6th) was stationed in the Gaza Strip. Behind it was 3rd Infantry Division with one brigade (5th) at the key position of Rafah, another at the equally important one of Umm Katef–Abu Ageila, and a third (4th) at Al Arish, standing in reserve to support the others. Thus the two northernmost roads leading into the Sinai, one running along the coast and the other from Nitsana to Bir Gafgafa, were effectively blocked. Farther south, however, the third road—which led from Nitsana southwest to Mitla Pass—was defended by only one battalion at Kusseima; even less well defended was the fourth road, in reality a desert track that ran from Elat to Mitla Pass. South of Elat, the terrain was so inhospitable that there were hardly any forces at all. Only Sharm al-Sheikh, forming the extreme southern tip of the peninsula, was occupied by two additional battalions.

The rationale behind the Egyptians' deployment was probably their troops' peculiar weakness in maneuver warfare. As one Israeli officer later wrote, fighting them was like playing chess against an opponent who could only make one move against each two of one's own.[65] Based on a thorough study of all avenues of approach, their defenses were designed to block the roads; the fortifications were probably as good as could be made. They were, however, located too close to the Israeli border—none more than fifteen miles or so away—and, particularly south of the main defensive perimeter at Umm Katef–Abu Ageila, incapable of receiving support either from each other or from the rear. In fact the main Egyptian reserves, two infantry divisions plus an armored brigade, were stationed west of the canal. At best it would take forward units two days to reach the battlefield.

In the event the initial Israeli offensive bypassed the main Egyptian fortifications completely—with the result, however, that it led them nowhere in particular. During late afternoon on October 29 sixteen Dakota transport aircraft took off. Escorted by IAF fighters, they carried a paratrooper battalion of 395 men commanded by Lieutenant Colonel Eytan. They dropped in an undefended area 120 miles inside Egyptian territory east of Mitla Pass. So remote was the area selected—upon hearing of it, Nasser exclaimed that the Israelis were "attacking sand"[66]—that the landing itself went unopposed and even unobserved by the Egyptians. However, later on the same day the paratroopers fired at three Egyptian vehicles, two of which got away and alerted superiors.

Reacting swiftly that evening, the Egyptian high command took countermeasures. Starting from Fayid, 1st Armored Brigade took the road by way of Giddi Pass toward Bir Gafgafa; once there it would have been able either to proceed toward the Israeli border or, turning south, take Eytan's paratroopers opposite Mitla Pass in the flank. The 2nd Infantry Brigade was sent directly from Suez toward Mitla Pass. In spite of being slowed by Nasser's insistence that commercial traffic through the canal not be halted,[67] this brigade made good progress, and early next morning its leading forces, having driven all night, debouched from the eastern end of Mitla Pass. There they were met by wave after wave of strafing IAF fighters that together with the paratroopers halted the Egyptian counterattack.

The Israelis quickly brought up the remainder of the paratrooper brigade from its assembly area at En Chatseva on the Israel-Jordan border, a location deliberately selected in order to mislead the Arab intelligence services concerning the true direction of the attack. In the event its progress was governed more by the shortage of transport than by enemy resistance. The brigade did not have enough military trucks to carry all the troops; the rest had to be packed into civilian lorries unsuitable for driving over the atrocious roads. Having crossed into the Sinai during late afternoon on October 29, 202nd Brigade overran Kuntilla, far south of the main Egyptian positions, without undue difficulty (its garrison had run away). Then it was the turn of Thamed where two companies barred the way; once that position fell, however, the third Egyptian position, at Nakhl, was captured without loss. At 2200 hours on October 30, Eytan's men could see the headlights of the approaching column; shortly afterwards Sharon and his men linked up with them. The paratroopers had not yet fought their fill, however, which would cost them dearly the next day.

These events had little impact on the Egyptian main defenses, which as noted were located in several different fortified perimeters not far from the Israeli border. Made wise by the War of Independence, Ben Gurion, fearing heavy casualties, had instructed Dayan that the IDF attack these perimeters only *after* England and France had issued their ultimatum, were refused, and started military operations against the Egyptians. Israel's allies did not prove true to their words, however, and everything proceeded much more slowly than expected. In the end they opened their campaign during late afternoon on October 31, which meant that during the first two days Israel was on its own.

To the north of Sharon's little expedition, breaking through the main Egyptian defensive positions (the Abu Ageila–Umm Katef–Kusseima complex), was the task of 38th *Ugda* (division-sized task force). It had under its command one armored brigade (in reality mechanized, since the unit in question, the 37th, had only one armored battalion) and two infantry brigades plus a reserve (7th Armored Brigade with its full complement of two armored battalions). Against this force (approximately 12,000 men) the combined Egyptian force mounted a single brigade (6th); the Israeli advantage in armor was much greater still since the Egyptians had no tanks, relying on artillery and antitank guns to stop opponents.[68] Even so, the Israelis were prevented from concentrating all of their forces owing to the need to capture Kusseima, at the southern edge of the Egyptian perimeter, so as to open up another road to Mitla Pass in case Sharon and his paratroopers failed to link up with their comrades. In addition Dayan, heeding Ben Gurion's instructions to delay, insisted on *not* using his armored brigades for the initial attack, thus depriving 38th *Ugda* from what might have constituted its main striking force.

One of the infantry brigades, the 4th, opened the attack against the southern edge of the Egyptian perimeter at Kusseima when it was suddenly joined by the tanks of 7th Armored Brigade. The latter had been thrown into the battle by the commander of the southern front, Brig. Gen. Asaf Simchoni, who, knowing nothing of political considerations at the top, acted against Dayan's explicit instructions in sending out his armor on October 30. Kusseima fell to 4th Brigade even before the tanks arrived; still, Simchoni's decision proved fortunate, because the main attack, launched simultaneously by 10th Brigade against the principal defenses farther northwest, had stalled. As had also happened, for example, to the Germans during their 1944 Ardennes offensive, when Gen. Hasso-Eccard von Manteuffel's attack on the south suddenly found itself getting ahead of Dietrich's 6th S.S. Panzer Army to its right, what had originally been planned as an auxiliary thrust was suddenly turned into the main thrust. The difference being that the Israelis proved sufficiently flexible to recognize what was happening and change their plans and also had another card up their sleeve.

The defenders of Abu Ageila and Umm Katef fought well enough, repulsing one assault after another. Even after 37th Armored Brigade had been brought up and joined the attack on October 31, they continued to resist, causing Dayan, who was thoroughly dissatisfied with the performance of his forces, to replace the commander of 10th Brigade midbattle. However, the fall of Kusseima changed the situation. Though 4th Brigade rested on its laurels, 7th Armored did not. Having successfully made their way through some difficult defiles, its tanks soon began to outflank the Egyptians from the south and threaten them from the rear. By the evening of October 31 the situation of the defenders was becoming quite difficult, but they still held out.

That morning the Egyptian reserve brigade, stationed at Al Arish, made an attempt to come to their aid; however, its leading battalion was attacked by Israeli fighter-bombers and was halted before it could get within effective range. That very evening the Egyptian high command—engaged in hostilities with the Anglo-French forces and fearful that its forces in the Sinai would become "isolated"—decided to withdraw to the canal.[69] As the last potential reinforcements disappeared the garrison at Abu Ageila too had no choice but to evacuate, which it did most successfully during the night of November 1–2. Not noticing, the Israelis renewed the attack the next day and found the position empty.

The fall of Abu Ageila meant that the principal road leading west into the central Sinai was wide open to the Israelis. With 7th Armored and its energetic commander, Col. Uri Ben Ari, firmly in the lead the latter drove on to Bir Gafgafa. There, Ben Ari had been informed by the IAF to expect to meet 1st Egyptian Armored Brigade, which was coming up from Fayid; however, by the time the encounter took place on the afternoon of November 2 the Egyptians had followed their orders and were already falling back on the canal. Only two companies, one consisting of T–34 tanks and the other of Su–100 tank destroyers, were caught and destroyed by the Israeli Shermans in the largest single armored battle of the war. Their defeat opened the road farther west, and by evening Ben Ari had reached his intended objective ten miles east of the canal.

The Israeli offensive proceeded from south to north—first the paratroopers, then Abu Ageila, then finally Rafah, which Dayan considered the most difficult objective as well as the decisive one.[70] Against the Egyptian brigade at Rafah he had concentrated the IDF's 77th *Ugda*, consisting of 1st Infantry Brigade and 27th Armored Brigade (the latter deploying only about half its tanks). The offensive started on the night of October 31–November 1 and at first made little progress since the air force and navy (the latter reinforced by a French six-inch gun cruiser[71]) were unable to pinpoint their targets in the dark; instead of hitting the Egyptian positions, they almost killed the *ugda* commander.[72] After this fiasco—"a giant sprat," to quote Dayan (who had attached himself to 27th Brigade)—heavy ground fighting started at 0300 hours. It proceeded hour after hour as Egyptians, well protected by mines and barbed wire, clung to their positions. Nevertheless by 0900 the town of Rafah, including the vital crossroads at which the road coming from Nitsana branched out to the right and left toward the towns of Gaza and Al Arish respectively, had fallen.

The Gaza Strip thus having been cut off from the Sinai, the Israeli forces split. With Dayan still following in its wake, 27th Brigade, having rested a few hours, turned southwest along the coastal road. Meeting no more than halfhearted opposition, they passed through the Jirardi Defile and reached Al Arish by evening; by the time they were ready to renew the assault next morning (November 2), however, the Egyptian brigade had obeyed its orders and evacuated the town. Meanwhile 1st Infantry Brigade had turned in the opposite direction, working northeast toward the town of Gaza. There they linked up with the 11th Infantry Brigade coming up from Israel proper, that is, from the west. Together the two brigades had little difficulty in overcoming the Egyptian (in fact, Palestinian) forces in the area—made up of units that, as Dayan noted, had not been issued with heavy weapons by their Egyptian masters and had never been intended for anything more than purely holding operations.

Having echeloned their offensive in three successive stages, by the end of the fourth day (counting from October 29) the Israelis had effectively broken the Egyptian army in the Sinai. What remained were three sideshows, two of which took place during the critical days (October 30–November 2) and one after everything else was over. On October 31 Sharon, claiming the need to improve his positions against the anticipated counterattack from the north[73] but defying Dayan's orders, sent his men into Mitla Pass. Three companies under Lt. Col. Mordechai Gur mounted their half-tracks and drove forward without attempting reconnaissance or securing the hills on both sides. Contrary to expectations they found the latter occupied by units belonging to Egyptian 2nd Brigade, which had not retreated the previous day. They came under heavy fire from invisible caves and had to be extricated, leading to a murderous battle in which the brigade's remaining forces outflanked the Egyptians by climbing the hills and then, descending the slopes into the pass itself, flushed them out from their positions among the rocks. This action cost the Israelis thirty-eight dead, almost a quarter of the number killed in the entire campaign. Furthermore, no sooner had the paratroopers cleared the pass than Sharon ordered them to evacuate.

The second sideshow also occurred on October 31 and took place at sea. At 0330 hours an Egyptian destroyer, *Ibrahim al Awwal*, appeared opposite the coast of Haifa and opened fire; though it fired 200 four-inch rounds, damage was slight. Initially the Egyptian vessel came under fire from a French ship, the destroyer *Kersaint*.[74] Then, retreating (as it was running out of ammunition and considered its mission accomplished), it was engaged by two Israeli destroyers, which positioned themselves between it and its base. Soon the Israeli vessels were joined by a couple of IAF Ouragans. Whether it was the destroyers that hit the Egyptian ship or rockets fired from the air- craft is immaterial. At any rate the steering gear was put out of action and *Ibrahim al Awwal* hoisted a white flag after its crew tried unsuccessfully to sink it by opening the valves. Strategically this action was entirely without significance. It did, however, serve to raise Israeli morale to new heights— after all it is not every day that an enemy warship surrenders, captain and all.

Finally, it remained to accomplish Israel's one real strategic objective for the entire campaign, that is, to seize Sharm al-Sheikh so as to break the Egyptian blockade and open the straits to shipping and overflight. Citing a shortage of transport, the local Egyptian commander had persuaded his superiors that evacuation was not practicable; with his naval support also gone (one Egyptian frigate was sunk by the British and another took refuge in a Saudi Port)[75] he and his two battalions were left entirely to their own devices. On the Israeli side a motorized brigade, the 9th, had been ear- marked for the task and was concentrated at Ras en Nakb just south of Elat. On the morning of November 2 it received orders to proceed down the coast. There was, however, no metalled road, and driving through the sands that covered part of the track proved to be grueling. Meanwhile two companies of paratroopers had been dropped at A-Tur on the southwest- ern coast of the Sinai. Having secured the airport, they were joined by an airborne infantry battalion and a battalion of comrades who made their way by land; commanded by Eytan, the combined force drove south.

Coming from two directions at once, the offensive against Sharm al- Sheikh now developed into a race between 9th Brigade and Eytan's men. In the event 9th Brigade arrived first. Supported by the IAF's fighter-bombers, which strafed and rocketed, it opened the attack during the night of November 4–5. As usual when fighting from prepared positions, the Egyp- tian troops put on a fierce resistance even when the situation was hopeless; the Israelis made slow progress. In the end it took almost twelve hours' fight- ing to break the outnumbered, outgunned, and isolated Egyptian battalions, and then it was Eytan's force, coming from the other side, that brought about the decision. Being told by Dayan that the campaign was over, Ben Gurion retorted: "And I suppose you can't bear that, can you?"[76]

At the time the Israelis went to war, about half of the Egyptian garrison normally stationed in the Sinai had already been withdrawn, giving the IDF considerable superiority in numbers of men and, even more so, armor. It is true that, having issued their ultimatum, the French and the British delayed the beginning of "Operation Musketeer"; yet only for the first forty-eight hours—until 1900 hours on October 31, to be precise—was the IDF on its own. At that time, out of the three main Israeli attacks, only the southernmost was a complete success. And that one was little more than a feint, mounted against an undefended sector with the aid of a single brigade that could be withdrawn if necessary. By contrast, the central Israeli advance, though it had already captured Kusseima and was threatening to take the main Egyptian positions in the flank and rear, had as yet made no impression on those positions. At that time the "critical" offensive (Dayan's term) against the Rafah junction had not even begun.

Even disregarding the difficulties experienced on the central axis, whether the IDF would have done as well had the British and the French not launched "Operation Musketeer" is open to some doubt. Much would have depended on the IAF's ability to identify and forestall Egyptian counterattacks; to judge from the episodes that did take place, like the successful interdiction of the Egyptian 2nd Brigade on October 30 and of the 4th on the next day, it was equal to the task. They were assisted by the three squadrons of French fighters that were stationed in Israel, strafed, dropped supplies, and even reached out as far as Luxor to bomb the Egyptian airfield there.[77] Still, and in large part owing to the entire way in which the campaign had been planned, the Egyptian air force was never defeated. After a somewhat slow start it fought back bravely enough, engaging in dogfights and launching several painful strafing attacks on the Israeli columns. Ultimately more than half its aircraft were destroyed by the British and the French;[78] but for "Operation Musketeer," a fight against the IAF alone might have been much more balanced.

However, the most remarkable aspect of the IDF's conduct of the campaign was its system of command and control.[79] Highly intelligent, easily bored, and something of a lone wolf—he hated committee work—Dayan himself was anything but an administrator. Having given his final orders prior to the campaign he spent his time away from headquarters, overflying the desert in a light aircraft, driving across it in his command car, and occasionally taking time to dig up archaeological finds. Attaching himself here to one force, there to another, much of the time he was out of radio contact with the General Staff and unable to influence the shape of the campaign. None of this was a surprise; instead it had been *planned* that way. Besides two *Ugda* headquarters, as in 1947–1949 the largest organic unit remained the brigade. Each brigade operated almost independently, having been assigned its objective, provided with supplies sufficient for forty-eight hours, and told to advance and fight continuously without paying heed to whatever happened to its right, left, or rear.[80] As two military historians have written, the "system" might have been well adapted for seizing fleeting opportunities in armored operations conducted against a mobile opponent[81]—except that no such operations took place.

Substituting morale for proper organization, the system was responsible for any number of "misfortunes," as Dayan euphemistically called them. The first took place even before the campaign started. Taking last-minute pictures of the designated landing zone of Eytan's paratroopers, the IAF mistook an Egyptian road construction crew for troops; consequently, instead of being dropped west of Mitla Pass as originally planned, they were landed in a more difficult-to-defend plain to the east. Even so, the pilots missed their objective by several miles so that the paratroopers had to march for two hours in order to reach their intended positions. Next Israeli pilots, having been sent to disrupt Egyptian telephone lines, found the tailhooks on their modified Mustangs were not up to the job and were forced to use their propellers and wings instead. While there could be no doubt concerning their bravery, clearly preparations had not been thorough enough.

These were only the beginnings. Driving toward Mitla Pass, Sharon's convoy lost numerous vehicles (as well as ten of thirteen tanks attached to it) and was almost brought to a halt because nobody thought to bring spanners that fit the nuts on the trucks' wheels. Once he arrived he sent his men to enter the pass against orders and in the most incompetent way possible, thus bringing about a totally unnecessary battle that also proved to be the bloodiest of the entire war. Farther east the 38th *Ugda*, consisting partly of elderly reservists who had not been given sufficient time to prepare, attacked the Umm Katef–Abu Ageila area without displaying the proper offensive spirit to satisfy Dayan. Ultimately not one but two out of its four brigade commanders, plus the *ugda* commander himself, had to go (nine years later he reemerged, this time as a professor of military history at Tel Aviv University).

Next, the officer commanding the southern front used the absence of the chief of staff in order to send armored forces into battle well ahead of time, a move so disruptive of everything the General Staff had planned that Dayan, who went to see a sick Ben Gurion late on October 30, did not even dare inform him that it had happened. Advancing toward Al-Agheila, units from Ben Ari's 7th Armored Brigade ran into others of 37th Brigade, opened fire on them, and knocked out several tanks before recognizing that their opponents were not Egyptians but other Israelis. True to Dayan's "system" of supply, the advance of Eytan's paratroopers from Mitla Pass to A-Tur was made without any logistic preparations at all so that they all but starved on the way. Bypassing the pass by way of En Sudar to the south, incidentally this move served as an additional proof that the battle for Mitla Pass had been totally unnecessary.

Last but not least, the IAF—apparently intent on filling *its* quota of blunders—opened fire on HMS *Crane*, which was patrolling Sharm al-Sheikh, causing a fire (according to the pilots' reports) but inflicting only superficial damage (according to the British captain).[82] What's more, on two different occasions IAF aircraft strafed their own forces, which in typical IDF fashion had taken over captured Egyptian vehicles without bothering to repaint them or even provide them with fresh insignia visible from the air. In this too, Dayan, who seemed to personify the IDF, set the example. Arriving at A-Tur on November 6, he found that somebody had blundered and that no arrangements to take him to Sharm al-Sheikh had been made. Accordingly he and his party commandeered an Egyptian car. Next they headed south and almost got themselves killed when they ran into Eytan's paratroopers, already on their way back.[83]

Had even one of these "misfortunes" taken place after 1985 or so, the resulting outcry would have been deafening. At the time, however, they were swallowed up by the combination of *en brera* on the one hand and censorship on the other. The inadequate performance of 38th *Ugda* and the resulting changes in command were known only to a select few, given that the IDF was not and still is not in the habit of disclosing the names of its division and brigade commanders. Inside the IDF, Sharon's unauthorized action at Mitla Pass was sharply criticized by his own men, who accused him of reputation-building at their expense.[84] Talking to Ben Gurion, Dayan was almost equally critical, but in his published account of the campaign he was content to write, "I regard the problem as grave when a unit fails to fulfill its battle task, not when it goes beyond the bounds of duty." Instead of the public attacking the IDF for taking unnecessary casualties, it took Dayan to task for disclosing the matter in "disregard [of] the feelings of widows, orphans and bereaved parents whose loved ones fought and died in the Mitla."[85] To blunt the impression, the story of one of Gur's paratroopers, Yehuda Ken-Dror, who sacrificed himself by deliberately drawing Egyptian fire, was given wide circulation—thus confirming the old adage that behind every hero there is a blunder.

The extent of Western involvement in the war, including the presence of three French fighter squadrons and one of transport, was also downplayed. With very few exceptions the Israeli public felt delirious with victory—telling itself that this five-day, two-division campaign had been "one of the most brilliant of all time" (Shimon Peres)[86] and "unequaled since the days when Hannibal crossed the snowy Alps and Genghis Khan, the mountains of Asia."[87] From cabinet ministers down, hordes of visitors descended on the Sinai in a holiday mood, seeking remains of the Exodus and using a passage from the sixth-century Byzantine author Procopius to convince themselves that it was somehow Israeli territory. Ben Gurion himself at one point ranted about his plans for retaining Sharm al-Sheikh and founding the "Third Kingdom of Israel"; whether this was seriously meant or merely represented a starting point for the inevitable negotiations remains immaterial.[88] The inevitable popular songs appeared as if out of nowhere, were broadcast on the radio, and sold on records. "This is neither legend nor dream my friends," the best known among them thundered, "this is the people of Israel face to face with Mount Sinai." Having defeated its enemy, the IDF, riding sky-high, felt it could face its future with confidence.

Building a Modern Army: motorized column on maneuver, 1965.

CHAPTER 10

BUILDING A MODERN ARMY

A LTOUGH MILITARILY a success, the Suez campaign of 1956 did not fundamentally change the balance of power between Israel and its neighbors.[1] If anything the opposite was the case; the war was one more demonstration of Israel's inability to translate military victory into political achievement. Not only was there no question of forcing the other side to change their policy and make peace; Israel was unable to retain any of its gains. Coming under heavy international pressure, it was compelled to withdraw early next year.

To be sure, the campaign was not altogether without benefits. The power of the IDF to defeat its enemies had been demonstrated. The objective of opening the Straits of Tyran to Israeli traffic, both naval and airborne, was achieved. The Sinai Peninsula was demilitarized, and a small UN peacekeeping force was inserted between Israel and its most powerful enemy. Moreover, Israel was allowed to remilitarize Nitsana, a small but strategically important border area opposite Abu Ageila. Once back to its own borders, however, the state reverted to being "a small island in an Arab sea." It also retained all the old vulnerabilities, including a long and wide-open border, an exceedingly narrow strategic "waist," and of course the overall disparity between it and its much larger enemies, who surrounded it on all sides except the western.

Against this geopolitical background, easily understandable to anybody who so much as bothered to glance at the map, the feeling of *en brera* not only survived but grew even stronger. As before, Israeli public opinion continued to see the IDF as the one great organization standing between it and death. Even more than before, it was prepared to do its utmost to ensure the army's success by providing the necessary resources in terms of materiel and the very best manpower at its disposal (that originating in the *kibbutsim*, which, rightly or not, was considered by themselves and others to constitute the crème de la crème.[2] The rejection of diaspora "cowardice" intensified; year in and year out the most important question tens of thousands of schoolchildren were asked when confronted with the

Holocaust was not how it could have happened but why "the Jews" had gone *ka-tson la-tevach* (like sheep to the slaughter). For those who joined the IDF as eighteen-year-old conscripts there was now a new generation of former Sinai heroes to emulate. Israeli-born and for the most part without religious sentiments, they were, in the words of the well-known writer Amos Oz, a race of "circumcised Cossacks."[3]

Under these circumstances, the highest praise one could bestow on anything was to say that it was *kmo mivtsa tsvai* (like a military operation). Far from doffing their uniforms when on leave, Israeli youngsters liked to wear them even on social occasions, when anybody sporting the insignia of an officer's rank considered himself at least a demigod. As Ezer Weizman wrote, combat aircraft were admired not just for their performance but for their supposed beauty,[4] an attitude that sometimes led to excess, as when air force mechanics set out to decorate planes at a financial cost that no military organization, let alone the IAF, could tolerate.[5] In the late 1960s the El Al Airlines office on London's Regent Street was even decorated with triangles suggestive of diving Mirage fighters. However, perhaps the best place to observe the difference in outlook between Israel and the rest of the world was the Four Days March. Held in the Netherlands each year, the march was a popular sporting event. To thousands of participants from various countries it was an innocuous occasion in which to walk and socialize. Not so the platoon of IDF men and women who participated each year, armed with Uzi submachine guns. They would storm the twenty-five-mile course as if their lives depended on it, always insisting on arriving first and, upon crossing the finish line, breaking into the mandatory *hora* dance to show what a lark it had all been.

The extremely high prestige of the IDF also made it possible to use the armed forces for achieving a variety of social goals. Germany, France, Italy, and Japan (from about 1870 on) and Russia (after the 1917 revolution) regarded their armies as "the school of the nation." Accordingly they entrusted them with all kinds of missions, from acquainting workers with the blessings of rural life by means of milking competitions (the German army before 1914) through technical training to political indoctrination in the virtues of republicanism or unity or Shinto or whatever. The same was true of the IDF, except that it went farther than most. Already in 1949, Ben Gurion had written that "the army must serve as an educational and pioneering center for Israeli youth—for both those born here and newcomers. It is the duty of the army to educate a pioneer generation, healthy in body and spirit, courageous and loyal, which will unite the broken tribes and diasporas to prepare itself to fulfill the historical tasks of the State of Israel through self-realization."[6] As late as 1991 a retired brigadier general argued that "the army is probably the last national framework within which it is possible to have an impact on Israeli youth and to influence the values that will accompany them throughout life."[7] In between the two dates similar ideas concerning the educational role of the military have been repeated a thousand times in every possible forum.

Like most modern armies, the IDF carries out its internal and external propaganda activities by various means, including countless lectures, "cultural events," shows, open days, a range of publications, and a radio station popular among young people in particular.[8] However, it has also developed a series of unique instruments that have no parallel in other countries and that need to be briefly discussed here. The first consisted of special courses for conscripts—most of them from Oriental countries—who did not know Hebrew or had not completed elementary education.[9] Somewhat similar courses were provided to civilians, often females and the mothers and sisters of those very soldiers, who had immigrated from Oriental countries and who, in addition to being even shorter on formal education than their menfolk, supposedly did not yet understand the meaning of Israeliness. The instructors were young female soldiers who after receiving a brief training course fulfilled their period of service in this way. In teaching civilians they were often sent to live in villages and townships.

The second program run by the IDF in its nation-building role is GADNA (Gdudei Noar, or Youth Battalions).[10] Originating in the prestate days when high-school students were often used for auxiliary tasks such as running messages, in principle GADNA was supposed to inculcate all Israeli youth with love of country, self-confidence, and a modicum of pre-military training that would make it easier to adjust to army life when the time came. Subjects taught included drill, fieldcraft, topography, and the firing of subcaliber weapons. From time to time hikes were organized, during which selected members proudly carried rifles and even light machine guns. Some youths spent a full month of their summer vacations taking a sort of basic training course, after which they would be formally appointed GADNA corporal. All these activities were fully incorporated into the school system, which set aside one hour each week for the purpose and even graded students on GADNA activities. Attempts were also made to reach youths who had dropped out of the formal education system, although on the whole they were less successful. The instructors and needed equipment were provided by the IDF.

The IDF's third major nation-building instrument was the previously mentioned NACHAL. The idea that settling the land also constituted a form of defense activity had deep roots in prestate days, when it was a question of "delivering" the land from its desolation and, as often as not, its Arab inhabitants. Between 1941 and 1948 it was embodied in PALMACH; indeed more so than the IDF would have liked, because many PALMACH personnel left the army after 1949 and returned to their *kibbutsim*. When Ben Gurion first proposed the Chok Sherut Bitachon (National Service Law) of 1949 to parliament he had in mind a system whereby every IDF soldier would spend a year doing agricultural work after receiving basic training.[11] This did not go over well with his centrist coalition partners, however, and in the end a compromise was struck. In theory, to this day every IDF conscript is liable for a year's agricultural work. In practice, NACHAL was limited to volunteers of both sexes (males were grouped in an elite infantry brigade). The number of volunteers, most of them *kibbuts* members or graduates of various youth movements, has proved sufficient to involve the IDF in a sustained colonization effort. Over the years it has produced dozens of settlements both inside the green line (the pre-1976 armistice line) and, since 1967, the Occupied Territories.

Militarily speaking none of these efforts amounted to much; then and later, NACHAL in particular was regarded by some as a waste of the country's best manpower, which went out to play with tractors instead of training for war. But socially they indicated the extent to which the Israeli public was prepared to regard the IDF as an educational institution par excellence, allowing it a role in settling the country as well as the indoctrination of youth and the integration of new immigrants. Rightly or not, the IDF was seen as a cardinal part of the nation-building effort—whereas conversely anybody who for one reason or another had *not* served might suffer discrimination in obtaining everything from public employment to a driver's license. All this fitted in rather nicely with the so-called development theory then current among sociologists in Israel and abroad.[12] Its central tenet was that, thanks to its cohesion and supposed familiarity with things technical, the military was one of the important institutions by which newly independent nations could pull themselves up by the bootstraps and achieve rapid modernization. Accordingly, and often backed by U.S. encouragement and finance, attempts were made to export IDF methods to numerous newly independent countries in Asia and Africa with whom Israel wished to establish good relations.[13]

The IDF's high social prestige apart, the other factors that permitted it to continue rapid development were the extraordinary rates of demographic and economic growth achieved during those years. At the time the War of Independence broke out, the *Yishuv* population stood at 650,000. Less than twenty years later it had more than trebled to about 2.4 million. About two-thirds of the increase consisted of new immigrants, most of whom entered the country during the first few years of independence; the remainder resulted from a comparatively high birthrate and rapidly improving standards of health, housing, social welfare, and the like. Compared with Western Europe and, a fortiori, the United States, Israel at the time remained a poor country, and life for many Oriental immigrants in particular was desperately hard. Still, between 1957 and 1965 a growing population enabled the economy to surge at close to 10 percent per year—remarkable even for the fast-growth 1960s and greater than that of any other country except Japan.

The upshot was that military expenditure rose from $141 million in 1957 (already twice the average spent annually during 1953–1955) to $458.5 million in 1966; from 1959 to 1965, moreover, expenditures were supplemented by substantial amounts of arms received free from West Germany. Although overall the Israeli-Arab economic balance remained heavily weighted in favor of the latter, relatively speaking the former was gaining. Thus, in 1951 the gross national product (GNP) of Egypt (the largest Arab country) exceeded that of Israel 4:1; in 1966 the gap had shrunk to 1.6:1. More significant still was per-capita income; Israel's advantage grew from approximately 3:1 to 7.5:1.[14] These were two entirely different societies, one increasingly modernized and forward looking and the other still largely agricultural and traditional.

After four years and one month during which he acted as the IDF's dynamo, the talented but controversial Dayan—he seldom accepted responsibility for his actions and was extraordinarily adept at turning his subordinates against each other—resigned in 1958. His replacement was Chayim Laskov, an almost equally experienced officer with no fewer than five terms as *aluf* (brigadier general) behind him. During the Sinai campaign he had commanded the northern *ugda* that took the Gaza Strip; until July 1957 his post was chief of the General Staff. By nature and temperament he was as different from his predecessor as could be: quiet, methodical, extremely honest, and inclined toward philosophical reflection (his favorite poem was Kipling's "If"). His appointment presaged the growing importance of the armored corps, armored forces being the prime instrument by which the Israelis and others have sought to wage blitzkrieg warfare since the late 1930s.

As noted earlier, Israel's armored corps originated during the War of Independence. During the first months it was a question of producing homemade armored cars—in reality, lorries with layers of steel plate with concrete in between—for use in the Battle of the Roads. Later what tanks, armored cars, half-tracks, and jeeps could be scraped together were used in various operations beginning with the abortive assaults on Latrun; on at least one occasion an immobilized Syrian tank was sent into battle by being

loaded on a truck, thus demonstrating both the IDF's poverty and its ingenuity.[15] Toward the end of the war Sadeh's 8th Armored Brigade was even
evincing clear signs of switching its tanks from an infantry-support role (as
at both Latrun and Iraq Suedan) toward mobile, deep-strike operations on
the models of military innovators Guderian, Manstein, Rommel, and Patton. On their side of the hill, the Arabs used their armor exclusively for
infantry support, as did the Jordanians at Latrun, the Syrians at Degania,
and the Egyptians in their attack against Negba. Thus *shin be-shin* (armor
against armor) warfare failed to develop even at this late stage (to which
must be added the plain fact that when the war ended, the IDF possessed
exactly four operational tanks).[16]

Although Dayan personally had successfully commanded "armor"—in
reality a battalion containing a variety of armored cars, half-tracks,
machine-gun carriers, and jeeps—during the operation against Ramla and
Lyddia, he remained an infantryman at heart. To him the ideal fighting
formation consisted of a self-contained brigade with artillery and tank support, the kind of formation that had been employed at Stalingrad and that,
had it only been available, might have been equally useful in the built-up
area of Jerusalem where he commanded during the second half of the war.
At Kalkiliya in October 1956, he had ruled out the use of armor, thereby
leading to unnecessary casualties;[17] when the first plans for the Sinai campaign were being drawn up he even raised the absurd proposal that the
tanks should be made to follow the infantry on transporters.[18] Indeed the
IDF's regard for the armored corps was so low that when Dayan offered
Laskov the commanding job in July 1956, the latter considered it a calculated insult (which it may well have been) and came close to tendering his
resignation.[19] In the event he was persuaded to stay, but only after Ben
Gurion intervened and promised that his position as Dayan's heir apparent
would not be affected by the appointment.

In September 1956 the question of armor versus infantry was thrashed
out at a top-level meeting presided over by Ben Gurion himself. The chief
of operations, Col. Uzi Narkis, and the chief of Northern Command, Brig.
Gen. Yitschak Rabin, allied with Dayan. Accordingly it is no wonder
Laskov got nowhere in his demand that the IDF's armored brigades be
concentrated in a single *ugda* and, instead of acting as a generalized pool
for vehicles, be assigned a critical role in the forthcoming Sinai campaign.
Still, until November 1956 Laskov managed to accomplish much. Of the
380 IDF tanks, 310 were organized in three brigades; the remainder were
distributed in three battalions among the commands.[20] He also tackled the
field of maintenance, where he instituted rigid order for the IDF's lack-
adaisical methods.

Came the campaign itself and armor—7th Armored Brigade above all—gave a dazzling demonstration of what it could do as even Dayan, who was capable of learning from an error, was later forced to admit.[21] From now on no holds were barred; comparing the 1957 budget to that of 1953, no component of the IDF increased its budget allocation nearly as much as the armored corps.[22] Some of the IDF's most promising officers, including in particular one David Elazar and one Yisrael Tal, were transferred to the armored corps. There they started learning their new business from the bottom up, going through every course from driver and mechanic to commander, etc. Later the IDF even overcame its reservations to the point of sending a few of them to study in Germany, though they were warned not to make passes at German girls.[23] In 1960 the first armored division was established and put through its paces, being made to cover 90 miles of desert terrain in 32 hours under conditions of simulated combat.[24]

By that time the IDF's upgraded, World War II–vintage U.S. Sherman and French AMX tanks—the latter a mere 13 tons, hardly suitable for real-life *shin be-shin* warfare—had been joined by the much heavier British Centurions, which led the IDF to develop armored doctrine that differed significantly from that of then-contemporary armies.[25] During their first appearance in World War I, tanks had been used as siege machines and worked closely with the infantry, acting as mobile shelters and pulling them across enemy trench systems. During the 1930s an attempt was made to turn them into a modern version of heavy and light cavalry, meaning a mobile striking force for independent operations directed deep into the enemy rear. The masters of this kind of thing were, of course, the Germans under Guderian, Manstein, Rommel, and the rest. Starting to develop their *Panzerwaffe* from 1935 on, in 1939–1942 their series of brilliant campaigns demonstrated what a modern armored force, properly organized and trained, could do; sometimes advancing dozens of miles a day, they caused entire countries to collapse in short order.

The Wehrmacht's run of deep-ranging victories did not last long. First at El Alamein in November 1942, then in Russia after the Battle of Kursk in July 1943, it increasingly reverted to defensive operations. Combined with a preference for quality over quantity, defense meant an emphasis on much heavier Panthers and Tigers (to say nothing of the monstrous Koenigstiger tanks). This, however, did not apply to the rest of the world, which had set itself the task of reconquering a continent. So much had the Wehrmacht's early victories captured the world's imagination that the American, Soviet, and French armed forces committed to mobility during the postwar years. Accordingly the tanks that they built were comparatively fast and lightly armored. The same applied to forces of the Bundeswehr when West German production resumed during the mid-1960s.

The IDF, however, found itself saddled with Centurions. They were fifty-ton machines originally built at the end of World War II with the specific objective of beating a path through the defensive screen of heavy German armor. Although the model acquired by the Israelis came equipped with, or was converted to, an excellent 105mm gun, it was not terribly fast; yet it was very well armored. At the hands of Tal, who commanded the armored corps from 1964 on, this combination of qualities was used to the best advantage. Contrary to the apostles of mobility who held court elsewhere, Tal insisted that the tank's most important quality was not simply its speed and cross-country capability but its ability to move and operate *under fire*. The factor that gave it this quality was, of course, its armor, and armor was something possessed by tanks alone and not by other forces such as artillery and motorized (and even, in Tal's reasoning, mechanized) infantry.

The Germans from the beginning,[26] and other armies from about 1943, emphasized the combined arms team in which tanks, antitank troops, self-propelled artillery, and an increasingly mechanized infantry are integrated to work together and protect each other. Not so in the IDF, which did not have modern mechanized infantry (as of the mid-1960s the latter still rode World War II M-3 half-tracks) and which tended to neglect its artillery. Accordingly the armored corps was organized in all-tank battalions: Centurions (at first) or the U.S. M-48 Patton, which was faster, easier to operate, but considerably less well armored (and bought secondhand from West Germany in 1965-1966 after the Bundeswehr itself had switched to the Leopard I). As to defense against short-range antitank weapons, Tal argued that this would not be much of a problem in the Middle East. There, in contrast with battlefields in central Europe, terrain tends to be open, cover scarce, and visibility excellent, thus enabling tanks, which possess advantages in armor and mobility, to see and hit enemies long before enemies hit them. A dogma (doctrine would be too complimentary) known as *helem ha-shiryon* (armored shock) coalesced and was even given poetic form and put to music in the armored corps' anthem of those years: "The track turns, the throat is dry . . . here come the tanks!" Confronted with *egrofei shiryon* (mailed fists) consisting of massed Israeli tanks galloping toward them, the enemy's troops were supposed to run away.[27]

Thus, compared to that of other armies, Israeli armored doctrine was backward; indeed when the 1967 war came the onslaught against Egypt in particular resembled nothing so much as a 1940-vintage blitzkrieg. Tal, however, also introduced other reforms, and here his contribution was perhaps more decisive. Training improved, both in individual fields—for example, gunners got so much practice that they accurately hit moving targets at an impressive range of 2.5 miles—and by systematically teaching all four crew members to perform each others' jobs so that they could form a cohesive team and take each other's place if someone was injured. Rigid operating and maintenance procedures were devised and enforced by means of strict discipline; not only did Tal expect orders to be obeyed without question but, mirabile dictu, each tank was given a logbook to meticulously record maintenance operations.[28] All this represented quite a change in an army that, perhaps because of its PALMACH background, had always boasted of being a *balagan meurgan* (organized mess). Though contemporary tanks with petrol engines were comparatively delicate affairs, when put to the test there could be no question of their breaking down en masse, as Sharon's vehicles had in 1956. Tremendous morale—exemplified by commanders who fought "exposed in the turret," as the title of one popular book had it—did the rest. In 1967, Israel's tankmen, so determined that they literally looked nowhere but straight ahead, easily carried the day in spite of their comparatively primitive tactics.

What applied to the armored corps was even more true of the other pillar of modern warfare, the air force. As we saw, the 1956 conflict had not been a proper test either of the IAF or of its Egyptian opponent. The former was made to operate against its professed doctrine; apart from the Israelis, the latter was engaged by the air forces of not one but *two* "great powers" of the time. In 1957, Ezer Weizman took over as air force commander. Young—he was born in 1924—brash, and charismatic, he too made a decisive contribution to morale by means of his reckless enthusiasm and leadership. In spite of his colorful language and occasional antics, however, Weizman was a thorough professional who had gone through every step, from fighter pilot to staff officer to base commander. He knew what he was doing and how to get his way, particularly in the face of a government inclined to be stingy.

With him at the helm, the last remaining piston-engine combat aircraft were withdrawn from service (later joined by the old British Meteors). The remainder of the Mystères purchased from France reached Israel, making the full contingent of seventy-two available. Later additional French aircraft were acquired, including Super Mystère and Mirage fighters as well as Vautour light bombers. Roughly equivalent to the American F–100 Super Saber and F–104 Star Fighter respectively, the former two were first-line combat aircraft even though their engines, following a well-established French tradition, tended to be weak and fuel-thirsty. They were thus less able to carry air-to-ground ordnance than, perhaps, they should have been; yet they were aerodynamically very well designed. Unlike the fighters, the twin-engine Vautour could exceed the speed of sound only while diving but could carry much more ordnance and had the range to reach the most distant Egyptian airfields—the precise reason it was purchased. The IAF also retained its Ouragans, smaller and lighter aircraft that, thanks to their straight wings (the others were swept-wing or delta-wing craft), possessed excellent maneuverability and provided very stable platforms for ordnance in the form of cannons and rockets. They in turn were supplemented by Fouga Magisters, the French training jets that were built in Israel under license and that, put into the ingenious hands of IAF technicians, were equipped with machine guns and rockets for air-to-ground work.

Having attended staff college in England, Ezer Weizman, according to his own subsequent account, came back convinced that the IAF had nothing to learn and should concentrate on doing things its own way.[29] In fact it molded itself into a tactical force (the order of battle comprised nothing heavier than twin-engine light bombers) and planned an offensive campaign centered on first strikes against enemy airfields. To make sure that the enemy air force stayed on the ground, a special runway-busting bomb was developed by the IAF's technical office and manufactured by the French company Breguet. Known as Durendal after Roland's sword, a parachute slowed it down, and a rocket engine drove it deep into runways.[30]

Planning for air-to-ground strikes, Weizman refused to equip his Mirages with first-generation air-to-air missiles then becoming available. Instead he insisted that they come equipped with older but trusted 30mm cannons more suitable for ground attack; to provide room, some of the more sophisticated electronic gear was removed (unnecessary in a geographical area where the weather is generally good and conditions clear). At the time, it should be noted, other air forces tended to neglect air-to-air combat training, considering it outdated. Not so the IAF, which was *compelled* to engage in this kind of training by its choice of equipment—a most important advantage, as it turned out.

As the plan for attacking Egyptian airfields was put together and perfected,[31] constant practice familiarized the pilots with their tasks. It also resulted in an extraordinarily rapid turnaround rate, which was essential if the offensive was to be sustained. Instead of one to two missions per day per aircraft the IAF, thanks partly to the excellence of its ground crews and partly to the short distances involved, was able to fly six to eight missions and sustain that pace for a number of days.[32] By 1967 enough planes were available, and the teething troubles that affected the Mirages had been overcome. The air force knew what it had to do and was ready to the last detail. This readiness meshed perversely with the manifest unreadiness on the Arab side.

When the day came the Egyptian radar proved defective; they did not even have teams of engineers standing by to repair their damaged runways. As the German chief of staff, Alfred von Schlieffen, had once put it, for a great victory to be won it is necessary for *two* sides to cooperate, "each in its own way."

Compared to the very great progress made by the air force and armored corps, the navy remained backwards. Just before 1956 a couple of old British destroyers had been purchased. Later they were supplemented by three German-built submarines as well as several smaller craft supplied by the same country. During the mid-sixties the inadequacy of the surface fleet came to be recognized, and plans were devised to revolutionize the navy by equipping it with French-built missile boats and new, Israeli-developed and -built Gavriel ship-to-ship missiles.[33] But bitter infighting developed between the ministry of defense, which pushed the missiles as hard as it could, and the IDF high command, which did not trust Israel's native military industries and operated under the motto *af mil la-til* (not a penny for the missiles).[34] Partly as a result, neither missiles nor boats were ready for the 1967 war, so the navy played only a minor role. Yet the upshot of the war was to increase the importance of the navy by lengthening greatly the coastline that had to be patrolled and defended. In October 1967 their negligence was to cost the Israelis dear, as one of their antiquated destroyers was sunk by Egyptian missile boats operating from Port Said—without being able to return fire, no less.

Though the borders with Jordan and Egypt calmed down considerably after the 1956 campaign, the atmosphere surrounding the IDF and Israel as a whole remained nervous. Typical was an incident on April 1, 1959, when the IDF proceeded to carry out a public mobilization exercise.[35] Inexplicably, no prior announcement was made in the newspapers; instead advance notice was served at 8:05 P.M. in the form of a radio broadcast that alerted people of an "important message" to follow. When the message came it interrupted a concert; all the state's dignitaries were attending a musical performance in Tel Aviv in honor of the queen of Belgium. The broadcast started in no fewer than nine languages—Hebrew, Arabic, English, French, Yiddish, Polish, Hungarian, Romanian, and Spanish—thus giving the impression that something dramatic was about to happen. Later, when the panic subsided it became clear that all the IDF had done was to call up three small reserve units. Since one of these happened to be code-named "water ducks," the expression "the night of the ducks" entered the Hebrew language as synonymous with much ado about nothing.

Then in February 1960 the Egyptian army, which since 1957 had been confined to its bases west of the Suez Canal, slipped one armored and one infantry division into the Sinai without Israeli intelligence noticing what was afoot. When the move was finally discovered, two Israeli brigades were rushed to the border and two more called up; made wise by their previous experience, however, this time the Israelis mobilized in secret as much as possible for such a small country. Perhaps the Egyptian intention had been to put pressure on Israel at a time when the latter was engaging the Syrians in a renewed series of border incidents around the Sea of Galilee (since 1958 the two Arab countries had been formally joined together in the so-called United Arab Republic, with Nasser acting as president of both). In any case on February 29, a mere five days after they had arrived, the Egyptians inexplicably turned tail and left.

Once again, in any other country the two episodes would have given rise to a major scandal. Not so in Israel, where the media cooperated in putting a damper on what had taken place and where the IDF was widely perceived as incapable of doing wrong. Did it not incorporate all that was best in society and state? After the first incident two of those responsible, the chief of the General Staff Division, Meir Zorea, and the chief of intelligence, Yehoshaphat Harkavi, were fired without public fuss. Laskov, a better-known figure, could not be treated in the same way, however, and when the time came Ben Gurion contented himself with refusing to extend Laskov's appointment for another year. Thus ended the military career of the most professional and most civilized chief of staff the IDF had ever possessed, albeit one who (perhaps for that very reason) never quite struck the chord in the public mind that his extroverted predecessor had.

Major General Tsvi Tsur, who took over in January 1961, made so little of an impression that his name is not even mentioned in *two* earlier accounts of the IDF's history, and a third merely says that he later became deputy minister of defense under Dayan.[36] These were the years when German scientists were active in Egypt, helping Nasser to develop two different surface-to-surface missiles, a small, delta jet fighter and a previously unheard-of contraption known as a cobalt bomb. In the event these efforts led to nothing more dangerous than a number of wooden mock-ups that were displayed on parade.[37] A few of the scientists involved in the program received parcel bombs, compliments of Mossad.[38] Others apparently went home under pressure from their own government. Shimon Peres, then serving as Israel's deputy minister of defense, was informed about the failure at an early date and believed that the Egyptian efforts represented a sheer waste of money.[39] Instead of disclosing his cards, however, he used the occasion to press the West German government into delivering additional arms[40]—then and later a typical Israeli gambit.

While the Egyptian program failed, Israel's own development efforts went ahead. To Ben Gurion the immense disparity between Israel and its

Arab neighbors had always been obvious.[41] Trusting to "Jewish genius"—after all, Albert Einstein was only the most famous of many leading twentieth-century physicists who were Jews—he sought solutions in the nuclear field. Immediately after the war in 1949 ended, prospecting for uranium started in the Negev. Later, Israeli scientists apparently developed indigenous processes for producing heavy water and enriching uranium; armed with these advances, as well as some outstanding work on computers, they were able to tempt the French government to cooperate.[42] From at least 1956 on, the latter engaged in negotiations about the supply of nuclear technology, and indeed Peres later claimed to have extracted a promise for such technology as part of the deal that led to the Suez campaign.[43]

In 1957–1958 there seems to have been some debate inside Israel's defense establishment as to whether a nuclear program was needed. The principal arguments in contra were as follows: First, developing nuclear capability would cause the Arabs to follow suit, thus possibly increasing the danger to Israel's security (the Arabs were regarded as irrational players) rather than reducing it. Second, the nuclear stalemate that would eventually emerge would rob Israel of its greatest single advantage, namely, the quality of its troops, which in turn rested on the socialist organization of the state and was responsible for its superiority in conventional warfare.[44] In the end, however, Ben Gurion and Peres prevailed. A horde of French technicians arrived, settled in Beer Sheva, and, relying on local labor, began work. In late 1960 the construction of Israel's nuclear reactor became public knowledge when the U.S. government used the *New York Times* to release pictures taken by high-flying U–2 spy planes.[45] Not disclosed until much later was the simultaneous construction of a plutonium separation facility concealed forty meters below the floor of a separate building.[46]

At the end of 1961, Egypt and Syria went their separate ways, though the former continued to call itself the United Arab Republic. Two years later the Egyptian armed forces became bogged down in Yemen, further relieving the immediate threat to Israel. Whether accidentally or not, during the same year the long reign of Ben Gurion came to an end. For years he had been regarded by many as "the one and only" expert on defense (and everything else); in a dispute with his ruling MAPAI Party he resigned, remaining as a member of the Knesset. In June 1965 he founded his own party, known as RAFI (Reshimat Poalei Yisrael, or "Israeli Workers' List"). He took both Dayan—who was serving as minister of agriculture—and Peres, whose career as deputy minister of defense was thus brought to an abrupt end. Peres's place was taken by a competent but long-forgotten bureaucrat, Tsevi Dinstein; Levy Eshkol replaced Ben Gurion as prime minister and minister of defense.

Russian-born like the rest, Eshkol had immigrated to Palestine in 1914 and was an old Hagana veteran. However, his specialty had always been organization and finance; his operational experience was limited to one episode in 1948, when he had commanded a convoy that made its way from Tel Aviv to Jerusalem. Yet he was ready to learn. He systematically toured units and bases, immersed himself in the kind of detail that was beneath the dignity of his more visionary predecessor, and delighted in playing devil's advocate by asking questions that went against the conventional wisdom presented by the IDF's intelligence division.[47] He also took a personal interest in the appointment of each *aluf* on the General Staff—a good way to keep people on a tight leash.

Eshkol's years as minister of defense lasted from 1963 to 1967 and were perhaps the best that the IDF, and the state of Israel, ever had. Always tending to be vindictive, Ben Gurion had never forgotten the long period of prestate conflicts when, not being in charge of a government organization, he had been unable to impose his authority and deal with "the dissenters" (ETSEL and LECHI) as he wanted. Perhaps in reaction, he had developed a fierce, high-handed style of leadership; he would fire people without so much as telling them of his decision, leaving them dangling in a vacuum and often making for acerbity and tension. Not so Eshkol, who was blessed with a refreshing sense of humor and whose methods were much more relaxed. He eased restrictions on the freedom of the press and depoliticized the security services; in 1966 he even felt sufficiently confident to cancel the system of military government under which Israel's Arab minority had been living in a sort of permanent curfew. But the 1967 war had not yet broken out, and so the terrible political dilemmas arising out of conquest—whether to regard the Occupied Territories as sacred, and thus to be retained at any price, or simply as bargaining chips—were still in the future. Precisely because the consensus was largely unspoken, more than ever (before or after) there existed consensus among the Israeli public concerning the objectives of the state and its military instrument, namely, to ensure survival at all costs.

Dictated by geopolitical circumstances, the IDF's basic doctrine, which staked everything on a short, rapid offensive, remained very much as it had been. What changed was the thoroughness and professionalism the high command undertook in its day-to-day work of planning, training, and preparation. Much had already been achieved under Laskov and Tsur, the former quiet and methodical and the latter more technically minded. Still, the real harbinger of change was Yitschak Rabin, whose term as chief of staff opened on January 1, 1964. Born in 1922, Rabin was the neglected son of "Red Rose," one of those Socialist Party activists who preferred dabbling in politics to looking after her family.

Having joined PALMACH in 1941, during the first months of 1948 he, commanded a brigade. Later, as Allon's chief of staff, he took a critical part in the operations that eventually led to the defeat of the Egyptian army. During the immediate postwar years he held various training posts; if Peres may be believed, Dayan prior to the Sinai campaign had appointed Rabin CIC Northern Command, "so he won't get in our way."[48] Later he served as chief of the General Staff Division under both Laskov and Tsur. By 1963 he had become the IDF's most experienced soldier (some would say even more so than the chief of staff himself).

Like Laskov, Rabin was uncharismatic—almost to the point of autism, his enemies said—clearheaded, and methodical. Unlike Laskov, who with his Oxford education and pipe tried to act the British gentleman, Rabin affected neither high culture nor foreign mannerisms but was native through and through with the kind of *dugri* (unsophisticated bluntness) many Israelis admire. Later in life his experience with politics was to turn him into a hard man who could be remarkably callous to the suffering of others. (Acting as minister of defense and "Mr. Security," he combated the Palestinian Uprising in 1987–1990 by ordering troops "to break the arms and legs" of unarmed demonstrators.) But during his tenure as chief of staff he did not yet have that quality and if anything was inclined to be bashful. By all accounts he worked well with Eshkol, who saw him as a sort of military oracle.[49] Rabin's main mission was to take the IDF, which at that time still consisted of independent brigades (a proposal for establishing permanent *ugdas* had been considered in 1959 but was rejected) as well as the various arms and services, and mold it into a single, cohesive fighting force.

In any large human organization, the two conditions essential for the proper functioning of the command system are clarity concerning overall objectives on the one hand and good mutual understanding—much of it not explicit but tacit—on the other. At the time, the former was provided to the IDF by *en brera*; to quote Dr. Samuel Johnson, the prospect of the hangman's noose makes for wonderful concentration of the mind. The latter was the natural product of a small, cohesive army in which everybody knew everybody else and whose members commonly addressed each other by first names if not nicknames. But that army was not yet too sophisticated, from a technological point of view, many of its weapons (particularly those of the ground forces and the navy) coming straight out of World War II. As a result, its members did not engage in excessive specialization or "churning" and were thus granted the time in which to get to know and trust each other.[50]

The organization itself was now functioning regularly enough. During 1947–1949 probably none of its members had gone through anything more advanced than a company commanders course, and since the PALMACH platoon commanders course did not produce enough person- nel, many veteran squad commanders had to be commissioned in the field.[51] Now it possessed an extensive training system, the outline of which was created during Rabin's tenure as head of training during 1954–1956. It ran up all the way from basic training (differentiated by arm and service and lasting from five weeks to six months) through the squad commanders course ("the rock-bottom on which everything rests," according to Rabin in a lecture just before the 1973 war) and various professional courses ear- marked for every kind of personnel from pioneers to corpsmen. Those who did well and passed the necessary exams—there was still no military academy—were taken into officers school and the various arms schools by which it was followed. All courses were run somewhat spartanly: An IDF battalion commander might inhabit quarters and eat in dining rooms, which in the armed forces of developed countries were not even consid- ered fit for enlisted men. Yet the courses were often staffed by the IDF's best and most charismatic officers on their way to the top. As important, given the pride that the public took in its army, they were able to take in the best Israeli youth.

Occupying one rung below on the ladder, the command and staff college was much less impressive. Located in an old British camp north of Tel Aviv, it was operated, as it still is, by the ground forces on behalf of the IDF as a whole. In addition, air force and navy ran supplementary courses for their own personnel; surprisingly, though, it was only after the October War that the first joint courses for company- and battalion-grade officers were insti- tuted.[52] Depending on their arm and service, officers would remain in the college between three and ten months. They listened to lectures on military and nonmilitary subjects, visited other bases, and engaged in exercises. However, given their own ignorance of English and the almost nonexistent library, they did precious little serious reading and almost no writing—with the result that, compared with their colleagues in other countries, they remained almost entirely unfamiliar with the theory and history of their own profession, Israeli military history specifically included. Furthermore, the "two- career" system meant that students were considerably younger than comrades in other countries. Since the borders were seldom silent, study took place against a background of constant "current security" operations in which field officers were given an opportunity to earn their spurs. All this may explain why the college was never able to overcome the IDF's strong prejudice against classroom learning in favor of practical, hands-on experience.

In 1963 a national defense college was started, but it never amounted to much. Senior officers were reluctant to spend a year studying at an unaccredited institution;[53] consequently, instead of being used as a vehicle for selecting future commanders, it acted as a holding pen for those with no immediate assignment. Shortly before the 1967 war it was closed by Eshkol, who considered the benefit not worth the expense. The gap was breached to some extent by sending some officers abroad for more or less extended periods of study; over time they included (besides Weizman) Laskov, Rabin, Bar Lev (the subsequent chief of staff), Sharon, and Eytan. In the IDF itself, however, the highest course was the battalion commanders course. Thus, officers beyond that grade could serve their last fifteen years without any formal instruction[54]—which actually happened to General Elazar (who served as chief of staff from 1972 to 1974). As General Tal once told a visiting French writer, in the IDF senior officers advanced by "natural selection."[55] By this, presumably, he meant to explain how he himself had succeeded.

By the 1960s the army had also largely overcome its remaining teething problems. On the one hand it was no longer unorganized and inexperienced. On the other hand, the system of "solving" the ethnic diversity by putting Ashkenazim (meaning the group of eastern European Yiddish-speaking Jews and their descendants) at the top of the pecking order and Sephardim (Jews from Arab-speaking countries) at the bottom (the latter, IDF experts told Ben Gurion, did not make suitable officer material[56]) did not yet give rise to protests, as it would later. With this exceptionally cohesive instrument at his disposal Rabin was able to institute, or perhaps one should say institutionalize, his system of optional control.[57] Not that this was unprecedented, but the IDF seems to have developed without reference to foreign models, if only because the best of the lot—German *Auftragstaktik* (mission-type orders)—could never be acknowledged. As under Dayan, each commander was assigned an objective and a geographical zone inside which his troops were to operate. He was then told to position himself with his troops (rather than in the rear, as with many other armies) and given the greatest latitude to achieve the objectives as it saw fit while leaving administrative detail to a rear headquarters.

At the same time there could be no question of a "hands-off" approach. When war broke out in 1967, Rabin did not join any particular unit, let alone go for extended tours. Rather (aside from brief visits to the front) he remained in Tel Aviv, where he was able to consult with the government and issue orders to the front commanders and those of the air force and navy. Farther down the chain of command, and taking Southern Command as our example, Yeshayahu Gavish attached himself to that headquarters that he considered critical in order to supervise the battle as closely as possible. Meanwhile control over the rest was assured by setting up a "directed telescope" in the form of special units to monitor the radio traffic of subordinate formations. Gavish thus created for himself a picture of the battlefield that was independent from, and supplementary to, those formations' own reports.

The upshot was a mixture of independence *and* control. IDF units were given the latitude needed to seize fleeting opportunities characteristic of mobile warfare while remaining part of a preconceived plan. The concept was first tested in the great maneuvers of 1960, which as it happened were directed by none other than Rabin as chief of the General Staff Division. In his postmaneuver summary he said that IDF commanders had to be capable of working out plans and giving orders while on the move—the shortcomings of communications notwithstanding.[58] Thereafter it was rehearsed during annual exercises; when the time came it served the IDF well.

While the IDF was thus preparing for another round of full-scale warfare against the Arab states, it also had to look after the usual "current security" problems along the border. In comparison with those incidents of 1950–1956, their significance and number declined. Yet even during the best years approximately one incident per week was registered, involving shootings, border crossings, mine planting, sabotage, and the like. As before, many were launched on local initiative and had no wider significance. However, a turning point of sorts was reached in 1965. Leadership of the Palestine Liberation Organization (PLO), founded the previous year, was snatched by Yasser Arafat and a number of his comrades in Cairo. Militarily, the incidents still did not amount to much (some of them were even imaginary as the PLO and its central military arm, al Fatach, exaggerated successes). Yet now they took on a clear political objective.[59] The PLO knew it could not defeat Israel on its own but hoped that its actions would lead to escalation and thus to eventual war between Israel and its Arab neighbors. The largest IDF punitive operation took place at Samua, near Hebron, on November 13, 1966. In full daylight, and with fighters circling overhead, an armored battalion took the village and blew up no fewer than 105 houses. When the Jordanian army rushed to the scene it was ambushed, leading to the deaths of two dozen of its troops.[60]

"More complicated and more serious" (Rabin, in his memoirs)[61] was the situation on the Syrian frontier. One question was fishing rights in Lake Galilee, which the Israelis insisted were exclusive to them; another bone of contention was formed by a number of small demilitarized areas that remained since 1948. Known by such quaint names as the Beetroot Lot and De Gaulle's Nose, their total area did not exceed a few hundred acres, yet the Israelis insisted the areas were sovereign territory they had the right to farm. The Syrians, not unexpectedly, objected and made their opposition felt by firing on fishermen and laborers, which over the years led to many minor skirmishes.

Still the entire matter might not have gotten out of hand if it had not merged into the so-called Battle of the Water. Already during the late fifties, Israel, having failed to reach agreement with its neighbors in dividing the River Jordan's waters, started work on a major project designed to pump water away from the Sea of Galilee and into the Negev. Faced with the project's imminent completion, Arabs, at the first Arab summit in January 1964, decided to respond by diverting the sources of the River Jordan. A detailed program for the project was drawn up and submitted to the second Arab summit in September. Three months later large-scale work— plans called for no fewer than forty miles of canal plus more than three miles of tunnels—got under way.

The first major incident involving the demilitarized areas took place at Tel Dan north of the Sea of Galilee on November 3.[62] An Israeli half-track was sent to patrol a disputed dirt road and, as had been planned, came under attack. Northern Command under its new commanding officer, Brig. Gen. David Elazar, returned fire, attempting to use the opportunity to knock out Syrian earth-moving equipment and tanks at long range but failing to register any hits.[63] Ten days later a similar incident, also deliberately staged by the Israelis, took place. This time the Syrian tanks were hit but not their artillery positions, which from elevated positions on the Golan Heights shelled the Israeli settlements below. In the end it became necessary to call in the IAF for strafing and bombing operations. After three and a half hours of fighting a cease-fire was arranged, but not before four IDF soldiers had been killed and damage suffered by two Israeli settlements.

Additional incidents took place in December 1964 as well as the spring and summer of 1965. By the latter time the IDF's armored corps was much better prepared. Tal's men proved capable of hitting the Syrians despite the difference in altitude between the two sides and even though the Syrians had changed the course of the canal being constructed to increase the range to seven miles. Unable to match the Israeli Centurions' accurate 105mm cannons, Syrian tanks responded by shelling the settlements in the upper Jordan Valley, holding them hostage. When the Syrians extended the range to as much as thirteen miles Israel called in the air force. In July 1966 it bombed the earth-moving equipment and also shot down its first Syrian aircraft (next month another one was destroyed as the Syrians tried to interfere with the IDF's attempts to salvage a boat that had run aground). There were major incidents in January and April 1967.

By this time, by Rabin's own subsequent admission, the Syrians had already given up their attempts to divert the sources of the River Jordan.[64]

Thus the last incidents were deliberately provoked by the Israelis, who, determined "to exercise their sovereignty," continued to send tractors into the disputed plots even though they knew full well that the Syrians would respond.[65] In retrospect, perhaps the most remarkable thing about these incidents was the fact that they could take place at all. To fight for a few small plots of land was entirely irrational; as a Northern Command officer pointed out at the time,[66] it would have been much cheaper to airlift individual grains of corn from California—packing, insurance, and all. Yet possibly because of decades of efforts to create the new Jewish fighting man, possibly owing to the effect of always living under the gun, by and large this was not how things were regarded either in the IDF, or by the government, or indeed by the Israeli public. Almost without exception, the country backed Northern Command. It did so even at the price of taking casualties and even though Dayan, then an ordinary Knesset member, repeatedly warned his former subordinates in the army that they were "out of their minds" in leading the country to full-scale war.[67]

The largest single incident took place in April 1967. As usual, the chain of events was started by an Israeli tractor attempting to work a disputed field (at one point the Syrians suggested that Israel work half of the field while they worked the rest, but this proposal was rejected). As usual, the Syrians responded by raining down artillery shells from their Golan positions, this time mainly on *kibbuts* Gaddot, which suffered considerable material destruction but no fatalities. Once again the range was too great and the topography too difficult for the Centurions, so the IAF was called in. Syria's air force rose to the challenge and scrambled, six of its fighters being shot down in air-to-air combat. Having received permission to pursue their prey,[68] Israeli Mirages flew over Damascus, which the pilots reported looked like "an overgrown Arab village."[69] Whether deliberately or not, the chain of events that led to the Six Day War had been set in motion.

In the absence of Arab documentation—not that Israeli material relating to the period has been released—the exact origins of the Six Day War will probably never be known. Clearly the IDF under Rabin, more cohesive and better trained than ever before, was spoiling for a fight and willing to go to considerable lengths to provoke it. Clearly there was talk of a full-scale Israeli attack on Syria, which the Soviets, ally to both Syria and Egypt, did nothing to discourage.[70] Nasser's decision to violate the agreements of 1957 by sending forces in May 1967 into the Sinai may have been a response to this threat. As self-appointed leader of the Arab world he could hardly be expected to sit by as the balance of power between Israel and its neighbors fundamentally changed; indeed for months he was attacked verbally for doing nothing while the Jordanians (at Samua) and the Syrians clashed with Israel. Yet he was provided with an excuse to disentangle himself from his commitment in Yemen, where his forces had been fighting to aid the Yemenite revolution for four years without achieving anything in particular. Yet another question—little written about, yet perhaps at least equally important—was Israel's nuclear program during those years.

As far as can be reconstructed, things developed as follows: French-assisted Israeli efforts to build a reactor went into high gear during the late fifties. From the beginning, they had been overshadowed by the possibility they would lead the Arabs to launch a preventive war or try to obtain a weapon of their own. For this reason, but also in order to avoid irritating the Americans (who then as always opposed the attempt of any country to obtain nuclear arms), the Israeli project was kept secret as much as possible. When news of the reactor being built at Dimona leaked—as it was bound to—Pres. John F. Kennedy put pressure on Ben Gurion to desist. After Kennedy was succeeded by Lyndon B. Johnson and Ben Gurion by Eshkol, an informal deal was apparently worked out. It is claimed that the Americans, having been allowed to inspect Dimona, pretended not to notice what was going on (a hoax they did their best to foist upon their incredulous British allies).[71] In return, Israel was to continue its confidence trick.[72] As part of the deal Eshkol may also have promised not to conduct a test.[73]

The Arabs, however, were not misled. Even if their intelligence services had not been able to warn them, they could have, along with everybody else, got the news from the *New York Times*. Already during the first half of the sixties various Lebanese, Jordanian, and Iraqi commentators had referred to the matter, expressing fear that an Israeli bomb would lead to the "freezing" of the conflict—and thus the end of any hope for defeating the Zionist entity and liberating Palestine.[74] From 1965 on, scarcely a week passed without some Arab commentator or other raising the issue. Among those who took note of the developing "Jewish threat" and discussed possible reactions to it were some of the highest-ranking personalities in the Arab world. They included Egyptian Prime Minister Ali Sabri; the president of Egypt's national assembly, Anwar Sadat; King Hussein of Jordan; Syrian President Zain; and Syrian Foreign Minister Ibrahim Machus.

But whereas the weaker and peripheral countries could afford to acquiesce—if only against their will—to the eventual existence of an Israeli bomb, Nasser, the self-styled leader of the Arab world, could not. He referred to the question in several public speeches, stating that Egypt would not resign itself to the existence of an Israeli bomb but would launch "a preventive war" against it—a pronouncement that reflected a resolution passed by the third Arab summit in Casablanca in September 1965 and confirmed by the Palestinian national council a few months later. Apparently he asked the USSR to provide him with nuclear arms but was rebuffed.[75] Equally unsuccessful was the attempt by his top aides to persuade Washington, London, and Paris to put pressure on Israel to stop their program. Just how these issues meshed with the origins of the June 1967 Six Day War we do not know, but the closer one looks the stronger the suspicion that they did in fact play a role.

During the first half of 1966, Nasser had apparently reached the conclusion that the Americans were not only going to do nothing to stop Israel from developing the bomb but also sell A–4 Skyhawk attack aircraft capable, if suitably modified, of delivering it. By this time the term *preventive war* was common throughout the Arab world; everybody, including the U.S. State Department,[76] knew just what it stood for.[77] Expecting the bomb to be ready in 1968,[78] the Egyptians knew it was now or never. When, in May 1967, the Soviets informed them that a dozen or so Israeli brigades were concentrated on the Syrian border they probably took the situation as a pretext for action and stuck to it even though a week or so later they knew that the Soviet reports were unfounded.[79] While Israel was celebrating its nineteenth Independence Day on May 15, Egyptian forces began crossing the Suez Canal into the Sinai, not secretly as they had in 1960 but in paradelike manner and with the greatest possible fanfare. On the next day Egypt asked for the UN forces stationed in the Peninsula to be withdrawn; a day later (May 17) its forces reoccupied Sharm al-Sheikh. On the same day, Dimona became the target of an Egyptian reconnaissance flight. On May 23 the Straits of Tyran were blockaded, and again an Egyptian aircraft flew over Dimona.

For obvious reasons, historically no country has ever admitted to surrendering to nuclear blackmail. Hence, even if the Egyptian archives should one day be opened, it is not to be expected that the Egyptian train of thought will ever be made clear. The flights over Dimona may have been intended as preparation for a military strike, as some have claimed.[80] However, and given the way they coincided with the moves at Sharm al-Sheikh, they may also have been meant as a signal to Israel. The latter interpretation is perhaps more likely, because attack aircraft would have come up against the IAF as well as Hawk antiaircraft batteries already positioned to protect the reactor.

Thus much points to the possibility that Nasser's real intent was to press Israel into halting the bomb's development—just as Pres. John F. Kennedy, five years earlier, had blockaded Cuba to put pressure on the Soviets. Whether Israel did in fact possess the bomb at the time is unknown, though at least one source suggests that such was in fact the case and that two devices were available.[81] This question has recently been put in an entirely new light when Shimon Peres wrote in his memoirs that if Israel had only adopted "a certain proposal" of his "that I cannot write about for reasons of state security" then the Arabs would have been "deterred" and the war "prevented."[82]

Thus Israel appears to have fallen into a trap of its own making when, bowing to U.S. pressure, it declined to tell the world how advanced its nuclear program really was. However, there is another possibility Peres also hints at,[83] namely, that Rabin, with Eshkol's backing, had wanted war against Syria all along and was doing his best to bring it about. Thus, on May 11 Eshkol said that Israeli action "larger than that of April 7" might be necessary. Three days later Rabin chimed in, giving four different interviews to different newspapers in which he said that more IDF operations might be necessary to change the regime in Damascus and make Syria stop supporting the PLO.[84]

By this interpretation Rabin, acting on the advice of his chief of intelligence, Aharon Yariv, had trusted in the fact that the Egyptian was busy in Yemen.[85] When Nasser, contrary to expectations, used the opportunity to extricate himself from that country, his action "struck Israel like a thunderbolt" (Moshe Dayan's words).[86] Not only that, but when the crisis materialized the Egyptians were able to carry with them both Jordan and Iraq. Although the former had been negotiating with Israel for years,[87] now suddenly it concluded an alliance and put its forces under an Egyptian general; the latter mobilized and prepared to send an expeditionary force to Jordan's aid. Taken aback by the consequences of his own actions, Rabin, recalling the events of 1960, at first hoped that things would calm down.[88] When that failed to happen he went to see Ben Gurion in the hope of finding encouragement but instead was castigated for playing with Israel's future and provoking an unnecessary war. Thereupon the chief of staff either panicked and offered to resign (as his detractors claim)[89] or suffered from exhaustion and nicotine poisoning (says he, seconded by his wife).[90] At any rate on May 24 he was under sedation and was hors de combat. Then he collected himself and went on to win the war.

Note, too, that nuclear weapons were never even mentioned in the public exchange of inflammatory messages between Israel and its neighbors during the crisis that preceded the war. On the Arab side this was probably because, had they been mentioned, any major military undertaking against Israel would at once have been seen to be impossible; on the Israeli side, they would have made it unnecessary. In the event it was precisely the fact that both sides—each for its own reasons—kept the nuclear genie in its bottle, which enabled the various military moves and countermoves to take place.

When the entry of Egyptian forces into the Sinai became known, the IDF's first response was to put some units on alert and send others into the Negev. Next, on May 19, the decision to mobilize the reserves was made. Once Nasser had committed himself by getting rid of the UN forces and blocking the Straits of Tyran, war was inevitable. As it happened, the crisis found the IDF at the peak of preparedness. Mobilization brought its strength to approximately 250,000 men, some 180,000 being reservists.[91] The three-week waiting period that followed proved fortunate: Whereas in 1956 parts of 38th *Ugda* in particular had been far from ready, now the IDF was given time to hone its edge. Having spent years preparing for exactly this eventuality, the air force, its two hundred modern combat aircraft at the ready, was eager to put its plans into practice. Since 1956, the ground forces too had been heavily reinforced until they numbered perhaps twenty-one brigades. According to a recently published account by Gen. Yisrael Tal, ten were armored and organized in four division-sized task forces. Between them they had 746 artillery barrels plus 1,300 tanks[92]—far above the figures mentioned in contemporary or near-contemporary accounts of the war.[93] Much later, Rabin explained that people at the time did not understand how powerful the IDF had become and "really believed" that Israel had been in danger.[94]

Meanwhile, not being informed as to the true state of its own defenses, the Israeli public panicked before the twelve or so Arab divisions surrounding them. The feeling in Israel during those awful days was as if the world was coming to an end and a second Holocaust just around the corner. Full mobilization caused the economy to come to a near halt and men up to middle age inclusive to disappear from the streets. Steeling themselves to losses, the Israelis prepared three times as many hospital beds (14,000) than were eventually needed; meanwhile, fearing that the regular burial services would break down, Tel Aviv parks were ritually designated as cemeteries. Prime Minister Eshkol's May 28 radio address did not help; he used IDF-ese and began to stutter as a result.[95] A "Government of National Unity" was set up, with Begin and one of his cronies as ministers without portfolio. More important, Eshkol—who had once referred to the one-eyed general as Abu Jilda, after an Arab bandleader of the 1930s—was forced by public opinion to relinquish the defense portfolio and entrust it to Dayan (a lasting blow to his self-confidence). Dayan spent the few remaining days holding speeches and touring the front. As Weizman told Eshkol at the time, the IDF was perfectly capable of winning the war without him.[96] Yet when victory came he would garner much of the glory.

To sum up, the IDF was confident in its power and extremely aggressive. Led by Rabin, it had done what it could to provoke the Syrians, even though by June 1967 it was at least one year since the latter had desisted from their attempt to divert the sources of the Jordan. Why Nasser chose to support Damascus at the time and in the form that he did also remains a mystery, but it very likely had something to do with his fear that Israel was about to develop nuclear weapons. When the crisis came it took the Israelis by surprise. From Ben Gurion on down, at least some of Israel's leaders were left in the dark concerning the IDF's true strength. If the real and alleged number of tanks is any indication, the underestimate may have been as much as 60 percent; one source even has Rabin tell the Cabinet that, in number of troops, Israel could match Egypt and Syria combined.[97] Still more important was the effect on the Israeli public and the IDF rank and file—with the welcome result that during the tense weeks that preceded the war both thought of nothing but fighting for their very lives. As it turned out, fighting for its very life is precisely what the IDF would do.

The Apogee of Blitzkrieg: Israeli landing craft unloading supplies at Sharm al-Sheikh, June 1967.

CHAPTER II

The Apogee of Blitzkrieg

T HE IDF HAD NOT been idle since 1956, building up a formidable order of battle, and neither had its Arab enemies. In 1967, as eleven years earlier, the strongest country was Egypt. Egypt's air force was deployed in some nineteen airfields, most located west of the Suez Canal. It had 385 combat aircraft, all of them Soviet-built (in contrast to 1956, when some were British) and including MIG–17, MIG–19, and MIG–21 fighters; Su–7 attack aircraft; as well as T–16 medium and Il–28 light bombers. As in the IAF, some aircraft were more modern than others, but none were obsolete. They provided cover to Egypt's forces in the Sinai Peninsula: approximately 100,000 men armed with 900 tanks, 200 assault guns, and 900 artillery barrels. As in 1956 there was a Palestinian division, the 20th, in the Gaza Strip. As in 1956, too, the Egyptian formations were deployed along the main roads leading into the Sinai with an eye to blocking them—forming a "shield" with a "sword" behind ready to counterattack (see Map 11.1).

From north to south, 7th Infantry Division was at Al Arish, 2nd Infantry Division in the Abu Ageila–Umm Katef area, and 6th Infantry Division at Kuntilla; besides the usual artillery regiment, each unit was reinforced by an armored battalion. On the central axis, 3rd Infantry Division stood behind 2nd Infantry Division in reserve. It was backed up by two armored formations, 4th Armored Division at Bir Gafgafa and "Force Shazly"—actually a heavily reinforced brigade—far south at Nakhl. During the days just before the Six Day War, the Palestinians in Gaza exchanged fire with the Israelis; of the remaining Egyptian forces only Force Shazly could have been quickly redeployed for advancing into southern Negev Desert. Even this threat does not seem to have caused Rabin any loss of sleep, for the forces he allocated for the defense of Elat were absolutely minimal. As he later wrote, "We were informed about Egypt's defensive plans . . . but we did not have their offensive ones, if any."[1]

What was true of the Egyptians also seems to have applied to the Jordanians (see Map 11.2). King Hussein having been forced into the confrontation by public opinion,[2] his army found itself geographically well positioned to cut Israel in half; however, with an overall strength of 55,000 men it was much too weak to accomplish anything of the sort. The air force had only twenty-one subsonic, 1950s-vintage Hawker Hunter fighters (on the eve of the war six new F–104s were spirited to Turkey)[3] and no bombers of any kind. The ground forces, with 100 artillery pieces and some 300 tanks, were reasonably well armed; still they could not match the IDF, which had received more advanced versions of the same tanks (M–48 Pattons and Centurions). Nine of eleven brigades were deployed in the West Bank in "a forward defense posture to ensure that not an inch of the Holy Land was abandoned without a fight";[4] of those, again the two armored ones were stationed in the rear, that is, the Jordan Valley, with the idea of forming an operational reserve and counterattack. As already mentioned, when the crisis erupted the Jordanians allowed an Egyptian general to take charge of their army and also admitted two Egyptian commando battalions; on the night of June 4–5 they were further reinforced by an Iraqi armored brigade (the 8th), which entered the country from the east. Coming under attack by the IAF, however, it never even approached the River Jordan, let alone crossed it.

Judging by their subsequent behavior, the Syrians were even less offensive-minded than the Jordanians.[5] As mentioned earlier, in 1948 two different Syrian forces had penetrated perhaps two miles into Erets Yisrael before being defeated and contained at Degania and Mishmar Ha-yarden, respectively. Since then they had often clashed with the IDF by firing at various Israeli military and civilian targets along the border. Not once did they try to cross that border, however, and indeed during the mid-sixties Damascus often claimed that the way to deal with the Zionist entity was not by means of conventional warfare but of guerrilla warfare on the lines of Algeria and Vietnam.[6] By supporting terrorist activities inside Israel, Syrian intelligence did its bit to raise tensions, thus helping to trigger the process that led to war.

At that time the Syrian armed forces had 65,000 men. The air force had slightly under 100 Soviet-built combat aircraft and was judged capable of carrying out "simple" operations; the ground forces consisted of the equivalent of ten brigades (including two armored and two mechanized) with 300 tanks and 300 artillery barrels.[7] Three infantry brigades occupied the slopes; three more, plus the two armored and one mechanized brigades, were stationed on the plateau itself, with Kuneitra, on the road to Damascus, as their main base. In his 1966 annual report to London, the British military attaché wrote that he "shuddered to think" what the army's "proletarian" officers and mostly "illiterate" rank and file would do with the advanced equipment at their disposal.[8]

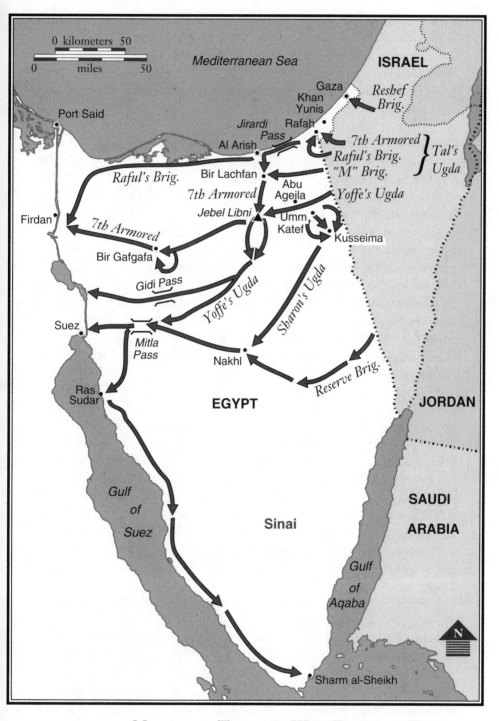

MAP 11.1   THE 1967 WAR, EGYPTIAN FRONT

Preparing for the worst case—a simultaneous clash with all these forces—the IDF had distributed its forces between its Southern, Central, and Northern Commands.[9] Facing the Egyptians, Brig. Gen. Yeshayahu Gavish had under him three *ugdas* with, from north to south, three, two, and four brigades. Of the nine, five were armored, three consisted of more or less motorized infantry (the available vehicles ranged from World War II half-tracks to civilian trucks), and one of heliborne paratroopers; in addition Gavish had three independent brigades (including one armored) standing by as an operational reserve. Central Command, under Brig. Gen. Uzi Narkis, had five brigades. Of these, one (the "Jerusalem Brigade") was already in Jerusalem; three were in the coastal plain and were brought up to participate in the battles around Jerusalem; one was to attack Nablus from the west. Finally, Brigadier General Elazar's Northern Command was split in two. Deployed in the Valley of Esdraelon and facing the Jordanians was an *ugda* under Brig. Gen. Elad Peled with one armored, one mechanized, and one infantry brigade. Left to face the Syrians under Brig. Gen. David Lanner were two infantry and one mechanized brigades. However, the IDF did not expect serious trouble on that front. On June 4 Dayan told a frustrated Elazar to "resign himself" to the fact that the war would be waged "against Egypt and not against others"; he even doubted whether the Syrians would enter the war at all.[10]

Having blocked the Straits of Tyran on May 23, Nasser and his allies seem to have been content to make warlike noises and wait. Not so Israel, which, owing to its system of mobilization, could not afford to do the same—and where people believed themselves in mortal danger. Arguing that time would enable the Egyptians to reinforce their hold on the Sinai, many of the *alufim* on the General Staff pressed for action (some calculated that each passing day would result in two hundred additional IDF casualties).[11] Still more eager to go was the chief of the General Staff, Ezer Weizman. A former air force commander, he feared lest waiting would compromise the plan for a first strike against the Egyptian airfields on which he and his successor, Brig. Gen. Mordechai Hod, had worked for so long. Roaring and bellowing, as was his wont, he went so far as to throw his epaulets on the table in front of a vacillating Eshkol,[12] this probably being the closest thing to a coup that Israel has ever experienced.

Faithful to its strategic approach, the IDF under Rabin had developed a number of plans, all of which envisaged taking the offensive at the earliest possible moment.[13] Though there was never any doubt about Egypt being the main enemy, initially it was not clear whether the attack against it would be limited, aiming at the occupation of the Gaza Strip and/or Sharm al-Sheikh, or full-scale, smashing the Egyptian army and overrunning the entire Sinai Peninsula; once the latter had been adopted it was still necessary to decide whether the main effort would be made by the northern *ugda* breaking through to Al Arish or the central one driving through ground the Egyptians regarded as impassable to attack the rear. There was also some debate whether to use the opportunity to launch an attack against Jordan. The events at Samua in 1966 demonstrated to the General Staff how easily the IDF could overrun the West Bank,[14] thus setting right the "historical error" of 1948. That idea, however, was rejected. In fact, for hours after the Jordanians opened fire on June 5, the government of Israel was still sending messages calling for mediation in an attempt to avoid a large-scale confrontation with its neighbor to the east.[15]

As the slide toward war continued, much depended on making sure the United States would not object, as it had in 1956. During the last week of May, there was a flurry of diplomatic activity as Foreign Minister Abba Eban attempted to hold the three Western powers (United States, Great Britain, and France) to their 1957 promise to open the Straits of Tyran if blocked by Egypt.[16] He failed, but at any rate his highly publicized visits reinforced the Israeli public's feeling that it was alone and thus strengthened its determination to fight for its life—probably the most decisive factor in the war.

On June 3 the head of Mossad, Brigadier General (ret.) Amit, returned home from talks with U.S. Secretary of Defense Robert McNamara. He brought the clear impression that the United States would not mind if "Nasser's bones were broken" and certainly would do nothing to prevent it. That evening the final decision to go to war was made.[17] Two days later, at 0750 hours, the air-raid sirens sounded in towns and settlements all over Israel. Those who switched on their radios could hear the announcer say that the IAF had gone to war in order to intercept Egyptian aircraft approaching Israel—a flat lie, no such approach having taken place. Five minutes previously, at 0845 hours Egyptian time, the first IAF flights had reached their targets. Excellent intelligence enabled the Israelis to pinpoint the entire order of battle of Egypt's air force, down to the names of individual pilots. More significant, the locations of individual squadrons and their types of aircraft were also known,[18] thus enabling the IAF to select and strike the most dangerous Egyptian forces first.

Of the IAF's 200 combat aircraft only twelve stayed behind to defend the homeland, either on airborne patrol or sitting at the edge of runways. Some of the attacking planes were loaded with few bombs and lots of fuel—many were operating at extreme range—and flew in low over the Mediterranean, maintaining radio silence and presumably using electronic countermeasures (ECM) to avoid the dozens of Egyptian, Soviet, and U.S. radars that might have detected them.[19] Other aircraft were sent against bases located in the Sinai itself and thus made straight for their targets. The first wave hit nine bases, knocking out many modern MIG–21 fighters and launching ground-penetrating Durendals into the runways to render them unserviceable. Some of the bombs exploded immediately, creating craters, whereas delayed fuses were set on others to obstruct attempts to clear and repair the runways. Then, for two hours and fifty minutes, one wave after another followed up until no fewer than nineteen Egyptian airfields had been attacked and 286 machines of various types turned into smoldering wrecks.[20]

The offensive had been carefully timed to hit its targets after the Egyptian predawn patrols landed but before senior commanders reached their desks. The enemy was taken totally by surprise, what with the majority of senior officers not yet at their desks and most planes sitting neatly on the runways, waiting to be strafed. Designed to shoot planes that flew at high altitudes, the Egyptians' Soviet-made SAM–2 surface-to-air missiles proved little threat, as did the fire of antiaircraft guns, which tended to be uncoordinated and overall lighter than anticipated. A couple of the Israeli aircraft in the first wave were shot down by Egyptian MIGs, which managed to take off but were themselves promptly downed. It was a nearly letter-perfect operation, carried out with zest and determination. By 1100 hours Israeli time Ezer Weizman could be heard bellowing on the telephone that the war had been won[21]—which indeed was the case.

Simultaneously on the ground, the principal thrust was made in the north by Brigadier General Tal's *ugda* with three brigades and Fouga ground-support light aircraft. But the Egyptian understanding of the terrain proved better than that of the Israelis, two of whose brigades floundered in the sands when they tried to outflank Rafah on the left. As they tried to advance through the dunes, Eytan's paratroopers, riding half-tracks, lost their way as well as contact with their own attached tanks. Next they came under an Egyptian counterattack, supported by heavy JS III tanks, and suffered losses; by late afternoon they could be found slowly grinding toward Rafah from the south. From there they drove back into the Gaza Strip, thus crossing the communications of the rest of their own *ugda* at the cost of considerable confusion;[22] in the Strip itself they linked up with "Force Reshef" (one of Gavish's reserve brigades), which had been standing by but was now unleashed.

Though Eytan's advance had been disorderly and uncoordinated, he finally reached his objective. Not so "M" Armored Brigade, with its reservists riding out-of-date Sherman and AMX–13 tanks. Throughout the day it attempted to pass the impassable stretch of dunes assigned to it; by evening it had yet to fire a shot. This meant that Tal's real thrust had to be delivered by a single brigade, 7th Armored, a crack formation consisting of conscripts riding Centurions. Coming from the west, first they captured Khan Yunis. Next, and overrunning the Palestinians on the way, they drove south to Rafah, where their accurate fire, delivered at long range, proved more than a match for the Egyptian antitank guns and thus vindicated Tal's theories (the more so because they were being supported by Fougas from the air). Having barely avoided firing at Eytan's paratroopers (who were reaching for the same objective from the south), they next headed for the Jirardi Defile. The leading tank battalion got through easily enough but found the road blocked behind it; approaching in its turn, the second one also got through but took heavy losses on the way. Still the Egyptians resisted, blocking the defile for the second time until 7th Brigade's mechanized infantry arrived and mopped up.

As fought—conducted would be too complimentary, since only one out of Tal's three brigades responded to his orders while carrying out its mission—the battle for the northeastern Sinai was misunderstood by the Israelis. It should have taught them that tank advances against unbroken infantry were risky business. Instead they took them as the supreme proof of the virtues of tanks driving forward in *egrofei shiryon*. "Tankomania" (in the words of Ariel Sharon) was carried to the point where the force was nicknamed *Ugdat Ha-plada* (Steel Division), and Tal became the only Israeli officer ever to have a serenade written in his honor: "On the fifth of June/The armored battalion broke through . . . just as you wanted, Tal." The hero of the day was the commander of 7th Brigade, Col. Shmuel Gonen, known for the martinetlike antics he inflicted on his unfortunate troops. Now he found the road to promotion open to him until, as we shall see, he came up against the "Peter Principle" and was cut down to size.

Farther south, Brig. Gen. Avraham Yoffe's two-brigade *ugda* had an easier task of it. This time the Israelis' confidence in their ability to get through terrain the Egyptians considered impassable proved well founded; although the struggle against the sand proved difficult, there was no opposition. By late afternoon the Centurions of the leading "I" Brigade had penetrated some thirty miles into Egyptian territory, thus interposing themselves between the two main Egyptian fortified areas to the north and south. They were refueled from the air—their own *dragim* (trains) got stuck in the dunes—took up positions along the road leading northeast from Jebel Livni, and waited. That same evening the leading elements of the Egyptian 4th Armored Division appeared in front of them as if on a peacetime march. Their objective was Al Arish, some twenty miles away, where they were supposed to counterattack Tal's forces; suddenly the sky lit up as the Israelis fired flares. The 4th Egyptian fell easy prey to the Centurions, with their long-range guns firing from concealed positions. Early next morning, the survivors turned back.

Still farther south, the IDF's third *ugda* found itself facing the Abu Ageila–Kusseima fortified zone, which had stymied their predecessors eleven years earlier. The Egyptians had learned from their experience: Not only was 2nd Infantry Division, which held the position, reinforced to approximately 16,000 men; it was provided with a mobile counterattack force in the form of a tank regiment (sixty-six T–34 tanks with 85mm guns) and a battalion of tank destroyers (twenty-two Su–100s with 100mm guns). The Egyptian reserves were, however, stationed too far west, and their commander did not have authority to act on his own. In the end, this deficiency in command would bring about their defeat.[23]

On the Israeli side, the commander in charge was Ariel Sharon. After 1956 he had been put on hold, first commanding a reserve infantry brigade and later serving as chief of staff, Northern Command. Once Rabin became chief of the General Staff, Sharon was brought back into the center of things as director of military training; in wartime he was to command an *ugda*. On the basis of detailed air photos he proceeded to draw up a meticulous plan for capturing the Abu Ageila–Kusseima area by way of a concentric attack.[24] One brigade was to capture Kusseima on the south, thus creating a diversion while also preventing any attempt by Force Shazly at Kuntilla to intervene. While the main assault was carried out by two armored brigades coming from the north, a force of paratroopers would land west of Abu Ageila, thus cutting off the position from its operational reserve.

Driving west against comparatively light opposition, by late afternoon both of Sharon's landborne prongs reached their jumping-off positions north and south of Abu Ageila. A message from Southern Command arrived and suggested that the attack be postponed until the next morning to enable the IAF to take part; Sharon, however, decided to go ahead. At 2200 hours artillery from two brigades opened up on the Egyptians from the north. Next, Col. Danny Matt's paratroopers used the confusion to enter the Egyptian artillery positions from the west. In the north, Sharon's two remaining brigades—one armored, one infantry—brought in mine-clearing equipment. Carrying colored identification lights and forming narrow wedges, they advanced closely behind their own artillery barrage and straight into the main defenses. As Sharon noted at one point, "It was all working like a Swiss watch." Though Matt's paratroopers took heavy casualties, by 1100 hours or so on the morning of June 6 the battle was over.

Perhaps the decisive factor in the Egyptian defeat had been the inactivity of their local reserves, which, since they did not come under attack, stood idly throughout the night until surrounded in the morning.[25] The same inactivity now overtook Sharon's own forces, either because of exhaustion or because they received no orders from headquarters. Dayan's daughter Yael was attached to Sharon's headquarters as a journalist; she reported[26] that they laid themselves down in the desert. They thus enabled Force Shazly to slip away and its commander to make a name for himself as the only Egyptian officer who escaped defeat; rising up the ladder of promotion, in 1973 he was chief of staff and in charge of crossing the canal.

Even at the height of the battle for Abu Ageila, however, Yoffe had already asked and received permission to send his second armored brigade across the road cleared by Sharon north of the perimeter westward into the central Sinai. On the morning of June 6 there were thus four armored brigades ready to carry out the second phase of the campaign: two under Yoffe, two under Tal (who also made Eytan's paratroopers reverse direction and join the attack). Coming from the north, Gonen drove south toward Jebel Livni, where on the morning of June 6 he linked up with Yoffe's "I" Brigade, thus building a pocket and trapping inside all the Egyptian forces (two divisions) defending the northeastern Sinai. With 2nd Egyptian Division at Abu Ageila broken, 4th Armored bloodied, and Force Shazly isolated far to the south, the lone main force remaining was the Egyptian 3rd Division.

When news of the fall of Abu Ageila arrived the minister of defense, Field Marshal Abdel Hakim Amer, panicked. Without so much as consulting the chief of staff, he ordered all remaining formations to retreat, with the result that command and control collapsed and the Egyptians ceased to represent a cohesive force. At about the same time as this order was being given (1630) Gavish met with his division commanders. Quickly surveying the latest developments, the Israelis decided not to pursue but to drive straight *through* the retreating Egyptians to reach the passes ahead of them.[27] Only Yoffe's forces succeeded in this task. Driving all night (and engaged retreating Egyptian tanks at point-blank range along the road) the Centurions of "I" Brigade reached the Giddi on the morning of June 8. They took up positions and opened fire on the approaching columns of 3rd Infantry Division, wreaking vast destruction.

Meanwhile to the north along the coastal road, Tal's "M" Brigade—the one that had not fired a shot on June 5—pursued from Al Arish, reaching the Suez Canal on June 7. At Bir Gafgafa on the same day, the campaign's only major *shin be-shin* battle was fought between Gonen's 7th Armored Brigade and elements of the Egyptian 4th Armored Division with its T–54 and T–55 tanks.[28] Like the Allies at Falaise in 1944 (albeit on a much smaller scale), the Israelis went for an encirclement and tried to outflank the enemy from the south. Also like the Allies at Falaise in 1944, they were only partly successful, since the jaws snapped shut too late; at least part of 4th

Armored Division managed to escape. Finally, and even though he was now being attacked from two directions (in addition to Sharon coming from the north, he was being pursued by Gavish's remaining reserve brigade, which drove at him from Kuntilla), Shazly, as already related, gave them both the slip. Only *after* he had passed through Giddi Pass did some of "I" Brigade's Centurions arrive on their last drop of fuel, holding it for eighteen hours before Sharon could reach them, bagging little but stragglers.

It remained to secure Sharm al-Sheikh. Committing his last available reserve, Gavish carried out the operation on June 7 by means of a para-trooper drop—but when the men landed they found the navy waiting for them. On June 8 the Israelis mopped up, sending forces north to south along the Suez Canal and from there on farther south along the peninsula's western coast. By that time, however, attention had long shifted to the central front. Despite the fact that King Hussein had put his forces under the command of an Egyptian general, Israel did not expect him to enter the war. The king's reasoning is hard to figure. If it were true, as was later claimed, that he was "almost certain" to be attacked by Israel following its eventual victory over both Egypt and Syria,[29] he should have hit out as hard as he could on the first day with his armored brigades. But he made only two symbolic thrusts at Jerusalem's Mount Scopus and the Mount of Evil Council (both of them totally unimportant objectives), fired a few long-range 155mm artillery shells in the general direction of Tel Aviv, and mounted a few air attacks against Israeli airfields. Perhaps Hussein felt that he had no choice but to do something, all the while hoping to avoid serious retaliation.

On the afternoon of June 5, after several hours trying to bring about a cease-fire, Israel and the IDF had had enough antics from the "little king." The IAF went into action, wiping out Jordan's small air force (they had one radar station) in its bases, also paying a visit to the old, British-built H–3 air base in western Iraq; when the balance of the first day's fighting was summed up on the radio late that night, the IAF could boast of having destroyed no fewer than four hundred Arab aircraft in all. Meanwhile a crack brigade of Israeli paratroopers (the 55th) had been standing ready to take Al Arish in conjunction with Tal's forces. When that town fell ahead of time, the brigade was diverted to confront the Jordanians.

To the south of Jerusalem, Narkis's Jerusalem Brigade was holding on to the area around UN headquarters while the paratroopers of Mordechai Gur—he had entered Mitla Pass in 1956—prepared to envelop the city from the north.[30] Late that night, the paratroopers fought an extremely tough engagement in a fortified area known as Ammunition Hill over-looking the road from West Jerusalem to Mount Scopus and Mount

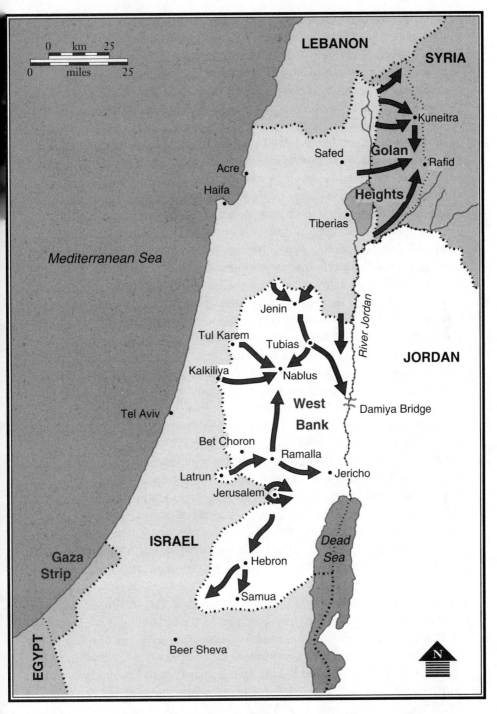

MAP 11.2   THE 1967 WAR, JORDANIAN AND SYRIAN FRONTS

Olives. When the latter fell, the Jordanians in East Jerusalem found themselves encircled. Moreover, since the main highway runs through town, communication between the two main parts of the West Bank—the northern and the southern—had also been cut.

That same evening (June 5) another mechanized brigade belonging to Central Command drove up the Tel Aviv–Jerusalem highway. Before reaching Mount Kastel they turned north, however, using a dirt road that ran parallel to the highway. Although the topography was the same, this time there could be no question of the Israelis attacking mainly with light arms, as Rabin's men had done in 1948; instead they used their Super Sherman tanks in close support, quickly breaking through several defended Arab positions before debouching at Tel Ful north of Jerusalem on the morning of June 6. As a third brigade reached Ramalla, farther north, by way of Latrun and Bet Choron, there were now no fewer than three IDF brigades stationed along the north-south watershed and cutting the West Bank in half. Any hope that the situation might still change was soon ended. With its hands freed by the destruction of the Arab air forces the previous day, the IAF intercepted Jordanian 60th Armored Brigade on the road from Jericho—where burned-out tanks and other armored vehicles could be seen strewn about for years to come.

On June 7 the great drama was complete. Jerusalem Brigade turned south, driving toward Hebron and sending the Jordanian brigade deployed around the city—they had been sent in hope of linking up with the Egyptians!³¹—into a hasty retreat. Gur's paratroopers broke through Jerusalem's Lions' Gate and were soon mopping up in the Old City; of Narkis's two mechanized brigades stationed on the Jerusalem-Ramalla Road, one took the old road toward the Jordan Valley and Jericho, whereas the other turned north to link up with the forces of Brigadier General Peled. That *ugda* had been engaged in heavy fighting since the afternoon of June 5. One armored battalion drove down to Bet Shean, from where it probed the Jordanian part of the Jordan Valley from the north, thus threatening to take 40th Armored Brigade in the rear. Three brigades (one minus a battalion) converged on Jenin. Farther southwest, Narkis's 5th Brigade entered the West Bank by a different road and made directly toward Nablus.

To defend the area in question the Jordanians had three infantry brigades plus the elite 40th Armored Brigade, which, disregarding the threat to its communications, moved up to Jenin by way of Tubias on June 6, meaning that the two sides were approximately equal in numbers. Riding dissimilar vehicles—the Israelis relied on their Super Shermans and half-tracks, the Jordanians on M–47s, M–48s, and M–113 armored personnel carriers (APCs)—they slugged it out at close quarters among the narrow mountain valleys. Israeli accounts emphasize the excellence of the Jordanian troops so long as they stayed put and were not called upon to counterattack;[32] per Jordanian accounts, the decisive nature of the air strikes rained down on their "hapless" troops.[33] Hitting fortified positions located on mountain slopes from the air with the equipment then used by the IAF—they wouldn't deploy precision-guided munitions (PGMs) and computerized navigation attack avionics till later—is difficult even for the best pilots. Perhaps, then, the two accounts can be made to dovetail by assuming that the Jordanian counterattacks failed *because* whenever their armor broke camouflage and got moving it would come under air attack.

Be that as it may, after thirty-six hours of tough fighting the Israelis prevailed. By the evening of June 7 their right-wing brigade had crossed through Nablus (where they were initially mistaken for Iraqis and welcomed by the population) and linked up with the one coming up from Jerusalem. The other three took Jenin and proceeded south and east, occupying the Jordan Valley and blocking the escape routes of whatever Jordanian units had remained intact. Though the Arab Legion fought well, its forces had been shattered, and only stragglers made it across the river; the Israelis, who also had a vast stream of refugees on their hands, did not try to stop them so long as they left their arms behind. In the confusion one of Narkis's brigades had actually crossed to the East Bank without orders.[34] According to Rabin, he learned of the move only when the United States, prompted by Hussein, ordered Israel to desist.[35] Thereupon the 10th Brigade, having crossed into the East Bank, was told to retreat and did so, blowing up the bridges as it went.

It remained to deal with the Syrians, who, in contrast to their bellicose actions during the years leading up to the war, scarcely lifted a finger while their allies were being pulverized. On June 6 and 7 they fired at the settlements in the Jordan Valley, inflicting considerable material damage ("205 houses, 9 chicken-coops, 2 tractor-sheds, 3 clubs, 1 dining hall, 6 haystacks, 30 tractors, 15 cars"[36] according to a meticulous Israeli account) but killing no more than two and wounding sixteen. What offensive plans they may have had never materialized; at any rate any talk of an offensive was absurd, given that by the evening of June 6 most of their air force had been destroyed by the IAF. Israel and the IDF, however, were bent on revenge against the Syrians, whom they regarded as the most implacable enemy of all.

Relying on the excellent intelligence on the Golan fortifications provided by spy Eli Cohen prior to the war, Northern Command drafted several plans for dealing with the Syrians. Thus "Makevet (Sledgehammer) North" provided an offensive against the northern part of the heights; "Makevet South" for an attack on the center; and "Makevet Center" for a purely holding operation. Once the war had started and a decision had to be made, how-ever, the Eshkol-Dayan-Rabin–Bar Lev (Rabin's deputy)–Elazar chain of command proved less than perfect. At first, on June 6, Elazar was given per-mission to attack on the next afternoon. Next, waiting for reinforcements—he had only two brigades left, having lost one to the West Bank—and for the sky to clear, he decided to postpone for twenty-four hours. Around noon on June 7 Bar Lev was still telling him to go ahead; but at 1000 hours on June 8 Rabin came on the phone and informed his front commander that the IDF "did not have permission" to attack.[37]

Flying to Tel Aviv, an outraged Elazar met with Eshkol (for some rea-son all the prime minister's secretaries had disappeared and his wife was answering the telephone); unable to change his mind, he went back to his command post. That same evening a Cabinet meeting was held and Dayan, seeking to restrain the aggressive tendencies of Rabin, Allon, and Eshkol himself, explained his reasoning. The war against Egypt was not yet over; the Soviets were making threatening noises and might intervene; the Israeli canary had swallowed two cats—Egypt and Jordan—enough of a meal even without also adding Syria.[38] That night, however, Dayan changed his mind. As he later explained, the Egyptians had agreed to a cease-fire, which in turn poured cold water on the Soviet threats. At 0400 hours on June 9, informing neither the prime minister nor the chief of staff, both out of reach (or so he later claimed), Dayan called Elazar. The CO Northern Command was ordered to storm the Golan Heights that day. So much for command, optional or otherwise.

Once unleashed, Elazar proved as aggressive as his fellow commanders. Already on June 6 the Syrian positions had come under heavy attack at the hands of the IAF. Elazar now postponed his assault from early to late morn-ing—thus enabling Hod's pilots to fly another two hundred sorties and rain down four hundred tons of bombs, a tremendous amount of firepower by standards of the day; as it turned out the effort was insufficiently accurate to knock out the well-sited Syrian artillery positions.[39] Originally the Israeli plan was to take the Golan Heights from each end. Against the southern end they planned to bring up a variety of paratrooper and mechanized infantry units; these had previously been fighting against the Jordanians, however, and had to be brought up first. At this time Israeli lack of traffic discipline made itself felt, creating a jam that delayed the effort an entire day. As a result the main Israeli effort was made by the two brigades (one armored, one infantry) deployed facing the northern end of the Golan Heights. Opposite the central Golan, Elazar had a brigade of mechanized infantry and "U" Armored Brigade. The latter had already been bloodied by the Jordanians at Jenin but arrived in time to lead the effort in this sector.

On the face of it four brigades (discounting the force in the south) were not much to confront the Syrians. But the topography made lateral movement along the slopes impossible, so the three Syrian brigades who occupied positions on those slopes were stationary. As the IDF concentrated all its forces in two narrow wedges, only the units immediately facing them were actually hit and could fight back, whereas the remainder could not come to their support without making huge detours. The six Syrian brigades stationed on the plateau, including most of their armor, never intervened in the battle—the reason presumably being that doing so would make them easy targets for the IAF.

At 1130 hours on June 9 the advance started. The narrow approaches allowed little room for tactical, much less operational finesse; proceeding under cover of heavy air and artillery bombardment, and in some places preceded by bulldozers, teams of tanks and infantry advanced separately on the northern and central axes. The Syrian lines had been built so as to overlook each other, each successive line supported by the line behind. Now they mismanaged the battle, failing to redirect their guns; thus the farther up the slopes the IDF units climbed, the less artillery fire they received.

Ideally the attack would have been delivered by tanks and infantry working together, the former using their cannons to deliver direct fire and covering the latter's approach. Such had been the IDF's modus operandi as long ago as the last successful attack on Iraq Suedan in 1948. By 1967, however, that hard-learned lesson had long been forgotten. From 1956 on, the IDF was organized almost exclusively for mobile warfare, what with the armored corps looking at the infantry as an encumbrance and devising derogatory nicknames for them. Consequently the infantrymen of Golani in particular found themselves advancing very much on their own. On their way up they got involved in several hand-to-hand fights for individual positions. The positions were taken for a heavy price in blood and might have been avoided if Elazar (and Rabin) paid more attention to the peculiar conditions on this front.

Nevertheless, on the evening of June 9 the most important positions—bearing names that still strike a chord among Israelis familiar with the war, such as Tel Azaziyat and Tel Fachar—had been taken, and the IDF was standing on the escarpment. On the northern axis stood Golani Infantry Brigade and Col. Albert Mandler's armored brigade, both of them thoroughly exhausted but about to be reinforced by another armored brigade ("B" Brigade, which had been brought back from the Jenin area). In the center the forward unit ("U" Brigade) had also been overtaken by the mechanized brigade that had been standing by in this sector and was sent up the plateau during the night. Thus Elazar had available a total of five brigades (one entirely fresh) against the remnants of the Syrian forces trying to escape from the slopes and the six uncommitted brigades that, indeed, were ordered to retreat that very night. However, at this point the IDF's lack of previous planning made itself felt. Apparently there had been no thought given by the General Staff to the campaign's final objectives. Nor were there any topographical features that could have forced a halt or at least a delay.

In face of this uncertainty, and expecting a UN-imposed cease-fire to come into effect at any moment, the Israelis advanced rather gingerly. In the south, Brig. Gen. Elad Peled, with various units forming an improvised *ugda*, climbed up the winding road that leads from Tsemach to the plateau, meeting no opposition. A paratrooper battalion belonging to this force was landed by helicopter but, arriving at Fiq (where the Syrians had their base), found it empty. In the center, "U" Brigade made toward Kuneitra on the main road to Damascus, hoping to catch the Syrians in a trap as "B" Brigade came down from the north. The night having been largely wasted, however, the pincer movement planned by Elazar came too late. Resistance was scattered; meanwhile the Syrian operational reserves (along with two-thirds with all available tanks) escaped, as did some of the forces stationed on the slopes. The decision where to halt was left to the discretion of junior commanders who captured this position or that as it suited them. It is a tribute to their tactical sense that the line that eventually emerged was defensible, including the southern slopes of Mount Hermon as well as two critical hills—Chermonit and Booster—in the center. Still, and as Brigadier General Elazar was forced to concede during his postmortem analysis, the Syrian army had not been annihilated.[40]

Owing to geographical circumstances and the lack of enterprise shown by the Arab navies, the Six Day War was fought above all in the air and on land. The Israeli navy at that time still consisted of two World War II destroyers (a third, the former Egyptian *Ibrahim al Awwal*, was hurriedly recommissioned and rechristened *Haifa*), three submarines, and a number of smaller vessels such as torpedo boats and landing craft—not much of a force to face seven Egyptian destroyers, twelve submarines, and eighteen Soviet-built *Komar*- and *Ossa*-class missile boats. Yet in practice the disparity was less than the figures would indicate, one-third of the Egyptian navy having been moved to the Red Sea in the wake of a successful Israeli feint. Torpedo boats were brought up by day, withdrawn by night, and returned the next day, thus creating the impression of a much larger force.

On June 5 the Israeli navy at once took the initiative, sending out submarines that in turn launched frogmen into the Egyptian bases of Alexandria and Port Said. Six frogmen were forced to the surface and captured; in return all they had to show for their sacrifice was the sinking of a small dredging vessel.[41] On the next day, June 6, the Egyptians in turn sent two destroyers with some escorting vessels against Elat, one submarine against Haifa, and one submarine against Ashdod. In the event the task force in the Red Sea never made it to Elat, turning back after its presence had been detected by the IAF—a wise decision, some would say.[42] The submarines were located by Israeli sonar, attacked with depth charges, and forced to retreat without having achieved anything in particular.

At the time and for years thereafter, the Six Day War was represented as an almost flawless victory; "a superb application of the strategy of indirect approach,"[43] enthused Basil Liddell Hart. A great victory it had undeniably been, and much of it was due to the IAF. Properly equipped and properly commanded, it attacked without warning, taking Egypt's air force (its strongest enemy) totally by surprise and all but annihilating it before it could respond. During the next few days the IAF roamed over the area at will, using open terrain (there was little cover to be found in the Sinai or on the slopes of the Golan Heights) and clear skies to rain destruction upon stationary and moving targets. The IAF helped Tal's and Yoffe's Centurions demolish the Egyptian antitank "shields" they faced; the IAF, too, was responsible for most of the vast destruction inflicted on the retreating Egyptians at Mitla Pass. Yet victory did not come cheap: some 40 aircraft,[44] almost all lost to antiaircraft fire. The short turnaround time of its aircraft, plus the fact that many more pilots than planes were available, enabled the IAF to fly far more sorties than its order of battle could be expected to deliver (as many as 1,000 a day).[45] Still, had the campaign lasted longer inevitably the pace of operations would have slowed as aircraft suffered damage or required maintenance, pilots became exhausted, and the like.

Thanks in large part to the IAF's command of the sky, the IDF's ability to switch units from one front to another also commands respect, acting as a force multiplier and playing a critical role in its victory. In all, about one-quarter of its forces had been engaged on more than one front. Not so its Arab enemies, who were operating on external lines and without unity of command. In spite of the appointment of an Egyptian general to command the Jordanian army, cooperation with the Egyptians was tenuous in the extreme. In their turn, the Syrians cooperated with nobody at all and, apart from shelling the settlements, merely stood by with arms folded as their allies were destroyed.

The picture on each individual front was similar. With commanders riding along, Israeli brigades went where they were sent. They did what they were told promptly, without hesitation, and as Eytan's paratroopers south of Rafah demonstrated, even when communications were difficult or absent. Not so on the Arab side, where perhaps two-thirds to three-quarters of all units involved were intended for stationary defense only, occupying positions and sometimes holding them but being unable to support one another. When directly attacked, Arab units generally fought well. However, as in 1956 they proved not to have the flexibility to respond to threats directed against them from unexpected directions—or even to shift artillery fire with sufficient speed.⁴⁶ To make things worse, except for the Jordanians most commanders positioned themselves in the rear; indeed not seldom the officers were the first to flee.

Thus in the Sinai a combination of faulty command arrangements and a lack of initiative on the part of subordinate commanders was largely responsible for the rapid fall of Abu Ageila. Probably because King Hussein had not yet made up his mind whether to enter the war in earnest, the crack Jordanian 60th Armored Brigade spent the whole of June 5 in the Jordan Valley doing nothing at a time when, the IAF being occupied elsewhere, it might have come to Jerusalem's aid. The Syrians also failed to use the night of June 9–10 to organize a counterattack against the exhausted Israelis who just reached the escarpment (something they might well have done given the IAF's limited night capability).

As to Israeli strategy and operational art, Liddell Hart's claim that this had been "the most brilliant application of the indirect approach in history" was clearly nonsensical. Contrary to the usual interpretation, the Egyptians were not deceived as to the direction from which the main Israeli assault would come—from north to south—and positioned their forces to meet it at Rafah, Al Arish, and Abu Ageila; to the south was only the Shazly Force, not even attacked by the IDF. There was nothing particularly indirect about 7th Armored Brigade's thrust into the northern Sinai or Elazar's battle against the Syrians. As we saw, the one "indirect" part of that operation, a heliborne landing on the southern edge of the Golan Heights, had to be postponed as the paratroopers were stuck in traffic. When it finally came, the bird had already flown.

Mounted as it was from the north and rear, the attack at Abu Ageila was in some sense "indirect." Still, its success was due above all to the operational genius of Ariel Sharon in precisely planning the battle and coordinating his forces; once it had been won, however, he failed to exploit. In fact it might be argued that the most "indirect" ground operation was the one by Yoffe's *ugda*. Refusing to be stopped by "impassable" terrain, it penetrated between two Egyptian strongholds. Next one of its brigades bottled up the Egyptian forces in the northeastern Sinai; the other, in an even more daring maneuver, reached out to block Giddi and Mitla Passes. Yoffe, however, was a reserve officer, as was the commander of his "I" Brigade, Col. Yissaschar Shadmi. Neither was any longer in the promotion game. Perhaps for this reason their achievement tended to be underplayed; after all, it would hardly do for regulars to admit that civilians could do as well.

Passing from the operational level to the tactical level: It could be argued that the most important fault that would become evident in 1973— namely, insufficient cooperation between the tanks and the rest of the ground forces—was present in 1967. Only Sharon, a bona fide tactical and operational genius, knew how to "orchestrate" every unit at his disposal, using the strengths of one to cover the weakness of another and vice versa; elsewhere it was a different story (as at the Jirardi Defile). So too the Golani infantrymen on the Golan Heights.[47] In contrast the mechanized brigade that outflanked Jerusalem from the north did much better against the Jordanians, driving as it did over terrain unsuitable for armor but making proper use of its attached Sherman tanks and consequently suffering fewer casualties. However, the Israelis were reluctant to recognize this shortcoming. Instead they stuck to the "all-tank" approach fully three decades after it had been abandoned by every other leading army in the world—with grave consequences (see Chapter 12).

In war morale is to materiel as three to one. To the Israelis, this was not an instrumental, Clausewitzian war. Far from a continuation of policy by other means, the war broke out at the precise moment when policy, in the form of Abba Eban's humiliating requests for Western aid in opening the Straits of Tyran, broke down. It seemed unable to guarantee Israel's continued existence, with the result that, among a people who had always been rather trigger happy, *en brera* took over and ends and means became fused.[48] The fact that Elazar, on Rabin's orders and with Eshkol's consent, had consistently provoked the Syrians was known only to a very few. Nor was it until almost thirty years later that Shimon Peres stated that, in his opinion, Israel in 1967 had possessed whatever it would have taken to deter the war.[49] Though perhaps unjustified in retrospect, the raw fear that gripped the Israeli public during the waiting period was real enough. It led to an iron consensus or, to put it in a different way, one of those rare instances when the political objectives of the state all but coincide with the feelings of its people.

As often written and said at the time, when the IDF finally broke loose it was like a tremendous spring being released. Nothing mattered any longer, not even the fear of incurring casualties. Was not Nasser a second Hitler? Was not another Holocaust just around the corner? Thus motivated, the Israelis fought like demons. In the Jirardi Defile, at Ammunition Hill, and in front of some of the stronger Syrian positions they "stared death in the eye until *he* looked away" (in the words of Col. Shmuel Gonen at 7th Armored Brigade's victory parade), freely giving their lives even when more thought and less brawn might have dictated different, and better, tactics. The same is true of the air force, most of its losses due to pilots flying very low to hit targets accurately with the comparatively primitive equipment available.

In general, the outcome of the Six Day War was welcomed with great fanfare not only in Israel but in the West as a whole. In part this was because the victory was seen as a defeat for the Soviet Union during the Cold War; after all, *Western* arms and *Western* doctrines triumphed over *Eastern* ones, even if the latter had been executed by Arabs and even though the former had often been obtained by Israel with great difficulty and in spite of the owners' reluctance to sell. Then, too, Israel's lightning victory saved the West from the horns of a dilemma: either come to its aid in accordance with the American-British-French declaration of 1957 or stand by as it went down to defeat. At bottom, though, the war was perhaps seen not so much as a triumph of Jew over Arab as of modernity over backwardness.[50] The war happened to take place toward the end of a twenty-odd-year period during which the armed forces of one "Western" country after another had suffered defeat at the hands of insurgents in their former colonies—and when those of the largest "Western" country of all were being first halted and then defeated by little brown men (and women) wearing black pajamas. Thus it helped reaffirm those countries in the feeling of their own superiority. As *The Economist* trumpeted: "They did it!"[51]

In Israel itself the IDF and its victory were also celebrated by all possible means. During the war the media, especially the publicly owned radio stations (there was no television), had been relatively restrained. Once it was over, however, all caution was thrown to the wind, and the feeling prevailed that a miracle had just occurred. Such a victory, many felt, could only have come about as a result of divine intervention. A crop of new popular songs sprouted almost immediately. The most famous (actually written just before the war but quickly modified to suit the circumstances) was devoted to "Golden Jerusalem"; others, less well known, serenaded everything from the beauties of Sharm al-Sheikh ("which is always in our hearts") to the "thousands of men" (in reality, a battalion) who had assaulted Ammunition Hill and, shedding their blood, turned it into "sacred" ground. Dozens of coffee table books were published; some even included some empty pages so heroes could write down reminiscences for grandchildren to read and profit from.

Referring to Germany's victory over France in the Franco-Russian War of 1870–1871, Nietzsche had warned his countrymen against the fallacy that a military victory constituted proof of superior culture.[52] After 1967

Israelis (and others) cast his advice to the wind, looking for and dully finding "underlying" causes that explained their victory while also "proving" that it could not have happened otherwise and would happen again in the next war. Thus entire books were produced to show that Israel had "The Power of Quality" on its side.[53] Statistical comparisons were made showing that Israeli academics outpublished all their colleagues in the Arab countries combined. Even if their output only consisted of purely theoretical studies—a charge often leveled at Israeli scientists during those years[54]—such superiority presumably translated into achievement on the battlefield.

Israelis were not content to attribute victory to intellectual qualities alone. From his post as professor of international relations at Hebrew University, Yehoshaphat Harkavi, the intelligence chief who had been fired in 1960, explained that the Arab rank and file were "amoral familists." Thousands of years of oppression at the hands of their betters made them unable to understand the meaning of any organization larger than the family; consequently they would not fight for it.[55] As chief of military intelligence, Brig. Gen. Aharon Yariv told a French writer that the "Western person" found it difficult to penetrate Arab mentality. The latter was characterized by "weakness and his lack of logic, tenacity, and faith. There is no cause that he does not wholeheartedly embrace and that he cannot betray with the same good faith, without ceasing to believe in it. . . . Most of the reports of officers to their colonels, of colonels to their generals, and of generals to Nasser are full of lies." By contrast, in the IDF "we never cheat on results. We tell the truth, however painful it may be at times . . . no matter how vanity is damaged." That was what Col. Shmuel Gonen said to the same writer[56]—and he undoubtedly believed it too!

As Nietzsche also wrote,[57] war makes the victor stupid. In retrospect, the smashing victory of 1967 was probably the worst thing that ever happened to Israel. It turned "a small but brave" people (Dayan's words during his radio address on the morning of June 5),[58] who with considerable justification believed itself fighting an overwhelmingly powerful coalition of enemies for dear life, into an occupying force, complete with all the corrupting moral influences that this entails. The military lessons of the "feat of arms unparalleled in all modern history"[59] began to be studied almost immediately. Not so its moral consequences, which were clear only to a very few—among them, rumor has it, Prime Minister Eshkol, who within days of the capture of East Jerusalem was wondering how one would ever "crawl out again." In the event Israel and the IDF refused to crawl out, and before long they were confronted with new challenges that they found difficult to overcome.

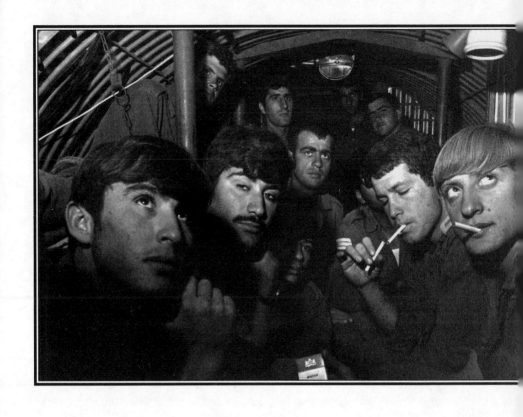

At Bay: troops cowering in a stronghold along the Suez Canal, 1969.

CHAPTER 12

AT BAY

ALTHOUGH RABIN, Weizman, and other Israeli leaders had been aware of the IDF's strength, the ease and rapidity of the June 1967 victory seem to have taken the Israeli public and government by surprise. This, after all, was experienced as a war for survival; hence absolutely no thought had been devoted to the question of how to terminate the war itself or to the fate of territories that might be occupied. Another factor was the fear that events of 1956 would be repeated, with Israel being compelled to withdraw against its will.[1]

On June 9 Dayan was handed the very first position paper that grappled with the problem. Its author, Col. Shlomo Gazit, headed the planning branch of IDF intelligence. It argued that, in return for peace and but for a few border adjustments, Israel should be prepared to hand the Golan Heights back to Syria and the Sinai Peninsula back to Egypt. The Palestinian refugee problem was to be solved by setting up an independent, though demilitarized, Palestinian state in Gaza and the West Bank. This was not the view of the other person Dayan consulted: a former intelligence colonel, Yuval Neeman, who following retirement developed into a world-renowned nuclear physicist. Israel, according to Neeman's paper (submitted to Dayan on June 11), should seek to keep the territories it had just captured. The West Bank and Gaza Strip were to be given autonomy but not statehood. As to the problem of the Palestinian refugees, it could be solved by settling them at the town of Al Arish in the Sinai.

Facing these two extremes—roughly reflecting the division between doves and hawks, a split that persists in Israel today—the Cabinet hesitated. On June 19 it met and voted for the evacuation of practically the entire Golan and the Sinai Peninsula (both of which were to be demilitarized) but excluded the Gaza Strip; in return Syria and Egypt were to agree to a formal peace, no further interference with the sources of the River Jordan, and freedom of overflight and navigation in the Straits of Tyran. However, the government was unable to make up its mind in regard to the problem of the West Bank, that is, whether to deal with one or two Arab entities—either King Hussein or some kind of local Palestinian leadership (though the latter did not yet exist). Given Israel's geographical configuration the West Bank was much more vital to security than the Golan Heights and the Sinai; finally (again unlike the Golan and the Sinai), the West Bank was considered by many to be sacred territory unjustly cut off from Erets Yisrael during the War of Independence of 1947–1949. Therefore it was not just security but ideological considerations that demanded it be retained—including the greatest prize of all, Jerusalem.

In the absence of serious pressure from abroad and in the wake of the Arab decision not to deal with Israel (no negotiations, no recognition, no peace, ran the resolution of the Arab summit at Khartoum), negotiations could not get under way, and Israel's government and public gradually found their positions hardening. For Israel, at the time under Labor government, ideological and religious considerations, however noisily they were presented, played only so much of a role among key decisionmakers such as Dayan, Allon (the minister of labor), and Prime Minister Eshkol. Yet recently published documentation shows that the importance of the Occupied Territories to preventing another Arab attack against Israel was taken very seriously—as if the war had not demonstrated how easily the Arabs might be attacked and defeated by Israel.

In fact, the war totally transformed Israel's strategic situation. In the international arena, it brought Israel squarely into the Cold War. The June 1967 victory had been against Soviet allies who were armed with Soviet weapons, supported by Soviet military advisers (the IDF claimed to have overheard them chattering on radio networks), and to some extent under Soviet political protection. As Israel's relations with the Soviet Union, heretofore decent more or less, deteriorated—immediately after the war all the Eastern Bloc countries broke diplomatic ties—the country found itself more dependent on the West and more welcome to the bosom of its leading member, the United States. Whatever the political disagreements between Washington and Jerusalem, within months after the war the IDF began to receive a trickle of U.S. weapons, which soon grew to a flood. Now, whenever Israel clashed with Syria or Egypt the superpowers would be facing off eyeball-to-eyeball—thus placing the IDF's military activities under much tighter constraints.

In the Middle East the demographic relationship between Israel and its neighbors remained as it had been. Consequently, any chance that Israel had of imposing peace on its neighbors remained as remote as ever; however, the war transformed the borders and made them much easier to defend.[2] In the north, occupation of the Golan Heights ended the Syrians' ability to shell Israeli settlements and secured the sources of the River Jordan. It also denied the Syrian army the advantage of height, a most important consideration in an age when the kind of accurate hits necessary to stop an advancing armored column could only be achieved by means of direct-fire weapons. In the east the Jordan Valley was considerably shorter and much easier to defend compared to the old armistice line, the more so because the topography made it almost impossible for any attacker to cross the river in front of a defender holding the hills. In the south the capture of the Sinai, besides leaving Sharm al-Sheikh in Israeli hands, replaced the land border between Israel and Egypt with a water border—"the most formidable antitank trench in the world," as common wisdom had it. On all three fronts, considerable room for strategic maneuver had been created. The Arab armies were now much farther away, "Old" Israel was beyond the range of hostile artillery fire, and even the air force had gained precious warning time—in the south, at any rate.

Though they were much easier to defend, the new borders paradoxically vitiated the strategic and operational doctrines heretofore at the heart of the IDF and that, indeed, were largely responsible for its success. Until now it had been clear to general headquarters (GHQ) that, the country being impossible to defend, the IDF would have to take the initiative in any war so as to campaign on enemy territory and break the forces of the other side by means of blitzkrieg. Now, however, the possibility of conducting defensive operations presented itself, at least until the reserves arrived and enabled the counteroffensive to begin; therefore, although preemption was still often talked about, in practice it did not take place. If troops actually in place were to hold out until reserves could be deployed, then fortifications would have to be built, another deviation from pre-1967 theory and practice. Furthermore, to counter the enemy's numerical superiority over the IDF's mobilized forces at the outset of any future war it was proposed to employ the IAF. This in turn meant that the IAF had to abandon its doctrine of obtaining air superiority first and instead act as "flying artillery."

As we saw, one of the critical factors in the June 1967 victory was the IDF's ability to operate on internal lines, which, compared with Arabs, increased its force by as much as 25 percent. Following the occupation of the Sinai, however, Israel's communications from Mount Chermon to the Suez Canal were more than twice as long as before; given there was no proper railnet, this was longer than the ground forces and the IAF could sustain. Thus Israel, though still fighting on internal lines and thus making it impossible for the Arabs to concentrate their forces, would no longer be able to shift forces from one front to another as easily as before. Add to this increased costs in supplying and maintaining forces deployed some two hundred miles away from the demographic, industrial, and transportation centers.

Last but not least, the 1967 victory revived the debate concerning the relative importance of the IDF and civilian settlements in defending the country. This debate had a political and a military aspect, as it still does.
Politically, and as had been the case before 1948, it was argued that only settlements could assure a continued Israeli presence; but for them the government
would have found it much harder to resist international pressure in favor of
withdrawal. Militarily it was expected that settlements, although unable to
resist an invading regular army (as, albeit with aid from PALMACH, some
of them *had* done in 1947–1948), would occupy territory and play a role in
combating guerrilla warfare and terrorism. Depending on the area in question, these conflicting views led to different solutions.3 Thus, in the Golan,
the initiative to settle was taken by the Jordan Valley *kibbutsim* almost immediately after the war had ended; only ex post facto did the government rat-
ify their action and provide support. In the West Bank, Dayan wanted to hold
the watershed but, given this was a densely populated region, thought that
a purely military presence would be enough. His views were rejected in favor
of those of Yigal Allon, who demanded that Israel hold the virtually empty
Jordan Valley and, to reinforce its hold, settle it as well.4 Only in the vast
expanses of the Sinai was there no question of using settlements in order to
create political facts on the ground (although a few feeble attempts to settle
were made). Still, even there the area adjacent to the Gaza Strip, which Israel
did not intend to return to Egypt, was settled from 1974 on.

On the face of it the decision whether and where to settle was a purely
political one that involved civilians. In practice, though, the dominant
question was always "security" considered in its broadest sense—the more
so because it was often the IDF (by means of NACHAL) that provided
"cores" for the new settlements. The result was that the role of the defense
establishment in the national decisionmaking process, which compared to
other countries had always been large, was increased still further.5 Nor did
this situation change in March 1969, when Eshkol died and was replaced by
the formidable Ms. Meir. Having made her way to the top via the Jewish
Agency's political department and later the MAPAI Party apparatus, she
knew less about defense than either of her predecessors. Willy-nilly she
retained Dayan, whose position as the idol of public opinion was unassailed
and unassailable, but she also leaned heavily on her old crony, the hawkish
Yisrael Galili, who served as minister without portfolio. Galili in turn was
closely allied with fellow left-winger Allon. When the agenda turned to
defense these three would be joined by Foreign Minister Eban, the IDF
chief of staff, and perhaps the chief of military intelligence. Together they
formed Golda's famous "kitchen Cabinet," where, over homemade cookies
and with dishes in the sink, all the most important decisions were made.

In Israel, most Cabinet ministers had never been privy to classified defense information. Now confronted with the prestige of a defense minister and military machine who supposedly had just saved the country from oblivion by winning one of the most smashing victories in history, even fewer were inclined to argue. On a lower level the same was true, owing to the greatly increased portion of national resources that now went the IDF's way. In 1966, the last year of "normalcy," that portion had stood at 12.4 percent of GNP;[6] by 1971 (the year after the 1969–1970 War of Attrition and thus one of relative peace) the figure had doubled to 24.7 percent. In terms of foreign currency spent on arms the increase was even greater, from $200 million to $670 million.[7] The country's heretofore modest arms manufacturing capabilities were also expanding into a true military-industrial complex (see Chapter 16). Much more than had been the case under Ben Gurion and Eshkol before 1967, Israel became like a sailing boat with an oversized keel—difficult to steer in any direction not first approved by, and serving the interests of, the defense establishment.

Against this double background of growing resources and an increasingly powerful voice in national affairs, it is no wonder that the mean, lean fighting machine of pre-1967 days became transformed. One of the first decisions was to increase the period of conscript service to three years for men and two and a half for women, thereby considerably augmenting the number of personnel available for setting up new units and for undertaking "current" security operations along the borders and in the Occupied Territories. By 1973 the twenty-one brigades the IDF had possessed in 1967 increased to twenty-six to thirty (with several of the former mechanized infantry ones converted to armor).[8] Moreover, the task forces of old were now consolidated into permanent divisions complete with their own headquarters, staffs, divisional troops, and the like. To solve the resulting organizational problems another rank, that of *tat-aluf* (brigadier), was inserted between that of *aluf mishne* (colonel) and *aluf* (brigadier general). The outcome was that the COS, as the highest-ranking officer, went up from major general to lieutenant general; his immediate subordinates, the brigadier generals, became major generals.

Even more important than numerical expansion was the improvement in materiel that took place. Whether because of financial difficulties or because various states refused to sell it arms, the IDF prior to 1967 had been a relatively poor army, to the point that in 1964 more men were available than arms and the decision was made to cut back the length of conscript service from thirty to twenty-six months[9] (after a year, with new arms coming from West Germany, the IDF reversed itself). Almost all arms had been provided by France and Britain, with only a trickle of U.S.

arms coming in the form of Hawk antiaircraft missiles and M–48 Patton tanks. Immediately after the Six Day War, however, French Pres. Charles de Gaulle blocked the delivery of fifty Mirage V fighter-bombers already paid for; in January 1969 the prohibition was transformed into a total embargo (though individual French officials and firms sometimes defied their government and continued supplying Israel as best they could for as long as they could). With its entire order of battle consisting of French-built machines, the IAF felt a particularly heavy blow. For a time it was desperate for new aircraft and spare parts.

In the event, the French embargo resulted not in the gradual suffocation of the IDF but, on the contrary, in its transformation into a modern army well armed from the much larger U.S. arsenals. Among the first weapons to arrive were the A–4 Skyhawk attack aircraft, which had been promised before the war.[10] Then, after considerable bargaining, the much more powerful F–4 Phantom fighter-bombers arrived during the winter of 1969–1970. By October 1973 the IAF had some 150 of the former and 100 of the latter; the total number of first-line combat aircraft had been doubled to somewhat over 400. Even these figures underestimate the magnitude of the change, however, since Skyhawks and Phantoms could carry four to six times more ordnance than older French aircraft and deliver it much more accurately. Aided by South Africa, whose air force also used the Mirage III, the IAF was able to keep some of its own Mirages flying. In addition it started building its own version of the Mirage V on the basis of stolen blueprints, although the operational number in October 1973 is not clear.

On the ground the problems created by the French embargo were less serious, yet the transformation that took place was no less far-reaching. In 1966 a couple of the new British Chieftain tanks were brought over for tests. Although Tal, commander of the armored corps, liked them, they were deemed too expensive, and in the end it was decided to develop a native tank.[11] In the interim TSAHAL pressed some 200 captured T–54 and T–55 tanks into service; with twenty tons less armor than the Centurion, these tanks were not a satisfactory solution. It also purchased M–60 tanks from the United States, bringing the total order of battle to little short of 2,000. Though the old Shermans retained their dangerously flammable gasoline engines, the rest came with diesel engines or, in the case of the Centurions and M–48s, were converted to diesel. They also carried or were converted to carry the redoubtable 105mm gun.

While the air force and armored corps were being allocated more than 80 percent of all available resources,[12] the equipment of the ground forces was less satisfactory. U.S.-built M–109 and M–107 self-propelled cannons (155mm and 175mm respectively) were purchased and took their place alongside the self-manufactured 105mm guns atop Sherman chassis, known as "Priests"; the IDF also had available locally manufactured 160mm mortars. Yet quantitatively, artillery, although no longer towed and thus capable of keeping up with the tanks, was still suffering from neglect (when war came in 1973 the ratio of tanks to self-propelled guns was approximately 5:1[13] instead of 2–3:1 as it ought to have been if each armored division had been provided with its full artillery complement). The situation of the mechanized infantry was even worse, only about one-seventh being converted from the antiquated M–3 half-tracks to the more modern M–113 APCs. Even in the field of small arms progress was limited. The USSR saw to it that every Egyptian and Syrian infantryman was equipped with the excellent Kalashnikov assault rifle, but its Israeli-made equal, the Galil, began to be issued to some units only in the last months before October 1973. Most still carried their old FN automatic rifles and Uzi submachine guns. Incredible as it sounds, some even had model 98 Mauser rifles, the "98" referring to 1898, the first year they were produced.

With its forces thus undergoing rebuilding and expansion, the IDF also transferred a growing part of its deployment to the Occupied Territories. On the Golan Heights, in the West Bank, and in Gaza and the Sinai some of the former Arab armies' bases were taken intact; this included the enormous former Egyptian base at Bir Gafgafa, airfield and all. Elsewhere new headquarters, training bases, depots, and of course fortifications were built at great cost. Military intelligence also moved into the Territories, setting up its characteristic electronic listening posts; as a result, from the Sinai through the Jordan Valley all the way to the Golan many of the tallest hills were soon festooned with mysterious antennae, their exact function being clear only to the initiated. Other buildings housed the military government that had been instituted to look after—according to the Israelis—or hold down—according to their enemies—the populations of the West Bank and Gaza Strip. Like the rest they had to be linked by means of roads, electric and telephone wires, water pipes, and so on, representing a huge investment that necessarily subtracted from monies for combat arms.

These were the years when IDF prestige was at its zenith. In this situation it had no trouble attracting and retaining high-quality manpower for the professional army. As one survey showed, two out of three officer candidates thought that "being a combat officer will make me rise in the estimation of the past generation"; a similar percentage thought that "being a good soldier is a proof that one is worth something."[14] Youngsters who for one reason or another were disqualified for service felt deeply hurt, sometimes mounting wild escapades to prove their worth to themselves and peers. Conversely the handful[15] who refused to accept the common view of the IDF as the glory of creation and did not want to serve were regarded as psychiatric cases. Every time a commander returned from a raid the media automatically characterized him as *yeffe toar* (handsome); meanwhile announcements coming out of the IDF's public relations office were believed as if holy writ. Despite these facts the growth in the army's size, the increase in the number and variety of its missions, and the fourfold extension of the territory over which it was deployed probably led to decreased cohesion—a fact that became obvious during the October War, when there suddenly appeared large numbers of psychiatric casualties.[16] No longer could everybody know everybody else, a fact the General Staff recognized when, on top of the old system of Tsiyun Le-shevach (literally honorary mention, referring to Mentioning in Dispatches) it decided to institute a regular system of decorations as in other armies.

In January 1968 Rabin's term ended. His replacement was Maj. Gen. Chayim Bar Lev (later a lieutenant general), an officer whose calm and deliberate professionalism (he spoke v-e-r-y s-l-o-w-l-y) helped him win the job against his main competitor, "wild" Ezer Weizman.[17] Reflecting the war's supposed lessons, he was the first COS since Laskov to have served as commander of the armored corps, but unlike Laskov (the perfect all-arounder) he was an armored specialist. He was a comparatively gentle character, and the future would show he did not really have whatever it takes to succeed in the rough-and-tumble of Israeli politics. He was an effective commander, however, and when brought back into service as a reservist in 1973 he proved able to create order out of chaos while keeping even the most difficult subordinates in check. During his four-year term the transformation of the IDF—from an army with an almost exclusively offensive orientation to one that, initially at least, expected to defend and hold out—was completed.

There was, in fact, a lot to defend. Up and down the new lines the cease-fire proved tenuous, and one incident followed another. Opposite Lebanon, a troublesome frontier for the first time in many years, the PLO fired mortar rounds and Katyusha rockets into Galilee. On the Golan Heights infiltrators planted mines and blew up installations. More trouble was caused by the Syrian army, which from time to time engaged the IDF in artillery and tank battles (although on the whole its size remained strictly limited). In the Jordan Valley the PLO, rapidly building a state within a state in the refugee camps, also fired rockets and repeatedly tried to infiltrate parties into the West Bank. Their objectives were to sow mines, attack patrols and settlements, and reach into the interior to stir the indigenous population to resistance. Finally, on the Suez Canal the Egyptian army sent raiding parties across and engaged in occasional artillery duels. On the northern and southern fronts the incidents sometimes escalated, causing one or both sides to call in their air forces, usually with sad results for the Arabs as the IAF shot down their planes. Israel also used its navy in its operations against Lebanon and Egypt.

A blow-by-blow account of these hundreds of incidents would be tedious. Tactically many of them displayed a brilliance that was sans pareil; given the feeling of *en brera* and the IDF's exalted status in the eyes of the Israeli public, it was not yet constrained by the need to minimize casualties (as it later would be). Perhaps the single most spectacular operation was the December 1969 raid against Beirut International Airport, following several terrorist attacks on El Al aircraft.[18] Excellent intelligence provided information on the type and location of each aircraft, making possible meticulous planning and training. Helicopters carrying commandos knifed in undetected, landing at four different spots. They blocked the road leading to the airport with caltrops. In a perfectly coordinated action the commandos blew up thirteen aircraft belonging to various airlines. The operation took exactly twenty-nine minutes, not a single casualty being caused or suffered.

Less successful was the earlier operation mounted against the PLO in Jordan (March 1969). Once again the motivating factor was terrorism, this time a mine planted north of Elat; riding a bus, two Israelis were killed and twenty-seven wounded.[19] In response the IDF organized two raids, one south of the Dead Sea at Tsaffi and one north of the sea, across the Jordan at Karameh. Whereas the former went without a hitch, the latter, directed against a PLO base, ran into stiff opposition. Morning fog delayed the planned heliborne landing, enabling Yasser Arafat and many of his guerrillas to escape.[20] Then the two Israeli brigades (one armored, one mechanized) came under accurate fire from the Jordanian army. At the end of the day they withdrew, having lost some thirty killed and almost one hundred wounded[21] as well as four tanks (one of which remains on display at the military museum in Amman). Though Jordanian and PLO losses were considerably larger, the operation achieved nothing and was not repeated.

Even so, the IDF's attempts to seal off the Jordan Valley against infiltrators gradually bore fruit. First under Eytan, then under Col. Moshe Levy (the subsequent chief of staff), elite infantry units patrolled, mounted ambushes, and used helicopters to detect parties that had crossed the river into Israeli-held territory; once they were detected it was a question of tracking, cornering, and destroying the infiltrators. During the early days these troops were reckless. Geared up and seeking to justify their reputation for heroism, they assaulted enemies head-on and suffered unnecessary casualties as a result. Later, after a brigade commander had been killed and

Levy himself severely wounded, they learned to be more deliberate, carefully sealing off an area before bringing up—if the terrain permitted—tanks. The tanks finished off the guerrillas within their hiding places at point-blank range.

As the PLO increased the size of the parties it sent across, the IDF's countermeasures expanded. Along the river itself stretches of vegetation were cut away or burned, thus depriving the guerrillas of much-needed cover. Eventually the entire border was protected by minefields, a dirt road that showed footprints of those who tried to cross it, and a *gader maarechet* (security fence) that sounded the alarm when touched or cut. In later years the fence was reinforced by adding closed-circuit TV cameras and various kinds of electronic sensors. As a result of the fencing effort an Israeli firm, Magal Ltd., would grow into the world's largest manufacturer of security fences.

Still, after some three years of skirmishing, the decisive blow that put an end to *tkufat ha-mirdafim* (the period of pursuits) was delivered not by the IDF but by the Jordanian army. Ever since the Six Day War the PLO had been building its forces in the Kingdom until they numbered thousands of well-armed men. In September 1970 one faction hijacked no fewer than three Western civilian airliners to Jordan's northern desert; after releasing passengers and crews they blew up the planes. To King Hussein this was the last straw. He had to act or risk losing the country to Arafat. On the morning of September 15 he struck, using artillery and tanks to drive into the refugee camps. His troops mercilessly butchered the Palestinians and sent them fleeing—ironically enough across the River Jordan into the IDF's arms.

Three days later the Syrians intervened, sending a "small force" (according to the Israelis) or a full division with two armored brigades and one mechanized brigade (according to the Jordanians) to invade northern Jordan, where the Palestinians had "liberated" the town of Irbid. Advancing, they ran into a trap, and after some fighting the Jordanians (with Centurion tanks, their 105mm guns far outranging the Syrian T–55s) prevailed.[22] Backed by the U.S. Sixth Fleet, the IDF's role in this episode was to provide the Jordanians with air cover and, at night, illumination.[23] It also concentrated reserves in the Bet Shean sector to deter the Syrians (apparently with success, judging by what Minister of Defense Hafez Assad later told his biographer).[24]

On the Syrian and Jordanian borders, the numerous military clashes that took place during these years remained rather limited. Not so along the Suez Canal, where the massive forces deployed by both sides threatened to draw in the superpowers. Dayan, reviewing Rabin's plans for the 1967 campaign, had not wanted the IDF to reach the waterline;[25] then and later he argued that an Israeli presence there constituted an intolerable affront to the Egyptians and would only lead to further confrontations. However, when his forces once again exceeded his orders the minister of defense did not have what it took to recall them; nor, after Ms. Meir took over, did he carry his point of view in the Cabinet. Meanwhile, since the Egyptians would not allow Israeli boats to use the canal, the Israelis in turn fired on Egyptian shipping. Thus, by accident rather than design, the two sides glowered across a 150-yard waterway itself blocked by sunken ships.

Lavishly supported by the Soviets, who not only sent in arms but eventually activated 20,000 military advisers in the country, the Egyptian army recovered from its defeat with astonishing speed. Fewer than eighteen months after June 1967 its order of battle had been substantially rebuilt,[26] though restoring the self-confidence of commanders and men in the face of the supposedly invincible Israelis took much longer.[27] As mentioned above, in October 1967, Egyptian missile boats hit and sunk the old Israeli destroyer *Elat*, a sitting duck if ever there was one.[28] The IDF's response was to mount a massive artillery bombardment of Egyptian oil refineries along the canal. While Dayan boasted that "nothing is burning" (Hebrew slang for "there is no problem") except the refineries, 500,000–750,000 Egyptian civilians fled their homes, and the canal towns of Ismailia, Kantara, and Suez were turned into empty shells.

On September 8, 1968, the Egyptians in turn opened fire along the northern part of the canal, catching the IDF by surprise—some of the troops were playing football—and killing ten. Additional bombardments followed and served as cover for parties of Egyptian commandos; repeatedly, the latter crossed the canal and inflicted casualties on the Israelis. In retaliation the IDF sent aircraft to attack two bridges crossing the Nile River. Meanwhile a heliborne force landed at Naj Hamadi, far to the south, and blew up a power transmission station. The raid, which took place on the night of October 31–November 1, seems to have shocked the Egyptians, as it exposed how the entire country, not just the canal front, was wide open to attack.[29] In any case, the next few months were a lull.

Within the IDF a debate had been developing concerning the best way to defend the Sinai. One school, headed by Yisrael Tal (now in charge of developing an Israeli tank) and Ariel Sharon (in charge of training and doctrine), argued in favor of relying on counteroffensives of *egrofei shiryon* (mailed fists) concentrated in the rear, out of Egyptian artillery range; the forward area itself would be lightly held by patrols.[30] The other school differed in that it wanted, in addition to the armored reserves, a system of permanent strongholds constructed on the waterline itself. This second school, whose principal advocate was Chief of Staff Chayim Bar Lev, prevailed. His reasoning was mainly political, centering on the need to prevent the Egyptians from establishing a toehold that might be made permanent by UN Security Council resolution. Hence it was essential that a forward defense be adopted, even at the cost of putting Israeli troops under the barrels of Egypt's superior artillery and abandoning the IDF's traditional offensive doctrine.

Though Egyptian military strength had been rebuilt, the high command in Cairo well understood it did not have the capability to launch a general war with the objective of forcing the IDF out of the Sinai. It therefore opted for a limited "war of attrition" (Nasser's term) with the objective of inflicting as many casualties as possible to the enemy's limited manpower and creating political momentum to force Israel to negotiate an acceptable solution (i.e., withdraw from the Sinai and end the Arab-Israeli conflict).[31] The IDF raids, which took place in late 1968, had proved Egypt's vulnerability and forced a delay; this in turn was utilized by the IDF to build fortifications along the canal. Eventually thirty-one *meozim* (strongholds) were built at intervals all the way from the northern coast of Sinai to the city of Suez. Each was designed to provide cover for fifteen to sixty troops; positioned nearby were earthen ramps designed to serve as cover for tanks. All were linked to the rear by specially built roads that, in turn, would carry the reserves for a counterattack.

On March 8, 1969, five days after the Egyptians announced they no longer recognized the cease-fire, the War of Attrition opened with a bang. Scarcely a day passed without clashes between the two sides. The number of so-called incidents rose from 84 in March to 475 in April before falling back to 231 in May; during that period the IDF suffered forty-three killed and 103 wounded.[32] The clashes ranged from light-arms and mortar fire to artillery bombardments by dozens of guns raining hundreds of shells (mainly the trusted World War II–vintage 122mm and 130mm towed guns but also including heavier models). As the Israelis cowered in their shelters Egyptian commandos repeatedly crossed the canal and attacked the *meozim*, occasionally penetrating them and raising a flag, though they never succeeded in actually capturing any stronghold. From time to time Egypt's air force also participated. Flying its MIG–21s and Su–7s it attempted to strike targets in the Sinai but enjoyed limited success since IAF pilots almost always proved superior.

On the Israeli side the IDF's engineering corps seems to have done a credible job; except among lookouts, casualties in the *meozim* were limited. However, the troops needed to be relieved and supplied; since the gaps between them were rather large, the roads had to be patrolled. While doing this IDF units were targeted by ambushes and sudden bombardments—the latter often very accurate, directed by Egyptian observation officers who had infiltrated the area. The former IDF quartermaster, Maj. Gen. Matityahu Peled, wrote that men were being sacrificed for the sake of transporting tomatoes,[33] that staple of Israeli diets without which no meal seems to be complete (in or out of the military). The best that can be said for Bar Lev's strategy—Dayan, as usual, found a way to shift responsibility to others—is that it was dictated by political constraints. Militarily, though, the Egyptians had presented the IDF with a challenge to which it had no effective answer.

On July 20, toward the end of a particularly bad period in which IDF casualties seemed to be higher than ever, Dayan, in a measure of desperation, activated the IAF. Day and night the Mirages, Vautours, and Skyhawks screamed over Egyptian artillery positions, knocking out many but failing to inflict as much damage on the remaining enemy troops who now took over the burden of the fighting.[34] Two large air-to-air battles also took place, with twelve Egyptian aircraft being shot down; undeterred by such casualties they kept coming. IDF ground, naval, and heliborne commando units mounted operation after operation. On July 19 they raided the well-defended Island of Green in the Gulf of Suez. On September 19 they crossed over to the east bank of the Red Sea and mounted a major raid in which as many as 200 (Weizman says 300) Egyptian troops were killed.[35] On December 26 they captured and successfully took home an entire Soviet-built radar installation; on January 22–23, 1970, they temporarily took an island in the Suez Canal itself from its garrison. Tactically each raid was more brilliant than the last,[36] which, as one of the officers involved wrote in his memoirs, "led to much rejoicing."[37] But none was nearly sufficient to make the Egyptians desist.[38] In fact, from August to December 1969, 180 Israelis were killed. On November 29 the Egyptians mounted their largest raid so far, sending a company-sized force across and attacking a *maoz*.

Thus perhaps for the first time, the IDF found itself without a spare arrow in its quiver. Given the difficult situation, it was decided to activate the air force against not only front-line targets but also Egypt's economic and industrial infrastructures. Given that the IAF had always been a tactical service and did not have anything like the means needed for conducting a sustained strategic bombing campaign, just what the Israelis hoped to achieve is not entirely clear. Rabin, who was serving as ambassador to Washington, hoped to topple Nasser, and his theories seem to have found some support at home.[39] The possibility that the Soviets would respond by deepening their involvement was apparently considered but rejected as unlikely.

Its confidence bolstered by the F-4 Phantoms, the first of which had just begun to arrive, the IAF on December 25, 1969, mounted its largest operation since June 1967. It rained bombs into a fifteen-mile zone along the canal's east bank, hitting many targets including twelve SAM–2 batteries. On January 7, 1970, the campaign escalated, concentrating on military targets such as bases and depots around Cairo as well as the area of the Nile Delta but occasionally missing its objectives and inflicting damage on nonmilitary installations and causing heavy civilian casualties. Nasser refused to surrender, instead visiting Soviet patrons and inducing them to send over fighter pilots—of which the Egyptians were desperately short[40]—personnel to operate antiaircraft defenses, and batteries of SAM–3s, which were more effective against low-flying aircraft than the older, larger SAM–2s. Both types of missiles were familiar to the Americans from the Vietnam War. Now the United States provided its protégé with pods of avionics to mount on aircraft and counter the new threat.

Thus, what later would be termed the first electronic war began to develop. In fact electronics had been used in wartime at least from the time of the Blitz; the British pioneered radar (and, later, the means for countering it) and the Germans pioneered use of radio signals for navigation (which in turn were countered by the British).[41] Vietnam and the Israeli-Egyptian struggle were, however, the first occasions when modern combat aircraft were faced by electronically guided missiles in addition to older antiaircraft artillery. Equipment provided the IAF during this period included gear designed to register the pulse of radar beams guiding the missiles, warning pilots and enabling them to break away in time. It may also have included jamming equipment[42] but almost certainly did not include as yet undeveloped homing missiles capable of using radar beams to lock on targets.

In the spring of 1970 the battle climaxed. Soviet pilots had arrived, and their presence was soon detected by the Israelis, who listened to them chattering Russian on the radio; as a result, from the end of March the Israelis no longer tried to penetrate in depth but limited operations to targets along the canal. As the artillery battle raged below, the IAF concentrated on preventing the Egyptians from rebuilding their antiaircraft defenses. They rained a hail of bombs—although probably not the 20,000 tons that Egypt's minister of war, Mohammed Fauzi, claimed had been dropped during a two-day period.[43] Yet bombing did not prevent the Egyptians from laboriously constructing a vast defensive zone of sixty by twenty miles. The zone held no fewer than 1,000 concrete shelters for the thirty antiaircraft missile regiments deployed—to say nothing of the 1,000 antiaircraft guns.[44]

Late in April 1970 the end run got under way. The IDF, with the air force as its spearhead, was desperately fighting the missiles. The figures given by different sources—Arab and Israeli—differ by as large a factor as eight; clearly more Israeli aircraft were being destroyed, including some of the vaunted Phantoms (with a top speed of mach 2.4). Meanwhile the Egyptians were steadily extending defenses westward toward the canal. More and more, those defenses were being operated by the Soviets, who not only sent advisers into every Egyptian unit down to that battalion level but also maintained entire combat units of their own.[45] They manned antiaircraft batteries and flew missions, including combat, reconnaissance, and electronic warfare. Under such circumstances a clash was inevitable, and on July 25 it came. Soviet pilots flying MIG–21s pursued a flight of Israeli Skyhawks into the Sinai; when they tried a repeat five days later, they were jumped by the IAF, which shot down five. Next day the commander of the Soviet Air Force arrived in Egypt.[46]

The precise sequence of diplomatic moves that led to the cease-fire of August 7, 1970—just more than a month after this episode—need not concern us.[47] Suffice it to say that pressure had been building since March; key roles were played by the patrons, the United States and the USSR. Under the terms of the cease-fire both sides undertook to maintain a stand-down over a thirty-mile strip on both sides of the canal. Nevertheless, the Egyptians violated the agreement immediately and openly, moving antiaircraft defenses forward.[48] The missiles' "slant range" made it extremely perilous for the air force to operate not only over Egypt proper but also the canal and the western Sinai. Yet the Israelis did not react. During the next few weeks there was some desultory talk of renewing the offensive to punish the Egyptians for the violation—but desultory talk it remained.

To sum up the precise outcome of the War of Attrition is anything but easy. Clearly there could be no question of Israel being forced to relinquish the Sinai; as the next three years proved, even the more modest Egyptian objective, namely, destabilizing the Middle East to the point that serious political negotiations would get under way, was not achieved. Yet the IDF had not broken the Egyptian will to pursue the struggle; given its failure to tackle the advanced missiles after the cease-fire, Israel arguably found itself in a worse position. As Ezer Weizman wrote—many years before he converted to a dove—it was the first time since 1948 that the IDF had failed to achieve its objectives. "It is no more than foolishness to claim that we won the War of Attrition. On the contrary, for all their casualties it was the Egyptians who got the best of it. . . . We, with our own hands, smoothed Israel's path to the Yom Kippur War."[49]

In 1970, though, the October War was as yet far off. Having experienced an impending sense of doom during spring 1970—when the Soviet Union seemed poised to intervene in the struggle—Israel greeted the cease-fire with a deep sigh of relief. Weizman's remained a voice in the wilderness. Both inside and outside the IDF most people preferred to believe that the brave Israelis had once again trounced their opponents, if not decisively then at least sufficiently to force them to desist. The element of reality in this assessment cannot be denied. Equally true, however, is that outside a very narrow circle the so-called victory was misinterpreted. Instead of inducing second thoughts it led to confidence, which in turn grew into overconfidence and a determination to hang on to the Occupied Territories at any cost. Thus, even as guns fell silent, the countdown toward the next war had already begun.

CHAPTER 13

OCTOBER EARTHQUAKE

T HE WAR OF ATTRITION over, from 1970 to 1973 the borders
with Egypt, Jordan, and Syria were relatively quiet. The number
killed and wounded—always a sensitive issue in Israel where
manpower is scarce and the sense of "one big family"[1] strong—fell very
sharply. To be sure, Palestinian terrorism was beginning to raise its head.
From 1968 on there had been sporadic clashes along the northern border;
later, having been ejected from Jordan, the PLO moved to Lebanon, where
it set up a quasi-independent enclave on the slopes of Mount Chermon
known as Fatachland. From there, supported by Syria, they often rocketed,
shelled, and sent raiding parties across the border.

Also, these were the years when the air lanes to and from Israel were
coming under attack. One El Al airliner was hijacked to Algiers and set free
only after Israel surrendered some of its Palestinian prisoners. There was
an attack on an El Al plane at Zurich's Kloten Airport, and on several occasions in various countries passengers waiting to board or deplane were
attacked with guns or hand grenades. In 1972 a hijacked Sabena airliner
landed at Lyddia Airport and had to be stormed by a commando party led
by Maj. Ehud Barak. Later that year a couple of Japanese terrorists arrived
at the same airport, opened their luggage, took out submachine guns, and
killed dozens before one was killed and the other captured.[2]

In spite of these and other attacks—including that against the Israeli
team at the 1972 Olympic Games in Munich—on the whole these were
years of heady optimism fueled by strong demographic growth. A quarter-
million new immigrants arrived from Russia, helping stimulate the economy and causing new neighborhoods to grow out of thin air. Even as the
country received increasing foreign aid, during the two years after 1971
the fraction of GNP devoted to defense declined significantly, from 24.1
to 16.3 percent.[3] By 1973, Israel, along with much of the Western world,
was experiencing an economic boom that in turn led to some social tensions as heretofore underprivileged groups demanded their shares. There
were also clear signs of overheating as inflation, which throughout the sixties had been modest, reached 13 percent.

October Earthquake: Israeli bus crossing the Suez Canal soon after the war.

At the end of 1971 Bar Lev left office, the Cabinet having declined to extend his term another year. His successor was David Elazar, who during the previous two years had served as chief of the General Staff Division. Dayan's preferred candidate for *that* job had been Yeshayahu Gavish, but the minister of defense did not have it in him to enforce his views, the more so because he was distracted by his many romantic affairs (at this very time one of his paramours was trying to blackmail him by releasing tapes of his telephone conversations with her). A former commander of the armored corps, Elazar appointed, as his second in command, Gen. Yisrael Tal. The continuing tilt toward armor gathered momentum when Sharon was replaced by Shmuel Gonen, the former 7th Armored Brigade commander who in 1967 had looked straight forward. Sharon did not leave the army altogether, becoming a reserve division commander; in this way he reflected the dilemma created by victory. In 1973 the IDF was saddled with a galaxy of supposedly brilliant generals, all of whom insisted on lending a "helping" hand and many of whom got their way in one capacity or another.

Though the IDF's order of battle expanded considerably since 1967, it did not grow as much as planned. When Elazar entered office he inherited an extremely detailed acquisition plan known as "Goshen," which started with the assumption that the Arabs in 1976 would be able to confront Israel with no fewer than fifteen divisions (of which eleven would be Egyptian) and 5,000 tanks.[4] However, in the spring of 1972 it was decided to replace Goshen by a smaller plan, "Ofek I." The establishment of new formations was postponed until 1977. Of greater immediate significance were decisions such as canceling the purchase of additional naval vessels, bridging equipment, tank transporters, and APCs; the IDF was so "tanko-manic" by this time that it considered the possibility of setting up an armored division without an organic artillery regiment. The cuts were not limited to major systems. When the IDF mobilized for war in 1973, the YAMACHim did not have enough binoculars (for tank commanders) and stretchers.[5] Then and later the cuts were justified on financial grounds— the burden of defense was just too heavy for Israel's economy to carry. That was certainly one reason, and yet the decision owed as much to overconfidence in the IDF's might.

Six weeks after the War of Attrition Nasser died of a heart attack. His replacement, Anwar Sadat, did not command respect; in Egypt his nickname was the "Black Ass" for his dark skin (which he inherited from his mother, a Sudanese slave). During his first year or so in office he often spoke of 1971 as the "Year of Decision" and of his own determination to liberate the Sinai even at the cost of "a million" Egyptian lives; when the "32nd of December" (a term invented by the Israelis to derogate Sadat) passed and the promised offensive did not materialize, however, he was seen as a clown. That estimate was reinforced during the summer of 1972 when Sadat, in a surprise move, ordered the army's Soviet advisers to depart. Whatever the diplomatic implications—Sadat's move was meant to appease the United States and make it put pressure on Israel[6]—militarily the decision was considered to have "greatly eased" Israel's situation.[7] After all, was it not obvious that the Egyptians were too incompetent to operate sophisticated equipment on their own?

Came 1973 and Israeli self-confidence peaked—"our [defense] situation has never been better" was the common wisdom spread by the IDF, accepted by Golda Meir,[8] and reflected in public opinion. Independence Day 1973 witnessed a parade, the first one in five years. With Ms. Meir and Dayan on the stand and a beaming Elazar taking the salute, Israelis and foreigners were given an impressive display of the IDF's might—including the new Phantoms, M–60 tanks, M–113 APCs, and self-propelled cannons. Yet about the same time there was brief panic as the Egyptian offensive appeared imminent; some of the reserves were mobilized. The IDF's chief of intelligence at the time, Maj. Gen. Eliyahu Zeira, discounted war as unlikely, and events proved him right (those who had contradicted him were left red-faced and had to account for nearly $10 million wasted in mobilizing).[9] From then on the views of this brilliant but opinionated officer prevailed to the point that, as late as September 1973, the ministry of defense—instead of working to expand the IDF—was studying the possibility of cutting the period of conscript service from three years to two and a half years.[10]

While Israel, supported by the Nixon administration, refused to evacuate the Occupied Territories and lulled itself to sleep, the Egyptians and the Syrians were busy. According to Sadat's memoirs, the decision to go to war was made on November 30, 1972.[11] Still there could be no question of attempting to liberate the entire Sinai: Not only were the IDF and the IAF in particular much too strong; there was no reason to believe that Egypt's weakness in conducting maneuver warfare had been corrected. Even more decisive, back in 1967 Nasser probably operated on the assumption that Israel did not yet possess nuclear weapons. That was a luxury which Sadat did not have, although Israel had not tested or admitted to possessing a nuclear weapon.

As will be remembered, during the years before June 1967 the Egyptian media in particular had often referred to an Israeli bomb, and numerous urgent attempts were made to bring the matter to the attention of the superpowers. Now that their problem was presumably to launch the war while minimizing the danger of escalation, however, Egyptian attitudes changed. The entire subject disappeared; on rare occasions it was mentioned only in stating that Israel *might* be working on the bomb. From Nasser and Sadat on down, Egyptian spokesmen claimed that reports it already existed—such as that printed in the *New York Times* on November 21, 1968—were no more than part of "a psychological campaign" designed to intimidate the Arabs.[12] It is thus fairly clear that, in sticking to its arrangement with the U.S. pressure and not admitting the state of affairs, Israel created a window of opportunity and helped Sadat prepare his war. Although, to be sure, a hair-raising gamble it was and remained.

Feeling fairly certain that a limited offensive would not provoke Israel to use the six to ten bombs that, as they later claimed, they believed were available,[13] the Egyptian high command went to work. Under the direction of the minister of defense, Gen. Ismael Fahmi, and the chief of staff, General Shazly, detailed plans were drawn up.[14] To cover preparations the Egyptians constructed a tall earthen ramp along the canal. Behind it they built up forces until they numbered 200,000 men distributed between two armies; 2nd Army (north) had 110,000 men and 3rd Army (south) had 90,000. Between them the two armies possessed five infantry divisions and two mechanized divisions; two additional armored divisions came under GHQ. The intention was that the infantry should cross first while the mechanized and armored formations remained in reserve. Even so, by attaching 200 to each infantry division the Egyptians had more than 1,000 tanks ready to participate in the first attack alone.

Crossing a major waterway being one of the most difficult of all military operations, this was prepared meticulously and rehearsed many times. First, teams of commandos were to block a series of petrol pipes the Israelis laid with the intention of igniting the canal (although they later claimed that the system never reached operational status). Under cover of air strikes and a massive artillery bombardment by more than 1,000 guns of various kinds, the leading infantry assault waves were to cross in rubber boats. Heavily loaded with antitank missiles in addition to their personal weapons, webbing, and gear, they were to take up positions to head off the first counterattacks. The earthen ramp the Israelis constructed on their side of the canal was to be breached by means of high-pressure water cannons mounted on rafts floating in the water. Once pontoon bridges had been laid opposite the breaches, the vehicles and armor would cross.

Though provided with a number of mobile SAM–6 antiaircraft missiles, the Egyptian high command intended to stay within slant range of their SAM–2 and SAM–3 batteries, which remained in position west of the canal. Just how far this would allow them to advance is not clear; it cannot have been much more than six to seven miles. There they intended to consolidate and defend, the objective being—as in 1969–1970—to set in motion a political process that would lead to the liberation of the Sinai. To make sure that they would be able to carry out even this limited plan the Egyptians coordinated their offensive with the Syrians. Rather less is known about Syrian intentions. Assuming they read the *New York Times* along with everybody else, however, it is likely they did not plan an advance into Israel proper but would be content with recapturing much or most of the Golan.

Presided over by Hafez Assad (who had taken power in October 1970 in a coup), the Syrians built up a formidable array of forces between Damascus and the 1967 cease-fire line. Ultimately there were to be five divisions of which three were mechanized and two armored; in addition there were several independent brigades, including one sent over by the king of Morocco. The approximately 1,300 tanks and 600 artillery pieces were covered by some 400 antiaircraft guns and more than 200 batteries of antiaircraft missiles—to say nothing of the air force's 300 or so combat aircraft. Like the Egyptians, the Syrians intended to open the offensive with a brief but intense barrage using all means, including air strikes and heliborne raids. Like the Egyptians, too, they split their advance into two main efforts, divided by the hill known as Booster. While the armored divisions stood in reserve—one for each sector of the front—two mechanized divisions were to attack in the north, one in the south. The defenses having been breached, the reserves would be thrown in. On each of the two sectors one division was to drive straight down the slopes to the River Jordan bridges. One, the 9th, was to stay in place and hold the Israelis; the two remaining ones would wheel inward on the heights themselves, thus building a pocket to trap the Israelis.

In Israel the arms shipments from the USSR and the Arab buildup along its own borders did not go unnoticed.[15] In particular, the spring of 1973 was characterized by nervousness; for example, Dayan on May 21 met with the "gentlemen of the General Staff" and ordered them "to be ready for War in June."[16] When that month came and went, however, the wind changed. In July the mercurial minister of defense was telling *Time* that no "large" war was likely during the next ten years and that, as a result, Israel's borders would remain frozen.[17] Should the Arabs decide to attack nevertheless, then the chief of military intelligence felt sure in his ability to present the government with the requisite advance warning. This in turn would enable the IDF to mobilize its reserves and deploy them on the canal and the Golan Heights. There, according to one general, it would repulse the offensive "in no time."[18]

Whether or not it had been planned that way by the Arabs, two incidents that took place in September tended to reinforce that assessment and distract attention away from the gathering storm. One grew out of a routine photo reconnaissance mission flown by the IAF over the Golan Heights on September 13; contrary to their habit the Syrians sent up Migs to intercept, and in the ensuing air-to-air battle thirteen Syrian planes and one Israeli plane were shot down.[19] The other was a terrorist attack against a train carrying Soviet Jewish immigrants from the Czech border to a transit camp at Schoenau, Austria. The Austrian government reacted by closing the camp—which in turn induced Ms. Meir to fly to Austria at the end of September in an unsuccessful attempt to make Chancellor Bruno Kreisky change his mind.[20]

By this time Israel's system of media self-censorship had begun to backfire. To be sure, the Arab buildup on both fronts did not escape notice. Feeling confident that the Arabs were incapable of going to war, however, Israeli military intelligence continued to misread the signs; the media, voluntarily refraining from publishing the news,[21] helped the IDF in its own assessment and put the public to sleep. The Syrian deployment was interpreted as a precautionary move against an *Israeli* attack,[22] whereas the Egyptian troop concentration was mistaken—as Shazly had intended it to be[23]—for another routine exercise that took place every year.[24] Still, on September 26 Dayan and Elazar felt nervous. Orders were given for an additional 4,000 mines to be laid, and four miles of antitank ditches dug, on the Golan Heights. The order of battle was doubled by flying up men of the crack 7th Armored Brigade and marrying them with tanks in storage; when war came the IDF on that front deployed almost 200 tanks divided between two brigades. While there was no last-minute attempt to reinforce the Bar Lev line, on that front too additional crews were brought in, raising the number of tanks available for immediate action to 300.

More meetings of the IDF General Staff, with Dayan present, took place on October 4 and 5. Each time the warning signs were more ominous, including, besides the state of alert that had been declared in the Arab armies and the vast military buildup revealed by continuing photo reconnaissance, the sudden withdrawal of dependents of Soviet military personnel from Egypt and Syria.[25] Still, the chief of intelligence, opinionated as ever, withheld critical evidence in his possession[26] and insisted that "the Egyptians and Syrians are not going to attack but are afraid of us."[27] Misled by his subordinate, Elazar did no more than order some additional precautions. On both fronts, all leave was canceled. For the first time since 1967, State of Readiness "C" was declared; all arrangements for the prompt mobilization of men and materiel were now in place. Last but not least, the air force was put on full alert and told to prepare for launching a preemptive strike if required. Yet when the last meeting dispersed at 1230 hours on October 5, the participants felt that a total of just under 500 tanks

available on both fronts were enough to repel any aggression;[28] indeed
Elazar wondered whether he overreacted in proclaiming the state of alert.

At 0430 hours on October 6, according to Ms. Meir's military secretary,
Yisrael Lior, he was awakened by a phone call.[29] The voice on the other side,
a senior intelligence official, announced that "this evening Egypt and Syria
will start a war." At 0800 Golda met with Galili, Allon, Dayan, and Elazar.
The last two had already met; failing to agree on the measures to be taken,
they left the final decision to Ms. Meir. The two most important issues were
the number of reserves to mobilize—*whether* to mobilize was no longer an
issue—and whether to launch a preemptive strike. A gray-faced Ms. Meir
overruled Dayan and on Elazar's advice decided that the IDF mobilize all
reserves, four divisions rather than only two. Political considerations
caused her to reject the chief of staff's demand that the IAF launch an
immediate preemptive strike against the Arab airfields and antiaircraft
defenses. Since then the question of whether such a strike might have
changed the face of the war has often been debated. War is a continuation
of policy by other means, however, and given Israel's financial and military
dependence on the United States, both decisions were definitely correct.

The day the Arabs selected—for their own reasons, those being the state
of the moon and tides in the Suez Canal[30]—also happened to be Yom Kippur. Normally this is a day of eerie quiet; those who do not pray in syna-
gogue fast at home, and there is no vehicular traffic in the streets. However,
at around 0800 hours the peace was interrupted by a pair of Phantom fighters roaring over central Israel, alerting the population that something
unusual was afoot. Since broadcasting services had been closed for the day
the call-up had to be carried out by teams of soldiers going house to house.
At the time, much was made of the "perfidious" nature of the Arab attack,
taking place as it did on the holiest of holy days. In fact that timing probably accelerated mobilization, given that everybody could be found at home
or in the immediate neighborhood and that there was no traffic clogging the
roads.

But the Egyptians and Syrians never gave the IDF time to complete
mobilization. At 1400 they opened fire, the hour being a compromise, the
two partners attacking from different directions yet each wanting the sun
to be in the enemy's eyes. On both fronts the offensive was covered by battery upon battery of antiaircraft missiles and guns. On both fronts it
opened with air strikes as well as tremendous artillery barrages. But owing
to a combination of geographical circumstance and the different objectives
Sadat and Assad set their armies, that is where the resemblance ended. In
the south it was a question of methodical and deliberate advance by
infantry and tanks toward a line that was to be held against counterattack.

In the north, by contrast, the Syrians planned to overrun as much of the Golan as possible as fast as possible and accordingly went for a classic offensive operation spearheaded by armor.

On the Egyptian front, the first shots found the IDF in a state of manifest unreadiness (see Map 13.1). When Elazar replaced Bar Lev at the end of 1971, the debate concerning the best way to defend the Sinai was renewed. In the absence of agreement a new compromise was struck: Out of thirty-one *meozim* along the canal about half were closed, leaving the front line occupied by no more than 450 or so troops. To reinforce them a second line of defense—using positions known as *taozim* and located some ten miles in the rear—was constructed. They in turn were linked by the so-called artillery road, a north-to-south artery for moving reserves laterally along the front. The mobile forces consisted of a reinforced armored division with three brigades in all. Of those one was in readiness approximately twenty miles behind the canal; from there it could link up with the *meozim*. Still fearing to provoke the Egyptians, however, Gonen on the morning of October 6 misunderstood or disobeyed an order to deploy a second brigade along the lateral road.[31] Instead, both his remaining brigades remained at Bir Gafgafa, far in the rear. As a result, the Egyptians' crossing was resisted by exactly *three* tanks; the early counterattacks were mounted with one brigade rather than two.

The IDF's plan for repelling an invasion was known as "Shovach Yonim (Dovecote)" and had been rehearsed many times.[32] It assumed forty-eight hours' warning, enough time to enable the armored forces in the Sinai to take up forward positions in support of the *meozim* while the reserves arrived. Next, using as their base one of the special marshaling yards that had been constructed out of earth along the canal and relying on ferries as well as specially developed bridging equipment, they were to cross to the other side. In the event the forty-eight-hour warning did not materialize. Given the fact that the canal is separated from Israel by more than 100 miles of desert, the IDF could easily have afforded to let the Egyptians advance until they were beyond antiaircraft missile range. However, such a course would have implied abandoning the *meozim*. It also ran counter to the IDF's plans—which did not envisage surrendering any territory—not to mention its instincts.

Thus, during the first few hours Gonen's objective (which he sought to attain with one brigade instead of two as originally planned) was to reestablish the situation that, *if* warning had been served and *if* everything had gone according to plan, ought to have served as the starting point for the crossing operation. At first he tried to command the battle from as far away as Beer Sheva, but even when he had advanced his headquarters to

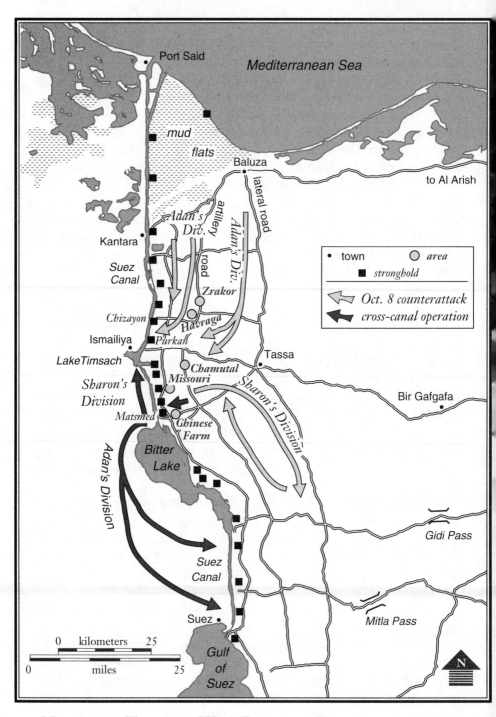

MAP 13.1   THE 1973 WAR, EGYPTIAN FRONT

Um Hasheiba, some twenty-five miles east of the canal, he still could not obtain a clear picture of unfolding events. At one per ten miles of front there was no question of the *meozim* performing their function as lookouts, to say nothing of men driven from observation posts by one of the heaviest artillery bombardments in modern history. Throwing themselves at the pontoon bridges the Egyptians were constructing across the canal, the IAF's planes met with very heavy antiaircraft fire and were unable to bring back information.33 With no information about the Egyptian center of gravity, and distracted by the *meozim*'s desperate calls for help, Gonen's tankers drove forward in dribs and drabs along the roads to the canal. The first to go were the tanks of the forward brigade; during the night they were joined by the two others. The Egyptian *chiri biri* (rotten infantry) was expected to run. Instead it stood its ground and "nailed"34 Israeli tanks— an unheard-of event that was somehow felt to be unfair.

When morning dawned on October 7, all the *meozim* along the canal had already either fallen or been surrounded; two-thirds of the Israeli tanks originally in the Sinai had been lost. Gonen, however, was beginning to feel optimistic, given that the reserves were arriving faster than expected. He divided the front into three sectors, each to be occupied by an armored division: General Adan's in the north, General Sharon's in the center (both of these consisted of reservists), and General Mandler in the south with the remains of two regular armored brigades (the ones previously at Bir Gafgafa). Admittedly not all the reserve units were in top shape, Sharon's tanks having driven all the way on their tracks and Adan's arriving without organic artillery and after having been mauled by Egyptian commandos on the way from Al Arish.35 All were somewhat disorganized and suffered from shortages, including the vehicles carrying the technical and medical services.36 Still, and although his leading forces were situated some six miles to the rear of the starting positions they should have occupied to carry out Shovach Yonim, Gonen felt the time had come to think about a counterattack.

During the afternoon the plan was worked out in a meeting among Elazar, Gonen, and Adan (Sharon arrived late and had to be briefed separately).37 The dominant factor was the IDF's lack of reserves: Between the canal and Tel Aviv there were no more than three divisions. Accordingly, instead of attacking with all forces united as classical armored doctrine would dictate, it was decided to proceed in echelon. While Mandler stood by, Adan was to attack early in the morning while Sharon joined later. Adan himself was not to attack from east to west, as Gonen's regular brigades had the previous day; instead he was to proceed north to south, rolling up the Egyptians but staying two miles away from the earthen ramp on the west side of the canal, which was "swarming with [Egyptian] infantry equipped with antitank weapons." Still, he was to rescue as many of the remaining *meozim* as possible. Arriving near the area known as Chamutal, about midway down the canal and just north of the Great Bitter Lake, he was to link up with Sharon. Together the two divisions were to effect a crossing.

How Adan could expect to stay out of range *and* rescue the *meozim*—let alone expect to cross the canal—remains a mystery. The plan was not clarified despite a series of conversations that took place that night; Dayan, Elazar, Tal (Elazar's deputy), Gonen, Magen (Gonen's deputy), Adan, and Sharon all contributed to increase the confusion by suggesting various alternatives and corrections.[38] In the end, the only clear directive came from Elazar, who felt a lively distrust of his "wild" subordinates, Gonen and Sharon, and forbade a canal crossing without his prior permission. As we shall presently see, even that directive was destined to be violated, though admittedly only thanks to the overheated imagination of a junior IDF officer who was listening to the communications network.

At 0800 hours on October 8, Adan, supported by exactly four artillery barrels instead of the several dozen he should have had and receiving only a small fraction of the air support promised,[39] started his advance from the area around Kantara. His men were farther away from the canal than they believed, however, and consequently made very good progress while meeting hardly any Egyptians. Arriving opposite Chamutal as agreed, they found the last of Sharon's forces about to move away to the south—having been ordered to do so by Gonen for reasons that remain unclear today.[40] Nevertheless Adan's division performed its right turn and charged west toward the canal. Ordered not to cross without permission, Gonen, Adan, and Col. Natan Nir—who commanded Adan's leading brigade—all took care to stay in the rear so they might stay in contact with superiors despite Egyptian interference with the radio network. Somehow rumor spread that a crossing had taken place—which, if true, would have been a violation of orders. While the chief of staff, in the middle of a Cabinet meeting, tried to find out what was going on, his subordinates "down south" lost control of their forces. Of the two battalions that attacked separately (instead of together, as armored doctrine would have dictated), the first was thrown back with heavy losses. The second was all but annihilated; its commander, along with many of his men, was captured.[41]

Up until then Elazar and the rest, grossly underestimating the Egyptians (there was talk of "waving" them across the canal), had expected to win the war with comparative ease. The failure of the first counteroffensive plunged GHQ into gloom, however, and that evening a stunned public listened to Brigadier General (ret.) Yariv, the former intelligence chief, explain on radio and TV that this was a war and not a picnic. The defeat of October 8 was not the last. Having wasted the afternoon driving south in pursuit of some imaginary "disaster" that never took place,[42] Sharon's division returned to the area that evening. On the morning of October 9 one of his brigades tried its luck against Chamutal but met with the usual hail of antitank missiles and was repulsed with losses.[43]

On the positive side, that evening Sharon's reconnaissance battalion was able to locate the seam between Egypt's 3rd and 2nd Armies.[44] Driving into it, it reached the canal just north of the Greater Bitter Lake without firing a shot. His tactical instincts aroused—he had always believed in taking the enemy from the rear—Sharon called Elazar's deputy, Tal, and requested permission to cross.[45] However, GHQ had been chastened by the previous day's experience and wanted to wait until after the Egyptians had committed their armored reserves to the east bank. On the next day a frustrated Elazar sent out General Bar Lev to take charge of the southern front from Gonen, leaving the latter in place but reducing him to a figurehead.[46] With that the Egyptian front calmed down for a few days as events on the Golan took priority.

Although hampered by its decision to defend the *meozim*, the IDF in the Sinai possessed considerable room for strategic maneuver. This was much less true on the Golan Heights, which are nowhere more than twenty miles wide. Here, too, a chain of fifteen strongholds had been constructed along the purple (cease-fire) line. In the event the most important stronghold, located on Mount Chermon and containing a variety of electronic sensors, was captured during the first hours by Syrian commandos who arrived by helicopter. The rest were bypassed and, though none of them fell, played no further role in the war (see Map 13.2).

To defend against the three-division Syrian attack the IDF initially deployed just one armored brigade, the "Barak Brigade." Whether because of its previous experience or because of some misunderstanding with the CIC Northern Command, Barak's commander, Col. Benyamin Shoham, initially assumed that the "war" about which he had been warned that morning was just another border clash.[47] Accordingly, instead of keeping his forces together for a counterattack, he sent them forward to their dispersed firing positions all along the line. During the afternoon he was reinforced by 7th Armored Brigade, previously standing in reserve but now moved to take over the northern sector. This move came too late to save the Barak, whose tanks had come under antitank missile fire and then were bypassed by the advancing enemy columns (unlike the Syrians, the Israelis did not have proper night-fighting equipment). By the afternoon of October 7 Shoham had been killed and his brigade all but annihilated.

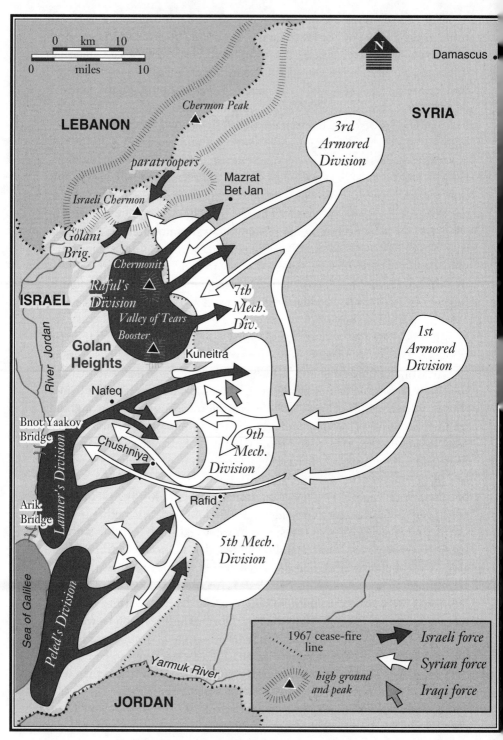

MAP 13.2   THE 1973 WAR, SYRIAN FRONT

With 7th Armored Brigade now opposing it in the north, the Syrian offensive was most successful in the south. On the morning of October 7 the Syrians recognized this fact, sending in the armored division standing in reserve for precisely that eventuality. Advancing under a heavy artillery barrage it drove on Nafeq, where the Israeli forces on the Golan had their headquarters, forcing their commander—Major General Eytan—to evacuate.[48] By afternoon the only force facing the Syrians was the IAF, its Skyhawks heroically throwing themselves at the enemy and being shot down in significant numbers.[49] CO Northern Command, Gen. Yitschak Choffi, had left the Golan Heights during the afternoon of October 6; now he ordered that the Jordan bridges be prepared for demolition.[50] At that point the first reserve units began to arrive. They belonged to a division under Maj. Gen. Moshe Peled that had previously been facing Jordan. Relations with King Hussein, however, were tolerably good, and Elazar was gambling that he would not intervene.[51] This enabled Peled to make his way to the southern part of the Golan Heights, and by morning on October 8 he took over the main burden of the defense in that sector.

Meanwhile Eytan's other brigade, 7th Armored, was fighting for its life in the north. Its men, though highly trained, were untested in combat; carefully maneuvering their fifty-ton Centurions to skirt the irrigation pipes that laced the terrain, they took up positions. Minutes later they found themselves fighting for their lives as tungsten bolts smashed into them in a hail of artillery fire. Col. Avigdor Ben Gal's men had the advantage of the terrain, which slopes gently downward from west to east, enabling them to bear down with their guns on the advancing Syrians. Still, as they came under attack by two divisions, by the evening of October 8 the situation looked bad enough—the more so because they did not have night-vision equipment and on occasion were reduced to silencing their engines to discover who was who in the dark.[52]

On the morning of October 9 the situation of 7th Armored Brigade became desperate when the Syrians committed their other reserve armored division in an effort to break through to the Jordan bridges. Unlike the remaining Syrian forces this division was equipped with T–62 tanks, the most powerful in the Arab arsenal and the only ones with guns matching the Israeli 105mm guns. As the Syrians also started landing commandos in the Israeli rear, around noon that day everything appeared to be lost. In particular, the tanks of one battalion—Col. Avigdor Kahalani's 77th—were down to their last few rounds of ammunition and being pushed back step by step toward the escarpment in their rear.[53] Then suddenly the Syrian rear echelons turned around and retreated, followed by the tanks in the forward line.

The reasons for the Syrian retreat, which, judging from the way it proceeded, must have been ordered from above, have never been made clear. It could be that their forces were being threatened on their left (south) flank, but even the Israelis seem unable to agree as to which of their units could have been responsible for the critical move. One source identifies an improvised task force numbering fifteen tanks from the defeated Barak Brigade; another identifies the advance units of a second reserve division under Maj. Gen. Dan Lanner that had climbed up the center of the Golan Heights and was turning north.54 In view of this confusion, a second and perhaps more credible explanation is that Israel, which on the evening of October 8 felt that the battle was being lost, had threatened Syria by rattling its nuclear saber (or so claimed a *Time* story published several years after these events).55

Whatever the reason for the decision, from this point on, the situation was stabilized. In the north the enemy in front of 7th Armored Brigade melted away, leaving the so-called Valley of Tears strewn with hundreds of burned-out tanks and combat vehicles. Farther south, the two divisions that had formed part of the Syrian left-wing drive were caught between Peled driving along the purple cease-fire line and Lanner. Once they had been annihilated—which took place on October 9 and 10—the time had come to mount a counterattack. It started on October 11 and consisted of 7th Armored Brigade, the three brigades of Lanner's division, and an additional brigade transferred from Peled.

Before the war the IDF's planning branch under Brig. Gen. Avraham Tamir had warned that the Arabs possessed thousands of antitank missiles.56 Yet somehow the significance of this fact had failed to sink in, leading to the futile counterattacks of the first few days. Now, however, the Israelis proved able to learn from experience—perhaps their single greatest advantage in the entire war. No longer did the tanks charge on their own; instead they moved inside an artillery "box" formed by thousands of exploding shells while they and their accompanying APCs raked every rock capable of offering shelter with machine-gun fire. Early on October 13 they met a thrust by the advance brigade of a 60,000-man Iraqi expeditionary force. Coming from the south, the brigade's tanks were driving with their hatches closed when they entered a killing ground and were all but annihilated by Lanner's tanks.57 Still, this distraction, plus fierce Syrian resistance, sufficed to slow down the advance until it petered out twenty miles short of Damascus.

According to Elazar's biographer, the chief of staff's real objective in mounting this offensive had been to make the Syrians scurry to Cairo and, by pressing the Egyptians to send their forces across the canal, facilitate an

IDF offensive on that front too.[58] If so—and hindsight may well be involved—the trick worked, since Syrian appeals for help did reach Egypt and became ever sharper in tone.[59] Whether or not the original Egyptian plan also included an advance to the passes is moot; if so, it is not clear why they allowed the days between October 10 and 14 to be wasted.[60] In any case the two armored divisions crossed the canal on Saturday, October 13. This was precisely the kind of battle the IDF liked best. For the first time in the war it was not they who had to rush forward into waiting antitank weapons; instead it was their tanks, constituting the best antitank weapons of all, that shot up the advancing enemy while themselves moving from one shelter to another to evade the Egyptian artillery. By late afternoon Adan's and Sharon's men were looking over a sight as unbelievable as it was welcome. The entire plain at their feet was dotted by hundreds of "bonfires," with Egyptian tank losses alone numbering around 250.[61] They themselves claimed to have lost no more than four tanks—though this does not include several dozen more that were hit but proved capable of being repaired.

October 14 also marked a change in the role played by the IAF. On the morning of October 6, hoping to obtain permission for a preemptive strike, Elazar had kept his aircraft armed and ready for that purpose; thus, when hostilities started and the Golan front in particular appeared under threat, many planes carried the wrong armaments and had to be rearmed before going into action. Once the war got under way they successfully maintained air superiority over Israel proper, a vitally important feat that enabled mobilization to proceed swiftly and without interruption. That accomplished, however, they divided their efforts between attacks on the canal bridges and a desperate attempt to stop the Syrian columns on the Golan—causing their commander, Maj. Gen. Benjamin Peled, to complain that his forces were being frittered away.[62]

In spite of command-and-control problems and faulty coordination with the ground forces,[63] the sorties flown in the north played a critical role in halting the Syrian columns. Not so over the Suez Canal, where the IAF achieved little, as the Egyptians quickly repaired whatever bridges were hit. On both fronts losses were extremely heavy. Between October 6 and 9 they amounted to almost one hundred aircraft destroyed or damaged,[64] a rate that, had it been sustained, would quickly have brought the force to the point where it could no longer guarantee air superiority over Israel.[65] Therefore, on the next day the IAF changed its tactics. Instead of trying to cover the entire country, it was effectively divided in two, with Maj. Gen. (ret.) Mordechai Hod commanding the northern front. Instead of trying to provide close support to the forces on the Golan Heights, it now concentrated on targets in the Syrian rear, including bridges (to interdict the approaching Iraqi expeditionary force), fuel farms, power plants, and the ports and airports where Soviet equipment was being unloaded. After Syrian surface-to-surface missiles missed their target, an airfield in northern Israel, and landed on a nearby *kibbuts*, the IAF even attacked Broadcasting House in Damascus (with the gratifying result that the announcer could be heard screaming with fear in the middle of a transmission). Still, its effect on the ground operations remained limited.

Then came the Egyptian offensive of October 14, which for the first time took the Egyptians out of the range of their antiaircraft missiles.[66] In particular, a column of vehicles tried to make its way south along the Gulf of Suez toward Sharm al-Sheikh but was caught on the way and massacred in a scene reminiscent of Mitla Pass in 1967. The day's events thus served to demonstrate the limits of Arab power. As Sharon supposedly put it to Bar Lev, "They were no different than in 1967: they came, they got killed, they ran."[67]

With the Syrians repulsed if not beaten, it became possible to shift forces from the Golan front to the Sinai. Southern Command hastily scraped together another division to take over the northern sector of the canal, thereby freeing two divisions—the ones commanded by Adan and Sharon—for the crossing. On the night of October 15–16 the operation started. As some of Sharon's forces held 3rd Egyptian Army in check by mounting demonstrations against it in the south, others were sent to secure a corridor in the seam between the two Egyptian armies that had been discovered a few days before. The corridor in turn was used by a brigade of paratroopers under Col. Danny Matt who brought along rubber boats. The crossing proceeded in absolute silence and went undetected by the Egyptians. By morning, a small foothold had been established.

This, however, was only the beginning. On October 16 the paratroopers were followed by a battalion of tanks that were transported on motorized rafts known as *timsachim* (crocodiles). After crossing they fanned out, shooting up the first Egyptian antiaircraft missile batteries and preparing for a more massive operation to come. While Sharon and Dayan—of all the senior commanders Dayan alone visited the front—pressed for as many forces as possible to be ferried across immediately, Elazar and Bar Lev hesitated. Rafts and rubber boats are totally inadequate to maintain armored divisions, which when going full-blast need hundreds of tons of supplies every day; whereas the Egyptians had been provided with Soviet-made river-crossing gear, the Israelis, to economize, had manufactured their own. Once again the man in charge was the technically minded General Tal. His efforts resulted in a monstrous contraption known as *gesher haglilim* (the roller bridge). Supported by Styrofoam-filled rollers—hence the name—it was more than 150 yards long and weighed about four hundred tons. It could be dragged forward only by tanks, and then only under specially trained crews over suitable terrain.

Initially the Egyptians had been slow to react to the creation of the Israeli bridgehead. By the night of October 16–17 they had woken up, however, and the two southernmost brigades of 2nd Egyptian Army were bearing down on Sharon's corridor. In the area known as "Chinese Farm" some of the heaviest battles of the war developed as first Adan's armor and then a battalion of paratroopers fought off the Egyptian attack; meanwhile, in their earthen "yard" along the canal, Sharon along with the forward troops of his division were being subjected to the artillery bombardment of their lives. As two divisions converged on the crossing site, the tank company that had been specially trained for dragging the roller bridge disappeared, and the work had to be carried out by another, unprepared unit. Next it was caught in a huge traffic jam. As a result of these mishaps, the bridge was not in place until the evening of October 17.

As Sharon's division took over the task of holding the corridor, it was Adan's turn to cross. With his forces decimated and blackened by previous fighting, he crossed during the night of October 17–18; on his right-rear fierce battles were still ongoing near Chinese Farm. Next, Sharon was relieved by the IDF's division to his left, now commanded by Brigadier General Magen after its original commander, Mandler, had been killed. This permitted the IDF on the west bank—known as "Africa"—to operate in two directions, north and south. As on the Golan Heights, the Israelis proved able to learn from their experiences, perhaps their greatest strength in the entire war. Instead of charging blindly forward with tanks, they used them to probe for Egyptian infantry with antitank weapons in the dense vegetation along the so-called freshwater canal that ran west of the main canal. Once that infantry had revealed its position, it was subjected to heavy artillery fire.

On the night of October 19, Egyptian General Shazly, who had been pressing for the return of the Egyptian armor from the east bank to the west bank in order to meet the Israeli threat, was relieved by Sadat.[68] Politically the decision to stick to the east bank was probably correct; it meant that, when the cease-fire came, Egypt was still holding on to its conquests in the Sinai and was thus able to claim a victory of sorts. Militarily it left the west bank forces open to the offensive by Sharon, Adan, and Magen (who had also crossed, leaving only one improvised division on the east bank). But while Sharon met with fierce resistance and made little progress on the right, Adan and Magen did much better on the left, driving south in several columns toward Suez in an all-out effort to encircle 3rd Egyp-

tian Army. By this time the Egyptian antiaircraft defenses, which throughout the crossing operation had prevented the IAF from providing effective
assistance, were finally coming under ground attack by artillery and tanks
and beginning to crack. This in turn compelled the Egyptians to send up
their own air force to provide cover, resulting in heavy air-to-air battles
with (the Israelis claim) the usual bad results for the Egyptians.

When a UN Security Council–mandated cease-fire went into effect on
the evening of October 22, the IDF had not yet completed its drive to surround 3rd Egyptian Army. However, both sides accused the other of
resuming hostilities, and the cease-fire was broken. This gave the southern
prong an extra two days to complete encirclement, albeit at heavy cost, as
one battalion of paratroopers, operating with the habitual lack of reconnaissance, entered the town of Suez at the mouth of the gulf, ran into a
trap, and had to be extricated after fierce fighting. By way of grand finale,
on the last day of the war the Israelis also set out to recapture the "Eyes of
the State" on Mount Chermon. This was done by means of a very costly
combined assault by infantry and heliborne paratroopers.

It remains to provide a brief outline of naval operations in this, the most
difficult of the major campaigns fought by the IDF and—as it turned out—
almost certainly the last.[69] Since 1967 the Israeli navy had been completely
renovated; instead of World War II–vintage destroyers its main strength now
consisted of twelve 250-ton Saar-class missile boats, to which were added
two of the newer and somewhat larger Reshef class. All were armed with the
Israeli-designed and -produced Gavriel sea-to-sea missile. With a range of
approximately fifteen miles, more importantly they possessed electronic
countermeasures that enabled them to evade the salvos of Soviet-made Styx
missiles of longer range carried by the Komar- and Ossa-class missile boats
of the Egyptian and Syrian navies. In the event there were no major clashes
with the Egyptians (at least none that have been reported). Not so in the
north, where clashes took place on October 6, 10, 11, 14, and 19. In each
case the Israelis rushed the Syrian boats before firing their Gavriels. They
claimed several Syrian vessels sunk at no loss of their own. With their
76mm and 40mm guns, the Israeli missile boats also shelled Syrian installations along the coast, probably only inflicting minor damage.

When the guns finally fell silent the IDF on the Golan Heights had
recaptured all the territory lost to the Syrians during the first days of the
war and then some, enabling its long-range artillery to shell Damascus. In
the south, though the Egyptians were still holding on to a narrow strip of
land in the Sinai, the 3rd Egyptian Army—still a major fighting formation
with two small divisions—had been encircled and was saved only by the
timely imposition of a cease-fire. Though the Egyptian air defense system

had not been annihilated, it had been weakened; had hostilities resumed, this would have enabled the IAF to operate effectively against the remaining ground forces, as it had in 1967. Yet their achievements in gaining territory had been limited, and on both fronts the Arabs had fought considerably better than during any previous conflict. The Egyptian and Syrian armies were not broken by the IDF, nor did they panic or self-disintegrate.

These facts were reflected in the separation of forces agreements signed in January and May 1974. The agreement with Egypt provided for the evacuation of "Africa" and the withdrawal of the IDF to a line twenty miles east of the canal. In return the Egyptians undertook to reopen the canal and resettle the towns alongside it—thus gaining a very strong incentive to refrain from reopening hostilities. By contrast, in the north, Israel surrendered only a very narrow and strategically insignificant strip of land along the previous cease-fire line but retained the critically important hills of Booster and Chermonit as well as its outpost atop Mount Chermon (two outposts higher up, captured by the IDF during the winter, had to be exchanged for Israeli POWs). The Syrians were now Israel's most dangerous enemy, although over the last twenty-something years the Syrians have given few signs of wanting a fresh conventional war.

The Reckoning: repatriated Israeli POWs in hospital, November 1973.

CHAPTER 14

THE RECKONING

I N 1973, as in 1967 and 1956, the factor that more than any other shaped the war was the surprise achieved by one side—in this case, the Arabs. As pointed out in several studies,[1] there was no lack of advance warning: The concentration of 300,000 men with thousands of tanks and guns as well as heavy bridging equipment simply could not escape notice. And neither was there a lack of other indications, from canal-crossing exercises to heightened states of alert to the sudden departure of the Soviet dependents less than forty-eight hours before the offensive. The alarms being sounded by individual officials at various levels were, however, all misinterpreted, ignored, or suppressed. Though subject to various degrees of nervousness, those who mattered—Dayan, Tsur (Dayan's deputy), and Elazar—were misled by Zeira, who thought he knew there would be no war. Even then, however, it is difficult to imagine that one officer alone could have had such an influence had not many of his underlying assumptions been shared by the rest.[2] Relatively ignorant about military matters and feeling isolated among her own defense experts, Ms. Meir, according to her own account,[3] acquiesced.

Compared to 1967 the IDF in 1973 started the war while holding excellent lines that were easy to defend—but that (thanks to the fact there no longer was any space separating the opponents) enabled the Arabs to take it by surprise. Once that surprise had been overcome, on the Golan Heights it was able to exploit its forte and engage on maneuver warfare vis-à-vis the Syrians and Iraqis. Not so in the Sinai, where the existence of the Bar Lev Line caused that advantage to be thrown away. The original decision, made in 1968, to hold on to the waterline was probably justified on political grounds; however, when the full-scale Egyptian attack came in 1973 it proved disastrous. On the one hand the line was occupied only by half as many men as it had been during the War of Attrition and with hardly any tanks or artillery to back up the *meozim*. On the other hand, IDF forces were frittered away in an effort to rescue the troops in their fortifications.

The effects of surprise also explain why, on both fronts during the first few days, IDF command and control was as bad as it could be. This caused entire units (Barak in the north, the advanced regular armored brigade in the south) to be sacrificed as other units stood by and did nothing (the two other regular armored brigades in the Sinai on October 6), acted on their own initiative (7th Armored in the north), or wasted time in purposeless maneuvering (Sharon's division on October 8). In the north, where personal relations among commanders were good, order was restored from October 8 on. Not so in the south, where Elazar's distrust of his subordinates resulted in a sort of "reverse optional control" as commanders, compelled to wait for his orders, positioned themselves too far to the rear while their units went on the offensive and consequently lost touch.[4] Ultimately it took the failure of a major counteroffensive to bring the IDF to its senses. Even so, Bar Lev, Adan, and Sharon continued to quarrel until the end of the war—and beyond.

Some of the problems were due to the fact that Israel had a surplus of supposedly excellent generals who were veterans of 1967. Whereas one reservist, Major General Lanner, had given a sterling performance, back in Tel Aviv, Elazar found himself surrounded by characters like Yadin, Rabin, Weizman, and Zeevi, former commander of the central front who had just doffed his uniform but came back to serve as a "special assistant" to the chief of staff. They crowded into the *Bor* (literally hole, the central command bunker), filling it with cigarette smoke and making it almost impossible for Elazar to perform his duties. Others appointed themselves as unofficial "eyes" for GHQ and hitched rides to the fronts. Gonen's position was the worst of all. The jumped-up 1967 colonel was considered a first-class fighter who, however, was still thinking like a division commander. Unfortunately he had under him not one but *two* generals (Adan and Sharon) who at one point had been superiors and over whom he was able to exercise little authority. Of the two, Sharon was not only a notoriously difficult subordinate but also affiliated with the opposition Likud Party, which meant that he could not be dismissed without risking a major political uproar. To the extent that henceforward no reservist was allowed to command a unit larger than a brigade, the lesson was learned. However, as we shall see, when Israel next went to war (in 1982) its top-level command structure was in some ways even more rickety than before.

Though the 1973 lines were easier to defend, they did not permit Israel to use its position between the Arab countries to the same extent as in 1967. The fronts were now much farther away, allowing only a few units to be transferred from the Golan Heights to the Sinai while hostilities lasted. Even the air force discovered that it was unable to operate as a unified force and during the initial days found itself trying to stem the Arabs on two fronts simultaneously; later it was virtually split into independent forces, each half concentrating on a front. In this way much of the advantage of occupying additional space was wasted, the more so because the attempt to hold on to every last inch of territory took away available room for maneuver.

The confusion at the front was matched by the disorder in the emergency depots. For example, one of Sharon's armored battalions found that not one of its half-tracks would start. By the time the war ended it had still not received the mortars that figured on the tables of organization and that would have been, had they been available, a great help in combating the Egyptian infantry.[5] One armored battalion went to war with twenty-five tanks, a mere two half-tracks, and practically none of its soft vehicles;[6] yet another did so without turret-mounted machine guns and, pushing toward the canal on October 8, was reduced to using Uzis instead.[7] Nevertheless, having worked through the night of October 6–7, the IDF rank and file mobilized more quickly than expected. In spite of shortages in everything from small arms (which were often inferior to those carried by the Arabs) through night-vision equipment, they fought very well, and calculations have shown that, on a man-to-man basis and in comparison to the 1967 war, the gap between them and their enemies had widened.[8] Particularly on the nearby Syrian front, it was a question of hold on or die; in the event of defeat the Israeli public, kept ignorant of whatever it was Peres in 1967 had thought could deter the Arabs, expected no mercy from their enemies. Though obviously not everybody could be equally heroic, the spirit of the times was exemplified by General Eytan. Forced to evacuate Nafeq on October 7, he swore he would not leave the Golan Heights alive.[9]

Though the IDF found its organization and equipment deficient in some respects, in others it had the advantage. The all-tank doctrine with which it entered the war proved a disaster, but after the first few days it was spontaneously abandoned as individual commanders and units adapted to fighting in an environment that was filled chock-a-block with antitank weapons. Once the initial problems had been overcome, on both fronts the IDF showed itself more adept in maneuver warfare than its enemies. Tank for tank, APC for APC, and gun for gun its heavy weapons proved as good as those of the enemy or better,[10] and although Egyptian bridging equipment was easier to handle and repair, that developed by the IDF compensated by carrying the much greater weight of Western-built tanks. The war also provided the IDF with a host of technical and tactical lessons that it incorporated during the following years.

What was true on the ground was even more true in the air and at sea. Thanks in large part to its superior U.S. aircraft, the IAF was able to keep absolute command of the air over Israel proper. This advantage was not as complete over the Golan Heights and the Sinai; on both fronts the short distances enabled air strikes and heliborne strikes against the Israeli ground forces to take place, though their effect was limited. Nevertheless, the IAF was unable to significantly dent the Syrian and Egyptian antiair-craft defenses. Attempts to carry out its missions in the teeth of those defenses proved well-nigh suicidal; during the war it lost as much as one-quarter of its strength. Once the first few desperate days were over, the IAF accordingly found itself constrained to change its objectives, as in the case of Syria, or else was limited to using those rare opportunities when the Arabs left their missile cover. Only during the last few days of the war was it able to play a greater role, and then it was largely thanks to the operations of Sharon's and Adan's forces on the ground.

In view of these considerations, perhaps the most impressive performance took place at sea. Much that happened remains classified; in particular, it is hard to believe that the Israeli submarines stayed in port and did not operate against enemy bases, particularly for intelligence-gathering purposes. Though the Soviet-made Styx missiles had twice the range of the Israeli Gavriel, the Israelis' better electronics, a well-thought-out doctrine, and thorough training gave them a decisive edge over their enemies, enabling them to sink several Syrian vessels without loss to themselves. Yet the Israelis, not having stationed major warships in the Red Sea and without a long-range airborne strike capability at their disposal, were helpless in front of the Egyptian blockade of the Straits of Bab al Mandeb. This was a shortcoming that they took to heart and set out to correct in the years to come.

Overall the balance of strength in this war was much worse than in 1956—when the Israelis fought on a single front and enjoyed superiority over the Egyptian forces in the Sinai—and not too different from what it had been in 1967 (although, of course, both sides had reinforced their forces very considerably).[11] Losses also increased to 2,800 killed and 8,300 wounded, as against 980 and 4,500 in 1967 and 190 and 900 in 1956. The average number of dead amounted to a little more than one hundred per day compared to fifteen in 1947–1948. However, the War of Independence had been fought by a population one-fifth as large, leading to the surprising conclusion that despite the vast advance in the quality of weapons and the amount of firepower, the intensity of the two conflicts in terms of daily losses per capita was not radically different. Calculated on the basis of Israelis killed in action per Arab division encountered, the figures for the three campaigns were 76:1 in 1956, 98:1 in 1967, and 200:1 in 1973 (against the PLO and Syrians during the first week in Lebanon they were to be around 113:1). By this rough measure it is clear that militarily speaking the October War was by far the most difficult and costliest ever fought by the IDF.

Yet once again statistics cannot convey the shock to Israel, which for the first time since 1948 saw its armed forces reeling and unable to decisively defeat the enemy. The public felt betrayed, and its belief in the IDF's superiority was shattered. This feeling was reflected in spontaneous antigovernment demonstrations as well as horrible jokes, such as the one that had children welcoming their father, just back from the front, with the words *od avinu chai* (and yet our father lives, a traditional Hebrew phrase referring to the Lord). Before the war Israelis had become overconfident and even arrogant, but not, it must be stated, without encouragement from the Western world, much of which liked to see the Arabs beaten and humiliated. They referred to the enemy as *Arabushim* (roughly translatable as despicable Arabs), and adopted Dayan's so-called bird theory, which, following his early experiences with the Syrians at Degania, envisaged the Arab armies scattering after a few bangs, like birds. Once again it was a poet, Jonathan Gefen, who best described the atmosphere that characterized the years before the war and the shock that followed:[12]

> *I am going to look at the sea, hoping*
> *It is still great and blue, at least the sea.*
> *Lonely and defeated I returned from the desert*
> *Everything that was close seems so far away.*
> *I am going to look at the sea.*

III

RUNNING OUT OF STEAM,
1974–1997

T HE END OF THE October War saw the IDF in a state of considerable demoralization. Public faith in it, as well as its own self-image, suffered badly. Commanders accustomed to being treated as demigods suddenly saw their professional expertise questioned and their social status steeply declining. The title of the very first book published about the war said it all: *Ha-mechdal* (The Oversight). The cover showed a weeping Ms. Meir, and the term *mechdal* gave rise to a family of related terms such as *mechdalnik* (an officer who by virtue of his affiliation with the IDF was regarded as sharing responsibility for the *mechdal*) and *mechdalit* (the car IDF officers drove). Previously any attempt to criticize the IDF had resulted in protest, as in 1971 when a play named *Malkat Ambatia* (Bathroom Queen) caused its audience to run wild and had to be withdrawn. Now, however, and for the first time in Israel's history, it became possible for people to make a name for themselves by touring the country and explaining all the things that the IDF had *not* done right.

More seriously, the months immediately after the war saw pressure build for an investigation. The government, which at first tried to resist, was forced to give in. A commission of inquiry was put together with the state comptroller and two former chiefs of staff (Yadin and Laskov) as its members; its chairman was High Court Justice Shimon Agranat, and the fifth member also a High Court justice. The commission was given a mandate to examine the events that led to the war as well as the first three days of operations. In its report it subjected the IDF to scathing criticism, including the failure to build up sufficient stores and to properly maintain those available. The chief of intelligence, the CO Southern Command, and the chief of staff were pilloried: the first for having failed to serve advance warning; the second for his conduct of operations during the first three critical days; and the third for having failed to order mobilization in good time. All three were forced to resign, and Elazar died soon after. Much to the former chief of staff's chagrin, the commission exonerated Dayan, who thereby gave one last display of his knack for avoiding responsibility. However, the former national idol was crucified by public opinion. When Ms. Meir resigned in April and was replaced by Yitschak Rabin, Dayan was left out of the government.

Meanwhile, even as the "First Separation of Forces Agreement" was signed with Egypt in January 1974, the work of reconstruction got under way. At first sight it was highly successful; as we shall see, a combination of massive U.S. aid (financial and technological), plus the mobilization of Israeli resources to an extent never previously attained in peacetime, resulted in the creation of a true juggernaut not only in regional terms but even on a worldwide scale. This army was still capable of spectacular feats, such as the Entebbe raid in 1976 and the bombing of the Iraqi nuclear reactor in 1981. When it invaded Lebanon in June 1982 its early victories—especially those of the IAF over Syria's air force and antiaircraft defenses—astonished the world.

Yet something of the earlier enthusiasm was gone. Particularly in the years immediately following 1967, war had been regarded almost as a lighthearted adventure in which heroic Israeli tankmen crashed into (*nich-nesu be-*, Israeli slang meaning, literally, "entered") second-rate opponents while they themselves were "exposed in the turret." In 1973 many tankmen had been killed and others suffered horrible burns, however, causing the tanks' hatches to be closed tight. All at once, war ceased to be a glamorous occasion honored by popular songs; instead it became a bloody, serious business in which many people were killed and others mutilated, wounded, and bereaved. Over time, graffiti reading *kol ha-kavod le*-TSAHAL (doff your hat to TSAHAL) tended to disappear from the streets. In 1978 Prime

Minister Begin tried to turn back the clock by proposing to hold a military parade on Independence Day with himself on the stand and taking the salute; however, neither the public nor the IDF were enthusiastic, and the idea had to be dropped. To substitute for the departed glamour, "strategy" in its Western, intellectual, and instrumental sense invaded Israel, which hitherto had been remarkably free of it. Israel still had no "defense community" to speak of—the IDF being much too proud to take outside advice—so the Center of Strategic Studies was opened as an affiliate of Tel Aviv University, and over the years has done useful if not spectacular work. Books and monographs on the subject multiplied, as did professors who researched and taught it.

Except during moments when they got carried away, the leaders of Israel's defense establishment had always been well aware of the country's inability to achieve final victory by breaking the will of the Arab countries and forcing them to make peace.[1] Now, even as the IDF grew more and more powerful, the limits of its power were demonstrated time and again—against progressively weaker opponents, no less. First in Lebanon and then during the Palestinian uprising it failed to perform as well as expected. In between it showed that it could not protect Israel against missile attack and was made to stand idly by as others smashed Saddam Hussein's war machine. Even as its size peaked during the mid-1980s, it was becoming bloated and top-heavy. By the end of the decade the IDF's morale was beginning to decline; by the mid-1990s it was clearly in a bad way. In some important respects it was as if the story of the U.S. armed forces in Vietnam was being reenacted, with the ominous difference that Israel is a mere speck on the map and does not have the Pacific Ocean to separate it from its Arab and, above all, Palestinian opponents.

Recovery and Expansion: female tank instructors, 1979.

RECOVERY AND EXPANSION

W ITH MEIR AND Dayan both gone—the former into retirement, the latter having become an ordinary Knesset member and later foreign minister—Israel's defense was
entrusted to a new team. At its head was Prime Minister Rabin. The previous six years he served as Israel's ambassador to Washington and had lost
much of his wide-eyed, young-boy-from-the-provinces air. His minister of
defense was Shimon Peres, an old rival, an expert on secret negotiations,
and the acknowledged founder of Israel's military, aviation, and electronics
industries as well as the Dimona nuclear reactor. After Labor was thrown
out of office in the 1977 elections, Rabin and Peres vented their mutual
antipathy, each one going out of his way to tell the public how incompetent the other was in defense-related matters. Yet the fact remains that
together they knew more about, and had done more for, Israeli security
than anybody else. So long as they remained in power their rivalry did not
prevent the IDF from recovering and, later, increasing its might by leaps
and bounds.

Elazar's replacement as chief of staff was a paratrooper, "Motta" Gur.
Self-confident to the point of rudeness, he, like Dayan, could not leave the
members of the female sex alone, addressing any woman who came his way
as "Hi, sweetie!" Unlike Dayan, however, who owed some of his charisma
to his qualities as a litterateur, his greatest intellectual achievement consisted of a series of children's book about Azzit, a heroic shepherd she-dog
who accompanied the paratroopers on their exploits against feeble-minded
Arab opponents. Having served as CO Northern Command from 1969 to
1972, he was then dispatched to Washington as military attaché, a post that
usually marks the end of an officer's career.[1] Thus he was fortunate not to
have shared in the *mechdal*, which of course was the real reason behind his
appointment. Also, unlike his immediate predecessors (and also unlike
General Tal, who as Elazar's chief of the General Staff was the natural candidate for the job) he was *not* an armored corps man; neither, to the present day, was any of his successors.

The "October Earthquake" notwithstanding, Israel's top-level security decisionmaking machinery remained as rickety as ever. In 1976 the Knesset passed a new law that sought to define the relationships between prime minister, minister of defense, and chief of staff. In practice an exact division of responsibilities proved impossible to set down, and much continued to depend on the way personalities interacted. Since the Knesset still did not have subpoena power, Israel's defense and foreign policy remained in the hands of a kitchen Cabinet—the above-mentioned trio plus Yigal Allon, who was serving Rabin as foreign minister. Depending on the occasion, these four were joined by others such as the commander of the air force, the chief of intelligence, the chief of Mossad, and other high-ranking security personnel. Later several prime ministers played with the idea of establishing a ministerial committee for defense, which never materialized. On other occasions the entire Cabinet was made to sit as the Ministerial Committee for Defense. But this arrangement did not work either, for twenty-odd ministers sworn to secrecy could never be trusted to keep their mouths shut.

From time to time the question of setting up a national security council was debated. The arguments in its favor were compelling: After all, the prime minister remained the sole juncture into which all channels fed, yet he did not have his own machinery to look into what he heard. From Peres to Mordechai, successive ministers of defense regarded the idea as harmful to their own authority, however, and went out of their way to torpedo it. But the ministry of defense did not succeed in constructing its own independent research and planning capability. Peres's attempt to make the IDF planning division—it had been upgraded from branch to division—serve him as well as the chief of staff did not work well. When Sharon took over the ministry in 1981 he tried to solve the problem by setting up the National Security Unit (NSU) in the Ministry of Defense, the upshot being a sort of parallel General Staff with one major general, one brigadier general, and twenty colonels.[2] Understandably the NSU excited the animosity of Chief of Staff Eytan[3]—as indeed it was supposed to, since he and Sharon were old rivals. When Arens in turn replaced Sharon, one of his first actions was to abolish the NSU for the sake of harmony with the IDF.

Thus, as before, neither prime minister nor minister of defense—let alone the Cabinet or the Knesset Foreign Affairs and Defense Committee— succeeded in setting up a strong organization capable of doing independent research and exercising effective oversight. Also, and contrary to the recommendations of the Agranat Commission of Investigation, the IDF retained its grip over the national intelligence estimate. To be sure, there were a few cosmetic changes. During the first year or two after the war an attempt was made to get the research department of the Foreign Office to duplicate the work of the IDF's intelligence research branch. A number of bright young men were recruited for the job, but after a while the research department languished. Though the IDF now commanded some of the world's most advanced sensors and early-warning systems, the fear that another Arab attack would catch it by surprise continued to haunt both GHQ and individual intelligence officers. Over time, this fear led to a great outpouring of works about intelligence, its possibilities, and its limitations.[4]

By way of correcting the inability of civilian and military decisionmakers to communicate with one another—in plain words, ensuring that the former should know exactly what a division is—the long-dead National Defense College was revived in 1976–1977. Its first commander was Maj. Gen. Menachem Meron. A Tal protégé, he had been responsible for the Sharm al-Sheikh area in 1973; by way of preparation he spent a year with the Royal College of Defense Studies in London. However, and as in its previous incarnation, the college never succeeded either in building up a first-rate faculty or in turning itself into a vehicle for selection. Intellectually its stature was reflected by the almost nonexistent library and the fact that, conspiring with Haifa University, it handed out M.A. degrees in a mere eight months (as against a minimum of two years in any other program). Functionally it acted as a pool for unemployed lieutenant colonels with the occasional civilian thrown in. The war also persuaded the IDF that its brigade commanders were unprepared for the job and led to the establishment of a special course for them. In 1994 the first higher command and general staff course (for brigadier generals) was held. However, the fact that most of them did not have good command of English precluded non-Israelis from being invited to speak; they mainly listened to their own former superiors.

With Rabin in the saddle, the country started pulling itself out of its confusion. Though there was constant trouble on the Lebanon border, the separation of forces agreements with Egypt and Syria proved their worth and enabled the IDF to rebuild. This was even more true after the "Second Separation of Forces Agreement" was concluded with Egypt in September 1975. Representing a real step toward peace, the agreement made war on the Egypt front much less likely. Should Egypt decide to go to war, however, it would have to do so in the teeth of U.S.-manned early-warning stations located in the Sinai passes. It also implied moving the forces across a twenty-mile demilitarized zone, thus simultaneously serving warning and getting out of antiaircraft missile range. Last but not least, the agreement opened the road for the IDF to receive even more U.S. weapons than before.

Yet economically speaking these were extremely difficult years. The war itself was said to have cost Israel the equivalent of a full year's GNP. No sooner was it over than it was followed by the energy crisis, which first doubled and then quadrupled the price of oil. From 1967 on, Israel had taken about half its oil from the fields at Abu Rhodeis, but in 1975 they were returned to Egypt. Together with the need to pay for rearmament, the effect was to quadruple the gap in the balance of payments between 1972 and 1981.[5] Inflation rose to dizzying heights. At no time during the decade after 1973 did it fall below 37 percent, and in 1985 it even exceeded 400 percent.

Had it not been for U.S. economic assistance, Israel might not have weathered the crisis. Before 1967, U.S. aid to Israel, mostly for civilian projects such as building the national water carrier, had been limited to no more than perhaps $50 million annually.[6] Between 1968 and 1973 it quintupled, reaching an average of $250 million (to which should be added the much-augmented proceeds of the bonds sold by the government of Israel to American Jewry).[7] In 1973–1974 it was increased to $2.2 *billion* per year—and even this sum later grew to $3 billion. Of the $3 billion, $1.8 billion consisted of outright military aid that, much to the IDF's sorrow, could only be spent by buying weapons in the United States.[8] The rest was provided in the form of loans for civilian purposes and could be converted into Israeli pounds and shekels; however, in 1984 the loans were converted into grants that were renewed by Congress in October each year. Thus the Israeli lobby in Washington has been spectacularly successful—never did so few receive so much free aid for so long.

As Rabin in particular never tired of saying, in part the U.S. assistance to Israel's defense may have been based on genuine sympathy for an embattled ally. In part it was governed by considerations pertaining to the so-called Second Cold War, and in part it was designed to prevent Israel from raising its nuclear profile (in plain words, endangering world peace by using unconventional weapons to defend against much more powerful enemies). In any case it made possible a very great increase in defense spending, which rose from $1.247 billion in 1972[9] to $4.27 billion in 1977[10] and as much as $7.34 billion in 1981.[11] In fairness, the increase was not paid for only by the Americans, who accounted for no more than just under half of Israel's military outlay.[12] The remainder was obtained by starving the civilian economy of funds, bringing growth to a near halt, a nightmarish balance of payments problem, and an exceedingly heavy tax burden on its own population—including the introduction of a new value-added tax that started at 6 percent and rose to 19 percent. The magnitude of the effort may be deduced from the fact that the share of defense out of gross domestic product (GDP) shot up from an average of 8.7 percent between 1957 and 1966 to 21.3 percent in 1968–1972 to 26.3 percent in 1974–1981—this after having peaked at a whopping 32.7 percent in 1973.[13]

In 1973, even after the reserves had arrived, on each of the fronts the IDF had found itself outnumbered 2.5–3:1.[14] Early in the war only three divisions had stood between the Egyptians and Tel Aviv; of those, one had been badly attrited, whereas another received a beating on October 8. Accordingly GHQ's first priority was to increase the size of the army, the twin objective being to maintain the balance of forces vis-à-vis the Arabs and to have more formations available for maneuver. The two main methods were to increase the size of the regular forces (*keva* plus conscripts) and to reclassify all manpower in the country. Results came soon. By the best available figures the regular army increased from 115,000 in 1973 to 164,000 in 1977 to 170,000 in 1982.[15] The total force (including reservists) expanded even faster, going from somewhat more than 300,000 to 400,000 to 540,000 during the same period. Since the number of divisions is a closely guarded secret, it had to be calculated on the basis of brigade equivalents, as they are listed in internationally published sources. It seems to have gone up from seven to thirteen to about sixteen—though the latter figure also includes a number of brigades suitable for local defense only. By comparison, the U.S. Army in 1982 also had sixteen divisions and the Bundeswehr, the second strongest army in the North Atlantic Treaty Organization (NATO), had twelve. But then again Israel's Jewish population was only around 3.5 million, its per-capita GNP perhaps one-third of that of the developed states.[16]

In point of doctrine there was little change from the period before 1973.[17] Although some ground had been lost both in the north and the south—on the Golan Heights, this amounted to only a mile or so—compared to the period before 1967 the borders remained much easier to defend. Accordingly the IDF prepared to "absorb" and "brake" an Arab first strike by means of the enlarged standing army and the air force. Next, as reserves arrived, it expected to go on the offensive, smash as much of the opponent's armed forces as possible before the UN Security Council arranged for a cease-fire, and seize territory that could be used as a bargaining chip. Owing to the availability of strategic depth, the doctrine was more easily applied in the south than along the River Jordan and on the Golan Heights; on both fronts a heavy investment was made in building strongholds, minefields, antitank ditches, and the like so as to hold off the initial assaults and buy time. Finally, to placate those who still insisted on using settlements for defense (in 1973, the Golan settlements had been evacuated before the first shot) a plan was hatched to revive *hagana mer-*

chavit by fortifying them and providing them with antitank weapons.[18] In practice, though, little came of this; indeed it is hard to envisage women and children slugging it out with invading Syrian and Jordanian forces while their menfolk were presumably away serving in the reserves.

Organizationally speaking there were several changes in the ground forces. The divisions were organized into permanent corps. The latter stood under front commanders; however, the IDF avoided inserting another rank between that of division commander and front commander, with the result that, in 1982, an *aluf* acting as CO Northern Command commanded another *aluf* acting as corps commander. Elite infantry brigades apart, practically the entire ground forces now consisted of armored divisions. The jettisoning of the all-tank doctrine was reflected inside each division by providing each armored battalion with a company of APC-riding infantry; they in turn were equipped with machine guns, mortars, and antitank missiles and were ready to support the tanks as they went into battle. Another change was to abolish the divisions' organic reconnaissance battalions, the rationale being that the task would be carried out by new technology then under development and that whatever remained of it could be entrusted to *any* battalion. This move was regarded by many officers as an error,[19] and indeed it may explain some of the IDF's ham-handedness during "Operation Peace for Galilee."

Reflecting the IDF's origins in prestate days, traditionally its General Staff had also acted as headquarters of the ground forces, but after the October War this arrangement came under critical fire. Some argued that the burden on the chief of staff was excessive and that the ground forces needed their own headquarters parallel to those of the air force and navy; others argued that new headquarters was needed in order to overcome problems in interarm cooperation. After several plans for resolving the problem had been proposed and rejected, in August 1977 Ezer Weizman asked Major General (ret.) Tal, who was then in charge of developing Israel's home-built tank, to present a detailed blueprint. It was promptly turned down by the General Staff, which discerned an attempt to reduce its own authority, and by the remaining ground arms, which suspected Tal of attempting to subordinate all of them to his beloved armored corps.

In the event neither Gur nor Eytan saw any need for organizational reform. Consequently the bickering went on throughout the late seventies and early eighties; it was not until after the invasion of Lebanon, which brought to light glaring shortages in the cooperation of armor, artillery, infantry, and engineers, that the scheme finally found favor. In 1983 the slot of CO of the armored corps was reduced from major general to brigadier general, thus depriving the corps of its status as first among equals, which it had enjoyed since the midfifties, and putting it on a par with the remaining ground arms. A new headquarters known as MAFCHASH (Mifkedet Kochot Ha-sadeh, Ground Forces Headquarters) and commanded by a major general was established.[20] Even so, the hopes of those who had advocated a ground forces headquarters similar to the semi-independent headquarters of the air force and navy were disappointed. MAFCHASH remained a mere inspectorate, responsible for coordinating peacetime organization, force development, and training but without an operational function in war.

Between 1967, when it suddenly burst on the world scene, and 1973 the IDF was widely admired for its fighting qualities. In spite of the modernization that took place, however, equipment-wise it was still the army of a comparatively small and poor country and was wanting in many respects. Since it was able to draw on 50 percent of the total military budget the IAF was better armed than the rest, but even here the order of battle still included obsolescent aircraft left over from the 1967 war, and there was a shortage of modern ground-to-air missiles and air-to-ground missiles. The situation of the land forces was much worse. Some of the armor consisted of upgraded Sherman tanks, and the majority of troops rode World War II–vintage M–3 half-tracks; for antitank work the IDF still relied on jeep-mounted recoilless rifles as well as limited numbers of 1950s-vintage, French-made SS–10 and SS–11 missiles. Some of the shortcomings were due to the financial constraints affecting a small country with a comparatively huge military establishment. Others reflected the IDF's obstinate refusal to adopt a combined arms doctrine as well as the kind of organization that this implies.

Already during the October War America's arsenals began to open as Pres. Richard M. Nixon and his principal advisers, Henry Kissinger and James Schlesinger, organized a massive air-sea lift. Its importance in raising Israeli morale is undoubted; bonbons were literally dropping from the sky. Yet its significance in assisting the IDF's war effort became moot. During the ten days that passed from the time it got under way until the cease-fire came into effect, only about 200 aircraft were able to make the journey and land. Though a handful of tanks and self-propelled cannons were flown in by way of demonstrating capability, clearly there could be no question of the airlift replacing hundreds of major weapon systems lost and tens of thousands of tons of ammunition expended. Of the total number of sorties flown by the U.S. Air Force Transport Command, about two-thirds took place after October 24; even so the bulk of the aid was sent by sea and thus arrived weeks after the war was over. Yet there is no denying that certain critically important items arrived during hostilities. The list included some fifty Phantom fighter-bombers, which, with midair refueling, could be flown in on their own power. It also included 155mm and 175mm artillery rounds—of which there was a shortage[21]—as well as air-to-air, air-to-ground, and antitank missiles and electronic equipment for radar jamming and the like.

Once the buildup began in earnest the results were nothing short of dramatic. According to internationally published figures, between 1973 and 1982 the number of main battle tanks went up from 1,700 (which may have been an underestimate)[22] to 3,600; armored fighting vehicles (AFVs) went from 3,000 to no fewer than 8,000. Of those about one-quarter consisted of the new M–113Æs,[23] meaning that Israel now had a truly mechanized army instead of one that was merely motorized, as previously. The old Super Shermans were finally discarded, and the ground forces received additional M–60 tanks of the most advanced model. They in turn were joined by Israeli-made Merkava tanks (for details, see Chapter 15), as well as additional T–54, T–55, and T–62 tanks, which had been captured during the war and reconditioned.

In keeping with the diminished status of the tanks the artillery if anything benefited even more, the total number of barrels rising to 2,000 or so.[24] The M–107 and M–109 guns that had been available before 1973 were joined by Israeli-made 155mm pieces, some U.S.-made M–110 heavy 203mm pieces, and multiple rocket launchers ranging from 122mm to 290mm in size. Still not content, the IDF paid its enemies the compliment of imitation by purchasing modern TOW (tube-launched, optically tracked, wire-guided) and Dragon antitank missiles. They replaced the old junk, thereby providing Israeli infantry with an effective antiarmor capability that could be deployed from the top of light vehicles or, if necessary, by small groups moving on foot. As numbers of U.S. M–16 rifles arrived and the production of the Israeli Galil gathered steam, for the first time in history all IDF troops could be issued first-rate personal arms. Finally, the engineering corps received new equipment such as bridge-laying tanks and minefield crossing systems.

The IAF's order of battle, which in 1973 was somewhat more than 400 first-line combat aircraft, expanded to almost 700. Previously the most powerful platform had been the F–4 Phantom, allegedly the best fighter-bomber ever built; for all its speed and ordnance payload, however, it was difficult to maintain, heavy, and, owing to its lack of maneuverability, not really suitable for air-to-air combat. Now the Phantoms were supplemented by growing numbers of the nimble new Kfirs, the Israeli-built version of the French Mirage V to which several refinements had been added. By the early eighties, though, pilots considered having to fly the Kfir almost as an insult. Instead all eyes were turned to the new generation of U.S.-built F–15 fighters and F–16 fighter-bombers. Introduced in 1977, their maneuverability and electronics (i.e., target-acquisition and weapon-guiding capabilities) outclassed anything the Arabs had; when the first arrived, Chief of Staff Gur went on record as saying that "a state with F–15's no longer resembles one without them."[25] To help these aircraft locate and track opponents the IAF received six EC–2 Hawkeyes, a U.S.-built airborne electronic warfare (AEW) platform to which the Arabs also had no answer. Properly integrated into the chain of command, it was to prove very effective during the Lebanon War.

These aircraft were joined by two different types of TOW-carrying helicopters, the AH–1G/S Cobra and the lighter MD–500 Defender. The former in particular was a highly specialized antitank platform. It formed part of the IAF and was not part of the ground forces as in many other countries; it constituted the IDF's very first line of defense in case of attack. During the October War the IDF had carried out a small number of heliborne raids against various targets, including Syrian bridges (to delay the Iraqi expeditionary force) and Egyptian communications centers.[26] For this mission as well as to increase its capacity for carrying out large-scale airborne operations, U.S.-built CH–53 helicopters joined the old French Super Frelons in 1974 to provide additional lift for troops. Traditionally the IDF had trusted its air force to maintain air superiority and consequently neglected its antiaircraft defenses. Now this shortcoming was corrected to some extent by purchasing multiple-barrel Chaparral guns and Redeye missiles, both of them U.S.-manufactured and intended for close-in defense of military targets.

At sea, the navy's missile boats had proved themselves in the October War. During the seventies the older Saar I–class boats were withdrawn and replaced by the larger Saar II and Saar III class. Later these in turn were joined by no fewer than nine of the newer Reshef class, bringing the total number up to a very respectable nineteen. Not only did the Gavriel missile give birth to the Mark 2 and Mark 3 missiles (with larger warheads, better electronics, and longer ranges), but it was joined by the U.S. Harpoon and the Israeli Barak—the former an over-the-horizon surface-to-surface missile and the latter a vertical-launch missile intended for antiaircraft and antimissile defense. In addition the navy provided some of its ships with formidable, radar-controlled, 20mm Vulcan-Phalanx guns, enabling them to shoot down sea-skimming surface-to-surface missiles. Finally, although it still did not amount to much, sea-to-shore operating capability was reinforced by the purchase of two hovercrafts.

As before, the navy and IAF were manned largely by professionals, the latter in particular in a state of hair-trigger readiness suitable for a country whose main enemies were only minutes away by air. Not so the ground forces, which also as before, continued to consist very largely of reservists. To ensure that the reserve units would reach the front as fast as possible several changes were made. To correct the deficiencies in maintenance and preparation the new Inspectorate for Maintenance was set up in 1975 and took over responsibility for the YAMACHim. Besides being much larger— they now contained stores and ammunition for many more days of fighting—the depots were better organized as the gradual introduction of computers improved inventory control. Another reform was the introduction of the so-called dry storage system, which meant that in the future precious hours would not be wasted greasing the tanks or finding batteries for those that would not start. Many additional trucks and tank transporters were purchased, thus if war came the tanks, self-propelled guns, and APCs would not have to reach the fronts on their tracks. Though the mobilization of civilian transport in an emergency could not be entirely dispensed, its importance was greatly reduced. The so-called Blue Band trucks, which in previous wars had done their best to follow the troops, all but disappeared.

As we saw, from 1936 on, volunteers and even entire units from countries as far away as Iraq and Morocco had taken part in various Arab-Israeli wars. Nevertheless neither the IDF nor its air force ever developed a true long-range striking arm capable of acting against the countries in question, contenting itself with interdicting enemy forces on their way to the front. As a result, when an El Al civilian airliner was hijacked to Algiers in 1969 the possibility of mounting some kind of rescue operation came up but had to be rejected for want of means.[27] And when the Egyptians closed the Straits of Bab al Mandeb during the October War, Israel was unable to respond. For a time it stood helplessly as its supply of Iranian oil was cut.

With this bitter lesson learned, during the next few years much was done to correct the problem. The old squadrons of DC–3 Dakota and Nord Atlas transports remained in service. However, the backbone of the service was formed by modern C–130 Hercules transports, with much greater range and payload. For flying missions to friendly countries the IAF had long possessed some old Boeing 707 passenger aircraft. Now a few of them were converted into tankers and provided with air-to-air refueling systems; others were modified to serve as flying command posts for ground troops, and others were adopted for intelligence-gathering purposes. Had it been up to Peres, always something of a visionary, Israel would have asked the United States during the mid-seventies to provide surveillance, reconnaissance, and early-warning satellites. However, Rabin in his memoirs claimed he saw no need for such hardware and accused the minister of defense of not knowing what he was talking about.[28]

The worth of the IDF's newly acquired long-range capability was put to the test for the first time in July 1976 when an Air France airliner on its way from Athens (its previous stop had been Tel Aviv) to Paris was hijacked to Entebbe, Uganda. Once on the ground the Ugandans allowed the non-Israeli passengers to go free; ninety-eight Israelis and the French crew were made to stay behind and then herded into the old terminal. After a few days' debating whether a military option even existed, the Israeli Cabinet decided to act. Fortunately information about the airfield was available from Israelis who had participated in its construction, and intelligence as to the hostages and the way they were guarded was provided by Mossad agents on the ground. On the night of July 2 four Hercules aircraft loaded with commandos took off from Sharm al-Sheikh and headed south, flying over Ethiopia on the way to Uganda. Approaching Entebbe, they apparently used electronic warfare to trick airport control[29]—the details are still classified—and landed, taking Idi Amin's troops totally by surprise.

As a command-and-control aircraft circled overhead, the commandos, preceded by a black Mercedes brought in to mislead the Ugandan guards, stormed the terminal, shot the hijackers dead, and liberated the hostages. Thirty minutes after it had landed, the first Hercules, carrying the hostages, was back in the air. The others remained a little longer, the commandos systematically shooting up the airport's control tower and blowing up the Migs of Uganda's air force so they could not pursue. During the return the transports landed in Nairobi, where they were refueled. Carried out at the cost of one dead and one wounded among the commandos (three hostages were also killed, and another who had been in hospital was later executed by the Ugandans), the operation was a brilliant success. When the heroes returned, people welcomed them by dancing in the streets—not just because the hostages were safe but because it was felt that the IDF had reasserted its superiority.

In May 1977, elections took place. For the first time in Israel's history Labor was defeated, the upshot being the emergence of a right-wing nationalist coalition with Menachem Begin as prime minister. Having joined the Cabinet as a minister without portfolio on the eve of the 1967 war, the former ETSEL commander had resigned three years later in protest of Ms. Meir's announcement in the Knesset that Israel might be prepared to give up some of the Occupied Territories. Since then he had systematically opposed the various separation-of-forces agreements with Egypt and Syria, denouncing the government for weakness. Now this man, with the glowering eyes and old-fashioned manners of a would-be Polish aristocrat—only a few weeks earlier Rabin had described him as an "archaeological exhibit"—found himself heading the country and its formidable fighting machine.

Begin's minister of defense was Ezer Weizman, now in his fifties. Having masterminded the propaganda campaign that brought Begin's Likud Party to power, on the surface Weizman remained as hawkish as ever; underneath he may have already started his slow evolution into a moderate dove. Certainly he had no use for the mystic-religious arguments that, at least to Begin and even more so to his coalition partners, belonging to the National Religious Party constituted the rationale behind the demand to retain all of Erets Yisrael; instead he was at one with the defeated Labor Party in regarding the Occupied Territories in almost purely strategic terms. Entering office, he was taken aback by the enormous growth of the IDF since he had doffed his uniform in 1969. Later he continued the accelerated buildup of the army as well as Israel's defense industries.

Militarily speaking perhaps more important than the substitution of Weizman for Peres was Eytan's replacement of Gur. In 1956 both of them had been battalion commanders under Sharon; since 1973, when his division had absorbed the first Syrian offensive on the Golan Heights, Eytan had served first as CO Northern Command and then as head of the General Staff Division. Like Gur he was and is a soldier's soldier: blunt, thorough, and obstinate to the point of mulishness. He was also not without a certain sly sense of humor, a quality that enabled him to form a good rapport with common soldiers and, later, voters. Before his appointment he had been famous for his curt and clipped speaking style. Now he developed a loquacity that caused Begin to label him—in all seriousness, it seems—the new Demosthenes.

As the Entebbe raid proved, some IDF services and units were as good or better than ever, capable of extremely rapid planning followed by equally decisive, precise action. This probably did not apply to the entire army, however, given that its breakneck expansion had resulted in internal changes. In 1987, something of the nature of these changes came to light following the publication of what came to be known as the Wald Report. Emmanuel Wald was a former infantry NCO who had gone on to earn a Ph.D. in systems analysis from an American university. Commissioned into the IDF as a colonel, he worked for the manpower division but soon got into trouble with his superiors and was put into the freezer by being moved to the National Defense College. There he wrote his report on the basis of classified documents obtained by somewhat unconventional means (at the time there were rumors that he had persuaded a female soldier to let him into the office of the chief of the planning division). Its publication caused a furor in the military and among the public, which wanted to believe that the IDF was still the best army in the world.

According to Wald, between 1973 and 1982 the IDF had become increasingly cumbersome. The combat echelon's share in the ground forces' order of battle dropped by 6 percent, from 35 percent of the total to 33 percent; by contrast the number of overhead slots rose by 33 percent. Of every 100 regular ground slots added, 50 were allocated to logistical and administrative services, 16 to the headquarters and units dealing with force construction, and 8 to the General Staff—against only the 24 that were left for the combat forces proper. The structure of the officer corps was also being altered as the number of lieutenants dropped and that of more senior officers—particularly captain to colonel—increased.[30] Thus the essence of Wald's findings was that the IDF was becoming bloated and top-heavy with supernumerary senior commanders. In addition he described organizational confusion and duplication of responsibilities among various headquarters, particularly in the ground forces. At the time they were made, his charges were furiously denied and the author came close to trial for the unauthorized use of classified material. Yet subsequent statements by several chiefs of staff lead one to suspect that he was right and his critics wrong; indeed, one source has it that by 1996 the percentage of IDF manpower serving in combat units was down to 20 percent.[31]

In part the changes may have been due to the very great infusion of modern weapons systems and other technologies during those years. This led to the growth of logistic and maintenance echelons as well as increased specialization, rotation of personnel ("churning"), and the fragmentation of careers that became increasingly dissimilar to each other (e.g., one brigade had five commanders in six years).[32] In part it was the result of numerical growth. Whereas previously everybody had known each other, now there probably took place a decrease in tacit understanding. This in turn made additional organization necessary; in particular, the increase in the size of the General Staff is explained by the fact that the IDF during these years set up an entire series of new inspectorates for maintenance, intelligence, administration, and replacements, among others.[33] Reduced cohesion, greater size, and more technology were slowly making the IDF more cumbersome and less flexible.

In other ways, too, breakneck expansion probably led to a drop in quality. To bring in additional troops Peres and Gur had scraped the bottom of the manpower barrel, reclassifying personnel who had previously been regarded as below par. Eytan in turn went farther still, taking up Ben Gurion's old view that the army was not merely a military instrument but an educational institution with duties toward society at large.[34] Accordingly he decided to start conscripting marginal youths and even petty criminals with the intent of reforming them and teaching skills useful in civilian life. As in the case of Robert McNamara's infamous and failed Project 100,000 (which used the military to help underprivileged youths), the experiment resulted in disciplinary problems from drug abuse to threats toward superiors.[35] After Eytan left office it was quietly dropped, and the money raised through voluntary contributions was diverted to other purposes such as general soldiers' welfare.

On the face of things the officer selection and training system remained the same. Though a second school for cadets was opened, the great majority of officers were still selected from among the more successful conscripts, put through various tests, and sent to officer school, after which they would specialize by branch and service. Yet wishing to get more officer for the time and money spent—in other words, to increase the period of commissioned service relative to the period of preparation and training—it was decided to make cadets sign on for an additional year as a condition of acceptance to officer school. Heralding a change in the significance of conscription—those willing to become officers were being penalized—the new system was initially resisted. During the mid- to late seventies a shortage of junior officers developed; in a country where parents had traditionally taken pride in their children being commissioned it became necessary to punish soldiers who refused to attend officer school.[36] Later this problem was corrected as officer salaries were raised—one explanation behind the sudden drop in the number of lieutenants and the rise in the number of captains. Even for those who did not intend to stay in the military, signing on for another year became an acceptable way to save some money in preparation for going to university or starting a career.

At a higher level, the combination of war losses and rapid expansion naturally meant additional opportunities for promotion. The average age at which officers occupied their designated slots dropped still farther—not necessarily a good thing for an army where officers were already younger than almost everywhere else, probably leading to a drop in quality.[37] Thus in the United States an officer would probably get his first battalion (or equivalent) at the age of thirty-seven or so after having gone through command and general staff college; IDF battalion commanders were appointed in their late twenties often *without* having spent a year attending POUM (Pikkud U-mateh, the IDF Command and General Staff College). An officer might command a brigade while in his early to mid-thirties, a division short of forty, and—unless promoted to major general and thus to a seat on the General Staff—be out at forty-two or forty-three when colleagues elsewhere were yet lieutenant colonels. As long as they *did* stay in the army, officers' time was spent fighting guerrillas along the borders and terrorists inside the Occupied Territories. Consequently officers never had the time to reflect and study; indeed their careers were over almost before they began.

Unlike predecessors who had started careers in prestate days, Israeli officers during this period spent their entire professional lives in the IDF. Systematically rotated, developed, and—if the necessary time was available and their progress not too rapid—taught, they were probably more professional than their predecessors. But they also developed the shortcomings of professionalism, including specialization and a certain narrow-mindedness.[38] The perfect example, of course, was Eytan, for whom wider cultural horizons simply do not exist. For the reasons just outlined and for others rooted in culture and tradition the IDF had never been a studious army.[39] To be sure, it did not develop a genial, easygoing, wine-drinking, *Papa Joffre*-type officer. Yet had its members included as intellectual an officer as Moltke—who at one point supplemented his income by translating Gibbons into German—then probably he would never have risen to senior rank.

As always, a special chapter in the history of the IDF during these years tells of female soldiers. In the 1967 war one woman was killed. In 1973 there were a handful of female casualties as the base at Bir Gafgafa, some fifty miles behind the Suez Canal, was hit by Egyptian surface-to-surface missiles. Those episodes apart, in both wars the vast majority of Israeli women conscripts served they always had. The *pkiddot plugatiyot* (company clerks) cleaned briefing rooms and served cookies in the rear;[40] there could be no question of having them join male units going into combat. A small number of reservists apart, Israeli women who were neither conscripts nor members of the standing army remained home. They did their jobs, looked after their families, and—according to legend—welcomed their returning menfolk with the words *yaale ve-yavo* (mount and enter, an adaptation of a traditional Jewish blessing). As the IDF remained mobilized during the months after the war, a handful of women were taken on as bus and lorry drivers. However, since time was relatively short and special qualifications were needed the size of the effort to substitute them for men was limited.

During the period of postwar reconstruction the IDF, desperately short of manpower, took another look at what it could and could not do with women. The number in each age group that was drafted rose sharply, from 50 percent in 1974 to 70 percent in 1993;[41] whereas in 1976 women could occupy only 210 out of 796 military occupation specialties, four years later the figure stood at 296.[42] As before, women continued to be administered by CHEN so that there could be no question of straightforward integration. Yet the MOS now open to women included drivers, maintenance personnel, radar operators, and instructors in a variety of fields from which they had heretofore been excluded. Traditionally the only female conscripts in charge of males were those who served in the IDF's education corps, teaching basics to underprivileged youths, one notable exception being Esther Shuchamarov, an Olympic-class athlete who was actually allowed to act as a MADASit (physical training instructor). Now, however, they were also supposed to teach such subjects as firing a rifle, driving a tank, and even operating an artillery piece.

These were the years when the U.S. armed forces, on orders from Congress, were preparing to take in women and accordingly conducted large-scale studies of the differences—if any—between them and men. Dutifully—and in contrast to work done in the fifties and sixties that often claimed to have discovered marked differences in the mental capacities of men and women—they concluded that the minds of the two sexes were the same; it was only in regard to physical strength, especially upper body strength, that differences existed.[43] Whether the IDF, before expanding the number of MOS open to women, also carried out similar studies is not known, but doing so would have been entirely out of character. Among the establishment, mostly of Ashkenazi origin, there never was any doubt that in regard to mental and technical qualities women were as capable of handling rifles, tanks, and other kinds of equipment as men.

Still, the use of women as instructors for men was not without its problems. For one thing even their supporters admitted that physically they were not up to par, thus imposing limitations in such jobs as artillery instruction, where the work is often hard and the loads heavy. Conversely, when they *were* used the result was to put an unfair burden on male comrades who had to do more than their fair share. Furthermore, for a nineteen- or twenty-year-old female NCO to gain the respect of conscripts—more than half of them from Sephardic backgrounds and thus still more or less influenced by their elders' ideas about a woman's place—was much harder than for male counterparts and often led to lax discipline if not to outright rebellion.[44] Last but not least the women, though they had been properly prepared for their jobs, never received basic training equal to that of their charges. Nor would they ever command units or go into combat. They knew it and so did the recruits. Thus being taught by females might be compared to taking driving lessons from an instructor who was experienced on simulators but never actually drove a car.

As Margaret Mead once wrote, in any society it is what the men do that matters. Conversely, the very fact that a field is occupied or a job is done predominantly by women will lead to a decline in social prestige,[45] and, after a while, ability to command material rewards and attract first-class people. In the IDF, women had traditionally been members of their own separate corps. As a result, they were seldom promoted beyond the rank of major and were excluded from most command jobs, let alone combat-related ones. Since the IDF was overwhelmingly combat-oriented this segregation and discrimination worked in its favor; they were precisely the factors that permitted IDF to use women *and* avoid the consequences of

Mead's law. In the mid- to late seventies, however, there were clear signs that the IDF's position in the eyes of Israeli society was no longer as secure as before. Primarily due to the fallout from the October War, it was probably not unrelated to the expansion of female roles.

Naturally some parts of the IDF suffered more than others. Probably the least affected was the air force, with its combination of strong professionalism and high technology. In the summer of 1981 it provided a dazzling display of new capabilities, using F–15s and F–16s to bomb and destroy the nuclear reactor the Iraqis were constructing near Baghdad.[46] Needless to say there were no women among the pilots, nor any women in the various *sayarot* (commando units) that had carried out the Entebbe raid and similar operations. The prestige of the *sayarot* and their ability to attract top-notch manpower was if anything enhanced by the fact that many of their officers found themselves on the fast lane to promotion; indeed they turned into a hotbed for future chiefs of staff.[47] Elsewhere, however, the growing presence of women; the drop in quality, cohesion, and experience that was the inevitable outcome of overly rapid expansion; and the ensuing organizational problems probably led to a force that, on a man-for-man basis, was not quite as good as its predecessor and certainly did not enjoy as high prestige.

Though he would be the last man to tolerate anybody criticizing the instrument he commanded, Eytan as chief of staff was clearly aware of some of these problems. While continuing to expand the IDF during the three and a half years that led up to the Lebanon War, he did what he could to restructure the somewhat dilapidated force he inherited from Gur. By Israeli standards, if not by those in many other armies, discipline was tightened. Units were made to train until they knew their weapons and missions by heart, even at the cost of sleep deprivation, which in turn led to growing numbers of accidents.[48] To show his determination to kick the army into shape Eytan insisted that uniforms be kept neat. He also sent out military police to make sure that soldiers wore their berets—a hopeless task, as it turned out, that ended in a compromise permitting personnel to carry them on the left shoulder. Since IDF officers seldom wear caps Eytan himself took the field in a slouch hat that became his trademark. Thus attired, he sought to set a personal example of parsimony by going out into the firing range to gather up the cartridges of spent artillery rounds. He even picked discarded crusts of bread from dustbins, had them fried, and forced his subordinates to eat them.[49] Although typical of the man, the performance did not win friends in the media or public.

In May 1980 Weizman resigned. Along with Dayan, who had served as Begin's foreign minister but left seven months earlier, he played a key role in negotiating the Camp David peace agreements with Egypt and the subsequent retreat from Sinai. As both men saw it, the accord left Israel in a stronger position than ever and should have opened the way to negotiations with Syria and the Palestinians; not so Begin who, taking the opposite tack, saw them as a means of holding on to the rest of the Occupied Territories. The prime minister's understanding of military matters was rudimentary, and he could not devote more than one day a week to them. Still he decided not to appoint a successor, serving as his own minister of defense and relying on a deputy, Brig. Gen. (ret.) Moredechai Tsippori, to do the day-to-day work. Inevitably the change meant that Eytan drew closer to the prime minister. Though their backgrounds were as different as could be—Begin the would-be aristocratic lawyer from Warsaw, Eytan the peasant from the Valley of Esdraelon—the two worked well together, and Eytan even felt that Begin liked him.[50]

A year later the defense portfolio went to Sharon. Having left the army for politics in 1974, Sharon had done much to fuse Begin's Cherut Party with some other right-wing parties, building Likud and helping it win the 1977 elections.[51] His reward was the ministry of agriculture, a position that to the uninitiated might look relatively unimportant but one that he used to build as many Jewish settlements in the Occupied Territories as possible and, in general, to strengthen Israel's hold on them.[52] Always distinguished by his brutal determination—the man who did not stop at the red light, as the title of his biography has it—in the meantime he had grown even more formidable. He was certainly not an easy person to stand up to, and in the end he was able to pressure a reluctant Begin into entrusting the defense post to him.[53]

With Sharon at the helm, the IDF's might peaked. As to organization and to quality of manpower, the officer corps specifically included, it may no longer have been quite as good as previously. Yet thanks partly to U.S. aid and partly to Israel's own efforts, quantitatively speaking the losses suffered in the October War had been made good several times over. An enormous military machine was built; it has been remarked that to equal Israel on a per-capita basis China, for example, would have had to deploy no fewer than 1 million tanks.[54] According to one set of figures, during the period 1954–1979 the ratio between the annual defense outlay of Egypt, Syria, and Jordan (the three so-called confrontation states) and that of Israel changed from 3:1 to 1.25:1.[55] According to another, as late as 1973 the relation between Israel's accumulated military capital and that of the same three countries had been as high as 1:3. From then on it began to tilt in Israel's favor, reaching 1:1.17 in 1979 and 1:1.1 in 1984.[56]

Moreover, and in contrast to the situation before 1973 (let alone before 1967), when only parts of the IDF had been equipped with modern arms, technologically this army was up to par in most respects and, as the Lebanese campaign would soon show, ahead of the pack in some. And its reach was no longer limited to the country's immediate borders. A long-range strike capability had been built. The navy with its larger missile boats and submarines was now capable of launching commando operations not just against nearby ports but against targets more than a thousand miles away. Still more important was the IAF's newly acquired airlift capability. Although its exact size is classified, already in 1976 it was massive enough for Air Force Commander Benjamin Peled to suggest that paratroopers be sent to "conquer" Uganda or, at least, the city of Entebbe.[57]

Considering the extremely difficult circumstances under which it had been constructed from 1973 on, this army was probably about as good as it could have been made. Some of its components, notably the air force and *sayarot*, were superb. Though the IDF was massively supported by U.S. technology and money, in large part its excellence was due to Israel's own efforts and, in particular, its burgeoning defense industries. Accordingly, before continuing with our history of the IDF proper, it is necessary to give a short account of the evolution of those industries.

Grenades into Mushroom Clouds: Israeli missile boats on maneuver, 1979.

CHAPTER 16

GRENADES INTO MUSHROOM CLOUDS

ISRAEL'S MILITARY industries originated during prestate days.[1] During World War I attempts were made to manufacture hand grenades, the necessary molds having been stolen from the Ottoman army. During the period 1919–1939 Hagana also made more or less sporadic efforts to manufacture explosives, small arms ammunition, copies of the Sten submachine gun, and more hand grenades—though some of them were so primitive that they scarcely deserved the name, having casings of concrete instead of steel.[2] From the beginning, manufacture was inseparable from repair and maintenance. Not only were many of the arms smuggled in defective, but once reconditioned they had to be kept in good order. All of this required setting up a certain infrastructure of engineers and technicians that, however, had to operate clandestinely and away from prying British eyes.

As British troops flooded Erets Yisrael during World War II, Jewish industry was given a tremendous boost. The number of workshops more than doubled to about 1,800; during the war their output was $180,000,000, with military orders accounting for two-thirds.[3] Compared to production in the main industrialized countries at the time, these figures counted for nothing, the more so because heavy industry was almost entirely absent. Compared to local Palestinians, however, the *Yishuv* was already beginning to draw light-years ahead. Thus in 1947 some 27 percent of the Jewish labor force was engaged in industry and another 60 percent in construction and services, leaving only 13 percent to till the land. At a time when Europe (including the USSR) and the United States still enjoyed a near monopoly on world higher education, much of the Jewish population was European-educated. In the form of the Hebrew University, the Technion, and the Weizman Institute the *Yishuv* possessed institutes of higher learning capable of training first-class engineers and scientists. By contrast, among the Arab population fully 60 percent of the employed population was in agriculture,[4] mostly *felaheen* living in hundreds of miserable villages without a penny to their name, with some Bedouins possessing even less.

As the War for Independence appeared on the horizon during the last years of the mandate, Hagana's arms industry expanded. In 1948 it was already manufacturing explosives, fuses, percussion caps, rifle grenades, PIATs, mortars, crude submachine guns, flamethrowers, mortars, various types of mines, and every kind of small arms ammunition used by the IDF. Yet the limits of its capacity are indicated by the fact that it could not undertake to produce a "complex" weapon such as the British Bren medium machine gun, let alone crew-operated weapons systems with internal combustion engines and transmissions consisting of thousands of precision parts. As important as production, repair and maintenance of the arms that now flowed into the country from abroad were required. Not all could be successfully absorbed: Some tanks and artillery arrived in such poor shape that they were never deployed, and the serviceability of IAF aircraft in particular was always rather low. Still it was higher than among the enemy and, at any rate, sufficient to win the war.

This is hardly the place to follow the growth of the military industries during the fifties and sixties, progressing as they did at an equal rate with the Israeli economy as a whole. Suffice it to say that, although by world standards it was still a pygmy, TAAS at the time of the October War was manufacturing most types of ammunition in use by the IDF, from small arms bullets to rockets and bombs for aircraft to 105mm rounds for tank guns, 106mm rounds for recoilless rifles, and 155mm artillery shells.[5] Barrels for these guns, as well as the 30mm aircraft gun used by the IAF, were just beginning to be manufactured by Soltam, a privately owned heavy-metal-working company. Yet another company was using German know-how in order to produce gasmasks.

In addition to TAAS the ministry of defense turned to RAFAEL (Rashut Le-pituach Emtsaei Luchama, the Weapon Development Authority). Founded during the fifties, it at first had built primitive radio-guided motorboats for use against shipping. When the 1967 crisis broke, it was hard at work on the first generation of Shafrir air-to-air missiles as well as the Gavriel sea-to-sea missile; however, a short-range surface-to-surface missile it tried to develop suffered from guidance problems and was not a success.[6] Israel Aircraft Industries (IAI), founded by Shimon Peres during the mid-fifties,[7] was doing maintenance work and manufacturing the Fouga Magister trainer under license from France, adding rockets and machine guns so it could double as a light close-support aircraft. A few years later Peres also helped set up a variety of electronics industries. Starting with batteries and transistors, they progressed over time to greater things. Among them were communications gear, radar, computers, and, increasingly, guidance systems for families of missiles.

Many kinds of equipment being produced were standard issue and could be purchased elsewhere. Others, particularly the runway-busting Durendal bomb (see Chapter 11), various types of missiles, and the Uzi submachine gun, were original—the latter even became something of a national symbol. Long before 1967 some equipment was being exported, including, besides the Uzi, mortars, ammunition, and detachable fuel tanks developed to increase the range of IAF fighters.[8] Even more important for the future (as there still could be no question of manufacturing major weapons such as tanks or combat aircraft), the ministry of defense was acquiring an impressive capability for modifying and upgrading the systems it possessed. Perhaps the most visible achievements in this field were the upgraded Super Sherman tanks—ultimately provided with a French low-velocity 105mm gun instead of the original 75mm gun—as well as the 105mm self-propelled "Priest" artillery piece. The former probably explains the vast discrepancy between the size of the armored corps as it appears in published international sources and its actual strength as given by General Tal—if that was in fact its actual strength. The latter played an important role in the capture of Abu Ageila during the June 1967 war and thus in bringing about the Egyptians' collapse.

By that time, according to an official statement, Israel was self-producing about one-fifth of its defense requirements.[9] This does not mean that building up the military industries was always easy. During the fifties and sixties Israel was—and regarded itself—as a small, dirt-poor, out-of-the-way country, with the result that those trying to build a native manufacturing capability were often perceived as visionaries or worse. The IDF itself was not always cooperative; from the Gavriel missile in the sixties through the Lavi fighter in the eighties to the Chets antiballistic missile in the early nineties, it doubted the ability of native industry to provide it and preferred to look abroad for its requirements. Other bones of contention that arose included the division of tasks between the IDF and industry; for example, whether third-echelon maintenance should be carried out by the IAF or IAI and whether RAFAEL should be allowed to go into manufacturing and thereby occupy a niche competing with other firms. Finally, as the arms industry expanded and became more sophisticated during the seventies and eighties, it sometimes excited the ire of its U.S. counterpart. The Americans feared, not entirely without justification, that by helping the Israelis develop technology, the United States was simply financing its own competition.[10]

Yet the factor that caused the greatest expansion of the arms industry was the Six Day War of June 1967, which left the IDF with a large amount of captured Soviet weapons including tanks, light armored vehicles, artillery, and small arms—not to mention mountains of miscellaneous equipment. Not all proved suitable for Israeli use, but some did, and soon after the war TAAS started producing ammunition for Kalashnikov assault rifles as well as shells for 130mm field guns; by 1970, according to Peres, self-sufficiency in all sorts of ammunition had been achieved.[11] Adapting captured T-54 and T-55 tanks to carry the armored corps's standard 105mm gun was more difficult; it too was accomplished, albeit at the cost of reducing the tanks' already limited ammunition payload. Other major tasks carried out in the wake of the Six Day War included the conversion of gasoline-engine tanks to diesel and 90mm guns to 105mm guns.

From the industry's point of view, an even more important outcome of the Six Day War was the imposition of a French arms embargo, which was later extended to near total. This gave the proponents of native development the rationale they had been looking for.[12] Israel and the IDF, it was argued, constituted a large enough market to justify efforts aimed at attaining self-sufficiency in a very large number of fields, from webbing and ammunition to spare parts to small and even medium arms. As to major weapons systems, complete autonomy clearly was out of reach; even much larger and richer countries such as Britain, Italy, and Germany began pooling their resources during the seventies to develop such systems as the Tornado fighter-bomber. With outside help, however, it might be possible to develop one major weapons system for each field. Since Israeli labor costs remained lower than elsewhere the price was expected to be bearable. Apart from the political advantages of extending the country's breadth in case of embargo, it would develop the economy, provide employment, and save hard currency (Israel was always short).

In fact, Israel during these years was flexing its military manufacturing muscle on a scale that had a very significant impact on its own economy (although still small by world standards). As a result, between 1966 and 1968, TAAS's sales alone rose 74 percent.[13] By 1972 investment in the arms industry was three and a half times greater than in 1967, and between 1968 and 1974 the electronics and metal-working industries together absorbed one-third of all industrial investments made in Israel.[14] Simultaneously the proportion of industrial workers employed in defense doubled from under 10 percent to 19 percent. Even this was nothing compared to what followed: The value of military industrial output rose from $500 million in 1974 to $1,400 million in 1980 to $2,250 million in 1984.[15] By that time defense took up 40 percent of metal demand and 50 percent of electronics demand;[16] having doubled since 1972, the number of employees reached 62,500 and accounted for one-quarter of all employees in industry.[17]

Compared to its foreign competitors, Israel's military industries enjoyed several advantages. Though tucked away in the Middle East and by no means a First World country, from an educational and professional point of view Israel was far ahead of the developing world. Its scientific and engineering elite was better than anything to be found between Rome and Tokyo but cost much less to train and maintain than its counterparts in the West.[18] General conscription, the existence of the reserve system, and the country's small size meant that this elite was not detached from military affairs, often the case in Western countries in particular. Instead it was intimately involved with the defense establishment; if the scientist or engineer no longer served in the IDF, his or her children almost certainly did. Finally, the October War in 1973 and the numerous skirmishes that followed provided combat experience unmatched by other countries in scale and modernity. In effect, Israel during the mid- to late seventies had become one huge military laboratory.

Owing to the high cost of research and development, which has to be spread among as many products as possible, the modern economics of arms production often depends on the ability to export. However, exporting major weapons systems from Israel was difficult given its position as a pariah state; after the 1973 war so many countries had severed diplomatic relations with Israel that the number of foreign embassies fell to around thirty. In the event a handful of Kfir fighter-bombers were sold to several bargain-hunting Latin American countries. A few more Kfirs went to the United States, which substituted them for MIG–21s in air-to-air combat simulations, the characteristics of the two being remarkably similar. That apart, the fact that many foreign military establishments simply could not afford to display the "Made in Israel" label placed a damper on the export of major weapons systems.

But these factors did not apply with the same force to sale of other military equipment. The list of direct customers included dozens of countries on every continent; the list of products, everything from patrol boats, missiles, and electronic equipment down to humble small arms, pistols, and ammunition.[19] Like the notorious arms dealer Sir Basil Zaharoff decades earlier, Israel often did business with both sides of a conflict: Taiwan and Communist China, Chile and Argentina, and Peru and Ecuador, for example.[20] The upgrade kits that Israeli industry developed for aircraft and tanks also showed a potential for export. They appealed to Third World countries, which sought to modernize their own order of battle without breaking the bank; for example, providing active armor for an old tank cost only $10,000, compared to $1–2 million for a new unit.[21] Quantitatively speaking the total export sales in question are said to have risen from $200 million in 1974 to $1,200 million in 1980 (how this may be reconciled with the previously cited *total* output of $1,400 million in the same year is not clear) to $1,400 million in 1984. By that time defense accounted for 40 percent of all industrial exports, excluding diamonds.[22]

The first complete major weapons system to be produced in Israel was the Kfir in the early seventies, which was not original or able to match the new generation of U.S. combat aircraft then coming into service, the F–15s and F–16s. Seeking the ability to design and develop aircraft from scratch, IAI during the late sixties started work on two other machines, the Arava and the Westwind. The former was a light transport aircraft especially adapted to operating from the short, primitive runways that might be found near the battlefield or in less-developed countries. The latter was a twin-engine executive jet, its design having been purchased from a U.S. firm; IAI converted it to a naval patrol aircraft by adding complex electronics in the nose. It was intended that both aircraft would also be exported, but in the event sales proved disappointing; by 1976 neither plane had even remotely approached the break-even point and the huge losses that ensued led to the resignation of IAI's founder, Al Schwimmer.[23] All the while the company was sinking money into the design of an advanced Israeli-designed fighter-bomber. The idea that the IAF's combat structure should have two tiers—a few high-performance aircraft and many less sophisticated machines—had originated with Ezer Weizman when he commanded the air force in the 1960s. As minister of defense, he pushed for its realization.

Originally, the Lavi, as the aircraft was called, was a small, lightweight fighter-bomber intended to replace the nearly obsolete Skyhawks and Kfirs at reasonable cost. Later, though, technical considerations caused refinement after refinement. Like counterparts elsewhere, Israeli engineers found it difficult to resist building the best and most advanced machine; but whenever they thought they had achieved it a new and even more promising technical advance appeared on the horizon, begging to be incorporated.[24] Consequently the aircraft grew until it became something like a little brother of the F–16; one can imagine Begin's bemusement when, during his term as minister of defense, he was called upon to decide whether the two aircraft should share the same engine. Under Sharon its prospects continued to look good, and in 1983 they improved again when the defense portfolio was taken over by Moshe Arens. Former IAI director, he liked the Lavi for its own qualities and for the potential impact its development would have on Israel's high-tech industry.

At this point the project ran into problems. The United States much preferred that the IAF purchase U.S.-made aircraft, and consequently it limited, though never completely prohibited, the conversion of military aid into Israeli currency. As Israel went into an economic recession in

1983–1984, the IAF was forced to cut back the number of Lavis it intended to purchase by more than one-half, from 350–400 to 150–200. As a result, per-unit price shot up, and it became imperative that the aircraft be exported so as to recover the development costs. However, the United States controlled much of the technology earmarked for the Lavi, including besides the engine the advanced composite materials for the airframe and wings. Hence prospects for exporting the Lavi, if completed, depended entirely on U.S. approval. When Rabin, who was strongly pro-American and since the sixties had opposed many native arms production projects, took over from Arens in 1984, the writing was on the wall. A year into office, he decided to cancel the Lavi and purchase F–16s instead.[25]

Although efforts to build a fighter-bomber did not yield fruit, Israel did produce a major weapons system, the Merkava tank. Tal in the sixties had developed an armored doctrine that differed significantly from that of other armies. The latter regarded mobility as the key and talked about using tanks on the offensive (although they never actually did so until 1991). Not so the IDF, which, considering the tank's greatest advantage to be protection under fire, preferred to fight defensively behind cover whenever possible. However, the U.S. M–60 was one of the tallest tanks ever produced and thus was not really suitable for that purpose. It had several other weaknesses, among them comparatively weak armor; a large and therefore easy-to-hit turret; and a tendency, which it shared with older U.S. tanks, to go up in flames when hit.

Accordingly, when the Merkava was unveiled it displayed some highly unusual features. The engine, the same 900-horsepower one as used in the M–60, was located in the front instead of the rear, thus placing several extra tons of steel between glacis and crew. The extra room allowed for a large compartment that, for the sake of rapid turnover, was capable of being loaded with ammunition from a forklift; it could also be used to transport several infantrymen or to carry a casualty or two. The turret was exceptionally well designed, flat and tapered. Like the Uzi in its time, the fifty-something–ton monster could almost stand as a metaphor for the IDF; wits claimed that it had a big body, a small head, and a gigantic. . . .

The Merkava, with its 105mm gun, laser range finder, computerized fire-control system, and TAAS-designed, elongated "Arrow" armor-piercing ammunition, was able to take on any enemy tank, including the Soviet-made T–72 with its enormous 125mm gun. Even so, it merely was the centerpiece of Israel's effort to upgrade its armor by means of native industries. In 1956 and 1967 the ratio of forces to space in the Middle East had been relatively low, permitting the IDF to wend through the less mobile Arab formations and attack from unexpected directions. This was much less the case in 1973 when the Golan front in particular had been crowded chock-a-block with units and weapons, leaving no gap uncovered and forcing the advance on Damascus to be made in the teeth of tenacious Syrian resistance. Considering its own subsequent growth and that of the enemy the IDF expected the future battlefield to be more crowded still; it would, to use a favorite phrase of the time, be "saturated with fire."[26] Accordingly it was necessary to find new means for protecting not only the Merkavas but the other tanks as well.

When they were put on display in the early eighties, the IDF's U.S.-built M–48s and M–60s had sprouted curious protrusions, like short horns with holes. The mystery was solved when Israel invaded Lebanon. A major surprise of the October War was the Sagger antitank guided missiles, used by Egyptian and Syrian infantry to stop the previously unstoppable Israeli tanks. The Israeli armor was designed to resist tungsten bolts fired from high-velocity guns, but it proved vulnerable to the "hollow" warheads that tipped the Saggers. Whereas the Merkava had been designed to overcome that problem, the IDF's other tanks had to be adapted by adding "active" armor. Active armor used explosives inside flat boxes made of thin steel; they were designed to deflect the jet of gas that resulted when a hollow warhead hit its target. Screwed onto the above-mentioned protrusions, active armor made the tanks look like a man in an inflatable swimsuit.

When the IDF marched into Lebanon, only the tanks and self-propelled artillery had received the new protection. Not so the mechanized infantry; with aluminum-covered M–113s, the men discovered they were death traps—when hit by a hollow warhead they would burst into flame. Accordingly the APCs received a layer of Israeli-made active armor, which added weight and in time made it necessary to re-engine them. Not content with this, Tal pushed for the adoption of heavier carriers truly capable of marching alongside tanks on the fire-soaked battlefield. The result was the NAGMASHA (the feminine of NAGMASH, the Hebrew acronym for APC), a unique Israeli contraption with no foreign equivalent. Its hull consisted of a modified Centurion tank with the turret removed and the interior adapted to carry infantry and their weapons (e.g., machine guns and antitank missiles).

Less visible than combat aircraft and tanks, the systems developed to counter the Arab antiaircraft defenses represented revolutionary technology. Understandably, not much was said about the subject during the seventies, but when the IDF next went into action it unveiled a series of new technologies. They ranged from humble flares—designed to mislead heat-seeking air-to-ground missiles—to electronic jammers to ground-to-air missiles that locked on enemy radar and stayed locked even after the radar was switched off. Some older planes were fitted with new radar built by Elta, others with modern navigation and computerized ordnance-dropping systems. To orchestrate this technology the IAF needed an entirely new network of command, communications, and control. That, too, was accomplished, with the result that in 1982 the gigantic system functioned like clockwork.

Another product that attracted attention during the Lebanon War was remotely piloted vehicles (RPVs). In 1973 the Israelis often suffered from lack of tactical intelligence as heavy enemy fire prevented aircraft and ground units from gathering it. Thus two different companies, IAI and Tadiran, started work on two different RPVs. In some ways the contraptions exemplified Israel's defense industry at its best; developed in close cooperation with the IDF, they were simple, robust, and well adapted for use under field conditions; owing to the use of off-the-shelf components (such as wheels taken from baby carriages) they were also cheap. The original models carried television cameras that relayed pictures to the operators, literally enabling them to see events on the other side of the hill. Later models were provided with laser range finders, which permitted them to act as artillery spotters. Other models carried radar-jamming equipment or carried out kamikaze strikes against enemy radar stations. The RPV family of weapons proved a hit, and many models were exported.

A shipping industry had long been developing near Haifa, Israel's major port and largest industrial center. Though it never had the capacity to construct large oceangoing vessels, it was capable of overhauling the navy's missile boats and building small vessels from scratch. During the seventies and early eighties it constructed hulls for the second- and third-generation missile boats. The engines still had to be imported, as were some of the weapons systems. Other systems, including of course the new versions of the Gavriel missile, were produced in Israel, as were the radar, computers, and electronic countermeasures designed to protect ships from enemy missiles such as the French Exocet, made famous during the Anglo-Argentine Falklands War. With Israel's navy supplying most all of its workload, the company that built the missile boats, Mispenot Yisael, later went bankrupt. This did not prevent other companies, such as MABAT (Mifalim Bitchoniyim, an IAI subsidiary), from manufacturing smaller patrol boats, some of which were exported.

Perhaps the most important component of Israel's arms manufacturing was also the least visible. This book, based mostly on non-Israeli sources, has already discussed the acquisition of nuclear weapons, an objective apparently achieved by 1967 (even though the devices at the time may have been too crude for operational use).[27] Based on calculations pertaining to the size of the reactor that had been provided by France, during the decade or so after 1973, foreign experts assumed that Israel was capable of producing enough plutonium for approximately two or three devices per year. By the mid-eighties this should have resulted in a modest arsenal numbering perhaps thirty to forty bombs[28] (although Israel, in a formula first developed under Eshkol, still insisted that it would not be the first to introduce them into the Middle East). In 1979 a flash in the Indian Ocean picked up by a U.S. satellite was widely interpreted as a joint Israeli–South African nuclear test. The Israelis, however, denied that they had tested a weapon, and the United States backed them up, saying the satellite might have been faulty.[29]

Aside from occasional references, matters rested until 1986. That year the experts were sent scurrying back to their figures by the defection of Mordechai Vanunu, a technician at the Dimona plant. From the point of view of the mass media, Vanunu's greatest significance consisted in that he made available the first pictures of Israel's highly sophisticated plutonium separation plant, thus filling in a critical gap in the puzzle that had mystified experts since the sixties. To those in the know, however, two other points were more important.[30] First, it appeared that the capacity of the reactor had been enlarged at least once. Based on these calculations, it should have been able to produce much more plutonium than originally thought; this caused the estimate of the number of bombs already built to be revised, up to as many as 100–200.[31] Second, Israel apparently had been interested in lithium deutride; indeed heavy isotopes of hydrogen were later said to have been among the materials Israel provided South Africa.[32] This in turn indicated plans to build hydrogen bombs (either true fusion devices or so-called boosted fission devices with lithium cores), neutron bombs, or tactical nuclear weapons. Supposing it weighed about a half-ton, a warhead belonging to any one of the three types would have explained the Rabin government's decision to purchase short-range but deadly accurate Lance missiles from the United States.[33] At any rate, in principle Israel should have been able to pursue all three courses simultaneously had it wanted to.

If Israel, as foreign reports have claimed, did in fact acquire its first nuclear devices before the Six Day War, then its only delivery vehicle would have been the French-made Vautour light bombers available at the time (assuming, that is, a bomb weighing no more than a ton and also that IAI would have had the capacity to carry out the necessary modifications). In 1968–1970 these aircraft were joined by Skyhawks and Phantoms, both of which possessed much larger ordnance payloads. At any rate, and in light of the losses it took during the war, the IAF cannot have felt comfortable with aircraft as the only delivery vehicle.

Long before, in fact, Israel had started work on the development of surface-to-surface missiles.[34] From the late fifties on, RAFAEL was designing and building a solid-fuel, two-stage meteorological rocket capable of carrying a five-pound (two-kg) payload to an altitude of sixty-five miles. A test-firing took place in July 1961, the timing dictated by the need to forestall the Egyptians displaying *their* missiles (which did not work) on Revolution Day. Observers outside Israel were left to speculate on what would happen if the Israelis succeeded in marrying their rocket to a nuclear warhead. In fact the subsequent fate of Shavit (Comet) 2, as the rocket was known, is not clear (published accounts of its development end with the test launch). It cannot have been judged a great success, or else Shimon Peres in September 1962 would scarcely have signed a contract with the French company Dassault to develop a 280-mile-range, two-stage surface-to-surface missile capable of carrying a 750-kg warhead.

According to journalist Seymour Hersh, work on the missiles' underground storage tubes was approaching completion in December 1967 when Dayan gave orders for Yigal Allon to be allowed to visit them—the idea being to convert the minister who previously had been among the bomb's staunchest opponents.[35] A recent Dassault publication claims that when de Gaulle imposed his embargo in January 1969, only prototypes and parts were ready and were subsequently delivered to Israel in spite of the French president's orders.[36] At the time the October War broke out, some of the missiles may or may not have been operational,[37] but for our purpose it matters little. The main point is that if foreign sources may be believed, at some moment during the seventies Israel's efforts led to the deployment at Chirbet Zachariya, a remote area in the Judean foothills, of nuclear-tipped surface-to-surface missiles. They had the range to reach the capitals of each neighbor (although, in the case of Cairo, with little to spare).

Against this background, the entire character of the Arab-Israeli conflict began to change. Already in the early sixties some Arab commentators had concluded that stalemate would ensue should Israel obtain nuclear weapons; any hope of wiping the Zionist entity off the map would vanish forever. Faced with the need to recover lost territory, between 1967 and 1973 the Egyptians in particular did their best to close their eyes to the strong probability that an Israeli bomb already existed, going so far as to insist that any reports on the matter were merely part of an Israeli psychological warfare campaign. In the wake of the October War, however, such an attitude became more and more difficult to sustain. What is more, if it *had* been sustained it would have begged the real question: Why did the "victorious" Arabs not husband all their resources and launch another war modeled on the 1973 one (as was demanded, for example, by the former Egyptian chief of staff, Saad Shazly)?

For its part, Israel during these years maintained its official line and continued to insist that it would not be the first to introduce the bomb into the Middle East. Nevertheless, from time to time hints concerning Israel's nuclear capability were dropped as if by accident. Thus, in December 1974 Pres. Efrayim Katsir—a founder of TAAS and former member of Israel's Atomic Energy Commission—answered a question concerning the existence of nuclear weapons by saying that civilian and nuclear energy were inseparable.[38] In March 1976 a story concerning a state of nuclear alert that Israel had allegedly proclaimed during the October War surfaced in *Time* and was reprinted word for word on the front page of Israel's daily (itself a remarkable occurrence since the IDF censor has the power to prevent such publication and often used it in the past). On both occasions relations with Syria happened to be particularly tense, and the IDF mobilized its reserves. I leave it to the reader to guess whether there are grounds for assuming these facts are connected.

According to two Israeli specialists who have studied the matter, "The period between 1977 and 1986 [the Vanunu revelations] was characterized above all by the elimination of any doubt in the Arab world as to the existence of an Israeli bomb and the possibility that Israel might use it in case of an existential threat."[39] In fact, references to the question began to multiply almost immediately after the October War; thus the editor of Egypt's *Al Aharam* (and Nasser's former minister of information), Muhamad Heikal, wrote that Israel's "defeat" in that conflict would cause it to place greater reliance on nuclear weapons.[40] Writing in a Lebanese newspaper toward the middle of 1974, a retired Syrian intelligence officer, Mohammed Ayubi, presented a similar line of thought. In his opinion the October War had shattered Tel Aviv's belief in the superiority of its conventional arms. Accordingly, should there be another clash it might well resort to the use of chemical, biological, and nuclear weapons.[41]

Although spokesmen in both Cairo and Damascus thus agreed on the danger of launching another 1973-style attack on Israel, the conclusions they drew differed. In the case of Egypt, the near certainties that an Israeli bomb existed and that its use could not be ruled out seem to have played important roles in the events that led to the Camp David Accords (even though this could never be acknowledged since it would make peace look very much like a surrender).[42] The position of Syria was more difficult. Rabin's government had shown itself prepared to move toward peace with Egypt by relinquishing part of the Sinai. However, Foreign Minister Yigal Allon was a representative of the Jordan Valley settlements; coming from

Ginossar on the shore of Lake Galilee, he vehemently opposed any return of the Golan Heights. Besides, the Israelis reserved special hatred for the Syrians, regarded as the most implacable of their enemies. Had not Israeli prisoners taken during the fifties been savagely tortured and finally returned as madmen? Begin, who took over from Rabin in 1977, was even more determined to retain the Golan Heights. In 1980 he passed a law through the Knesset, formally annexing it to Israel.

Thus, since Israel's attachment to the Golan was stronger than to the Sinai, even had the Syrians wanted to—which was and remains doubtful—they would have found the road to peace more difficult than for the Egyptians. While Sadat was taking that road, Assad on various occasions still talked about the need for a military solution that, he claimed, was being prepared. To do so he had to convince himself and his audience that a way existed to implement such a solution without risking nuclear war. A careful reading of his statements between the mid-seventies and late eighties shows him toying with several possibilities.[43] At times he returned to the pre-1967 notion of a popular war, using Algeria, Vietnam, "and other countries which I do not wish to mention" as analogous cases.[44] At times he insisted that since Israel was such a small country it would not be able to use any nuclear weapons it had.[45] At other times he referred to something called "strategic parity," either announcing that the Arabs too would acquire nuclear weapons or appearing to put his trust in chemical warfare as a means for offsetting the Israeli nuclear threat.[46] Finally, in 1985 he seems to have tried to obtain a nuclear guarantee from the Soviet Union.[47] Judging by the fact that new hostilities have not broken out a quarter-century after the 1973 October War, none of these "solutions" seems to have been satisfactory. Moreover, there is no reason to think that the Arabs are more capable of finding their way out of the nuclear predicament than were the superpowers during the Cold War.

Partly because of the looming if unacknowledged nuclear factor, partly for other reasons, in the late seventies Israel's strategic position was becoming "completely different" (in the words of Ezer Weizman).[48] First came the peace talks with Egypt, which were crowned by the Camp David Accords. Following the Israeli withdrawal from the Sinai, the peninsula was demilitarized and the pre-1967 situation restored in many respects. The Israelis no longer confronted the Egyptians eyeball-to-eyeball; instead more than one hundred miles of desert terrain and a small UN force separated the former enemies in the south. Last but not least, Israel was able to retain the Gaza Strip. Consequently it no longer had Egypt's army standing within fifty miles of Tel Aviv.

To replace the two modern airfields that the IAF had to return to Egypt (not allowed to be used for military purposes) the United States financed and helped build two better ones inside the Negev Desert. Though Sharm al-Sheikh had to be surrendered, so long as peace lasted the opening of the Suez Canal enabled Israel's navy to transfer warships between the Mediterranean and the Red Sea for the first time. Militarily Egypt was now more or less out of the picture; although its army remains strong in regional terms, it is difficult to imagine it engaging in major hostilities against Israel without the support of a superpower, which, of course, it no longer has. To be sure, it was still necessary to take some precautions. But when the Israelis invaded Lebanon, Sadat's successor, Hosni Mubaraq, did not stir.

On the eastern front, the same was true of Iraq. Its nuclear potential aside, throughout the seventies its growing conventional power had bothered the IDF. The latter did not forget how Iraqi expeditionary forces had participated in most wars from 1948 through 1973. Some IDF commanders even argued that it had been the Iraqi expeditionary force that had stopped the drive toward Damascus in 1973,[49] although how so few (one brigade) could have achieved so much against so many (two divisions) remains unclear. Be this as it may, in 1980 Saddam Hussein engaged in a murderous war against Iran and for several years thereafter appeared to be on the brink of defeat. Israel for its part did not conceal its delight: Chief of Staff Eytan at one point said that "both sides are so stubborn—may they go on [fighting each other]." This left Syria and, at a pinch, Jordan with whose king Begin was unable to establish the kind of rapport that Rabin and Allon had enjoyed.[50] However, by 1979, Israel was outspending both countries combined by a ratio of 3:2;[51] measured in terms of accumulation of military capital, the ratio was 1.46:1.[52]

Traditionally Israel had regarded itself, not without justification, as a small island amid an Arab sea. Whatever the underlying "strategic" realities, its public can be excused for regarding itself as subject to destruction at the hands of pitiless Arab hordes bent not only on eliminating the state but also on physically killing its people. In 1948 this feeling motivated the young Rabin when he had made "an inner resolution to devote my life so that never again will Israel be caught unprepared for war which may be forced on us, but will be prepared to fight back with well-trained soldiers and the best available weapons."[53] The feeling of imminent disaster prevailed during the horrible weeks preceding the 1967 Six Day War and again during April–May 1970 (when there were ominous signs that the USSR might intervene in the War of Attrition while the West, judging by its record in Czechoslovakia in 1968, would do nothing). The climax came during and immediately after the 1973 October War, when there was much talk of the Holocaust syndrome and the Masada complex.

But during the years under discussion, this feeling began to fade away. Some, among them Bar Lev and Weizman, felt that the seemingly unending cycle of wars was finally about to be broken.54 Others, such as Ariel Sharon, were less optimistic but basked in the IDF's newly found power; during his tenure as minister of defense he stated that Israel was capable of overrunning the entire Arab Middle East from the Atlantic Ocean to the Persian Gulf.55 Always tending to be stout, by now he had developed almost preternatural girth. The minister of defense appeared to personify the new IDF; perhaps no longer lean, it was definitely mean. However, in this case as in so many others the outcome of hubris was tragedy. In June 1982 the mighty military machine Israel had built was destined to be thrown away in the one country, and against the one opponent, where it stood no chance and was foredoomed to defeat.

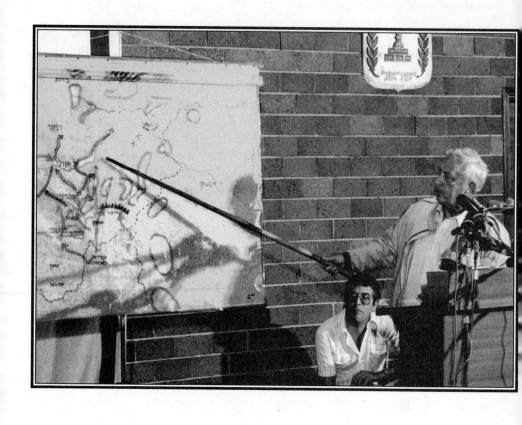

"The Lebanese Morass": "I went to Beirut a-Hunting Arabs."

"THE LEBANESE MORASS"

NTIL 1968 the Israel-Lebanon border had been the most peaceful. Indeed Israeli politicians often said that Lebanon would be the second Arab country to conclude peace with Israel, presumably after a larger neighbor showed the way. In that year, however, the quiet was interrupted when the Palestine Liberation Organization started using the country's southern districts—including in particular the difficult terrain on the foothills of Mount Chermon—as a base for terrorist operations against Israel. Over the next year or two a dreary pattern emerged.[1] Various Arab guerrilla organizations such as al Fatach, the Popular Front for the Liberation of Palestine (PFLP), and the Syrian-supported al Saiqa would rocket and infiltrate and ambush and plant mines. Not then or later did they achieve any strategic gains, but they did inflict military and civilian casualties.

Seeking to counter the threat, IDF Northern Command would patrol, shell, bomb, and raid. Some of its operations were aimed directly at the guerrillas in the field. Others sought to hit the villages and refugee camps that gave them shelter and in which their headquarters, recruitment areas, training grounds, and arms stores were allegedly located. From time to time an exasperated Israel sought to counter the threat with larger measures, using the IAF and navy to strike deep into Lebanon or mounting miniature invasions. For example, on May 12, 1969, two columns of some one hundred vehicles crossed the border. Supported from the air, they occupied a forty-five-square-mile area opposite Kiryat Shmona, held it for thirty-four hours, and screened the population of the six villages it contained. After killing twenty presumed guerrillas, the Israelis withdrew. The enemy remained undaunted, however, and less than twelve hours later, mortar rounds and rockets were again falling on Israeli soil.

Then and later, some of the attacks were launched by Palestinian organizations on their own initiative. Others were assisted by Syria's army, which provided weapons and used the Palestinians as proxies. The Lebanese government was ambivalent. Lebanon was and remains a country divided among numerous ethnic groups such as Christians, Druze, Shiites, and Sunnis. All were further divided into subgroups, and many were being manipulated to one extent or another by the powerful Syrian neighbor on the east—not to mention other Arab rulers who, if only to thwart Syria, also had a finger in the pie. Depending on the momentary balance of power among the various parties, the prime minister would attempt to suppress the guerrillas or allow them a free hand or cooperate with them or pretend to do one of these three while in fact doing something else. Coming under Israeli attack, the Lebanese would loudly complain that they were not to blame. And in fact theirs is less a unified state than a beehive of competing peoples and factions, all heavily armed and with a tradition of mutual hatred.

In May 1973, following one particularly vicious Israeli raid into the center of Beirut, Lebanon's slide into civil war began. As riots broke out in the refugee camps, Christian Pres. Suleyman Franjiyeh ordered Lebanon's army and air force into action against the Palestinians. They soon discovered that the latter had allied with the Druze and Shiites, both of whom feared the move might herald a Christian attempt to achieve supremacy at their expense. Beset on all sides at once, the army simply melted away. By 1975 the country was in chaos as an astounding number of militias fought each other tooth and nail. The Christians alone fielded four different militias: Bashir Gemayel's Phalange, Kamel Chamoun's Tigers, and two smaller forces belonging to Franjiyeh and George Kassis. Counting the various religious and Palestinian militias, the total number must have come to more than fifty.

As Lebanon disintegrated Israel acted. Although cross-border activity never ceased, compared to what was going on in the north and center of Lebanon the south was an oasis of quiet and attracted many refugees. Guided by Shimon Peres as minister of defense,[2] Israel sought to establish a kind of protectorate over the area. It would help the local Shiites set up their own armed force; paid for, trained, and equipped by the IDF, it would do its bit in protecting the border against attack. The policy was known as the "Good Fence," after the heavily guarded fence separating Israel and Lebanon. From 1976 on, the gates in the fence became as important as the fence itself. Through them passed Israeli supplies and military advisers in one direction, Lebanese civilians seeking work and medical treatment in the other.

During the first period of civil war Syrian intervention was generally limited to manipulating the various sides and providing arms. In June 1976, Syria invaded Lebanon, however, ostensibly to help Palestinians against their enemies and make sure they would be in a position to continue their struggle against Israel. The story of subsequent Syrian involvement is immensely complicated; suffice it to say they allied now with one side, then with another, taking on militia after militia and invariably defeating them in short, sharp encounters. How they managed this without falling apart, as would virtually every other army caught in a similar situation since 1945, has never been properly studied. All the while they were obviously determined to extend their own influence and by 1982 ended up dominating Lebanon's eastern and central regions.

In the face of the Syrian threat, Israel's initial response had been to issue stern warnings against an invasion.[3] When that did not work, first Rabin and then Begin sought to draw "red lines," which the Syrians were not supposed to cross. In fact an understanding was reached by which the Syrians undertook not to activate their air force against the IAF—which had been roaming over Lebanon for years—and not to station antiaircraft missiles in the country. Above all, they were to remain north of a line stretching from the mouth of the Zaharani River on the Mediterranean to the village of Mashki in the Beqa Valley to the east,[4] thereby leaving a sort of no-man's-land where PLO, supported by Syria, fought for domination against Israel and its Shiite allies.

Against this background of continual skirmishes, March 11, 1978, was a particularly bad day. A PLO party left Damour (in northern Lebanon) by sea, landed south of Haifa, and killed an American woman tourist they met on the beach. Next they hijacked a bus that was driving south along the coastal highway; thanks to deficient coordination between the IDF and the Israeli police, they were able to get as far as the northern outskirts of Tel Aviv before they were stopped. By the time the incident was terminated, thirty-seven Israelis were dead, the majority having been killed by the terrorists but some apparently by the security forces as they stormed the bus. Previously Begin as opposition leader had repeatedly chided Rabin for not being tough enough on Lebanese-based terrorism. Now he and Weizman organized two brigades—some 7,000 troops with artillery and tanks—and, after a weeklong weather delay, sent them rolling into southern Lebanon.

How Chief of Staff Gur, who during his term as CO Northern Command had been in charge of several similar operations, could have hoped to beat the PLO by such cumbersome means remains a mystery. Possibly he had learned nothing from the lessons of Vietnam, where countless similar operations had failed; more likely he and his masters just wanted to assuage outraged Israeli public opinion. In any event local Lebanese paid the price as dozens were killed, hundreds had their homes demolished, and tens of thousands fled north to escape the shelling and aerial bombardment. Needless to say the guerrillas, having had plenty of warning, also fled, some with their arms and others without (then again, outside the Occupied Territories acquiring additional light arms never constituted a problem for the PLO). Having suffered more than thirty dead, the IDF, five days after "Operation Litani" began, was back at its starting line. The only tangible result, if it may be called that, was the creation of a small UN observation force, which took up positions north of the border.

In retrospect "Operation Litani" constituted a turning point. It not only proved that the IDF did not know how to deal with the PLO but also boosted PLO confidence. Accordingly, even as skirmishes proceeded apace Arafat and his men set out to transform the guerrillas in southern Lebanon into a semiregular force. Syria and some other Arab countries, mainly Libya, helped; by summer 1981 this had resulted in the creation of three fledgling infantry brigades named Karameh, Yarmuk, and Kastel. They were supported by some one hundred artillery barrels and a number of old T–34 tanks.[5] The Palestinians acquired in addition astounding quantities of small arms, various antiaircraft guns, and antitank weapons in the form of Soviet-manufactured RPG–7 rockets. Many of the arms were stored in the extensive system of underground bunkers that honeycombed the refugee camps; when the time for invasion came, the IDF would find them wrapped in their plastic covers.

By that time Israel, hoping to counter the Syrians, had become heavily involved with the Lebanese Christians concentrated in the north. The first direct contact between the two sides took place while Rabin was prime minister; he was, however, dubious and unwilling to do more than provide weapons, ammunition, fuel, and training.[6] Begin, too, was initially cautious but later persuaded himself that the Syrians were genocidal, so he determined to do more. Mossad took up contact with the most important Christian militia, the Phalange, whose leaders made use of truly scrumptious feasts in order to recruit the Israelis for their cause.[7] The ultimate goal was to form an alliance and drive the Syrians out of the country. Clashes between Phalange commander Bashir Gemayel and the Syrians multiplied. Syrian army helicopters were used against the Phalange, two being downed by the IAF; in April 1981 the Syrians responded by moving antiaircraft missiles into Lebanon.[8]

Thus, during a period of several years the elements that would combine to create the IDF's greatest folly were being assembled one by one. In summer 1981 the border between Israel and Lebanon flared up as the IDF answered fresh Katyusha rocket attacks by means of an unprecedented heavy artillery bombardment and a heliborne raid against PLO bases on the Zaharani River. Still Begin held back; after about two weeks of fighting a cease-fire was concluded and during the next year was to be observed fairly

scrupulously by both sides. A month later Sharon's appointment as minister of defense marked the beginning of the end run. Since 1973 the hawkish former general had often castigated the government for being soft on
the Arabs; he even voted against the Camp David Accords. Now that the
Lebanon border was almost completely quiet he, Eytan, and other members of the General Staff, every time some incident took place anywhere in
the country, would descend on it like vultures, looking hard to see whether
it was their excuse to invade. During the winter and spring of 1982, the plans
were repeatedly set in motion and the tank transporters loaded and sent on
their way. They were always recalled for one reason or another.

In truth, the IDF's planning for Lebanon simply was not a rational
response to PLO attacks. Perhaps because he had never been a soldier,
Begin saw war in romantic terms. According to Arye Naor, who served as
secretary to the Cabinet, for Begin the idea of Jews taking military action
against their enemies struck a deep emotional chord; after all, the state of
Israel had been established specifically to put an end to the pogroms that
made them the hapless victims.[9] Even among those who did not share this
vision, the October War had caused a trauma that the Entebbe raid and the
operation against the Iraqi reactor could only do so much to heal. Constantly harassed by guerrillas in Lebanon and the Occupied Territories,
army commanders were raring to go—had they not spent years building
the most enormous force ever fielded by such a small country? Above all,
the air force was seeking revenge for the losses it had suffered in 1973,
which had induced its former commander, Ezer Weizman, to say that "the
missiles had bent the wing of the airplane." When the next clash came, it
was a question of pitting "our best against theirs" to see who would come
out on top.[10]

In any event Israel's excuse for launching "Operation Peace for
Galilee"—the name dreamed up by Begin personally—proved paper-thin
(see Map 17.1). On June 3, 1982, Israel's ambassador to London, Shlomo
Argov, was shot in the head and gravely wounded. The PLO disclaimed
responsibility; there were indications that the perpetrators belonged to
Abu Nidal's group, intending to put Arafat out on a limb.[11] Yet Sharon
ordered the IAF to bomb Palestinian bases in the camps near Beirut,
knowing full well that the response would be renewed rocket attacks on
northern Israel. The attacks duly took place, and the tank transporters
were set rolling toward the frontier. This time they did not stop, however,
and on June 6, exactly fifteen years after the Six Day War, Israel found
itself embroiled in large-scale hostilities against an Arab neighbor.

Officially the campaign's objective was to overrun the PLO strongholds
and throw the guerrillas back to a line twenty-five miles (forty kilometers)

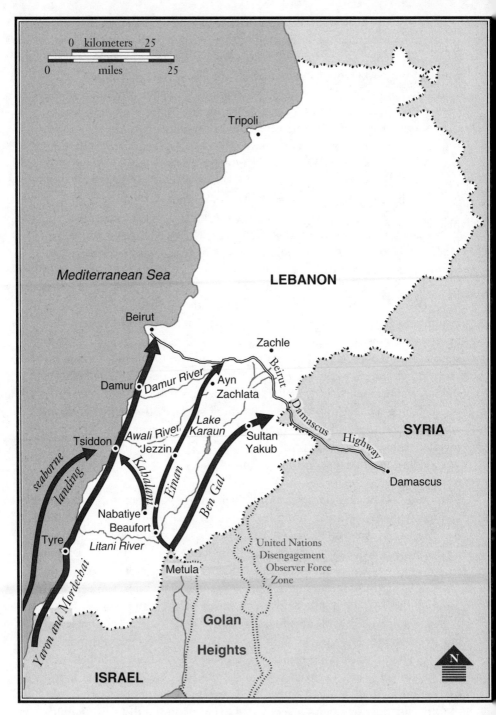

MAP 17.1 "OPERATION PEACE FOR GALILEE," 1982

north of the border, thereby putting them beyond the range of their Katyusha rockets. As early as October 1981 a much larger operation had been hatched, however, aiming to link with the Christians in Beirut to break the PLO; it was in Lebanon that the fate of the Occupied Territories was to be decided.[12] Since the Syrian forward positions in the eastern sector were located only fourteen miles or so from Israel's border, a clash with them was inevitable.

Sharon may have been acting in the hope that the Syrians would abandon their positions as the IDF, bypassing them on the west, cut the Beirut-Damascus Road, which served as their main line of communications with the Lebanese capital. More likely, though, a clash with the Syrians was planned from the beginning; certainly when the time came ample forces for the purpose were available, ready, and willing. Whether Begin's Cabinet was informed of the larger plan (as Sharon claims) or whether the former paratrooper commander was once again preparing to exceed instructions (as Begin's son, Benyamin, says on the strength of alleged conversations he had with his father) is immaterial and almost certainly will never be known.[13] Another possibility that cannot be excluded: Begin, far from being misled, was using Sharon to do much more than he could reveal in public; whatever the prime minister's faults, a fool he was not.

To carry out the operation Sharon had concentrated an enormous force, no fewer than six and a half divisions and yet another standing in readiness on the Golan Heights in case the Syrians should make a move on that front. Of those earmarked for Lebanon proper, and proceeding from west to east, two were positioned along the coastal road. Commanded by Brigadier Generals Mordechai (later to become minister of defense under Netanyahu) and Yaron, their mission was to link up with another brigade scheduled to carry out a landing at the mouth of the Awali River some thirty miles north of the border. Having done so, the combined force was to drive straight for Beirut, reaching the outskirts after only three days.

In the center a third division under Brigadier General Kahalani—in 1973 he stopped the Syrians at the Valley of Tears—stood ready to take the central route that led through the mountains toward Nabatiye and then toward Siddon on the road to Beirut. Behind him was positioned yet another division under Brigadier General Einan, the intent being to push through the road cleared by Kahalani to advance from Nabatiye and Jezzin toward the road from Beirut to Damascus; had he reached it the Syrian forces in Beirut and the Beqa Valley would have been cut off. Finally, in the Galilee panhandle near Metulla there was concentrated the IDF's most powerful striking force, a two-division corps commanded by Major General Ben Gal. In October 1973 he had been highly successful as CO of 7th Armored Brigade on the Golan Heights; later he had served as CO Northern Command before going on study-leave. Shaggy, dour, subject to violent outbreaks of temper, he was regarded by Eytan as the IDF's best field commander and a candidate for chief of staff. Now his mission was to advance toward the Syrian forces deployed in the Beqa Valley.

Otherwise put, the IDF's plan of operations provided for the deployment of four independent divisions, an amphibious brigade, and a two-division corps (with yet another division standing in reserve). In charge of the whole machine—about twice as large as that in 1973, which had stopped Egypt's entire army!—was the CO Northern Command, Maj. Gen. Amir Drori. Since this, unlike 1973, was a war on a single front, Eytan was free to control his forces at close quarters. Behind Eytan again stood Sharon, who also had a free hand and, between briefings to the Cabinet, kept visiting the front and acting as a kind of super chief of staff.

Thus the IDF's command organization was top-heavy, what with Drori, Drori's deputy, intelligence chief Yehosua Saguy, former intelligence chief Aharon Yariv (who was serving as "head of Northern Command's think tank"), Refael Eytan, Moshe Levy (Eytan's deputy), Maj. Gen. (ret.) Yona Efrat (Eytan's assistant), and Sharon—and during the first two days Begin himself—crowding into the operations room of Northern Command for "Marathonian discussions" that went into the small hours of the night.[14] Remarkably enough it also succeeded in being insufficiently thought through at the lower level since the span of control proved too large for Drori to handle. As in 1973, generals who had nothing to do with the campaign butted in. The most important one was Yekutiel Adam, former chief of the General Staff Division who was away on study-leave in New York. When war broke out he flew home, packed his gear, marched into Lebanon on some unspecified mission, and ended up getting killed under circumstances that remain unclear.

In part, the use of such huge forces in Lebanon—the country is mountainous and, except along the coast, has hardly any first-class highways—may have been dictated by the need to show the USSR, as Syria's supporter, that any intervention would have to be massive and costly. In part, too, it may have resulted from a dispute between Sharon and Eytan as to where the operation's center of gravity ought to be—west or east—and a consequent decision to be strong on both axes. Be this as it may, the result was overcrowding: Fuel convoys could not get through, the wounded could not be evacuated, and commanders who went forward to observe got caught in traffic jams and were unable to return to headquarters. Fearing casualties, the IDF did not use its helicopters for seizing key points such as bridges, defiles, and the like that might have enabled it to trap the PLO's main forces. The latter's retreat was facilitated by terrain that, except in the Beqa Valley, was either built up or mountainous and heavily wooded.

Along the coast Yaron's and Mordechai's forces drove forward ponderously. Whether because of stronger-than-expected Palestinian resistance (as the PLO claims) or because they wanted to save civilian lives by not using all the firepower of their artillery (as they claim), they got entangled in the maze of refugee camps surrounding Tyre and Siddon. Originally they were supposed to reach the Awali after one day;[15] in fact it took them the better part of three. The extra time was burned up in attempts to flush out guerrillas from among the civilian population, which was done by concentrating the latter on the beach and screening them. Eventually several thousand suspects were captured and brought to so-called detainee camps. Since the PLO did not constitute a state, the IDF insisted that its men did not deserve to be treated as POWs; yet since PLO members normally wore uniforms while fighting and had not been captured on Israeli territory, the IDF could not treat them as criminals either. This is as good a sign as any that something was very, very wrong with this war.

During the night of June 6–7, Israel's navy, covered by as many as seventeen missile boats and two submarines,[16] started landing what would eventually grow into a brigade at the mouth of the Awali. The landing was carried out practically without opposition; however, in the absence of surprise[17] it achieved little. Moreover, once on the beach the brigade, not having enough vehicles to carry all its troops, was slow to move, and during the next twenty-four hours it could do no more than extend its hold some nine miles to the north. Thereupon it halted, simply waiting for the ground forces to reach it. By the time the linkup was achieved on the morning of the fourth day of the campaign, the Palestinian bird, albeit plucked of its largest feathers, had long since flown. The two divisions then continued driving toward Beirut, reaching the southern outskirts after six days instead of three as planned.

Progress along the central axis was also much slower than expected. First, it was necessary for a commando unit of the Golani Infantry Brigade to take the dominant Beaufort Crusader Castle, an operation that started during the late afternoon of June 6 and took most of the night before finally succeeding.[18] On the morning of June 7 Begin arrived by helicopter to inspect the "awesome monster," as he called it. He told an Israeli TV audience that the assault had been carried out without loss, which turned out to be untrue (six soldiers had been killed and a number wounded), the result of a misunderstanding between him and GHQ. Then the feckless prime minister was overheard asking whether the guerrillas possessed machine guns, thus showing the world that he was still thinking in terms of the Poland of his youth, where such sophisticated weapons had presumably been few and far between.

The fortress taken, Kahalani's advance in this sector was held up less by enemy resistance (there was hardly any) than by the narrow, twisting road his division was navigating. Every time a few machine guns and bazookas opened up, the huge column—with several thousand vehicles to a division—halted; on other occasions delays were caused by tanks overturning and commanders being hit.[19] Behind Kahalani, Einan was on his way by June 8 but lost twelve hours because Kahalani had misunderstood his orders and failed to evacuate a bridge in time—a failure that would cost him his military career. Einan himself fought only one minor engagement against a Syrian commando battalion at Ayn Zachlata. Having crawled forward for three days, he discovered that resistance was becoming more tenacious. When the cease-fire went into effect he was still well short of the Beirut-Damascus highway as ordered; strategically speaking his achievement amounted to nothing.

Starting at Metulla, Ben Gal's corps drove northeast toward the Beqa Valley where the Syrians maintained a reinforced division (another division was stationed west of Damascus and was to start moving into Lebanon on June 10).[20] Even without Einan on his left he enjoyed 2:1 superiority; now he advanced gingerly, overrunning "Fatachland" and driving the PLO before him. However, even more so than along the coast (where there was at least an attempt to provide a blocking force in the form of the amphibious operation and the linkup with Kahalani) there could be no question of preventing hundreds of guerrillas from making good their escape into the Syrian lines. From there they continued to harass the IDF columns advancing from the south and seeking to outflank them from the west. As Palestinians and Syrians became intermixed a clash between the latter and the IDF became inevitable. On June 9 it came, regardless of whether it had been planned by Sharon.

Throughout these days the IAF had been taking an active part in the campaign. It strafed and bombed targets along the coastal highway in particular but left little impression, for the enemy, having for the most part abandoned all vehicles, walked north in small parties. Now it was presented with the opportunity to show its mettle against the Syrian antiaircraft defenses in the Beqa: nineteen batteries of surface-to-air missiles with the usual support of deadly ZSU 23–4 (meaning four 23mm barrels), capable of spitting out four thousand shells per minute. The IAF for its part had been preparing at least a year, overflying the area in a cat-and-mouse game in order to pinpoint the batteries and discover the Syrian radar operating frequencies.

The details of the attack that began on the afternoon of June 9 have never been divulged.[21] Certainly there must have been a combination of various weapons, including RPVs (sent up to force the Syrians to switch on their radars) and Phantoms and F–16 fighter-bombers, which launched homing missiles at the sites; the missile batteries were probably attacked with cluster bombs, the proper weapon against such soft targets. Long-range artillery may have carried part of the load, the Israelis having developed a rocket-assisted round for the M–107 175mm guns that extended range to as far as twenty-five miles. As the attack began, Syria's air force scrambled to intercept but found that its planes were identified ahead of time by IAF Hawkeyes and shot down. On June 9 and 10 there accordingly developed a series of massive air-to-air battles during which almost one hundred Syrian fighters were shot down against a single Israeli plane.

The IAF destroyed the Syrian antiaircraft defense system in Lebanon and eliminated approximately one-fifth of Syria's air force, which illustrates the IAF's spectacularly successful engagements. The 100:1 kill-to-loss ratio was better than that in 1967 (30:1) and 1973 (50:1).[22] Yet the IAF's ability to influence operations on the ground was limited. In the west and center its bombing and strafing sorties were fundamentally irrelevant owing to the nature of the terrain and the nature of the enemy. In the east it did somewhat better, preventing Assad from sending in another division to reinforce troops in the Beqa. Even there, however, the closed terrain apparently prevented the IAF from offering close support, its one attempt to do so ending in disaster on June 10 as its aircraft hit an Israeli armored battalion and thoroughly demolished it. The IAF was also unable to prevent the Syrians in this sector from successfully withdrawing their forces when the time came.

Meanwhile, cooped up as his corps was between the central massif on the left and the foothills of Mount Chermon on the right, Major General Ben Gal displayed little of the tactical finesse that had earned him his spurs on the Golan Heights in 1973. During the first three days he merely crawled forward, apparently so as not to involve the Syrians in an all-out clash. The Syrian antiaircraft defenses having been eliminated on the afternoon of the fourth day (June 9), he was finally given his head by Northern Command—with Sharon listening to the network and breaking in to tell Ben Gal that the Syrian border should on no account be crossed.[23] Though the IDF's shortcomings in night-vision equipment had been corrected during the preceding years, evidently corps HQ did not feel it could move in darkness. Instead it allowed the night to be wasted before finally engaging Syrian 1st Division near Lake Karoun on the morning of June 10, destroying some of its tanks and pushing it back.

Next, Ben Gal's attention was distracted by the above-mentioned bombing of one of his tank battalions by the IAF; later that afternoon a forward battalion drove forward without reconnaissance at Sultan Yakub, ran into an ambush, and had to be extricated at heavy loss. Though Drori did his best to put fire into Ben Gal, the latter complained that his troops were tired (after a mere single day of fighting) and his vehicles short on fuel;[24] consequently the second night was largely wasted. Granted a respite, the Syrians were able to withdraw in good order, for which Assad later awarded his commander a medal. When the cease-fire went into effect at noon on Friday, June 11, Ben Gal, like his remaining colleagues to the left, still had not reached the vital Beirut-Damascus highway.

Had the IDF been serious in its attempt to annihilate the Syrians, then it should have used Ben Gal (and the IAF) to fix them in place while Einan descended from the mountains in the west and took them in the rear. Whether because of the need to conceal the plan for a clash with the Syrians from the government's eyes or because of other reasons, three days plus one night were wasted before Ben Gal even came to grips with his adversary. When he finally did engage the Syrians, on the afternoon of June 9, he merely pushed them backward slowly while Einan, stuck in the mountains, did nothing to help. In part Einan's slowness is explained by his ponderous armament; whereas in earlier wars the IDF had often operated at night, the tracks leading through the Shouf Mountains were no place to maneuver armored formations in the dark. Following the October War, the IDF order of battle had been designed to take on heavily armed Egyptian and Syrian forces in the open terrain of the Sinai and the Golan Heights. When the test came, the IDF was destined to be thrown away in a country to which it was much less suited.

To look at it in another way, the IDF's performance in this war—the first major war in which it possessed a clear numerical advantage and undisputed technological superiority—varied according to the opponent at hand. Against Syria's air force and missiles it performed magnificently, given the lack of civilians and topographic obstacles to clutter up the environment and limit its weapons and weapon systems. Although the incident at Sultan Yakub represented a major failure, against the Syrian ground forces the IDF performed quite well, using its Merkavas and "Arrow" ammunition to destroy the most advanced T–72 tanks, push them steadily back, and capture much equipment. As the experience of "Operation Litani" should have told (as well as that of virtually every other army since 1945), however, their armored columns were almost irrelevant against guerrillas in the west. Although the PLO brigades were quickly scattered, those units were never meant to take on the IDF in a frontal battle; indeed so long as they remained intact they merely presented convenient targets for Israeli artillery and tanks. Once scattered (and their heavy equipment captured) they were if anything more able to harass the Israelis.

If there was one moment when the IDF appeared capable of winning the campaign, it came on June 11, when the first cease-fire went into effect under U.S. pressure. When that cease-fire was broken and hostilities resumed, it should have been clear that all was lost and that the only prospect was for a war of attrition, which the IDF was doomed to lose. In fact that is what happened. As both sides accused the other of violating the cease-fire, Sharon ordered his forces to "crawl" north toward the Beirut-Damascus highway, an objective finally achieved at the cost of dozens of casualties. Recalling their experience in October 1973 when a battalion of paratroopers had tried to capture the city of Suez and had to be extricated at heavy loss, the Israelis were wary of moving into Beirut proper; instead they contented themselves with artillery fire and thousands of tons of bombs, which the IAF rained on the city (officially with the aim of hitting terrorist centers but very often hitting civilians). Come August Beirut was in shambles: running out of food and medicines; electricity cut off; and water supplies so short that the inhabitants used artesian wells. Yet the skirmishes, instead of subsiding, spread into the center of the country where many villages had initially welcomed the Israeli troops by throwing rice at them.

Toward the end of August the Israelis were able to book one last success. With U.S. mediation, talks over evacuating the PLO from Beirut to save what remained of the city got under way. Agreement was finally reached and a small international force assembled to observe the proceedings; under watchful eyes (the UN's and the IDF's) some 14,500 persons left Beirut including, besides PLO members and their dependents, about 3,500 Syrian troops permitted to retreat to the Beqa Valley. The Israelis were unable to reap the benefit of their victory, however, since on September 14 their principal Christian ally, Bashir Gemayel, fell victim to a bomb presumably planted by Syrian intelligence.

Then and later, Sharon and other Israelis tried to make out as if Bashir's death—just elected president, he was due to take office in nine days when the assassination occurred—constituted the turning point in "Operation Peace for Galilee."[25] In fact his death was just one of countless incidents during which the Israelis, the Syrians, and the myriad Lebanese militias clashed and during which the IDF took a continuous trickle of casualties to no apparent gain. Whatever the IDF did, at every twist it found another Lebanese preparing to take another potshot. Despite the enormous booty the Israelis had captured,[26] the Lebanese would not run out of weapons, given that the country was saturated with them and that the Syrians were always ready with replacements. As one bitter joke had it, now that the IDF had overrun the place from where the Katyusha rockets were fired, it ought to go ahead and capture the place where they were made (presumably in the Ural Mountains). Israel's situation did not improve one iota after it decided to occupy western Beirut, a move carried out on September 15 and one that led directly to the greatest tragedy of the war.

Even before June 1982 the IDF's intelligence service had assessed the Phalange's real military capabilities as weak.[27] To avoid a situation in which they would have to come to the Phalange's aid (with its main forces concentrated north of Beirut, this would have extended lines even farther) the Israelis asked their ally to refrain from clashing with the Syrians. Now it was decided to use the Phalange to screen the refugee camps for PLO suspects, a mission more suited to the Phalangists with their supposedly thorough knowledge of the country and language.[28] After coordinating with Drori and Yaron (the commander on the spot) Phalangists moved into the Sabra and Shatilla camps—in reality, dense areas of concrete houses, some several stories tall, and a mass of narrow, winding alleys connected by underground shelters and surrounded by a wall. Once inside they started a massacre. It lasted from the evening of September 16 to the morning of September 18, killing several hundred unarmed Palestinian civilians including many women and children. The IDF stood guard at the gates and averted its eyes even though unofficial reports of the horrific events trickled in during the first evening. Some troops even aided the Christians, providing earth-moving equipment and firing illumination rounds into the sky.

When the Israeli invasion started, 93.3 percent of Israelis regarded it as either definitely or reservedly justified.[29] Within a month, however, the mood began to shift, and support was down to 66 percent.[30] Surprisingly, in a country where grassroots movements had always been rare the change started below and gradually found an echo in the Knesset. Traditionally Israel had grown accustomed to fighting much stronger or, at any rate, larger enemies; now the fact that Israel's PLO opponents were too weak to do more than harass, the northern Galilee region began to act against the government. "Operation Peace for Galilee" was denounced as an instrumental *milchemet brera* (war of choice), the implication being that it went against the entire tradition of Israel's defense and was almost criminal by nature. Already by the end of August Prime Minister Begin felt sufficiently pressed to defend himself in an address to the Command and Staff College. In one of the strangest performances of his demagogic career, he turned the concept of *en brera* on its head. He argued that most of Israel's previous wars had also been wars of choice; the more "choice" was involved, the fewer the casualties. In this way he made them look less like episodes in a prolonged, desperate struggle for survival and more like aggressive acts intended to achieve this or that political objective.[31]

When facts about the Sabra-Shatilla massacre emerged a political storm broke. On the evening of September 25 hundreds of thousands—the police estimated 400,000, one-ninth of Israel's Jewish population—demonstrated in a Tel Aviv square. Much against its will, the government was compelled to set up a commission of investigation; this time it was clear that IDF commanders as well as Israel's political leaders would be accountable. As the commission started deliberating, support for the war continued to drop. It was down to 45 percent in October and 34 percent in December, more and more people beginning to see it as a "morass" (in the words of Shimon Peres) in which the IDF floundered helplessly without end in sight.

Inside the military, too, the mood was changing. When the war opened, an easy victory was expected and cynicism prevailed: "I went to Lebanon a-hunting Arabs, hei-ho hei-ho a-hunting Arabs," as one popular song had it. However, already during the summer individual soldiers began to vent their frustration. The best-known case was that of Col. Eli Geva, a brigade commander and the son of a 1950s-vintage IDF general. Previously he had been on the fast track to promotion; now, ordered to advance, he refused orders to open fire in his sector of Beirut where he expected numerous civilians to be killed. Several attempts by Sharon and Eytan to make him change his mind having failed, he had to be discharged.[32] Meanwhile, inside Israel, groups of reservists joined together in a variety of ad hoc movements, all of which had this in common: Their members questioned the war and insisted they would rather go to prison than participate.[33] Eventually the number refusing to serve reached several hundred, of whom about 170 were tried and imprisoned; these numbers were unprecedented in the history of the IDF.

Of those who went to prison the majority was between twenty-six and thirty-two years old, from urban rather than rural areas, and well educated. About one-fifth consisted of officers (who were thus overrepresented in comparison with their number in the army).[34] Thousands more probably avoided service by inventing excuses; indeed in one case a Knesset member bribed his way out of serving. Though there is no evidence that the protest movement ever gained sufficient strength to make the government change course, repeated demonstrations and remonstrances certainly left their imprint. Come winter the troops in their dugouts were singing words and melody adapted from a well-known Israeli children's ditty:

Aircraft come down from the clouds
Take us far to Lebanon
We shall fight for Mr. Sharon
And come back, wrapped in shrouds.

Yet another indication of the army's state of mind was the growing number of psychiatric casualties.[35] Born and bred to defend their country against great odds, and enjoying near-unanimous public support in doing so, Israelis were not supposed to suffer mental problems as a result of war. In 1947–1949 there had been cases, known in PALMACH slang as *deggim* (shortened from *degeneratim*, degenerates). Some, having been slapped by commanders, pulled themselves together.[36] Others, perhaps less fortunate, were treated in the psychiatric wards of several hospitals; their fates are unknown. A few more cases came to light in 1956 and 1967. Given that both campaigns were over almost before they had begun, the numbers were small.

Then in October 1973 the roof fell in. Hundreds—perhaps 700 to 2,300 or even more[37]—of weeping, screaming, trembling, bed-wetting, and paralyzed soldiers presented themselves. Having neglected to profit from past experience or to study other armies,[38] the IDF medical establishment was taken by surprise. Instead of treating the men with a regime of sedation, rest, exercise, and suggestion at collecting points near the front, it committed the classic error of evacuating them to special installations in the rear.[39] There some of them are said to remain to the present day.

When the time for analysis came the IDF's psychiatrists attributed the large number of cases to the swift switch from peace to war and the intensity of the combat. However, deficient unit cohesion also played its part: 40 percent of psychiatric casualties studied said their unit had morale problems, as against only 10 percent in a control group.[40] By 1982 the medical branch had provided itself with the appropriate doctrine as well as an organization consisting of teams of psychiatrists, who were attached to each division and ready to step in when and where needed. Yet opening the field to the so-called KABANim (*ktsinei briut nefesh*, mental health officers) was a double-edged sword. To a considerable extent the ability to keep going among the horrors of war is a question of will. Hence troops who know that psychiatric help is available—in other words, if they know that there is an easy way to get out of combat—may become inclined to use it.

In fact that is what happened. Except perhaps for a couple of days in the Beqa Valley, "Operation Peace for Galilee" was scarcely high-intensity combat. Victory was never in doubt, the IDF dominated the sky, and ground troops overran the PLO like a steamroller. Physically speaking, conditions were relatively good, the weather perfect, and creature comforts were carried to the point that mobile banks accompanied the troops to the field to enable them to speculate on the stock exchange. Yet from June to August about six hundred cases of "battle shock"—a misnomer, as many served in second-line units and never saw intense fire—appeared. They formed 18 percent of all wounded, as much as 55 percent in some battalions.[41] Later as many again were diagnosed with posttraumatic stress disorder (PTSD);[42] this time inexperience could *not* be blamed.

In February 1983 the Kahn Commission investigating the horrific events at the Sabra and Shatilla camps published its report.[43] No evidence was found that IDF senior officers had known of the massacre, let alone conspired with Phalange commanders to carry it out; indeed Sharon later successfully sued *Time* for claiming he had done so. Still, the commission maintained that they ought to have foreseen it and, since they as representatives of the occupation force were responsible for whatever went on in the Beirut area, prevented it from taking place. Amos Yaron, the commander on the spot, was asked to resign, as were the chief of intelligence (Major General Saguy) and Ariel Sharon. As for Eytan, his term of office was about to end. Therefore the commission, though treating him with undisguised contempt, did not demand his resignation.

To replace Sharon, Begin selected Moshe Arens, a longtime Likud member with no military experience to speak of. By profession he was an aviation engineer who had once received the Israel Defense Award for his role in developing the Kfir; as such he was the only true technocrat ever to hold the defense portfolio. Eytan's deputy, Maj. Gen. Moshe Levy, succeeded him. Previously known mainly for his tall stature, his principal qualification (like Gur before him) was his slight involvement in the current debacle. Moreover, whereas Sharon and Eytan had constantly been at loggerheads, the dry, humorless Arens and the bland, undemonstrative Levy made a good team. Though it took time, they started guiding Israel back to something resembling sanity.

In May, after weeks of negotiations, a last-ditch attempt was made to salvage what could be salvaged by signing a peace agreement with Lebanon's new president, Amin Gemayel (who happened to be Bashir's brother). Though Sharon described it as "a tremendous achievement," within days it turned out not to be worth the paper on which it was written; later it was formally disavowed by the Lebanese government. All the while, guerrilla warfare in Lebanon was picking up. Except in the Beqa Valley, much of the terrain occupied by the IDF was either built up or mountainous and densely wooded, dotted with villages perched on the hills and winding tracks that led among them. From Galilee to Beirut it was more than sixty miles, hopelessly exposed to mines and ambushes with small arms, antitank rockets, and mines.

According to one source, the first three weeks of the war had cost the IDF 260 dead and 1,270 wounded.[44] Now Lebanon's civil war, dormant since the invasion, flared up as Druze, Shiites, Sunnis, Christians, and Palestinians infiltrating back from Damascus battled each other and the

IDF. Even when hostilities were not directed against them, Israeli soldiers often got caught in the crossfire while fulfilling their duty as an occupation force and protecting one side against another. "They all hate each other and they all hate me," one sad Israeli commentary went. Casualties mounted by the week, including a particularly horrible episode when sixty or so people, thirty of them Israelis, were killed when their Tyre head-quarters was demolished by a car bomb.

A confirmed hawk, Arens tried to defend the IDF's continued presence in Lebanon as best he could, arguing that any change in deployment ought to be coordinated with the Lebanese government (whose power, however, was confined almost entirely to the presidential palace) and the United States.[45] In September 1983 he was forced to give way, recalling the IDF out of Beirut back to central Lebanon, where it occupied a new line from the mouth of the Awali River to Mount Dov on the Syrian border. Just more than a year had passed since Begin, posing as a conquering hero, had visited Beirut. By now he was a cripple—he had fallen in the bathroom and broken his hip—and recently widowed. Always something of a manic-depressive, now he fell victim to the blackest of black moods. He resigned, hid himself in a residence near Jerusalem, and hardly left it until he died.

The retreat to the Awali still left some 1,200 square miles, with a popu-lation of more than 500,000, under Israeli control. Though the army did its best to protect its soldiers by providing their vehicles with addi-tional armor—this was the period when the first reinforced APCs and NAGMASHot (*noset geyasot meshuryenet*, the heavy armored personnel car-riers mounted on tank chassis) were coming into service—there was no way to cope with the increasing guerrilla attacks along the lines of com-munications. Like late-twentieth-century armies elsewhere, the IDF floundered, vainly trying to sort out combatants from noncombatants and hitting thin air when it tried to bring tormentors to heel. Like late-twen-tieth-century armies elsewhere, too, the heavy-handed punitive operations it sometimes mounted left a legacy of hatred and, if anything, played into the opposition's hands. By the time Shimon Peres, appointed prime min-ister in winter 1984, finally decided to put an end to the agony the num-ber of dead had risen to more than 650, with almost 3,000 wounded. The cost of the adventure was estimated at $2–5 billion[46]—this at a time when the country's GNP amounted only to about $23 billion. All supposedly in a good cause, and all to absolutely no avail.

As Ben Gal wrote in retrospect, of all Israeli wars the one in Lebanon was probably the best prepared, down to the most minute detail.[47] Every tank was ready to start; every inch of the terrain had been reconnoitered many times; even the characteristics of every Syrian antiaircraft missile were sufficiently well known for a counter to be readied and put into action with flawless precision. As Ben Gal also wrote, however, of all Israeli wars, it was based on the most profound misunderstanding of what the IDF could and could not achieve. For the first time it had entered the capital of an Arab country. This done, however, there could be no question of imposing a political settlement; indeed during the days before his death Bashir Gemayel had been quarreling with Begin and Sharon over precisely this issue.[48] Economically speaking, so strong are Lebanon's ties with the rest of the Arab world that trade never halted even during the worst days of the war. The country simply could not afford to make a separate peace with Israel. This is true regardless of who rules and regardless of the ruler's relations with the factions.

Furthermore, though there had always been some terrorism in the Occupied Territories, in Lebanon the IDF for the first time came up against true guerrilla warfare. Given Lebanon's fragmented political system, the ubiquitous militias, the nature of the terrain, and the long border with Syria, it ought to have been clear from the beginning that the country was ideal for guerrilla tactics. Had not Machiavelli written that decentralized states were easy to overrun but difficult to hold?[49] The Israelis were blind to the political realities of the country and their own unpopularity in the Arab world. So much so that these difficulties were not foreseen, and no available source gives any reason to believe they were seriously considered.

In 1985, Peres, along with Rabin as minister of defense, finally ended the agony by recalling the IDF from Lebanon. However, the question of renewed rocket attacks and border raids remained unanswered. The solution was to leave Israel a narrow strip of land, some three to six miles wide, as a security zone. As before 1982, part of the job of defending the strip was entrusted to approximately 2,000 local militiamen paid, trained, and equipped by Israel. They were supported by a number of strongholds that Israel retained, each providing shelter to one company. Behind them the full resources of Northern Command with its artillery and tanks as well as the air force and navy were deployed, called upon as occasion demanded. The border was strongly fortified. A security fence runs along its entire length even today, liberally fitted with searchlights, radar, and other kinds of electronic sensors.

Though Palestinian guerrillas had been returning to Lebanon in small numbers, the main PLO forces in the country were gone. This scarcely took the pressure off the IDF, however, for Shiite militias moved in—first Amal and then, increasingly, Hizbullah (Party of God). The last in particular was a political movement as well as a military one. It operates a network of religious and welfare institutions over much of Lebanon and even has representatives in the Lebanese parliament; hence there could be no question of eradicating it simply by attacking its 400 or so[50] hard-core fighters concentrated in the south. Furthermore, as long as it directed its efforts against Israel, Hizbullah could count on Syrian support. Behind Syria again stood Iran, which provided money and arms to the tune of $50–100 million per year.

Considered a native Lebanese movement, Hizbullah's declared objective has always been to remove the Israeli presence from "conquered" Lebanese soil. Considered a proxy for Syria and Iran, its objectives presumably were more far-reaching. Over time, that prevented Israel from putting an end to the matter by withdrawing completely. In plain words, the Syrians were using Hizbullah to press for the return of the Golan Heights. Hence there exists no guarantee that it would halt attacks even if the last inch of Lebanese territory were evacuated; indeed its leaders have consistently refused to promise anything of the sort.[51] Moreover, given its dependence on the Syrians and the weakness of its own armed forces, the Lebanese government cannot be trusted to maintain peace.

Unable to withdraw, the IDF did about as well as could be expected. During the seventies PLO guerrillas crossed the border many times to plant mines and ambush patrols. At least once they mounted a major hostage-taking operation, seizing a school in the town of Maalot and holding it until they were ousted with considerable loss of life. Since the security zone was established, however, there have been no penetrations into Israel proper, and very few guerrillas are even able to reach as far as the fence itself. Recognizing this fact, guerrillas on several occasions have used motorized hang gliders for transportation. Since there is no way to return, those who make it across are doomed; presumably for this reason the number of these incidents has remained small.

The IDF's efforts to protect Israeli territory were thus largely successful. However, the IDF could not prevent Hizbullah from harassing the "Army of Southern Lebanon"—as the militias were grandiloquently called—and IDF troops in the security zone. In addition to the usual fire from small arms, bazookas, and antitank missiles, there were mines—autonomous and remote-controlled—as well as car bombs and booby traps of every kind. To counter this the IDF over years developed extremely detailed procedures, with every move carried out exactly to regulations to forestall the formation of yet another commission of investigation, which seemed immediately to follow every snafu. IDF companies reacting to the approach of a car on a dirt road in Lebanon are akin to players in a ballet. Like pirouetting ballerinas troops take up positions in preparation for the attack, which rarely occurs. Yet such precautions only minimize the damage Hizbullah causes and do not silence it.

Strongly supported from the air—over time there was a growing tendency to rely on attack helicopters rather than the faster, less maneuverable fighter-bombers—the IDF on occasion took the initiative. Brilliant intelligence enabled the IDF to pinpoint leaders and target them at home or while they rode in cars. Several were killed or captured by commando teams; however, invariably the results were disappointing as new leaders replaced the old. More often the IDF would retaliate by "returning fire to the sources of fire," as the standard formula has it. Since southern Lebanon is a heavily populated area, civilian casualties ensued (the more so because guerrillas often operated bases near or inside villages to obtain shelter). When civilians were killed, as inevitably they would be, Hizbullah retaliated by firing Katyusha rockets at Israeli settlements, which thus were held hostage.

On two occasions—summer 1993 and spring 1996—Israel sought to answer the Katyushas by deploying massive firepower against the guerrillas. Both times some of the world's most modern weapons systems were put on display. On the ground, RPVs, artillery radar, and laser range finders fed coordinates directly to computers that now equipped every big gun, enabling them to locate Katyusha launch sites while the rockets were still in the air and to shift from one target to the next in seconds. At sea, Israeli missile boats shelled the coastal highway. The performance of IAF attack helicopters—including now the Apache—was even more impressive; they launched missiles through windows in high-rises amid a densely populated city. To the initiated the firepower put on display during "Operation Grapes of Wrath" (April 1996) was nothing short of awe-inspiring, the more so because it was carried out uninterrupted day and night. In the air and on the ground, in many ways it was more sophisticated than anything the Coalition forces deployed as recently as 1991 in the Persian Gulf.

Had the targets been Syrian armored divisions attempting to drive down from the Golan Heights into the Jordan Valley, no doubt they would have been annihilated. After sixteen days during which 13,000 rounds were fired and hundreds of strikes by fighter-bombers and attack helicopters took place, between six (says Hizbullah) and fifty (says the IDF) persons were killed.[52] Meanwhile the Katyushas, though perhaps no longer as numerous or well-aimed as during the first days of the operation, kept coming, bringing life along the border to a halt, demolishing hundreds of houses, and causing damage of approximately $30 million. Above all, Israel did not succeed in using the operation to achieve its declared aim of pressing the population of southern Lebanon to press the Lebanese government to press the Syrians to press the guerrillas (the formula known as "circular pressure," dreamed up by Rabin before his assassination). On the contrary, if anything it was Prime Minister Peres who came under domestic and international pressure after a round missed its target and hit a UN compound serving as an assembly point for refugees, killing some 100 people and forcing Israel to call a halt.

At the time of this writing hostilities in Lebanon continue and cost the Israelis one or two casualties every fortnight. Countless raids by some of the world's best troops—including commandos who serve as long as a year in the area[53]—two massive invasions, and the repeated use of some of the most technologically advanced weapons in history have failed to silence the guerrillas. Hence, according to press reports,[54] the IDF is now much more careful not to target civilians, even if that means fire cannot be returned to the source. Meanwhile the relationship between the number of casualties on both sides has begun to change. It stood at 1:5.2 in the IDF's favor in 1990, 1:2 in 1991, and was down to 1:1.71 in 1992 and the first months of 1993.[55] Since then, reliable figures have been impossible to obtain; it is worth noting that from 1992 to 1993 the number of incidents more than doubled.[56]

On the positive side, Israeli public opinion recognizes the fact that its army in southern Lebanon is to some extent being held hostage by the Syrians.[57] Hence, and in spite of voices to the contrary, it seems resigned to continuing the struggle as long as necessary and did not waver in its determination following a helicopter crash in February 1997 that killed 73 troops. Above all, in Lebanon the IDF is facing an opponent who, although numerically weak and falling well short of a regular army, consists of uniformed, armed troops rather than of unarmed civilians—many of them women and children, as was usually the case in the Occupied Territories. Therefore, if fighting them is scarcely glorious, at any rate it is not demeaning, and morale, though perhaps not great, has not declined to the point where it constitutes an insuperable problem.[58] Judging by its own past performance as well as that of other armies, the IDF will almost certainly be unable to win. Then again, barring a crisis of confidence inside Israel there is no reason why it should lose.

CHAPTER 18

AN INDIAN SUMMER

DURING ITS three-year adventure in Lebanon, the IDF suffered approximately 650 fatalities, approximately one in 1,700 of the Jewish population per year. During its eight-year adventure in Afghanistan the Soviet army suffered approximately 13,000 fatalities, approximately one in 18,000 of the population per year.[1] Following the withdrawal from Afghanistan the Red Army and the USSR disintegrated. Following withdrawal from Lebanon the IDF, though it had taken a beating, survived and, for a time at any rate, appeared to prosper. That it did so is a tribute to its sound structure and, even more so, the patriotism of the Israeli people.

Israel's efforts to put the Lebanese debacle behind were facilitated by a marked improvement in the international situation. Viewing Israel as an ally in its global fight against communism as well as that against fundamentalist Islam as spread by Iran, the U.S. administration under Pres. Ronald Reagan was as friendly as any since 1948 and much more friendly than Jimmy Carter's preceding administration. In 1981 it signed the "Agreement for Strategic Cooperation," undertaking to pre-position some arms on Israeli soil, conduct joint exercises, share some types of intelligence, engage in joint research and development on selected weapons systems, and purchase $200 million (later raised to $300 million) in military equipment each year from the Israeli arms industry.[2] The political significance of the agreement was perhaps even greater, for it marked the first time Israel, long accustomed to isolation, entered into something like a formal alliance with another country.

Three years later, foreign aid peaked at $4.5 billion per year, which at the time represented no less than 20 percent of Israel's GNP.[3] U.S. support also helped Israel start emerging from its post-1973 isolation as a pariah state. Meanwhile, during much of the 1980s, Egyptian military power stagnated as the country concentrated on combating the internal threat posed by fundamentalist Islam. As for Syria, between 1982 and 1985 it rebuilt its forces with Soviet support. Syria's grip on Lebanon if anything became

*An Indian Summer: While the Palestinian uprising was brewing,
the IAF practiced air-to-air refueling.*

even stronger as Assad's forces destroyed or disarmed the militias of Michel Aoun and Samir Jaja, brought civil war to an end, and made the Arab countries recognize their presence. However, after 1987, Syria found itself increasingly isolated as new Soviet leader Mikhail Gorbachev signaled that he would not support another war in the Middle East.[4] As a result, sources of cheap military technology dried up and Syria's armed forces became increasingly obsolete. Finally, the ongoing Iran-Iraq War showed no signs of abating, thus taking what was fast becoming the strongest Arab state (Iraq) clean out of the equation.

In Israel, following the July 1984 elections, the Government of National Unity was set up. First Shimon Peres, then Yitschak Shamir, became prime minister. Whereas Peres was an excellent diplomat who did much to improve Israel's international status, Shamir was an introverted, ever suspicious former LECHI member who had risen through the ranks of Mossad and served as minister of foreign affairs under Begin. Whatever their differences, both supported Yitschak Rabin as minister of defense: Peres because he had no choice—as number two on the Labor list Rabin had almost as many adherents as himself—and Shamir because he was aware of his own inexperience in military affairs and because he greatly respected the former chief of staff's abilities.[5] Later, having spent two years in the opposition—during 1990 to 1992—Rabin took over as prime minister while acting as his own minister of defense. Thus, with the exception of those two years, Rabin dominated Israeli defense for a full decade.

As before, Rabin's ability to get along with the Americans on whom so much depended was an important asset and represented a welcome change from the time when Ariel Sharon, trying to get his way in Lebanon, pounded the table in front of Reagan's secretary of defense, Caspar Weinberger. As before, by and large Rabin and Peres used this renewed goodwill to the best effect, obtaining first an extra $1.5 billion in aid to fight inflation (in 1985) and then no less than $10 billion in loan guarantees approved by Congress (in autumn 1992). Assisted by falling oil prices from 1986 on, economic growth resumed. In particular, high-tech industries were given a tremendous boost; by the early 1990s the sixty-mile corridor between Tel Aviv and Haifa boasted the second largest concentration of software firms in the world. By 1996, GDP stood at $99.3 billion and per-capita income had reached $16,980. A strong shekel, held up by the U.S. loan guarantees as well as high interest rates, encouraged a flood of imports. For the first time Israel began to feel and look more or less like a Western developed country. Compared to events in neighboring countries, Israel's economic transformation was dramatic. It produced more than Jordan, Syria, and Egypt combined; the gap in per-capita product stood at 9:1, 14:1, and 15:1 respectively.[6]

As the economy expanded, the military budget was cut. Its share of GNP fell from 21.8 percent in 1985 to 19.4 percent in 1987, 16.4 percent in 1988, and 14 percent in 1989. Since then it has continued to decline until it leveled out at approximately 11–12 percent during the early 1990s.[7] The share of defense imports went down from 8 percent to 1.5 percent of GNP,[8] that of military pay from 40.4 percent of all public salaries (1980) to 34 percent (1995).[9] To be sure, these figures tend to underestimate the true cost because they exclude "hidden" factors such as the cost of servicing military debts and the pay of reservists, which is provided by Social Security; it is also not clear if, and where, the cost of the nuclear establishment is tucked in. By international standards the share of defense in GNP and per-capita military expenditures have remained rather high, the latter at $1,300 (1992), roughly equal to the U.S. figure and twice that of a typical West European country.[10]

Against this background, the breakneck expansion that characterized the military from 1973 to 1982 could not be sustained. Relative to its neighbors the size of the IDF declined somewhat as progress toward peace lessened the threat of war; in absolute terms, the size of the ground forces steadied as did the number of major formations.[11] The air force order of battle also stagnated as older aircraft (Skyhawks) were sold or put into storage.[12] The end to growth was accompanied by a spectacular rise in the sizes of the age groups available for service. Between 1960 and 1974 the Jewish population grew by a third, from about 2.2 million to 2.9 million. During the same years the annual birthrate per thousand increased from 22.9 to 36.3.[13] Assuming all other factors remained unchanged, this meant that the class of 1992 was twice as large as that of 1978. This does not even account for some 750,000 immigrants who entered the country from 1989 on, about 20 percent being of a military age.

As a result, during the late eighties the manpower shortage that existed during the seventies was transforming into a glut. Though there are no published data, presumably standards rose as it was no longer necessary to scrape the bottom of the barrel and conscript the unwilling, the mentally marginal, and the physically unfit.[14] Obtaining a discharge became much easier, and some of the social stigma attached to it lessened as did various restrictions incurred by those who are exempt. Entire groups that used to be called up no longer were (for example, male and female immigrants more than twenty-four and seventeen years old, respectively).[15] Moreover, the surplus of young people made it possible to release older classes of reservists, leading to a rejuvenation of the army.[16]

The increase in the number of youths inducted each year has had certain negative consequences. From the sixties on, most developed countries have been moving away from universal service toward some form of all-volunteer army because their security was guaranteed by nuclear capability and because such a force structure is more suitable to a modern world where high technology requires lengthy training.[17] On the face of it both considerations apply to Israel. On the one hand it too is a nuclear country whose ultimate security rests not with the IDF but with a very few technicians who sit at consoles, fingers on the keys or triggers or whatever. On the other hand the conventional technology is becoming much more sophisticated and tends to demand better training. Although the question has been extensively debated,[18] so far a change has been prevented by the desire to retain a large force of trained reservists.

Cynics would add that from the army's point of view both reservists and conscripts have the extra advantage of being cheap. The fact that reserve pay is provided not by the military but by Social Security has often come under critical fire; it means that IDF commanders do not have to worry about financial consequences when calling up men for duty. Most conscripts so long as they live are paid only around $90 per month. Should they die during active service, rarely are there widows or orphans to support. Apart from the expense of burial—a plot of land, a headstone, and a platoon firing blank cartridges—the state's cost is substantially limited to $17,000 or so in life insurance. Thus a conscript's life is valued at two months' pay of a major general (without benefits); the premium is even deducted from their pay.[19]

In theory the problem of surplus manpower could have been met by switching to selective service, a system used by many countries particularly during the nineteenth century. Alternatively, the conscript service period could be cut, as in 1964–1965. Against a background of declining willingness to serve, in practice the first alternative is impossible thanks to the need to maintain "the equality of carrying the burden"; the second is impossible thanks to the lopsided relationship between training time and operational utilization that follows. Unable to escape the dilemma, the IDF during the late eighties and early nineties became enormously wasteful of manpower; its supporting services (the combat units, as we shall see, are a different story) are overflowing with conscripts without work. Judging from the fact that in 1995 it was proposed to cut the period of service of soldiers in noncombat units from three to two years, the surplus may be on the order of 30 percent. That proposal having been rejected, some soldiers spend as much as nine of fourteen days at home—a system colloquially known as "5/9." Apparently it is welcomed by the IDF because it shifts the burden of supporting them to their parents.

The basic training that most troops receive is pared down to one month or less, which at one time was not even considered sufficient for women;

while it lasts, they might fire perhaps one hundred rounds from small arms. Next they take assignments in a very large variety of slots, such as administrative or guard duty. Many of these positions probably could be better filled by regulars who stay longer on the job and can master it thoroughly. Others, such as construction, dental treatment, psychological testing, and looking after medical stores, could and should be civilianized as in other countries around the world.[20] From 1994 on, the surplus has been so great that some recruits are transferred into the police and the border guard, thereby making those services younger and less professional—just the opposite required for coping with the *Intifada*, where self-control and discipline count for everything.[21] Had it been up to that great democrat, Yitschak Rabin, conscripts would have fulfilled active duty working for either the Frontier Guard or for Shin Bet, without their consent. Only protests in parliament prevented him from instituting such an arrangement.

Once completing conscript service, IDF soldiers are assigned to reserve units. Here the surplus of second-echelon troops is even greater than in the standing army; as much as 40 percent of those on the rolls never serve.[22] Yet those who *are* called up for their annual stint often find themselves assigned to low-level "current security" tasks such as patrolling the border and mounting guard, even though they are not really suited for combat duty. As long as nothing untoward happens these assignments pass without comment; the men, having spent time with comrades in something like a holiday camp, go home happily enough. From time to time, however, some unexpected incident takes place. For instance, in February 1992 three Arab terrorists armed with knives and axes entered a base in the center of the country, killing three soldiers and wounding three others before making good their escape. In July 1996 a patrol of reservists was ambushed along the Jordan border, losing three killed and two wounded. This time reinforcements were summoned but failed to arrive on time; the guerrillas escaped with the squad's .50-caliber machine gun.[23] Each time a *fashla* (blunder) occurs a furor arises, and the troops' low state of training, particularly refresher training, is blamed. The incident is soon forgotten—until the next one.

Traditionally the IDF avoided assigning women to combat areas and evacuated women serving in field units as soon as hostilities flared up. However, during the later stages of the Lebanese adventure the IDF confronted growing unwillingness among male reservists to serve in a conflict with neither purpose nor end. To prevent discontent from spreading, female conscripts were sent into the breach. For the first time since the days of PALMACH, women could be found serving in combat zones as communicators, medical orderlies, and administrators; the IDF, aware of the public-relations disaster that could ensue, ensured that none became casualties, and in fact no woman is known to have been killed or wounded.[24] To CHEN proponents the experiment constituted more proof that the army had been underutilizing women all along.[25] Perhaps a more correct interpretation would be to say that when morale began to falter the IDF, with the connivance of its female commanders—who remained safely in the rear—took the path of least resistance. It turned to its pool of defenseless girls, making them do work older men were increasingly reluctant to perform.

Reaching Israel a decade or so late, feminist pressures started during the eighties, a possible reason being that as *en brera* faded away, society felt it could engage in all kinds of experiments. From 1980 to 1991 the number of MOS formally open to female soldiers was increased by an additional 60 percent, from 296 to 500.[26] The number of those working in intelligence, communications, military police, the medical professions, and training rose, though each of these fields separately only accounted for less than 10 percent of all women. The number of women working as secretaries dropped, though at 39 percent secretaries still remained by far the largest group of female soldiers.[27] As before, using women who would never see combat to instruct men expected to do so gave rise to problems. In some instances it created a situation whereby commanders no longer knew how to instruct, or instructors to command.[28]

In practice, as of 1991, women occupied only 234 out of the 500 MOS open to them. Feminist commanders steered females away from such jobs as truck driving, which, partly because of their low prestige and partly because they required physical force, were supposed to be more suited to males.[29] The discrepancy led to a vast surplus of female recruits. Efforts to solve the problem by cutting the period of service (now around twenty-one months) tend to make it worse; understandably the army is reluctant to train personnel who will spend only a brief period applying skills before being released.[30] The upshot is that many female conscripts are even more underemployed than male counterparts; a chief of manpower/planning put the surplus at 50 percent.[31] Many acquire no useful skills and spend the better part of two years marking time. Others are used as cheap labor in civilian-type jobs, controlling passports, minding pilots' children, and serving under what has been called "semiservile" conditions.[32]

The increased presence of female soldiers also changed the face of the officer corps. Whereas from 1983 to 1993 the number of male officers increased by only 29 percent, that of female ones doubled. Rank by rank, the percentage of female captains rose from 14 percent to 23 percent of the total; that of majors, from 13 to 18 percent; and that of lieutenant colonels,

from 6 to 11 percent.[33] Many of these newly promoted women were said
to be overqualified for their jobs.[34] Take the lieutenant colonel who acts as
secretary to the Command and General Staff College. Factoring in benefits, separation pay, and pension, the cost of filling the slot must be three
or four times as high than if the IDF, following the example of other armies
around the world, had filled it with a civilian.

The IDF's use—or, depending on one's point of view, abuse—of female
personnel stands out more strongly against the background of Israeli labor
law and the experience of Western armed forces. At least on paper, Israel's
labor law is among the world's most advanced; it prohibits discrimination
(except for some forms that work in women's favor, such as tax breaks and
shorter hours for working mothers) and imposes near-complete equality
on the sexes.[35] Western armed forces have gone far to integrate women in
the various MOS, including use aboard ships and as combat pilots. Not so
the IDF, which had to be forced in court to accept women pilot trainees.
The IDF also retains CHEN as a separate women's corps, though recently
its significance has been reduced as commanders, in what is officially
described as a sign of trust, were given greater disciplinary authority over
female subordinates. Although some women who are assigned to the border guard now receive combat training, they are assigned to such rear echelon duties as patrolling the streets of Israeli cities, guarding shopping
centers, and the like. The result is to unfairly increase the burden on men;
women who run the risk of contacting the enemy (such as those policing
Jewish settlers in Hebron) remain sufficiently exceptional to be known as
"the eleven viragoes."[36]

The IDF's tendency to fall behind civilian society is not limited to its
treatment of women. To cite just two examples: In Israel as in many other
Western countries public education is slowly giving way to private schooling. Teachers in private schools are paid more, and attendance is voluntary;
since there are virtually no disciplinary problems, often they are able to
provide a superior education and even to pass students through the state-
run exams ahead of public-school counterparts. Perhaps because Israel has
been a socialist country for so long, however, the IDF manpower division
adheres to the old idea that "public" is good and "private" is bad, a fallback
for those who could not make it under ordinary circumstances. When they
join the army the graduates of so-called extramural schools automatically
lose points in the exam that determines a recruit's KABA (*kvutsat echut*, or
"quality group"); this results not only in discrimination but also inefficient
use of manpower.

The second example, which took place at the end of 1996, is even more
interesting. In Israel as in many other developed welfare states the institu-

tion of marriage has been losing ground in favor of other forms of cohabitation, formal and informal. Thus, when an Israeli woman decided to marry her non-Jewish boyfriend by means of a so-called Paraguay wedding—in fact the only way in which she could have done so, given that Israel's rabbinate would have refused to perform the ceremony—she was doing nothing very exceptional. The IDF manpower division refused to recognize the marriage, however, so when the young woman in question claimed to be exempted from service she found herself behind bars. She was released within twenty-four hours after the matter became public, but the IDF's inability or unwillingness to adapt to changing social norms had been put on display for all to see.[37]

The most flagrant failure to adapt to new social realities concerns the education of officers. Unlike armed forces elsewhere, the IDF never maintained a military academy; a few special groups apart, the great majority of future commanders enter officer training school straight from the ranks without benefit of higher education. As long as officers were regarded as an elite and Israeli society at large remained comparatively backward, this did not present a disadvantage. For example, as late as 1969 only 10 percent of Israelis twenty to twenty-four years old studied, far behind the United States (43 percent) and Japan (36 percent).[38] As in other developed countries, though, Israeli higher education has exploded. By 1992 the percentage of high-school graduates who went on to some kind of higher education stood at 47.1 percent (Israel), 64.8 percent (United States), and 54.9 percent (Japan).[39]

During most of the IDF's history, only those officers who went through the Academic Reserve received a full university education before being commissioned. The rest either attended an institution of higher learning during their period of *keva* service or, particularly if they were members of the combat arms, remained without. Now it can be argued that as far as military qualifications are concerned a lieutenant in command of a platoon does not really need a college degree.[40] After all, as victories have proved, the quality of Israel's junior officers has been superb. However, by and large the higher that one rises the more difficult the problems. This is even more so in the IDF than elsewhere, for its professional officers are much less well educated than reservist comrades. Almost all of the latter attend university after the end of their conscript service. Regardless of whether they work for government or for business or in the professions, they will represent the flower of Israeli society.

Possibly because it trusted to its own high prestige—after all, nowhere else are the armed services so vital to the state's very existence—the IDF has been extremely slow to respond to these developments. As far back as 1957, Ben Gurion (who studied law at Constantinople but never received his degree) argued that every officer needed a higher education and that it should be provided by the army as a matter of right.[41] His call went unheeded, and for decades thereafter "professor" was a derogatory reference in the IDF. Although some outstanding officers studied abroad, the quality and prestige of the army's Command and General Staff College remained low. Some officers, notably Lt. Gen. Ehud Barak (chief of staff, 1992–1994), managed to avoid the staff college altogether, evidently regarding it as a waste of time, intended for those less bright than himself; he preferred to study systems analysis at Stanford University instead.

It was not until the second half of the eighties that the army woke up to the educational deficiencies of its officer corps, not least because the officers often found they were unemployable after being discharged. Efforts to bring them up to civilian standards were made. However, from the beginning it was not a question of serious education so much as finding ways to issue degrees (which in turn resulted in significant pay raises).[42] Seeking to increase student intake, which formed the basis for allocation of government funds, most of Israel's universities closed an eye and cooperated.

Ironically, some of the officers who became university students did not even have their high school diplomas.[43] Others, despite scoring poorly on the "psychometric" entrance test governing civilian admissions, were admitted nevertheless. Still others, having spent careers rushing from one incident to the next, might not have read a book in years; the great majority did not have a sufficient command of English to get along in a country where, owing to its small size, almost all readings at the university level are in that language. To get around these difficulties universities often crammed officers through courses specifically designed for them. Alternatively, they granted accreditation for some staff college courses.

Though officers had the road thus smoothed, problems remained. Many who attended university classes en bloc would not take them seriously; instead of learning from teachers they tended to conspire against them. Meanwhile employers, knowing the score, frequently continued to treat discharged soldiers as second-class applicants. After years of half-measures, in 1997 every company-grade officer who signs up for the required number of years of continued service in the standing army is given the right to attend the university of choice,[44] spending two and a half years studying for a bachelor of arts degree. This should lead to a corresponding rise in the age of commanders at all levels from battalion up.

In theory, attending university ought to make officers more like civilians,[45] and indeed anyone who watches the Kirya (the Tel Aviv neighborhood that houses the general staff) will be amazed at the number of uniformed, briefcase-carrying, thirty-something clerks running about. In practice there is some reason to believe that many IDF officers were mov-ing away from the mainstream, into places where the majority of Israelis do not want to follow. Traditionally it drew more than its share of *kibbuts* members; indeed, during the post-1967 years of glory learned treatises were written to explain the reasons behind *kibbuts*niks' exceptional military qualities.[46] During the eighties, however, the *kibbuts* movement had long passed its prime. Not only was its share among the population falling; instead of being regarded (and regarding itself) as a social elite it gradually adapted bourgeois values (for instance, ending communal dining rooms and introducing wage scales).

Nor were *kibbuts*niks the only ones to distance themselves from a mili-tary career. Against the background of growing economic prosperity and the decline of socialist ideas, the military life held less attraction for Israel's urban socioeconomic elite, which preferred to go into business or the pro-fessions. More and more the place of both groups is being taken by reli-gious youths, so-called *kippot sruggot* (hand-knit yarmulkes, after their fashion in headgear, which differs from that of the non-Zionist orthodox). Many are graduates of the thirty *yeshivot hesder* (Talmudic high schools with a strong right-wing nationalist orientation). By virtue of a special arrangement with the IDF, these schools combine military service with study. They provide it to some 3,000 soldiers a year, with no fewer than 750 being considered officer material.[47]

Like the *kibbuts*niks in their heyday, *kippot sruggot* view themselves as an elite selflessly sacrificing individual goals for the sake of wider social goals, which in their case come divinely inspired. Whereas the *kibbuts*niks in their heyday were generally admired by Israeli society, *kippot sruggot* are often disliked. Their religious lifestyle is entirely different from that of the sec-ular majority; for them, it is difficult if not impossible to brook such minor matters as operating automatic vending machines on the Sabbath or orga-nizing a singsong (the reason being that under strict Jewish religious law "a female voice is shameful"). Traditionally no great ideological barrier separated the IDF officer corps from civilian society at large.[48] However, both *kippot sruggot* and *yeshivot hesder* are affiliated with the right-wing MAFDAL Party, which seeks to combine religion with Zionism and regards every inch of Erets Yisrael as sacred, God-given territory to which Israel has an eternal right.

Whereas until the late seventies religious commanders had been as rare as winged cows, in 1996 they constituted almost 50 percent of company-grade officers in combat units.[49] From 1995 to 1996 alone the number undergoing pilot training doubled; by one account *kippot sruggot* are said to make up no less than 30 percent of troops in some combat units.[50] The effect is to set up social and ideological barriers between the officers and their secular-minded men, who understandably resent being subjected to all sorts of religious restrictions, as well as between them and society at large. Worse, there have been recent cases where at least some religious officers became torn between the orders of their superiors and rabbinical teachings (for example, during the evacuation of Hebron). Yet as long as the IDF retains its traditional character as an army of short-time conscripts and reservists, any danger this will lead to a coup remains minimal, since presumably the troops would not know whether to open fire for Labor and against Likud or the other way around. However, it is not impossible to imagine a day when a mainly right-wing, orthodox, nationalist officer corps will command an all-volunteer rank and file consisting, as tends to be the case in so many developed countries, primarily of the down-and-out. Should that come about, the handwriting clearly will be on the wall.

Until the shift to an all-volunteer army takes place, the combination of universal conscription, a surplus of manpower, and a stagnant order of battle has produced a soft, bloated, frequently undisciplined, and under-trained military instrument that bears little resemblance to the superb fighting machine it once was. The disclosures of the Wald Report, which accused the IDF of having become bloated and were widely denounced when first published, are now regarded almost as holy writ;[51] indeed from 1986 on, *every* successive chief of staff has talked about the need to build a "small and naughty" (Hebrew for lean and mean) army.[52] However, each successive chief of staff has failed to pay off on the promise. From 1984 to 1994 the number of major generals went up nineteen to twenty-six, an increase of 36 percent. In the same period, according to a set of figures released by the Knesset Foreign Affairs and Defense Commitee, the number of brigadier generals rose 30 percent, that of colonels 17 percent, that of lieutenant colonels 31 percent, and that of majors almost 100 percent.[53] Such was the inflation in ranks that by 1997 it might take a battalion commander to lead a squad of commandos in Lebanon; by comparison, the German officer commanding the eighty commandos who captured the critical fortress of Eben Emael in 1940 was a first lieutenant.[54] Farther down the ladder, the number of captains and lieutenants was almost halved. Asked to comment, the IDF spokesmen claimed the problem was being taken care of.[55] All this in an army that has always been justly proud of the quality of its junior officers and that regarded their courage and readiness for self-sacrifice as the real cause behind its success.

Thanks partly to the scandalously low pay the IDF doled out to conscripts—$14 per month—and partly to the fact that Israeli wages were low compared to those of developed countries, in 1974 salaries and personnel expenditures (exclusive of reservists) accounted for a mere 10 percent of the defense budget.[56] Twenty years later conscripts were still being scandalously underpaid, but so many officers were receiving such high salaries and retirement pay that the share of personnel expenditures (exclusive of U.S. aid) grew to 50 percent.[57] When benefits such as housing, free study, recreation allowances, tax rebates, and exceptionally generous separation payments and pension schemes are factored in, Israeli officers were not underpaid compared to foreign counterparts. Officers from the rank of major up are assigned a car, all expenses paid (a privilege in a country where vehicles and spare parts are taxed 150 percent ad valorem and fuel costs almost $4 per gallon).[58] Much of the change reflects the declining attractiveness of the military life. In a rapidly modernizing society, the way to retain high-quality personnel, especially technical and medical, is to pay salaries roughly equivalent to those in the civilian sector.

With its structure in some disarray and its fighting spirit clearly declining, the IDF understandably turned toward high technology. The cancellation of the homegrown Lavi fighter proved to be a blessing in disguise. Initially thousands of IAI employees were let go, as well as subcontractors. Over time, however, the cancellation freed up resources for products that, though perhaps less suitable as objects of national pride, were better matched with the size of the economy, faster to develop, and easier to export. This was all the more important because, along with counterparts elsewhere, Israel's arms industry suffered from changes in the global economic climate resulting from the end of the Cold War. Some companies, notably Bet Shemesh Jet Engines and Soltam's artillery manufacturing division, went bankrupt and had to close their doors (the latter even though it just completed developing a revolutionary gun). The majority pared their labor force by up to two-thirds and, thanks to as much as $1 billion in state aid,[59] survived. Having done so, they set out in directions that involved less hubris but promised more profit.

In 1996, with the Lavi gone, IAI (the largest single firm by far) was dependent on no fewer than 1,300 different contracts for a turnover of $1.4 billion.[60] Most of the contracts were focused in three areas. First, there were upgrades to old machines. They included Super Frelon helicopters and the F–4 Phantom; the latter were provided with new engines and converted to an anti-SAM role by the addition of modern electronics and missiles. Based on the avionics originally developed for the Lavi, IAI has also produced modernization kits for MIG–21s and early-model F–16s. Some of these had export potential as other countries such as India, China, and Turkey sought to extend *their* older planes (a typical phenomenon in the post–Cold War era when any country with a modern military can acquire nuclear weapons and the usefulness of conventional weapons is declining).

Second, IAI and competitor Tadiran continued to expand their lines of RPVs, the objective being to produce smaller, more robust models with greater endurance and improved electronics packages for surveillance, reconnaissance, and target acquisition. In particular, great attention is being paid to the difficult problem of separating targets from surroundings such as wadis, depressions in the ground, overhanging cliffs, and vegetation. A new generation of long-range unmanned airborne vehicles (UAVs) is also under development. The RPVs also proved exportable and are now seeing service in many armed forces around the world. More so than the aircraft, they have civilian uses in policing coastlines and the like, which in the long run probably assures them of greater development potential and a better market.

Third, IAI and RAFAEL have continued working on missiles, where software is critically important and where Israel's technological forte could therefore be exploited to the limit. The list of missiles known to exist includes the Popeye, a long-range, highly accurate surface-to-ground missile exported to U.S. forces during the Gulf War; an advanced air-to-air missile known as the Pithon III; and the Chets, an antiballistic missile now under development and intended to bring down Scuds the next time they are launched at Israel.[61] In late 1988, Israel gave proof of its technological prowess by launching Ofek I, an earth-circling satellite. The first stage of the launcher is said to have consisted of the Jericho II missile. Though details on throw weight are scarce, a missile that can boost a satellite into space should easily be capable of landing a small nuclear warhead on enemy capitals as far away as Tripoli and Tehran. When the nineteen F–15Is on order are delivered in 1998, the IAF will be able to reach Iranian and Libyan targets without having to refuel on the way.

During the early nineties several countries started work on a new generation of RPV-directed ground-to-ground missiles on mobile launchers. These are not ballistic missiles but guided and homing ones, intended for tactical use against field targets; once enough become operational they should make armored divisions obsolete. Assuming Israel will one day be able to acquire or produce similar weapons, its over-the-horizon capability should very largely nullify the advantage that topography currently gives Syria. Thus it would become much easier to give back that area as part of an eventual peace settlement with Damascus.

Until the new weapons materialize and become operational, the pièce de résistance of Israel's arms industry continues to be the Merkava tank, considered "a national asset" and progressing into Marks II, III, and IV. The

Mark II has an upgraded engine, a turret-mounted mortar for dealing with enemy infantry, and an improved suspension system for a cross-country capability second to none. The Mark III sports a formidable 120mm gun firing armor-piercing, sabot-discarding, fin-stabilized (APSDFS) ammunition with greatly improved muzzle velocity and range; an all-electric mechanism for slewing the turret around makes it much less vulnerable to fire than earlier models. The modified Merkava is the equal of any tank in Arab hands, including the U.S. M–1 Abrams produced by the Egyptians under license. It is clearly superior to anything in the hands of Israel's main enemy, Syria; in early 1997, Syria was said to be in the market for new fire-control systems to reequip their obsolescent T–72s.[62]

Though these are impressive achievements, like other arms-exporting countries Israel discovered that some of its exported systems were falling into enemy hands by way of third parties. Furthermore, the systems reflected a more realistic approach to the ideal of self-sufficiency than was the case during the feverish period from 1973 to 1985. At a time when most major arms manufacturers worldwide are suffering from overcapacity and entering joint ventures,[63] for Israel with its population of fewer than 6 million, swimming against the tide is pointless; when it tried in the early nineties such losses mounted that Rabin, as prime minister, suggested giving the defense industries away "for free." If only because the United States continues to limit the sums that may be converted into shekels and spent locally, critically important and expensive weapon systems are being purchased abroad. Besides the F–15Is just mentioned—at $100 million each, they alone account for a full year's military assistance—this has included additional F–16 fighter-bombers, Apache attack helicopters, and fifth-generation missile boats. At 1,200 tons, the latter are considerably larger than their predecessors, which enables them to carry helicopters and thus launch Harpoon missiles (also U.S.-manufactured) at targets over the horizon. The Apache is the best of its kind, and with Hellfire missiles and FLIR (forward-looking infrared) equipment, it is especially well suited for repelling the next Syrian armored assault, by day or by night.

As it had done in previous wars, Israel pressed the West for more weapons during the 1991 Gulf War. Most visible were the Patriot antiaircraft missiles used to intercept incoming Scuds (with mixed results). Partly because German firms had apparently been involved in building poison-gas plants for Saddam Hussein, partly because arming Israel was a politically acceptable way for Germany to help pay for the Gulf War, Israel also succeeded in getting aid from that quarter. Besides the transfer of Fuchs poison-gas identification and decontamination vehicles, it led to the construction of three submarines at no cost to Israel (at $250 million each, that's no mean advantage). The land forces acquired the U.S.-built MRLS (multiple rocket launching system), a weapon specifically designed for breaking up massed armored assaults. Last but not least, Israel's antiaircraft radar system was modernized and a permanent link was established between the IAF operations center and the U.S. Air Force (USAF) Space Command early-warning center at Cheyenne Mountain, Colorado. Should another missile attack take place from the direction of Iraq, this link should increase warning time from two to approximately seven minutes.[64]

Thus, overall the decade after 1985 witnessed two conflicting trends. With Rabin and Arens at the helm, the IDF continued transforming from the lean, superbly motivated fighting army of a small country bent on survival into an organization bloated with surplus manpower, supernumerary officers, and inflated headquarters. In the wake of its failure to prevail in Lebanon, this army lost much of its aura: It was no longer as highly respected and found its ability to attract top-level manpower increasingly in doubt. Yet the period also witnessed a tremendous enhancement of Israel's military and technological capabilities, whether imported or home-grown. As in modern armed forces elsewhere, the occasional voice warned against overreliance on technology but was left a cry in the wilderness.[65] And as in other modern forces, the result has been to shift the balance from fighters in favor of technicians.[66]

These twin developments took place against the background of an improving international situation as well as very great cuts in military procurement on both sides of the former Iron Curtain. Although Israel's military industries went through their period of downsizing and reorganization, globally speaking the effect was to make the IDF perhaps the most modern armed force, behind only that of the United States. Relative to the country's size and resources the IDF continued to command a vast pool of free manpower and to attract a very large share of GDP—to say nothing of the greatest amount of free financial aid provided to any country since Lend Lease and the Marshall Plan. Yet the next two tests came, and the IDF failed to defend the country against Saddam's missiles and against the much smaller but potentially far more dangerous threat posed by the Palestinian uprising.

CHAPTER 19

IMPOTENT AT THE GULF

F OR DECADES ON END Iraq participated in most of Israel's wars. In 1936 a force of Iraqi volunteers helped organize the Palestinian revolt. In 1948 a division-sized Iraqi expeditionary force entered the West Bank and could only be prevented from reaching the Plain of Sharon, and thus cutting Israel in half, by dint of desperate fighting. Similarly in 1967 an Iraqi Tu–16 bombed targets inside Israel; Iraqi units were on their way across Jordan when they were met and forced to turn back by the IAF. Iraqi units remained in Jordan until 1970, when they withdrew; however, in 1973 the lead brigade of a 60,000-strong Iraqi expeditionary force clashed with the Israelis on the Golan Heights, suffering losses but helping to halt the IDF's advance on Damascus. During the next seven years there was much speculation concerning the creation of a so-called eastern front consisting of Syria, Jordan, and Iraq. Had it come about, it would have deployed military resources more than equal to those of the coalition that faced Israel in the 1973 October War.[1] In the event the outbreak of the Iran-Iraq War nullified any such plans. So long as it lasted, Israel was more secure than at any time in history.

In late spring 1988 the situation changed. After eight years of war in which it suffered horrendous casualties to superior Iraqi firepower and saw its cities bombarded by Iraqi missiles, Iran, ruled by the Mullahs, appeared ready to give up. A cease-fire was signed, confirming Iraq's original goals by giving it control over the entire Shatt al Arab Channel instead of drawing the border along the middle of the waterway, which according to the Iranians was the rightful thing under international law. This freed the hands of Saddam Hussein, whose military machine according to the best available estimates now consisted of as many as 1.25 million men, 60–65 divisions, 6,000 tanks, 5,000–8,000 APCs, 4,500–5,000 artillery barrels, more than 700 combat aircraft, and almost 500 helicopters of which some 200 were armed.[2] To be sure, not all of the equipment was up to date, and much of the Iraqi force consisted of low-grade infantry units suitable only for stationary defense. Yet despite the protracted war with Iran it was con-

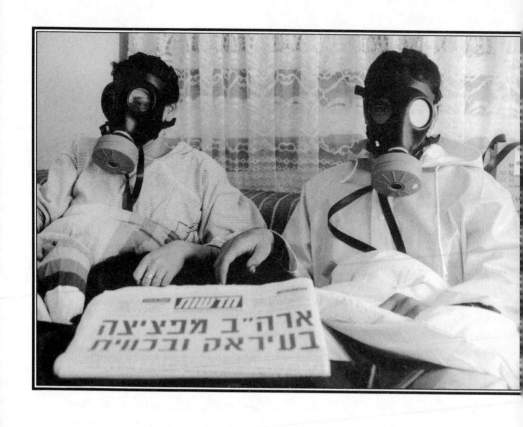

Impotent at the Gulf: Israelis wearing gas masks inside "sealed room."
The newspaper headline reads: "US bombing Iraq and Kuwait."

sidered to be, if not really up to NATO or Warsaw Pact standards, then at any rate tough and experienced in the conduct of defensive operations in particular.[3]

What was more, following the destruction of his nuclear reactor by the IAF in 1981, the Iraqi dictator was known to have engaged in an extensive, very expensive effort to acquire weapons of mass destruction. In their war against Iran the Iraqis had repeatedly resorted to poison gas. Then and later they also used it against Iraq's Kurdish population, spraying it over villages and killing hundreds if not thousands. Even more serious, there were signs that Baghdad was attempting to revive its nuclear program. Though Iraq consistently denied any intention to build nuclear weapons, and though the country is in fact a signatory of the Non-Proliferation Treaty, understandably these denials were not given much credence in Israel or elsewhere.

Just what Saddam Hussein intended to do with his steadily growing military might was not clear. Certainly Israel was only one factor in his calculations and by no means the most important; after all, Iraq has other concerns closer at hand including, besides Iran and the Gulf countries with Saudi Arabia at their head, the long-standing Kurdish ulcer that from time to time threatened to deprive it of some of its most important oil-producing provinces. Whatever Saddam's intentions, in April there was a fierce verbal clash with Israel when he used the occasion of Baath Party Day to announce that "if Israel attacked a certain metal-working plant of ours" he in turn would "burn half of Israel."[4] The threat must have referred to a possible repetition of the 1981 reactor attack, the "burning" to the use of chemical weapons Iraq was known to be producing on a large scale. For what it was worth, Shamir as Israeli prime minister responded by reassuring Saddam that he had no intention of attacking Iraq.[5] In truth a 1981-style attack would not have been practical at the time. The Iraqis never rebuilt their reactor for the production of plutonium; their effort to produce enriched Uranium-235 was dispersed at several sites and carefully concealed. Moreover, this time the vital element of surprise was lacking.

So far as Israel was concerned, there matters rested. No more than its counterparts in other countries did the IDF intelligence service—headed at the time by Maj. Gen. Amnon Shachak, the subsequent chief of staff—succeed in keeping abreast of Saddam's plans for occupying Kuwait. If anything the feeling was that Iraq's need for economic recovery "was bound to inject a measure of moderation into [its] foreign policy"; it was expected to be "largely preoccupied with domestic problems" while "moderat[ing] its position on the Arab-Israeli conflict."[6] More than its counterparts in other countries, however, Israel could justify complacency by the fact it does not share a border with Iraq and that the latter, so long as it stayed out of Jordan, was not considered a "confrontation state." The gulf is approximately a thousand miles away, so that a clash there need not affect Israeli interests directly.

As the diplomatic process for building a coalition against Iraq got into gear and as U.S. and other armed forces poured into the Persian Gulf region, some precautions were taken. In particular, additional gas masks were purchased from abroad. King Hussein of Jordan was permitting Iraqi aircraft to overfly his country and mount reconnaissance flights along Israel's eastern border, so the IAF stepped up patrols. That apart, life went on more or less as usual. During autumn 1990, Israel's attention was distracted first by a series of bloody terrorist knife attacks and then by a major clash on Jerusalem's Temple Mount. In the latter no fewer than nineteen protesting Palestinians lost their lives and another 100 or so were wounded, the former being the largest single-day figure during the *Intifada* till then.

As 1990 drew to an end, indications that an eventual war in the Persian Gulf would involve Israel multiplied. In the face of mounting international pressure Saddam Hussein regarded an attack on Tel Aviv as his best means for breaking up the Coalition, now formalized and gathering against him; his spokesmen insisted that in case conflict broke out, Iraqi missiles would "definitely" be launched against Israel.[7] The atmosphere in Israel grew increasingly nervous; by October popular pressure forced the government to start distributing gas masks even though the minister of defense and the IDF high command felt that was premature.[8] In a country supposedly accustomed to living under an existential threat, the extent to which people had become estranged from the deadly serious business of war was revealed when orthodox Jews successfully insisted that they should not be obliged to cut off their beards but be provided with special gas masks instead.

In other respects, too, preparations for the attack did not proceed as smoothly as they should have. In Beer Sheba, so nervous was the population in its attempt to lay hands on gas masks that female soldiers responsible for distributing them were beaten.[9] Not only was IDF intelligence unable to provide the government with hard data on the size and nature of the threat (e.g., how many missiles Saddam possessed and whether he had chemical warheads for them);[10] it turned out that authorities had overlooked the problem of protecting the young. In the end it was necessary to improvise by designing a sort of incubator suit, made of plastic sheets and provided with a filter.

As the clock ticked toward war, the mood inside Israel grew increasingly weird. The *Intifada* having already caused tourism to fall, now many foreign residents also left. Furthermore, an IDF "closure" prevented the Palestinians from leaving the Occupied Territories, thus slowing or even halting many kinds of economic activities. In a country noted for its exceptional dynamism and bustling atmosphere a strange quiet prevailed. Meanwhile a survey showed that the public shelters built throughout the country beginning in the fifties were all but useless. Not only were they too far away to be reached by the population in case of a missile alarm, but they could not be rendered gasproof and thus constituted death traps rather than refuges. Though all private houses built since the late sixties had to be constructed with shelters, they too had not been designed to withstand gas.[11]

Acting on instructions from their government, people went to work preparing so-called sealed rooms. The idea was that poison gas is heavier than air; therefore, in case of attack it was necessary to gather in the highest possible room, out of the wind's way, and hermetically sealed against the outside. To accomplish this the population was told to use masking tape and plastic sheets for their windows; any cracks between doors and floors were to be closed with the aid of wet rags. The rooms were to be provided with food, water, and children's games, and occupants were to don gas masks when ordered to do so. How valuable these preparations would have been if put to the test nobody knows. Perhaps the best that can be said is that so long as preparations were made they gave the population the feeling that there was *something* it could do.

Meanwhile Western statesmen and politicians, seeking to prevent any crack in the Coalition, avoided Jerusalem as if it had already come under attack. For the same reason the Israelis were unable to coordinate with the United States or even to obtain precise information as to the latter's military plans for dealing with the threat. In the absence of reliable information about Iraqi capabilities, speculation abounded; each day produced a fresh crop of experts, some in uniform and others not. Some, on the basis of calculations taken from the Iran-Iraq War, forecasted thousands of casualties in the event of a major Iraqi chemical attack; others insisted that not one of Saddam's missiles would get through the hail of U.S. firepower directed against them.[12]

Talks in Geneva having failed to solve the crisis,[13] on the night of January 16–17 the Coalition forces attacked. Understandably most of the effort was concentrated against Iraqi strategic targets, such as command centers, communications nodes, radars, antiaircraft defenses, and airfields. However, a substantial number of sorties were also flown against western Iraq where the missiles threatening Israel were suspected to be hidden. Early reports originating in the headquarters of U.S. Gen. Norman Schwarzkopf seemed to indicate that all Iraqi missile launchers had been destroyed, though whether the Americans believed this or were deliberately attempting to mislead their Israeli (and Saudi) allies is not clear. In any case the mood in Israel during the first forty-eight hours tended to be confident if not self-congratulatory. At 2 A.M. during the night of Friday, January 18, however, the quiet was broken as the wail of sirens was heard in Israel for the first time since the opening minutes of the 1973 October War. Two minutes later five missiles landed in Tel Aviv and another three in Haifa, and the country found itself in what is best described as a one-sided war.

During the months immediately preceding the outbreak of hostilities the question as to what Israel should do in case it came under Iraqi attack was often debated.[14] As Arens later explained, a modern military unit can cover 500 miles in twenty-four hours;[15] hence he considered the most serious threat to consist of an Iraqi invasion of Jordan[16] and set into motion a contingency plan for landing a complete airborne division in the eastern Jordanian desert. Supported from the air, the paratroopers were to occupy one of several ridges (apparently the operation was canceled before it was necessary to decide just which one). With other forces presumably standing by to ward off eventual threats from Egypt or Syria, an IDF ground corps would break loose. It would cross the River Jordan, climb the escarpment to the east, and link up with the paratroopers in forty-eight to seventy-two hours. Jordan's air force with its handful of obsolescent aircraft was not seen as a serious threat, and its army was too small to do much more than show how bravely it could fight. Regarded from an operational point of view the plans were probably sound. Strategically, though, they rested on a gross overestimate of the ability of the Iraq army, already under some of the heaviest air attacks in history, to move and operate so far from its bases.

Details concerning the Israeli plans for attacking Iraqi missile launchers are, understandably, even more scarce. Like the Coalition the Israelis intended to rely on their air force. More than the Coalition they would be operating at extreme range. Unlike the Coalition, they did not possess satellite reconnaissance of the area over which they would operate but depended on their own planes flying photo-intelligence missions (plus whatever the Americans would be kind enough to provide). Finally, and again like the Coalition, the IDF was planning to put teams of commandos on the ground. Whether the IAF would have been more successful in targeting launchers than the Coalition—who, it was later revealed, never hit even *one* launcher—is immaterial. At least one former IAF commander, the redoubtable Major General Peled, is on record as saying that it would not have.[17]

As matters stood, Israel's ability to retaliate against the Iraqi attacks by striking targets other than missile launchers was also in doubt. Unlike the USAF, the IAF is mainly an operational service and has never acquired strategic bombers capable of carrying heavy bomb loads over thousands of miles. To be sure, some of its fighters would be able to reach Baghdad and other strategic locations; operating at extreme range, however, their capacity to inflict damage would be limited. Compared to the rain of ordnance already coming down on Iraq it would almost certainly amount to mere pinpricks; the lack of bombers could not be compensated with precision-guided munitions with their relatively small warheads. To produce a real impression on a country of 170,000 square miles and almost 18 million inhabitants Israel would have to resort to weapons of mass destruction. Though not unimaginable, this course would have been considered only in retaliation if Saddam resorted to such weapons.

According to his published memoirs, Minister of Defense Moshe Arens was firmly in favor of retaliation. However, he was being held back by Prime Minister Shamir who for once took a more moderate line. In the event, each time the issue became urgent—meaning each time the Iraqis fired a salvo—some obstacle would come up and prevent the IAF from taking action.[18] At first it was lack of up-to-date photo intelligence. Then it was the Americans refusing to provide the necessary identification friend-foe codes, without which Israeli and U.S. aircraft risked getting in each other's way (the Israelis could not know that had they attacked, the Americans planned to withdraw their aircraft from western Iraq to create a corridor for IAF forces).[19] The next several days were allegedly wasted while the United States sent over a two-star Air Force general, Tom Olson, to discuss the matter; then again when the weather over the theater of operations became cloudy and prevented the IAF from taking action on its own. Dispatched to Washington in order to tell the Americans that Israel was "determined to take military action even without coordinating with them," Generals Barak and David Ivri (the latter as director general of the ministry of defense) returned without having persuaded Secretary of Defense Richard Cheney of the seriousness of the threat. Thus Arens, by his own account, was like an athlete going after an opponent on the field while shouting "Hold me back!" For weeks on end one excuse followed another until finally one day the war was over and the opportunity, if one ever existed, had passed.

Whatever Arens might do or say, Israel's population was well aware of the IDF's limitations. "Don't we have an Army? An Air Force? An atomic bomb? Special Forces?" asks the heroine in a best-selling novel published soon after the war; "They cannot do nothing," answers the paratrooper captain (res.), stretched out on the sofa.[20] But once the euphoria of the first two days wore off, Israelis resigned to life under threat of missile attack. Doing so was easier thanks to Coalition dominance of the skies over western Iraq, which permitted Saddam's military to leave hideaways and operate only at night. During the day Israel was safe, and life, although considerably subdued by the fact that schools had been closed and mothers could not go to work, continued more or less as normal.

The missiles being fired at Israel and Saudi Arabia were the El Hussein type, a stretched-out version of the Soviet Scud (itself based on the German World War II–vintage V–2) with a liquid-fuel engine and a high-explosive payload of 250–300 kg. Before the war there had been considerable speculation concerning Iraqi ability to launch them in rapid succession from mobile launchers while under attack by Coalition air forces; in the event, these difficulties appear to have been overcome. Arriving at several times the speed of sound, the missiles, provided they exploded (not all did), could cause considerable damage at the point of impact. Yet the effectiveness of their already primitive guidance systems had been further reduced by modifications the Iraqis introduced to increase range. Accordingly they did not have the accuracy to threaten anything but area targets the size of cities, and several hit unpopulated areas or, falling short, the West Bank.

Militarily, and from the point of view of the casualties that it caused, the Iraqi missile threat was negligible. Psychologically it was very considerable, however, the more so because it soon turned out that preparations by HAGA (Hagana Ezrachit, Civil Defense Organization) had been inadequate. When the war started it was discovered that not all areas had been provided with air-raid sirens and that some existing ones did not work. Dividing the country into regions in accordance with the extent of the threat (outlying rural areas were considered to be in less danger than central urban areas) proved crude and repeatedly caused hundreds of thousands of people to be confined to sealed rooms without any good reason and for longer than necessary. According to the state comptroller's subsequent report, one-third of the gas masks distributed did not fit; had they been put to the test, the children's incubators would have proved all but useless.[21] As if to emphasize that they did not know what they were doing, the IDF at first used codes (*nachash tsefa*, or "viper snake") to refer to incoming missiles. Soon after, realizing that it was opening itself to ridicule by trying to conceal what everybody knew, it abandoned the practice.

Above all, the longer the war lasted the clearer it became that the authorities had no answer to the high-explosive/gas dilemma—though in fairness it should be added that finding such an answer is all but impossible. At first each alarm was followed by orders to enter sealed rooms, don gas masks, and wait, the assumption being that a chemical attack could not be ruled out and that it was the more dangerous of the two. However, as the days went on and no chemical attack materialized, more and more people started wondering whether this was the right thing to do. Instead of improving with experience, HAGA's instructions tended to become more confused. At one point it even recommended a "sealed stairwell,"[22] an oxymoron if ever one there was. Feeling they had been left unprotected, a growing number of people of Tel Aviv—which suffered more than any city—took matters into their own hands. Some went up to the sealed rooms, others down into their basement shelters, others first up and then down. Others remained in bed or defied officialdom by climbing atop roofs to watched the spectacular sight of antiballistic missiles being launched.[23] Apparently the largest number by far deserted their homes every night. They went to stay with relatives elsewhere in the country or took up residence in hotels; the mayor, Maj. Gen. (ret.) Shlomo Lahat, denounced them as "traitors" who had abandoned their posts.

Prior to the war, calculations based on the Iran-Iraq War had led the IAF to speculate that three persons would be killed per missile fired.[24] In fact, whether because nightly migrations left the cities empty or due to pure luck, the number of casualties was very small. Throughout the war only one person was killed by a direct Iraqi hit, though two more later died of injuries and another ten of heart attacks following near-misses or of suffocation as they failed to unscrew the filters on their gas masks. The number of those requiring medical attention was slightly more than a thousand. Of those, about one-quarter visited the emergency rooms after having sustained actual physical injury; the rest either suffered from shock (one-half of the total) or because they had injected themselves with atropine (a poison-gas antidote provided with the masks) and had to be treated.[25] Some two hundred houses were demolished and up to two thousand more damaged. Though property losses were estimated at approximately $100 million, this was more than made up for by U.S. and West German aid.

Militarily speaking the IDF's only weapon against the Iraqi missiles consisted of U.S. Patriot antiaircraft missiles. Hurriedly provided during the first days of the war, they were positioned in locations designed to cover Tel Aviv and Haifa and operated by U.S. crews; later, as additional batteries arrived, Israeli crews took over some. Not having been designed for antimissile work, the Patriots were almost useless for intercepting incoming warheads, though the precise reasons for this poor performance remain disputed. The Americans in Saudi Arabia claimed a much higher success rate against incoming missiles, thus indirectly blaming the Israelis for ineptitude in operating the missiles and modifying the software.[26] The Israelis in turn pointed out that the performance of the batteries in Saudi Arabia had never been subject to a systematic inquiry by an independent team, thus making it impossible to establish actual success rates. The failure of the Israeli Patriots was blamed on the Iraqi missiles wobbling or disintegrating during reentry into the atmosphere. Thus, even when a Patriot did score a hit—meaning that its warhead exploded near one of the Scud's parts—the latter's warhead was not necessarily affected but was capable of going on and hitting a target the size of a city. Furthermore, the Patriot is a short-range, close-defense weapon. As a result, Patriot parts could cause damage when they dropped from the sky.

When everything was over and the time for a balanced assessment had come it was clear that whatever successes had been scored in the war against the missiles—that is, the fact that no more were launched against Israel—were due to the USAF patrolling the sky over western Iraq. By contrast, Israeli attempts to organize passive air defenses had been almost entirely useless, its active ones, if anything, even more so. Patriot's poor performance apart, the most important reason for failure was the inability of HAGA to make up its mind whether chemical or conventional attacks formed the greatest danger; even after Israel's alert system was linked up with U.S. satellites, warning times were often too short for those who did not have home shelters or lived in modern high-rises. As the IDF later admitted,[27] people took matters into their own hands. In the event, it was their spontaneous decision to desert homes during the night that prevented far larger casualties.

Once the war was over, the decision was made to change priorities and spend more on civil defense. As a first step overall responsibility was transferred from HAGA to the new Home Defense Command, headed by a major general.[28] Henceforward lookout and evacuation services were to be operated by the IDF, a most necessary change since during the war some parties that had been stationed on rooftops to identify the location of hits had deserted their posts.[29] Additional gas masks were purchased and the entire population was issued new ones in exchange for the old—although their quality remained in doubt and, six years later, 2 million people have not bothered to show up at the distribution stations.[30] New regulations required every new house and apartment building to be fitted with a room of reinforced concrete and rendered more or less blast- and gasproof by the addition of steel windows and doors. From time to time air alarm exercises are held to train police forces, municipal workers, operators of heavy equipment, fire brigades, medical evacuation parties, and the like.

With U.S. financial support, Israel also speeded development of its Chets (Arrow) antiballistic missile. Unlike the hapless Patriot, the Chets is designed to bring down ballistic missiles rather than aircraft. Unlike the hapless Patriot, too, its range—approximately fifty miles—is long enough to prevent remnant parts of incoming or outgoing missiles from falling anywhere near protected zones; indeed, assuming the next attack comes from Iraq or Iran the endangered areas would probably be well east of the Jordan Valley. To provide maximum security it was planned to fire the Chets in salvos of three. This, its designers claim, should result in a better than 99-percent chance of hitting the target.[31]

Not only is it unclear whether the Chets will be able to identify the warhead and destroy it[32] (which is more than the Patriots did); designing countermeasures that will mislead the defense ought not to be too difficult.[33] Even if the enormous investment in early warning radar, fire-control radar, and command and control is discounted, each Chets is expected to cost ten times more than a Scud. To obtain 99-percent probability of obtaining a hit, the cost-exchange ratio would be 30:1. Hence a determined attacker should always be able to get through the defense simply by increasing the number of missiles; as of late 1997 there were signs that the Syrians were preparing to put additional missiles in position.[34] In other words so long as it is a question of countering a conventional attack the Chets appears extremely wasteful. Yet the Gulf War points to the lesson that the best response to a potential chemical attack is probably not to spend billions on antimissile defenses but to threaten retaliation of a similar kind.[35] A fortiori the same applies to a nuclear threat, which may one day emerge. Indeed so large is the nuclear threat that any attempt to build a "reliable" defense against it would almost certainly represent an oxymoron.

Given the many failures attending development of the Chets,[36] clearly the deployment of an antimissile defense system capable of providing full protection—whatever that may mean—is still some years in the future (the same for other systems being planned or developed). According to newspaper reports, among the latter are a long-range UAV known as Moav that will loiter over the area and locate and destroy missiles at the launching phase, as well as a laser gun known as Nautilus jointly developed with the United States and recently brought to Israel for operational tests.[37] Unless and until these projects materialize, should another war take place any time soon, the IDF will be able to do precious little to protect the country and its population against missile attack. Even then it will be risky business.

Judging from past performance and barring an attack with weapons of mass destruction, the mortality and physical damage resulting from such an eventuality ought not to be so large as to seriously interfere with the country's ability to wage war. What *does* appear serious is the psychological aspect of the matter. During World War II, English and German cities regularly absorbed thousands of tons of bombs and suffered tens of thousands of casualties without ceasing to function for longer than was necessary to repair the worst damage.[38] During Israel's War of Independence Ben Gurion felt encouraged by the population's apparent determination to cope with air attacks and carry on life as usual.[39] In 1991, however, and as Rabin later noted,[40] Israelis did not take well to missile attacks. A total of thirty-nine—some say forty—Iraqi missiles were fired during a period of six weeks. Even counting those that completely missed their targets, the total payload of around ten tons was less than the combined payloads of two modern fighter-bombers. Yet initially this small-scale attack was enough to bring civilian life to a halt. Even later, though the economy recovered somewhat, semiparalysis prevailed.

Although luck played its part, Israel in 1991 had the dubious distinction of becoming the first country in history to go through a war in which the number of those who had died of fear exceeded those who had been killed by enemy action by a ratio of 10:1 (or 3:1, if one includes those who later died of injuries). It was also the first war in history to produce a hero who was not a soldier but rather a baby-faced public relations man, Nachman Shai. A journalist who had been drafted for the occasion and festooned with the rank of an IDF brigadier general, he became the darling of the Israeli public. In the manner of Hollywood stars, he would be flooded with letters from female admirers proposing anything from marriage down.

During the years between 1956 and 1982 the armed forces of the Western world in particular often stood by and watched, not without muted envy, as the Israelis proved their military prowess by smashing the Arabs. Now the roles were reversed, and the IDF watched helplessly as others did the job, deploying firepower that Israel could never hope to match. Not only were they helpless; judging from the signs, the war gave the first clear warning that the people of Israel were losing courage in the face of adversity and turning into a nation of cowards who no longer had what it takes to endure and fight. For anyone with a rudimentary understanding of military psychology, that lesson should not have come as a surprise but followed as a natural result of years of trying to cope with the Palestinian uprising. Therefore, we turn our attention to the IDF's experience with the *Intifada*.

CHAPTER 20

COPING WITH *Intifada*

D URING THE Gulf War the West Bank and Gaza Strip were almost absolutely quiet. For several months before January 15, 1991, the number of incidents had been declining sharply; whereas in July 1990 the wail of police sirens could be heard about every thirty minutes on Jerusalem's Mount Scopus, now entire days and even weeks passed without a single case of rock-throwing or tire-burning along the road to Jericho. When Iraqi Scud missiles started coming down on Israeli cities during the war itself, the population of the Occupied Territories registered its approval by climbing to their roofs to watch and cheer. At the same time, however, the Palestinians were clearly aware that any careless move on their side might well lead to a repeat of events of 1948 and 1967 when hundreds of thousands were expelled or simply fled. For this reason, and also because the border between Israel and the Occupied Territories had been closed, an eerie calm prevailed. Armed and unarmed clashes between Israelis and Palestinians all but ceased.

Since 1967, when it first became an occupation force, the IDF's involvement in the Occupied Territories had been gradually expanding. During the early weeks it had been a question of setting up a military government and helping civilian life back on its feet by restoring such services as electricity and water, ensuring food was available, reopening schools, and the like. At the same time it was necessary to look after Israel's own security by eliminating dozens of known PLO members, a task that was left to the Israeli Shin Bet and carried out with ruthless efficiency. No plans having been made for a permanent occupation, at first these and other arrangements bore a makeshift character. Unable to envisage a political settlement with the Jordanians or the Palestinians, the Israelis apparently hoped to postpone the need for it by creating a tolerable day-to-day life. This led Dayan in particular to insist that Israel should limit its interference with the population's life to the indispensable minimum.[1]

As weeks lengthened into months and years, however, Israel's involvement in policing and governing the population deepened. Functioning as

Coping with Intifada: *Israeli trooper and Palestinian Woman, 1994.*

the government, army officers built roads and assumed control over natural resources such as water. They licensed every kind of business and exercised censorship over newspapers and schools, determining what could be published (and not seldom closing newspapers and arresting editors) and what could be studied. Others took control over the bridges that crossed the Jordan, supervising the movement of people and goods in both directions as well as attempting to prevent sabotage, terrorism, and smuggling. Army personnel were used to levy customs and to force the population to pay taxes; since there was a growing tendency to import goods and services (including energy and electricity) from Israel, in case of a default in payment IDF soldiers acted as the collectors. Army units provided security when the authorities carried out activities such as confiscating land and demolishing unauthorized houses; indeed the bulldozers used were painted in IDF colors.

The inhabitants of the Occupied Territories certainly never resigned themselves to Israeli rule. Still, and as also happened in other countries that were conquered, during the years immediately after the Six Day War their resistance tended to be muted. Early on, the efficient operations of Shin Bet had destroyed terrorist bands that might have emerged, killing potential leaders or forcing them to take refuge across the borders. Yet in Gaza and the West Bank the early period of Israeli occupation often came as a relief to populations long accustomed to the brutally repressive methods previously employed by the Jordanian and Egyptian governments. To this must be added economic prosperity. From 1967 to 1973 the Israeli boom tended to spill over into the Occupied Territories; later they benefited from the oil crisis as Palestinian workers abroad sent their remittances home. With tens of thousands working in Israel unemployment dropped; tourism increased. The gangs of barefoot, runny-eyed children who used to infest the streets of Jerusalem during the early years of the occupation disappeared and have not returned. Finally, the Palestinians during these years were as much under the impression of Israeli military might as anybody else. They were, literally, paralyzed by shock.

Under these circumstances armed resistance—other manifestations of it, such as political organization and literary activity, do not concern us here—to occupation differed from one area to the other. The principal regions to be discussed here are the West Bank and the Gaza Strip. The former had been integrated into Jordan for nineteen years. It still contained numerous supporters of King Hussein—the more so since he continued to pay the salaries of administrators and teachers. Accordingly, although there were always occasional strikes, demonstrations, knifings, and bombings, on the whole indigenous resistance to the occupation was relatively unimportant, and the population kept waiting for external help and guidance. During the first years of the occupation the PLO and other Palestinian guerrilla movements did their best to provide that guidance and that help by sending parties of heavily armed men across the River Jordan (see Chapter 12). Most of them were intercepted, however, with the result that resistance remained sporadic and a true people's war never got off the ground.

Compared to the West Bank, the Gaza Strip was much more densely populated (although the population was probably only half as large), economically less developed, and with a less well-educated population. It was also much smaller, virtually devoid of natural obstacles, and bordered by the Mediterranean on the west and the Sinai Desert on the southwest. These factors made it easy to cut it off from the external world, yet the combination of poverty and religious extremism made for an explosive mixture that soon translated into a vicious war of Arab versus Arab. The war's objective was not so much to combat the Israeli security forces as to prevent the population from cooperating with the occupation by dealing with the military government or going to work in Israel. Among the densely populated slums so-called action committees, many of them self-appointed and not belonging to any larger organization, were organized. Armed mainly with knives and axes but also with firearms left behind by Egypt's army, they sought out "collaborators" of both sexes. If the latter refused to comply, they were subjected to forms of torture as ingenious as they were horrible.

The Israeli man on the spot at the time was CIC South, Maj. Gen. Ariel Sharon. In his memoirs he describes how he went about pacifying the Gaza Strip.[2] His first step, as he tells us, was to walk every inch of the territory to get to know it as well as the terrorists did. After a few weeks of doing this a plan emerged, the idea being that the terrorists depended on movement for their operations; it was a question of communicating between central headquarters, local headquarters, hideouts, arms depots, and of course the places where the actual acts of terror occurred. Elite infantry units, some in uniform and some in Arab dress,[3] could, given time, learn the area and population well enough to distinguish "ordinary" movements from suspicious ones. Having done so, they could ambush the terrorists.

To this purpose the Gaza Strip was divided into little squares, each one only a mile or so in size. Each was patrolled day and night; other troops were stationed for longer periods, taking up covert positions and simply waiting for something to happen. Troops carried ropes to measure the internal dimensions of houses against their external ones as well as ladders for climbing on roofs and taking inhabitants by surprise; on other occasions bulldozers were used to remove physical obstacles such as cactus fences and to destroy bunkers. The objective was always to force the terrorists into the open where they could be faced and destroyed by superior Israeli firepower. There were numerous firefights; the better-trained Israelis usually came out on top although there were often casualties on both sides.

Sharon's measures, which also included razing as many as two thousand4 houses in the refugee camps to make way for wider roads, were largely successful. Terror in the Gaza Strip abated to some extent, and the IDF's ability to hold on to the Occupied Territories was never in doubt, even during the October War and its aftermath. Even as late as the early eighties it was not yet necessary to reinforce the forces to the point that occupation duties seriously interfered with the IDF's preparations for waging large-scale war; though terrorism was never entirely put down, it was as if the Palestinians' grievances had been put inside a pressure cooker, with occasional hissing sounds portending the great explosion to come.

The 1973 war over, the nature of Israel's commitment to the West Bank in particular underwent a not so subtle change. So long as Eshkol and Ms. Meir had been in power, and with the exception of East Jerusalem, Jewish settlement of the Occupied Territories was driven mainly by strategic considerations. Accordingly it was carried out either by the *kibbuts* movement or directly by the IDF at the hands of NACHAL; either way, and with the partial exception of the Golan settlements, the decision had always been made at the top. Now, however, the balance shifted. Though Rabin also headed the Labor government, more and more he saw the initiative seized, and his own hand forced, by the movement Gush Emunim. Politically speaking, Gush Emunim was one of the organized expressions of the previously mentioned *kippot sruggot*, the other one being the MAFDAL Party, which backed it in the Knesset. Then and later its core was formed by a number of nationalist-minded *yeshivot*. Their rabbis, headed by one Tsvi Yehuda Kook, distinguished themselves by preaching a fanatical belief in the Jews' divinely inspired *duty* to settle every inch of the holy land. Then and later the movement enjoyed considerable financial support from abroad, primarily the United States. It also exercised a powerful attraction on the kind of diaspora Jew (including, to name but two, Rabbi Meir Kahane and Dr. Baruch Goldstein)5 who, perhaps because of anti-Semitism suffered during youth, hoped to act out aggressive fantasies on defenseless Arabs.

Already in April 1968 a small group of Gush Emunim forerunners led by Rabbis Nachum Waldman and Moshe Levinger had taken up residence in the old city of Hebron, seeking to repossess houses from which the Jewish population had been expelled during the 1929 Arab revolt. From then on the movement prospered, "putting new settlements on the ground" (as the saying went) in the face of government disapproval and insisting, usually with success, that they be allowed to stay put. Prime Minister Rabin tried to stop the settlers, but his coalition included MAFDAL and his efforts were hesitant and ineffective. Yet the settlements they set up were not seen as a major problem given that only a small minority of Israelis participated in the movement and that any kind of political agreement with Jordan or the PLO was still distant.

When Likud came to power in May 1977, the situation changed again. Like Rabin, Begin depended on MAFDAL for maintaining his majority in parliament. Although he personally was not religious, unlike Rabin he shared the belief that the whole of Erets Yisrael belonged to Israel as a matter of right and should be settled by Jews. Immediately after coming to power he announced that there would be "many Allon Morehs" (the name of a settlement Gush Emunim, evading IDF roadblocks, had established in 1974). With Sharon as chief executive for the Occupied Territories, Begin soon proved true to his word, engaging in a massive building program not only of rural settlements but of entire townships.[6] Nor was the population of these new settlements limited any longer to orthodox, right-wing fanatics. In a country where housing costs have traditionally been astronomical, the government promised cheap Palestinian land, generous loans, and various amenities such as shopping centers and country clubs. Consequently the program proved much more able than previously to attract secular, run-of-the-mill Israelis looking for a good deal.

Ever since 1967, along with the establishment of a military government, Israel's "security arms"—a term that includes the IDF, the police, the Frontier Guard, and Shin Bet—had perfected the instruments of repression. By world standards their rule may not have been of the harshest; never were hostages taken, or terrorists executed by formal court order, or entire villages demolished (as the French did in the Algerian War). Still, from the point of view of those affected it was bad enough. During the first months after the Six Day War the Israelis sought to rid themselves of as many Arabs as possible, pressuring them to migrate across the River Jordan and refusing reentry when they tried to return.[7] When that failed to produce any considerable results they built up an elaborate licensing system. Palestinians were required to obtain permission for virtually anything from opening a business to obtaining a telephone to working in Israel to traveling abroad; as Chief of Staff Eytan once put it in his blunt way, the objective of all this "chicanery" was to "make the Arabs run about like drugged bugs in a bottle." Gradually roadblocks, curfews, searches, and arrests multiplied. Organizations that seemed to pose a threat were banned, strikes prohibited, demonstrations broken up, and the houses of people accused of sheltering terrorists sealed or demolished—all in addition to constant overt and covert surveillance for locating and breaking up terrorist cells.

In 1974 the Rabat Summit of Arab leaders recognized the PLO as "the sole legitimate representative of the Palestinian People," a position that received the support of the world community when Yasser Arafat was later permitted to address the UN General Assembly. The Israelis, however, regarded the PLO as a terrorist organization and steadfastly refused to negotiate, leaving no partner for an eventual solution. Under Labor and Likud, from time to time feeble attempts were made to bypass the PLO by engaging the local Palestinian population in talks to leave occupation in place while relieving Israelis of the burden of day-to-day administration. In 1977, municipal elections were held; when they failed to produce a crop of "moderate" leaders the Israelis turned from the towns to the villages, feeling that villagers were more conservative (read: less well educated and therefore less susceptible to radical PLO propaganda) and that some kind of deal could be struck with them. Instigated by Sharon with the aid of a Hebrew University professor of Arab literature, Menachem Milson, the experimental "Rural Leagues" also ended in failure. Either the Israelis did not offer a sufficient measure of autonomy to satisfy even the most backward Arab, or their own leaders came under PLO pressure, quarreled among themselves, and, when they did not resign, often ended up being murdered.

These were the years of the Camp David Accords and, of course, the invasion of Lebanon. In Sharon's view they formed two sides of the same coin. The peace accords were deliberately formulated to sever any "linkage" between peace with Egypt and the Occupied Territories, which still remained under Israeli control; the invasion was designed to "break" the PLO and secure that control forever.[8] In the event the invasion misfired, exposing the IDF to effective guerrilla warfare for the first time and revealing the limits of its power. The spectacle of the mighty IDF with its thousands of tanks and vehicles reeling from Lebanon was not lost on the Palestinians. It was accompanied by intense frustration as more land in the West Bank and Gaza Strip continued to be expropriated for the purpose of settling additional Jews. Excluding East Jerusalem, its municipal boundaries vastly enlarged after 1967, the number rose from 4,200 in 1977 to little short of 100,000 ten years later. Add the severe economic downturn that started in 1983, and the background to the outbreak of the *Intifada*— literally, "a shaking off"—becomes understandable.

Throughout 1987 the writing was on the wall as incidents in which Palestinians clashed with Israeli troops—riots, tire burnings, rock throwings, and roadblocks—increased by leaps and bounds.9 Yet the Israelis failed to realize the significance; according to a lecture delivered by the coordinator of activities in the Occupied Territories, Shmuel Goren, on the eve of the revolt, their rule had been "a brilliant success."10 The signal was given on December 8, 1987, when a road accident involving an Israeli truck killed four Gaza residents. The funeral was accompanied by the usual violent demonstrations; this time unlike previous occasions they did not die down when night fell. Instead the next morning saw renewed demonstrations on an even larger scale. By noon small parties of Israeli troops scattered all over the Gaza Strip came under attack from thousands who sought to burn or overturn vehicles and injure the men with steel rods, axes, rocks, and Molotov cocktails.

Israel's minister of defense at the time was Yitschak Rabin. He was scheduled to leave for Washington, D.C., in order to discuss such vital issues as the sale of additional F–16s and the U.S. purchase of Israeli arms. In light of the uprising he did not see fit to change his schedule, so he took off as planned on December 10. The riots spread from Gaza to the West Bank, taking the Israeli authorities totally by surprise and leaving them without a prepared response. The PLO was equally surprised, although of course its activists had been organizing and carrying out propaganda for years. Now based in Tunis following its expulsion from Lebanon, the PLO also sought to gain control. It was only partly successful, however, as other Palestinian organizations took a hand, including the socialist-oriented People's Front for the Liberation of Palestine and the Democratic Front for the Liberation of Palestine (DFLP) as well as fundamentalist Hamas and Islamic Jihad. Moreover, some hurried Israeli research among detainees during the early days of the *Intifada* showed that many of the incidents were spontaneous. They did not involve an organization or centralized command but individual actions venting frustration at the continuing Israeli occupation or some other personal gripe.11

As during the British mandate, when the boot was on the other foot, the fact that the *Intifada* was never completely subject to central control was both a strength and weakness. It was a weakness insofar as there was no question of widespread, coordinated violence in the territories against the Israelis, who of course controlled all the roads and most telecommunications. It was a strength insofar as it left the Israelis without a clear military target as well as a supreme Palestinian leadership with which to negotiate. The more activists were killed or arrested or incarcerated or deported, the more the ranks of the uprising were replenished from below; indeed, very often relatives of those killed or imprisoned took action against their tormentors.

From the first the Israeli military authorities were at a loss in dealing with an uprising that had no central leadership and in which the "enemy" usually consisted of unarmed civilians, including many women as well as children as young as five. Although occasional demonstrations of force were held, especially during the early days, in this struggle 95 percent of the firepower it had often deployed against regular Arab armies was irrelevant; neither the fighter-bombers nor the tanks nor the heavy artillery (let alone warships and submarines) were of any use when it came to controlling crowds or chasing small parties of teenagers over the limestone hills of Judaea or down the alleys of the Gaza Strip refugee camps. Perhaps a small fraction of the firepower in question *would* have been decisive if it had been deployed during the very first days in the way Napoleon used "a whiff of grapeshot" to disperse the mob that attacked the French National Assembly in 1795. In the event the IDF either did not have the stomach for such measures or (as likely) failed to implement them owing to a fundamental misunderstanding of the situation.

Within weeks a dreary routine established itself. Dozens of incidents took place daily (according to one source, at the end of three and a half months there had been no fewer than 6,840).[12] Although most were small they were punctuated by clashes in which hundreds and even thousands of people participated. Demonstrations were held in the vicinity of military installations, roadblocks, and settlements, often degenerating into riots as crowds threw or brandished every conceivable object that could inflict damage on their opponents. Israeli soldiers and civilians in the Occupied Territories were attacked, cars and other targets stoned, tires burned, and prohibited Palestinian flags displayed. Much of the violence took place at random; other incidents tended to cluster around special occasions such as "hero" funerals, a variety of Moslem and PLO-established memorial days, and visits from foreign dignitaries. Often it was accompanied by strikes, some protracted, some brief, but all instigated and enforced by the PLO or some other terrorist organization with the aim of demonstrating to the world that the general population sympathized with the uprising.

Having failed to bring the situation under control at the outset, the Israelis fought back with a mixture of secret service methods, ordinary police methods, and riot police methods. The most visible were units of army and Frontier Guard troops—dressed in the same uniforms, the two had become all but interchangeable—battling demonstrators with truncheons and tear gas while obeying Rabin's orders "to break arms and legs." Similar units manned roadblocks, carried out spot searches, imposed curfews, and mounted patrols in the streets of towns, villages, and refugee camps. Other units raided various Palestinian organizations suspected of acting as cover for the PLO and searched the houses of leaders, arresting suspects and taking them to the headquarters of the military government for interrogation and, frequently enough, torture. Schools and universities were closed, merchants who refused to break the strikes were fined, and whole districts were subjected to repeated curfews that sometimes kept inhabitants confined to their homes for weeks on end.

More sinister than the overt activities, which soon developed a ritualistic character, were the covert ones. Using classic secret police methods, Shin Bet agents had been chasing and eliminating "terrorists" and "instigators" for years. Now they were joined by two units of "Arabists"—one for the West Bank, one for the Gaza Strip—whose task was to go after individual suspects and arrest or kill them. Dressed and acting as Arabs—although the local population once warned was usually able to make out fake Arabs in a crowd—they acted like death squads, arresting suspects and often killing them when they tried or did not try to flee. Counting from the beginning of the uprising to September 1993 the total number of Palestinians killed was around 1,200. Tens of thousands were wounded or imprisoned without trial in special camps in the Negev Desert. The disruption of economic activity by repeated curfews, the closure of markets and borders, the cutting of electricity and water, and periods during which Palestinians were forbidden to work in Israel caused living standards in the Occupied Territories to decline almost 40 percent.[13]

Never known for its discipline, the IDF's traditional strengths—originating in the *Yishuv*'s prestate military organizations—had been initiative and aggressiveness in defeating larger Arab armies in short, sharp wars. Now those very qualities started turning against it in a prolonged conflict that demanded patience, professionalism, and restraint. At various times during the uprising Rabin, and after him Arens as well as their subordinates on the General Staff, experimented with different solutions to the problem. Sometimes they sought to break the demonstrations might and main; sometimes they considered a more relaxed, less brutal approach. Sometimes they brought in older reservists (the spectacle of heavily laden, often potbellied Israeli troops chasing graceful Palestinian youngsters was to become familiar around the world) in the hope that they would be less easily provoked. Sometimes they replaced them with border guards, who were supposedly more professional but, alas, more brutal than the rest.[14] Sometimes they sought to break up strikes by intimidation, whereas they allowed others to unfold hoping that the other side would simply give up. Sometimes they deported "instigators" (deportation was frequently used as a weapon against Palestinians who, for lack of sufficient evidence, could not be put on trial) and sometimes they made "gestures" allowing them to return. And so on and so in an endless stop-and-go process characteristic of leaders at their wits' end.

Beginning with the homemade mortars of 1948, the IDF has a record of technical ingenuity that often enabled it to upgrade existing weapons and develop original ones. Thus it came as no surprise that the defense industries were called upon to help cope with the *Intifada* too, resulting in all kinds of gadgets that seemed to come out of a disturbed child's imagination. Particularly memorable was the *chatsatsit* (gravel thrower), a contraption mounted atop a half-track that pelted demonstrators with gravel in the manner of a machine gun. Then there was special paint that could be sprayed from helicopters, the idea being to mark demonstrators so they could be arrested later on. After several incidents in which Palestinians were electrocuted while carrying out orders from IDF soldiers to remove Palestinian flags hanging from electricity wires, RAFAEL, a world-class high-tech organization, was asked to design a nonconducting telescopic flag-removal pole; one does not know whether to laugh or to cry.

Early in the *Intifada*, Chief of Staff Shomron declared that the Palestinian outburst merely showed that the measures taken by the IDF were working(!) and that calm would be restored "within two or three weeks."[15] His superior, Rabin, was even more sanguine. In a perfect demonstration of the Peter Principle, the former chief of staff and onetime prime minister spoke and acted as if he were still a young member of FOSH on a punitive expedition against some Arab village, insisting that "to see the white in the enemy's eyes" was good for soldiers' training and morale.[16] Having won so many victories and enjoyed such high prestige for so long, perhaps the IDF felt that it had nothing to learn from others. At any rate there is no indication that the significance of such difficult struggles as those in Algeria, Vietnam, and Afghanistan had been grasped or even so much as studied; even though coping with *Intifada* constituted the army's main activity between 1988 and 1995, *Maarachot*, its flagship publication, did not carry a single article about it. Given Israel's own experience in confronting the British in 1946–1948, the relevant lessons were ready at hand. Begin, who as the leader of ETSEL did as much as anybody to make life unbearable for the British troops in Palestine, had written in *The Revolt:*

> The very existence of an underground, which oppression, hangings, torture and deportations fail to crush or to weaken, must, in the end, undermine the prestige of a colonial regime that lives by the legend of its omnipotence. Every attack which it fails to prevent is a blow at its standing. Even if the attack does not succeed, it makes a dent in that prestige, and that dent widens into a crack which is extended with every succeeding attack.[17]

By the time the Palestinian revolt got under way, however, Begin had turned himself into a living mummy, and few if any members of the IDF's General Staff had read his book. Like their colleagues around the developed world on both sides of the Iron Curtain, IDF commanders thought of war primarily in terms of a struggle between the armed forces of opposing states. Also like colleagues around the world, they were hardheaded strategists who carried out the instructions of political masters and paid little attention to the *moral* implications of a prolonged struggle against much weaker opponents. Yet experience would soon prove that the IDF was no more capable of standing up to this kind of warfare than were most other modern armies. In fact it was considerably less so, given that the intensity of "operations" against largely unarmed demonstrators was always rather low and the number of military dead during the entire six years between the outbreak of *Intifada* and the signing of the first Oslo Agreement limited to a few dozen.

On the first day of the uprising unfortunate Israeli troops in the Gaza Strip were complaining that they had been left without clear orders. On that day a young lieutenant named Offer, together with three men, found himself amid rioting crowds, opened fire, and killed a demonstrator. His reward for doing as best he could in this hair-raising situation was to be sent home in disgrace by the CO Southern Command, Maj. Gen. Yitschak Mordechai, who felt that the troops had erred in judgment (they had entered a house while trying to arrest a stone-throwing demonstrator) and used excessive force while trying to extricate themselves. Yet Offer's men, feeling he had been unjustly treated, demanded his reinstatement in writing; when this was refused several other officers in the company resigned.[18] (He was fortunate to be let off lightly. The longer the uprising lasted, the more IDF personnel caught in similar situations were abandoned by superiors, subordinates, and colleagues. Rather than being relieved, they were put on trial and punished if found guilty.)

Like armed forces caught in similar situations elsewhere, the IDF was at risk of committing crimes by using "excessive" force against lightly armed or unarmed opponents. Like armed forces elsewhere, it tried to cope by developing extremely detailed rules of engagement that spelled out what the troops could and could not do. Depending on circumstances—whether, for example, they were being pelted with rocks or Molotov cocktails, by "adults" older than twelve or by children, at close range or at long range—truncheons, tear gas, rubber bullets, plastic bullets, and live ammunition were to be used. In turn, ammunition was to be fired first into the air, then at demonstrators' legs, and straight ahead only as a last resort to kill. Demonstrators and rioters were to be handled firmly and dispersed with the appropriate amount of force; random brutality and unnecessary friction with the local population were to be avoided. Provided they were old enough and of the proper sex those who resisted were to be taught a lesson; once resistance ceased captured Palestinians were not to be mishandled. "Our Jewish moral legacy" and "respect for human honor and human life" were to be maintained at all times.[19] And so on in literally thousands of *tadrichim* (briefings), some in writing but the vast majority oral, which, circumstances permitting, were held each time a unit went into action.

In practice, needless to say, the rules of engagement were constantly broken. Sometimes this was deliberate, the handiwork of such scoundrels who are always present in any army and enjoy that kind of thing. More often it was a question of soldiers and even recruits being sent into the territories with short notice and poor training; once there they vented frustrations on hapless Arabs. Now they opened fire at the wrong persons under the wrong circumstances and in the wrong manner; now they administered beatings, either "authorized" or "extracurricular"; now they inflicted humiliations such as forbidding captives to relieve themselves or making them hop around on one leg and sing Israeli songs while cursing their own Palestinian leadership; now they invented ingenious forms of torture, as when one party of soldiers used a bulldozer to bury captured demonstrators (they came out alive). Perhaps more often still, the *chariggim* (excesses) were the result of stress as the troops panicked and used "excessive force" in situations they considered life-threatening—but that their superiors, prompted by the growing presence of reporters and TV cameras, thought should have been handled with greater care.

As it happened the late eighties were the years when cable TV entered Israel. In a country where citizens traditionally were limited to two Hebrew-language, government-supervised channels (one is government-owned), by 1996 an estimated 800,000 households were exposed to numerous American, British, German, French, Italian, and Russian programs; news in Turkish and Arabic is even available. Owing to diplomatic considerations the IDF's censorship authority over foreign correspondents has always been limited. During the Gulf War it was not even able to prevent pictures of neighborhoods hit by Scuds from being broadcast, thus potentially aiding the Iraqis in aiming their missiles more accurately. Now, with cellular telephones and video cameras and satellite dishes proliferating among the media and the general population (including the Occupied Territories, often the site of some of the best material), it lost much of what power remained.

Moreover, the Israeli media were galvanized by foreign competition. To be sure, 1988 saw the passing of a new and comprehensive censorship law. It obliged "any person who prints or publishes material relevant to the security of the state, whether in Israel or abroad," "to submit it to the censor in advance ... even if the information in question has already been published before."[20] Yet a year later the case of *Schnizter v. The State of Israel* resulted in a landmark ruling. Not only did the High Court rule that the IDF censor came under its own jurisdiction (i.e., the office did not enjoy the "executive prerogative" claimed); his authority to prevent publication was limited to cases in which there was "fair certainty" that state security would be endangered.[21] Since then, although the censor's formal powers have not been curtailed, he has become much more careful in exercising them. Conversely the media insist on their own right to publish, repeatedly threatening to take him to court if necessary.

Even in the age of satellite dishes and video cameras it is obvious that the vast majority of *chariggim* were never reported. Often this was because brutality had become routine; often it was not considered sufficiently newsworthy or perhaps the right witness was absent or those involved on the Israeli side swore to maintain silence. Of the thousands of published reports (Israeli publications and non-Israeli groups concerned with human rights) only very few were ever properly investigated. Only a handful of investigations led to trial and the rare conviction. Yet each trial was fully covered by the national and international media. The accused contended they just followed orders from superiors; the superiors in turn disclaimed responsibility, testifying that the accused had exceeded or misinterpreted orders. Since 1987 there has been only *one* case in which an officer, Maj. (res.) Gideon Levite, voluntarily chose to stand by his men and was convicted alongside them. All the rest, including Major Levite's own commander, Lt. Col. Efrayim Fein, wriggled out as best they could, usually with success since to date, no officer higher than colonel has been convicted of maltreating Arabs.

As the IDF's own history illustrates so well, an army fighting an opponent as strong or stronger than itself will be able to suffer setbacks, take casualties, bite its lip, and carry on. As Vietnam veterans will recall, however, when an army that is ostensibly much stronger than its opponent takes casualties and suffers setbacks something must be wrong by definition, thereby causing people inside and outside the forces to start looking for an explanation. Investigations will be launched and, inevitably, culprits will be found. Once found they are blamed for *mechdalim*, negligence, lack of professionalism, or *fashla*. The upshot is that those who use "excessive" force and "unnecessarily" kill or wound Palestinian demonstrators find themselves at risk of being treated as criminals; those who did not use enough force and lost lives, as fools.

This dilemma is one that no armed force can withstand in the long run: "A sword, plunged into salt water, will rust"—Lao Tsu. In the IDF's case it was made worse by Rabin's policy of deliberately passing as many ground units through the Occupied Territories as possible, often on short notice and with little or no specialized training.[22] No wonder they often lost their heads: Between 1987 and the end of 1994 some three hundred officers and men have been investigated, subjected to disciplinary proceedings, or put on trial.[23] Of those found guilty, the vast majority were let off lightly with transfers, reprimands (which might or might not entail permanent damage to one's career), deprivation of rank, and tiny, symbolic fines. A few were sentenced to prison, yet none seems to have actually served time, as sentences were either suspended or commuted.[24] At one time or another the list of implicated officers was tantamount to a *Who's Who* of senior commanders of Northern Command.[25] No fewer than seven out of ten commanders of the two "Arabist" units have been put on trial.[26]

Seeking to defend themselves, the officers in question have hired civilian lawyers. The latter accused the IDF attorney general of acting with malicious intent and of violating their clients' rights, threatening to take their cases to the High Court. In March 1997 the chain of accusations and counteraccusations became so bad that the former chief of staff, Lt. Gen. Moshe Levy, along with thirteen major generals on active duty, wrote the attorney general demanding that the IDF back up its officers and the trials be stopped (to no avail, as the attorney general also fears being taken to the High Court by various human rights groups and the relatives of IDF soldiers who were killed in accidents).[27] As always in Israel, a small and intimate society where most people listen to the news several times a day, a repertoire of would-be comic acronyms has sprung up out of nowhere to describe the situation. It opens with KASTACH (cover your . . .) and ends with ODATS (the lawyer who serves as the cover).

In theory *fashlot* that occur in the field should not necessarily affect the spirit and readiness of rear units engaged in training. In practice it has created a situation where serious training has become almost impossible for fear of committing errors that may lead to trials. At first it was curtailed by the *Intifada* as units constantly were alerted and had courses interrupted to act as firehoses whenever the territories "went up in flames." For example, the period of officer training had to be cut; the system in which each member of a tank crew is trained to perform all functions was brought to an end.[28] Later training was made even more difficult when Chief of Staff Ehud Barak (himself present at and blamed for failing to participate in the evacuation of several soldiers who were killed in one major accident) put in place a new network of "safety officers." Since then unit commanders have been obliged to submit plans in advance, and exercises are closely supervised at every step. The number of accidents has indeed dropped very sharply, as has the quality and quantity of training, according to those in the know.

Amid the constant accusations and counteraccusations the various groups that during the later period of the Lebanese War had announced their refusal to serve reasserted themselves. By the end of 1992 almost two hundred soldiers[29] had done or were doing time, including a high percentage of officers. One reservist, Rami Chasson, was sentenced to four consecutive prison terms of thirty-five days each until Rabin, realizing that his victim was being turned into a hero, gave up. Constantly harassed by the media and occasionally by the courts, the IDF did not dare resort to harsher measures. Instead unit commanders were instructed to solve the problem without bothering superiors with statistics, which in practice meant that anyone could avoid serving in the Occupied Territories by inventing an excuse. Since the end of 1992 very few soldiers, almost all of them conscripts, have been sentenced for this offense. Thus Rabin's directive swept under the carpet a problem that was literally beginning to tear the IDF apart. In an army that once prided itself on truthfulness, lying had become institutionalized.

Owing to the IDF's relative numerical weakness, for decades on end morale acted as the real engine behind the IDF's outstanding performances, and now it began to crack. Surprisingly, surveys taken between 1988 and 1991 still showed that an overwhelming majority of youngsters trusted the IDF's combat proficiency (87–90 percent), claimed that they would have been prepared to enlist voluntarily even if conscription had not existed (94 percent), and were willing to serve in elite units (78 percent).[30] Such attitudes did not by any means turn out to be *Intifada*-proof. As early as 1988 Chief of Staff Shomron is reported to have refused to meet with subordinates who had researched the problem and generated uncomplimentary findings concerning the uprising's effects on unit morale and the men's willingness to serve.[31] Later the IDF high command, feeling the ground under its feet slipping away, banned surveys and prevented those that may have been held from being published. Officers who looked facts in the face, such as a colonel in charge of manpower/behavioral science, were forbidden to speak up and relieved from their posts.[32]

Since systematic evidence has been deliberately suppressed for years[33]— as one former chief of manpower belatedly admitted[34]—spot reports will have to do. During the nineties the growing numbers of people in each age group caused rear-service units to be flooded with troops. Against a background of sharply rising living standards and steadily improving medical care, the conscripts ought to have been stronger and healthier than ever; yet the percentage of those examined and found fit for combat declined from 76 percent in 1986 to 64 percent a decade later.[35] Year after year, the IDF experienced great difficulty in finding sufficient "quality" manpower to fill its frontline units.[36] The paradox is explained by the fact that soldiers and their parents no longer trust the IDF to take care of any medical problems that may arise during the period of service.[37] As Chief of Staff Shachak told the Knesset Foreign Affairs and Defense Committee,[38] many obtain doctored doctors' reports concerning all kinds of imaginary and semi-imaginary diseases. What he failed to mention, or perhaps did not know, is that some doctors will gladly provide recruits with such reports without being asked.

In 1995, according to one survey that was leaked to the press, 72 percent of troops interviewed felt that serving in the Occupied Territories was "very demoralizing"; no fewer than 46 percent had witnessed "inappropriate behavior" toward Palestinian civilians.[39] Visiting fresh recruits in the IDF's central depot for newly conscripted manpower (BAKUM) in the summer of 1996, Minister of Defense Mordechai was taken aback when all but a handful told him that they did not want to serve in combat units;[40] by that time 10 percent of recruits destined for combat training had to be physically manhandled to get onto the transports, whereas another 4 percent were preferring imprisonment to service.[41] Furthermore, out of every hundred conscripts who enter the army, twenty are prematurely discharged either honorably or dishonorably.[42] According to the chief of manpower, 40 percent of those whose age and military background qualify them for reserve service do not even appear on the lists. Another 30 percent have succeeded in evading service by various means, so that only 30 percent actually serve.[43] Finally, among those who are called up, only about 50 percent bother to report.[44] As of late 1996, Chief of Staff Shachak described their morale as "critical."[45]

In response the IDF has placed greater reliance on conscripts rather than reservists. It has also increased the salaries of soldiers in combat units, although conscripts who risk their lives in Lebanon are still paid only about $180 per month and numerous forms of bureaucratic intimidation are used to deprive newly discharged conscripts of the grants to which they are formally entitled. Various schemes for bonuses, such as free enrollment in courses that prepare Israelis to enter the universities, have been proposed; some that are not too outrageous (one would have required the universities to pass students absent owing to military service) are actually being implemented.[46] As of early 1997 there also existed a scheme for reclassifying manpower so that personnel who had previously been exempt would be called up; to ensure that the mental cases among them would present no danger to themselves and to others, it was proposed to make them serve without arms.[47] Though the *Intifada* has abated to some extent, so far there is scant evidence of these measures having any effect. Judging by the experience of the U.S. armed forces in Vietnam,[48] as long as the army remains in the Occupied Territories and continues to conduct police operations against much weaker opponents, a fundamental change is not likely to take place.

War by definition is a two-sided activity. It is also an imitative activity in which, given sufficient time, the two sides will learn from each other and tend to resemble each other. Thus he who fights the weak will himself become weak; he who by "fighting" the weak behaves like a coward will end up turning into one, suffering one humiliation after another and losing the will to fight. From the beginning of the *Intifada* to the present day the number of Israeli soldiers killed by Palestinians during active counterinsurgency operations does not exceed a few dozen. Even including all civilians who lost their lives by stabbings, bomb explosions, and the like, during nine years the number of victims is only about 350, or forty per year, which equals the number of those killed on Israel's roads in *three weeks*. For the overwhelming majority who do not live in the Occupied Territories—more than 95 percent—the impact on day-to-day life has been negligible.

By the mid-1990s the effect of trying to put down the *Intifada* had become plain for all to see. The fighting power of Israel's once-heroic army steeply declined in front of opponents who are numerically and materially incomparably less powerful than itself but, as they have repeatedly proven, determined to the point that there is no shortage of volunteers ready to commit suicide for their cause. Given the lamentable state to which the army has been reduced, there is no prospect of the old fighting spirit reasserting itself.

CHAPTER 21

THE BETRAYAL OF FAITH

H IM WHOM THE gods wish to destroy they first strike blind. From the day that Rabin ordered the IDF to put down the *Intifada*, possibly even from the day TSAHAL mounted "Operation Peace for Galilee," the tragedy unfolded and the decline in its morale became inevitable. Worse still, in a country whose military consists very largely of conscripts and reservists the distrust eating it up from inside could not but spread to civilian society. Early on it was a question of a few dissenters who refused to go along, as well as relatives and friends standing by soldiers accused of using too much or not enough force. Later, growing distrust meant that with every incident the army found itself accused not only of negligence but also of deliberately covering up the truth; the number of cases it promised but failed to investigate must run into the thousands. Things have deteriorated so far that most of the Israeli written media will publish only negative stories about the IDF. Those who try to put in a word to the contrary risk having phone receivers slammed in their ears.

It was not merely a question of isolated individuals venting frustration or of sensation-hungry journalists echoing their claims. The parents of many conscripts now see the army as a greater danger to their children's welfare (including, specifically, their moral welfare) than are the Arabs. The result has been constant interference on their part,[1] culminating in one bizarre case in early 1997 when a mother was discovered hiding on base, having spent four days videotaping the activities of recruits to make sure her daughter came to no harm. To better allow parents to monitor their children Israeli technical ingenuity has come up with specially designed cellular telephones. Known as "mangos," they are popular presents and allow recruits to call parents at the latter's expense—much to the army's chagrin, which sees discipline undermined and has tried to ban their use in the field.

In 1978, when Chief of Staff Eytan relieved the commander of the navy's frogmen after one of his men had been killed in a training accident, the rest of the unit came close to mutiny.[2] By contrast, after two young commandos were killed in 1995—the cable by which they were being lifted

The Betrayal of Faith: Israelis demonstrating against the continued occupation of the Territories, Tel Aviv, March 1988.

onto a hovering helicopter snapped—their parents accused the air force of covering up. To make their point they went on a hunger strike. Next they turned to the High Court, which considered the matter and appeared ready to rule in their favor. Fearing as much, Minister of Defense Yitschak Mordechai beat a hasty retreat the following autumn. For the first time in Israel's history he agreed to the appointment of an independent (i.e., non-military) commission to look into the affair.[3]

Since then, though the IDF has been waging a rearguard action to prevent every statement made by an officer during a *tachkir* (debriefing) from being recognized as evidence in court,[4] the writing has been on the wall. As the chief of manpower put it in a seventeen-page staff paper that was leaked to the press, there exists "a growing gap" between the demands of relatives for a thorough investigation of each and every accident and the declining ability of the IDF to provide it.[5] This is not surprising; in any army, commanders are a precious asset into which much time, effort, and resources are invested. Prevented by the courts and public opinion from backing them up yet unwilling to let them go, the IDF has played a ghastly game of musical chairs. In at least one case, an air force squadron commander cashiered for allowing a major accident to happen was replaced by another who had previously been reprimanded for the same reason.[6]

Meanwhile the public's loss of faith in its army began to spread from the living to the dead. In contrast to premodern fighting organizations, but like its opposite numbers in other countries, the IDF has always insisted that it owns its fallen heroes. It buries them in dedicated military cemeteries and, in the name of equality, dictates a standard formula that is inscribed on their graves. Of late, however, some bereaved families have refused to go along with this policy. They insist that all kinds of other details be recorded (including, in a number of cases, the fact that their sons and daughters were killed by accident rather than "while performing their duty"). Predictably meeting with a refusal on the authorities' part, they too have threatened to take the matter to the courts. On this and other matters the IDF, fearing courts will side with the plaintiffs and change the legal status quo, has been forced to retreat. For example, the parents of some of the seventy-three soldiers killed in the early 1997 helicopter accident successfully pushed through their demand that the words "died on the way to Lebanon" be engraved on their sons' tombs.

"The difference between the Six Day War and subsequent ones," according to Ariel Sharon in early 1997, "is that IDF commanders and their decisions were trusted."[7] "TSAHAL," according to Chief of Staff Shachak while addressing an audience of thousands on the anniversary of Yitschak Rabin's assassination, "that TSAHAL which you [i.e., Rabin] led to victory and which you loved and cherished and respected so much, is losing its social standing. . . . Direct contact between it and civilian society is being broken."[8] "The IDF," he added on another occasion, "has been turned into a national punching bag."[9]

Two decades after public pressure caused *Bathroom Queen* to be taken off stage, a play named *Gorodish*, which portrayed the man who commanded Southern Command in 1973 as a brutal megalomaniac, became a smash hit. With so many negative things being published about the army each day, inevitably people began to believe it had always been that way, causing the past as well as the present to be dragged through the mud. The years since 1985 have witnessed the rise of the so-called New Historians—actually a very small group of persons armed with word processors. Relying on the archival sources that are now available for the period to 1956, Benny Morris,[10] Avi Shlaim,[11] and a handful of others have started casting doubt on Israel's long-time self-perception as a peace-loving society surrounded by bloodthirsty enemies who seek to destroy it. Instead they brought to light an unflattering picture of a bellicose country with a cocksure and trigger-happy defense establishment. Time after time the latter went behind the civilian authorities' backs. It exceeded its orders and used more force than authorized, almost always to no avail and sometimes with results that were counterproductive as Israel's neighbors, instead of ceasing their attacks, saw themselves constrained to rearm and react. From time to time it also committed atrocities, whether against fleeing refugees (as in 1948–1949), unarmed infiltrators (1950–1955), or prisoners of war (1956, 1967, and 1978).[12]

Thus, not only is the IDF losing the battle for the present, but it stands in danger of being robbed of its past—that quasi-mythological past that is essential to the morale of any army, new or old. Long gone are the days when soldiers were proud to wear uniforms off-duty[13] and when people sent each other pictures of TSAHAL on New Year's cards. All but forgotten is the fact that this high-tech but soft, bloated, strife-ridden, responsibility-shy, and dishonest army was once the superb fighting force of "a small but brave" people; spokesmen's declarations were believed as if they were gospel truth. Swamped with almost daily reports concerning *fashlot* and demands that they be investigated, few people in Israel can recall the last time the military booked a success; in the eyes of the young, even brilliant operations such as the Entebbe raid are memorable chiefly, if at all, because of the few casualties that the commandos took. As to the ongoing campaign to resist Palestinian progress toward a sovereign state, like similar efforts elsewhere it can only end in disgraceful failure while wrecking the IDF in the process. To quote the title of one popular book that records the experiences of individual Israelis during the uprising,[14] about *this* struggle "poets will remain silent."

The Good and the Evil

I N 1971 the well-known Israeli sculptor Yigael Tumarkin received a commission to erect a monument.[1] It was to be built in honor of the *mirdafim*, the Jordan Valley skirmishes that cost the Israelis considerable effort and blood during 1967–1970 and were finally brought to an end by the intervention of King Hussein's army in September 1970. The design he selected, approved by the overseeing committee, consisted of a sixty-foot Kalashnikov-like barrel pointing toward the sky, made entirely of bits and pieces of steel taken from various weapons. Mounted atop a large concrete pedestal overlooking the Jordan Valley, the monument evokes the rough nature of the countryside as well as the toughness of combat at close quarters. It is a splendid construction, provided fighting is what you like.

The years after 1973 have seen the erection of many additional monuments to the IDF's fallen heroes. Only one, built in 1977 to commemorate the battle for Rafah in 1967, was nearly as dramatic as Tumarkin's, and *that* one had to be moved back into Israel a few years later as part of the Camp David Accords. Most of the rest consist of simple stones or tables that record the names of those who died on this occasion or that, sometimes in alphabetical order but often by rank as if God in Heaven cared about the insignia that men and women carry on their shoulders. Memorials established in honor of the October War tend to be surrounded by Israeli and captured Arab weapons in various states of disrepair, thus presenting the destruction that war wrought in no uncertain terms. Many small memorials commemorate people who were killed by terrorists; indeed, erecting them has turned into a cottage industry as relatives and friends insist that the least their loved ones deserve is some sort of marker, however humble. None, however, celebrate the IDF "victories" over the PLO and its successor organizations in Lebanon or over the inhabitants of the Occupied Territories—the countless cases when guerrillas were intercepted and killed, acts of terrorism allegedly preempted, arms caches uncovered, and the like. It is as if the army and the people to whom it belongs have lost their pride, leaving behind little more than sorrow, pain, and regret.

TOP: *The Good: Rabin and Arafat shake hands at the White House,* 1993.
BOTTOM: *And the Evil: Israeli military cemetery,* 1998.

The armed forces of other developed countries were usually created pari passu with their states, a process that took hundreds of years. Not so the IDF, which grew out of illegal and semilegal self-defense organizations such as Ha-shomer, Hagana, FOSH, CHISH, and PALMACH. Thus far it resembles the armed forces of many other former colonial countries that also had to fight for their independence, but here the similarity stops. Unlike so many others, the IDF grew into an exceptionally cohesive force that, however large the role it played in national affairs, normally ended up obeying its political masters. Unlike them it never got even near the point where it might launch a coup—although, as we saw, that may change in the future. A rapidly expanding, comparatively well-educated population; the growing foreign technological and economic aid, first from France and then, in the years after 1967, the United States; and the pervasive feeling of *en brera*, which in turn translated into high motivation and a clearly defined doctrine; all these permitted phenomenal quantitative and, above all, qualitative growth. To this must be added the typical Israeli qualities of *tushia* (resourcefulness) and *iltur* (improvisation). Systematically inculcated into the army, they helped produce one of the best militaries of the twentieth century and, as many people in and out of Israel once believed, of all time.

Looked at from a different perspective, Israel's army is not so much a unique creation but a typical modern force that has traveled, and is still traveling, along the trajectory taken by other modern armed forces—albeit at much greater speed. At first, in 1948–1949, it was mainly an infantry force slugging it out with enemies at a slow pace and heavy cost. In 1956–1967 mechanization came; centering around the fighter-bomber and the tank and guided by the system of optional command, it resulted in a blitzkrieg campaign as typical of its kind as it was brilliant. Having been caught with its pants down, the IDF was compelled to adopt combined arms warfare by the October 1973 earthquake. Finally, the mid- to late seventies initiated the age of electronics, missiles, and long-range strike forces capable of operating far beyond the country's borders.

Even as Israel's conventional military might increased during the late seventies and early eighties, its entire strategic position was being revolutionized by the widely reported introduction of nuclear weapons and their delivery vehicles. Though their existence has never been officially acknowledged, from the early sixties on, the widespread expectation that they would be introduced into the region represented one factor in the strategic calculus both of Israel and its neighbors. By 1973, at the latest, they were playing a critical part in shaping the plans of the Egyptians and the Syrians; subsequently, and as has also happened in *every* other part of the world where states possess nuclear weapons, their presence made the outbreak of another large-scale interstate war less and less likely. During the early nineties it even led to the first tentative exchange of views concerning eventual arms control.[2]

Following the economic crisis that struck Israel in the mid-eighties, the IDF's quantitative growth in terms of formations and hardware has ended. Not so qualitative progress; although during the years since 1986 the research and development budget has been cut almost in half,[3] continuing U.S. assistance and burgeoning native defense industries still allowed the introduction of many new weapons and weapons systems, some of which are the envy of the world. Yet when the Gulf War came it turned out that some of Israel's security problems were simply beyond the IDF's reach. They could be solved, if at all, only within a larger framework of an alliance with the United States, which alone possessed the necessary means for surveillance, reconnaissance, early warning, and command and control, and which, as the Gulf War demonstrated, might or might not be inclined to put them at Israel's disposal.[4] Since then, not only has the number and sophistication of surface-to-surface missiles available to various Arab countries grown; the Iranians too were reported to be experimenting with missiles capable of reaching Israel.[5] The development of the Chets notwithstanding, one may conclude as Rabin did[6] that Israel will almost certainly never again enjoy the luxury of waging a war against one or more of its neighbors without its rear being threatened by weapons of mass destruction; indeed in 1997 there were disturbing reports about as many as 120 Syrian missiles standing ready for near-instantaneous launch as well as attempts to develop a new poison gas for them.[7]

At the time of this writing the size of the IDF and the weaponry at its disposal remain very impressive, both absolutely and, even more so, relative to the country's size. Since Egypt and Jordan are at peace with Israel, on paper it has little to fear from its principal remaining enemy, Syria; underneath, though, it is affected by dry rot. Hindsight allows us to identify the beginning of the decline during the mid- to late seventies. Breakneck expansion, triggered by the 1973 October War, was causing the available manpower resources to be stretched to the limit—and beyond. The rate of "churning" increased; organization became more complex and more cumbersome. The results showed themselves in 1982. The Lebanese adventure saw a superbly prepared and equipped but clumsy and heavy-handed armed force that, except in the air, failed to perform as well as expected. Next that force floundered helplessly in the face of a nasty guerrilla war, one that (no doubt because it trusted to a short "operation") it had neither foreseen nor prepared to counter. This in turn was followed by the IDF's Indian summer, lasting from the late eighties to the early nineties. As three successive chiefs

of staff have admitted, it was during this period that TSAHAL was transformed into a soft, bloated, top-heavy force brimming with surplus and
underemployed manpower.

One of the causes as well as symptoms of the decline was the evolving
position of female soldiers. As has happened in countless uprisings that
took place in other countries, even Muslim ones, so long as it was a matter
of fighting the mighty British occupant, the participation of women in the
struggle presented no problem. As in other countries, too, no sooner had
open warfare broken out before Israeli women were withdrawn from combat units and sent to the rear. Later Israel became the only country in history to subject women to conscription, which, supposing the purpose of
waging war is to protect the weak, constitutes a doubtful honor. What
saved the situation was the fact that until the late seventies women were
secluded in CHEN and their position was marginal. This permitted the
IDF to have the best of both worlds, in other words, to make use of women
and maintain itself as a high-prestige (i.e., male-dominated) institution.

From the late seventies on, manpower shortages and then feminist pressures—which, as in other Western countries, were supported by the
courts—caused women to become more prominent. By 1997 even the air
force was beginning to suffer as female pilot trainees who, despite having
been given special privileges (bathing, etc.) failed to complete the course,
accused the IDF of discriminating against them and enlisted the support of
the Knesset women's lobby.[8] Elsewhere the growing use of women in non-
traditional roles caused all sorts of problems. Pressed from outside, the
IDF even experimented with putting women and men destined for noncombat slots into mixed companies and passing them through the same
basic training.[9] Should this experiment be judged a success and extended,
then it can only lead to a situation where the majority of the IDF's troops
are as well prepared to fight as its women used to be.

Developing from humble beginnings into a magnificent instrument of
war, for many years after 1948 the IDF met every military challenge the
Arabs presented. Either it won great victories—as in 1956 and 1967—or at
least it fought its enemies to a standstill, as in 1969–1970 and (arguably)
1973. During the first week of "Operation Peace for Galilee" it still did
fairly well, but not so during the rest of that ill-fated campaign. Much
worse was the effect of its attempt to put down the Palestinian *Intifada* that
began in late 1987 and in one way or another continues today. Here
numerical strength and technical superiority in weapons and weapons systems conferred no considerable advantage. On the contrary: Precisely
because it was incomparably stronger than its opponents, the IDF was
caught in moral dilemmas with which it could not cope and which con-

tinue to haunt it day and night. Though some of the dirtiest work was shifted to Shin Bet and the Frontier Guard, as could have been foreseen and should have been foreseen and was foreseen by some, the longer the struggle, the greater the impact on fighting power.

In a country that had always prided itself on its citizens' patriotism, beginning in the early eighties hundreds simply refused to serve and declared themselves prepared to accept the consequences. In addition tens of thousands evaded service by one means or another without the state feeling powerful enough to do something; instead of being denounced, they saw growing social approval of their actions.[10] By 1996 the number of the medically and mentally fit who did not join the conscript force had grown to 7 percent of each age group.[11] Yet for years on end the army averted its eyes, insisting that things were going well and even going so far as to fire officers who called attention to the facts. Cover-ups—real and alleged—trials, accusations, and counteraccusations multiplied; one popular joke even claimed that the reason why retired generals so often served on commissions of investigation was they were used to *fashlot*. All this was to the benefit of nobody but a growing host of lawyers, who proved (not for the first time) that the acronym LIC (low-intensity conflict) really stood for lawyer-infested conflict.

By the mid-nineties the faith of Israeli society in its military had been broken. As every move came under the closest scrutiny, serious training often became all but impossible, and commanders were afraid of taking responsibility;[12] things got to the point that each time the IDF warned about a possible war with Syria the media took it as an attempt by commanders to protect salaries and benefits against possible cuts.[13] In response to the barrage of criticism the sons and daughters of the social elite no longer wanted to join the corps of professionals, leaving the field to the less well educated and to the *kippot sruggot*. Those already on active service huddled together and adopted a defensive attitude to the outside world. They closed their eyes to evidence that might have revealed the IDF's declining prestige,[14] took care to avoid attending civilian symposia dealing with the army and its problems, and hired public-relations experts to make their case for them. In this way the development theory of the sixties was stood on its head. A military that used to regard itself—and was regarded by others—as the vanguard of the nation in many ways has turned into a social anachronism.

Worst of all, there is every reason to believe that ten years of trying to deal with the *Intifada* has sapped the IDF's strength by causing troops and commanders to adapt to the enemy. The troops now look upon mostly empty-handed Palestinian men, women, and children as if they were in fact a serious military threat.[15] Among the commanders, the great majority can barely remember when they trained for and engaged in anything more dangerous than police-type operations; in the entire IDF there is now hardly an officer left who has commanded so much as a brigade in a *real* war. Taking the behavior of the Argentines in the Falklands as our example, one shudders to think what IDF commanders and troops would do if under full-scale attack by real-life soldiers armed not with rocks and knives but with missiles, cannons, and tanks.

Finally, the internal problems that IDF experiences have not spared Israeli society as a whole—if, indeed, the process has not worked the other way around. Along with faith in the military, faith in the state itself is being undermined.[16] This is shown inter alia by the phenomenal number of injunctions served by citizens against the government in the High Court, as well as the latter's growing tendency to act as a kind of unelected super-government. None of this should come as a surprise. After all, the Soviets' war in Afghanistan was one of the main factors that led to the disintegration of the USSR. Following the Christmas bombings of December 1972 during the Vietnam War, 250,000 people tried to storm the Pentagon, and the credibility gap that arose from that war has never since closed.[17] In 1958 the Algerian conflict brought France to the verge of civil war, which was averted only by de Gaulle and the establishment of the Fifth Republic. Three years later the generals commanding the army in Algeria rose in revolt. To protect the National Assembly in Paris against an eventual landing by the paras, tanks had to be stationed in front.

Rabin's assassination was the warning light. Should Israel persist on its current course of trying to hold on to the Occupied Territories and their inhabitants, in the long run it very likely will come down to civil war, not only of Jew against Jew but of some Jews and some Arabs against some other Jews and some other Arabs; unlike France and the United States, it has neither the Mediterranean Sea nor the Pacific Ocean to provide space and save it from its fate. He who is wise should never engage the weak for any length of time. He who, whether through his fault or that of others, already is involved in such a situation should consider ways to end it as fast as possible. One thinks of *Deuteronomy*, chapter 3, 15–20:

> Lo I set before thee today life and the good, death and evil . . . and thou shalt choose the good . . . so that thou and thine offspring mayest live . . . in the country which God the Lord has sworn unto thine fathers Abraham and Yitschak and Yakov to give unto thee.

NOTES

PART I

1. D. Ben Gurion, *Yoman Ha-milchama, 1948–1949* [War Diary, 1948–1949] (Tel Aviv: Ministry of Defense, 1982), vol. 3, p. 1019.

CHAPTER 1

1. M. Naor, ed., *Al Saf Mea Chadasha: Erets Yisrael Ba-shanim 1897–1902* [On the Threshold of a New Century: Palestine in the Years 1897–1902] (Tel Aviv: Ministry of Defense, 1979), p. 39.
2. Such a journey is described in A. Krinitsi, *Be-Koach Ha-maase* [By the Deed] (Tel Aviv: Masada, 1959), pp. 45–46.
3. B. Jaffe, *Djokana shel Erets-Yisrael 1840–1914* [A Portrait of Palestine, 1840–1914] (Tel Aviv: Dvir, 1983), p. 200.
4. Lord Kinross, *The Ottoman Centuries: The Rise and Fall of the Turkish Empire* (New York: Morrow Quill, 1977), p. 381.
5. A. Blumberg, *Zion Before Zionism, 1838–1880* (Syracuse: Syracuse University Press, 1985), p. 139.
6. G. Biger, *An Empire in the Holy Land: Historical Geography of the British Administration in Palestine, 1917–1919* (New York: St. Martin's, 1994), p. 154.
7. This and subsequent figures on Jewish demography from M. Eliav, *Erets Yisrael Ve-yishuvah Ba-mea Ha-tshaesre* [The Settlement of the Land of Israel During the Nineteenth Century] (Jerusalem: Keter, 1978), p. 335.
8. The size of the Arab population is discussed in detail in M. Asaf, *Ha-yechasim ben Aravim Ve-yehudim Be-erets Yisrael, 1860–1948* [The Relationships Between Arabs and Jews in Palestine, 1860–1948] (Tel Aviv: Tarbut Ve-chinuch, 1967), p. 121 ff.
9. This description of conditions in Palestine is based on S. Avitsur, *Chaye Yom Yom Be-erets Yisrael Ba-mea Ha-tshaesre* [Daily Life in the Land of Israel During the Nineteenth Century] (Tel Aviv: Am Hasefer, 1972), p. 129 ff.
10. For the pogroms' role in driving the Jews to Palestine see S. Laskov, *Ha-biluyim* [The Biluyim] (Jerusalem: Zionist Organization, 1979), introduction; also A. Shapira, *Cherev Ha-yona* [The Dove's Sword] (Tel Aviv: Am Oved, 1992), p. 58 ff.
11. Cf. A. L. Avneri, *Ha-hityashvut Ha-yehudit Ve-teanat Ha-nishul, 1878–1948* [Jewish Settlement and the Myth of Expropriation, 1878–1948] (Efal: Tavenkin Institute, 1980), p. 13 ff.
12. On the Ottoman landowning system see Ph. E. Schoenberg, "Palestine in the Year 1914" (Ph.D. thesis, New York University, 1978), pp. 23–32.
13. Ibid., pp. 94–95.

14. E.g., Y. L. Pinsker, *Autoemancipatsia* [Autoemancipation, 1881], M. Yoeli, ed. (Tel Aviv: Ministry of Education, 1970), is one long tirade against the bad qualities that Jews supposedly acquired in the diaspora.

15. Y. Doron, "Ha-tsiyonut Ha-klasit Ve-ha-antishemiut Ha-modernit: Hakbalot Ve-hashpaot, 1883–1914" [Classical Zionism and Modern Anti-Semitism: Parallels and Influences, 1883–1914], *Ha-tsionut* 8 (1989): 57–103.

16. See G. Israel, *The Jews in Russia* (New York: St. Martin's, 1975), for a short account.

17. S. A. Cohen, "The Bible and Intra-Jewish Portraits of King David," *Jewish Political Studies Review* 3 (1991): 49–66.

18. Y. Klausner, *Ha-ktavim Ha-Tsioniyim shel Ha-rav Tsvi Kalisher* [The Zionist Writings of Rebbe Kalisher] (Jerusalem: Kuk, 1947), p. 36; J. H. Alkelai, "Minchat Yehuda" [Juda's Offering], in *Ketavim* [Writings] (Jerusalem: Kuk, 1944), vol. 1.

19. Ts. H. Kalisher, *Drishat Tsion*, in G. Kresel, ed., *Rabbi Yehuda Alklai—Rabbi Tsvi Hirsch Kalisher, Mivchar Ktavim* [Rabbi Yhuda Alkalai and Rabbi Tsvi Hirsch Kalisher, Selected Writings] (Tel Aviv: Shreberk, n.d.), p. 138.

20. The first modern mention is in M. Y. Berdichevsky, *Machshavot Ve-torot* [Thoughts and Doctrines] (Leipzig: private printing, 1922), pp. 34–38. See also B. Schwartz and others, "The Recovery of Masada: A Study in Collective Memory," *The Sociological Quarterly* 27:2 (1986): 147–164.

21. The document is pretend in M. Berslevsky, *Tnuat Ha-poalim Ha-erets Yisraelit* [The Workers' Movement of *Erets Yisrael*] (Tel Aviv: Ha-kibbuts Ha-meuchad, 1967), pp. 293–296.

22. *Shire Yaakov Cohen* [The Poems of Y. Cohen] (Tel Aviv: Dvir, n.d.), pp. 75–76.

23. The Jewish-German paper, *Selbtstemancipation*, No. 1, 1880, quoted by Doron, "Ha-tsiyonut Ha-klasit," p. 68.

24. Th. Herzl, *The Jewish State* (London: The Zionist Organization, 1934 [1896]), p. 72.

25. Cf. R. Wistrich, "Tsiyonuto shel Herzl ben Mitos Le-utopia" [Herzl's Zionism between Myth and Utopia], in D. Ochana and R Wistrich, eds., *Mitos Ve-zikaron* [Myth and Memory] (Tel Aviv: Ha-kibbuts Ha-meuchad, 1996), p. 111.

26. Th. Herzl, *Ha-yoman* [The Diary] (Tel Aviv: Sifriya Tsiyonit, 1978–1991), vol. 1, pp. 50–51, entry for June 9, 1985.

27. R. Patai, ed., *The Complete Diaries of Theodor Herzl* (New York: Herzl Press, 1960), vol. 1, pp. 27, 33, 43, 77.

28. Y. Slutsky, *Mavo Le-Toldot Tnuat Ha-avoda Ha-yisraelit* [Introduction to the History of the Israeli Labor Movement] (Tel Aviv: Am Oved, 1973), p. 160 ff.

29. The customs that prevailed in the *madfa* are described in Ts. Nadav, *Bi-yme Shmira Ve-hagana* [In the Days of Guarding and Defending] (Tel Aviv: Maarachot, 1954), pp. 74–76.

30. I. Ivri (pseud. for Y. Klausner), *Chashash* [Fear], *Ha-shiloach* 17 (1907); J. Aharonovitsh, *Klape Pnim* [Turning Inward], *Ha-poel Ha-tsair*, November 1, 1912.

31. The death-threatening document, dated January 1914, is printed in Y. Goldstein, *Chavurat-Ha-roim* [The Shepherds' Association] (Tel Aviv: Ministry of Defense, 1993), p. 21.

32. Ibid., p. 127.

33. A. Pialkov and Y. Rabinovitsh, eds., *Yitschak Tabenkin, Pirke Chayim* [Yitschak Tabenkin, a Life] (Kibbuts Beeri: Yad Tabenkin, 1982), p. 54.

34. A typical contract is printed in S. Shva, *Shevet Ha-noazim: Korot Maniya Ve-Yisrael Shochet Ve-Chavrehem Be-"Ha-shomer"* [The Daring Tribe: The Story of Manya and Yisrael Shochet and Their Comrades in "Ha-shomer"] (Tel Aviv: Sifriyat Ha-poalim, 1970), pp. 138–139.

35. A typical episode of this sort is described in G. Gra, *Ha-shomer* [Ha-shomer] (Tel Aviv: Ministry of Defense, 1985), p. 96.

36. It is described in Y. Ben Tsvi et al., eds., *Sefer Ha-shomer* [The Book of Ha-shomer] (Tel Aviv: Dvir, n.d.), p. 21.

37. The role played by women in *Ha-shomer* is discussed by Gra, *Ha-shomer*, p. 66 ff.; also Y. Goldstein, *Ba-derech el Ha-yaad: "Bar Giora" Ve-"Ha-shomer" 1907–1935* [Toward the Objective: "Bar Giora" and "Hashomer," 1907–1935] (Tel Aviv: Ministry of Defense, 1994), pp. 62–71.

38. Avneri, *Ha-hityashvut*, p. 87.

39. B. Ts. Di-Nur, ed., *Sefer Toldot Ha-hagana* [The History of the Hagana] (Tel Aviv: Maarachot, 1954), vol. 1, pt. 1, p. 227.

40. Ben Tsvi, *Sefer Ha-shomer*, p. 38.

41. There is an English translation of Shochet's memorandum in Y. Allon, *The Making of Israel's Army* (London: Sphere Books, 1971), pp. 116–118.

42. Ben Tsvi, *Sefer Ha-shomer*, vol. 1, pp. 36–37.

43. Cf. N. Efrati, "Ha-yishuv Ha-yehudi Be-erets Yisrael Bi-tkufat Milchemet Ha-olam Ha-rishona" [The Jewish Settlement in Palestine During World War I] (Ph.D. thesis, Hebrew University, Jerusalem, 1986), p. 270 ff.

44. Cf. Goldstein, *Ba-derech el Ha-yaad*, p. 45 ff.

45. Ben Tsvi, *Sefer Ha-shomer*, vol. 1, pp. 39–40.

46. A typical session is described in *Kovets Ha-shomer* [Ha-shomer File] (Tel Aviv: Archion Ha-avoda, 1938), pp. 484–489.

CHAPTER 2

1. The relationships that prevailed are described in A. Druyanov, *Ktavim Le-Toldot Chibat-Tsion Ve-Yishuv Erets Yisrael* [Writings on the History of the Chibat-Tsion Movement and the Settlement of Palestine], S. Laskov ed. (Tel Aviv: Tel Aviv University, 1982), document nos. 791, 798.

2. Ibid., pp. 28, 59.

3. D. R. Divine, *Politics and Society in Ottoman Palestine: The Arab Struggle for Survival and Power* (Boulder: Lynne Rienner, 1994), p. 145 ff.

4. Quoted in H. M. Kalvarisky, "Ha-Yechasim ben Ha-Yehudim Ve-ha-Aravim Lifne Ha-milchama" [Relationships Between Jews and Arabs Before the War], *Sheifotenu* 2 (1931): 54.

5. Y. Porath, *The Emergence of the Palestinian-Arab National Movement, 1918–1929* (London: Cass, 1974), pp. 28–29.

6. The most authoritative account of this episode is S. Laskov, *Trumpeldor: Sippur Chayav* [Trumpeldor: Story of His Life] (Jerusalem: Keter, n.d.), p. 228 ff.; for the subsequent legend see A. Shapira, *Cherev Ha-yona* [The Dove's Sword] (Tel Aviv: Am Oved, 1992), p. 141 ff.

7. For statistics see A. L. Avneri, *Ha-hityashvut Ha-yehudit Ve-teanat Ha-nishul, 1878–1948* [Jewish Settlement and the Myth of Expropriation, 1878–1948] (Efal: Tavenkin Institute, 1980), p. 224 ff.

8. The activities of these battalions are described in Y. Elam, *Ha-gdudim Ha-ivriyim* [The Jewish Battalions] (Tel Aviv: Zmora Bitan, 1984).

9. The sufferings of *Ha-shomer* women are emphasized in G. Gra, *Ha-shomer* [Ha-shomer] (Tel Aviv: Ministry of Defense, 1985), p. 66 ff.

10. E. Talmi, *Ma U-mi Ba-shmira U-ba-Hitgonenut* [Who Is Who in Guarding and Defense] (Tel Aviv: Davar, 1978).

11. U. Ben Eliezer, *Derech Ha-kavenet: Hivatsruto shel Ha-militarizm Ha-yisraeli, 1936–1956* [Through the Gunsight: The Emergence of Israeli Militarism, 1936–1956] (Tel Aviv: Dvir, 1995), pp. 105–106.

12. Cf. Porath, *The Emergence*, pp. 110–111.

13. *Census of Palestine, 1931* (London: His Majesty's Stationary Office, 1932), summary.

14. Term used by Y. Ratner, the organization's future chief of staff, and quoted in M. Pail, *Min Ha-hagana Li-Tsva Hagana* [From the Hagana to the IDF] (Tel Aviv: Zmora Bitan, 1979), p. 19.

15. On the Hagana forces in Haifa see A. Lubrani, *Darko shel Adam; Kovets Le-Zichro shel Yakov Pat* [A Pamphlet in Memory of Yakov Pat] (Herzliya: private edition, 1958), p. 76; also B. Ts. Di-Nur, ed., *Sefer Toldot Ha-hagana* [The History of the Hagana] (Tel Aviv: Maarachot, 1954), vol. 1, pt. 2, pp. 422–423.

16. The largest "ex" took place in November 1923 and is described in ibid., pp. 227–228.

17. Ibid., p. 230.

18. Ts. Nadav, *Bi-yme Shmira Ve-hagana* [In the Days of Guarding and Defending] (Tel Aviv: Maarachot, 1954), p. 307.

19. Di-nur, *Sefer Toldot Ha-hagana*, vol. 1, pt. 2, p. 628.

20. See Porath, *The Emergence*, p. 265 ff.

21. G. Biger, *An Empire in the Holy Land: Historical Geography of the British Administration in Palestine, 1917–1929* (New York: St. Martin's, 1994), pp. 158–159.

22. Di-nur, *Sefer Toldot Ha-hagana*, vol. 1, pt. 2, pp. 313, 404.

23. Ts. Eshel, *Maarchot Ha-hagana Be-Chefa* [The Hagana's Campaigns in Haifa] (Tel Aviv: Ministry of Defense, 1978), p. 163 ff.

24. Y. Ben Tsvi et al., eds., *Sefer Ha-shomer* [The Book of Ha-shomer] (Tel Aviv: Dvir, n.d.), pp. 77 and 408, has two firsthand accounts of this mission.

25. Di-nur, *Sefer Toldot Ha-hagana*, vol. 1, pt. 2, p. 387.

Chapter 3

1. For the details of this plan see B. Ts. Di-Nur, ed., *Sefer Toldot Ha-hagana* [The History of the Hagana] (Tel Aviv: Maarachot, 1954), vol. 1, pt. 2, p. 407 ff.

2. Z. Abramovitsh and Y. Glaft, *Ha-meshek Ha-aravi Be-erets Yisrael U-be-artsot Ha-mizrach Ha-tichon* [The Arab Economy in Palestine and the Middle East] (Tel Aviv: Ha-kibbuts Ha-meuchad, 1944), p. 39.

3. Di-nur, *Sefer Toldot Ha-hagana*, vol. 1, pt. 2, p. 479.

4. For a vivid account of Tel Aviv as it appeared during those years see S. Peres, *Battling for Peace* (London: Weidenfeld and Nicolson, 1995), p. 17 ff.

5. These and other figures are from M. Asaf, *Ha-yechasim ben Aravim Ve-yehudim Be-erets Yisrael, 1860–1948* [The Relationships Between Arabs and Jews in Palestine, 1860–1948] (Tel Aviv: Tarbut Ve-chinuch, 1967), p. 121 ff.

6. Y. Ratner, *Chayai Ve-ani* [My Life and I] (Tel Aviv: Schocken, 1978), p. 262.

7. A facsimile of the document is printed in Di-nur, *Sefer Toldot Ha-hagana*, vol. 1, pt. 2, p. 527.

8. Y. Elam, *Ha-gdudim Ha-ivriyim* [The Jewish Battalions] (Tel Aviv: Zmora Bitan, 1984), pp. 259–266.

9. See on this phenomenon A. Kadish, *La-meshek Ve-la-neshek* [To Farms and Arms] (Tel Aviv: Tag, 1995), pp. 190–191.

10. A. Gorali, Judge-Advocate General, Report, September 5, 1948, TSAHAL Archive, file 121/50/221.

11. Y. Horowitz, *Mah Chidesh Ha-FOSH* [FOSH Innovations] (Ranana: Snunit, 1985), p. 18.

12. What little is known about the *nodedot* is summarized in M. Pail, *Min Ha-hagana Li-Tsva Hagana* [From Hagana to IDF] (Tel Aviv: Zmora Bitan, 1979), p. 133 ff.

13. See on this entire question A. Shapira, *Cherev Ha-yona* [The Dove's Sword] (Tel Aviv: Am Oved, 1992), p. 156 ff.

14. Th. Herzl, *Old-New Land* (New York: Bloch, 1960 [1898]), p. 116.

15. E.g., Sh. Yavnieli, *Bi-yme Ha-keev* [In the Days of Pain], *Igeret* (May 1921); Y. Aharonovitsh, *Le-achar Ha-praot* [After the Pogroms], *Ha-poel Ha-tsair* (May 13, 1921).

16. E.g., Y. Brenner, *Mi-Pinkas* [From the Notebook], *Kontras* (April 1921); D. Ben Gurion, *Anachnu Ve-shchenenu* [We and Our Neighbors] (Tel Aviv: Davar, 1931), p. 61. For a low-level English-language exposition of the same idea see D. Duff, *Palestine Picture* (London: Hodder and Stoughton, 1936), p. 295 ff.

17. The Sheik's story is told in Ch. Knaan, *Be-enei Shoter Palestinai* [Through the Eyes of a Palestinian Policeman] (Tel Aviv: Masada, 1980), pp. 7–32.

18. On the beginning of the uprising see Ts. El-Peleg, "Ha-mered Ha-aravi, Hearot Mashlimot" [The Arab Uprising: Supplementary Remarks], in Ministry of Defense, ed., *Tsva Ha-medina Ba-derech* [Army on the Way to the State] (Tel Aviv: Ministry of Defense, 1988), p. 106 ff.

19. Based on Knaan, *Be-enei Shoter Palestinai*, p. 79 ff., which constitutes an eyewitness account.

20. The best source for Kauji's activities is E. Danin, ed., *Ha-knufiot Ha-araviot Bi-Meoraot 1936–1939* [The Arab Gangs in the Events of 1936–1939] (Jerusalem: Magnes, 1981), pp. 1–8.

21. Figures on casualties may be found in W. Khalidi, ed., *From Haven to Conquest: Readings in Zionism and the Palestine Problem Until 1948* (Beirut: Institute for Palestine Studies, 1971), app. 4, pp. 846–849.

22. Data from S. Slutski, *Kitsur Toldot Ha-hagana* [Concise History of Hagana] (Tel Aviv: Ministry of Defense, 1986), p. 181.

23. Y. Avidar, *Ba-derech Le-TSAHAL* [On the Way to TSAHAL] (Tel Aviv: Maarachot, 1970), p. 115.

24. A convenient account of British-Jewish military cooperation during this time was written by Ben Gurion and published in *Jewish Observer and the Middle East Review* (September 20, 1963): 13–14.

25. An English translation of his article, "Our Friend: What Wingate Did for Us" (1963), may be found in Khalidi, *From Haven to Conquest*, pp. 382–388.

26. See the colorful account in L. Mosley, *Gideon Goes to War* (London: Barker, 1955), pp. 55–64.

27. Details on Sadeh's life to this point may be found in Ts. Dror, *Matsbi Le-lo Srara: Sipur-Chayav shel Yitschak Sadeh* (Commander Without Power: The Life of Yitschak Sadeh] (Tel Aviv: Ha-kibbuts Ha-meuchad, 1996), pp. 1–124.

28. Abdu testimony, Hagana Archive, No. 1829.

29. The decision is printed in Khalidi, *From Haven to Conquest*, pp. 331–333.

30. Cf. figures in Asaf, *Ha-yechasim ben Yehudim Le-aravim*, p. 216.

31. Y. Horowitz, *Ma Chidesh Ha-FOSH*, p. 25.

32. Cf. ibid., pp. 164–165; also Pail, *Min Ha-hagana Li-tsva Hagana*, pp. 154–160.

33. There is a list of its operations in Pail, *Min Ha-hagana Li-tsva Hagana*, pp. 176–177.

34. An account of the *Patria* episode may be found in M. Merdor, *Shlichut Aluma: Pirke Mivtsaim Meyuchadim Be-maarchot Ha-hagana* [Secret Mission: Special Operations in the History of Hagana] (Tel Aviv: Maarachot, 1957), pp. 23–25.

35. For the importance of this episode in Dayan's own life see S. Teveth, *Moshe Dayan: The Soldier, the Man, the Legend* (London: Quartet, 1972), chap. 8.

36. For this and other attempts to curtail Hagana see Slutski, *Kitsur Toldot Ha-hagana*, pp. 297–300.

37. Cf. Y. Avigur, *Ba-derech Le-TSAHAL: Zichronot* [Memoirs on the Road to TSAHAL] (Tel Aviv: Maarachot, 1970), pp. 154–155.

38. Figures from Ben Gurion, *Jewish Observer and Middle East Review* (September 27, 1963): 17–18.

CHAPTER 4

1. The episode is described in Y. Sadeh, "Im Zecher Ha-sira: Ech Naflu Giborim" [In Memory of the Boat: How Heroes Fell], *Maarachot* 33:4 (May 1946); also D. Hacohen, *Et Le-saper* [A Time to Tell] (Tel Aviv: Am Oved, 1974), pp. 165–174.

2. On this episode see S. Teveth, *Moshe Dayan: The Soldier, the Man, the Legend* (London: Quartet, 1972), p. 137 ff.; also G. Warner, *Iraq and Syria, 1941* (London: Davis-Poynter, 1974), chap. 5.

3. The precise figures were: training: 9 days per month; work: 13.6 days; leave and sickness: 2.6 days; total: 25.2, Saturdays excluded. A day's labor was valued at 0.5 Palestinian pounds, the PALMACHniks' maintenance budget stood at rather less than 7 pounds per month—paltry even by the standards of those days. U. Brenner, *Le-tsava Yehudi Atsmai: Ha-kibbuts Ha-meuchad Ba-hagana 1939–1945* [Toward an Independent Jewish Army: The United *Kibbuts* Movement in Defense 1939–1945] (Efal: Yad Tabenkin, 1985), p. 148.

4. U. Narkis, *Chayal shel Yerushalayim* [A Soldier for Jerusalem] (Tel Aviv: Ministry of Defense, 1991), p. 52.

5. The best recent work on PALMACH ideology is A. Kadish, *La-meshek Ve-la-neshek* [To Farms and Arms] (Tel Aviv: Tag, 1995), particularly chap. 7.

6. Ts. Dror, *Matsbi Le-lo Srara: Sipur-Chayav shel Yitschak Sadeh* (Commander Without Power: The Life of Yitschak Sadeh] (Tel Aviv: Ha-kibbuts Ha-meuchad, 1996), p. 210.

7. The best source for the plan is U. Brenner, *Le-nochach Iyum Ha-plisha Ha-germanit Le-erets Yisrael, 1940–1942* [Confronting the Menace of a German Invasion of Palestine, 1940–1942] (Efal: Yad Tabenkin, 1985).

8. Dror, *Matsbi Le-lo Srara*, p. 214; Ch. Knaan, *Matayim Yeme Charada* [Two Hundred Days of Fear] (Tel Aviv: Art, 1975), pp. 245–247.

9. Y. Gelber, "Ha-mediniyut Ha-britit Ve-hatsiyonit, 1942–1944" [British and Zionist Policy, 1942–1944], *Ha-tsiyonut* 7 (1981): 335 ff.

10. S. Slutski, *Kitsur Toldot Ha-hagana* [Concise History of Hagana] (Tel Aviv: Ministry of Defense, 1986), p. 304.

11. H. Gofer, *Ha-mishmar al Ha-chof* [The Guard on the Shore] (Tel Aviv: TAG, 1995).

12. For a breakdown of those who served in the various forces see ibid., p. 376.

13. For the attempts to set up a Jewish brigade and the authorities' attempts to frustrate them, see Y. Gelber, "Mekomah shel Ha-hitnadvut La-tsava Ha-briti Ba-mediniyut Hatsiyonit, 1939–1942" [The Role of the Volunteer Movement to the British Army in Zionist Policy, 1939–1942] (Ph.D. thesis, Haifa University, 1977).

14. The differences are discussed in U. Ben Eliezer, *Derech Ha-kavenet: Hivatsruto shel Ha-militarizm Ha-yisraeli, 1936–1956* [Through the Gunsight: The Emergence of Israeli Militarism, 1936–1956] (Tel Aviv: Dvir, 1995), p. 117 ff.

15. M. Dayan, *Avnei Derech* [Memoirs] (Tel Aviv: Dvir, 1976), p. 39.

16. A. Koestler, *Thieves in the Night: Chronicle of an Experiment* (New York: MacMillan, 1946), p. 152. The full quote runs: "These stumpy, dumpy girls with their rather coarse features, big buttocks and heavy breasts, psychically precocious, mentally retarded, over ripe and immature at the same time; and these raw, arse-slapping youngsters, callow, dumb and heavy, with their aggressive laughter and unmodulated voices."

17. M. Naor, *Laskov: Lochem, Adam, Chaver* [Laskov: The Soldier, the Man, the Friend] (Jerusalem: Keter, 1988), p. 128.

18. The 1939 figures: investment: 14,475 pounds; employees: 25; production 5,508 pounds. The 1944 figures: 97,500 pounds; employees: 140; production: 32,577 pounds. Source: Y. Evron, *Ha-Taasiya Ha-bitchonit* [The Defense Industries] (Tel Aviv: Ministry of Defense, 1980), pp. 61–62.

19. U. Milstein, *Toldot Milchemet Ha-atsmaut* [The War of Independence] (Tel Aviv: Zmora Bitan, 1989), vol. 1, p. 232.

20. Slutski, *Kitsur Toldot Ha-hagana*, p. 463.
21. Y. Arnon-Ochana, "Ha-machane Ha-aravi Bi-meoraot 1936–1939" [The Arabs During the Events of 1936–1939], in Ministry of Defense, ed., *Tsva Ha-medina Ba-derech* [Army on the Way to the State] (Tel Aviv: Ministry of Defense, 1988), pp. 96–105.
22. These operations are described in detail in Y. Avidar, *Ba-derech Le-TSAHAL* [On the Way to TSAHAL] (Tel Aviv: Maarachot, 1970), pp. 115., 233–237.
23. Cf. above all L. Pyenson, *Civilizing Mission: Exact Science and French Expansion, 1870–1940* (Baltimore: Johns Hopkins University Press, 1993).
24. For Jabotinsky's views see R. Bilski-Ben Hur, *Every Individual a King: The Social and Political Thought of Zeev Vladimir Jabotinsky* (Washington, D.C.: Bnai Brith, 1993), p. 111 ff. (the Arab question), pp. 46 ff. and 214 ff. (militarism).
25. Lecture by Dr. Y. Eldad, Tel Aviv, September 1, 1989 (eyewitness account).
26. Cf. J. Heller, *The Stern Gang: Ideology, Politics, and Terror, 1940–1949* (London: Frank Cass, 1993), particularly pp. 289–296.
27. On the so-called season see Y. Bauer, *Diplomatya U-Machteret Ba-mediniyut Ha-tsiyonit, 1939–1945* [Diplomacy and Underground in Zionism, 1939–1945] (Tel Aviv: Sifriyat Ha-poalim, 1966), pp. 275–283.
28. R. Crossman, *Palestine Mission* (London: Hamilton, 1947), p. 139.
29. For the debates that led Hagana in particular to follow this policy see J. Heller, "'Neither Masada nor Vichy': Diplomacy and Resistance in Zionist Politics, 1945–1947," *The International Historical Review* 3:4 (October 1981): 517–539.
30. D. A. Charters, *The British Army and the Jewish Insurgency in Palestine, 1945–1947* (London: MacMillan, 1989), p. 196.
31. A. Dankner, *Dan Ben Amots, Biographia* [Dan Ben Amots—a Biography] (Jerusalem: Keter, 1992), pp. 92, 98. Dan Ben Amots was a PALYAM member who later became a well-known journalist and satirist.
32. A detailed analysis of the attempts at illegal immigration, and their interception by the British, is presented in N. Bogner, *Sfinot Ha-meri* [The Ships of the Revolt] (Efal: Yad Tabenkin, 1993).
33. *The Star*, September 8, 1947, p. 11; *The Daily Telegraph*, September 8, 1947, p. 12; and *The News Chronicle*, September 8, 1947, pp. 1 and 7.
34. Hagana's activities in Cyprus are described in N. Bogner, "Shurot Ha-meginim" [The Defenders], in G. Rivlin, ed., *Ale-Zayit Ve-cherev: Mekorot U-mechkarim Be-ginze Ha-hagana* [Olive Leaves and Sword: Sources and Studies in the Hagana Archives] (Tel Aviv: Ministry of Defense, 1990), pp. 177–205.
35. For a breakdown see H. Lebenberg, *The Military Preparations of the Arab Community in Palestine, 1945–1948* (London: Cass, 1993), p. 94.
36. Cf. L. James, *Imperial Rearguard: Wars of Empire, 1919–1985* (London: Brassey's, 1988), p. 94.
37. A. Horne, *A Savage War for Peace* (London: MacMillan, 1979), p. 566.
38. Field Marshal John Dill, Chief of the General Staff, 1941, quoted in James, *Imperial Rearguard*, p. 96.
39. Cf. R. D. Wilson, *Cordon and Search: With 6th Airborne Division in Palestine* (Aldershot: Gale and Polden, 1949), app. K, pp. 230–246.
40. Charters, *The British Army*, p. 87.
41. Field Marshal Montgomery to General Dempsey, Commander, British Forces, Middle East, June 27, 1946, quoted in A. Nachmani, "Generals at Bay in Post-War Palestine," *Journal of Strategic Studies* 4:6 (December 1983): 68.
42. Life in the camp is described by A. Krinitsi, *Be-Koach Ha-maase* [By the Deed] (Tel Aviv: Masada, 1959), pp. 182–190. In the end, since nothing could be definitely proven against them, almost all the detainees were released.
43. Figures from Slutski, *Kitsur Toldot Ha-hagana*, p. 426.
44. Avidar, *Ba-derech Le-TSAHAL*, pp. 238–239.

45. Cf. J. Heller, "Neither Masada—Nor Vichy: Diplomacy and Resistance in Zionist Politics, 1945–1947," *The International History Review* 3:4 (October 1981): 558–559.
46. M. Begin, *The Revolt* (New York: Dell, 1977), pp. 285–287.
47. LECHI poster printed in Y. Nedavah, *Mi Geresh et Ha-Britim Me-erets Yisrael* [Who Expelled the British from the Land of Israel] (Tel Aviv: Ha-amuta Le-hafatsat Todaah Leumit, 1988), p. 60.
48. A book-length account of this episode is A. Eshel, *Shvirat Ha-gadromim: Parashat Chatifatam Ve-tliyatam shel Ha-serjentim im Chasifat Mismechei Ha-hagana* [Breaking the Gallows: The Kidnapping and Hanging of the British Sergeants in the Light of Hagana Documents] (Tel Aviv: Zmora Bitan, 1990).
49. Cf. M. J. Cohen, *Palestine and the Great Powers, 1945–1948* (Princeton: Princeton University Press, 1982).
50. Charters, *The British Army*, chap. 5; Nachmani, "Generals at Bay," p. 70 ff.
51. B. L. Montgomery, *The Memoirs of Montgomery of Alamein* (London: Collins, 1958), p. 468.
52. C. von Clausewitz, *On War* (Princeton: Princeton University Press, 1976), p. 127.
53. House of Commons (HC) Debates, vol. 441. The same source puts the number of soldiers, policemen, and civilians killed and wounded at 79/40, 16/180, and 69/10 respectively.
54. Lord Davies as quoted in A. Koestler, *Promise and Fulfillment: Palestine, 1917–1949* (London: MacMillan, 1949), p. 62.
55. Cf. B. J. Evensen, *Truman, Palestine, and the Press: Shaping Conventional Wisdom at the Beginning of the Cold War* (Westport, Conn.: Greenwood Press, 1992), for the effect on American public opinion in particular.
56. Quoted in James, *Imperial Rearguard*, p. 100.
57. Quoted in Begin, *The Revolt*, p. 313.
58. Thucydides, *The Peloponnesian War* (Harmondsworth, Middlesex: Penguin, 1954), p. 360.

CHAPTER 5

1. This and the following paragraphs based on Z. Ostfeld, *Tsava Nolad: Shlavim Ikariyim Bi-bniyat Ha-tsava Be-hanhagato shel Ben Gurion* [An Army Is Born: Main Stages in the Buildup of the Army Under the Leadership of Ben Gurion] (Tel Aviv: Ministry of Defense, 1993), vol. 1, p. 18 ff.
2. The committee's establishment is described in D. Almog, *Ha-rechesh Be-artsot Ha-brit, 1945–1949* [Arms Acquisition in the U.S., 1945–1949] (Tel Aviv: Maarachot, 1987), pp. 30–31.
3. The reasons for the change are discussed in Y. Gelber, *Lamah Perku et Ha-PALMACH?* [Why Did They Abolish PALMACH?] (Tel Aviv: Schoken, 1986), chap. 8; also, at much greater length, in M. Pail and A. Ronen, *Maavake Koach Ba-tsameret Ba-derech Le-nitsachon Be-milchemet Ha-atsmaut* [Trials of Strength at the Top on the Way to Victory in the War of Independence] (Efal: Yad Galili, 1991).
4. The article, called "Hatsaa Chashuva" [An Important Proposal], was published in *Le-achdut Ha-avoda* 113 (October 15, 1946). Cf. also Ts. Dror, *Matsbi Le-lo Srara: Sipur-Chayav shel Yitschak Sadeh* (Commander Without Power: The Life of Yitschak Sadeh] (Tel Aviv: Ha-kibbuts Ha-meuchad, 1996), chap. 18.
5. For the differences between the two systems see M. van Creveld, *Fighting Power: German and U.S. Army Performance, 1939–1945* (Westport, Conn.: Greenwood Press, 1982), chap. 6.
6. Figures in Ostfeld, *Tsava Nolad*, vol. 1, p. 54.

7. COS note, January 13, 1948, TSAHAL Archive, 5205/49/14, quoting British document.

8. Data on these forces in Y. Shimoni, *Arviye Erets Yisrael* [The Arabs of Erets Yisrael] (Tel Aviv: Am Oved, 1947), pp. 376–377.

9. IDF, Historical Department, *Toldot Milchemet Ha-komemiyut* [History of the War of Independence] (Tel Aviv: Ministry of Defense, 1959), p. 69.

10. Quoted in A. Koestler, *Promise and Fulfillment: Palestine, 1917–1949* (London: MacMillan, 1949), p. 156. Lebenberg, *The Military Preparations of the Arab Community in Palestine, 1945–1948* (London: Cass, 1993), p. 200, puts the number at 6,000.

11. On the early history of the Arab Legion see J. B. Glubb, *The Story of the Arab Legion* (London: Hodder and Stoughton, 1948), chaps. 1–11.

12. On the strength and organization of the Arab Legion see Abdullah al Tal, *Zichronot* [Memoirs] (Tel Aviv: Maarachot, 1960), pp. 66–67. According to him the Arab Legion forces in Palestine had 84 armored cars and 131 guns of various calibers.

13. The negotiations were summed up by Ms. Meir's assistant, E. Danin, in Zionist Archive Doc. No. S 25/4004. See also G. Meir, *My Life* (Jerusalem: Steimatzky, 1975), p. 176, which, however, is much less specific.

14. Lists of these atrocities, together with expressions of satisfaction at their success, may be found in IDF, *Toldot Milchemet Ha-komemiyut*, p. 86; and al Tal, *Zichronot*, pp. 18–20.

15. Y. Rabin, *Pinkas Sherut* [A Service Record] (Tel Aviv: Maariv), vol. 1, p. 51.

16. D. Ben Gurion, *Yoman Ha-milchama, 1948–1949* [War Diary, 1948–1949] (Tel Aviv: Ministry of Defense, 1982), vol. 1, p. 67.

17. See in particular U. Milstein, *Toldot Milchemet Ha-atsmaut* [The War of Independence] (Tel Aviv: Zmora Bitan, 1989), vol. 3.

18. M. Asaf, *Ha-yechasim ben Aravim Ve-yehudim Be-erets Yisrael, 1860–1948* [The Relationships Between Arabs and Jews in Palestine, 1860–1948] (Tel Aviv: Tarbut Vechinuch, 1964), p. 217.

19. Shimoni, *Arviye Erets Yisrael*, p. 205.

20. M. Begin, *The Revolt* (New York: Dell, 1977), p. 224 ff.

21. This short account of the exodus, as well as the figures, is based on B. Morris, *Ledatah shel Baayat Ha-plitim Ha-palestinaim, 1947–1949* [The Birth of the Palestinian Refugee Problem, 1947–1949] (Tel Aviv: Am Oved, 1986).

22. Elazar's account of the episode may be found in N. Bar Tov, *Dado: Arbaim U-smoneh Shanim Ve-esrim Yom* [Dado: Forty-Eight Years and Twenty Days] (Tel Aviv: Maariv, 1978), vol. 1, pp. 40–43; that of Eytan in R. Eytan, *Sippur shel Chayal* [A Soldier's Story] (Tel Aviv: Maariv, 1991), pp. 38–41.

23. For the role played by the Arab Legion in the fighting for Jerusalem see S. Ali El-Edroos, *The Hashemite Arab Army, 1909–1979* (Amman: The Publishing Committee, 1980), pp. 253–254.

24. A book-length account of the fighting for Kfar Etsion is presented in D. Knohl, ed., *Gush Etsion Be-milchamto* [Gush Etsion at War] (Jerusalem: Jewish Agency, 1957).

25. The operations around Mishmar Ha-emek are described in Dror, *Matsbi Le-lo Srara*, p. 349 ff.; also N. Lorch, *The Edge of the Sword: Israel's War of Independence, 1947–1949* (Toronto: Longmans, 1961), pp. 93–95.

26. IDF, *Toldot Milchemet Ha-komemiyut*, p. 135.

27. Cf. his own description quoted in Lorch, *The Edge of the Sword*, p. 280.

28. Cf. Begin, *The Revolt*, p. 451 ff.

CHAPTER 6

1. For the planning that took place see Z. Ostfeld, *Tsava Nolad: Shlavim Ikariyim Bi-bniyat Ha-tsva Be-hanhagato shel Ben Gurion* [An Army Is Born: Main Stages in the

Buildup of the Army Under the Leadership of Ben Gurion] (Tel Aviv: Ministry of Defense, 1993), vol. 1, pp. 5–14.

2. D. Ben Gurion, *Yoman* [Diary], unpublished, Ben Gurion Archive, Sdeh Boker, entry for May 4, 1947. Like other intelligence data these seem to have been far from accurate, and different figures—mostly lower ones—can be found at other places in the diary.

3. A. Ilan, *The Origins of the Arab-Israeli Arms Race* (New York: New York University Press, 1996), p. 67, table 2.

4. The 1948 figures were: *Yishuv*: 0.65 million; Egypt: 19 million; Iraq: 4.8 million; Syria: 2.9 million; Lebanon: 1.1 million; Jordan: 1 million; total Arab: 28.8 million. Figures from M. Brecher, *The Foreign Policy System of Israel* (New York: Yale University Press, 1972), p. 68.

5. Ilan, *The Origins of the Arab-Israeli Arms Race*, table 3.

6. Y. Beer, *Be-maagal Beayot Bitachon* [In the Circle of Security Problems] (Tel Aviv: Am Oved, 1957), pp. 166–167. Roughly similar figures are given by Ilan, *The Origins*, tables on p. 67.

7. Figure from M. Merdor, "Ha-rechesh Ba-shanim 1947–1948," in Ministry of Defense, ed., *Tsva Ha-medina Ba-derech* [Army on the Way to the State] (Tel Aviv: Ministry of Defense, 1988), p. 206.

8. Figures from ibid., tables 5 and 6, pp. 212–213.

9. Cf. tables 2 and 9 in ibid., pp. 209, 216; also Ilan, *The Origins*, p. 67.

10. The best account of the origins of the IAF is B. Cull and others, *Spitfires over Israel* (London: Grub Street, 1994), which also contains plenty of information on the Arab air forces of the time.

11. Cf. his own account in *On Eagle's Wings* (Tel Aviv: Steimatzky's, 1979), chap. 2.

12. Manpower data in D. Ben Gurion, *Yoman Ha-milchama, 1948–1949* [War Diary, 1948–1949] (Tel Aviv: Ministry of Defense, 1982), entry for February 8, 1948, p. 220.

13. An English version of the agreement may be found in N. Lorch, *The Edge of the Sword: Israel's War of Independence, 1947–1949* (Toronto: Longmans, 1961), p. 239.

14. More details on this episode in M. Begin, *The Revolt* (New York: Dell, 1977), chap. 9; Ben Gurion's account may be found in his *Be-hilachem Yisrael* [When Israel Went to War] (Tel Aviv: Am Oved, 1975 ed.), pp. 165–178. There is a book-length account in S. Nakdimon, *Altalena* (Jerusalem: Idanim, 1978).

15. Jenkins to Ambassador, British Embassy, December 30, 1947, Public Record Office (PRO), 371–68366-e458/11/65g.

16. Cf. Golda Meir, *My Life* (Jerusalem: Steimatzky, 1975), pp. 178–179.

17. Cf. S. Ali El-Edroos, *The Hassemite Arab Army, 1909–1979* (Amman: The Publishing Committee, 1980), pp. 244–245.

18. M. Dayan, *Avnei Derech* [Memoirs] (Tel Aviv: Dvir, 1976), pp. 58–61.

19. Ben Gurion, *Yoman Ha-milchama*, vol. 2, p. 431, entry for May 16, 1948.

20. Lecture by Ariel Sharon, on the site, May 5, 1993.

21. N. Ben Yehuda, *Ke-she-partsa Ha-medina* [When the State Broke Out] (Jerusalem: Keter, 1991), p. 32 ff., provides a firsthand account of these events.

22. The battles for Latrun are analyzed at great length in S. Shamir, *"Be-chol Mechir"— Li-yerushalayim; Ha-maaracha Be-latrun—Hachraa Be-derech 7* ["At Any Price"—to Jerusalem; Decision on Route Seven] (Tel Aviv: Maarachot, 1994).

23. D. Almog, *Ha-rechesh Be-artsot Ha-brit, 1945–1949* [Arms Acquisition in the U.S., 1945–1949] (Tel Aviv: Maarachot, 1987), p. 73.

24. Cf. Lorch, *The Edge of the Sword*, p. 250 ff.

25. Ben Gurion, *Yoman Ha-milchama*, entry for May 8, 1948, p. 401.

26. Ostfeld, *Tsava Nolad*, vol. 1, p. 561 ff.

27. For a list and explanation cf. E. N. Luttwak and D. Horowitz, *The Israeli Army* (London: Allen Lane, 1975), p. 45.

28. Cf. his own account in *Avnei Derech*, pp. 67–71.
29. This operation is analyzed in A. Yitschaki, *Latrun: Ha-maaracha al Ha-derech Li-yerushalayim* [Latrun: The Battle for the Road to Jerusalem] (Jerusalem: Kanah, 1982), pp. 417–430.
30. Ben Gurion, *Yoman Ha-milchama*, entry for July 17, 1948, p. 597, has Ben Gurion's message to Shealtiel.
31. There were five dead and sixteen wounded; IDF, Historical Department, *Toldot Milchemet Ha-komemiyut* [History of the War of Independence] (Tel Aviv: Ministry of Defense, 1959), p. 272.
32. Z. Gilad, ed., *Sefer Ha-PALMACH* [The Book of PALMACH] (Jerusalem: Jewish Agency, 1953), p. 460.
33. Y. Gelber, *Lama Perku et Ha-PALMACH* [Why Was PALMACH Dissolved?] (Jerusalem: Schocken, 1986), pp. 161–162.
34. Shamir, *"Be-chol Mechir,"* p. 80.
35. Y. Levi, *Tisha Kavin: Yerushalayim Bi-kravot Milchemet Ha-atsmaut* [Nine Measures: Jerusalem in the War of Independence] (Tel Aviv: Maarachot, 1986), pp. 292–293; also U. Narkis, *Chayal shel Yerushalayim* [A Soldier for Jerusalem] (Tel Aviv: Ministry of Defense, 1991), p. 99.
36. Quoted in Ts. Dror, *Matsbi Le-lo Srara: Sipur-Chayav shel Yitschak Sadeh* (Commander Without Power: The Life of Yitschak Sadeh] (Tel Aviv: Ha-kibbuts Ha-meuchad, 1996), p. 345.
37. On the background to this decision see U. Bar Joseph, *The Best of Enemies: Israel and Transjordan in the War of 1948* (London: Cass, 1987), p. 112 ff.
38. IDF, *Toldot Milchemet Ha-atsmaut*, pp. 298–299.
39. Cf. T. Ben Moshe, "Liddell Hart and the Israel Defence Forces," *Journal of Contemporary History* 16 (1981): 369–391; B. Bond, *Liddell Hart: A Study of His Military Thought* (London: Cassell, 1977), p. 252.
40. Dror, *Matsbi Le-lo Srara*, p. 373; Y. Tal, "Yitschak Sadeh, Kavim Li-demuto Ke-ish Shiryon" [Yitschak Sadeh: Portrait of an Armor Man], *Maarachot* 224 (July 1972): 17–20.
41. Cf. C. Barnet, *The Desert Generals* (London: Kimber, 1963), p. 177 ff.
42. Cf. Sadeh's own description in his *Ketsad Nilkeda Ha-metsuda* [How the Fort Was Captured], in Y. Sadeh, *Ktavim* [Writings] (Tel Aviv: Ha-kibbuts Ha-meuchad, 1980), vol. 3, pp. 114–129.
43. Ben Gurion, *Yoman Ha-milchama*, December 31, 1948, vol. 3, pp. 314–318.

CHAPTER 7

1. E. Oren, "Ha-hityashvut Be-milchemet Ha-atsmaut" [The Settling Movement in the War of Independence], in G. Rivlin, ed., *Ale-Zayit Ve-cherev: Mekorot U-mechkarim Be-ginze Ha-hagana* [Olive Leaves and Sword: Sources and Studies in the Hagana Archives] (Tel Aviv: Ministry of Defense, 1990), p. 151.
2. Office of the Chief of the General Staff Division, "Arab Artillery in the War of Independence," November 16, 1949, TSAHAL Archive, file 64/137/1953.
3. A. Ilan, *The Origins of the Arab-Israeli Arms Race* (New York: New York University Press, 1996), p. 67.
4. Office of the Chief of the General Staff Division, "Arab Artillery in the War of Independence," November 16, 1949, TSAHAL Archive, file 64/137/1953.
5. A. Shatkai, "Solele Ha-atsmaut Ba-avir" [Pioneers of Air Independence], *Chel-Ha-avir* no. 44 (1955).
6. Ariel Sharon, lecture, May 5, 1993.
7. D. Ben Gurion, *Yoman Ha-milchama, 1948–1949* [War Diary, 1948–1949] (Tel Aviv: Ministry of Defense, 1982), vol. 3, p. 755, entry for October 18, 1948.

8. Cf. O. Azoulay-Katz, *Ha-ish She-lo Yada Le-natseach: Shimon Peres Be-malkodet Sysipus* [The Man Who Did Not Know How to Win: Shimon Peres in the Sysipus Catch] (Tel Aviv: Yediot Acharonot, 1996).
9. A. Lieblich, *Kibbuts Makom: Report from an Israeli Kibbuts* (New York: Pantheon, 1981), pp. 34–39; also U. Ben Eliezer, *Derech Ha-kavenet: Hivatsruto shel Ha-militarizm Ha-yisraeli, 1936–1956* [Through the Gunsight: The Emergence of Israeli Militarism, 1936–1956] (Tel Aviv: Dvir, 1995), p. 73.
10. A. Koestler, *Thieves in the Night: Chronicle of an Experiment* (New York: MacMillan, 1946), pp. 152, 153.
11. Y. Tabenkin, "Bet Ha-sefer Ve-ha-milchama" [School and the War], *Devarim* 3 (1942): 105.
12. These and subsequent figures and calculations from E. Sivan, *Dor TASHACH: Mitos, Dyokan Ve-zikaron* [The Generation of 1948: Myth, a Portrait, and Memory] (Tel Aviv: Ministry of Defense, 1991), p. 21 ff.
13. Cf. M. van Creveld, *Fighting Power: German and U.S. Army Performance, 1939–1945* (Westport, Conn.: Greenwood Press, 1982), pp. 155–159.
14. A. Yitschaki, *Latrun: Ha-maaracha al Ha-derech Li-yerushalayim* [Latrun: The Battle for the Road to Jerusalem] (Jerusalem: Kanah, 1982), pp. 564–571.
15. M. Azaryahu, "War Memorials and the Commemoration of the Israeli War of Independence," *Studies in Zionism* 13:1 (Spring 1992): 64.

PART II

1. Cf. U. Bialer, *Between East and West: Israel's Foreign Policy Orientation, 1948–1956* (Cambridge: Cambridge University Press, 1990), particularly chap. 10.
2. During the period of the British mandate the Palestinian pound was worth a British pound sterling but carried different marks. When Israel became independent the British simply declared that a Palestinian pound could no longer be exchanged for a British one, with the result that the currency holdings were wiped out.
3. Cf. M. van Creveld, *Nuclear Weapons and the Future of Conflict* (New York: Free Press, 1993), chap. 2.

CHAPTER 8

1. For Jordan and Syria see A. Shlaim, *Collusion Across the Jordan: King Abdullah, the Zionist Movement, and the Partition of Palestine* (New York: Oxford University Press, 1988); and, in response, I. Rabinovitsh, *Ha-shalom She-chamak* [The Elusive Peace] (Jerusalem: Keter, 1991). For Egypt see M. B. Oren, *Origins of the Second Arab-Israel War* (London: Cass, 1992), chap. 5.
2. D. Ben Gurion, *Yichud Ve-yeud: Devarim al Bitchon Yisrael* [A Unique Destiny: Notes on Israeli Defense] (Tel Aviv: Maarachot, 1971), p. 145.
3. E.g., M. K. M. Begin, June 15, 1949, *Divrei Ha-knesset* [Parliamentary Record] (Jerusalem: Government Printer, 1950), vol. 1, p. 728; M. K. Ch. Landau, November 30, 1953, ibid., vol. 4, p. 279.
4. Allon to Ben Gurion, March 24, 1949, quoted in Z. Tsur, *Mi-pulmus Ha-chaluka ad Le-tochnit Allon* [From the Debate About Partition to the Allon Plan] (Efal: Yad Tabenkin, 1982), p. 73.
5. See Dayan quotations in Morris, *Milchamot Ha-gvul shel Yisrael* (Tel Aviv: Am Oved, 1996), pp. 27–28.
6. There are several such plans in TSAHAL Archive, file 13/636/1956.
7. See A. Levite, *Offense and Defense in Israeli Military Doctrine* (Boulder: Westview Press, 1989), chap. 2.

8. Cf. R. Garthoff, *Soviet Military Doctrine* (Glencoe, Ill.: Free Press, 1953), pp. 34–35. The factors were the stability of the home front, the morale of the army, its size, the quality of the weapons, and the organizing skills of the General Staff.

9. Y. Yadin, "Avot Ha-lekach" [The Fathers of All Lessons], *Maarachot* 16 (July 1950): i–ii. See also Yadin's recapitulation of his ideas in "Ba-yamim Ha-hem U-ba-zman Hazeh" [In Those Days and Now] *Maarachot* 33 (May 1959): 37–42.

10. The best short exposition of the early years of Israeli defense planning remains M. Handel, *Israel's Political-Military Doctrine* (Center for International Affairs, Harvard University, Occasional Papers in International Affairs, No. 30, 1973), chaps. 2 and 3.

11. E.g., Y. Tal, "Torat Ha-bitachon—Reka Ve-dinamika" [Defense Doctrine—Background and Dynamics] *Maarachot* 253 (December 1976): 2–9.

12. J. Luvaas, *Frederick the Great on the Art of War* (New York: Free Press, 1966), p. 21 ff.; cf. also Gerhard von Scharnhorst: "Prussia cannot wage a defensive war . . . her geographic position and lack of natural and artificial defensive means do not permit it." Quoted in P. Paret, *Clausewitz and the State* (Princeton: Princeton University Press, 1985), p. 111.

13. This entire question is discussed in E. Oren, "Ha-hityashvut Be-milchemet Ha-atsmaut" [The Settlement Movement in the War of Independence], in G. Rivlin, ed., *Ale-Zayit Ve-cherev: Mekorot U-mechkarim Be-ginze Ha-hagana* [Olive Leaves and Sword: Sources and Studies in the Hagana Archives] (Tel Aviv: Ministry of Defense, 1990), pp. 145–153.

14. Ben Gurion, Yoman (unpublished diary), Ben Gurion Archive, September 30, 1949.

15. *Chuke Medinat Yisrael* [Laws of the State of Israel] (Jerusalem: Government Printer, 1975–1976), vol. 30, pp. 150–151. An English translation of the most important parts of this law may be found in Y. Ben Meir, *Civil-Military Relations in Israel* (New York: Columbia University Press, 1996), p. 35.

16. Cf. the discussion in Ben Meir, *Civil-Military Relations in Israel*, chap. 3.

17. Eyewitness account in *Vaadat Ha-chakira—Milechement Yom Hakippurim* [Commission of Investigation—the Yom Kippur War, henceforward Agranat Report] (Jerusalem: Government Printing Office, 1975), pp. 27–28.

18. E. Haber, *Ha-yom Tifrots Milchama* [Today War Will Break Out] (Tel Aviv: Idanim, 1987), pp. 16, 28.

19. Ben Meir, *Civil-Military Relations in Israel*, p. 159.

20. Y. Greenberg, "Misrad Ha-bitachon Ve-ha-mateh Ha-klali: Ha-pulmus Bi-sheelat Taktsiv Ha-bitachon" [The Ministry of Defense and the General Staff: The Debate over the Defense Budget], *Medina, Memshal Ve-yachasim Ben-leumiyim* 38 (Spring–Summer 1993): 58, 68.

21. A. Braun, *Moshe Dayan Be-milchemt Yom Ha-kippurim* [Moshe Dayan in the Yom Kippur War] (Tel Aviv: Idanim, 1993), p. 348.

22. For this entire subject see R. Gabizon and Ch. Shneidor, eds., *Zechuyot Ha-adam Ve-ha-Ezrach Be-yisrael, Mikraah* [Human Rights and Civil Liberties in Israel—a Reader] (Jerusalem: Agudah Li-zechuyot Ha-ezrach, 1991), vol. 2, pp. 37–85.

23. A good explanation of the working of Vaadat Ha-orchim is provided by M. Hofnung, *Yisrael—Drishot Ha-bitachon mul Shilton Ha-chok* [Israel—the Demands of Security Versus the Rule of Law], Ph.D. thesis, the Hebrew University, Jerusalem, 1989, p. 128 ff.

24. M. Zak, *Hussein Osse Shalom* [Hussein Makes Peace] (Ramat Gan: Bar Illan University Press), pp. 127–128.

25. On this entire question see Ben Meir, *Civil-Military Relations in Israel*, p. 81 ff.

26. Levite, *Offense and Defense in Israeli Military Doctrine*, p. 51.

27. Cf. M. van Creveld, *Air Power and Maneuver Warfare* (Maxwell Air Force Base, Ala.: Air University Press, 1994), chap. 1.

28. Y. Steigman, *Me-atsmaut Le-kadesh, Chel Ha-avir Ba-shanim, 1949–1956* [The IAF from the War of Independence to Suez, 1949–1956] (Tel Aviv: Ministry of Defense, 1990), pp. 29, 96.

29. Cf. Ezer Weizman, *On Eagle's Wings* (Tel Aviv: Steimatzky's, 1979), p. 100; also M. Naor, *Laskov: Lochem, Adam, Chaver* [Laskov: The Soldier, the Man, the Friend] (Jerusalem: Keter, 1988), p. 230 ff.

30. The infighting that went on in this context is documented in Steigman, *Me-atsmaut Le-kadesh*, chap. 3.

31. Y. Ratner, *Chayai Ve-ani* [My Life and I] (Tel Aviv: Schocken, 1978), p. 382.

32. Ben Gurion in the Knesset, August 15, 1949, *Divre Ha-knesset* [Knesset Record], August 15, 1949.

33. There is a good English-language discussion of the law in E. N. Luttwak and D. Horowitz, *The Israeli Army* (London: Allen Lane, 1975), app. 2, pp. 424–426. See also M. van Creveld, "Conscription Warfare: The Israeli Experience," in R. G. Foerster, ed., *Die Wehrplicht: Entstehung, Erscheinungsformen und politisch-militaerische Wirkung* (Munich: Oldenburg, 1994), p. 227 ff.

34. On the most important tests see R. Gal, *A Portrait of the Israeli Soldier* (Westport, Conn.: Greenwood Press, 1986), p. 76 ff.

35. Figures on strength in T. Segev, *Ha-yisraelim Ha-rishonim* [The First Israelis] (Jerusalem: Domino, 1984), p. 251.

36. On the kind of cohesion that develops inside Israeli reserve units see M. Bar On, "Ruach Ha-lechima Be-maarechet Kadesh" [Fighting Power During the Suez Campaign], *Maarachot* 140 (1962): 8; and, at much greater length, E. Ben Ari, "Mastering Soldiers: Conflict, Emotions, and the Enemy in an Israeli Military Unit," unpublished study, the Harry S. Truam Institute, the Hebrew University, Jerusalem, 1996, particularly chaps. 4–8.

37. E. Shor, ed., *Derech Ha-mitla* [By Way of the Mitla] (Ramat Gan: Massada, 1967), p. 78.

38. In 1991, e.g., Israel had 0.18 motor vehicles and 0.45 telephones per member of the population; the corresponding Arab figures were 0.02 and 0.25 (Egypt), 0.066 and 0.21 (Jordan), and 0.019 and 0.22 (Syria). Figures calculated from *Britannica Book of the Year* (Chicago: Encylopaedia Britannica, 1993), pp. 633, 600, 640, 724.

39. On the U.S. system for selecting officer-candidates as it originally developed see S. E. Ambrose, *Duty, Honor, Country: A History of West Point* (Baltimore, Md.: Johns Hopkins University Press, 1966), p. 18 ff.

40. For a detailed discussion of the way these things were and, to a large extent, still are being done see Gal, *A Portrait of the Israeli Soldier*, p. 115 ff.

41. In 1955, e.g., 500 out of 4,300 had not even achieved a high school diploma; of university studies there could be scarcely any question. Moshe Dayan, *Avnei Derech* (Tel Aviv: Dvir, 1976), p. 147.

42. Cf. S. Teveth, *Moshe Dayan: The Soldier, the Man, the Legend* (London: Quartet, 1972), pp. 257–258, for the origins of this system.

43. For a professional breakdown of retired officers as of 1966 cf. A. Perlmutter, *Military and Politics in Israel* (London: Cass, 1969), p. 76, table 8.

44. Y. Allon, *The Making of Israel's Army* (London: Sphere Books, 1971), p. 256.

45. Cf. G. J. DeGroot, "Whose Finger on the Trigger? Mixed Anti-Aircraft Batteries and the Female Combat Taboo," in *War in History* 4:4 (November 1997): 434–453; and A. Noggle, *Dance with Death: Soviet Airwomen in World War II* (College Station: Texas University Press, 1994).

46. I. Jerby, *Ha-mechir Ha-kaful: Maamad Ha-isha Ba-chevra Ha-yisraelit Ve-sherut Ha-nashim Be-TSAHAL* [The Double Price: Women's Status and Military Service in Israel] (Tel Aviv: Ramot, 1996), p. 66.

47. Ratner, *Chayai Ve-ani*, p. 259.

48. The most detailed figures are in PALMACH Hq., memo of February 1, 1948, PALMACH Archive, file H.109, No. 5; also D. Ben Gurion to H. Tsadok, April 26, 1948, Galili Archive, box 2, file C.

49. Cf. Allon lecture on the subject, 1945, quoted in A. Kadish, *La-meshek Ve-la-neshek* [To Farms and Arms] (Tel Aviv: Tag, 1995), p. 121.

50. Cf. the description of one such operation in U. Narkis, *Chayal shel Yerushalayim* [A Soldier for Jerusalem] (Tel Aviv: Ministry of Defense, 1991), p. 57 ff.

51. N. Ben Yehuda, *Ke-she-partsa Ha-medina* [When the State Broke Out] (Jerusalem: Keter, 1991), p. 1; Kadish, *La-meshek Ve-la-neshek*, p. 234.

52. E.g., one company of Harel Brigade is known to have had three women among 140 men; U. Ben Ari, *Acharai* [Follow Me] (Tel Aviv: Maariv, 1994), p. 169 ff.

53. H. Avigdori-Avidav, *Ba-derech She-halachnu: Mi-yomana shel Melavat Shayarot* [The Road We Took: From the Diary of a Convoy-Escort] (Tel Aviv: Ministry of Defense, 1988); Narkis, *Chayal shel Yerushalayim*, p. 78.

54. Figure from L. Tiger and J. Shepher, *Women in the Kibbutz* (Harmondsworth, Middlesex: Penguin, 1975), p. 185. Here it should be added that in PALMACH as a whole women formed up to 20 percent of strength.

55. Kadish, *La-meshek Ve-la-neshek*, p. 238 ff.

56. The major categories were 3,200 secretaries and clerks, 1,360 cleaning ladies (the second largest category), 1,220 doctors and nurses, 730 communicators, 600 food-service workers, 600 telephone operators, and 480 commanders and instructors. Z. Ostfeld, *Tsava Nolad: Shlavim Ikariyim Bi-bniyat Ha-tsava Be-hanhagato shel Ben Gurion* [An Army Is Born: Main Stages in the Buildup of the Army Under the Leadership of Ben Gurion] (Tel Aviv: Ministry of Defense, 1993), vol. 2, p. 819.

57. Women's Corps memoranda, January 31, 1949, February 11, 1949, quoted in Ostfeld, *Tsava Nolad*, vol. 1, pp. 444–445.

58. Ben Gurion, *Yichud Ve-yeud*, p. 79.

59. Ostfeld, *Tsava Nolad*, vol. 1, p. 442 ff. On the British origins of CHEN see also A. R. Bloom, "Women in the Defense Forces," in B. Swirski and M. P. Safir, eds., *Calling the Equality Bluff: Women in Israel* (New York: Pergamon Press, 1991), p. 134.

60. Avigdori-Avidav, *Ba-derech She-halachnu*, p. 154 ff.

61. Cf. Kadish, *La-meshek Ve-la-neshek*, p. 285.

62. Term used by CHEN commander, Col. Stella Levy, quoted in J. Larteguy, *The Walls of Israel* (New York: Evans, 1969), p. 195.

63. Jerby, *Ha-mechir Ha-kaful*, p. 139.

64. Gal, *A Portrait of the Israeli Soldier*, p. 49.

65. Israel Women's Lobby, "Nahsim Ve-sherut Be-TSAHAL: Metsiut, Ratson Ve-chazon" [Women in the IDF: Reality, Will, and Vision] (Tel Aviv University: mimeographed, 1995), p. 41.

66. The attempt to train female divers was made in 1974. A. Peled, "Lochamot Ha-shayetet" [The Naval Commando's She-Fighters], *Yediot Acharonot* weekend magazine, April 26, 1994, pp. 6–13.

67. On the eve of Independence Day 1997, a third woman was promoted to brigadier general as a "special gesture." *Maariv*, May 8, 1997, p. 5.

68. Prime Minister's Office, *DOCH al Matsav Ha-isha* [Report on the Status of Women] (Jerusalem: Government Printer, 1978), pp. 8–10.

69. Cf. A. Shapira, "Labour Zionism and the October Revolution," *Journal of Contemporary History* 24 (1989): 623–656.

70. For example, see C. von Der Goltz, *The Nation in Arms* (London: Allen, 1887 [originally published 1883]), perhaps the most thorough discussion of the system ever.

71. Cf. M. van Creveld, *Fighting Power: German and U.S. Army Performance, 1939–1945* (Westport, Conn.: Greenwood Press, 1982), chap. 3.

72. Cf. A. Oz, "Derech Haruach" [By the Wind], in Oz, *Artsot Ha-tan* [The Lands of the Jackal] (Tel Aviv: Am Oved, 1965), pp. 41–59.

73. The unseemly proceedings are described in Segev, *Ha-yisraelim Ha-rishonim*, pp. 244–245.

74. Herzl Rosenblum in *Yediot Acharonot*, August 16, 1949, p. 2.
75. Cf. M. Azaryahu, *Pulchanei Medina: Chagigot Ha-atsmaut Ve-hantshachat Ha-noflim, 1948–1956* [State Cults: Independence Day Festivities and Commemorating the Dead, 1948–1956) (Sde Boker: Ben Gurion University, 1995), p. 115.
76. O. Almog, *Ha-tsabar—Djokan* [Portrait of the Sabra] (Tel Aviv: Am Oved, 1997), pp. 365–366.
77. A. Dankner, *Dan Ben Amots, Biographia* [Dan Ben Amots—a Biography] (Jerusalem: Keter, 1992), p. 165.
78. Ben Gurion, *Yichud Ve-yeud*, pp. 182–183.
79. D. Ben Gurion, "Le-baayot ha-bitachon" [Re. Defense Problems], lecture held on January 5, 1955, in Ben Gurion, *Yichud Ve-yeud*, p. 205 ff.; also Z. Tsachor, "Ben Gurion Kimeatsev Mitos" [Ben Gurion as Mythmaker], in D. Ochana and R. Wistrich, eds., *Mitos Ve-zikaron* [Myth and Memory] (Tel Aviv: Ha-kibbuts Ha-meuchad, 1996), p. 150; also S. I. Troen, "The Sinai Campaign as a 'War of No Alternative': Ben Gurion's View of the Israel-Egyptian Conflict," in S. I. Troen and M. Shemesh, eds., *The Suez-Sinai Crisis 1956, Retroperspective and Reappraisal* (London: Cass, 1990), pp. 180–195.

CHAPTER 9

1. By far the best account is B. Morris, *Milchamot Ha-gevul shel Yisrael, 1949–1956* [Israel's Border Wars, 1949–1956] (Tel Aviv: Ofakim, 1996), chap. 2.
2. Figures on the extent of infiltration in ibid., p. 154 ff.
3. Ibid., pp. 443, 445.
4. For some figures see ibid., chap. 4.
5. Ben Gurion, "Nochach Ha-metach Ba-gevulot" [Vis-à-vis the Tension Along the Borders], Knesset speech, January 2, 1956, in D. Ben Gurion, *Yichud Ve-yeud: Devarim al Bitchon Yisrael* [A Unique Destiny: Notes on Israeli Defense] (Tel Aviv: Maarachot, 1971), p. 235.
6. Ben Gurion, Yoman (unpublished diary), Ben Gurion Archive, September 21 and November 14, 1949.
7. Dayan talk to MAPAI leaders, June 18, 1950, MAPAI (Labor Party) Archive.
8. Dayan according to Moshe Sharet circular, October 26, 1954, quoted in M. Sharet, *Yoman Ishi* [A Personal Diary] (Tel Aviv: Maariv, 1978), No. 22, p. 595.
9. Morris, *Milchamot Ha-gvul shel Yisrael* (Tel Aviv: Am Oved, 1996), p. 208 ff.
10. M. Bar Kochva, *Merkevot Ha-plada* [Steel Chariots] (Tel Aviv: Maarachot, 1989), pp. 105–111.
11. Unsigned IDF memo, "Infiltration to Israel, 1952," undated but apparently written early in 1953, Foreign Ministry Papers, State Archive, Jerusalem, file 2428 A.
12. Record of Meeting in the Foreign Minister's Office, February 2, 1953, ibid., No. 4373/15.
13. M. Bar Zohar and Ch. Haber, *Sefer Ha-tsanchanim* [The Book of the Paratroopers] (Tel Aviv: Levin-Epstein, 1969), p. 60.
14. U. Beeri to Y. Ben Aharon, June 4, 1953, Ha-shomer Ha-tsair Archive, file K 90-4/5.
15. Listed in Chief of Staff's Office, "Report on Operational Activity Since 1953," July 1954, TSAHAL Archive, file 13/636/1956.
16. Quoted in S. Teveth, *Moshe Dayan: The Soldier, the Man, the Legend* (London: Quartet, 1972), p. 239.
17. For his early years cf. U. Benziman, *Sharon: Lo Otser Be-adom* [Sharon: Does Not Stop at the Red Light] (Tel Aviv: Adam, 1985), p. 13 ff.
18. Quoted in Teveth, *Moshe Dayan*, p. 244.
19. There is a Jordanian report on the incident in Jordanian Foreign Ministry to British Foreign Ministry, undated (late October 1953?), Public Record Office (PRO), FO/816/193.

20. M. Dayan, *Avnei Derech* [Memoirs] (Tel Aviv: Dvir, 1976), p. 115.
21. M. Sharet, "Yisrael Ve-arav—Milchama Ve-shalom" [Israel and the Arabs—War and Peace], *Ot* (September 1966), published version of an October 1957 lecture.
22. Eliav report, "Retaliation Along the Borders," Foreign Ministry Papers, State Archive, No. 2448/15.
23. Brigadier General Gibli (Intelligence) to M. Dayan, June 20, 1954, TSAHAL Archive, file 13/656/1956.
24. Cf. E. N. Luttwak and D. Horowitz, *The Israeli Army* (London: Allen Lane, 1975), pp. 113–116.
25. Chief of Staff's Office, "Report on Operational Activity Since 1953," July 1954, TSAHAL Archive, file 16/636/1956.
26. From Morris, *Milchamot Ha-gevul shel Ysrael*, p. 327 ff.
27. Ibid., p. 361.
28. A. Sharon, *Warrior* (New York: Simon and Schuster, 1989), p. 98.
29. Dayan, *Avnei Derech*, p. 147, note for July 3, 1955.
30. M. Har Tsion, *Pirke Yoman* [Chapters in a Diary] (Tel Aviv: Levin-Epstein, n.d.), pp. 162, 164.
31. A. Sharon, *Warrior*, pp. 133–134.
32. J. E. Talbott, "The Myth and Reality of the Paratrooper in the Algerian War," *Armed Forces and Society* 3:1 (Fall 1976): 69–86.
33. S. Peres, "Ha-kumta Ha-aduma" [The Red Beret], in S. Peres, *Ha-shalav Ha-ba* [The Next Stage] (Tel Aviv: Am Ha-sefer, 1965), p. 126.
34. The attempts to negotiate with Egypt are described at length in M. Bar On, *Be-shaare Aza: Mediniyut Ha-chuts Ve-habitachon shel Medinat Yisrael, 1955–1957* [At the Gates of Gaza: Israel's Defense and Foreign Policy, 1955–1957] (Tel Aviv: Am Oved, 1992), chaps. 7 and 8.
35. The most recent full-size account is S. Teveth, *KALABAN* [Shearing Time: KALABAN] (Israel: Ish-Dor, 1992).
36. Cf. Morris, *Milchamot Ha-gevul shel Yisrael*, p. 354 ff., for the details.
37. Ibid., p. 359 ff.
38. Cf. the discussion in Benziman, *Sharon*, pp. 57 ff., 66 ff.
39. Dayan, *Avnei Derech*, p. 148.
40. All figures from Bar On, *Be-shaare Aza*, pp. 30–31.
41. For evidence that Nasser was planning an attack on Israel see M. Oren, *The Origins of the Second Arab-Israeli War* (London: Cass, 1992), p. 137.
42. Including Ben Gurion's own talk, delivered to senior commanders on January 16, 1955, "Ha-yesh Makom Le-milchemet Mena Neged Mitsrayim?" [Should We Launch a Pre-emptive Attack on Egypt?] in Ben Gurion, *Yichud Ve-yeud*, pp. 218–225.
43. This is the thesis advanced by Morris, *Milchamot Ha-gevul shel Yisrael*, chap. 12.
44. The arguments in favor of *Hagana Merchavit* are summed up in Y. Ber, *Be-maagali Bitachon Yisrael* [Problems of Israeli Security] (Tel Aviv: Am Oved, 1957).
45. Bar On, *Be-shaare Aza*, p. 90 ff.
46. U. Ben Eliezer, *Derech Ha-kavenet: Hivatsruto shel Ha-militarizm Ha-yisraeli, 1936–1956* [Through the Gunsight: The Emergence of Israeli Militarism, 1936–1956] (Tel Aviv: Dvir, 1995), pp. 301–302.
47. Ibid., p. 171.
48. A. Eban to Foreign Ministry, March 29, 1956, Foreign Ministry Papers, State Archive, 5/2455.
49. Additional figures on weapons bought, and the sums paid for them, in Dayan, *Avnei Derech*, pp. 183–184.
50. Figures on the strength of the IAF in Moshe Dayan, *Diary of the Sinai Campaign* (London: Weidenfeld and Nicolson, 1957), p. 209.
51. Ezer Weizman, *On Eagle's Wings* (Tel Aviv: Steimatzky's, 1979), p. 135.

52. The most detailed account is M. Bar Zohar, *Suez: Ultra Secret* (Paris: Fayard, 1964); the most recent one, M. Bar On, "David Ben Gurion and the Sevres Collusion," in W. M. Roger Louis and R. Owen, eds., *Suez 1956* (Oxford: Clarendon Press, 1989), pp. 145–160.

53. Y. Serena, "Neshek Tmurat Chisulim" [Arms for Liquidations], *Yediot Acharonot* weekend magazine, October 25, 1996, pp. 13–14, 62.

54. D. Eisenhower to G. Mollet, July 31, 1956, Foreign Relations of the United States (FRUS), 1955–1957, Washington, D.C., Government Printing Office, 1990, vol. xvi, pp. 77–78, No. 39; D. Eisenhower to A. Eden, September 6, 1956, printed in A. Eden, *Full Circle: The Memoirs of Anthony Eden* (London: Cassell, 1960), pp. 466–467.

55. Bar On, *Be-shaare Aza*, p. 220, based on the diary of the chief of staff's office for which he himself was responsible.

56. Ibid., pp. 268–269.

57. Dayan, *Diary of the Sinai Campaign*, p. 43.

58. Cf. the details in Y. Steigman, *Me-atsmaut Le-kadesh, Chel Ha-avir Ba-shanim, 1949–1956* [The IAF from the War of Independence to Suez, 1949–1956] (Tel Aviv: Ministry of Defense, 1990), pp. 155, 173–175.

59. Bar On, *Be-shaare Aza*, pp. 295–296.

60. Steigman, *Me-atsmaut Le-kadesh*, p. 184.

61. See Sharon's description of the action in *Warrior*, pp. 136–140.

62. Dayan, *Avnei Derech*, pp. 250–251.

63. Dayan, *Diary of the Sinai Campaign*, p. 70.

64. K. Love, *Suez: The Twice Fought War* (New York: McGraw-Hill, 1969), p. 492.

65. M. Gur, "Nisayon Sinai" [The Experience of Sinai], *Maarachot* (October 1966): 17–22. Laskov, reporting to Ben Gurion shortly after the operation, felt as Gur did; M. Naor, *Laskov: Lochem, Adam, Chaver* [Laskov: The Soldier, the Man, the Friend] (Jerusalem: Keter, 1988), p. 263.

66. M. Heichal, *Cutting the Lion's Tail: Suez Through Egyptian Eyes* (New York: Arbor House, 1987), pp. 177–178.

67. G. W. Gawrych, *Key to the Sinai: The Battles for Abu Ageila in the 1956 and 1967 Arab-Israeli Wars* (Fort Leavenworth, Kan.: U.S. Army Command and General Staff College, 1990), p. 34.

68. Cf. ibid., p. 25, for the balance of forces as well as the most detailed account of these battles.

69. According to the diary of Egypt's minister of municipal affairs, Abd al Latif al Bagdadi, quoted in S. I. Troen and M. Shemesh, eds., *The Suez-Sinai Crisis 1956, Retroperspective and Reapparaisal* (London: Cass, 1990), p. 339.

70. Dayan, *Diary of the Sinai Campaign*, p. 116.

71. Bar Zohar, *Suez*, p. 196.

72. Cf. the detailed description of the battle in Dayan, *Diary of the Suez Campaign*, p. 128 ff.

73. Cf. Sharon, *Warrior*, p. 146 ff.; B. Amidror, "Ha-mitla: Malkodet Ha-esh" [The Mitla: The Fire Trap], *Ha-olam Ha-zeh*, October 9, 1974, pp. 16–17, 26.

74. Bar Zohar, *Suez*, pp. 193–195.

75. T. N. Dupuy, *Elusive Victory: The Arab-Israeli Wars, 1947–1974* (New York: Harper and Row, 1978), p. 181.

76. Teveth, *Moshe Dayan*, p. 323.

77. R. Eytan, *Sippur shel Chayal* [A Soldier's Story] (Tel Aviv: Maariv, 1991), p. 66; Bar Zohar, *Suez*, p. 188 ff. Bar Zohar, incidentally, mistook the French F–84s for F–86s.

78. Steigman, *Me-atsmaut Le-kadesh*, p. 290.

79. Cf. M. van Creveld, *Command in War* (Cambridge, Mass.: Harvard University Press, 1985), pp. 196–198.

80. Dayan, *Diary of the Sinai Campaign*, pp. 39–40.

81. Luttwak and Horowitz, *The Israeli Army*, pp. 161–163.
82. The episode is described in Steigman, *Me-atsmaut Le-kadesh*, pp. 281–282.
83. Eytan, *Sippur shel Chayal*, p. 70.
84. Benziman, *Sharon: Lo Otser Be-adom*, pp. 78–79.
85. Teveth, *Moshe Dayan*, p. 315.
86. Peres, "Ha-kumta Ha-aduma," p. 125.
87. *Ba-machane*, October 29, 1957, p. 11.
88. *Ha-arets*, November 7, 1956; S. Peres, "The Road to Sevres: Franco-Israeli Strategic Cooperation," in Troen and Shemesh, eds., *The Suez-Sinai Crisis*, p. 145.

CHAPTER 10

1. Cf. E. Orren, "The Changes in Israel's Concept of Security After Kadesh," in S. I. Troen and M. Shemesh, eds., *The Suez-Sinai Crisis 1956, Retroperspective and Reappraisal* (London: Cass, 1990), pp. 218–229.
2. For data on the proportionally very high number of *kibbuts* members among IDF officers, and their quality, see Y. Amir, "Bnei Kibbutsim Be-TSAHAL," *Megamot* 15:2–3 (August 1967): 250–258.
3. A. Oz, *Menucha Nechona* [Perfect Peace] (Tel Aviv: Am Oved, 1981), p. 167.
4. Ezer Weizman, *On Eagle's Wings* (Tel Aviv: Steimatzky's, 1979), p. 169.
5. Y. Tsiddon-Chatto, *Ba-yom, B-layil, Ba-arafel* [By Day, by Night, in Fog] (Or Yehuda: Maariv, 1995), pp. 177–178.
6. A. Perlmutter, *Military and Politics in Israel* (London: Cass, 1969), p. 66.
7. E. Gross, "The IDF Education Corps," in D. Ashkenazy, ed., *The Military in the Service of Society and Democracy* (Westport, Conn.: Greenwood Press, 1994), p. 57.
8. Cf. N. Eytan, "The *Hasbara* Branch of the IDF Education Corps," and D. Novack, "The Cultural Branch of the IDF Education Corps," in ibid., pp. 65–80.
9. For details on the program see R. Gal, *A Portrait of the Israeli Soldier* (Westport, Conn.: Greenwood Press, 1986), p. 54; also M. Bar On, "The Process of Integrating Ethnic Groups in TSAHAL," offprint, n.p., n.d., the Hebrew University Library, Jerusalem.
10. For a brief English-language account of its activities see J. Larteguy, *The Walls of Israel* (New York: Evans, 1969), pp. 196–201; also V. Azarya, "Israeli Armed Forces," in M. Janowitz and S. U. Westbroad, eds., *Civic Education in the Military* (London: Sage, 1989), pp. 115–116.
11. Cf. Z. Drori, "Utopia in Uniform," in I. Troen and N. Lucas, eds., *Israel: The First Decade of Independence* (New York: State University of New York, 1995), p. 600 ff.
12. A typical example is M. Lissak, *Military Roles in Modernization: Civil-Military Relations in Thailand and Burma* (Beverly Hills, Calif.: Sage, 1976).
13. Cf. L. Laufer, *Israel and the Developing Countries: New Approaches in Cooperation* (New York: Twentieth Century Fund, 1967), pp. 30–31, 167–172; M. Kreinin, *Israel and Africa—A Study in Technical Cooperation* (New York: Praeger, 1964).
14. All figures from N. Safran, *From War to War: The Arab-Israeli Confrontation, 1948–1967* (New York: Pegasus, 1969), p. 156 ff.
15. M. Bar Kochva, *Merkevot Ha-plada* [Steel Chariots] (Tel Aviv: Maarachot, 1989), p. 31.
16. A. Brezner, *Nistane Ha-shiryon* [The Origins of the Israeli Armored Corps] (Tel Aviv: Ministry of Defense, 1995), p. 8.
17. A. Sharon, *Warrior* (New York: Simon and Schuster, 1989), pp. 136–138.
18. Moshe Dayan, *Diary of the Sinai Campaign* (London: Weidenfeld and Nicolson, 1957), p. 61.
19. M. Naor, *Laskov: Lochem, Adam, Chaver* [Laskov: The Soldier, the Man, the Friend] (Jerusalem: Keter, 1988), pp. 248–249.

20. M. Bar On, *Be-shaare Aza: Mediniyut Ha-chuts Ve-habitachon shel Medinat Yisrael, 1955–1957* [At the Gates of Gaza: Israel's Defense and Foreign Policy, 1955–1957] (Tel Aviv: Am Oved, 1992), p. 222.

21. Naor, *Laskov*, p. 264, quoting interview with Brig. Gen. Meir Zorea, who in 1956 was Laskov's second in command.

22. M. Dayan, *Avnei Derech* [Memoirs] (Tel Aviv: Dvir, 1976), p. 149. The figures were: armored corps: 324 percent increase; air force: 123 percent; navy: 224 percent (mostly spent purchasing two World War II destroyers); ground forces as a whole: 39 percent.

23. A. Kahalani, *A Warrior's Way* (New York: Shaplovsky, 1994), p. 71.

24. Z. Levkovits, "Ha-vikuach al Ha-ugda Ha-meshuryenet, 1953–1960" [The Debate About the Armored Division, 1953–1960], *Maarachot* 329 (June–July 1992): 30–39.

25. Cf. E. N. Luttwak and D. Horowitz, *The Israeli Army* (London: Allen Lane, 1975), p. 186 ff.

26. Cf. R. L. Dinardo, "German Armor Doctrine: Correcting the Myths," *War in History* 3:4 (November 1966): 384–397.

27. Bar Kochva, *Merkevot-Ha-plada*, p. 36.

28. For Tal's training methods see S. Teveth, *The Tanks of Tammuz* (London: Sphere Books, 1970), p. 66 ff.

29. Weizman, *On Eagle's Wings*, p. 101.

30. For details see Tsiddon, *Ba-yom, Ba-layil, Ba-arafel*, pp. 322–324. Tsiddon, incidentally, claims to have developed the weapon himself.

31. For the mechanics see Luttwak and Horowitz, *The Israeli Army*, pp. 196–197.

32. Cf. R. S. and W. S. Churchill, *The Six Day War* (London: Heinemann, 1967), p. 66, for a graphic description of the IAF's methods.

33. E. Haber, *Ha-yom Tifrots Milchama* [Today War Will Break Out] (Tel Aviv: Idanim, 1987), p. 125.

34. S. Peres, *Lech im Anashim* [Go with People] (Jerusalem: Idanim, 1978), p. 47.

35. This and the following episode are described in Naor, *Laskov*, p. 283 ff.

36. S. Rolbant, *The Israeli Soldier: Profile of an Army* (New York: Barnes, 1970); Z. Schiff, *A History of the Israeli Army* (San Francisco: Straight Arrow Books, 1974); J. Larteguy, *The Walls of Israel*, p. 161.

37. For the failure of the Egyptian efforts see Saad el Shazly, *The Crossing of the Suez* (San Francisco: American Mideast Research, 1980), pp. 79–80.

38. Y. Melman and D. Raviv, *Meraglim lo Mushlamim* [Imperfect Spies] (Tel Aviv: Maariv, 1990), pp. 117–120.

39. Haber, *Ha-yom Tifrots Milchama*, p. 61.

40. Peres interview with *Der Spiegel*, February 24, 1965.

41. For an account of his reasoning see S. Aronson, *The Politics and Strategy of Nuclear Weapons in the Middle East* (New York: State University of New York, 1992), p. 48 ff.

42. Cf. S. Hersh, *The Samson Option: Israel's Nuclear Arsenal and American Foreign Policy* (New York: Random House, 1991), chap. 2.

43. Peres on Israel TV, October 30, 1996.

44. Cf. Y. Allon, *Masach shel Chol* [A Curtain of Sand] (Tel Aviv: Ha-kibbuts Ha-meuchad, 1959). This is the most sustained argument in favor of a conventional strategy ever written by an Israeli.

45. Hersh, *The Samson Option*, p. 71 ff.

46. P. Pean, *Les deux bombes* (Paris: Fayard, 1982), pp. 113–121.

47. For discussions of Eshkol's performance as minister of defense see Haber, *Ha-yom Tifrots Milchama*, pp. 42, 48, 133; Y. Rabin, *Pinkas Sherut* [A Service Record] (Tel Aviv: Maariv), vol. 1, pp. 112–114, 121; Perlmutter, *Military and Politics in Israel*, pp. 106–107.

48. S. Peres, *Battling for Peace* (London: Weidenfeld and Nicolson, 1995), p. 166.

49. Haber, *Ha-yom Tifrots Milchama*, p. 42; M. Brecher, *The Foreign Policy System of Israel* (London: Oxford University Press, 1972), pp. 215, 220.

50. Cf. Y. Chasdai, *Emet Be-tsel Ha-milchama* [Truth in the Shadow of War] (Tel Aviv: Zmora Bitan, 1978), p. 19.

51. D. Ben Gurion, *Yoman Ha-milchama, 1948–1949* [War Diary, 1948–1949] (Tel Aviv: Ministry of Defense, 1982), vol. 1, p. 270, entry for March 29, 1948.

52. Bar Kochva, *Merkevot Ha-plada*, p. 515.

53. U. Narkis, *Chayal shel Yerushalayim* [A Soldier for Jerusalem] (Tel Aviv: Ministry of Defense, 1991), p. 297.

54. Chasdai, *Emet Be-tsel Ha-milchama*, p. 21.

55. Larteguy, *The Walls of Israel*, p. 145.

56. D. Ben Gurion, *Yichud Ve-yeud: Devarim al Bitchon Yisrael* [A Unique Destiny: Notes on Israeli Defense] (Tel Aviv: Maarachot, 1971), p. 176.

57. Cf. D. Horowitz, "Flexible Responsiveness and Military Strategy: The Case of the Israeli Army," *Policy Science* 1 (1970): 191–205; also M. van Creveld, *Command in War* (Cambridge, Mass.: Harvard University Press, 1985), pp. 198–199.

58. Y. Rabin, "Acharei Ha-timron Ha-gadol" [After the Great Maneuvers], *Maarachot* special issue (August 1960): 6–9.

59. Cf. W. Laqueur, *The Road to War 1967: The Origins of the Arab-Israel Conflict* (London: Weidenfeld and Nicolson, 1969 ed.), chap. 2.

60. The Samua raid is analyzed in great detail in A. Ayalon, "Mivtsa Magressa" [Operation Shredder], *Maarachot* 261/262 (March–April 1978): 27–38.

61. Rabin, *Pinkas Sherut*, vol. 1, p. 121.

62. A blow-by-blow description of this and the following incidents may be found in O. Bull, *War and Peace in the Middle East: The Experience and Views of a U.N. Observer* (London: Cooper, 1973), p. 75 ff.

63. The incidents are described in Rabin, *Pinkas Sherut*, vol. 1, pp. 121–123; cf. also S. Teveth, *The Tanks of Tammuz* (London: Sphere Books, 1970), p. 56 ff., and N. Bar Tov, *Dado: Arbaim U-smoneh Shanim Ve-esrim Yom* [Dado: Forty-Eight Years and Twenty Days] (Tel Aviv: Maariv, 1978), vol. 1, pp. 106–107.

64. Rabin, *Pinkas Sherut*, vol. 1, p. 125. Here the chief of staff mistakenly says that the Syrians had given up *two* years before the 1967 war rather than one.

65. Bull, *War and Peace in the Middle East*, p. 101. In the last interview he ever gave, Dayan even claimed that 80 percent of the incidents had been deliberately provoked by Israel; *Yediot Acharonot*, April 27, 1997, p. 3.

66. Bull, *War and Peace in the Middle East*, pp. 109–110.

67. Weizman, *On Eagle's Wings*, p. 197; also Peres, *Battling for Peace*, p. 101.

68. Rabin, *Pinkas Sherut*, vol. 1, p. 125.

69. *Yediot Acharonot*, April 8, 1967, p. 5.

70. For the role played by the Soviets see Laqueur, *The Road to War*, pp. 40–41.

71. British Foreign Office memo, March 16, 1966, Public Record Office, Kew, FO/371/18684.

72. For the details see Hersh, *The Samson Option*, chaps. 8 and 9; also McG. Bundy, *Danger and Survival: The Political History of the Nuclear Weapon* (New York: Random House, 1988), p. 510.

73. The most detailed account of these events is O. Brosh, "Tfissot shel Ha-meimad Ha-garini Be-sichsuchim Ezoriyim Rav-Tsdadiyim Ve-emdot Be-inyanan" [Perceptions and Public Attitudes Toward the Nuclear Dimension in Multinational Regional Conflicts] (Ph.D. thesis, Hebrew University, Jersualem, 1990), vol. 1, pp. 63–66.

74. For these events, as well as the relevant sources, see M. van Creveld, *Nuclear Proliferation and the Future of Conflict* (New York: Free Press, 1993), pp. 107–108.

75. *Al-Difa* [Amman, Arabic], May 12, 1966; *New York Times*, January 4, 1966. The story was later confirmed by Ismail Fahmi in *Al Shab* [Cairo, Arabic], February 17, 1971, and in *Al Aharam* [Cairo, Arabic], February 26, 1971.

76. Telegram, U.S. Ambassador, Cairo, to State Department, April 11, 1964, No. A 737, LBJ Library, NSF Country File UAR, Box 158, item 39; quoted in Aronson, *The Politics and Strategy of Nuclear Weapons*, pp. 198–199.

77. E.g., *Al Achbar* [Cairo], February 5, 1965; *Al-Thwara Arabia* [Baghdad], February 7, 1966; Radio Baghdad, May 6 and 10, 1966; and *Al-Manar* [Amman], February 14, 1967.

78. *Al Nahar* [Beirut], May 21, 1963, quoted in *Maarachot* 155 (November 1963): 10; *Al Aharam* [Cairo], August 20, 1965 and January 8, 1966.

79. Cf. Abdel Ghani el Gamasy, *The October War* (Cairo: American University Press, 1993), p. 23; also A. E. Levite and E. B. Landau, *Be-einei Ha-aravim: Dimuya Ha-garini shel Yisrael* [In Arab Eyes: Israel's Nuclear Image] (Tel Aviv: Papyrus, 1994), p. 42, and the sources therein quoted.

80. Ibid., p. 41.

81. *Ha-arets*, August 8, 1996, p. 1. This is based on a statement by a TAAS man, M. Merdor.

82. Peres, *Battling for Peace*, p. 167.

83. Ibid., p. 101.

84. The various statements are summarized in M. Gilboa, *Shesh Shanim Ve-shisha Yamim: Mekoroteah Ve-koroteah shel Michlemet Sheshet Ha-yamim* [Six Years and Six Days: The Origins and Course of the Six Day War] (Tel Aviv: Am Oved, 1969), pp. 98 and 101.

85. Haber, *Ha-yom Tifrots Milchama*, p. 54.

86. Cf. Dayan, *Avnei Derech*, p. 396.

87. M. Zak, *Hussein Osse Shalom* [Hussein Makes Peace] (Ramat Gan: Bar Illan University Press), p. 35 ff.

88. Rabin, *Pinkas Sherut*, vol. 1, p. 136; Weizman, *On Eagle's Wings*, pp. 199–200.

89. Weizman, *On Eagle's Wings*, pp. 202–203.

90. L. Rabin, *Kol Ha-zman Ishto* [Always His Wife] (Tel Aviv: Idanim, 1988), p. 112.

91. Figures on the IDF's strength in this period range from 180,000 (Haber, *Ha-yom Tifrots Milchama*, p. 202) to 300,000 (S. Ali El-Edroos, *The Hassemite Arab Army, 1909–1979* [Amman: The Publishing Committee, 1980], p. 350). The last-named figure is probably inflated to show how heroic Jordan's army was; the former was understated in order to disguise Israel's true strength.

92. Y. Tal, *Bitachon Leumi—Meatim Mul Rabim* [National Defense—the Few Against the Many] (Tel Aviv: Dvir, 1996), p. 142. Some confirmation that this was indeed the true figure may be found in A. Braun, *Moshe Dayan Be-milchemt Yom Ha-kippurim* [Moshe Dayan in the Yom Kippur War] (Tel Aviv: Idanim, 1993), pp. 131, 137. According to him, Dayan on October 9, 1973, said that the IDF, having lost about 500 tanks (100 in the north, 400 in the south), was back to the number it had had in 1967.

93. E.g., R. S. and W. Churchill, *The Six Day War*, p. 27; Luttwak and Horowitz, *The Israeli Army*, p. 215; Laqueur, *The Road to War*, p. 68.

94. Rabin, *Pinkas Sherut*, vol. 1, p. 150.

95. For this episode see Gilboa, *Shesh Shanim Ve-shisha Yamim*, p. 168.

96. Haber, *Ha-yom Tifrots Milchama*, p. 203.

97. Ibid., p. 162.

CHAPTER 11

1. Y. Rabin, *Pinkas Sherut* [A Service Record] (Tel Aviv: Maariv), vol. 1, p. 142; also Abdel Ghani el Gamasy, *The October War* (Cairo: American University Press, 1993), p. 38.

2. Dr. S. Mutawi, Jordanian representative to a Washington, D.C., conference, June 1992, quoted in interview with Maj. Gen. (ret.) M. Amit, *Maarachot* 325 (June–July 1992): 15.

3. M. Zak, *Hussein Osse Shalom* [Hussein Makes Peace] (Ramat Gan: Bar Illan University Press), p. 106.

4. S. Ali El-Edroos, *The Hassemite Arab Army, 1909–1979* (Amman: The Publishing Committee, 1980), p. 362.

5. According to M. Dayan, *Avnei Derech* [Memoirs] (Tel Aviv: Dvir, 1976), p. 473, they did have a plan for invading the upper Jordan Valley but cancelled it during the night of June 5–6 when the extent of the Egyptian defeat became clear.

6. Damascus Radio, July 7, 1966; and the Syrian newspaper *Al-Mussawar*, December 16, 1966. On Syrian support for PLO terrorism inside Israel see also W. Laqueur, *The Road to War 1967: The Origins of the Arab-Israel Conflict* (London: Weidenfeld and Nicolson, 1969 ed.), p. 55 ff.

7. International Institute for Strategic Studies, *The Military Balance, 1967–1968* (London: IISS, 1968), pp. 40–41.

8. Military Attaché, Damascus, "Annual Report on Syrian Armed Forces," January 21, 1966, FO/371/186923.

9. Perhaps the best analysis of the Israeli deployment is T. N. Dupuy, *Elusive Victory: The Arab-Israeli Wars, 1947–1974* (New York: Harper and Row, 1978), p. 338.

10. Dayan, *Avnei Derech*, p. 430. The actual quote is from N. Bar Tov, *Dado: Arbaim U-smoneh Shanim Ve-esrim Yom* [Dado: Forty-Eight Years and Twenty Days] (Tel Aviv: Maariv, 1978), vol. 1, p. 125.

11. Rabin, *Pinkas Sherut*, vol. 1, pp. 156, 161, 169; Laqueur, *The Road to War*, p. 147.

12. E. Haber, *Ha-yom Tifrots Milchama* [Today War Will Break Out] (Tel Aviv: Idanim, 1987), p. 203.

13. Rabin, *Pinkas Sherut*, vol. 1, pp. 142–143.

14. M. Gilboa, *Shesh Shanim Ve-shisha Yamim: Mekoroteah Ve-koroteah shel Michlemet Sheshet Ha-yamim* [Six Years and Six Days: The Origins and Course of the Six Day War] (Tel Aviv: Am Oved, 1969), p. 75.

15. For these efforts cf. Zak, *Hussein Osse Shalom*, p. 112 ff.

16. For the details cf. Laqueur, *The Road to War*, chap. 5.

17. Dayan, *Avnei Derech*, pp. 426–430, and Haber, *Ha-yom Tifrots Milchama*, p. 216, describe the meeting that led to the decision.

18. Haber, *Ha-yom Tifrots Milchama*, p. 207.

19. Apparently the departing Israeli squadrons were detected by one radar, stationed in Jordan, but defective communications prevented it from sounding the alarm; Gamasy, *The October War*, p. 58.

20. A list of Egyptian losses was given by Brigadier General Hod on Israel Radio, June 6, 1967.

21. Ezer Weizman, *On Eagle's Wings* (Tel Aviv: Steimatzky's, 1979), p. 216.

22. Cf. his own account in R. Eytan, *Sippur shel Chayal* [A Soldier's Story] (Tel Aviv: Maariv, 1991), p. 92 ff.

23. The best analysis of the Egyptian dispositions is G. W. Gawrych, *Key to the Sinai: The Battles for Abu Ageila in the 1956 and 1967 Arab-Israeli Wars* (Fort Leavenworth, Kan.: U.S. Army Command and General Staff College, 1990), pp. 82–86.

24. See Sharon's own account in A. Sharon, *Warrior* (New York: Simon and Schuster, 1989), p. 188 ff.

25. Gawrych, *Key to the Sinai*, p. 116.

26. Y. Dayan, *Israel Journal: June 1967* (New York: McGraw Hill, 1967), pp. 65–70.

27. See the account in M. van Creveld, *Command in War* (Cambridge, Mass.: Harvard University Press, 1985), p. 201, which is based on an interview with General Gavish.

28. The battle is described in M. Naor and Z. Enar, eds., *Yemei Yuni: Teurim min Ha-milchama, 1967* [June Days: Episodes from the 1967 War] (Tel Aviv: Maarachot, 1967), p. 132 ff.

29. S. Ali El-Edroos, *The Hassemite Arab Army, 1909–1979* (Amman: The Publishing Committee, 1980), p. 374. For Hussein's reasons for entering the war see also Zak, *Hussein Osse Shalom*, p. 111; Hussein of Jordan, *My "War" with Israel* (London: Owen, 1969), pp. 125–126; and J. Lunt, *Hussein of Jordan* (London: MacMillan, 1989), p. 143.

30. For a blow-by-blow account of these battles see U. Narkis, *Achat Yerusahalayim* [Jerusalem Is One] (Tel Aviv: Am Oved, 1975); also M. Gur, *Har Ha-bayit Be-yadenu* [Mount Temple Is in Our Hands] (Tel Aviv: Maarachot, 1974).

31. Rooshdi, *The Hassemite Arab Army*, p. 366.

32. E. N. Luttwak and D. Horowitz, *The Israeli Army* (London: Allen Lane, 1975), p. 267; Bar Tov, *Dado*, vol. 1, p. 128; M. Bar Kochva, *Merkevot Ha-plada* [Steel Chariots] (Tel Aviv: Maarachot, 1989), p. 170.

33. Rooshdi, *The Hassemite Arab Army*, p. 386.

34. For this episode see U. Narkis, *Chayal shel Yerushalayim* [A Soldier for Jerusalem] (Tel Aviv: Ministry of Defense, 1991), pp. 330–331.

35. Rabin, *Pinkas Sherut*, vol. 1, p. 203.

36. Bar Tov, *Dado*, vol. 1, p. 131.

37. Ibid., vol. 1, pp. 131–136.

38. Dayan, *Avnei Derech*, p. 474; see also the recent account by S. Nakdimon in *Yediot Acharonot*, May 30, 1997, pp. 16–27.

39. Bar Kochva, *Merkevot Ha-plada*, p. 221.

40. Quoted in Bar Tov, *Dado*, vol. 1, p. 145.

41. Cf. M. Eldar, *Shayetet 11* [Flotilla 11] (Tel Aviv: Zmora Bitan, 1996), p. 40.

42. Dupuy, *Elusive Victory*, p. 331.

43. B. H. Liddell Hart, "The Strategy of a War," *Encounter* (February 1968): 18.

44. Figure from Dupuy, *Elusive Victory*, p. 40.

45. Haber, *Ha-yom Tifrots Milchama*, p. 208.

46. E. Shor, ed., *Derech Ha-mitla* [By Way of the Mitla] (Ramat Gan: Massada, 1967), p. 127, recounts the experiences of Yoffe's brigade; Bar Kochva, *Merkevot Ha-plada*, p. 219, recounts the experiences of his armored brigade against the Syrians.

47. Bar Kochva, *Merkevot Ha-plada*, p. 225.

48. Cf. the analysis of "war for existence" in M. van Creveld, *The Transformation of War* (New York: Free Press, 1991), pp. 142–149.

49. S. Peres, *Battling for Peace* (London: Weidenfeld and Nicolson, 1995), p. 167.

50. For an analysis of American press attitudes in particular see M. W. Suleiman, "American Mass Media and the June Conflict," in I. Abu Lughod, ed., *The Arab-Israeli Confrontation of June 1967: An Arab Perspective* (Evanston, Ill.: Northwestern University Press, 1970), pp. 146–147, table 4.

51. Number for June 10–16, cover.

52. F. Nietzsche, *The Twilight of the Idols* (Harmondsworth, Middlesex: Penguin, 1968), pp. 62–63.

53. G. Yakobi, *Otsmatah shel Echut* [The Power of Quality] (Haifa: Shikmona, 1972).

54. E.g., S. Peres, *Ha-shalav Ha-ba* [The Next Stage] (Tel Aviv: Am Ha-sefer, 1965), p. 181.

55. Y. Harkavi, "Basic Factors in the Arab Collapse During the Six Day War," *Orbis* 2 (1967): 677–691.

56. J. Larteguy, *The Walls of Israel* (New York: Evans, 1969), pp. 87 (interview with Yariv) and 146 (interview with Gonen).

57. F. Nietzsche, *Human, All Too Human* (Cambridge: Cambridge University Press, 1986), p. 163.

58. Cf. Dayan, *Avnei Derech*, p. 436.

59. R. S. and W. S. Churchill, *The Six Day War*, p. 191.

CHAPTER 12

1. For this and the following paragraphs see R. Pedatsur, *Nitschon Ha-mevucha: Mediniyut Memshelet Eshkol Ba-sthachim Le-achar Milchemet Sheshet Ha-yamim* [The Triumph of Embarrassment: The Eshkol Government and the Territories After the Six Days' War] (Tel Aviv: Zmora Bitan, 1996), p. 30 ff.

2. For some figures on the distances between Israel's major centers and the new and old borders see A. Levite, *Offense and Defense in Israeli Military Doctrine* (Boulder: Westview Press, 1989), p. 71.

3. For the complex processes that were involved in the decisionmaking process see Pedatsur, *Nitschon Ha-mevucha*, esp. pp. 145 ff., 177 ff., and 221 ff.

4. A later version of the so-called Allon Plan is Y. Allon, "The Case for Defensible Borders," *Foreign Affairs* 55:1 (October 1976): 38–55. A full-length discussion is Y. Cohen, *Tochnit Allon* [The Allon Plan] (Efal: Ha-kibbuts Ha-meuchad, 1973).

5. Cf. M. Brecher, *The Foreign Policy System of Israel* (London: Oxford University Press, 1972), p. 213 ff.

6. N. Safran, *From War to War: The Arab-Israeli Confrontation, 1948–1967* (New York: Pegasus, 1969), p. 158.

7. Figures from G. Yaakobi, *Otsmatah shel Echut* (Haifa: Shikmon, 1972), p. 120.

8. According to the order of battle in T. N. Dupuy, *Elusive Victory: The Arab-Israeli Wars, 1947–1974* (New York: Harper and Row, 1978), pp. 181., 612–613.

9. Cf. Y. Greenberg, "Ha-hachlata al Kitsur Sherut Ha-chova Be-TSAHAL Bi-shnat 1963" [The Decision to Cut Conscript Service in 1963], *Medina, Minhal Ve-yechasim Ben-leumiyim* 40 (Summer 1995): 67–77.

10. E. Haber, *Ha-yom Tifrots Milchama* [Today War Will Break Out] (Tel Aviv: Idanim, 1987), p. 125.

11. Ibid., p. 138. In contrast, Major General Meron once told this author that the decision resulted from the fact that the Chieftain's suspension system was too delicate for the rough terrain of the Middle East.

12. M. Dayan, *Avnei Derech* [Memoirs] (Tel Aviv: Dvir, 1976), p. 563.

13. Z. Levkovits, "Hebetim Be-logistika" [Logistic Aspects], *Maarachot* 332 (September–October 1992): 36.

14. S. Rolbant, *The Israeli Soldier: Profile of an Army* (New York: Barnes, 1970), p. 172.

15. Between 1976 and 1973 there were only nine, of whom four later changed their mind: R. Gal, *A Portrait of the Israeli Soldier* (Westport, Conn.: Greenwood Press, 1986), p. 256, n. 4.

16. On the link between unit cohesion and psychiatric casualties see M. van Creveld, *Fighting Power: German and U.S. Army Performance, 1939–1945* (Westport, Conn.: Greenwood Press, 1982), pp. 91–97.

17. Haber, *Ha-yom Tifrots Milchama*, p. 48 ff.

18. The raid is described in detail in R. Eytan, *Sippur shel Chayal* [A Soldier's Story] (Tel Aviv: Maariv, 1991), pp. 114–117; also Haber, *Ha-yom Tifrots Milchama*, pp. 322–334.

19. Dayan, *Avnei Derech*, pp. 531–532.

20. According to Eytan, *Sippur shel Chayal*, p. 108, the guerrillas' escape was due to the fact that the IDF had dropped leaflets to warn the civilian population.

21. Different, and much larger, figures are given by S. Ali El-Edroos, *The Hassemite Arab Army, 1909–1979* (Amman: The Publishing Committee, 1980), p. 440.

22. The Jordanian-Syrian clash, as well as Hussein's operations agaisnt the Palestinians, is analyzed in some detail by Rooshdi, *The Hassemite Arab Army*, pp. 449–460.

23. For the details see M. Zak, *Hussein Osse Shalom* [Hussein Makes Peace] (Ramat Gan: Bar Illan University Press), pp. 141–142, n. 2.

24. P. Seale, *Assad: The Struggle for the Middle East* (Berkeley: University of California Press, 1988), p. 166.

25. Dayan, *Avnei Derech*, p. 422.

26. For figures see International Institute for Strategic Studies, *The Military Balance, 1968–1969* (London: IISS, 1968), pp. 33–37.

27. See on this subject the Egyptian minister of defense, Muhammad Fawzi, as discussed in D. Schueftan, *Hatasha: Ha-astretegia Ha-medinit shel Mitsrayim Ha-natserit Be-ikvot Milchemet 1967* [Attrition: Egypt's Post-1967 Political Strategy] (Tel Aviv: Maarachot, 1989), pp. 107–109.

28. This episode has been analyzed at length in Y. Shoshan, *Ha-krav Ha-acharon shel Ha-maschetet Elat* [The Last Battle of the Destroyer Elat] (Tel Aviv: Maariv, 1984).

29. Cf. A. Sadat, *In Search of Identity* (New York: Harper and Row, 1978), p. 197.

30. Dayan, *Avnei Derech*, p. 515; A. Sharon, *Warrior* (New York: Simon and Schuster, 1989), pp. 220–221.

31. For Egypt's war aims see Schueftan, *Hatasha*, p. 201 ff.; also Y. Bar-Siman Tov, *The Israeli-Egyptian War of Attrition, 1969–1970* (New York: Columbia University Press, 1980), p. 47 ff.

32. Figures from Bar-Siman Tov, *The Israeli-Egyptian War of Attrition*, p. 92 (table 4.1) and p. 97 (table 4.4).

33. M. Peled, "Ech lo Hitkonena Yisrael Le-milchama" [How Israel Did Not Prepare for War], *Maarachot* 289/290 (October 1983): 25–28.

34. Cf. the calculations of Bar-Siman Tov, *The Israeli-Egyptian War of Attrition*, p. 91 ff., regarding the types of Egyptian fire and their relative effectiveness.

35. The operation is described in some detail in M. Eldar, *Shayetet 11* [Flotilla 11] (Tel Aviv: Zmora Bitan, 1996), pp. 55–59.

36. Some additional operations of the same kind are briefly described in Eytan, *Sippur shel Chayal*, pp. 113–114.

37. Ch. Nadel, "Hafalat Ha-kochot Ha-meyuchadim shel TSAHAL Be-milchemet Ha-hatasha" [Israel's Special Forces in the War of Attrition], M.A. thesis, Tel Aviv University, 1990. Nadel was a special forces officer who later rose to major general.

38. For Nasser's plans during this period see Schueftan, *Hatasha*, chap. 5.

39. Y. Rabin, *Pinkas Sherut* [A Service Record] (Tel Aviv: Maariv), vol. 1, pp. 261–263. For quotes from other key Israeli decisionmakers see Schueftan, *Hatasha*, p. 120 ff.

40. Schueftan, *Hatasha*, p. 250 ff., using a variety of Egyptian sources.

41. Cf. A. Price, *Instruments of Darkness: The History of Electronic Warfare* (London: Mac-donald's, 1967).

42. Cf. E. O'Ballance, *The Electronic War in the Middle East, 1968–1970* (London: Faber and Faber, 1974), pp. 123–124.

43. Quoted in Schueftan, *Hatasha*, p. 265.

44. Figure from E. N. Luttwak and D. Horowitz, *The Israeli Army* (London: Allen Lane, 1975), p. 325.

45. Bar Lev estimate, in G. Yaakobi, *Ke-chut Ha-seara* [By a Hair's Breadth] (Tel Aviv: Idanim, 1989), p. 157.

46. Schueftan, *Hatasha*, p. 365.

47. The best source is once again Schueftan, *Hatasha*, p. 267, which makes use of all the available Israeli, Egyptian, and U.S. sources.

48. For a blow-by-blow account of the way it was done see E. Zeira, *Milchemet Yom Ha-kippurim, Mitos mul Metsiut* [The Yom Kippur War: Myth Versus Reality] (Tel Aviv: Yediot Acharonot, 1993), p. 34 ff.

49. Ezer Weizman, *On Eagles' Wings* (Tel Aviv: Steimatzky's, 1979), p. 265.

CHAPTER 13

1. S. Rolbant, *The Israeli Soldier: Profile of an Army* (New York: Barnes, 1970), p. 244.

2. For a blow-by-blow account of terrorist activities and Israeli responses see E. O'Ballance, *Arab Guerrilla Power, 1968–1972* (London: Faber and Faber, 1974).

3. Dayan lecture, August 9, 1973, quoted in N. Bar Tov, *Dado: Arbaim U-smoneh Shanim Ve-esrim Yom* [Dado: Forty-Eight Years and Twenty Days] (Tel Aviv: Maariv, 1978), vol. 1, p. 274.

4. Bar Tov, *Dado*, vol. 1, pp. 179, 202–203. There are some additional details of the plan in E. N. Luttwak, "Defense Planning in Israel: A Brief Retroperspective," in S. G. Neuman, ed., *Defense-Planning in Less-Industrialized States* (Lexington, Mass.: D.C. Heath, 1984), p. 140.

5. Cf. the account in B. Kedar, *Sippuro shel Gdud Machats* [The Story of "Machats" Battalion] (Tel Aviv: Tamuz, 1975), p. 11.

6. Abdel Ghani el Gamasy, *The October War* (Cairo: American University Press, 1993), p. 148.

7. Dayan to *Yediot Acharonot*, August 18, 1972.

8. G. Yaakobi, *Ke-chut Ha-seara* [By a Hair's Breadth] (Tel Aviv: Idanim, 1989), p. 170.

9. For the preparations that were made on this occasion see Bar Tov, *Dado*, vol. 1, pp. 238–248.

10. E. Haber, *Ha-yom Tifrots Milchama* [Today War Will Break Out] (Tel Aviv: Idanim, 1987), p. 17.

11. A. Sadat, *In Search of Identity* (New York: Collins, 1978), p. 237.

12. Cf. M. van Creveld, *Nuclear Proliferation and the Future of Conflict* (New York: Free Press, 1993), p. 109; also Levite, *Be-einei Ha-aravim*, pp. 42, 76, plus the sources quoted in both works.

13. See the sources quoted in Levite, *Be-einei Ha-aravim*, p. 43.

14. Cf. his own account in Saad el Shazly, *The Crossing of the Suez* (San Francisco: American Mideast Research, 1980), p. 27 ff.

15. For some figures see Bar Tov, *Dado*, vol. 1, pp. 282, 286.

16. M. Dayan, *Avnei Derech* [Memoirs] (Tel Aviv: Dvir, 1976), p. 570.

17. *Time*, July 30, 1973.

18. Quotation from a GS meeting, September 17, 1973, in Bar Tov, *Dado*, vol. 1, p. 287.

19. For the details see Haber, *Ha-yom Tifrots Milchama*, pp. 15–16.

20. Cf. Meir, *My Life* (Jerusalem: Steimatzky, 1975, p. 347 ff.

21. Cf. M. Negbi, *Namer shel Niyar* [Paper Tiger] (Tel Aviv: Sifriyat Ha-poalim, 1985), pp. 87–88.

22. According to Brigadier General Shalev, head of IDF intelligence/research, and Zeira's own office manager, a lieutenant colonel whose name was also Shalev; see Bar Tov, *Dado*, vol. 1, p. 305.

23. Shazly, *The Crossing of the Suez*, pp. 206–207.

24. Haber, *Ha-yom Tifrots Milchama*, p. 20.

25. Shazly, *The Crossing of the Suez*, p. 213, says that the evacuation took the Egyptians by surprise and almost betrayed their plans.

26. Cf. U. Bar Joseph, "Israel's Intelligence Failure in 1973," *Security Studies* 4:3 (Spring 1995): 584–609.

27. Quoted in A. Braun, *Moshe Dayan Be-milchemt Yom Ha-kippurim* [Moshe Dayan in the Yom Kippur War] (Tel Aviv: Idanim, 1993), p. 58.

28. E. Zeira, *Milchemet Yom Ha-kippurim, Mitos mul Metsiut* [The Yom Kippur War: Myth Versus Reality] (Tel Aviv: Yediot Acharonot, 1993), p. 215.

29. For a blow-by-blow account see Haber, *Ha-yom Tifrots Milchama*, p. 11 ff.

30. Cf. Gamasy, *The October War*, p. 180.

31. Braun, *Moshe Dayan*, pp. 79, 81.

32. Cf. Bar Tov, *Dado*, vol. 1, pp. 177–178.

33. For the lack of information affecting Gonen at this time cf. M. van Creveld, *Command in War* (Cambridge, Mass.: Harvard University Press, 1985), pp. 205–206.

34. Brig. Gen. Emmanuel Shaked as quoted in Zeira, *Milchemet Yom Ha-kippurim*, p. 217. The verb *li-dfok* is normal IDF slang for "to kill" or "to fuck."

35. In these attacks Adan lost twenty-seven killed, five tanks, and eight half-tracks. Lt. Col. Nachum and Lt. Col. Tsvi, "Lechima Be-kommando Mitsri Be-milchemet Yom Ha-kippurim" [Fighting Egyptian Commandos During the 1973 War], *Maarachot* 327 (November–December 1992): 23.

36. E. Shimshi, *Seara Be-Oktober* [Storm in October] (Tel Aviv: Maarachot, 1986), p. 14.

37. No record of this meeting has ever come to light. It is, however, described in A. Adan, *On the Banks of the Suez* (London: Arms and Armor, 1980), pp. 95–100; and Bar Tov, *Dado*, vol. 2, pp. 73–75.

38. Cf. van Creveld, *Command in War*, pp. 213–218, for a blow-by-blow account of IDF "staff work" during these hours.

39. Adan, *On the Banks of the Suez*, p. 119.

40. Cf. Sharon's own account in A. Sharon, *Warrior* (New York: Simon and Schuster, 1989), pp. 301–302.

41. For that commander's own story see A. Yaguri, *Le-hiyot Itam, Kulam Sheli* [To Be with Them, They Are All Mine] (Tel Aviv: Idanim, 1979).

42. Kedar, *Sippuro shel Gdud Machats*, p. 23.

43. See the firsthand account in ibid., p. 28 ff.

44. The Egyptians later claimed that it was a U.S. reconnaissance aircraft that alerted the Israelis to the location of the seam; Gamasy, *The October War*, p. 278.

45. Sharon, *Warrior*, 307–309.

46. Details in Braun, *Moshe Dayan*, pp. 139–140.

47. Cf. the detailed account in E. Rozen, "Lama Hufkera Chativat Barak?" [Why Was "Barak" Brigade Abandoned to Its Fate?] *Maariv* weekend magazine, September 24, 1993, pp. 32–33.

48. See his own account in R. Eytan, *Sippur shel Chayal* [A Soldier's Story] (Tel Aviv: Maariv, 1991), p. 130.

49. Agranat Report (Jerusalem: Government Printing Office, 1975), p. 1035.

50. Braun, *Moshe Dayan*, p. 94.

51. See M. Zak, *Hussein Osse Shalom* [Hussein Makes Peace] (Ramat Gan: Bar Illan University Press), pp. 130–134, for the details.

52. Personal communication by Lt. Col. David Chillion.

53. A. Kahalani, *Oz 77* [Strength 77] (Tel Aviv: Schocken, 1977), p. 104 ff., is a blow-by-blow account of the battle.

54. Ch. Herzog, *The War of Atonement* (London: Futura, 1975), pp. 112–113.

55. For this interpretation see van Creveld, *Nuclear Proliferation*, pp. 101–102; S. Aronson, *The Politics and Strategy of Nuclear Weapons in the Middle East* (New York: State University of New York, 1992), pp. 143–149.

56. Tamir, lecture, Hebrew University, December 1974.

57. Personal communication from one of Lanner's battalion commanders, Lt. Col. Amram Lazar. The Iraqis have described this episode in Ts. Ofer, ed., *Tsva Iraq Be-milchemet Yom Hakippurim* [The Iraqi Army in the Yom Kippur War] (Tel Aviv: Maarachot, 1986), pp. 110–112; according to them it was this attack that saved Damascus.

58. Bar Tov, *Dado*, vol. 2, p. 147.

59. M. Heikal, *The Road to Ramadan* (London: Sphere Books, 1974), p. 224.

60. Gamasy, *The October War*, p. 266 ff.

61. Figures from Herzog, *The War of Atonement*, p. 206, and Gamasy, *The October War*, p. 277; for once, the Israeli and Egyptian accounts agree.

62. Braun, *Moshe Dayan*, p. 96.
63. E. Amber, "Chel Ha-avir Ha-yisraeli Bi-krav Ha-yabasha Be-milchemet Yom Hakip-purim" [The IAF's Participation in the Ground Battle in the Yom Kippur War], in U. Milstein, *Ha-tslicha she-lo Hayta* [The Crossing That Wasn't] (Tel Aviv: Golan, 1992), p. 284 ff.
64. Braun, *Moshe Dayan*, p. 141.
65. Peled lecture, Nevatim Air Base, January 16, 1988.
66. Shazly, *The Crossing of the Suez*, p. 248.
67. Bar Tov, *Dado*, vol. 2, p. 216.
68. See Shazly's own account in *The Crossing of the Suez*, p. 400 ff.
69. Cf. B. Telem, "Naval Lessons of the Yom Kippur War," in L. Williams, ed., *Military Aspects of the Israeli-Arab Conflict* (Tel Aviv: University Publishing Projects, 1975), p. 231 ff.

CHAPTER 14

1. The most detailed account is S. Nakdimon, *Svirut Nemucha* (Tel Aviv: Revivim, 1982), chaps. 1–10; also Y. Ben Porat, *Neila* [Lock-In] (Tel Aviv: Idanim, 1991). In 1973 Brig. Gen. Ben Porat was the Israeli intelligence officer in charge of signals intelligence (SIGINT).
2. J. G. Stein, "The 1973 Intelligence Failure: A Reconsideration," *Jerusalem Quarterly* 24 (Summer 1982): 41–54.
3. Meir, *My Life* (Jerusalem: Steimatzky, 1975), pp. 356–357.
4. Cf. M. van Creveld, *Command in War* (Cambridge, Mass.: Harvard University Press, 1985), pp. 218–229; there is an even more detailed account in U. Milstein, *Ha-tslicha she-lo Hayta* [The Crossing That Wasn't] (Tel Aviv: Golan, 1992), p. 142 ff.
5. B. Kedar, *Sippuro shel Gdud Machats* [The Story of "Machats" Battalion] (Tel Aviv: Tamuz, 1975), p. 11.
6. E. Shimshi, *Seara Be-Oktober* [Storm in October] (Tel Aviv: Maarachot, 1986), p. 15.
7. Lieutenant Colonel Adini as quoted in Milstein, *Ha-tslicha she-lo Hayta*, p. 183.
8. T. N. Dupuy, *Elusive Victory: The Arab-Israeli Wars, 1947–1974* (New York: Harper and Row, 1978), pp. 623–627.
9. R. Eytan, *Sippur shel Chayal* [A Soldier's Story] (Tel Aviv: Maariv, 1991), p. 131.
10. U. Eilam, "Weapons Systems and Technologies—East and West," in L. Williams, ed., *Military Aspects of the Israeli-Arab Conflict* (Tel Aviv: University Publishing Projects, 1975), pp. 22–27.
11. In 1967 it was six divisions and 200 combat aircraft against thirteen and 400 respectively; in 1973, seven against sixteen (counting Moroccan Iraqi and Jordanian forces that took part in the fighting) and 400 against 700 (counting Egyptian and Syrian ones only). More detailed figures in A. Adan, "Echut Ve-kamut Be-milchemet Yom Ha-kippurim" [Quality Versus Quantity in the Yom Kippur War], in A. Kover and A. Ofer, eds., *Echut mul Kamut* [Quality Versus Quantity] (Tel Aviv: Maarachot, 1985), p. 257, tables 1 and 2.
12. Y. Ben Porat et al., *Ha-mechdal* [The Oversight] (Tel Aviv: Private Edition, 1974), p. 283.

PART III

1. E.g., Y. Rabin, "Ha-hartaah Be-mivchan Milchamot Yisrael" [Deterrence in the Crucible of Israel's Wars], *Safra Ve-saifa* 4 (November 1981): 28–29.

CHAPTER 15

1. E. Weizman, *Ha-krav al Ha-shalom* [The Battle for Peace] (Jerusalem: Idanim, 1981), p. 190.
2. Y. Ben Meir, *Civil-Military Relations in Israel* (New York: Columbia University Press, 1996), p. 96.
3. R. Eytan, *Sippur shel Chayal* [A Soldier's Story] (Tel Aviv: Maariv, 1991), p. 197.
4. Eg., Ts. Lanir, *Ha-haftaa Ha-besisit: Modiin Be-mashber* [Basic Surprise: Intelligence in Crisis] (Tel Aviv: Jaffee Center, 1983); Ts. Ofer and A. Kover, eds., *Modiin U-bitachon Leumi* [Intelligence and National Security] (Tel Aviv: Maarachot, 1987); Y. Ben Yis-rael, *Dialogim al Mada U-modiin* [Dialogues About Science and Intelligence] (Tel Aviv: Maarachot, 1989).
5. Y. Kondor, *Kalkalat Yisrael* [The Israeli Economy] (Jerusalem: Schocken, 1984), p. 204, table 25.
6. M. Bentov, *Kalkalat Yisrael al Parashat Drachim* [The Israeli Economy at a Crossroad] (Tel Aviv: Sifriyat Poalim, 1965), p. 139.
7. Figures from D. Schueftan, *Hatasha: Ha-astretegia Ha-medinit shel Mitsrayim Ha-natserit Be-ikvot Milchemet 1967* [Attrition: Egypt's Post-1967 Political Strategy] (Tel Aviv: Maarachot, 1989), pp. 100–101, and G. Yakobi, *Otsmatah shel Echut* [The Power of Quality] (Haifa: Shikmona, 1972), p. 120; M. N. Barnett, *Confronting the Costs of War: Military Power, State, and Society in Egypt and Israel* (Princeton: Princeton University Press, 1992), p. 231, table 6.7.
8. More detailed statistics on U.S. military aid in M. Gazit, "Ha-rechesh Ha-tsvai shel Yisrael Be-arhav" [Israeli Military Procurement in the United States] (Jerusalem: Leonard Davis Institute for International Relations, 1983), pp. 55, 63.
9. International Institute for Strategic Studies, *The Military Balance, 1972–1973* (London: IISS, 1973), p. 31.
10. International Institute for Strategic Studies, *The Military Balance, 1977–1978* (London: IISS, 1978), p. 36.
11. International Institute for Strategic Studies, *The Military Balance, 1981–1982* (London: IISS, 1982), p. 52.
12. D. Kochav, "The Economics of Defense—Israel," in L. Williams, ed., *Military Aspects of the Israeli-Arab Conflict* (Tel Aviv: University Publishing Projects, 1975), p. 179.
13. Figures from Kondor, *Kalkalat Yisrael*, p. 24, table 4.
14. For a unit-by-unit, item-by-item comparison see M. Merdor, *RAFAEL: Bi-netivei Ha-mechkar Ve-ha-pituach Le-bitchon Yisrael* [Defense-Related Research and Development in Israel: The Story of RAFAEL] (Tel Aviv: Ministry of Defense, 1981), p. 21.
15. The 1973 and 1977 figures from IISS, *The Military Balance, 1973–1974*, and *The Military Balance, 1977–1978* (London: IISS), pp. 33 and 37 respectively. The 1982 figures from M. Heller, *The Military Balance in the Middle East* (Tel Aviv: Tel Aviv University, 1983), p. 115. For yet another set of figures see E. N. Luttwak, "Defense Planning in Israel: A Brief Retroperspective," in S. G. Neuman, ed., *Defense-Planning in Less-Industrialized States* (Lexington, Mass.: D.C. Heath, 1984), p. 143.
16. The 1980 figures were: Sweden $13,520, France $11,730, United States $11,360, Israel $4,500. Kondor, *Kalkalat Yisrael*, p. 52, table 7.
17. Cf. E. Inbar, "Israeli Strategic Thinking After 1973," *Journal of Strategic Studies* 6:1 (March 1983): 37–57.
18. Z. Schiff, "Mahapecha Be-hagana Merchavit" [A Revolution in Territorial Defense], *Ha-arets*, January 14, 1976, p. 2; A. Tamir, *Chayal Shocher Shalom* [A Soldier in Search of Peace] (Jerusalem: Idanim, 1988), pp. 309–310.
19. M. Bar Kochva, *Merkevot Ha-plada* [Steel Chariots] (Tel Aviv: Maarachot, 1989), p. 52.

20. Cf. Dudi Shalom, *Ech Ossim Chidush Irguni: Hakamat Mifkedet Chelot Ha-sadeh (MAFCHASH) Be-TSAHAL* [The Making of Organizational Innovation: Setting up MAFCHASH] (Tel Aviv: The Institute for Management, 1995), chap. 4.

21. Z. Levkovits, "Hebetim Be-logistika" [Logistic Aspects], *Maarachot* 332 (September–October 1992): 38.

22. Ibid., p. 36, puts the number at 2,029.

23. Figure of 2,000 M-113s from Luttwak, "Defense Planning," p. 142.

24. Figure from M. Levin and D. Halevy, "Israel," in R. A. Gabriel, *Fighting Armies: Antagonists in the Middle East, a Combat Assessment* (Westport, Conn.: Greenwood Press, 1983), p. 19.

25. Y. Rabin, *Pinkas Sherut* [A Service Record] (Tel Aviv: Maariv), vol. 2, p. 539.

26. The operations are listed in U. Milstein, *Ha-tslicha she-lo Hayta* [The Crossing That Wasn't] (Tel Aviv: Golan, 1992), p. 299 ff.

27. Eytan, *Sippur shel Chayal*, p. 114.

28. Rabin, *Pinkas Sherut*, vol. 2, pp. 497–498.

29. Y. Ben Porat et al., *Mivtsa Entebbe* [Operation Entebbe] (Tel Aviv: Zmora Bitan, 1991), p. 346.

30. For this and other figures cf. E. Wald, *The Wald Report: The Decline of Israeli National Security Since 1967* (Boulder: Westview Press, 1992), pp. 143–146, 151.

31. *Ha-arets*, January 19, 1996, p. 2.

32. N. Barnea, "MACHAT Givati Medaber" [The Commander of Givati Speaks Out], *Yediot Acharonot* weekend magazine, November 30, 1990, p. 21.

33. Shalom, *Ech Ossim Chidush Irguni*, p. 27.

34. Cf. his own account in *Sippur shel Chayal*, p. 167 ff.

35. G. Weissman, "Klitat Noar Shulayim Be-TSAHAL" [The Absorption of Marginal Youth in TSAHAL], *Maarachot* 260 (January 1978): 47.

36. On these problems cf. M. Pail, "The Israeli Defense Forces: A Social Aspect," *New Outlook* (January 1975): 40–44; also Ch. Laskov, *Manhiggut Tsvait* [Military Leadership] (Tel Aviv: Maarachot, 1985), pp. 45–49.

37. R. Gal, *A Portrait of the Israeli Soldier* (Westport, Conn.: Greenwood Press, 1986), pp. 254–255; Bar Kochva, *Merkevot Ha-plada*, p. 580; E. Wald, *Ha-yanshuf shel Minerva* [The Owl of Minverva] (Tel Aviv: Yediot Acharonot, 1994), p. 63.

38. Cf. Y. Chasdai, *Emet Be-tsel Ha-milchama* [Truth in the Shadow of War] (Tel Aviv: Zmora Bitan, 1979), pp. 13–27.

39. Cf. Z. Schiff, "Hitchaprut Pshuta" [Taking Cover], *Ha-arets*, September 19, 1980, p. 2.

40. M. Naor and Z. Enar, eds., *Yemei Yuni: Teurim min Ha-milchama, 1967* [June Days: Episodes from the 1967 War] (Tel Aviv: Maarachot, 1967), p. 49.

41. Israel Women's Lobby, "Nahsim Ve-sherut Be-TSAHAL: Metsiut, Ratson Ve-chazon" [Women in the IDF: Reality, Will, and Vision] (Tel Aviv University: mimeographed, 1995), p. 13.

42. A. R. Bloom, "Women in the Defense Forces," in B. Swirski and M. P. Safir, eds., *Calling the Equality Bluff: Women in Israel* (New York: Pergamon Press, 1991), p. 135.

43. R. F. Priest et al., "Education at West Point," *Armed Forces and Society* 4:4 (August 1978): 592–593, ref. 13.

44. Interview with Brig. Gen. Yisraela Oron, CO, CHEN, *Yediot Acharonot* weekend magazine, August 15, 1997, p. 68.

45. M. Mead, *Male and Female* (New York: William Morrow, 1949), pp. 159–160.

46. Cf. A. Perlmutter et al., *Two Minutes over Baghdad* (London: Valentine, 1982); also S. Nakdimon, *First Strike* (New York: Summit Books, 1987).

47. For a discussion of the *sayarot* and their impact on the IDF see S. A. Cohen, *Towards a New Portrait of a (New) Israeli Soldier* (Ramat Gan: BESA Center, 1997), p. 85.

48. Laskov, *Manhiggut Tsvait*, pp. 121–122.

49. Eytan, *Sippur shel Chayal*, p. 166.

50. On their relationship see Eytan, *Sippur shel Chayal*, pp. 191–194.

51. See his own account in A. Sharon, *Warrior* (New York: Simon and Schuster, 1989), chap. 23.

52. Cf. his own account in ibid., chap. 25.

53. Cf. U. Benziman, *Sharon: Lo Otser Be-adom* [Sharon: Does Not Stop at the Red Light] (Tel Aviv: Adam, 1985), p. 235 ff.

54. D. Horowitz, "Ha-kavua Ve-ha-mishtane Bi-tfisat Ha-bitachon Ha-yisraelit" [Permanence and Change in Israeli Defense] (Jerusalem: Leonard Davis Institute, 1982), p. 10.

55. Data from Y. Arnon, *Meshek Be-sichrur* [An Economy in Turmoil] (Tel Aviv: Hakibbuts Ha-meuchad, 1981), p. 43.

56. Data from A. Halperin, "Hitpatchut Melaei Ha-hon Ha-tsvaiyim shel Yisrael U-medinot Ha-imut" [The Development of Military Capital in Israel and the Confrontation States] (Jerusalem: Falk Institute for Economic Research, 1986), p. 23, table 15.

57. S. Peres, *Battling for Peace* (London: Weidenfeld and Nicolson, 1995), pp. 179–180; Ben Porat, *Mivtsa Entebbe*, pp. 235–237.

CHAPTER 16

1. For a short English-language account see S. Reiser, *The Israeli Arms Industry* (New York: Holmes and Meier, 1989), chap. 1.

2. Y. Evron, *Ha-Taasiya Ha-bitchonit Be-yisrael* [The Israeli Defense Industry] (Tel Aviv: Ministry of Defense, 1980), p. 9.

3. Reiser, *The Israeli Arms Industry*, p. 7.

4. H. Pack, *Structural Change and Economic Policy in Israel* (New Haven: Yale University Press, 1971), pp. 5–6.

5. For a list of the kinds of ammunition produced see Evron, *Ha-Taasiya Ha-bitchonit*, p. 191 ff.

6. M. Merdor, *RAFAEL: Bi-netivei Ha-mechkar Ve-ha-pituach Le-bitchon Yisrael* [Defense-Related Research and Development in Israel: The Story of RAFAEL] (Tel Aviv: Ministry of Defense, 1981), p. 241 ff.

7. See his own account in S. Peres, *Kela David* (Jerusalem: Weidenfeld and Nicolson, 1970), p. 98 ff.

8. E. Haber, *Ha-yom Tifrots Milchama* [Today War Will Break Out] (Tel Aviv: Idanim, 1987), p. 135.

9. M. Gilboa, *Shesh Shanim Ve-shisha Yamim: Mekoroteah Ve-koroteah shel Michlemet Sheshet Ha-yamim* [Six Years and Six Days: the Origins and Course of the Six Day War] (Tel Aviv: Am Oved, 1969), p. 65.

10. A. Klieman, *Cherev Pipiyot: Ha-yetsu Ha-bitchoni shel Yisrael Ve-shuk Ha-neshek Ha-olami* [Double-Edged Sword: Israel's Defense Exports and the World Arms Bazaar] (Tel Aviv: Am Oved, 1992), p. 277.

11. S. Peres, *Kela David*, p. 257.

12. Cf., e.g., G. Yakobi, *Otsmatah shel Echut* [The Power of Quality] (Haifa: Shikmona, 1972), p. 172, where a comparison is drawn between Israel and Sweden.

13. Evron, *Ha-Taasiya Ha-bitchonit*, pp. 210, 213.

14. N. Blumenthal, "The Influence of Defense Industry Investment on Israel's Economy," in Ts. Lanir, ed., *Israeli Security Planning in the 1980s: Its Politics and Economics* (Tel Aviv: Jaffee Center, 1986), p. 170, table 9.1.

15. N. Levi, "Memadim Optimaliyim shel Taasiyat Ha-bitachon" [Optimal Dimensions of the Defense Industry], *Technologiyot* 45 (September 1987): 21–23.

16. M. N. Barnett, *Confronting the Costs of War: Military Power, State, and Society in Egypt and Israel* (Princeton: Princeton University Press, 1992), p. 236.

17. A. Mintz, "Military Industrial Linkage in Israel," *Armed Forces and Society* 12:1 (Fall 1985): 14.

18. D. Kochav, "The Economics of Defense—Israel," in L. Williams, ed., *Military Aspects of the Israeli-Arab Conflict* (Tel Aviv: University Publishing Projects, 1975), p. 183.

19. Cf. A. Klieman, *Israel's Global Reach: Arms Sales as Diplomacy* (London: Brassey's, 1985).

20. See Reiser, *The Israeli Arms Industry*, p. 216 ff., for details.

21. H. Goodman and W. Seth Carus, *The Future Battlefield and the Arab-Israeli Conflict* (New Brunswick, N.J.: Transaction Publishers, 1990), p. 124.

22. Data from A. Klieman and R. Pedatzur, *Rearming Israel: Defense and Procurement Through the 1990s* (Boulder: Westview Press, 1991), p. 79.

23. *Aviation Week and Space Technology*, August 16, 1976, p. 19.

24. Z. Klein et al., *Ha-milchama Ba-terror U-mediniyut Ha-bitachon shel Yisrael* [The War Against Terrorism and Israel's Security Policy] (Tel Aviv: Ha-kibbuts Ha-meuchad, 1990), pp. 178–179.

25. For the Lavi's fall see Reiser, *The Israeli Arms Industry*, p. 179 ff.; also Rabin, in Klein et al., *Ha-milchama Ba-terror*, pp. 174–175.

26. Cf. A. Kover, "Hachraa Tsvait Be-milchama" [Military Decision in War] (Ph.D. thesis, Hebrew University, Jerusalem, 1995), pp. 372–373.

27. For the case against Israeli miniaturization of their weapons see P. Pry, *Israel's Nuclear Arsenal* (Boulder: Westview Press, 1984), pp. 88–89.

28. Pry, *Israel's Nuclear Arsenal*, p. 77.

29. For this episode see L. S. Spector, *The Undeclared Bomb: The Spread of Nuclear Weapons, 1987–1988* (Cambridge, Mass.: Ballinger, 1988), pp. 18, 166; also L. S. Spector and J. R. Smith, *Nuclear Ambitions: The Spread of Nuclear Weapons, 1989–1990* (Boulder: Westview Press, 1990), p. 161 ff.

30. For the significance of the Vanunu revelations see above all F. Barnaby, *The Invisible Bomb: The Nuclear Arms Race in the Middle East* (London: Tauris, 1989), chap. 3.

31. For the relevant calculations see A. Cordesman, *After the Storm: The Changing Military Balance in the Middle East* (Boulder: Westview Press, 1993), p. 242.

32. Cf. Y. Melman, "Ha-kesher Ha-garini shel Yisrael Ve-drom Africa" [The Israel–South Africa Nuclear Connection], *Ha-arets*, April 21, 1997, p. 4.

33. Pry, *Israel's Nuclear Arsenal*, p. 91.

34. The story is told by Merdor, *RAFAEL*, p. 319 ff.

35. S. Hersh, *The Samson Option: Israel's Nuclear Arsenal and American Foreign Policy* (New York: Random House, 1991), pp. 173–174.

36. *Le Monde*, December 10, 1996.

37. Hersh, *The Samson Option*, p. 231.

38. *Maariv*, December 12, 1974.

39. A. E. Levite and E. B. Landau, *Be-einei Ha-aravim: Dimuya Ha-garini shel Yisrael* [In Arab Eyes: Israel's Nuclear Image] (Tel Aviv: Papyrus, 1994), p. 44.

40. "The Bomb," *Al-Aharam*, November 23, 1973.

41. *Al Usbu el Arabi*, July 1 and 4, 1974.

42. Cf. Levite and Landau, *Be-einei Ha-aravim*, p. 76 ff.; M. van Creveld, *Nuclear Proliferation and the Future of Conflict* (New York: Free Press, 1993), p. 110 ff.; and S. Aronson, *The Politics and Strategy of Nuclear Weapons in the Middle East* (New York: State University of New York, 1992), pp. 151–166; also E. Weizman, *Ha-krav al Ha-shalom* [The Battle for Peace] (Jerusalem: Idanim, 1981), p. 42.

43. The various Syrian analyses are discussed in Levite and Landau, *Be-einei Ha-aravim*, p. 98 ff.

44. *Tishrin*, November 3, 1982; *Al Thwara*, November 24, 1982.

45. Radio Damascus, August 1, 1986.
46. For the sources, as well as an analysis of the Syrian concept of "strategic parity," cf. O. Brosh, "Tfissot shel Ha-meimad Ha-garini Be-sichsuchim Ezoriyim Rav-Tsdadiyim Ve-emdot Be-inyanan" [Perceptions and Public Attitudes Toward the Nuclear Dimension in Multinational Regional Conflicts] (Ph.D. thesis, Hebrew University, Jerusalem, 1990), pp. 186–187.
47. Syrian Minister of Defense Mustafa Tlas, as quoted in *Maariv*, June 2, 1985; Hafez Assad interview in *Al Najala*, December 12, 1985. For the entire question see also E. Karsh, "A Marriage of Convenience: The Soviet Union and Assad's Syria," *Jerusalem Journal of International Relations* 11:4 (December 1989): 9 ff.
48. Cf. Aronson, *The Politics and Strategy*, p. 161.
49. M. Bar Kochba, "Ha-maaracha neged Ha-irakim Be-milchemet Yom Ha-kippurim," *Maarachot* 258/259 (November 1977): 6.
50. M. Dayan, *Ha-lanetsach Tochal Cherev* [Will the Sword Bite Forever?] (Tel Aviv: Idanim, 1991), p. 36.
51. Cf. E. Sheffer, "The Economic Burden of the Arms Race Between the Confrontation States and Israel," in Lanir, ed., *Israeli Security Planning in the 1980s*, p. 147, table 8.2.
52. A. Halperin, "Hitpatchut Melaei Ha-hon Ha-tsvaiyim shel Yisrael U-medinot Ha-imut" [The Development of Military Capital in Israel and the Confrontation States] (Jerusalem: Falk Institute for Economic Research, 1986), p. 23, table 15.
53. Y. Rabin, *Pinkas Sherut* [A Service Record] (Tel Aviv: Maariv), vol. 1, p. 83.
54. Z. Schiff, "Bar lev-Be-hamtana" [Bar Lev on the Sidelines], *Ha-arets*, April 24, 1981, p. 2; E. Weizman, *Ha-krav al Ha-shalom* [The Battle for Peace] (Tel Aviv: Idanim, 1982), p. 41.
55. *Maariv*, February 18, 1982, p. 1.

CHAPTER 17

1. For a blow-by-blow account see E. O'Ballance, *Arab Guerrilla Power, 1968–1972* (London: Faber and Faber, 1974), chaps. 5 and 11.
2. Cf. his own account in S. Peres, *Battling for Peace* (London: Weidenfeld and Nicolson, 1995), p. 222.
3. Cf. statements by Peres, Rabin, and Allon, *Maariv*, November 8, 11, and 20, 1976.
4. The details of the agreement may be found in A. Yaniv, *Dilemmas of Security: Politics, Strategy, and the Israeli Experience in Lebanon* (Oxford: Oxford University Press, 1987), pp. 60–61.
5. For PLO strength and dispositions see T. N. Dupuy and P. Martell, *Flawed Victory: The Arab-Israeli Conflict and the 1982 War in Lebanon* (Fairax, Va.: HERO Books, 1986), pp. 86–88.
6. For these contacts see Z. Schiff and Y. Yaari, *Milchemet Sholal* [The Vain War] (Tel Aviv: Schocken, 1984), p. 40 ff.
7. *Ha-arets* weekend magazine, January 2, 1997, pp. 6–7.
8. Schiff and Yaari, *Milchemet Sholal*, p. 22 ff.; Syria's defense minister has described this episode in M. Tlas, *Ha-plisha Ha-yisraelit Li-lebanon* [Israel's Invasion of Lebanon] (Tel Aviv: Ministry of Defense, 1988), p. 69 ff.
9. A. Naor, *Memshala Be-milchama* [A Government at War] (Tel Aviv: Lahav, 1986), p. 47.
10. See M. Halperin and A. Lapidot, eds., *Chalifat Lachats* [Pressure Suit] (Tel Aviv: Ministry of Defense, 1987), p. 144 ff., for the atmosphere of those days.
11. Yaniv, *Dilemmas of Security*, pp. 109–110.
12. Naor, *Memshala Be-milchama*, p. 31.

13. Cf. on this question Schiff and Yaari, *Milchemet Sholal*, pp. 115–116; A. Sharon, *Warrior* (New York: Simon and Schuster, 1989), p. 460 ff.; S. Feldman and H. Rechnits-Kizinger, "Ha-hahataya, Ha-kontsenzus Ve-ha-milchama: Lebanon, 1982" [Confidence Tricks, Consensus, and War: Lebanon, 1982], in Y. Alper, ed., *Shnaton Astretegi* [Strategic Annual] (Tel Aviv: Jaffee Center for Strategic Studies, 1986), pp. 23–25.

14. Z. Klein et al., *Ha-milchama Ba-terror U-mediniyut Ha-bitachon shel Yisrael* [The War Against Terrorism and Israel's Security Policy] (Tel Aviv: Ha-kibbuts Ha-meuchad, 1990), p. 82.

15. T. Yair, *Iti Mi-levanon* [With Me from Lebanon] (Tel Aviv: Maarachot, 1990), p. 18.

16. M. Eldar, *Shayetet 11* [Flotilla 11] (Tel Aviv: Zmora Bitan, 1996), p. 216.

17. Radio Lebanon announced the landing in advance; ibid., p. 222.

18. Cf. A. Kahalani, *A Warrior's Way* (New York: Shaplovsky, 1994), p. 332 ff.

19. Ibid., p. 342 ff.

20. For the Syrian order of battle see Dupuy and Martell, *Flawed Victory*, p. 90.

21. One of the best accounts is W. S. Carus, "Military Lessons of the 1982 Israel-Syria Conflict," in R. Harkaby and S. Neuman, eds., *The Lessons of Recent Wars in the Third World* (Lexington, Mass.: Lexington Books, 1985), pp. 261–280.

22. Figures from Y. Rabin, *Ha-milchama Be-levanon* [The War in Lebanon] (Tel Aviv: Am Oved, 1983), p. 25.

23. E. Wald, *The Wald Report: The Decline of Israeli National Security Since 1967* (Boulder: Westview Press, 1992), pp. 45–46.

24. Drori, quoted in Klein, et al., *Ha-milchama Ba-terror*, p. 81.

25. Sharon, *Warrior*, p. 497 ff.

26. R. Eytan, *Sippur shel Chayal* [A Soldier's Story] (Tel Aviv: Maariv, 1991), p. 275, mentions 1,350 trucks, 113 armored fighting vehicles including 87 tanks, 250 other vehicles, 22,000 small arms, 650 antitank weapons, 12,000 rockets, 43 artillery barrels, and fabulous amounts of ammunition. *New York Times*, October 12, 1982, listed 420 armored combat vehicles, 636 other vehicles, 34,321 small arms, 1,193 antitank rockets (RPG–7s), 1,193 mortars and rocket launchers, and 150 antiaircraft guns.

27. Klein et al., *Ha-milchama Ba-terror*, pp. 113–114.

28. Sharon testimony in New York, quoted in D. Aharoni, *General Sharon's War Against Time Magazine* (New York: Shapolsy, 1985), pp. 165–166.

29. *Jerusalem Post*, July 2, 1982.

30. This and subsequent public opinion figures from various polls summed up in Yaniv, *Dilemmas of Security*, p. 316.

31. M. Begin, "Milchemet En Brera Ve-milchemet Brera" [No Choice War and Choice War], *Yediot Acharonot*, August 20, 1982, p. 2.

32. See on this episode R. Gal, "Commitment and Obedience in the Military: An Israeli Case Study," *Armed Forces and Society* 11:4 (Summer 1985): 558–559.

33. For these movements see Y. Yishai, "Dissent in Israel: Opinions on the Lebanon War," *Middle East Review* (Winter 1983): 38–44.

34. Data from R. Linn, "Sarvanut Mi-taamei Matspun" [Conscientious Objection], *Iyunim Be-chinuch* 49/50 (1989): 51–52.

35. For the link between an army's cohesion and psychiatric casualties see D. H. Marlowe, *Cohesion, Anticipated Breakdown, and Endurance in Battle: Considerations for Severe and High Intensity Combat* (Washington, D.C.: Walter Reed Army Institute of Research, 1979); Z. Solomon et al., "Effects of Social Support and Battle Intensity on Loneliness and Breakdown During Combat," *Journal of Personality and Social Psychology* 51:6 (1986): 1269–1277; also M. van Creveld, *Fighting Power: German and U.S. Army Performance, 1939–1945* (Westport, Conn.: Greenwood Press, 1982), pp. 91–96.

36. U. Ben Ari, *Acharai* [Follow Me] (Tel Aviv: Maariv, 1994), p. 174.

37. Sh. Noy, *Lo Yachol Yoter: Tguvot Le-lachats Krav* [Can't Go On: Combat Stress Reactions] (Tel Aviv: Ministry of Defense, 1991), p. 43.

38. A. Levy et al., "Tguvot Ha-krav Be-milchamot Yisrael, 1948–1982" [Reactions to Combat in Israel's Wars, 1948–1982], mimeograph, IDF, Chief Medical Officer, 1993, pp. 13–14, 19, and *passim*.

39. R. Gal, *A Portrait of the Israeli Soldier* (Westport, Conn.: Greenwood Press, 1986), p. 213.

40. R. Gal, "Mabat Nosaf al Helem Krav" [Another Look at Battle Shock], *Maarachot* 332 (September–October 1982): 40–45.

41. Noy, *Lo Yachol Yoter*, p. 44; also Gal, *A Portrait of the Israeli Soldier*, p. 220.

42. Levy, "Tguvot Ha-krav," p. 41.

43. *The Beirut Massacre: The Complete Kahan Commission Report* (New York: Karz-Cohl, 1983).

44. Dupuy and Martell, *Flawed Victory*, p. 140.

45. *Jerusalem Post*, June 9, 1983.

46. Lowest estimate in interview with Tsvi Eshet, financial adviser to the IDF chief of staff, *Yediot Acharonot* weekend magazine, May 31, 1985, p. 33; highest one in Ch. Barkai, "Reflections on the Economic Cost of the Lebanon War," *The Jerusalem Quarterly* 37 (1986): 95–106.

47. In Klein et al., *Ha-milchama Ba-terror*, p. 93.

48. Cf. Yaniv, *Dilemmas of Security*, pp. 152–153.

49. N. Machiavelli, *The Prince* (Harmondsworth, Middlesex: Penguin, 1961), p. 45.

50. Figure from E. Yaari, "Neighbourhood Watch," *The Jerusalem Report*, September 18, 1997, p. 26.

51. E.g., Sheik Nasrulla as quoted in *Yediot Acharonot*, February 14, 1997, p. 2.

52. *Yediot Acharonot*, April 26, 1996, p. 2.

53. The existence of this unit was disclosed for the first time on Israel TV, December 4, 1996.

54. R. Adelist and A. Lam, "Regel Poh, Regel Sham" [A Leg in Each Camp], *Yerushalayim*, November 22, 1996, p. 18.

55. Z. Schiff, "Ma Chadash Ba-tsafon?" [What Is New in the North?], *Ha-arets*, March 25, 1993, p. 2.

56. S. Gazit et al., eds., *The Middle East Military Balance, 1993–1994* (Tel Aviv: Jaffee Center, 1994), p. 146.

57. Y. Luts, "Levanon: Tomche Ha-nesiga Mitchazkim" [Lebanon: The Supporters of Withdrawal Get Stronger], *Anashim*, January 14, 1997, p. 5.

58. N. Barnea, "Not the Soldiers but the Parents Need Psychiatric Attention," *Yediot Acharonot* weekend magazine, June 6, 1997, p. 2.

CHAPTER 18

1. The figure for the United States, taking 220 million as its population base, is 1:2,400 per year of the Vietnam War.

2. Sh. Feldman, "Yachasei Mimshal Regan-Yisrael, Ha-kadentsia Ha-shnia" [The Reagan Administration and Israel, the Second Term], Monograph No. 14 (Tel Aviv: Jaffee Center, 1985), pp. 62–65.

3. S. Flotsker, "Atsmaut Kalkalit, 1986–1996" [Economic Self-Sufficiency, 1986–1996], *Yediot Acharonot*, December 27, 1996, p. 5.

4. For details of the Syrian buildup see H. Goodman and W. Seth Carus, *The Future Battlefield and the Arab-Israeli Conflict* (New Brunswick, N.J.: Transaction Publishers, 1990), pp. 29–36; also M. Heller, ed., *The Middle East Military Balance, 1984* (Tel Aviv: Jaffee Center, 1984), pp. 209–212.

5. Cf. Y. Shamir, *Sikumo shel Davar* [Summing Up] (Tel Aviv: Idanim, 1994), p. 202.

6. Figures on Israel, Jordan, Egypt, from The Economist, *The World in 1997* (London: The Economist, 1996), p. 100; figures on Syria kindly provided by Professor Moshe Maoz, the Hebrew University.

7. Data from A. Klieman and R. Pedatzur, *Rearming Israel: Defense and Procurement Through the 1990s* (Boulder: Westview Press, 1991), pp. 59–60.

8. Flotsker, "Atsmaut Kalkalit," p. 5.

9. *Yediot Acharonot*, November 22, 1996, p. 4.

10. Figure from Encyclopaedia Britannica, *1993 Britannica Book of the Year* (Chicago, Ill.: Britannica, 1993), p. 663. U.S. per-capita expenditure during the same year was comparable, but defense only formed 5.8 percent of GNP; ibid., p. 744. The corresponding figures for Germany were 4.9 percent and $544 (ibid., p. 613); for Britain, 4.2 percent and $605 (ibid., p. 740); for France, 3.7 percent and $628 (ibid., p. 608).

11. Comparison between 1984 and 1994 data based on tables in Sh. Gazit et al., eds., *The Middle East Military Balance, 1993–1994* (Tel Aviv: Jaffee Center, 1994), p. 498.

12. In 1984, inclusive of 180 Skyhawks, it stood at 520; in 1994, exclusive of 175 Skyhawks, it stood at 522.

13. Figures on fertility taken from Government of Israel, *Ha-shnaton Ha-statisti* [Statistical Yearbook] (Jerusalem: Government Printing Office, 1960, 1974).

14. As of 1996 17 percent of young males and 30 percent of young females were not drafted; *Yediot Acharonot*, September 2, 1996, p. 5.

15. A. Bernheimer, "Profil '96" [A Profile for 1996], *Yediot Acharonot* weekend magazine, April 19, 1996, p. 16; Israel Women's Lobby, "Nahsim Ve-sherut Be-TSAHAL: Metsiut, Ratson Ve-chazon" [Women in the IDF: Reality, Will, and Vision] (Tel Aviv University: mimeographed, 1995), p. 10.

16. Chief of the General Staff Division, Maj. Gen. Matan Vilnai, on Israel Radio, December 26, 1996.

17. See J. van Doorn, *The Soldier and Social Change* (Beverly Hills, Calif.: Sage, 1975), chap. 3.

18. See above all S. A. Cohen, "The Israel Defense Forces: From a 'People's Army' to a 'Professional Military,' Causes and Implications," *Armed Forces and Society* 21:2 (Winter 1995): 237–254; also S. Gordon, "Bi-zchut Giyus Barerani" [In Favor of Selective Service], *Maarachot* 328 (September 1993): 32–37.

19. Figure of $17,000 from Israel Radio, February 23, 1997; major general's pay from *Yediot Acharonot*, October 1, 1997, p. 29. One is reminded of the eighteenth-century tables for the ransoming of prisoners, which valued a private at 4 *livres* and a *Marechal de France* at 240,000.

20. Cf. *Maariv*, September 11, 1997, p. 14.

21. In 1996 no fewer than two-thirds of the 8,500 border guards were conscripts: *Yediot Acharonot* weekend magazine, November 21, 1996, p. 6.

22. *Haarets*, May 1, 1996, p. 6.

23. See for the details Y. Gvirts, "Lo Barachnu, Lo Nichnasnu Le-helem" [We Didn't Run, We Didn't Go into Shock"], *Yediot Acharonot* weekend magazine, July 19, 1996, pp. 14–15.

24. Interview with Brigadier General (ret.) Dotan, former chief, CHEN, in I. Jerby, *Ha-mechir Ha-kaful: Maamad Ha-isha Ba-chevra Ha-yisraelit Ve-sherut Ha-nashim Be-tsahal* [The Double Price: Women's Status and Military Service in Israel] (Tel Aviv: Ramot, 1996), p. 149.

25. Lt. Col. Margalit, "Nashim Be-TSAHAL—Mashav She-lo Mutsa" [Women in the IDF—an Underutilized Resource], in Ts. Ofer and A. Kover, eds., *Echut mul Kamut* [Quality Versus Quantity] (Tel Aviv: Maarachot, 1985), pp. 331–340.

26. Y. Knoller, "Yalda Yehudiya Lo Sholchim Le-shevi Ha-oyev" [A Jewish Girl Should Not Be Sent to Become a POW], *Ha-arets*, March 7, 1991, p. 4. In 1978 the total number of MOS was 709.

27. See table in Jerby, *Ha-mechir Ha-kaful*, p. 73; also Israel Women's Lobby, "Nashim Ve-sherut Be-TSAHAL," p. 19.

28. *Yediot Acharonot*, September 13, 1992, p. 26.

29. Interview with Brig. Gen. Chedva Almog, CO, CHEN, in A. R. Bloom, "Women in the Defense Forces," in B. Swirski and M. P. Safir, eds., *Calling the Equality Bluff: Women in Israel* (New York: Pergamon Press, 1991), p. 135; interview with Brig. Gen. Yisraela Oron, CO, CHEN, in *Yediot Acharonot* weekend magazine, August 15, 1997.

30. Israel's Women Lobby, "Nashim Ve-sherut Be-TSAHAL," p. 16.

31. U. Dayan quoted in S. Cohen and I. Soleyman, "Mi-tsva Ha-am Le-tsava Miktsoi?" [From a People's Army to a Professional Army?], *Maarachot* 341 (May–June 1995): 4.

32. *Yediot Acharonot*, January 10, 1997, p. 12; O. Petersburg, "Ha-shin gimmel shel Ha-medina Hizhir" [The State's M.P. Serves Warning], *Yediot Acharonot* weekend magazine, November 15, 1996.

33. Israel Women's Lobby, "Nashim Ve-sherut Be-TSAHAL," pp. 13, 19. However, women still constituted only 2 percent of colonels and brigadier generals; *Ha-arets*, April 25, 1995, p. 2.

34. Ch. Almog, "Sherut Ktisnot Be-TSAHAL—Tsipiyot Ve-efsharuyot" [Female Officers' Service in the IDF—Expectations and Possibilities], *Maarachot* 317 (October–November 1989): 40–43.

35. Cf. F. Raday, "Women, Work, and the Law," in Swirski and Safir, eds., *Calling the Equality Bluff*, pp. 178–186.

36. "Achat Esre Ha-muflaot," *Yediot Acharonot*, January 10, 1997, p. 12; also, at greater length, R. Shaked, "Achat-Esre Ha-Noazot," *Yediot Acharonot* weekend magazine, January 10, 1997, pp. 18–19.

37. *Yediot Acharonot*, December 13, 1996, p. 7.

38. S. Peres, *Kela David* (Jerusalem: Weidenfeld and Nicolson, 1970), p. 258. Note that in 1969 the United States also had the draft.

39. Higher Education Authority Information Bulletin 8 (August 1996): 8.

40. Cf. M. van Creveld, *The Training of Officers: From Military Professionalism to Irrelevance* (New York: Free Press, 1989), pp. 3–4.

41. D. Ben Gurion, *Yichud Ve-yeud: Devarim al Bitchon Yisrael* [A Unique Destiny: Notes on Israeli Defense] (Tel Aviv: Maarachot, 1971), p. 305.

42. Cf. A. Lori, "Toar Akademai Im Kritsa" [A Degree with a Wink], *Ha-arets* weekend magazine, March 28, 1997, pp. 19–24.

43. A. Kahalani, *A Warrior's Way* (New York: Shaplovsky, 1994), p. 409. At the time Kahalani was commandant of the staff college.

44. On September 15, 1997, Israel radio announced that the treasury was attempting to dissuade the IDF from implementing the program on grounds of cost.

45. Cf. M. Janowitz, *The Professional Soldier* (New York: Free Press, 1971).

46. Y. Amir, "Bnei Kibbutsim Be-TSAHAL" [*Kibbuts* Children in the IDF], *Megamot* 15:2–3 (August 1967): 250–258.

47. For details about the arrangement see S. Cohen, *The Scroll or the Sword? Dilemmas of Religion and Military Service in Israel* (Amsterdam: Harwood, 1997), p. 105 ff.

48. Y. Peri, "Ofyah Ha-idiologi shel Ha-elita Ha-tsvait Ha-yisraelit" [The Ideological Character of Israel's Military Elite], *Medina, Mimshal Ve-yechasim Benleumiyim* 6 (Autumn 1974): 146–155.

49. *Yediot Acharonot* weekend magazine, August 30, 1996, p. 5.

50. *Bitaon Chel Ha-avir* 103 (June 1995): 8, and ibid. 109 (June 1996): 12; interview with Brig. Gen. Yair Nave, chief infantry and parachute officer, *Ha-tsofe*, September 13, 1996, p. 2

51. E.g., cf. Dudi Shalom, *Ech Ossim Chidush Irguni: Hakamat Mifkedet Chelot Ha-sadeh (MAFCHASH) Be-TSAHAL* [The Making of Organizational Innovation: Setting up MAFCHASH] (Tel Aviv: The Institute for Management, 1995), pp. 40–41, 145.
52. For Dan Shomron's views on this subject see A. Levite, "Changes of the Guard in Israel," *Armed Forces Journal International* (June 1987): 50–51.
53. *Ha-arets*, February 7, 1996, p. 1.
54. *Yediot Acharonot*, September 7, 1997, p. 1. In fact, since a problem with a glider prevented the lieutenant from reaching the scene on time, the mission was carried out by a senior NCO.
55. A. Fishman, "Yoter Miday Generalim" [A Surfeit of Generals], *Yediot Acharonot* weekend magazine, October 6, 1995, pp. 12–13, 26. The existence of a problem is admitted in Brigadier X, "Koach Ha-adam Be-TSAHAL" [IDF Manpower], *Maarachot* 330 (May–June 1993): 2–4.
56. D. Kochav, "The Economics of Defense—Israel," in L. Williams, ed., *Military Aspects of the Israeli-Arab Conflict* (Tel Aviv: University Publishing Projects, 1975), p. 181.
57. Fishman, "Yoter Midday Generalim," p. 13; also Cohen, *Towards a New Portrait*, p. 109.
58. Data about the pay of Israeli officers in E. Blanche, "Middle East: Is the Myth Fading for the Israeli Army?" *Jane's Intelligence Review*, October 1, 1996.
59. E. Klein, "Taasiyot Bitchoniyot al Shulchan Ha-nituchim" [Defense Industries on the Operating Table], *Yediot Acharonot*, August 23, 1994, pp. 10–11.
60. A. Egozi, "Ech Mochrim 'Migim' le-Zambia" [Selling MIGs to Zambia], *Yediot Acharonot*, November 29, 1996.
61. The most recent list of Israeli-made missiles is A. Fishman, "Tilim Chachamim Le-lo Shlita" [Smart Missiles Out of Control], *Yediot Acharonot*, February 28, 1997, pp. 12–13.
62. Y. Melman, "Ha-shorashim Ha-polaniyim shel Ha-iska Ha-surit" [The Polish Roots of the Syrian Arms Deal], *Ha-arets*, February 26, 1997, p. B3.
63. See most recently anonymous, "European Defence," *Worldlink* (March–April 1997): 36–42.
64. See for these developments A. Cordesman, *After the Storm: The Changing Military Balance in the Middle East* (Boulder: Westview Press, 1993), p. 236 ff.
65. M. Pail, "Tachbulla, Ruach Lechima Ve-technologia" [Tactics, Fighting Spirit, and Technology), in Ofer and Kover, eds., *Echut Ve-kamut*, pp. 361–372.
66. Lt. Col. R., "Hearot La-manhigut Ha-technologit shel TSAHAL" [Notes re the IDF's Technological Leadership], *Maarachot* 323 (March 1992): 37.

Chapter 19

1. Cf. e.g., Z. Schiff, "Ha-kavim Ha-adumim shel Sharon" [Sharon's Red Lines], *Ha-arets*, November 22, 1981.
2. See Z. Eytan, "Ha-iyum Ha-iraqi al Yisrael Acahrei Milchemet Ha-mifrats" [The Iraqi Threat to Israel After the Gulf War], in Jaffee Center, ed., *Milchama Ba-mifrats, Hashlachot al-Yisrael* [The Gulf War, Implications for Israel] (Tel Aviv: Papyrus, 1991), p. 138, table 1; also A. Cordesman, *After the Storm: The Changing Military Balance in the Middle East* (Boulder: Westview Press, 1993), pp. 457–458.
3. A good appreciation of the Iraqi performance may be found in A. H. Cordesman, *The Gulf and the Search for Strategic Stability* (Boulder: Westview Press, 1984), p. 695 ff.
4. For the exchange see *Ha-arets*, April 4, 5, and 6, 1990.
5. *Ha-arets*, July 6, 1990, p. 1.
6. E. Karsh, "Regional Strategic Implications of the Iran-Iraq War," in S. Gazit et al., eds., *The Middle East Military Balance, 1988–1989* (Tel Aviv: Jaffee Center, 1989), pp. 106, 109–110.

7. Foreign Minster Tareq Abd'el Aziz, as quoted in *The Washington Post*, January 10, 1991.
8. M. Arens, *Milchama Ve-shalom Ba-mizrach Ha-tichon, 1988–1992* [War and Peace in the Middle East, 1988–1992] (Tel Aviv: Yediot Acharonot, 1995), pp. 163–164.
9. *Yediot Acharonot*, January 14, 1991, p. 4.
10. Y. Melman and D. Raviv, *Meraglim lo Mushlamim* [Imperfect Spies] (Tel Aviv: Maariv, 1990), p. 340; R. Pedatzur, "Milchemet Ha-mifrats, Iyun Bikorti Rishoni" [The Gulf War: A Preliminary Critical Assessment], *Maarachot* 321 (May–June 1991), p. 11; Y. Harkabi, "Rosh Ha-modiin Ke-ezer La-kvarnit" [The Chief of Intelligence as an Aid to the Decisionmaker], *Maarachot* 326 (August–September 1992), p. 49.
11. For these shortcomings see R. Pedatzur, "Milchemet Ha-mifrats," pp. 9–10.
12. M. Yaavets as quoted on Israel Radio, January 13, 1991. In fairness it should also be said that Yaavets was the only commentator who foresaw a quick, easy victory over Iraq with hardly any losses for the Coalition.
13. For the details see J. A. Baker III, *The Politics of Diplomacy, Revolution, War, and Peace, 1989–1992* (New York: Putnam's, 1995), pp. 355–365.
14. Cf. L. Freedman and E. Karsh, *The Gulf Conflict* (London: Faber and Faber, 1993), pp. 331–332.
15. Arens, *Milchama Ve-shalom*, p. 159. In fact, experience since 1940 has shown that no considerable modern armed force can get away more than 200 or so miles from base without running into serious logistic trouble.
16. *Yediot Acharonot*, August 8, 1990, p. 1.
17. Quoted in *Chadashot*, February 8, 1991, p. 7.
18. Arens, *Milchama Ve-shalom*, pp. 193–214.
19. According to M. R. Gordon and B. E. Trainor, *The General's War: The Inside Story of the Conflict in the Gulf* (Boston: Little, Brown, 1995), p. 238.
20. I. Linur, *Shirat Ha-sirena* [The Siren's Song] (Tel Aviv: Zmora Bitan, 1992), p. 223.
21. Ts. Gilat, interview with the state comptroller, *Yediot Acharonot*, January 15, 1993, p. 4.
22. *Yediot Acharonot*, February 12, 1991, p. 1.
23. Cf. R. Werman, *Notes from a Sealed Room: An Israeli View of the Gulf War* (Carbondale: Southern Illinois University Press, 1991), p. 135.
24. D. Leshem, "Tilei Karka-Karka Be-Iraq" [Iraqi Surface-to-Surface Missiles], Jaffee Center, Monograph No. 33, November 1990, p. 15.
25. Figures from Werman, *Notes from a Sealed Room*, pp. 173–174.
26. For this debate see R. Pedatzur, "Evolving Ballistic Missile Capabilities and Theater Missile Defense: The Israeli Predicament," *Security Studies* 3:3 (1994): 544–545.
27. Radio Israel, April 8, 1998.
28. A. Levite, "Lekachim Tsvaiyim Le-yisrael" [Israeli Military Lessons], in Jaffee Center, ed., *Milchama Ba-mifrats*, p. 142 ff., represents the best discussion.
29. Private information from a participant who has asked to remain unidentified.
30. State Comptroller's Report for 1996, as quoted in *Yediot Acharonot*, May 8, 1997, p. 2.
31. Dov Raviv, "father" of the Chets, in *Yediot Acharonot*, April 19, 1996, pp. 20–21.
32. In March 1997 one test successfully intercepted the target missile but failed to destroy it as the Chets warhead did not explode; A. Egozi, "Paga Bull" [A Bull's-Eye Hit], *Yediot Acharonot*, March 12, 1997, p. 9.
33. Pedatzur, "Evolving Ballistic Missile Capabilities," pp. 551–552.
34. H. Howe, "Suriya Mechina Optsia shel Mahalumat Peta Chimit al Arei Yisrael" [Syria Is Preparing for a Chemical Surprise Attack Against Israel's Cities], *Yediot Achanronot* weekend magazine, September 12, 1997, pp. 4–7.
35. Cf. Y. Evron, *Israel's Nuclear Dilemma* (London: Routledge, 1994), p. 211 ff.
36. On April 7, 1998, Israel TV announced an abortive launch of a Chets II. This failure was the sixth of its kind.

37. *Yediot Acharonot*, March 12, 1997, p. 9.
38. See above all D. Irving, *Und Deutschlands Staedte Starben Nicht* (Zurich: Schweizer Druck, 1963).
39. D. Ben Gurion, *Yoman Ha-milchama, 1948–1949* [War Diary, 1948–1949] (Tel Aviv: Ministry of Defense, 1982), vol. 2, p. 428, entry for 16.5.48.
40. Rabin speech to the Forum for Security, Judaism, and Society, Tel Aviv, January 8, 1995.

CHAPTER 20

1. For Dayan's ideas on administering the territories see S. Teveth, *Killelat Ha-bracha* [The Cursed Blessing] (Jerusalem: Schocken, 1968), p. 64 ff.
2. A. Sharon, *Warrior* (New York: Simon and Schuster, 1989), p. 251 ff.
3. On the undercover units engaged in Gaza see Y. Serena and G. Leshem, "Ha-chisulim Ha-rishonim" [The First Liquidations], *Yediot Acharonot*, September 26, 1997, pp. 1–12.
4. Figure from A. Hess, *Li-shtot Me-ha-yam shel Aza* [Drinking from Gaza's Sea] (Tel Aviv: Ha-kibbuts Ma-meuchad, 1996), p. 185.
5. He who killed thirty Muslim worshippers in Hebron before being killed himself.
6. For the building plan see E. Efrat, *Geography and Politics in Israel Since 1967* (London: Cass, 1988), chap. 6.
7. For this policy cf. M. Palumbo, *Imperial Israel* (London: Bloomsbury, 1990), pp. 40 ff., 82 ff.
8. Sharon speech as reported in *Yediot Acharonot*, June 18, 1982, p. 1.
9. Compared to 1986 the number of riots had grown by 133 percent, that of tire-burnings by 178 percent, that of rock-throwings by 140 percent, and that of road-blocks by 68 percent. The figures, which refer to the Gaza Strip only, are from Z. Schiff and E. Yaari, *Intifada* [Hebrew] (Jerusalem: Schocken, 1990), p. 26.
10. Quote from *Yediot Acharonot* special supplement, "Helem-Ha-shtachim" [The Shock of the Territories], January 14, 1988.
11. Schiff and Yaari, *Intifada*, p. 73 ff.
12. Figures from ibid., p. 6.
13. Figure from Schiff and Yaari, *Intifada*, p. 274; also Hess, *Li-shtot Me-ha-yam shel Aza*, p. 354.
14. A. Ringel Hoffman, "MAGAV Yatsu Sayeret" [The Border Guards as Commandos], *Yediot Acharonot*, October 4, 1966, pp. 6–10.
15. *Yediot Acharonot*, January 15, 1988, p. 4.
16. Quoted in *Yediot Acharonot* special supplement, January 14, 1988, p. 4.
17. M. Begin, *The Revolt* (New York: Dell, 1977), p. 92.
18. For this entire episode cf. Schiff and Yaari, *Intifada*, pp. 18–19.
19. Quote from chief of staff's directive on the use of physical force, IDF Chief Education Officer, November 1989, p. 16.
20. Quoted from Z. Segal, *Chofesh Ha-itonut: Ben Mitos Le-metsiut* [Freedom of the Press: Between Myth and Reality] (Tel Aviv: Papyrus, 1996), p. 63, n. 24.
21. On the nature and implications of this case see ibid., p. 75 ff.
22. R. Gal, "Aspektim Psychologiyim Ve-Musariyim Be-hitmodedut Chayalei-TSAHAL im Ha-intifada" [Psychological and Moral Aspects of the IDF's Struggle Against the *Intifada*], in R. Gal, ed., *Ha-milchama Ha-sheviit* [The Seventh War] (Tel Aviv: Ha-kibbuts Ha-meuchad, 1990), p. 143.
23. Figure from IDF spokesman, *Ha-arets*, November 29, 1994, p. 1.
24. A. Ringel Hoffman, "Tsahal Neged Tsahal" [IDF Versus IDF], part 2, *Yediot Acharonot* weekend magazine, January 24, 1997, p. 26.

25. J. Cohen, "Mi-Pikkud Tsafon Tetse Ha-raa" [From Northern Front Will Evil Start], *Kol Ha-ir*, October 20, 1995, pp. 27–30.

26. A. Ringel Hoffman, "Tsahal Neged Tsahal," part 1, *Yediot Acharonot* weekend magazine, January 17, 1997, pp. 62–66, 98.

27. A. Ringel-Hofman, "Hitkomemut Ha-alufim" [The Generals' Revolt], *Yediot Acharonot*, March 14, 1997, p. 18.

28. A. Klivnov, "Hirhurim Be-yom Huladeto Ha-shmonim shel Ha-tank" [Thoughts at the Tank's 80th Birthday], *Ba-shiryon* 1 (October 1996): 45.

29. Figure from S. A. Cohen, *Towards a New Portrait of a (New) Israeli Soldier* (Ramat Gan: BESA Center, 1997), p. 104.

30. See the various tables in D. Ashkenazy, *The Military in the Service of Society and Democracy* (Westport, Conn.: Greenwood Press, 1994), pp. 28–40.

31. E. Berkovits, "Ha-ish She-shaal Yoter Midai" [The Man Who Asked too Many Questions], *Kol Ha-ir*, August 25, 1995, p. 54.

32. Ibid., p. 52.

33. Bernheimer, "Profil '96" [A Profile for 1996], *Yediot Acharonot* weekend magazine, April 19, 1996, p. 16.

34. Maj. Gen. (ret.) Ran Goren, quoted in *Yediot Acharonot*, August 7, 1996, p. 10.

35. Report by chief of manpower division, *Ha-arets*, October 24, 1996, p. 1.

36. *Ha-arets*, March 22, 1995, p. 1; Deputy Chief of Staff Vilnai on Israel Radio, December 26, 1996; also *Yediot Acharonot*, November 22, 1996, p. 4.

37. Bernheimer, "Profil '96," p. 14.

38. *Yediot Acharonot*, August 15, 1996, p. 11.

39. E. Lebel, "Niflat Me-ha-sherut Be-shel Choser Hatama" [Discharged as Unfit], *Ha-arets* weekend magazine, April 4, 1997, p. 70.

40. *Yediot Acharonot*, August 7, 1996, p. 10.

41. Figures, based on interview with chief of manpower division, in Cohen, *Towards a New Portrait*, p. 107.

42. A. Fishman, "Echad Mi-kol Chamisha Chayalim Lo Mesayem Sherut Chova Maleh Be-TSAHAL" [One out of Five Soldiers Does Not Complete His Conscript Service], *Yediot Acharonot*, September 2, 1996, p. 5.

43. The figure of 30 percent was mentioned by Ran Cohen, member of the Knesset Foreign Affairs and Defense Committee, as quoted on Israel Radio, August 23, 1996; Israel TV, December 4, 1996; *Maariv*, December 17, 1996, p. 1.

44. *Yediot Acharonot*, October 24, 1996, p. 19. "Senior officers" quoted on IDF Radio on September 9, 1996, put the figure of those who actually serve at 16 percent.

45. *Yediot Acharonot*, May 4, 1997, p. 1.

46. *Yediot Acharonot*, October 24, 1996, p. 19.

47. *Ha-arets*, April 29, 1997, p. 1.

48. R. Gabriel and P. Savage, *Crisis in Command* (New York: Hill and Wang, 1976).

CHAPTER 21

1. A. Ringel-Hoffman, "Milchamtam shel Ha-horim Ha-shakulim Be-TAAL Shiff" [The Bereaved Parents' Battle Against Brigadier General Shiff], *Yediot Acharonot*, July 19, 1996, pp. 6–9; also S. A. Cohen, *Towards a New Portrait of a (New) Israeli Soldier* (Ramat Gan: BESA Center, 1997), p. 101.

2. M. Allon, "Ha-mered Ha-gadol Ba-Kommando Ha-yami" [The Great Revolt in the Naval Commando], *Yediot Acharonot* weekend magazine, December 6, 1996, pp. 7–10, 13.

3. *Yediot Acharonot*, October 7, 1996, p. 9.

4. Israel Radio, December 15, 1996.

5. *Ha-arets*, April 16, 1997, p. 1.

6. *Yediot-Acharonot*, April 18, 1997, p. 5.
7. *Ha-arets*, April 25, 1997, p. 4.
8. Quoted in *Yerushalayim*, November 2, 1996, p. 16.
9. Israel TV, October 29, 1996.
10. In particular, *The Birth of the Palestinian Refugee Problem, 1947–1949* (1986), and *Israel's Border Wars, 1949–1956* (1994).
11. *War and Peace in the Middle East* (New York: Whittle, 1994).
12. On this subject see E. Blanche, "Middle East: Is the Myth Fading for the Israeli Army?" *Jane's Intelligence Review*, October 1, 1996, pp. 5–6; A. Oren, "Mutar La-harog Shvuyim (Le-itim Rechokot)" [License to Kill Prisoners—Rarely], *Ha-arets*, March 28, 1997, p. 5; R. Eytan, *Sippur shel Chayal* [A Soldier's Story] (Tel Aviv: Maariv, 1991), p. 164; M. Allon, "Hereg-Ha-shvuyim" [Killing POWs], *Yediot Acharonot* weekend magazine, April 11, 1997, pp. 17–18.
13. The father of one soldier killed in Lebanon said his son, though forming part of an elite unit, would not wear his uniform while on leave for fear of being considered "a sucker"; *Yediot Acharonot*, May 18, 1997, p. 1.
14. R. Rosen and I. Hammerman, *Meshorerim lo Yichtevu Shirim* [Poets Will Remain Silent] (Tel Aviv: Am Oved, 1990).

The Good and the Evil

1. For details see I. Shamir, *Hantscaha Ve-zikaron* [Commemoration and Remembrance] (Tel Aviv: Am Oved, 1996), p. 104.
2. Cf. S. Feldman, *Nuclear Weapons and Arms Control in the Middle East* (Cambridge, Mass.: MIT Press, 1997).
3. *Ha-arets*, May 19, 1994, p. 2.
4. E. Inbar, *Contours of Israel's New Strategic Thinking* (Mideast Security and Policy Studies, BESA Center for Strategic Studies, Ramat Gan: Bar Illan University, 1996), pp. 57–63.
5. Israel Radio, April 14, 1997.
6. Y. Rabin in *Ba-machane*, September 23, 1992, p. 9.
7. *Ha-arets*, April 29, 1997, p. 1.
8. *Yediot Acharonot*, May 8, 1997, p. 17; May 9, 1997, p. 6; September 12, 1997, pp. 8–12.
9. *Yediot Acharonot*, March 31, 1997, pp. 14–15.
10. On the process of legitimization see A. D. Epstein, "Ha-sarvanut Ha-matspunit Ke-indikator Le-yachasei Medina-Tsava-Ha-chevra Ha-ezrachit Be-yisrael" [Conscientious Objection as an Indicator for Relations Between State, Military, and Civil Society in Israel], M.A. thesis, the Hebrew University, Jerusalem, 1997.
11. Major General Nativ, chief of manpower, as quoted in *Yediot Acharonot*, March 27, 1997, p. 2.
12. A. Fishman and Y. Adiram, "Achavat Ha-lochamim Nishberet" [Soldier's Solidarity Breaking Down], *Yediot Acharonot* weekend magazine, March 7, 1997, pp. 14–15.
13. *Yediot Acharonot*, May 5, 1997, p. 3.
14. A. Bernheimer, "Profil '96" [A Profile for 1996], *Yediot Acharonot* weekend magazine, April 19, 1996, p. 16.
15. E. Ben Ari, "Chayalim Be-masechot" [Soldiers in Masks], in R. Gal, ed., *Ha-milchama Ha-sheviit* [The Seventh War] (Tel Aviv: Ha-kibbuts Ha-meuchad, 1990), pp. 113–114, based on the author's experiences in his reserve paratrooper battalion.
16. D. Horowitz and M. Lissak, *Trouble in Utopia* (New York: University of New York Press, 1989).
17. Cf. S. M. Lipset, *The Confidence Gap* (Baltimore: Johns Hopkins University Press, 1987).

About the Author

Martin van Creveld was born in the Netherlands in 1946, has lived in Israel since 1950, and received his Ph.D. from the University of London. Since 1971 he has been a faculty member at the Hebrew University, Jerusalem, where he is an internationally acknowledged expert on military history and strategy. His best-known publications are *Supplying War* (1977), *Fighting Power* (1982), *Command in War* (1985), *Technology and War* (1988), and *The Transformation of War* (1991); they have been translated into eight languages including Japanese, Chinese, and Arabic. He has taught or lectured at virtually every center, civilian and military, of strategic learning in the Western world, and has consulted for the defense establishments of many governments.

Professor van Creveld's partner in life is Dvora Lewy, a painter. Four of their children serve, or have served, in the IDF.